Components of MACMILLAN ENGLISH

THINKING AND WRITING PROCESSES

Pupil's Edition
Teacher's Edition with Teacher's Manual
Teacher's Resource Book, which includes the following:

- Teacher's Professional Resources
- Overhead Transparencies
- Study and Composition Blackline Masters
- Practice Blackline Masters (also available in consumable format)
- Practice Teacher's Edition
- Test Blackline Masters (also available in consumable format)
- Test Teacher's Edition

PWR: Macmillan English Composition Software
Macmillan English Test Generator

Authors and Advisors

ELIZABETH ACKLEY
English Teacher
Indian Hill High School
Cincinnati, Ohio

PAULA A. CALABRESE
Assistant Principal
Ingomar Middle School
North Allegheny School District
Pittsburgh, Pennsylvania

SANDRA A. CAVENDER
English Teacher
Nathan Hale High School
West Allis, Wisconsin

SYLVIA COLLINS-KIMBELL
Supervisor of Language Arts
Hillsborough County Schools
Tampa, Florida

SONYA POHLMAN
English Teacher
Rangeview High School
Aurora, Colorado

JUDI PURVIS
Secondary Language Arts Appraiser
Carrollton–Farmers Branch School District
Texas

ROBERT RANTA
English Department Head
Lacey Township High School
Lanoka Harbor, New Jersey

MARJORY CARTER WILLIS
English Teacher
Midlothian High School
Midlothian, Virginia

Some material for Part 1 was prepared by Intentional Educations, Watertown, Massachusetts.

FOR "THINKING ABOUT THINKING"

SHARON FLITTERMAN-KING
Faculty Associate
Bard Institute for Writing and Thinking
Annandale-on-Hudson, New York

DAVID C. KING
Educational Writer
Director, Curriculum Design for
Tomorrow's World, Inc.

The Publisher would also like to thank the following educators for their contribution to the TEACHER'S PROFESSIONAL RESOURCES, which accompanies MACMILLAN ENGLISH:

EMILY B. BUTLER
Vanguard High School
Marion County, Florida

KAROL CAMP
Dixie Hollins High School
St. Petersburg, Florida

DELANIE B. FANT
Robert E. Lee Senior High School
Jacksonville, Florida

BRIAN ROWLAND
Western High School
Broward County, Florida

BARBARA S. WILSON
Lake Gibson Senior High School
Lakeland, Florida

Special Consultants

FRANKLIN E. HOROWITZ
Adjunct Assistant Professor of Education
Teacher's College, Columbia University
New York, New York

ROY PETER CLARK
Associate Director
The Poynter Institute for Media Studies
St. Petersburg, Florida

Contributing Writers

Harrison B. Bell, Robert A. Bell, Sally R. Bell, Larry and Susan Berliner, Sheila C. Crowell, Richard Foerster, Eleanor Franklin, Carol Goldman, Joan C. Gregory, Florence W. Harris, Paula R. Hartz, Barbara Klinger, Ellen D. Kolba, Christopher T. McMillan, William Maxey III, Cynthia Miller, Carroll Moulton, Eileen Hillary Oshinsky, Milton Polsky, John David Richardson, Derrick Tseng, Gail Schiller Tuchman, Sidney Zimmerman

MACMILLAN ENGLISH

THINKING AND WRITING PROCESSES

Scribner Laidlaw
New York
Collier Macmillan Publishers
London

Scribner Laidlaw
866 Third Avenue
New York, New York 10022
Collier Macmillan Canada, Inc.

Printed in the United States of America

Pupil's Edition ISBN 0-02-242530-6 Teacher's Edition ISBN 0-02-242570-5

9 8 7 6 5 4 3

Acknowledgments

Grateful acknowledgment is given authors, publishers, and agents for permission to reprint the following copyrighted material. In the case of any omissions, the Publisher will be pleased to make suitable acknowledgments in future editions.

STEVEN BIRNBAUM
"Beyond Rollercoasters" by Steven Birnbaum from *Games Magazine*, August 1986, Vol. 10, No. 8, issue 78, page 12. Reprinted by permission of the author.

LEO CARDENAS
Excerpt from "The Other Pioneers" by Roberto Felix Salazar originally appeared in *Lulac News*, 1939. Reprinted by permission.

CHAPPELL/INTERSONG Music Group USA
"A Cock-Eyed Optimist" by Richard Rodgers & Oscar Hammerstein II. Copyright © 1949 by Richard Rodgers & Oscar Hammerstein II, Copyright Renewed, Williamson Music, Co., owner of publication and allied rights. International Copyright Secured. *All Rights Reserved.* Used by permission.

EUGENIA COLLIER
Excerpt from "Marigolds" by Eugenia Collier. Reprinted from *Negro Digest*, October 1969. Copyright © 1969 by Johnson Publishing Company, Inc. Reprinted by permission of Eugenia Collier.

VICTOR HERNÁNDEZ CRUZ
Excerpt from "Slide 32" by Victor Hernández Cruz. Copyright © 1966 by Victor Hernández Cruz. Reprinted by permission of the author.

DODD, MEAD & COMPANY, INC.
Excerpt from "Harriet Tubman: The Moses of Her People" from *Famous American Negroes* by Langston Hughes. Copyright © 1954 by Langston Hughes. Reprinted by permission of Dodd, Mead & Company, Inc.

DOUBLEDAY & COMPANY
Excerpts from *The Diary of a Young Girl* by Anne Frank, translated by B. M. Mooyaart. Copyright 1952, Doubleday & Company. Reprinted by permission of the publisher.

PENELOPE FRANKLIN
Excerpt from "The Diary of Yvonne Blue" by Yvonne Blue. Copyright © 1986 by Yvonne Blue Skinner in *Private Pages: Diaries of American Women 1830s–1970s* edited by Penelope Franklin. Copyright © 1986 Penelope Franklin. Published by Ballantine Books, a division of Random House, Inc. Reprinted by permission of Penelope Franklin.

GRAFTON BOOKS LTD.
"maggie and milly and molly and may" from *Complete Poems 1913–1962* by E. E. Cummings. Copyright © 1956 by E. E. Cummings. Reprinted by permission of the publisher.

HARCOURT BRACE JOVANOVICH, INC.
"maggie and milly and molly and may" from *Complete Poems 1913–1962* by E. E. Cummings. Copyright © 1956 by E. E. Cummings.
"A Slander" by Anton Chekhov translated by Natalie Wollard. Copyright © 1970 by Harcourt Brace Jovanovich, Inc.
Excerpts from *The Diary of Virginia Woolf* by Virginia Woolf, Volume Two, 1920–1924 edited by A. O. Bell. Copyright © 1978 by Quentin Bell and Angelica Garnett.
All reprinted by permission of Harcourt Brace Jovanovich, Inc.

HARPER & ROW, PUBLISHERS, INC.
Excerpts from *Off the Record: The Private Papers of Harry S. Truman* edited by Robert H. Ferrell. Copyright © 1980 by Robert H. Ferrell.

HIRT MUSIC, INC.
Excerpt from "When I Think About Myself" from *The Poetry of Maya Angelou*. Copyright © 1969 Hirt Music, Inc. Reprinted by permission of the publisher.

THE HOGARTH PRESS, LTD.
Excerpt from *The Diary of Virginia Woolf*, Volume

BOOK DESIGN AND PRODUCTION: Textart Inc.
COVER DESIGN: Textart Inc.
TECHNICAL ART: Network Graphics

Photo Credits

ANIMALS ANIMALS: © Patti Murray p 45. © 1987 Beth Bergman, p 449. THE BETTMANN ARCHIVE, INC.: pp 35, 443. CULVER PICTURES, INC.: pp 95, 249, 311, 414, 533, 537. DUOMO: Steven E. Sutton p 418. EARTH SCENES: © Gary W. Griffen p 672. EKM-NEPENTHE: © Robert Eckert p 166. ESTO PHOTOGRAPHICS INC: © 1978 Ezra Stroller p 581. THE IMAGE BANK: M. Kimak 1982 p 553. © Ken Karp, pp 427, 527. LEO DE WYS INC.: p 403. MONKMEYER PRESS: © Rameshwar Das 1986 p 666; © Mimi Forsyth pp 209, 322, 645; © Leonard Lee Rue pp 457, 474. NASA: p 600. PHOTO RESEARCHERS INC.: © George Holton p 119; © Robert A. Isaacs 1982 p 652; © Ellan Young 1983 pp 512, 630; © Katherine Young p 111. PHOTOTHEQUÈ: p 256. THE PICTURE CUBE: © Read D. Brugger p 521; © Ellis Herwig p 234; © Franz Kraus p 70; © Jaye R. Phillips p 53; © 1983 Frank Siteman p 422; © Eric A. Roth p. 436. STOCK, BOSTON: © George Bellerose p 397; © Lionel J-M Delevingne p 25; © Clif Garboden p 159; © Ellis Herwig pp 409, 607; © 1985 Deborah Kahn p 433; © Ira Kirshenbaum p 543; © Jean-Claude Lejeune p 145; © Mike Mazzaschi p 689; © H. Morgan p 509; © Richard Pasley 1985 p 393; © Jack Prelutsky p 17; © Cary Wolinsky p 503. © 1987 Martha Swope, p 338. TAURUS PHOTOS: © 1982 Sid & Mary Nolan p 81. UPI/BETTMANN NEWSPHOTOS: p 288. WOODFIN CAMP & ASSOCIATES: © Marc & Evelyn Bernheim p 567; © Shelly Grossman 1980 p 486; © Michal Heron 1981 p 592; © David Hume Kennerly 1979/Contact p 179; © Bill Strode 1982 p 617.

Unit Opener Credits

ART RESOURCE: both: Henry Moore, *King and Queen* (bronze, 1952) (front view & back view), Hirshhorn Museum & Sculpture Garden, Smithsonian Institution/Joseph Martin/Scala pp 136–137. STOCK, BOSTON: © John A. Decindis pp 2–3; © Ira Kirschenbaum pp 92–93, 682–683; © Peter Menzel pp 224–225, 280–281; © Peter Vandermark pp 492–493; © Barbara Alper pp 604–605; © Frank Siteman pp 386–387. © Michal Heron 1986, p 561.

Part Opener Credits

PHOTO RESEARCHERS, INC.: © Mary M. Thacher p 1. RAINBOW: © Dan McCoy p 385. LEO DE WYS INC.: © Everett C. Johnson p 603.

Art Credits

MICHAEL ADAMS—141, 302, 317, 400, 434, 565, 590, 659
RICHARD LOEHLE—49, 573
STEPHEN MARCHESI—58, 98, 127, 334, 497, 549, 554, 671, 704
DONNA RUFF—289, 461, 685
SAMANTHA SMITH—14, 15, 62, 72, 196, 215, 238, 239, 267, 389, 413, 519, 615, 626, 676
EVA BURG VAGRETI—39, 113, 169, 479

For Writer's Sourcebook Credits see page 720.

Contents

UNIT IV *The Essay and the Research Report*

UNIT V
Writing Across the Curriculum

PART 2 Grammar, Usage, and Mechanics 385

UNIT VI Grammar

UNIT VII Usage

UNIT VIII
Mechanics

UNIT X Resources

Special Features

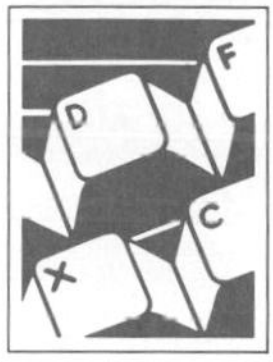

Writer's Choice

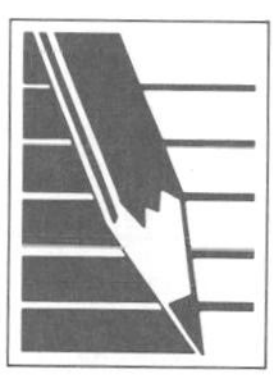

Revising Your Writing

Student Writers

Many models of student writing appear in this textbook. In the "Writers on Writing" feature, models and commentaries by the following student writers appear on the pages indicated.

Professional Writers

Excerpts from the work of many writers appear in this textbook. Here is a list of some of the writers included.

The "Writer's Sourcebook" contains the following literary selections:

Thinking Skills

Thinking About Thinking

Thinking and writing go hand in hand. Thinking is built into each stage of the writing process, and writing itself can be a tool of the thinking process. As you progress through this textbook, you will discover how applying certain thinking skills can help you become a better writer.

Each unit in *Macmillan English* opens with a special feature called "Thinking About Thinking." This feature defines one particular thinking skill that is part of a larger thinking process. Each skill is one you will find useful as you engage in the activities of that unit.

"Thinking About Thinking" helps you to become aware of what you do when you think. Each feature asks you to think in a certain way about a photograph. By becoming more aware of the way you think, you can gain greater mastery of the thinking skills you use as you write.

Here, in everyday language, are descriptions of the thinking skills you will apply at the start of each unit in this book.

UNIT I	THE PARAGRAPH AND THE WRITING PROCESS
THINKING PROCESS	*Invention*
THINKING SKILL	**Demonstrating Fluency** When you demonstrate fluency, you let words flow without stopping in order to help your thoughts flow more freely. This skill is most helpful during prewriting because it allows new ideas to surface.

UNIT II THE DEVELOPMENT OF A PERSONAL WRITING STYLE

THINKING PROCESS *Decision Making*

THINKING SKILL **Recognizing Alternatives**

Recognizing alternatives means seeing that choices are *possible* in a given situation. This skill helps you to see options, avoid dead ends, and make better informed decisions.

UNIT III THE MODES OF WRITING

THINKING PROCESS *Critical Analysis*

THINKING SKILL **Identifying Varying Perspectives**

This skill involves being aware of different angles or points of view from which something can be considered. It is helpful in the close examination, or critical analysis, that takes place in all the modes of writing.

UNIT IV THE ESSAY AND THE RESEARCH REPORT

THINKING PROCESS *Critical Analysis*

THINKING SKILL **Organizing Information**

Organizing means examining information closely and arranging it in a reasonable way. This is the skill of "making sense" of a body of information, putting data in order so that a pattern or meaning emerges.

UNIT V WRITING ACROSS THE CURRICULUM

THINKING PROCESS *Invention*

THINKING SKILL **Generating Ideas About a Topic**

This is the skill of creating ideas about a specific, predetermined topic in subjects that are part of the conventional school curriculum.

UNIT VI GRAMMAR

THINKING PROCESS *Logical Reasoning*

THINKING SKILL **Categorizing Information**

When you categorize, you group information according to common qualities. This skill helps you to deal logically with information by making it easier to see relationships and to make generalizations.

UNIT VII USAGE

THINKING PROCESS *Decision Making*

THINKING SKILL **Identifying Context**

Identifying context means being aware of the characteristics of a situation, noticing how something interacts with everything around it. This skill helps you make decisions that fit in with other decisions.

UNIT VIII MECHANICS

THINKING PROCESS *Problem Solving*

THINKING SKILL **Recognizing a Symbol System**

This skill involves seeing that people use symbols to clarify situations and solve problems. It is a skill that helps you to use the mechanics of English to achieve clear communication.

UNIT IX SKILLS

THINKING PROCESS *Problem Solving*

THINKING SKILL **Recalling**

Recalling is remembering information and situations you have experienced. This skill helps you to build on the past to solve problems you face in the present.

UNIT X RESOURCES

THINKING PROCESS *Problem Solving*

THINKING SKILL **Observing**

Observing means seeing and being aware of what you see. This skill helps you to focus your attention, describe what you see, and solve problems—not only writing problems—with greater ease and efficiency.

SPEAKING OF ENGLISH

Ralph Wiley, *a staff writer for* SPORTS ILLUSTRATED *magazine, combines an in-depth knowledge of sports with a vivid style. Born in Memphis, Tennessee, Mr. Wiley has lived in California, Chicago, Detroit, and Washington, D.C. Mr. Wiley recently talked with Danny White, a student at Dobbs Ferry High School in Westchester, New York. This interview sets the stage for the material on thinking and writing in the chapters ahead.*

Danny White: When you were in high school, were you first interested in *sports* or in *writing*? Which came first for you?

Ralph Wiley: I spent more time being involved in sports than being involved with writing. Really I was thinking of myself as a football player first. I was a wide receiver, and I had spent a lot of time doing that and playing other sports. And then one day, I had this tremendous knee injury. I remember while I was lying on the field, I was trying to describe in my mind, how does this feel, trying to find words to describe it. So when I got to the hospital I was lying there, and I said, wait a minute, maybe I'm approaching this all wrong. That's when I really started to go over to the *observer's* side of it.

White: So you feel that, before you became a writer, you really knew what you wanted to write about. The subject matter came first.

Wiley: Yes. And if there are any rules of journalism, the first one is to know your subject. On the one hand, it's not difficult, but on the other hand, it's the most difficult thing you can try to do because there is always so much to know. And that's why you have to simplify, which is the second rule of being a journalist —one, know your subject, and two, simplify. But remember that in sports we're talking about people. You know, scores come and go, but it's the people that are unique and can never be replaced. So what you try to do is to reflect individual people as much as they'll allow, as much as you can. At the same time, thinking always—simplicity, thinking—What can I tell the world about this person in a simple form?

White: How do you decide what to tell the world, what it is that people want to read about?

Wiley: Usually I won't make a decision like that before reaching my subject. I won't sit here in the office and say, well, I'm going to do a story on *x*, and I'm probably going to end up writing about *x*. No, I won't do that. I'll go out and *observe* the situation, talk to the subject, talk to the people around the subject, and I will let that dictate what I think will be most interesting. And there's a bit of entertaining going on too.

White: Does your audience dictate what you're going to say?

Wiley: To some degree. I do think that my audience expects a certain amount of entertainment in the writing. They appreciate a well-turned phrase, and they appreciate finding out things. But you've really got to write to please yourself. Because if you're a thinking, intelligent person and you find out what *you* want to know—what do I want to know about, what intrigues me—then basically you've got it. Sometimes you'll know you have it. You write it and you say, I've got it. This is it. And when you feel that, you learn to *trust* it and you trust that it's the best you can do.

White: What was the toughest thing that you had to learn to do to become a successful sportswriter?

Wiley: The two toughest things were to allow myself patience and to stay within myself. You need your ego, because there are going to be many people who tell you that you can't do something. They'll form a line to tell you how good you aren't or can't be. So you need that ego to say, Yes, I can do it. But you also need a great deal of humility. You must be prepared and ready to see and hear everything, but at the same time you can't go in with assumptions. In a sense you must almost be a blank page.

White: How does patience help you in a very nitty gritty sort of way, gathering material together, writing, rewriting?

Wiley: Well, first you have to realize that the story was there before you got there. All you're doing is finding it and letting it find you. After you get it and have all your notes and begin to pick out the quotes that are the best quotes, you have maybe a hundred pages of information, but there are ten pages in there that really make the point. And as you get better, you see that the best writing, the best stories, they all have a thread. There's a beginning, there's a middle, and there's a conclusion. And you shouldn't let that intimidate you. Because they will be there. You don't have to create them. If you have to create them, you really don't know enough about the subject. If you're *patient*, reading and rereading what you've done, the thread will present itself to you. And that's when it really becomes a joy.

White: How do you take notes? Do you use a tape recorder, do you use shorthand, do you keep a journal?

Wiley: All of those, in varying forms and in different situations. Usually I use my memory. I once lost a notebook that I had done a story in. I had all these great notes and quotes, and I lost the notebook and I sat there and I said, Wait—the good stuff stuck in my mind. It was still there. So really your mind is your greatest tool. And I hardly even pull out the notebook when I'm interviewing someone. Sometimes, if they say something that's really pungent, I'll jot that sentence down, so I'll have it precisely as they said it. But usually I won't depend on that.

White: After you have collected your notes, do you sit down and do a first draft and then go back and edit it?

Wiley: It would be nice to tell you that I was a Mozart—write a first draft that would be perfect and never touched again. But that occurs only in screenplays, I think. That's one of the beauties of technology now. We've got portable computers which are very easy to use to edit. And everything can be edited. Always, whatever you write, no matter how well it's written, it can always be adjusted. You wrote it and you say, this is "dead solid perfect," to use a phrase coined by a former *Sports Illustrated* writer, Dan Jenkins. Dead solid perfect. You had it, but in a week you're going to go back and look at it. A week has passed in your life—you've changed. And you look at your own words differently. Every writer is an editor. You get about a thousand lines of information, weed out what is least necessary, and give them the 180 lines that you think the people want to know. And no editing is really purely objective. You'll hear that word a lot in journalism. Objectivity. There's really no such thing as objectivity, because if you ask twenty questions and you use five of the answers that I give you, then you have chosen which five answers to give. It's a matter of being as open-minded and as fair as you can be in your reporting.

White: After you've got your notes, what do you do then?

Wiley: OK. Let's go through the whole process. Say the game's over. I already have an idea—I have the score. I know why the score is what it was. I go down to the locker room with one hundred other people. It's very difficult to have exclusivity in the locker room. It's very competitive. But you get some quotes. Then you go home or go back to the press box. I work mostly in hotel rooms. Set up your portable word processor. And then —it's a beautiful thing. It's almost like being a sculptor. I just throw clay out. It's like rain on a tin roof for about thirty minutes—rrrrrrrrrr. [Wiley motions as if he were typing at great speed.] I let it out. Pow! And then I bring it back up. I begin to chip away at it, make it more presentable, move things here, oh this would be better here, because you want to structure it. You want to capture the ear of the reader, because really what you are doing is reading it aloud in your mind. So once again, we're in my hotel room. And I cannot impress upon you the importance of being able to write on a deadline, because the most difficult thing about writing is facing a blank page. Newspaper writing taught me to adapt to a deadline. At 11:00 I had to have it in. So it was a great discipline. There's a basketball game at 7, and it's over at 9, we need a story by 11. That was my training, my proving ground. I found I tended to perform very well with—you know, 120 minutes and then boom, out. That's the moment of truth that you shouldn't linger over. You never linger over it. You never sit back. Attack. Rrrrrrrrr. Attack—because you can always change, you can always modify a draft. But think positively and attack the senses of the readers and sort of grab, reach out for them. Again, just go, go for it. And whatever struck you, put it out there.

White: Were you always able to do this, or was there some particular person, a teacher or an editor, who helped you?

Wiley: My twelfth-grade teacher, Mrs. Minnie V. Echols, a wonderful woman. She was tremendous in that she was always encouraging me. "Write, because that's the only way you're going to get better. Write and write and write."

It's like playing quarterback in the National Football League. No matter how good you are, as an athlete, if you go out there on your first day, there's *nothing* you can do. They will slap you silly. Because even though you can throw it through a brick wall at twenty-five yards and throw the next three through the hole you just made, you really don't know how fast those athletes are, how quickly they react. You don't know the terminology. You don't know the capabilities of your own men. There are no fairy tales in sports or in writing. I mean there is no automatic, "Whoa—here's my perfect first novel." No. It's a kind of gut-rattling experience and sometimes you fall and sometimes you have a block, but you just write through it. You just keep writing, just keep writing. And then after a while, you see that when you don't write, you begin to get that urge. And it all starts up again from that urge.

To be a good writer—what an advantage to have in life. I mean, you can do anything. You can translate that writing skill into a job. You can create so much. You can get your point across. Writing is a ticket to your wants. Being able to get your point across. That's basically what it comes down to. If you can't get your point across, well then you might as well not even have a point.

White: As you continue to develop, how would you say you want your writing to improve?

Wiley: My style is good for me, now, but the main thing I do want is more experience, more experience. The writing—I'll become a better writer. As time passes, you continue to develop your style, or you learn how to adapt a rule. Another thing about Mrs. Echols in high school: She told me about these rules, and I said, "Well, Mrs. Echols, rules are made to be broken." And she said, "No, rules are made to be broken by those who know how"—and she was right. Never break rules just for effect. Do it to communicate better.

Communicate. You know how you can go somewhere and your friend's not there. And you see something amazing. And you say, I wish so and so were here. Well, as a writer, you can say, hey, I'm going to show you where I was, so you can be there with me. You can understand what I understand.

MACMILLAN ENGLISH

THINKING AND WRITING PROCESSES

Composition

PART 1

Egyptian hieroglyphics: one of the earliest forms of written communication

UNIT I

The Paragraph and the Writing Process

Thinking About Thinking: Demonstrating Fluency

In this unit you will learn about the three parts of the writing process—prewriting, writing, and revising. Each stage of the writing process involves thinking. In fact, as a writer, you will find yourself engaged in thinking processes just as much as you are engaged in the writing process. For example, when you prewrite you invent new ideas, and you use a variety of thinking skills to help you be inventive.

Defining the Skill

Inventive thinkers and writers often demonstrate fluency. **DEMONSTRATING FLUENCY** means letting your ideas and words flow without interruption. Often, as you think or speak or write without stopping, you find yourself inventing a useful idea. The more you let your thoughts flow freely, the more opportunities you make for new thoughts to surface.

Applying the Skill

Look at the photograph. In order to demonstrate your fluency, write for one minute about the photo. Write whatever comes into your mind. You may want to ask yourself questions like these:

What is the girl thinking?
How can I describe her expression?
Does she remind me of someone? Why?

If you cannot think of anything to write, write that, but keep writing. What new or unusual ideas did you invent?

Introduction: Writing from Personal Experience

When you engage in personal writing, you are recording your thoughts, feelings, experiences, and observations. Personal writing comes in many forms, including the personal letter, the diary, the writer's journal, the autobiography or memoir, and the personal narrative or personal essay.

The Personal Letter

Before the age of modern technology, letters were the main form of communication between people who lived far away from one another. Letter writing was so common that sometimes novelists created whole books made up of fictional letters between fictional characters. Even with today's video cameras and computers, the personal letter remains a special way of recording and communicating ideas—perhaps because a letter is so private in a world that often is so public. (For a detailed study of *business* letters, see Chapter 30.)

Since a letter has a definite reader—or audience—you almost automatically select your ideas and wording for that reader in particular. Depending on how close you feel to your readers, you may "tell all" or "hold back." For example, former President Franklin D. Roosevelt began a letter to his wife, Eleanor, with "Gee! But these are the strenuous days!" and ended another with "Loads of love and I hope James' tummy is better." A letter from another former President, Harry S Truman, to his wife, Bess, reveals deeper feelings and carries with it a more serious tone.

> June 29, 1949
>
> Dear Bess:
>
> . . . Thirty years ago I hoped to make you a happy wife and a happy mother. Did I? I don't know. All I can say [is] I've tried. There is no one in the world anyway who can look down on you or your daughter. That means much to me, but I've never cared for social position or rank for myself except to see that those dear to me were not made to suffer for my shortcomings.

The personal letter can reflect the entire range of human emotions—from sadness to joy, from fear to relief, from longing to fulfillment.

Notice the different emotions expressed by Lewis Carroll (of *Alice's Adventures in Wonderland* fame) in the beginnings of two of his letters.

> Aggie Darling,
>
> I'm quite too low-spirited to write much. Why *did* you all go away so soon?

> My dear Edith,
>
> I'm very glad you are able, and willing, to pay me a visit; and I *hope* it will be as pleasant to *you* to be here, as it certainly will be to *me* to have you.

Many personal letters ask or answer questions. When Emily Dickinson, who was to become a famous poet, was sent to an exclusive boarding school in South Hadley, Massachusetts, she felt shut off from the real world and so wrote a letter full of questions to her brother. Here is part of that letter from 1847:

> Won't you please to tell me when you answer my letter who the candidate for President is? I have been trying to find out ever since I came here, and have not yet succeeded. I don't know anything more about affairs in the world than if I were in a trance, and you must imagine with all your "Sophomoric discernment" that it is but little and very faint. Has the Mexican War terminated yet, and how? Are we beaten? Do you know of any nation about to besiege South Hadley? If so, do inform me of it, for I would be glad of a chance to escape, if we are to be stormed.

As an established writer, James Thurber was often asked questions about how to achieve success in his field. This is how he answered one inquisitive, aspiring author in a letter dated February 23, 1961:

> Dear Robert:
>
> I always tell everybody who asks, "If you are a writer you write."
>
> O. Henry once said, "The only rule for writing short stories is that there is no rule." You should take all kinds of courses in high school and college, because a general education is the best foundation for a writing career.
>
> It is also important to read good books and nobody should try to be a writer until he reaches twenty-four years of age. I didn't get started on *The New Yorker* until I was thirty-two, and the first of my twenty-seven books came out when I was thirty-five.
>
> Good luck.

Notice that in his letter Thurber found it helpful to use a quotation to make his point. Whether you include a quotation, a rhyme, or even a little sketch, your personal letter should get your message across by reflecting the real you.

EXERCISE 1 **Writing to a Historical Person.** Pretend that you are a friend of a famous historical figure. Write a personal letter to him or her in which you discuss the person's accomplishments. You may offer compliments or criticism, as you would when writing to a close friend. You may also include answers to imaginary questions asked of you in an earlier letter and ask questions on the assumption that your historical friend will write back.

EXERCISE 2 **Beginning a Personal Letter Correspondence.** Now write a personal letter to someone who will actually receive and read it. Do you have a distant friend or relative from whom you have not heard in a while? Perhaps you would prefer to write to a classmate or family member who lives close to you. No matter to whom you choose to write, remember the following guidelines:

1. Date your letter.
2. Use a friendly greeting.
3. Ask or answer questions.
4. Adjust your content and language according to how close you feel to your reader.
5. Try to use a quotation, original rhyme, sketch, or other personal feature to get your message across.
6. End with a friendly closing.
7. Sign your name.

The Diary and the Writer's Journal

In a diary you can record your most personal thoughts, feelings, experiences, and observations. One particular type of diary that has gained popularity in English classes is the writer's journal.

You can think of the writer's journal as a diary with the specific purpose of being a storehouse of ideas to use later in writing assignments. Students and established writers alike have referred to their journals weeks, months, or even years after making an entry and found it an inspiration. Many professional writers have said that the ideas for their stories or plays came from incidents they experienced and recorded long ago.

You can also look upon your writer's journal as a place to practice your writing. Like any skill, your ability to write will improve with practice. Someone who wants to be a better painter, paints; someone who wants to excel in dancing, dances. If you want to improve your written expression, you must write—and your journal is a place where you should always feel free to write. Moreover, a journal enables you to write about the things that are most important and interesting to you.

Many people who keep diaries or journals like to make entries each day. In fact, the words *diary* and *journal* came from the Latin word *dies,* which means "day." Other people make diary or journal entries less frequently, perhaps once or twice each week or whenever they feel they have something they need to express or note.

Although diaries and journals are usually kept in bound books, you may prefer to make entries on loose sheets of paper, on index cards, or in a computer file. Where you make the entries is not important; what is important is that you have a place to record your thoughts, feelings, and observations

Perhaps the concept of the diary as a friend and confidant was described best by Anne Frank, a teen-ager who kept a personal record of her experience while she and her family hid from the Nazis in Holland during World War II. *Anne Frank: The Diary of a Young Girl,* published after her death, begins with these words:

> I hope I shall be able to confide in you completely, as I have never been able to do in anyone before, and I hope that you will be a great support and comfort to me.

Her diary was indeed a great comfort to her. Here, while confiding in her diary, Anne reveals a deep inner strength. After two years in hiding, she writes the following:

> I know my own faults and shortcomings better than anyone, but the difference is that I also know that I want to improve, shall improve, and have already improved a great deal.

Whether you want to reveal your strength or admit a weakness, your diary is there. Yvonne Blue, a twentieth-century teacher, artist, and writer, had serious doubts about herself when she was a teen-ager. This is how she began her diary entry of November 4, 1926:

> I wonder if anyone in the world has ever hated himself as I hate myself. It is just recently that I have. Formerly I thought more of myself. I thought I could write, and now that illusion too has been shattered. No one has said anything, but I have tried to write recently, and I can't—I can't. I never could. It was just illusion.

Despite these feelings, Yvonne Blue's ability proved to be no "illusion," as she grew up to achieve success as an adult. Part of her success doubtless grew out of her effort to come to terms with her doubts by writing about them. Because writing is really thinking recorded on a page, keeping a diary may help you to clarify important problems.

Ordinary events can furnish suitable diary material. Drew Pearson was already a world-famous journalist when he made this diary entry on November 2, 1957, during a visit to California:

> I took the children out to Disneyland. They had a wonderful time. It was a little tiring for their grandfather, however, who hasn't had much sleep lately. I can't seem to sleep out here, partly because of the change of time, partly because I wake up in the night to cover Joe. He gets uncovered every hour or so.

The way in which you record personal thoughts and emotions is entirely up to you. As you have seen, some people let their feelings pour out in sentences and paragraphs, but you may choose to make an entry in the form of a list, a poem, or a dialogue. Upon being elected governor of New York, Mario Cuomo reflected on what this achievement meant to his immigrant mother. His diary entry for December 27, 1982, includes an imaginary dialogue between his mother, as she arrived years before in the United States, and an immigration officer.

Q. Where are you from?
A. Salerno.
Q. What do you do?
A. Nothing, I'm going to meet my husband in New Jersey.
Q. What does he do?
A. Nothing, he's looking for work.
Q. What kind of work?
A. Any kind.
Q. But what can he do?
A. Well, he has no skill, he never was educated.
Q. Well, does he have any friends?
A. No.
Q. Any money?
A. No.
Q. What about you?
A. No, we have nothing, no friends, no money, just a baby.
Q. Well, with no friends, no money, what do you expect of this country?
A. Only one thing before I die. I want to see my son the governor of New York State.

The newly elected governor admits in his diary that the officials would have thought his mother crazy and would have locked her up, had she really had this conversation. He then admits in his diary, "I feel something but I don't understand it yet, the way I am expected to. Maybe later in the week." Although the writer has experienced a feeling he does not fully understand, he has nevertheless recorded it.

EXERCISE 3 **Understanding Diary Entries.** The following two diary entries were written by Hannah Senesh, a teen-age girl from Hungary. Read the entries and then write out your answers to the three questions that follow the selections.

November 24, 1936

I have a pupil, from today, in arithmetic. I've already given her the first lesson. She's a nice little girl, and I'm so glad I finally have a pupil this year. I'm in such a great mood I actually sang on my way home from school. It's really not because I'm earning money that I'm so happy, but because my wish has been fulfilled.

April 15, 1937

For days I've been experiencing a general dissatisfaction with myself, and I don't know what's causing it. Because actually nothing unusual has happened to me. And I've certainly done nothing wrong. I can't understand myself. Possibly I'm just tired; I've been very busy. I'm doing all sorts of things, and I'm rather sorry I undertook so many school activities. The only thing I don't regret, even for a moment, is the coaching I do.

1. Explain what Hannah was feeling in each of these entries. Cite specific words and phrases to support your opinion.
2. Which idea might she have had trouble expressing aloud? Why?
3. What type of person does Hannah seem to be, based on these diary entries?

EXERCISE 4 **Writing an Imaginary Diary Entry.** Historical figures, entertainers, and sports heroes have always been in the public eye. Therefore, many of these people have found it necessary to wear public faces. But what is behind each public face? How do you think people living in the spotlight really feel? Pretend you are a famous person and write a diary entry as you imagine that person might write one. Remember to adapt your writing style to the personality of the person you have chosen.

EXERCISE 5 **Writing a Personal Diary Entry.** Think over the events of this day. Make a personal diary entry. You need not show it to anyone. If something special has happened, describe how you feel about it. If it has been a day of ordinary events, pick one, describe it, and explain how it made you feel. You may want to maintain your diary for the next few weeks, months, or years. It may even become a lifelong experience.

Characteristics of a Writer's Journal

When an incident that you would like to record occurs, try to enter it into your journal as soon as possible—while it is still fresh—be it a happy incident or a sad one, an earthshaking incident or a trivial one. In his journal entry dated November 1, 1949, Harry S Truman tells us what it was like to eat dinner alone as President of the United States.

> Had dinner by myself tonight. Worked in the Lee House office until dinner time. A butler came in very formally and said "Mr. President, dinner is served." I walk into the dining room in the Blair House. Barnett in tails and white tie pulls out my chair, pushes me up to the table. John in tails and white tie brings me a fruit cup. Barnett takes away the empty cup. John brings me a plate, Barnett brings me a tenderloin, John brings me asparagus, Barnett brings me carrots and beets. I have to eat alone and in silence in candle lit room. I ring—Barnett takes the plate and butter plates. John comes in with a napkin and silver crumb tray—there are no crumbs but John has to brush them off the table anyway. Barnett brings me a plate with a finger bowl and doily on it—I remove finger bowl and doily and John puts a glass saucer and a little bowl on the plate. Barnett brings me some chocolate custard. John brings me a demitasse (at home a little cup of coffee—about two good gulps) and my dinner is over. I take a hand bath in the finger bowl and go back to work.
>
> What a life!

Truman's journal entry is a narrative; it tells a brief story. Descriptions are also good material for journal entries. One particular kind of description that you can practice in your journal is the character sketch.

These two character sketches by twentieth-century writer Virginia Woolf are part of her journal entry of November 16, 1923:

> . . . Indeed, I've been talking to Hugh Walpole—not an impressive man—a man who protests too much; an uneasy, prosperous vain man, who harbors some grudge against clever intellectuals & yet respects them, would like to be one. He has the look of a kindly solicitor [lawyer] or banker; red cheeks; very small bright eyes; a genial, but not profound or cordial manner. . . . There was old Lady Horner, with her gray big eyes very far apart in a face creased & crumpled like some old faded glove—an interesting subtle face; a mind worn down by society, into that kind of simple ease which enhances even small talk. I mean what she said was so freely & easily said that it had a manner with it. Spacious gardens & money have gone to it. Poor unhappy old woman.

A writer's journal can be a ready source of clever expressions and striking comparisons. Copy into your journal interesting word pictures that others have used, and refer to them from time to time. Creative uses of language occur all around you: in conversations, books, magazines, newspapers, movies, radio, and television. Alternatively, you can create your own special expressions and phrases, and your writer's journal is the place to preserve them until you can use them.

When the nineteenth-century philosopher Henry Thoreau wanted to describe slow-falling snowflakes, he did not use expressions such as "slow as molasses" or "slow as a snail." Instead, in his journal entry of January 9, 1858, he wrote, "The more distant flakes appear to loiter in the air as if uncertain how they will approach the earth. . . ." With this original description, Thoreau stimulates the mind to see the falling snow in a new and memorable way.

Journal Writing as a Prewriting Technique

Prewriting is an essential first ingredient in most forms of writing. It involves searching your mind for ideas and putting those ideas on paper. Often the quality of your finished product depends on the time you devote to the prewriting process.

Freewriting and brainstorming are two forms of prewriting. Each of these techniques will be discussed in detail in following chapters. A writer's journal is a perfect place to carry out experiments with freewriting and brainstorming. Anaïs Nin engaged in freewriting when she made the following entry in her journal (spring 1961). She wrote a free association about what she saw:

> New York.
> Women look like flowerpots, hats of lilies, poppies, cherries. Windows full of orange and shocking-pink dresses. An explosion of color. Dogs running away from their master in the park. Central Park much better for Piccolo [my poodle]. The Village is full of Bowery bums, beggars, staring tourists.

In her journal entry of February 14, 1975, May Sarton focused on the color blue in a freewriting sort of way:

> . . . And the ocean now dark bright blue, sequined by the sun in a great swath to the south toward the islands.
>
> Why is blue *the* color? Does any other excite in the same way? Blue flowers—gentians in an Alpine meadow, delphinium in the summer garden, forget-me-nots, bachelor's buttons among the annuals—always seem the most fabulous, the most precious. And I'm afraid I have always been drawn to blue-eyed people! Lapis lazuli; the much paler marvelous blues used by Fra Angelico ("Fra Angelico blue," I have heard it called by my mother); the very blue shadows on snow, bluebirds.

Starting and Maintaining a Writer's Journal

1. *Be prepared.* Keep a pad or notebook and pen or pencil handy. You can never be sure when or where you will discover material for your journal. If you are unable to record an idea or event immediately, then do so as soon as possible. Otherwise, detail and accuracy will suffer.
2. *Write all the time.* Do not be concerned with "overstuffing" your journal. Write as much as possible. Use *all* of your senses to experience the world around you.
3. *Keep what you write.* Try not to judge what is worth saving. What seems unimportant today might be tomorrow's inspiration.
4. *Set aside time for journal writing.* Of course, any time is a good time for making a journal entry. However, it might be helpful to set aside a certain time each day or each week to record special events and feelings or just to note your random thoughts and ideas.

EXERCISE 6 **Writing a Journal Entry: An Incident.** Write a journal entry narrating an incident you have experienced or witnessed recently. Include as many specific details as possible. Explain how the incident made you feel.

EXERCISE 7 **Writing a Journal Entry: A Character Sketch.** Decide on a subject for an original character sketch. Select a relative, a friend, or someone you hardly know—for example, a person you have observed on a bus, in a crowded department store, or at a party. Your sketch should include a detailed physical description, as well as examples of the person's actions and choice of words. Use specific language to bring your character to life.

CHAPTER 1

Overview: The Writing Process

I learned long ago that you cannot tell how you will end by how you start.

—*John Steinbeck*

Writing. You may think of it as an enjoyable activity. *Writing!* You may consider it an irksome chore. *Writing?* You may not think much about it at all. Whatever your thoughts about it may be, the act of writing is a process. When you engage in the **writing process,** you gradually learn what ideas you have about people and things. You then select ideas you want to express. Finally you put the ideas you choose into words and communicate them clearly to others. Consciously or unconsciously, all writers (including you) become deeply involved in this discovery process, whether they are writing informally (a humorous account of an unusual vacation) or formally (a school report on Greek myths).

Consider John Steinbeck's words at the beginning of this chapter. As this well-known American writer points out, you will rarely have a completely clear idea of where you are heading when you begin to write. After you finally get a start, you may hit dead ends, change your direction, or tear everything up and begin again, as even an experienced writer like Steinbeck certainly did. However, as you write, if you keep the three essential steps of the writing process in mind, you will never get completely lost. These three steps are outlined here. Take a few minutes now to familiarize yourself with them.

prewriting—preparing to write by generating ideas and by choosing possible subjects

writing a first draft, or **discovery draft**—getting your ideas down on paper in rough form

revising (also called **postwriting**)—questioning, rethinking, and editing your first, or discovery, draft until it says what you want it to say and is ready to be "published" and shared with your readers.

As you can see, prewriting, writing a draft, and revising are shown in straight chronological order in the outline. As you write, however, you may find that you hop, skip, and jump between one step and another. In the revising step, for example, you may change only one word that was in the first draft, but as a result you may come upon a whole new idea to explore. At that point, you may decide to go back and do some further prewriting, or you may choose to expand or even completely rewrite the first draft. In short, a picture of the writing process would show a constant moving back and forth between the three essential steps. The following flow chart gives you such a picture.

THE WRITING PROCESS

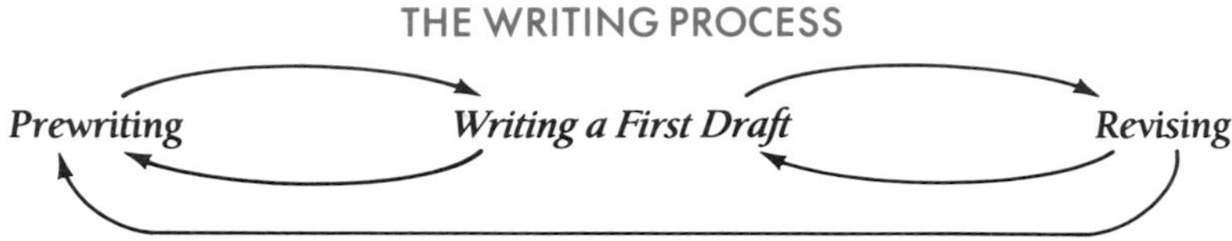

In studying the remaining pages of this chapter, you will observe one writer as she follows the three essential steps of the writing process on the way to writing a single paragraph. (Of course, the writing process can be used to create longer pieces of writing too.) Observing this writer will give you an overview of the three steps. In the next three chapters, you will examine each of the steps in greater detail and follow each of them yourself.

Prewriting

In the **prewriting** step of the writing process, you begin digging for the basic raw materials you need. You first look into your mind for subjects for writing. Once you unearth a promising subject, you gather, explore, and focus your ideas about it, keeping notes as you go along. You also consider your **audience**—the particular reader or readers you are writing for—and your **purpose**—the goal you hope to reach through your writing. Your general purpose may be to inform, to entertain, or to persuade your reader-audience. However, you may also decide on a more specific purpose: to share an experience, to express a strong feeling, to make your readers laugh or cry, or to do any of the countless other things people do when they communicate.

Prewriting will enrich your final product with specific, interesting facts and observations. On the other hand, if you skip the prewriting step, your final product is likely to be thin, repetitious, and directionless. For example, look at the following paragraph. The writer did no prewriting.

> [1]I have been interested in wild creatures since my first visit to a zoo at the age of five. [2]Many species of wildlife are now extinct and other species are on the verge of extinction. [3]I think zoos are unnatural places,

but a zoo is where I first became interested in wildlife. [4]Among the animals I like best are the ones that live in Africa. [5]Some species of wildlife there and in other parts of the world are extinct or nearly extinct. [6]I have found wildlife interesting most of my life, so I can't understand this. [7]Whenever I can, I read about wildlife. [8]I pick up any book I can find about animals, birds, reptiles, and insects and read it from cover to cover. [9]I wish I lived in a place where I could see wild creatures every day. [10]I find them extremely fascinating.

EXERCISE 1 **Thinking About Prewriting.** Reread the preceding paragraph. Then write sentences to answer the following questions.

1. The first sentence of a paragraph often gives you information that you can expect to find in the other sentences. After reading the first sentence of this paragraph, what types of information did you look for? Did you find that type of information?
2. What unrelated pieces of information about wildlife are mentioned in this paragraph?
3. Sentences 2 and 5 say about the same thing: Many species of wildlife are extinct or nearly extinct. Find two other places in which information given in one sentence is repeated in yet another sentence.

The writer about wildlife could have written a paragraph that included facts, experiences, and insights to inform and interest her readers. Because she did not go through the prewriting step of the writing process, she could not include such material. After she wrote her unsuccessful paragraph, she was asked to put it aside and start again with the important prewriting step. She noted the different topics, questions, and comments that occurred to her when she thought about wildlife. Here are some of the prewriting notes that the writer eventually prepared.

FIRST SET OF PREWRITING NOTES

wildlife of Africa
species in danger of extinction
how I got interested in wildlife
what careers are open to wildlife lovers?
wildlife in my city
my meeting with a bear (funny now, not then)
new plans for saving endangered wildlife?
my association of wildlife with faraway places
wildlife reserves
unusual wildlife in Australia

The writer then started thinking more carefully about the writing topics that the notes suggested to her. Her thinking resulted in the following new set of notes. Notice that she dropped some of her original notes because they were unsuitable for one reason or another. She also indicated which notes suggested topics that might interest particular audiences, and she gave some thought to possible purposes.

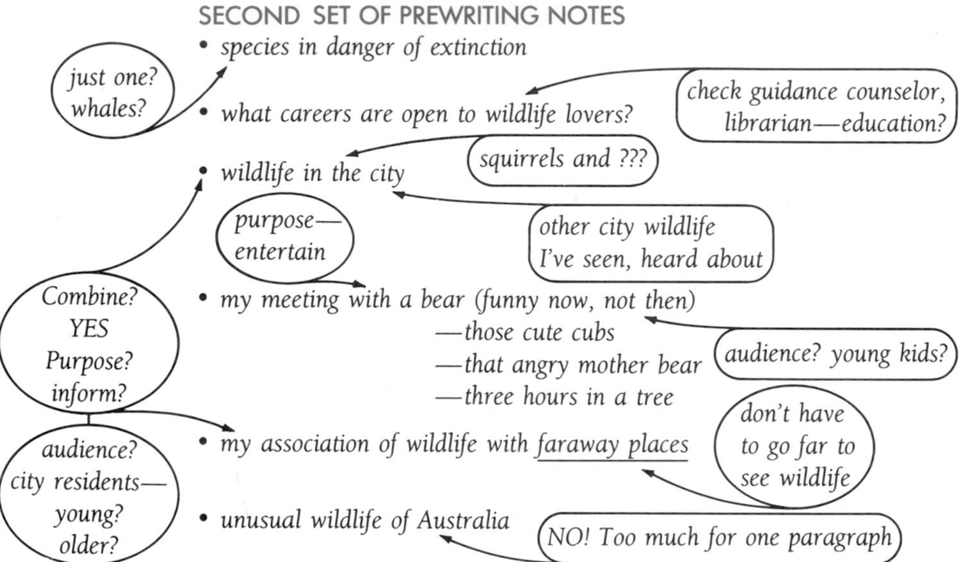

When she finished working over her second set of prewriting notes, the writer decided on one topic to develop in a new paragraph. Before she began writing the new paragraph, she also had to make a fairly definite decision about the audience and purpose of her paragraph. If you remember John Steinbeck's words at the beginning of this chapter, you will know that a writer can always change these decisions later.

EXERCISE 2 **Thinking About Prewriting.** Look again at the writer's two sets of prewriting notes. Then write responses to the following:

1. List the notes in the first set that seem to be based on the writer's personal experiences.
2. Point out one note in the first set that could be developed into a humorous paragraph.
3. Find one note in the first set that might be of special interest to wildlife specialists.
4. Imagine that the writer is a friend who has come to you for an opinion. From the second set of notes, pick out two notes that suggest promising writing ideas, and explain why you think so.

Writing a First Draft

Preparing a **first draft** is the second step in the writing process. The draft is your initial try at communicating in a series of related sentences the topic you chose in the prewriting step. The name **discovery draft** is a good one, for in this draft you begin to discover your ideas.

Some writers produce their first drafts quickly without stopping at all once they begin. Others take a longer time. They experiment with their drafts, changing words and sentences frequently.

Right now, however, let's rejoin the writer you have been following through this chapter. Remember, the writer has completed prewriting (the first step). She has written notes and, as you will see, has chosen a topic for her paragraph. In choosing her topic, she kept her intended audience and purpose in mind. Only then did she write the following draft, making changes along the way.

FIRST DRAFT

fascinated by since ~~a child~~ childhood.
~~Ever since I~~ I have been ~~very interested in~~ wildlife ~~for a long time now~~.
creatures distant A
Wild ~~animals~~ always remind me of the lands where they live. ~~and~~ ~~as~~ I
are creatures my own
grew older, I began to realize that there ~~were~~ wild ~~animals~~ in ~~the~~ city.
frisky less lovable
~~where I live~~. There are squirrels and ~~other~~ rodents such as rats and
There are (spelling?)
mice. ~~Also~~ birds such as pijuns, sparrows, and robins. Insects and snakes
more and more rural creatures (raccoons?)
~~lives~~ live in the city too. Lately, ~~even animals~~ like skunks and racoons are seen in the city.

EXERCISE 3 **Thinking About the First Draft.** Reread the draft of the preceding paragraph. Then write answers to the following questions.

1. Which notes in the second prewriting list did the writer use?
2. Point out one change in wording that the writer made as she wrote, and explain the effect of this change.
3. What do you think was the writer's purpose in writing this draft? Who do you think her audience was?

Revising

Revising, the third step in the writing process, involves two kinds of editing, preparing a final copy, and proofreading.

In one kind of editing, you make small-scale changes in your draft, reworking sentence structure and wording if necessary. In the other kind of editing, you may find that you have to make one or more large-scale changes. For example, you may decide that your first draft does not clearly make your main point. If so, you may decide to add, change, rearrange, even drop a sentence or several sentences. Occasionally, you may decide to rewrite the draft completely.

The next stage in revising is making your final copy. This copy will include all the changes you made in the two editing stages. Last, you should proofread your final copy for any mistakes in grammar, usage, capitalization, punctuation, and spelling.

On reading over the draft, the writer of the paragraph on wildlife discovered that she needed to make large-scale changes in order to emphasize an important point she made about wildlife.

FINAL VERSION

[1]It took me a long time to discover that wildlife thrive in cities, even in my own back yard. [2]I have been fascinated by wildlife since my first visit to a zoo when I was five. [3]Within a few years, I started to connect wild creatures with faraway places, and I yearned to go on safari in these places. [4]Then one day I saw a squirrel on the fire escape outside our apartment, and the realization hit me: Cities have wild creatures too! [5]After that, I began to go on "safaris" to find the wildlife in my own city. [6]Of course there were squirrels and other, less lovable rodents such as rats and mice. [7]The birds of the city were truly a joy to watch—pigeons, sparrows, robins, bluejays, sea gulls, and an occasional cardinal or oriole. [8]Houseflies, mosquitoes, butterflies, snakes, frogs, and toads are only a few of the insects and reptiles I found on my safaris. [9]More and more often I have come across skunks and raccoons too. [10]With all these exciting wild creatures so close to my home, I do not have much time to think about wildlife in faraway places anymore.

EXERCISE 4 **Thinking About Revision.** Compare the final copy with the first draft, and answer these questions.

1. What, specifically, has the writer done to emphasize her new realization about wildlife?
2. Find three small-scale changes in the final copy. Why do you think the writer made these changes?

Writer's Choice

You have followed one writer through the three essential steps of the writing process. Now it is your turn. Apply the writing process to one of the following assignments.

Writer's Choice #1

ASSIGNMENT To write a paragraph about a single daisy

LENGTH Five to ten sentences

AUDIENCE Young children who have been blind since birth and have never seen a daisy

PURPOSE To help the blind children "see" the daisy

PREWRITING Think about and jot down the parts and colors of a daisy. Then jot down ideas that would help you see a daisy.

WRITING Start your first draft by telling what you intend to do and then do it (write about a daisy).

REVISING Edit your draft, making any needed small-scale and large-scale changes in your final copy.

Writer's Choice #2

ASSIGNMENT To write a paragraph about a quality you look for in your friends

LENGTH Your choice

AUDIENCE Your choice

PURPOSE To identify a quality you think a friend should have and to explain why you think it is an important quality

PREWRITING List several qualities and select one to develop. Note your reasons for considering this quality desirable.

WRITING Name the quality in the first sentence of your draft. In the remaining sentences explain why you think a friend should have this quality.

REVISING Proofread and edit your draft. Ask yourself if the reasons you give really explain why the quality is desirable in a friend. Then write the final copy of your paragraph.

Writer's Choice #3

ASSIGNMENT To write a paragraph about a subject you choose

LENGTH Your choice

AUDIENCE Your choice

PURPOSE Your choice

OPTIONS You may want to look at the photographs in the Writer's Sourcebook on pages 354–357 for ideas.

CHAPTER 2

Prewriting

To write well it is first necessary to have something to say.

—Stephen Leacock

Prewriting • ***Writing*** • ***Revising***

American humorist James Thurber used to say that the hardest job he had as a writer was to convince his wife that he was working when he was staring out the window thinking. Thurber and Canadian humorist Stephen Leacock (quoted above) both knew that no one, not even the most talented writer, can simply sit down and start writing. While Leacock searched for "something to say" and Thurber stared out the window, each was involved in the first stage of the writing process—prewriting.

Prewriting is the part of the writing process that helps you discover a promising subject and then prepares you to write about the subject you have discovered.

In prewriting you experiment with all kinds of ideas. Logic, neatness, and accuracy do not concern you. Your only concern is to find a subject that you really want to write about. You let your ideas form a stream that gives life to your imagination.

As your ideas and imagination interact, writing subjects will begin to occur to you. It is important that you jot down ideas about these subjects as they occur. No matter what subject you finally choose, you will always have much to write about if you fill your prewriting notes with related facts, comments, questions, and opinions. Even if you do not use all of your notes, every one of them will bring color, depth, and breadth to your writing.

If you keep at these prewriting activities, you will eventually arrive at a focused writing topic and details that support the topic. You will, in Stephen Leacock's words, have "something to say." In addition, prewriting will stir excitement in you, an excitement that will show itself in your writing and will allow your writing to capture the attention of your readers.

In this chapter you will have the chance to examine the prewriting step of the writing process in some detail. You will follow three writers as they think their way through the following prewriting activities and prepare to write paragraphs. These same activities can also be used to help you prepare to write longer works—essays, research papers, and stories, for example. Familiarize yourself with these activities.

generating ideas
exploring subjects
focusing on a topic
forming a main idea
developing the main idea

Prewriting
GENERATING IDEAS
EXPLORING SUBJECTS
FOCUSING ON A TOPIC
FORMING A MAIN IDEA
DEVELOPING THE MAIN IDEA

Generating Ideas

Always write about something that is so interesting to you that you want to get started right away. Never settle for anything less than a topic that fully involves you. Writing topics can come from many sources—from your childhood memories and present experiences, from what you see in the movies and hear in conversations with others.

You can spark your imagination to generate writing ideas by applying any of these three techniques: **freewriting**, **brainstorming**, and **charting.** In the next few pages you will examine and experiment with each of these techniques to learn which work best for you. (Perhaps you will decide to invent your own methods for getting started.) As you experiment, be aware that you can apply each of the three techniques in at least two ways:

You can work alone, recording your ideas and feelings in a private journal or notebook.

You can exchange ideas with one or more classmates in a small group.

Freewriting

Freewriting is writing done continuously for a specified, but very brief, period of time.

When you freewrite, you give yourself a time limit. You begin to write about a subject at a signal and do not lift your pen from the paper until the time is up. Freewriting limbers up your writing and gets it flowing, just as jogging limbers up your muscles and gets your blood flowing. You let your mind and imagination jog for a few minutes, recording your ideas as they come to you, without concern for logic, grammar, or grace.

If your freewriting does not seem very free at first, do not worry. You will come up with some ideas before very long. Look at the following example of freewriting. It contains errors, and it wanders all over the place, but notice how many ideas and associations pop up in it.

FREEWRITING SAMPLE: A WRITER LOOKING FOR A SUBJECT (IDEAS SHADED)

Write on any subject you choose. Oh, sure! Whenever a teacher says that, every idea in my head vanishes. Let's see. Subject subject whose got the subject, not me. Not me and I could be sitting here for five years. But I got only 5 minutes. Can't waste time. Hold it. Waste. That's what the TV program the other night was about. Wasting resources like water and trees and so on. Really about saving resources for people of the future. Use but don't abuse resources. That's what the guy on the program said. The part about how forests, trees, could be all gone some day. Scary. Not a bad idea for a subject. Conserving natural resources. Important. Might as well give it a try.

This writer discovered something valuable about freewriting, and you will too: When you have been asked to think of a writing subject and you have no ideas, freewriting will get those wheels in your mind turning.

Freewriting is also valuable for discovering approaches to more definite writing assignments and for helping you find your way out of dead ends in the writing process. For example, a student assigned a paragraph about her career goals discovered several ideas about this subject in just a few minutes of freewriting. As you will see, the freewriting contains some errors, but—more important—it suggests some promising writing ideas.

FREEWRITING SAMPLE: A WRITER WITH A GENERAL SUBJECT

What do I want to be if the neighbors let me grow up? Be serious. The assigned writing subject is the career I'm aiming for. It would have to be a job that benefits people. A teacher? Always at the back of my mind Mrs. Curren, third grade, Mr. Leonard, sixth grade. Teach handicapped children? Challenging. What education, special training? Have I got what it takes? What do I know about it anyhow? Teachers, students I talk to at school for blind down the street from my house. The times I sat in on Miss Freneau's classes. What a teacher! Kids loved her. Could I teach blind children? What would my motives be? Think some more about it.

EXERCISE 1 **Generating Ideas in Freewriting.** Take another look at the sample of freewriting by the writer interested in identifying her career goals. On your paper identify one possible writing idea.

EXERCISE 2 **Freewriting in Pairs.** Work with another writer to freewrite on a subject that interests both of you. Agree on a time limit—say, five minutes. Then begin writing and do not stop until the time is up. After both of you have finished, read one another's freewriting, and list all the possible writing ideas that you find. (Even a scrap of an idea counts as long as you can justify it as a starting point for a paragraph.) Compare the ideas you developed from prewriting with the ideas that your partner developed. Save your notes for a composition that you will write later.

Brainstorming

Like freewriting, **brainstorming** can help you generate ideas through free association.

Brainstorming is different from freewriting. When you brainstorm, you do not write an uninterrupted stream of words. Instead, you jot down your thoughts in any order, pausing whenever you like and writing disconnected phrases if you choose. Different people feel comfortable with different brainstorming formats. Some writers like to make orderly lists like the following one. This list was created by the writer who did the freewriting on the general subject of career goals. She started with one of her original ideas and then listed a few more.

BRAINSTORMING SAMPLE: LIST FORMAT

1. *Teaching the blind—would benefit kids, but me even more? What are my motives? Right ones?*
2. *Annie Sullivan, Helen Keller's teacher—*The Miracle Worker *(play about Sullivan and Keller). Do I have her persistence?*
3. *Teachers of the blind I know—Miss Freneau.*
4. *Books by blind people (Tom Sullivan?)—what do they say about their teachers?*
5. *Qualifications needed?—check guidance counselor, librarian*
6. *Talk to kids at school for blind—what qualifications do they think their teachers need?*

Other writers prefer to brainstorm by using a more open format known as **clustering.** Look below at a sample of the clustering format created by the writer who did the freewriting on conserving resources. Notice that he wrote ideas and circled them. Then he drew lines between circles to show how the ideas could be connected.

BRAINSTORMING SAMPLE: CLUSTERING

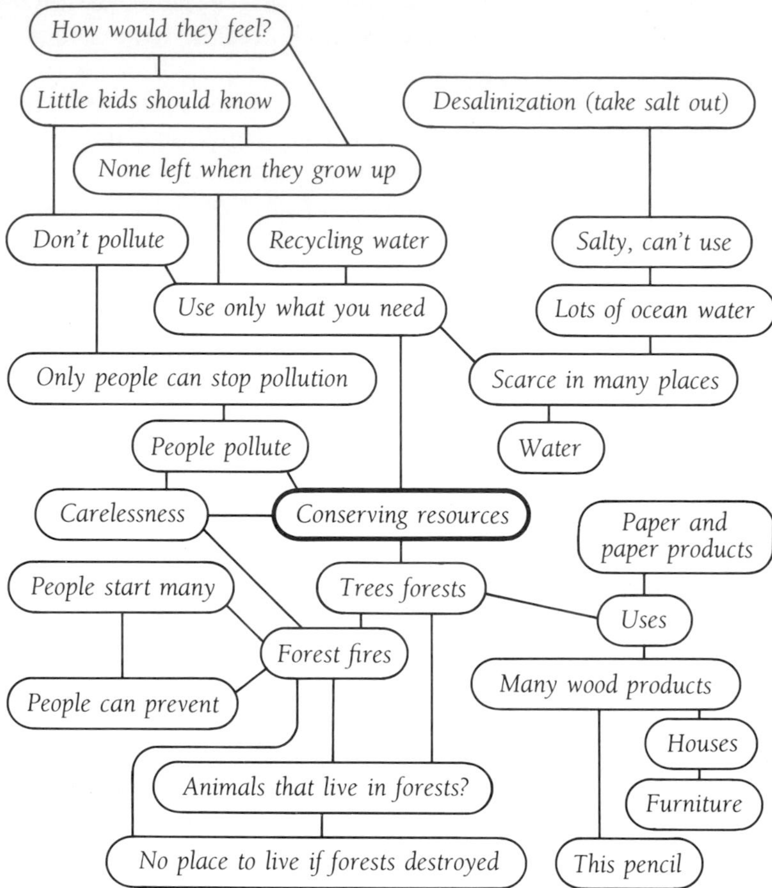

You have several options for using freewriting and brainstorming. You may choose to try freewriting first and follow it with brainstorming, or you may discover that brainstorming produces better results for you than freewriting. You may find freewriting effective for one writing task and brainstorming effective for another. You may even decide to brainstorm first and then freewrite on an idea that comes to you while brainstorming. Experiment with all these options. Then use what works best for you.

EXERCISE 3 **Brainstorming from a Photograph.** Carefully observe and study the photograph at the bottom of page 25. Take ten minutes to brainstorm about it. Use either the list or the clustering format to note all your writing ideas about the photograph. Be sure to indicate connections between these ideas. Save your notes for a composition.

EXERCISE 4 **Generating Ideas by Brainstorming.** Choose one of the items in the following list, or use an idea that you came up with while you were freewriting in Exercise 2. Spend ten minutes brainstorming about your idea, noting comments, issues, or questions that occur to you. Save your brainstorming notes for a composition.

1. winning and losing
2. imagination
3. a high school diploma
4. my favorite poem
5. my favorite holiday
6. election campaigns
7. a job I'd like to have
8. exercise fads
9. pro vs. amateur sports
10. writing
11. computers and me
12. TV commercials
13. taking a stand on . . .
14. the elderly
15. the future
16. conserving resources

Charting

Charting helps you focus on specific life experiences in order to generate writing ideas.

If you are asked to write on a subject of your choice, you may turn to your own life experiences for ideas. You can make a chart like the following one to help you sort through your experiences. The first column lists general areas of personal experience that might suggest writing ideas to any writer. In the second column the writer who completed the chart recorded specific examples of these general experiences from her own life. Then in the third column she noted writing ideas suggested by these examples.

SAMPLE CHART FOR GENERATING WRITING IDEAS

AREA OF EXPERIENCE	SPECIFIC EXAMPLE	WRITING IDEA
Childhood Memories	• *Fourth of July*	• *history of fireworks* • *early celebrations of July 4*
Family	• *being the "baby"* • *my great-grandfather*	• *is it harder to be the oldest?* • *his boyhood in Mexico*
Hobbies, Interests	• *figure skating* • *collecting stamps*	• *is it a sport or an art?* • *what it takes to be great* • *the most valuable U.S. stamps*
Pet Peeves	• *loud radios in public places* • *waiting in checkout lines at the supermarket*	• *what I'd like to do about people with loud radios* • *speeding up checkout lines*
Friends	• *the time Joe helped me out*	• *the value of friendship*
Current Events	• *weapons in outer space* • *space station*	• *should space weapons be banned?* • *the future of space exploration*
Interesting (funny, infuriating) Experiences	• *learning to ride a unicycle*	• *funny sketch?*
Assigned Reading, Classwork	• *biography of Amelia Earhart* • *taking tests*	• *her mysterious disappearance* • *are tests really necessary?*
Leisure Reading, Newspapers, Magazines	• *Art Buchwald's columns* • *magazine article on astronaut Sally Ride*	• *a career as a columnist* • *comparison of Earhart and Ride?*
Television, Radio, Films, Records, Tapes	• *TV commercials* • *old radio programs*	• *how many commercials should be allowed during 1 show?* • *weekly radio adventure serials*

EXERCISE 5 **Generating Ideas by Charting.** Create your own experience chart, using the previous one as a model. Copy the areas of experience from the first column of the model. (If you wish, replace some or all of these areas with other areas you create.) In the second column of your chart, write specific examples of your own. In the third column note writing ideas suggested by your examples. Save your completed charts for a composition.

EXERCISE 6 **Compiling Your Writing Ideas.** Review the prewriting notes and writing ideas that you generated in Exercises 2–5 as you practiced freewriting, brainstorming, and charting. Evaluate your writing ideas, and star five that you think you want to write about.

Prewriting

GENERATING IDEAS

EXPLORING SUBJECTS

FOCUSING ON A TOPIC

FORMING A MAIN IDEA

DEVELOPING THE MAIN IDEA

Exploring Subjects

You have come up with a number of possible writing ideas, some exciting, some not so exciting. You still may not know, however, exactly what you want to say about these writing ideas, or subjects. You can find out by exploring the most promising subject.

One of the best ways to explore a subject is to ask and answer specific questions about it. On the following pages, you will get an idea of two different types of questions you can use. At times you may want to ask questions of each type about your subject. However you decide to use these questions, be sure to adapt them to your subject.

Using Informational Questions

News reporters answer informational questions in lead paragraphs of news stories. An informational question begins with one of these words: *Who? What? Where? When? Why?* or *How?* (A good way to remember these questions is to remember the first letters of the words that begin them—five *Ws* and *H*.)

The informational questions that follow were created by the writer who made the experience chart shown earlier. As you examine her questions, notice that she has used them to explore one of the writing subjects she included in her experience chart.

INFORMATIONAL QUESTIONS TO EXPLORE A SUBJECT	SAMPLE ANSWERS
1. Who or what is my subject? What sort of person is my subject?	*Amelia Earhart—pioneer woman pilot; attractive woman, independent, courageous, dares to try new things, find new paths.*
2. What happened regarding my subject? What memorable incident(s) can I relate about my subject?	*First gained fame as first woman to fly Atlantic as passenger and later as pilot of solo flight; these daring flights made her familiar to newspaper readers around world. The disappearance of her plane on a round-the-world flight in 1937 remains a mystery.*
3. When did these events occur? In what ways did my subject change over time?	*First flight in 1928; soloed Atlantic in 1932; many other flights in 1930s; flight around world began in May of 1937, ended when her plane vanished in July 1937. Earhart grew increasingly determined to find out limits of airplanes and of herself.*
4. Where did all this happen?	*Cross-country flights in United States; ocean flights over Atlantic; attempted round-the-world flight began in Miami, ended near Howland Island in the mid-Pacific.*
5. How did it happen?	*Interest in airplanes and flying was high among people in late 1920s and 1930s; Earhart's own interest in flying became a fascination, leading her to try to reach ever more difficult goals.*
6. Why did it happen?	*Probably as much because of her personality and character; she was always looking for new challenges.*
7. To whom (what) can I compare my subject?	• *Pioneers of the early West in the United States* • *Another pioneer—Sally Ride, American astronaut (find out more about her).*

EXERCISE 7 **Exploring a Subject with Informational Questions.** Choose one subject that you starred in Exercise 6. Adapt the informational questions in the preceding chart to fit your subject. Then answer these questions. Save your notes for a composition.

Using Personal Questions

Personal questions are a second type you can use to explore a writing subject. You should use this type of question only if you have had direct personal experience with your subject. The writer working with the subject of teaching blind children used personal questions to explore her subject. Study her questions and answers.

PERSONAL QUESTIONS TO EXPLORE A SUBJECT	SAMPLE ANSWERS
1. What are my own experiences of the subject?	*Limited: talked with students at school for blind near my house—teachers too; sat in on some of Miss Freneau's classes there, saw the play about Annie Sullivan and Helen Keller.*
2. What sensations (sight, sound, smell, taste, and touch) do I associate with the subject?	*Visits to the school for blind made me appreciate my eyesight; made me aware of how important other senses are to blind people and how they develop these senses.*
3. What were my emotions during these experiences?	*I felt uncomfortable at first, then I felt admiration; Miss Freneau's classes made me feel excited about what a good teacher can do.*
4. What did I learn?	*That I was definitely interested in teaching blind children (Miss Freneau's class); that blind people accept their blindness as part of themselves and want sighted people to know this—they don't want pity.*
5. What problems did I have?	*I was uncomfortable with blind kids, afraid to say the word* blind*; had to learn to look at blind kids as people and to overcome picturing myself as a hero.*

EXERCISE 8 **Exploring a Subject Through Personal Questions.** Choose a subject, either one you starred in Exercise 6 or one from the following list. On a separate sheet of paper, explore the subject through personal questions. Save your notes for a composition.

1. a memorable day from a recent vacation
2. an incident that taught you something
3. a possession that means a great deal to you
4. an activity that you really enjoy
5. something about which you are knowledgeable
6. a challenge that you met
7. a person whom you really admire
8. a place that you like to visit
9. an experience that changed you
10. a truly remarkable character from a book or movie

Prewriting

GENERATING IDEAS
EXPLORING SUBJECTS
FOCUSING ON A TOPIC
FORMING A MAIN IDEA
DEVELOPING THE MAIN IDEA

Focusing on a Topic

In this chapter you generated writing ideas through various freewriting, brainstorming, and charting techniques. By using these techniques you found promising subjects. You explored the most promising subjects by asking and answering a number of informational and personal questions. Your goal was to find approaches to a broad subject.

Now you are ready to narrow your broad subject into a topic that you can cover in a single paragraph. As you begin to narrow your subject, remember that a "wide-angle shot" of the subject is not what you are after, since this will not show readers the kinds of details you want them to see. What you need is a "close-up" of the subject.

Consider how one writer chose a topic and narrowed it. Her original subject was Amelia Earhart. On reviewing answers to her informational questions, this writer decided that she wanted to compare Amelia Earhart and American astronaut Sally Ride. She had moved from a broad subject to a narrower topic, but this topic needed to be still narrower. Then one important similarity between the two women struck her: Each did a job that men ordinarily do, and each did it extremely well.

Here are two other examples that move from broad to narrow topics that could be covered in one paragraph.

TECHNIQUE	Identify specific procedures
BROAD SUBJECT	Conservation of natural resources
NARROWER TOPIC	Conserving forest resources
STILL NARROWER	How individuals can help conserve forests

TECHNIQUE	Use one incident to illustrate an idea
BROAD SUBJECT	Career goal—teaching
NARROWER TOPIC	Teaching handicapped children
STILL NARROWER	Teaching blind children

EXERCISE 9 **Narrowing Topics.** Number a paper from 1 through 4. Then write the narrowest topic in each group beside each number.

1. a. Lincoln's speech at Gettysburg
   b. The two administrations of Abraham Lincoln
   c. The political career of Abraham Lincoln
2. a. Egyptian sculptures
   b. The art of ancient Egypt
   c. The Great Sphinx at Giza, Egypt
3. a. The television broadcasting industry
   b. Fifty years with TV
   c. The first television program
4. a. Five steps to a healthy heart
   b. Fighting the "killer" diseases
   c. Diseases of the heart and lungs

EXERCISE 10 **Focusing on Your Topic.** Choose one of the broad subjects you explored in Exercises 7–8. Narrow it into a topic you can cover in a paragraph. Save your written response for a composition.

Prewriting

GENERATING IDEAS
EXPLORING SUBJECTS
FOCUSING ON A TOPIC
FORMING A MAIN IDEA
DEVELOPING THE MAIN IDEA

Forming a Main Idea

Take a minute to review your progress. You generated and explored several ideas to find a writing topic. Then you narrowed the scope of your topic so that you can cover it in a paragraph. Your next task is to form a **main idea** about your topic. You and your paragraph will both have more direction if you state that main idea in a complete sentence. Before you can state your main idea, however, you must consider your **purpose**—the goal you hope to accomplish in writing—and your **audience**—the person or persons who will read what you write.

Thinking About Purpose

While you were generating, exploring, and narrowing ideas, you were making decisions. The basis for each decision was a vague purpose at the back of your mind. It is time now to make that purpose clearer. You can do so by asking yourself the following questions.

1. Why do I want to write about this topic?
2. Is my purpose to **inform** readers of something or **explain** something to them?
3. Is my purpose to **persuade** them to change their thoughts and feelings about something or to take some action?
4. Is my purpose to **amuse** or **entertain** them?
5. Is my purpose to **narrate** a story of some kind?
6. Is my purpose to **describe** something or someone?
7. Do I have some other, more specific purpose in mind? For example, do I want to describe a movie in order to persuade my readers to see it?

The writer developing the topic of forest conservation chose the purpose shown in this chart.

BROAD SUBJECT	NARROWED TOPIC	POSSIBLE PURPOSE
conservation of natural resources	*how individuals can help conserve forests*	*to inform readers of ways thay can help conserve forests*

EXERCISE 11 **Thinking About Purpose.** Write one possible purpose for each of the following topics.

1. student council elections
2. raising mushrooms in a cellar
3. the day an elephant came into our back yard
4. the natural beauty of Colorado
5. progress made by the class picnic committee

Becoming Aware of an Audience

Whenever you write, you address a particular reader or group of readers—your audience. In school and later in life you will write for many audiences: classmates, teachers, readers of the school magazine or newspaper, family members, friends, people you work with, companies you do business with, government officials. No matter what your topic is, you will adapt what you say about it to your audience. For example, if you work for a large company, you would describe a business project one way to your boss and in another way in a letter to a friend.

The most skillful writers have learned to become sensitive to their audiences. An important part of their skill is their ability to sense how their readers will react to their writing. You can learn this important skill by asking yourself questions like the following. Your answers to such questions will help you remain aware of the kinds of people in your audience, the information they need to know about your topic, and the details that will capture and hold their interest. Notice the answers of the writer with the topic of teaching blind children.

QUESTIONS ABOUT AUDIENCE	SAMPLE ANSWERS
1. Am I writing for a general audience or a special audience (such as a group of experts or schoolchildren)?	*A general audience—members of my English class. (Maybe I could also read my paragraph to the kids at the school for the blind, to get their reactions.)*
2. What do I want to say to this particular audience?	*Why I want to teach blind children.*
3. How much does this audience know about my subject? What other information shall I give them?	*Probably not too much. Also, may have some uncomfortable feelings about working with the blind—I did at first.*
4. What details about my topic will interest this audience most?	*How blind people feel about being sightless; how they want sighted people to treat them.*
5. What preconceptions and objections might this audience have regarding my topic? How can I counter these?	*The idea that blind people have to be treated in a special way. I can counter by describing Miss Freneau's attitude.*
6. What techniques will help me accomplish my purpose?	*Humor not appropriate; give the facts.*

EXERCISE 12 **Thinking About Audience.** Write a sentence that identifies one appropriate audience for each topic below.

1. Willy, the friendly word processor
2. shortcuts for inputting text on a word processor
3. helpful books on how to choose your word processor
4. how a word processor can boost your grades
5. increased-capacity microchips for word processors

Stating the Main Idea

Once you have chosen and narrowed a topic for your paragraph, decided on your purpose, and considered your audience, you are ready to formulate the **main idea**—the one thought that you plan to develop in your paragraph. Your paragraph will be easier to write if you state your main idea in a sentence. This sentence may state a fact; it may express your opinion; it may present an overall impression of a scene; or it may summarize your reaction to an experience.

Before you can write such a sentence, however, you must first decide what the main idea of your paragraph will be. Here are some tips that may help you decide.

1. Your main idea should make *one* point about your topic.
2. You should be able to develop your main idea adequately in *one* paragraph.
3. Your main idea should "reach out and grab" you and make your audience eager to read your paragraph.
4. Your purpose should be clear from your main idea.

In this chapter you have been following the prewriting progress of three writers. Take a look now at the main ideas they formulated for their paragraphs.

ORIGINAL TOPIC	Conservation of natural resources
NARROWED TOPIC	How individuals can help conserve forests
PURPOSE	To inform
AUDIENCE	Young children
MAIN IDEA	If you want to help save the trees in our forests, here are some things that you can do.

ORIGINAL TOPIC	Why I want to teach the blind
NARROWED TOPIC	Sitting in on Miss Freneau's class
PURPOSE	To explain
AUDIENCE	Teacher and other students
MAIN IDEA	Miss Emma Freneau was the one who convinced me by her example that I should teach blind children.

ORIGINAL TOPIC How Amelia Earhart and Sally Ride are similar
NARROWED TOPIC Earhart and Ride—pioneers on the frontier of ideas
PURPOSE To inform
AUDIENCE General public
MAIN IDEA Both Amelia Earhart and Sally Ride have helped people to realize that women can perform as well as men in jobs that were thought of as "men's work."

EXERCISE 13 **Reflecting Purpose and Audience in a Main Idea.** For each general topic, select one purpose and one audience from the two choices given. Then write a sentence that expresses one main idea about the topic. Be sure that your main idea reflects your purpose and audience. In the example here, the underlined words represent the purpose and audience chosen by one writer and are reflected in the main idea.

GENERAL TOPIC The World Series
PURPOSE To inform *or* to narrate
AUDIENCE American baseball fans *or* friends who live abroad.
MAIN IDEA The World Series is an annual competition between the two best baseball teams in America.

1. GENERAL TOPIC Modern popular music
PURPOSE To persuade *or* to describe
AUDIENCE Parents and other adults *or* friends

2. GENERAL TOPIC The perils of camping out
PURPOSE To explain *or* to entertain
AUDIENCE General public *or* experienced campers

3. GENERAL TOPIC The solar system
PURPOSE To describe *or* to inform
AUDIENCE Astronomers *or* third-graders

EXERCISE 14 **Forming Your Main Idea.** Look at the topic you narrowed in Exercise 10. List two possible purposes and two possible audiences for the topic. Then write a main idea that you might develop in a paragraph for each purpose and audience.

Prewriting

GENERATING IDEAS
EXPLORING SUBJECTS
FOCUSING ON A TOPIC
FORMING A MAIN IDEA
DEVELOPING THE MAIN IDEA

Developing the Main Idea

When you write a paragraph of your own, it will include more than a statement of your main idea. It will also include *facts, details, examples, incidents,* and *reasons*. You will include items of this type to *develop*—express, prove, clarify, or expand upon—your main idea.

In looking over your prewriting notes, you may discover that they already contain some facts, details, examples, incidents, and reasons. If so, you can simply choose the items that relate to, or support, the main idea of your paragraph. If not, you may have to think of other items that will support the main idea. Sometimes this will mean consulting reference books to locate helpful details, for example. You should also consult reference books to check the accuracy of facts you use to support your main idea.

Specific supporting items will make your main idea convincing and will give your paragraph the individual flavor that only you can provide. In searching for such supporting items among your prewriting notes, you should watch in particular for the following:

facts—objective statements that can be proven by experience, observation, or study

sensory details—concrete, specific features that can be perceived by the five senses

examples—particular cases or instances of something

incidents—particular events

reasons—logical arguments used to support an opinion

Look over the items that one writer chose to support her main idea. She has listed mostly facts, but she has also included relevant reasons and incidents.

MAIN IDEA Both Amelia Earhart and Sally Ride have shown that women can perform as well as men in jobs that are ordinarily thought of as "men's work."

SUPPORTING ITEMS Earhart's daring exploits as an aviator thrilled the people of the world in the late 1920s and in the 1930s. [INCIDENT]

She was among the pioneers of flight through Earth's atmosphere. [INCIDENT]

Accomplishments: Several solo flights across the U.S.; a solo flight across the Atlantic; an attempt to fly around the world which ended in the disappearance of her plane and her presumed death. [FACTS]

Sally Ride, an American astronaut, captured the interest of the world in the early 1980s. [INCIDENT]

She helped push the frontier of flight into space. [FACTS]

Accomplishments: She became one of the first woman astronauts in 1978; she was the first American woman to travel in space in June 1983 as a crew member on board the space shuttle *Challenger*. [FACTS]

Both women were truly pioneers because they helped to push the frontier of flight farther and farther away from Earth. [REASON]

Both women can justly be called pioneers on the frontiers of ideas and attitudes; they helped people to realize that women can perform as well as men in jobs that were ordinarily thought of in our society as "men's work." [REASON]

EXERCISE 15 **Developing Your Main Idea with Specific Support.** List at least five supporting items for one of the main ideas that you formulated in Exercise 14. Use as many different kinds of supporting items—facts, incidents, sensory details, examples, and reasons—as you can.

Preparing to Write a First Draft

You have generated writing ideas, explored them, narrowed one into a topic, formed a main idea, and found specific support to develop that main idea in a paragraph. You should be ready now to use these basic ingredients in a first draft of your paragraph. If you have experimented and worked thoughtfully with your ideas during prewriting, preparing your first draft will be easier. What is more important, your final paragraph will be one that will make you proud.

Checklist for Prewriting

1. What writing ideas can I generate by freewriting, brainstorming, and charting? Can I combine any of these?
2. Would informational or personal questions, or some combination of these questions, work best to explore my subject?
3. Which topic appeals to me most? How can I narrow that topic?
4. What is my purpose? Who is my audience? What main idea about my topic will best accomplish my purpose and appeal to my audience?
5. What specific facts, sensory details, incidents, examples, and reasons can I use to develop and support my main idea?

The following paragraphs grew out of the prewriting done by the three writers you have been following through this chapter. For each writer, prewriting—generating ideas, exploring various subjects, narrowing a topic, and forming and developing a main idea—probably took no more than an hour or two. By spending this time thinking out what they had to say, these writers found that they were quite ready to write their first drafts.

HOW TO CONSERVE FORESTS (FIRST DRAFT)

If you want to help save the trees in our forests, here are some things you can do. The wood from trees is used to make the pencils, paper, and books you use in school. Take care of these supplies. Paper bags, paper towels, paper napkins, and paper tissues are all produced from wood too. Explain to your families why they should not waste these wood products, and use them carefully yourself. If you go camping, be sure your campfire is completely out when you are ready to leave. Otherwise, the fire could spread and burn the forest down. If you make a habit of doing all these things, you will be doing what you can to help save trees so that your children and their children can enjoy their beauty.

WHY I WANT TO TEACH BLIND CHILDREN (FIRST DRAFT)

I have always wanted to teach, and recently I have been wondering whether I could teach handicapped children. Miss Emma Freneau was the one who convinced me by her example that I should teach blind children. She is an English teacher at a school for the blind near my home, but she herself is not blind. Occasionally, I would talk briefly to some of the students at the school when I passed by. I never felt comfortable with them; maybe I was even a little afraid of them. I tried carefully never to mention blindness or eyes or seeing to the blind students because I did not want to offend them. Then one day Miss Freneau invited me to one of her classes, and so I went. I was quite surprised to notice that she demanded as much of her blind students as my teachers demanded of their sighted students—their best. That day (I am sure Miss Freneau arranged it this way) the students gave oral reports on Sighted People. Student after student made the same points: "My blindness is a part of who I am. I accept it. Why can't sighted people do the same?" "Why are sighted people so afraid of blind people? We don't bite." "I don't want the pity of sighted people. I don't need it." "Although I can't see, my other senses are sharper than a sighted person's." "I am, first of all, a person. It just happens that I'm a person who can't see." Thanks to Miss Freneau, I learned much about *myself* that day. For one thing, I knew I wanted to teach blind children, and I am now looking into doing that.

AMELIA EARHART AND SALLY RIDE (FIRST DRAFT)

In the 1920s and 1930s Amelia Earhart thrilled the world by her pioneering airplane flights. She soloed in nonstop trips across the United States and the Atlantic. Her last flight, during which she vanished, was an attempt to fly around the world. In all these flights she joined with other early pilots to extend the frontiers of flight through Earth's atmosphere. Sally Ride is a more recent pioneer. In June of 1983 she captured the interest of the world when she joined the crew of the space shuttle *Challenger* on a scientific Earth-orbital flight. She is among the American and Russian astronauts who are helping to push the frontiers of flight deeper and deeper into space. Both of these women can justly be called pioneers on a second, equally important frontier—the frontier of ideas and attitudes. Both Amelia Earhart and Sally Ride have helped people to realize that women can perform as well as men in jobs once considered "men's work."

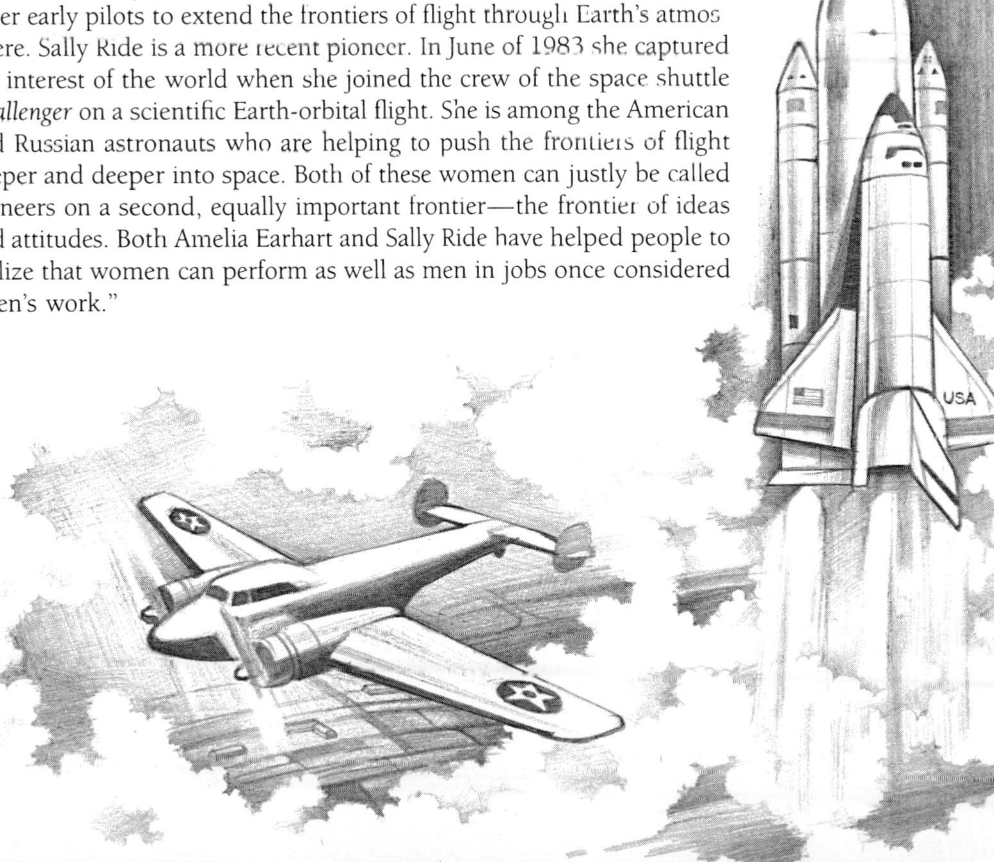

Writer's Choice

This chapter has given you activities in which you practiced—one at a time—skills that prepare you to write. Now you can put all these skills together by completing one or more of the following Writer's Choice assignments. Concentrate on prewriting, but, in addition, see how well you can channel your prewriting notes into a first draft and final copy.

Writer's Choice #1

ASSIGNMENT In this chapter you have done many exercises to acquaint you with various prewriting skills. To prepare Writer's Choice #1, you will have to go back and look at your notes from particular exercises. The assignment in Writer's Choice #1 is to write a paragraph using the main idea and support that you listed as your responses to Exercises 14 and 15.

LENGTH Eight to ten sentences

AUDIENCE One of the audiences that you selected in Exercise 14

PURPOSE One of the purposes that you selected in Exercise 14

PREWRITING Review your prewriting notes from Exercises 6–8, 10, 14, and 15 in this chapter.

WRITING Make your statement of your main idea the first sentence of your paragraph. Then choose your strongest supporting items, and write sentences expressing each. Try to end your paragraph by making an interesting observation or by drawing a conclusion.

REVISING Edit your paragraph to see if you have made full use of your prewriting notes. If something in your notes would improve your paragraph, use it. Continue editing by evaluating how well your paragraph gets across your main idea. Clarify any vague or otherwise unclear expressions. Then proofread your paragraph to check grammar, spelling, capitalization, and punctuation.

Writer's Choice #2

ASSIGNMENT To write a paragraph about a person who impresses you

LENGTH Five to seven sentences

AUDIENCE People who do not know the person

PURPOSE To describe

PREWRITING First prewrite briefly about a few people you know. Then choose the person who most impresses you. Explore your subject by asking and answering personal questions. Decide on a main idea—your overall impression of the person. Then list supporting details.

WRITING Identify the person in the first sentence of your paragraph. In the next few sentences describe your subject's physical appearance. Then describe his or her chief personality traits. Be sure to emphasize the qualities that most impress you.

REVISING Do you get a clear mental picture of your subject from your description? If not, add or change details in order to give more or better information about your subject.

Writer's Choice #3

ASSIGNMENT To write a one-paragraph editorial for the school newspaper about an activity in which you think students should take part

LENGTH Ten sentences

AUDIENCE The students in your school

PURPOSE To persuade

PREWRITING Decide on a worthwhile activity. You might explore your subject with *Who? What? Where? When? Why?* and *How?* questions similar to those on page 28. Note the important facts about the activity. List at least two reasons why you think students in your school should take part in the activity.

WRITING In the first sentence of your paragraph state what the activity is. Tell how this activity would be helpful. Then give reasons why students should take part in it.

REVISING Proofread your paragraph. Then edit it, making any changes and additions that will make it more convincing to the audience.

Writer's Choice #4

ASSIGNMENT Your choice

LENGTH Your choice

AUDIENCE Your choice

PURPOSE Your choice

OPTIONS Use one of the photographs in the Writer's Sourcebook on pages 354–357 to get you thinking.
Use any technique to generate and explore ideas.
Decide on an audience, a purpose, and a main idea.

Writers on Writing

Born in Salt Lake City, Utah, Tracy Anderson has lived in Washington State for most of her life. She has been swimming since the age of two and has competed in swimming and gymnastic events. She also likes to sing and she has written for the school newspaper.

THE PRODUCT

The following excerpt comes from a story of Tracy's entitled "The Grand Adventure," which she wrote when she was a student at Kentridge High School in Kent, Washington. Read Tracy's finished product, and then take a look at "The Process," in which she explains how she got the idea for her story.

> The sun rose like a big yellow beach ball flying through a clear summer sky. While the morning was cool, it promised to be another scorcher. Utah summers are like that. Six little boys, eyes bright with anticipation at the prospect of once more having a purpose, began to assemble at Murphy's garage. Bobby arrived first carrying his buggy wheels. He was easily the most excited—too many days of just hangin' around made this one all the more special.
>
> Joe came next with the wagon wheels, removed carefully and quietly while his little sister slept. Ace came dragging an old Model T windshield, followed close behind by Mack and John lugging a tractor seat and David proudly carrying a steering wheel. The boys came in breathless and red-faced from the morning's exertion.
>
> "Hey, what's he doing here?" growled Joe. "Dave wasn't invited to this project. He's not a member of our secret club, even."
>
> "He's just a baby," said Bobby. "He's only in the second grade."
>
> "Third grade in September," said Dave. "And you'll only be in the fourth."
>
> "Okay, you guys, knock it off. I can bring a friend if I want to," said Ace. "After all, Dave had this neat old junker car in his backyard, and he said we could have this stuff."
>
> "What are we going to do with a steering wheel? You know a soap box only uses ropes to guide it," said Joe.
>
> "But I got this great idea. We can wrap the rope around the steering post lots of times, and when we turn the wheel, the rope will move the wheels—you know, worm-drive," argued Ace.
>
> "The only worms around here are the ones in your brain," said Joe.
>
> "Hold on, Joe. That just might work," said Bobby. "Anyway, we've got to build the frame and attach the wheels and build a hood and all that stuff before we worry about a steering wheel."
>
> "What about brakes?" asked Dave. "We gotta have brakes."
>
> "Never mind, kid," said Joe. "We know how to make a car. Think we were born yesterday?"

THE PROCESS

My assignment was to write a story about anything I wanted. I felt sort of mindless that day, and so I just started jotting down ideas. I do have to say that most of my ideas were pretty crummy. Finally I remembered some of the stories that my father used to tell us about his childhood; they were so funny, just like the Our Gang comedies. I remembered his telling me this story about when he went down the biggest hill during rush hour in a go-cart. Of course, I had to add the building of the car and other bits to make the story more interesting.

Organizing the story wasn't difficult. I just followed a logical sequence of events. Whenever I needed a word, I looked it up in a thesaurus. I also had to put my words into the language of a bunch of little kids. I must have rewritten my story over ten times. Each time I read through it, I would add a new word or edit out a sentence. Finally I was satisfied. As it turned out, I won second place in the Northwest Writers' Contest.

I think I'd enjoy being a writer someday.

YOUR TURN *Writing About a Reminiscence*

Tracy took one of her father's reminiscences and built a story around it. Generate ideas of your own using an incident that one of your relatives has told you about his or her childhood. You may decide to embroider the real-life incident with details of your own, as Tracy did. Use any prewriting techniques that help you add to your ideas. Once you have planned what you are going to write, try a first draft, and show it to a friend.

CHAPTER 3

Writing the Paragraph

That's what makes it [a paragraph] interesting, because it comes alive as it's written. . . . It's like city planning. It's a vast work of architecture.

—Gore Vidal

Prewriting • *Writing* • *Revising*

The following passage appeared in a magazine article. As it was written originally, the passage was correct. As it appears here, however, it is incorrect in one important way. Read the passage now to decide what is wrong with it.

Chincoteague, Virginia, is a small town of 4,300 on Chincoteague Island, which measures seven miles in length and a mile and a half in width. The island is located off the Atlantic Virginia coast of the Delmarva Peninsula. Washington, D.C., is 110 miles away to the northwest, across the Chesapeake Bay, and Philadelphia is 140 miles due north. Chincoteague is a working island inhabited by working-class people, and it still has fishermen, clam boats, and a sense of independence that separates it from the outside world. What has brought the outside world closer to Chincoteague's door is the herd of wild ponies on the seaward island of Assateague, a long narrow barrier island that stands between Chincoteague and the Atlantic Ocean. Somehow, centuries ago the ponies appeared on Assateague. Perhaps a Spanish merchant ship foundered off the coast nearby, and the ancestors of today's ponies made it to shore. Or maybe English settlers set their ponies to pasture there, or just herded the ponies on to Assateague to keep them from damaging crops elsewhere. The Chincoteague Volunteer Fire Department bought nearly all the ponies in the 1940s, and every July at Pony Penning time, the firemen round up the Assateague ponies, swim them across the channel to Chincoteague, and march them up South Main Street to the carnival grounds. There the foals are auctioned off to the highest bidder. Ponies who aren't sold get herded back to Assateague to wait for next year. The ponies, the Pony Penning Carnival, and the two islands were made famous by a children's book called *Misty of Chincoteague* by Marguerite Henry, which was published in 1947. The movie version of *Misty* still plays every summer during Pony Penning at the town's only movie theater. Back in the late 1940s, it played everywhere, and drew the first large numbers of tourists to the island. A bridge erected between the islands in 1962 made the Assateague shore easy for tourists to reach, and that attracted even more people to Chincoteague. They have come in increasing numbers every summer.

—Roger MacBride Allen, "Chincoteague: A Hometown Island"

You may have had some difficulty reading this passage because you could not tell where the writer finished his discussion of one important idea and began his discussion of another. You probably recognized why the passage was difficult to read: It was not broken into paragraphs.

A **paragraph** is a group of sentences that develops one main idea.

Within each paragraph in the preceding passage, the writer aimed to achieve unity by making sure that all of the supporting sentences in each paragraph helped develop the main idea of the paragraph. He also aimed for coherence within each paragraph—using words and phrases to connect one sentence with another. Finally, the writer aimed for clear organization within each paragraph—making each sentence follow logically upon the preceding sentence. These qualities of the writer's work become clear when you realize that in the original passage the paragraphs began on lines 8, 16, and 21.

When you consider the steps taken by the writer of this passage, you will begin to understand the quotation at the beginning of this chapter. Studying this chapter will make you even more alert to the qualities of a good paragraph and will help you write some good ones yourself. You will focus on one of the three essential steps of the writing process—writing. You will also be involved in the two other steps—prewriting and revising—as you create your own complete paragraphs. These are the concerns on which you will concentrate:

topic sentences
developing a topic sentence into a paragraph
writing a unified paragraph
writing a coherent paragraph
organizing a paragraph

Writing the Paragraph

Topic Sentences

A **topic sentence** states the main idea of a paragraph and points the direction for the other sentences to follow.

Experienced writers keep the needs of their readers in mind. They are aware, for example, that a topic sentence should make the main idea of a paragraph immediately clear to readers and should also give readers help in following the supporting sentences easily. In short, writers recognize that a topic sentence should actually be a useful generalization or summary of the content of a paragraph. Consider the underlined topic sentence in this sample paragraph. Does it help you to understand the paragraph?

> Many shoppers select products from supermarket shelves solely because the packages are colorful and attractively designed. When questioned in consumer surveys, such shoppers say they recognize that what is inside the package should be a more important consideration in making buying decisions than what the package looks like on the outside. These shoppers also admit that they should base their buying decisions on such other factors as weight relative to price. Yet sales data consistently indicate that packaging is the chief influence on the product choices made by a large segment of the buying public.

Not every paragraph needs a topic sentence. In general, the narrative paragraphs of a story do not have topic sentences, nor does every expository paragraph, because the information in the sentences of the paragraph may suggest the main idea so clearly that the paragraph does not need a directly stated generalization or summary. Even though writers of narrative and expository paragraphs do not always use topic sentences, however, you should be aware of how helpful these sentences are to readers.

Some topic sentences are better than others. They are clearer, more direct, and more useful for establishing the organization of the paragraph. To understand the difference between a strong topic sentence and a weak one, compare the following two. Decide which would be better for the paragraph about packaging.

TOPIC SENTENCE A Many shoppers select products from supermarket shelves solely because the packages are colorful.

TOPIC SENTENCE B Shoppers are a strange breed.

Why is Sentence A the better topic sentence for the paragraph on product packaging? Consider the questions and sample answers on the following checklist.

Checklist for Evaluating Topic Sentences

1. What is the one main idea presented by the topic sentence?

   Sentence A presents one main idea—importance of packaging. Sentence B also presents one main idea—the strangeness of shoppers.

2. Is the topic sentence an overgeneralization; that is, does it make a statement too broad to be really useful in understanding the paragraph?

   Sentence A is a summary or generalization about the specific topic to be discussed in the paragraph. Sentence B, however, is an overgeneralization that is broader than necessary.

3. Do all of the other sentences in the paragraph take their direction and focus from the topic sentence?

   Only Sentence A, not Sentence B, gives a strong direction to the specific content of the other sentences in the paragraph.

Notice that you may use the questions in the checklist to test the adequacy of any topic sentence.

Two Kinds of Topic Sentences

Like all sentences, topic sentences should be appropriate to a writer's audience and purpose. Most topic sentences are declarative sentences, or statements. Some topic sentences, however, may be interrogative sentences, or questions.

A QUESTION AS THE TOPIC SENTENCE

Did you know that many shoppers select products from supermarket shelves solely because the packages are colorful and attractively designed? When questioned in consumer surveys, such shoppers say they recognize that what is inside the package should be a more important consideration in making buying decisions. These shoppers also admit that they should base their buying decisions on such other factors as weight relative to price. Yet sales data consistently indicate that packaging is the chief influence on the product choices made by a large segment of the buying public.

EXERCISE 1 **Writing Two Kinds of Topic Sentences.** Choose a topic of your own or one of the following topics. Write two different topic sentences for a paragraph on the topic you choose—one a statement and one a question. Clearly identify your purpose—to inform, persuade, amuse, entertain, narrate, or describe. Assume your class is your audience. Use the questions in the preceding checklist to help you evaluate your two topic sentences.

1. challenging jobs
2. today's heroes
3. science-fiction movies
4. rainy days
5. washing dishes
6. unusual kites

Placement of Topic Sentences

When a topic sentence appears at or near the beginning of a paragraph, it grabs a reader's attention and provides a general idea of what is to come in the remaining sentences. When a topic sentence appears in the middle of a paragraph, it unifies the sentences that come before and after it. When a topic sentence appears at the end of a paragraph, it summarizes the paragraph, serving as a clincher and ensuring that the reader has firmly grasped the main idea. Compare the effect of the topic sentences in the following two paragraphs. What changes in wording result from changing the position of the topic sentence?

TOPIC SENTENCE IN THE MIDDLE

When questioned in consumer surveys, many shoppers say they recognize that what is inside a package should be a more important consideration in making buying decisions than what the package looks like on the outside. They also admit that they should base their buying decisions on such other factors as weight relative to price. Nevertheless, many shoppers select products from supermarket shelves because the packages are colorful and attractively designed. Sales data consistently indicate that packaging is the chief influence on the product choices made by a large segment of the buying public.

TOPIC SENTENCE AT THE END

When questioned in consumer surveys, many shoppers say they recognize that what is inside a package should be a more important consideration in making buying decisions than what the package looks like on the outside. They also admit that they should base their buying decisions on such other factors as weight relative to price. Yet sales data consistently indicate that packaging is the chief influence on the product choices made by a large segment of the buying public. In other words, many shoppers select products from supermarket shelves solely because the packages are colorful and attractively designed.

EXERCISE 2 **Placing Topic Sentences.** Find a paragraph in a book or magazine. Be sure the paragraph has a topic sentence at the beginning. Copy the paragraph as it is. Underline the topic sentence. Then revise the paragraph twice. In the first revision move the topic sentence to the middle position. In the second revision move the topic sentence to the end. Change wording of sentences if necessary. Briefly evaluate the effect of the topic sentence in each of the three positions.

Developing a Topic Sentence into a Paragraph

Developing a paragraph means writing sentences that prove, clarify, and expand upon the main idea stated in the topic sentence—in short, supporting the main idea with specifics. Four of the most common kinds of support for a topic sentence are (1) concrete details, (2) examples or incidents, (3) facts or statistics, and (4) reasons.

While prewriting, one writer compiled a general list of notes about a walk through the city. Then, by placing these notes into four more focused lists—one for each kind of support—the writer came up with four different main ideas about that walk.

CONCRETE DETAILS

SIGHTS

the great number of vehicles on the streets
the throngs of people of all kinds
the unusual shadows of the tall buildings
the displays in store windows
the many pushcart "restaurants"
the parks, large and small
scruffy squirrels and birds
rapid movement of pedestrians and vehicles

SOUNDS

the noise of traffic	police and fire sirens
people talking	children playing in parks
planes passing over	jackhammers digging up streets
newspaper vendors	

SMELLS	TASTES
salty ocean breeze	pretzels with mustard
exhaust fumes	the Italian lemon ice
fresh tar on streets	freshly roasted peanuts

FEELINGS

the heat of the sun	the hard sidewalks
the coolness of shadows	the wetness of a shower

MAIN IDEA Every sense gets stimulated in the city.

EXAMPLES OR INCIDENTS

the ride on the subway
trying to cross the street
resting in the park
meeting an unfortunate lady
asking directions
the city police in action

MAIN IDEA I met an interesting woman in the park.

FACTS OR STATISTICS

the temperature—103°F
the number of city residents and visitors—6 conventions
the number of tourist attractions
the high prices—20% higher
the heights of the tallest buildings

MAIN IDEA The city was a collection of superlatives that day.

REASONS

the great variety
the feeling of excitement
the harsh beauty
the interesting people
the feeling of being a part of something wonderful

MAIN IDEA I want to go back to the city again.

After listing the supporting items in four different groups and thinking of a main idea based on each group, the writer was able to compose four different paragraphs, each of which contains a strong *topic sentence* and a number of *supporting sentences*.

Development with Concrete Details

Like most of us who live in this physical world, any reader is attracted to writing that describes the sights, sounds, smells, feelings, and tastes of that world. This attraction is reflected in the list of concrete details. In the following paragraph the writer begins with a strong topic sentence that states the main idea and uses several of the notes on sights in the city to develop the topic sentence.

> Walking through the city was like watching an action packed movie. Thousands of people moved nonstop in both directions on sidewalks and crosswalks, now and then vanishing into subway entrances, stores, restaurants, and high buildings. In the bright sunlight, the shadows of these buildings reached darkly across streets and climbed halfway up buildings on the other side. A confusion of cars, trucks, buses, motorcycles, and other vehicles crept or whizzed through these shadows and then briefly into alternating strips of sunlight. The gray-brown, uneven walls of buildings occasionally gave way to large and small patches of green—parks where joyful children, scruffy squirrels, and fluttering pigeons all contributed to the ceaseless and frantic motion of the city movie.

EXERCISE 3 **Developing a Topic Sentence with Concrete Details.** Write a paragraph about a city, using the concrete details listed under Sounds, Smells, Tastes, and Feelings in the writer's notes. If you prefer, write a paragraph using a topic sentence and concrete details of your choosing. Be sure to revise your paragraph and write a final copy.

Development with Examples or Incidents

Look again at the list headed *Examples or Incidents*. From this list the writer selected two related incidents as a topic and wrote the following paragraph. The writer's paragraph about these incidents invites readers not only to understand the main idea but to *experience* it as well.

> Who could ever forget Helen, the "bag lady" I met on my walk through the city? I met her on a bench in a small park where I stopped to rest. At first she said nothing, but I noticed that she kept watching me drink a can of soda. When I had drained the last drop of soda, Helen turned to me, held out her hand, and asked me for the empty can. When I nodded my head, she snatched the can and pushed it into one of the two shabby shopping bags beside her on the bench. Then she was ready for a limited conversation in which I learned that Helen was one of the city's homeless people. All that she owned was in the two shopping bags, which she continually replenished from the city's trash cans, dumpsters, alleys, gutters, and any other place where people discarded things they did not want. Helen was about to tell me more when she spotted a man tossing something into a trash basket down the path from the bench on which we sat. She was off to the basket in a flash, muttering, "I'll be back." But she never did return. Often, since that day, Helen comes into my mind, and, when she does, I find myself wondering what will happen to her and the other "discarded" people like her.

EXERCISE 4 **Developing a Topic Sentence with Examples or Incidents.** Write a paragraph about a city. Use at least one of the examples or incidents listed earlier or another example or incident you can think of related to a city. Draw ideas from your own experience, from discussion with others, or from your reading. Begin your paragraph with a strong topic sentence that will capture your readers' interest. Include other sentences that support the main idea stated in your topic sentence. Be sure to reread and revise your paragraph after writing it.

Development with Facts or Statistics

In the following paragraph the writer thought over the specific facts and statistics that he had jotted down to describe the city. A **fact** is a statement that has been proved by experience, observation, or study. **Statistics** are particular kinds of facts that give precise numerical information. Here the writer uses statistics to develop the main idea expressed in the topic sentence.

> The city was a collection of superlatives the day I visited it. In the first place, the temperature was 103°F, a fifty-year record high. In addition, the city was hosting six different conventions, increasing the population, at least temporarily, by about 10,000 people. Many of the stores were having "super sales" that day, too. These sales attracted many thousands of people from the surrounding areas. Low prices were not common in the city, however. That morning's newspaper headlined government findings that prices in the city were, on the average, 20 percent higher than in other cities of the nation. Finally, in the afternoon, I attended a ceremony in which the mayor officially opened a new building—the highest skyscraper in the world.

EXERCISE 5 **Developing a Topic Sentence with Facts or Statistics.** Write a paragraph, using facts or statistics to develop a topic sentence of your own. If you prefer, use one of the following topic sentences.

1. The space shuttle could eventually benefit the whole world.
2. Our city offers several recreation opportunities.
3. Poverty and hunger are increasing among some people on earth.

Development with Reasons

In the following paragraph the writer uses several reasons to support the main idea—a wish to return to the city. Why would the writer return? The people, the memories, and the environment itself provide powerful reasons. By the end the topic sentence has not been merely restated but has been *developed*.

I am eager to make a return trip to the city some day soon. I did not have time to see and do all the things I wanted to during the one day I spent there. The next time, I would visit more of the tourist attractions. Then I would take a closer look at some of the stores and shops I passed, and of course I would have dinner in one of the city's famous restaurants. On a return trip I would try to get to know the people who live there—what they do for work, how they feel about their city, who they are.

EXERCISE 6 **Developing a Topic Sentence with Reasons.** Write a paragraph to develop the main idea stated in the following sentence:

____________ is the one place I would most like to visit.

Use reasons to support the main idea. After writing your first draft, be sure to reread and revise your paragraph. Then write a final copy.

Writing a Closing Sentence

A well-developed paragraph often needs more than a strong topic sentence and several related supporting sentences. To be truly effective, a paragraph often needs a good closing sentence. A strong closing sentence gives the reader a sense of finality. It can clinch an argument, restate the idea of the topic sentence, announce a conclusion or decision, or give a personal opinion. A good closing sentence lets the reader know that a main idea has been expressed, supported, and given clear boundaries.

Notice, as you read on, the different kinds of closing sentences that can be used with the paragraph about product packaging. First, consider the underlined example, which you have already seen, of a closing sentence that clinches an argument by bringing additional evidence to bear—sales data.

Many shoppers select products from supermarket shelves solely because the packages are colorful and attractively designed. . . . Yet sales data consistently indicate that packaging is the chief influence on product choices made by a large segment of the buying public.

Here are a few other examples of kinds of sentences that can be used to close a paragraph.

RESTATING THE TOPIC SENTENCE

. . . In spite of their consciousness of these reasonable guidelines, some shoppers buy products simply because their packages are visually appealing.

ANNOUNCING A CONCLUSION OR DECISION

. . . Considering this, manufacturers would probably do well to invest more money in making the most attractive packages possible for their products.

GIVING A PERSONAL OPINION

. . . Perhaps this group of consumers will learn wiser buying practices when they end up with inferior products or empty wallets and pocketbooks.

EXERCISE 7 **Writing Closing Sentences.** Read the paragraph and closing sentences A, B, and C. Write the sentence that would make the best closing sentence for this paragraph. Then explain your choice.

For a long time now, people have been wasting or polluting life-giving resources and endangering the earth that provides them. Forests have been reduced to ashes in fires caused by careless campers or stripped bare by shortsighted manufacturers. Rivers, underground streams—even the vast oceans—are being poisoned and made unfit for people and the creatures that live in them. Wasteful farming practices have caused the erosion and loss of soil we need to grow the food that keeps us alive. Automobile exhausts and factory smokestacks fill the air we breathe with dangerous, health-threatening pollutants.

SENTENCE A Someone should take some action immediately.

SENTENCE B The earth will probably survive, but the people who live on it might not.

SENTENCE C It should be evident that the situation has reached terrible proportions and may be beyond repair.

Writer's Choice

Writer's Choice #1

ASSIGNMENT Write a topic sentence on a topic of your own choice, or use one of the following topics. Use concrete details to develop your topic sentence into a paragraph.

a platypus	a city in fog
a kitchen at mealtime	the skin of a squash
a flag in the wind	a sour lemon

LENGTH Five to seven sentences

AUDIENCE Your class

PURPOSE To describe

PREWRITING List concrete details that support your topic sentence, and group them according to the five senses (sight, hearing, taste, smell, and touch)

WRITING Develop your topic sentence by writing sentences using concrete details that appeal to the senses. Restate the topic sentence in a good closing sentence.

REVISING Make sure that each detail is clear, specific, and directly related to your topic. Use precise words.

Writer's Choice #2

ASSIGNMENT Using examples, facts, or reasons, write one paragraph developing a topic sentence of your own or one of the following topic sentences:

Making friends is a lifelong learning experience.
Keeping peace should be our politicians' first goal.

LENGTH Your choice

AUDIENCE Your choice

PURPOSE To state and support your opinion

OPTIONS Begin with a topic sentence that states your opinion directly. Decide which method of development you will use, and include only those sentences that use that method. Draw from your experience, from discussions with others, or from something you have read.

Writer's Choice #3

ASSIGNMENT Use examples, incidents, facts or statistics, or reasons to write a paragraph on any subject you choose.

OPTIONS Decide for yourself the length, audience, and purpose of the paragraph.
Make your topic sentence clear and direct, and develop it with specific concrete details.

Writing a Unified Paragraph

Before going on, take a minute or two to retrace your steps in this chapter. You have built two kinds of topic sentences to express main ideas of paragraphs. You have constructed paragraphs by using various kinds of supporting items to develop topic sentences. Now, reread the quotation at the beginning of this chapter. Are Gore Vidal's words more meaningful to you after coming this far?

As you continue in the chapter, you will discover that there is still more to the "architecture" of a paragraph. On the next few pages you will learn that a paragraph must be unified and how you go about making a paragraph unified.

A **unified paragraph** is a paragraph in which all the sentences belong together and develop one main idea.

Imagine that you have written a topic sentence for the first draft of a paragraph. You continue the draft by writing additional sentences. Each of these sentences should support, or be related directly to, the main idea expressed in the topic sentence. If the sentences are related, the paragraph will be unified. If they are not related, you will have too many ideas in the paragraph, and it will have less power and effect on readers. Read the following two paragraphs. Which is unified? Why?

PARAGRAPH A

Bicycle riders rank high among travelers in terms of efficiency. Over the same distance, they expend about one-fifth the energy of a person on foot. After a calculation converting calories into gasoline, bicycles are found to get close to 3,000 passenger miles per gallon. This wonderful machine can carry a payload ten times its weight. Its drive mechanism translates 95 percent of a rider's energy into usable output. Bicycles with world-class racers can attain speeds as high as 44 miles per hour.

—Thomas A. Bass

PARAGRAPH B

The wolf is an intensely social animal within its own pack which, with up to 12 members or so, is essential for hunting moose and other large prey. Wolves sometimes eat their prey before it is dead. Each pack is built around a dominant male and female, and these animals may sometimes mate for life. Their dominance is established within their respective litters as pups, and inferior animals learn to accept their position and demonstrate it often with deferential gestures and motions. . . . As the pups grow they depend on all members of the pack, indiscriminately demanding food by nuzzling any adult's muzzle. The adult obligingly regurgitates a meal (the only means of carrying it home) and the lesson is clear—the pack is family. Between 60 and 65 thousand wolves live in Canada, Alaska, and other parts of North America today.

—David Nevin

Paragraph B is not unified because the two underlined sentences do not relate directly to the main idea stated in the topic sentence. The two sentences are interesting, and they might make suitable sentences in other paragraphs. Here, however, they draw the reader's attention away from the main idea—the social habits of wolves in a pack.

As you write, remember that unity in a paragraph is largely a matter of keeping your supporting sentences concentrated on the main idea so that your readers will be able to do the same. Keep your supporting sentences on the target—your topic sentence.

Checklist for Writing a Unified Paragraph

1. In what specific way does each supporting sentence relate to the main idea stated in the topic sentence?
2. If a sentence is not directly related to the topic sentence, should I delete it, revise the topic sentence, or save the sentence for another paragraph?

EXERCISE 8 **Writing a Unified Paragraph.** Write a unified paragraph on any topic you choose. If you prefer, use one of the following topics:

1. the best day of my life
2. the name of my city [town]
3. last Sunday
4. the American flag

In your prewriting pay special attention to identifying those ideas directly related to your topic. When you revise, make sure each sentence in the paragraph is directly related to the main idea expressed in the topic sentence.

Writing the Paragraph

TOPIC SENTENCES

DEVELOPING A TOPIC SENTENCE INTO A PARAGRAPH

WRITING A UNIFIED PARAGRAPH

WRITING A COHERENT PARAGRAPH

ORGANIZING A PARAGRAPH

Writing a Coherent Paragraph

When you concentrate on writing a unified paragraph, you concern yourself with the relationship between the topic sentence and each of the other sentences. When you concentrate on writing a coherent paragraph, you concern yourself with the way each individual sentence is linked or connected to the sentences before and after it.

A **coherent paragraph** is a paragraph in which the sentences are clearly and logically connected to one another.

Notice how, in the following model paragraph, the writer links the individual sentences. As the connecting lines and boxes show, the writer uses repeated words, pronouns, and transitions to create a coherent paragraph.

> Millions of years ago, a volcano built a mountain on the floor of the Atlantic. In eruption after eruption, it pushed up a great pile of volcanic rock, until it had accumulated a mass a hundred miles across at its base, reaching upward toward the surface of the sea. Finally its cone emerged as an island with an area of about 200 square miles. Thousands of years passed, and thousands of thousands. Eventually the waves of the Atlantic cut down the cone and reduced it to a shoal—all of it, that is, but a small fragment which remained above water. This fragment we know as Bermuda.
>
> —Rachel Carson, *The Sea Around Us*

By using the same word in two sentences, or by using synonyms—words with similar meanings—you can forge strong links between sentences, as the following excerpt from the model paragraph shows.

> Eventually the waves of the Atlantic cut down the cone and reduced it to a shoal—all of it, that is, but a small fragment which remained above water. This fragment we know as Bermuda.

Remember to use repetition skillfully. If you overuse it, your readers may become bored or consider your writing immature. Use synonyms to introduce some variety while keeping the links between your sentences in place.

Use pronouns to refer to a word, a group of words, or an idea that appears in a preceding sentence.

> Millions of years ago a volcano built a mountain on the floor of the Atlantic. In eruption after eruption, it gushed up a great pile of volcanic rock, until it had accumulated a mass a hundred miles across at its base. . . .

Transitions are words and phrases that create coherence by making the movement from one sentence to another clear, smooth, and easy to follow. Transitions show how you are progressing from one idea to the next and help readers follow your train of thought. Here are some of the most commonly used transitions:

TRANSITIONS THAT SHOW TIME

after	finally	immediately	meanwhile	soon
always	first	last	now	then
eventually	following	later	sometimes	until

TRANSITIONS THAT SHOW PLACE AND POSITION

above	beneath	horizontally	opposite	there
ahead	down	inside	outside	under
around	far	near	over	vertically
below	here	next to	parallel	within

TRANSITIONS THAT SHOW CAUSE AND EFFECT

as a result	consequently	so	therefore
because	for that reason	so that	

TRANSITIONS THAT SHOW COMPARISON AND CONTRAST

but	in the same way	on the other hand	similarly
however	like	on the contrary	unlike

TRANSITIONS THAT SHOW EXAMPLES

for example	for instance	namely	that is

Checklist for Writing a Coherent Paragraph

1. What can I do to link all sentences in the paragraph clearly and logically?
2. Which words can I repeat and still give my sentences sufficient variety? What synonyms can I use?
3. Does each pronoun clearly refer to a word, a group of words, or an idea that appears in another sentence?
4. What are the best transitions I can use to link the sentences?

EXERCISE 9 **Identifying Kinds of Transitions.** Reread the paragraph by Rachel Carson. Identify each kind of transition that she uses.

EXERCISE 10 **Using Transitions to Achieve Coherence.** Write a fictitious and humorous newspaper story consisting of three short coherent paragraphs. Select notes from the following prewriting list as the basis for your paragraphs. Use a total of at least six different transitions to achieve coherence. Include a headline. Be sure to reread and revise your story before making a final copy of it.

PREWRITING LIST

Andrea Doreen Bruno completed the first nonstop crossing of the United States on roller skates.
Andrea is an American high school student.
Her roller skates were inherited from her grandmother.
Her skates were lined with a special foam rubber padding.
A van carrying skate wheels and other necessary supplies accompanied Andrea.
Andrea called her skates Hortense and Matilda.
Andrea left from Portland, Oregon.
Andrea skated for slightly more than 1,200 hours, or 50 days.
Andrea wore out six sets of wheels during her trip.
Andrea intended to end her ordeal in Palm Beach, Florida.
A freak ten-day blizzard in the South prevented her from getting to Palm Beach.
After waiting six days in Baltimore, Andrea decided to end her journey.
Five other people previously attempted the same feat.
One of the people was Andrea's grandmother.
Andrea's grandmother made it from Portland to Sioux Falls, Dakota.
Andrea got painful blisters and a touch of frostbite.
Andrea said she hardly noticed these afflictions.

EXERCISE 11 **Writing a Coherent Paragraph.** Write a coherent paragraph on a topic of your own choice or on one of the following topics:

1. inside my school locker
2. how to fly a kite

In your paragraph use and identify at least one example of *repeated words or synonyms* and one example of *pronouns,* and use at least two *transitions.* Be sure to reread and revise your paragraph before making a final copy of it.

Organizing a Paragraph

To write a unified paragraph, you must relate all the sentences to the main idea. To write a coherent paragraph, you must link the sentences together clearly. To write a well-organized paragraph, you must make sure that the sentences are presented according to a logical sequence of development.

A **well-organized paragraph** is one in which the order or sequence of sentences is logical.

When you write such a paragraph, your readers can sense your mind flowing without interruption toward a clearly established goal. As a result, your readers develop confidence in you as a writer and as a thinker.

Which of the following two paragraphs is well-organized?

PARAGRAPH A

Elizabeth Blackwell proved that American women could make contributions to society outside of the home. So did Rosa Parks, another outstanding American woman of the past. Blackwell was a doctor. In the past women were supposed to be seen and not heard. Women like Elizabeth Blackwell and Rosa Parks, who stood up for her rights on a bus, did not hold to this belief, however. Society tried to limit women. Amelia Earhart, a famous flyer, made many contributions outside the home. Another example of fighting stereotypes is Frances "Fanny" Wright. She did not believe women should be seen and not heard. She helped working people.

PARAGRAPH B

Not all American women of the past were willing to accept the limiting roles society tried to impose on them. Elizabeth Blackwell, against strong opposition, became the first licensed woman doctor in the United States. Frances "Fanny" Wright scandalized many people of her times by campaigning fearlessly and tirelessly for the rights of working people. Amelia Earhart's many daring flights, though considered "unwomanly," contributed greatly to the growth of civil aviation. Rosa Parks's courageous refusal to give up her seat to a white person on an Alabama city bus touched off a civil rights movement that brought American blacks closer to the equality long promised them by the Constitution.

Why is Paragraph B easier to follow than Paragraph A? The ideas in Paragraph A are presented in a disorderly way. It is difficult to follow the order or sequence of the sentences in Paragraph A. On the other hand, the sentences in Paragraph B are well-organized.

Chronological Order

Chronological order is time order, the order in which events take place in the real world.

Since people first started telling stories, chronological order has been the most popular way in which to relate an event, summarize an incident, or organize a narrative. Notice that the narrator, or storyteller, of the following model paragraph adds suspense to the narrative by telling it in chronological order. Notice also the underlined transitions.

> I did not at first hear the movement in the surrounding undergrowth because of the howling wind. Then the wind stopped, and my ears filled with the sound of someone or something moving through the bushes toward me. Memories of stories about a creature—half-human, half-animal—who roamed this part of the forest now flooded my mind. As the sound became louder, my apprehension surrendered to total panic. When the bushes in front of me parted, I turned and ran. Whatever had come out of the bushes pursued me. I ran until I could run no more and stopped frozen in my tracks. At the same instant, my pursuer stopped too. After a long moment of fearful indecision, I finally decided to confront whatever it was behind me. Breathing hard, I forced myself to turn. There, staring quizzically at me with gentle brown eyes was a fawn, a baby deer, that had apparently strayed from its mother and was as frightened as I was.

EXERCISE 12 **Using Chronological Order.** Write a paragraph on a topic of your own choice or on one of the following topics:

1. a mini-biography of ____________
2. my first plane ride
3. getting to school on time
4. training a dog

Use chronological order to organize the paragraph. When you revise, make sure that the order of events is clear.

Spatial Order

Spatial order is order in terms of space.

When you use spatial order to organize a paragraph, follow this one basic rule: Always let your reader know where you are as you describe

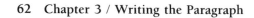

what you see. Are you standing in one spot looking at something? Are you moving through something, moving around it, or moving away from it? Be sure your readers can clearly envision your *position* and your *direction*, as the writer of the following paragraph does. As you read the paragraph, be aware of how the underlined words help you to know where the writer is and to follow the *direction* in which his eyes are moving.

> I was standing in front of a display of five paintings and drawings at the Art Fair, trying to decide which one I should buy. At the far left was a pastel drawing of one pink rose in a crystal vase. An oil painting of a pensive old man hung to the right of the pastel. At the center of the display was a watercolor scene of a quiet pond in the woods. Next to this delicate painting was a pen-and-ink sketch of a tumbledown barn. The picture at the far right was an unfinished pencil drawing of a horse's head.

EXERCISE 13 **Using Spatial Order.** Write a paragraph on a topic of your own choice or on one of these topics:

1. one shelf in a bookcase
2. a refrigerator
3. the view from a moving ferris wheel
4. the view into a tunnel

Use spatial order to organize the paragraph. When you revise, make sure that your position and direction are clear to your readers.

Cause and Effect

When you write a paragraph organized according to cause and effect, you want your readers to see that one event takes place *because* another event has taken place. A cause-and-effect paragraph is especially useful for writing about scientific or historical subjects, as in the following example. Notice the underlined transitions.

> Our treatment of loyal Japanese Americans at the beginning of World War II was an unfortunate error. Thousands of American citizens of Japanese ancestry found themselves imprisoned in detention camps. Japanese war planes attacked the naval base at Pearl Harbor, Hawaii, on December 7, 1941. For that reason, many people feared that Japanese Americans would support Japan through activities such as sabotage and spying, possibly with the purpose of preparing the way for an invasion of California, Oregon, and Washington by Japanese troops. Therefore, pressure was put on state and national government leaders to prevent Japanese Americans from engaging in such activities. Consequently, thousands of Japanese American men, women, and children were forced to leave their West Coast homes.

EXERCISE 14 **Using Order Based on Cause and Effect.** Write a paragraph on a topic of your own choice or on one of the following topics.

1. the game we lost
2. heart disease
3. happiness
4. pollution
5. wind
6. studying
7. forest fires
8. exercise

Use order based on cause and effect to organize the paragraph. When you revise, make sure that the cause-effect relationship between events is clear to your readers.

Comparison and Contrast

Comparison is writing that describes similarities; **contrast** is writing that describes differences.

By showing readers how someone or something is similar to or different from someone or something else, you can give a paragraph more precise definition and clearer boundaries. Consider the following example, in which the traits of two people are contrasted. As you read the paragraph, be aware of the underlined transitions and their effect on the flow and meaning of the paragraph. Observe how the paragraph moves from a discussion of physical to nonphysical traits.

> Unless someone told you, you would never guess that Roger and Peter are twins. Roger is over six feet tall and weighs about two hundred pounds. He has fair skin, blue eyes, and long, straight blond hair. Roger is a serious student, but he has a great sense of humor and a hearty, infectious laugh. Although he enjoys sports as a pastime, Roger does not play on any of the school teams because, between his part-time job and the many hours he spends studying, he cannot find the time. Peter is as different from his twin as as he can possibly be. Unlike Roger, Peter has olive skin and brown, almost black eyes. He has black, curly hair, which he keeps closely cropped. Peter is not the student that Roger is. He does have a sense of humor, but it is grimmer than his brother's. Peter's laugh is more like a snicker and sometimes makes people uncomfortable. Peter spends so much time at sports that he has little time left for anything else, including school.

Notice that the writer of the paragraph first describes *all* of Roger's traits and then contrasts them with *all* of Peter's traits. In other words, the structure of the paragraph is *AAABBB*. The *A*'s represent Roger's traits, and the *B*'s represent Peter's traits.

EXERCISE 15 **Using Order Based on Comparison and Contrast.** Write a paragraph on a topic of your own choice or on one of the following topics.

1. freshmen and sophomores
2. spring and fall
3. classical music and rock
4. two TV characters

Use order based on comparison and contrast to organize your paragraph. When you revise, make sure the specific points of comparison and contrast are clear to your readers.

Checklist for Organizing a Paragraph

1. Should this paragraph be organized in chronological order? If so, what is the sequence of events?
2. Should this paragraph be organized in spatial order? If so, how shall I let my readers know my position and direction?
3. Should this paragraph be organized in cause-and-effect order? If so, what is the cause? What is the effect?
4. Should this paragraph be organized in comparison-and-contrast order? If so, what similarities and differences should I relate?

Writer's Choice #1

ASSIGNMENT A paragraph of a friendly letter

LENGTH Six to seven sentences

AUDIENCE A relative who lives in a distant city

PURPOSE To relate an amusing incident that happened at a family reunion the relative could not attend

PREWRITING Review in chronological order the events that make up the incident.

WRITING Start your paragraph by explaining why your relative will be interested in reading about the incident. Continue by describing what happened in four or five sentences. Use concrete details, examples, or facts. Conclude with a sentence stating how the incident might have been different if your relative had been there.

REVISING Be sure to use transitions to make the time order of the events clear.

Writer's Choice #2

ASSIGNMENT A paragraph describing a trip you really want to make

LENGTH Six to seven sentences

AUDIENCE Your parents

PURPOSE To persuade your parents to let you go on the trip

PREWRITING Think of at least three or four reasons why you want to make the trip.

WRITING In your topic sentence identify the place you want to visit. Then write four or five sentences detailing your reasons for wanting to go there. End with a sentence describing how you think the trip will benefit your family as well as yourself.

REVISING Be sure the reasons you give are sensible and convincing. Evaluate your paragraph for correctness and neatness.

Writer's Choice #3

ASSIGNMENT A review of a performance

LENGTH Your choice

AUDIENCE Your choice

PURPOSE To evaluate a recent musical performance you have heard live, on TV, or on a recording

PREWRITING List information about the performance—the type of music, the musician or musicians, and how you heard it.

Describe the performance. Then state your opinion of the performance.

WRITING In your topic sentence give the title of the music performed and the name(s) of the musician(s) who performed it, adding your general opinion of the performance. Support your opinion with facts and concrete details about the performance. Perhaps you will want to compare this performance with another.

REVISING Check to see that the support you gave for your opinion does the job.

Writer's Choice #4

ASSIGNMENT A paragraph of any kind

LENGTH Your choice

AUDIENCE Your choice

PURPOSE To describe how your town or city five years ago was different from the town or city today

OPTIONS You might wish to focus on the physical aspects of the community or the people who made it up at the time.
You might use comparison-contrast or cause-and-effect, depending on what you say about your town or city.

Writer's Choice #5

ASSIGNMENT A paragraph of any kind

LENGTH Your choice

AUDIENCE Your choice

PURPOSE Your choice

OPTIONS Write on whatever topic you wish. You may be inspired by an illustration in the Writer's Sourcebook, pages 353–384.
Identify your audience and purpose at the top of your paper.
You may include a topic sentence or not, as you choose.
Use any method of organization you wish. Include transitions appropriate to the organization in order to give your paragraph coherence.

Writers on Writing

Richard Turner has lived in Virginia all his life, but he would like to try living in England after college.

THE PRODUCT

When he was a student at Midlothian High School in Midlothian, Virginia, Richard wrote the following paragraph.

Where in the world is Midlothian, Virginia? How could anyone ask that question! Why, Midlothian is the capital of the world—the center of everything that's going on! Why, you ask? Well . . . well . . . because Midlothian has two shopping malls! Not only that, but my family, best friend, and girlfriend all live there! What? Of *course* that's important! . . . Up until this past summer, that was my outlook on the world. My world revolved around myself, so I figured everyone else's world centered on me, too. But I soon found out that I couldn't have been more wrong. A trip to Europe with some classmates showed me just how big the world really is.

THE PROCESS

This is Richard's description of how he got his writing idea.

Writing a paper is a little like building a house. A house without a strong foundation might collapse; likewise, a paper without a solid main idea might not hold together.

When I wrote "Where in the World Is Midlothian, Virginia?" I came up with my basic idea first—I wanted to tell that my trip to Europe really opened my eyes. But I wanted to lead up to this idea, not state it right away. Also, I've found many of the things I've read in textbooks boring and monotonous, and I wanted *my* writing to be nonboring and exciting. So I decided to start out in a slightly different way, by asking questions. Then, after I grabbed my reader's attention, I set out my main idea.

By the way, I got my question "Where in the world is Midlothian, Virginia?" from a T-shirt my parents bought for my brother from a store in Midlothian. As soon as I saw the shirt, I knew I had found my attention-grabber.

YOUR TURN *Writing a Paragraph*

Write a paragraph that starts with a catchy opening and then leads up to your main idea, which you express in a topic sentence at the end of the paragraph.

CHAPTER 4

Revising the Paragraph

Every writer should own a wastebasket.

—E. M. Forster

Prewriting • Writing • Revising

Not all of a writer's first attempts are filed in the wastebasket to which the English novelist E. M. Forster refers. A few of these attempts may, indeed, belong in a wastebasket. However, some can be salvaged by careful revising.

Revising is "re-seeing." It is looking again at what you have done and seeing it as you have not seen it before. Revising is not simply one extra step tacked on at the end of the writing process: It is an essential part of that process.

Experienced writers recognize that writing *is* revising. Great writing, as novelist Forster makes clear, does not spring automatically or perfectly from a writer's mind. Revising to some degree is almost always necessary. Consider what Kurt Vonnegut, a contemporary American writer, has to say about it: "Be merciless on yourself. If a sentence, no matter how excellent, does not illuminate your subject in some new and useful way, scratch it out." Some writers have been known to go through dozens of drafts of a poem or story before deciding that their work was ready for publication. Two or three drafts may be sufficient for you, but your first draft will nearly always need more work. This is true no matter how experienced you are as a writer.

In this chapter you will become familiar with some practical techniques you can use to revise your writing. Some of these techniques will be more helpful to you than others, depending on the kind of writer you are. You must become your own critical reader and choose the techniques that will help you improve every paragraph you produce. The following is a list of revising activities that you will learn in this chapter:

revising for purpose and audience
revising the topic sentence
revising support, development, and organization
revising for coherence
revising word choice
editing, **proofreading**, and **publishing**

Revising for Purpose and Audience

Do not hesitate to make changes in your first draft if you discover that they will improve your work. Some student writers do not want to "mess up" what they have written. After all, they reason, it looks so neat, why ruin it with cross-outs and erasures? However, it is far more important to focus on *what* to say than to create a perfectly neat paper.

The purpose of your paragraph should be as clear to your reader as it is to you. When you are revising, identify for yourself the purpose of the paragraph by completing this sentence:

> The purpose of my paragraph is to ____________ [*inform, persuade, amuse, entertain, narrate, describe,* or *combine several purposes*].

After you have your purpose clearly in mind, read the paragraph from start to finish. If the paragraph *as a whole* does not seem to accomplish its purpose, reread each sentence *individually* to identify the sentence or sentences that do not fulfill your purpose.

To write successfully, you must always consider the particular needs of your audience so that you can help them to understand and enjoy what you are writing. For example, if you are telling the tale of Little Red Riding Hood to first-graders, you would not tell them that the little girl "unexpectedly encountered a member of the animal family Canidae, genus Canis, while embarked on a peripatetic journey one day." You would definitely have forgotten the needs of your audience! Do not write *at* your audience; write *to* them.

Checklist for Revising for Purpose and Audience

1. What is the purpose of the paragraph? Does it inform, persuade, amuse, entertain, narrate, describe, or does it combine several of these purposes?
2. Which sentence or sentences, if any, do not directly fulfill the purpose of the paragraph? What changes should be made to put every sentence on track?
3. Who is the audience for this paragraph? What changes should be made to make every sentence understandable or enjoyable?
4. What facts or details need to be added to help the audience understand me? If this is a specialized audience—people who share a particular body of knowledge—what can I assume they know?

EXERCISE 1 **Revising for Purpose and Audience.** Read the following paragraph, and then write answers to questions 1 through 4.

As famous mountains go, Vesuvius is not large. It slopes 4,000 feet above the sprawling Bay of Naples. (McKinley and Kilimanjaro are about five times as high, Everest more than seven times.) Its peak is flattened and slightly misshapen. Yet there is something impressive about Vesuvius, something that commands respect. The something, of course, is its notoriety. Look at Vesuvius and you see not a mountain but an awesome villain that has mercilessly laid waste to its neighbors a dozen and a half times during the 1,900 years since Pompeii and nearby villages were drowned in the volcano's greedy flow.

—Dan Carlinsky, "Bird's-Eye View of Vesuvius"

1. What do you think the purpose of this paragraph is?
2. The paragraph is a final draft and was published in a magazine article called "Bird's Eye View of Vesuvius." Suppose that an earlier draft included a few sentences about the two-car, twenty-passenger tourist railway that operates on Mount Vesuvius. Why would the writer have taken out those sentences when revising the paragraph?
3. Who is the audience for this paragraph?
4. Suppose also that in the first draft the author had included this sentence: "Vesuvius is a strato-volcano whose steep-sided form is determined by the angle at which the cinder and ash stands, whereas the layers of lava give strength and bulk." Why would the writer have omitted that sentence while revising?

Revising the Paragraph

REVISING FOR PURPOSE AND AUDIENCE

REVISING THE TOPIC SENTENCE

REVISING SUPPORT, DEVELOPMENT, AND ORGANIZATION

REVISING FOR COHERENCE

REVISING WORD CHOICE

EDITING, PROOFREADING, AND PUBLISHING

Revising the Topic Sentence

The **topic sentence** not only states the main idea of a paragraph; it also determines the scope and the direction of all the other sentences in the paragraph. Imagine you have been asked to revise the underlined topic sentence of the following paragraph:

> Today it is difficult to find a watch with only a minute hand and an hour hand. Modern people want different kinds of watches. At the very least, watches are expected to keep their owners informed not only of the hours and minutes but also of the passing of every second. Some people would not think of wearing a watch unless it showed the day of the week, the month, and the year. There are even people who require their watches to have musical alarms, to record the phases of the moon, or to show the time in the place they are visiting as well as the time back home.

If you want to revise any topic sentence, you should first decide whether it expresses the *main idea* of the paragraph. The topic sentence of this paragraph, *People want different kinds of watches,* does not really focus on the main idea. You might revise the sentence by refining the focus on the main idea.

> Modern people want different kinds of watches.
>
> ↓
>
> Modern people want their watches to do more.
>
> ↓
>
> Modern people want their watches to do more than give them the hour and minute.
>
> ↓
>
> In addition to telling the hour and minute, modern people expect their watches to provide a variety of information.

As you can see, the final revision of the original topic sentence focuses much more closely on the main idea of the paragraph.

Once the topic sentence has been focused, its placement within the paragraph should be considered. Where would it be most effective—at the beginning, in the middle, or at the end?

Checklist for Revising the Topic Sentence

1. If the topic sentence circles around the main idea without ever stating it directly, how can I revise it?
2. What noun or nouns would make the *subject* of the topic sentence more specific? What *verb* would express the action of the subject more accurately? What *adjective* or *adverb* would help express the main idea more precisely?
3. After reading the topic sentence, what will the reader expect the rest of the paragraph to say?
4. How, if at all, would the topic sentence improve the paragraph if I moved it elsewhere in the paragraph?

EXERCISE 2 **Revising the Topic Sentence.** Read the following paragraphs, and revise the underlined topic sentence in each. Move the topic sentence to a different position within the paragraph if this will improve the paragraph. In revising, ask yourself whether the topic sentence clearly expresses the main idea of the paragraph and whether it also appears to determine the scope and direction of the other sentences.

PARAGRAPH A

The cheetah is a member of the cat family. A spotted golden coat, a lean and streamlined body, and the deceptively gentle brown eyes of this hunting leopard combine to create its fierce beauty. When hunting, a cheetah can run as fast as 70 miles per hour. However, its speed has not saved it from hunters who sell its valuable hide to manufacturers of fashionable fur coats. These hunters have contributed to the decline of the number of cheetahs in Africa and the near extinction of these beautiful cats in Asia.

PARAGRAPH B

Making quilts is fun. The making of these padded bed covers began thousands of years ago in some parts of medieval Europe. Dutch and English women brought this art to North America when they came here in colonial times. Women in the colonies and later on the western frontier used to get together to make quilts at parties called quilting bees. They developed a variety of interesting and pleasing quilt designs. For example, some patterns featured events in American history. Others portrayed flowers, birds, animals, and geometric shapes. Many of these designs were passed from mothers to daughters over the years, and quilters today still use them.

Writer's Choice

Writer's Choice #1

ASSIGNMENT Write a paragraph on a topic of your own choice or on one of the following topics:

an interesting novel
a new design for a school building
what honesty means
sneezing

LENGTH Six sentences

AUDIENCE Readers of a school newspaper

PURPOSE To inform

PREWRITING Brainstorm to discover an interesting approach to your topic. (You will have to narrow the suggested topics before you begin writing.) Review your brainstorming notes, and decide on a main idea that will appeal to the readers in your audience.

WRITING First write a topic sentence that states the main idea. Then write four sentences that support your main idea with concrete details, facts, or reasons. Finally, write a closing sentence that will motivate your readers to learn more about your topic.

REVISING When revising the paragraph, give special attention to the purpose, audience, and topic sentence. Refer to the checklists presented earlier for help.

Writer's Choice #2

ASSIGNMENT Write a paragraph on a topic of your own choice or on one of the following topics:

"telephone-itis"
novel phone designs
the inventor of the telephone
a telephone dial

LENGTH Your choice

AUDIENCE Your choice

PURPOSE Your choice

OPTIONS Design your own prewriting strategy. As you revise, however, pay special attention to the purpose, audience, and topic sentence. Refer to the checklists presented earlier for help.

Revising Support, Development, and Organization

Supporting sentences form the body of a paragraph. If they are weak and vague, the paragraph will be weak and vague, too. As you revise, then, be sure your supporting sentences are strong and clear. Go back to your prewriting. Check to make sure that you have chosen the concrete details, facts, examples, or reasons that best support the main idea. Ask yourself what supporting sentences would best fulfill your purpose and have the greatest effect on your particular audience.

Developing a paragraph is something like keeping a promise to your readers. A topic sentence promises them that you are going to offer them a certain kind of information. For example, if your topic sentence is *The beauty of the view from the window of the jet gave me king-size goosebumps,* your readers have every right to expect that the supporting sentences will present exciting concrete details about the view. If your topic sentence is *You can bet that Jim will never again pet strange dogs,* your readers will be watching for supporting sentences with reasons *why* Jim will not pet strange dogs again.

Paragraphs written by inexperienced writers are often criticized because they "do not go anywhere." It is true that some inexperienced writers simply repeat the topic sentence or restate it in different words, assuming that they are developing the main idea. As the following model shows, *repetition is not development:*

> *The "down under" continent of Australia is noted for the unusual animals that live there.* Consider the duckbill platypus and the emu, for example. *These two Australian creatures are unique, to say the least.* Although tourists can see emus and platypuses in zoos, not many have been lucky enough to view them in their natural habitats. *If you are curious about things that are different, the bizarre wildlife of the "down under" continent will more than satisfy your curiosity.*

The three italicized sentences all state the same basic idea. The synonyms *creatures* and *wildlife* add no different meaning to *animals;* nor do the adjectives *unique* and *bizarre,* synonyms for *unusual,* provide any new information to readers. In revising this paragraph, the writer would make sure that each sentence makes a genuine contribution to the development of the main idea.

As you continue revising, make sure that the organization you have used for your paragraph is the one most suitable to your purpose. Consider alternate methods of organization. For example, you may have used chronological order to discuss an historical event, but perhaps an organization based on cause and effect would have been more effective.

If you decide to reorganize a paragraph, do not hesitate to *rewrite* the sentences in your first draft. Sometimes trying to rearrange sentences is more difficult than rewriting them. You may save yourself time and trouble by changing a few sentences instead of trying to force them into a different organization.

Checklist for Revising Support, Development, and Organization

1. Which concrete details, facts, examples, or reasons form the strongest support for the main idea?
2. Which sentence or sentences, if any, merely repeat the main idea instead of developing it?
3. Why is the method of organization used in the paragraph the most suitable one?

EXERCISE 3 **Revising Support, Development, and Organization.** Rewrite one of these paragraphs, revising it for correct support, sufficient development, and logical organization. Rewrite, reword, rearrange, or replace any sentence, if by doing so you can improve the paragraph.

A. Scientists have found a great many uses for the thin, intensified beams of light emitted by lasers. American physicists first suggested the idea for a laser, and an American engineer built the first laser. The pioneering work of these Americans opened the way for others to develop practical uses of laser light beams. In industry, the laser does a variety of jobs. For example, intense laser beams are used in welding the tiny parts of electronic machines, such as computers. The three types of lasers now in existence are solid lasers, gas lasers, and liquid lasers, all of which are extremely useful in different areas of life. A second field in which lasers are used beneficially is medicine. Surgeons can burn away diseased body tissue and perform delicate eye operations by skillfully manipulating these super-bright beams of light. The light from a laser, unlike light from electric bulbs, travels in only one direction. In addition, lasers are now commonly used by military strategists, research scientists, mapmakers, and astronauts. Although it is a comparatively recent discovery, laser light has already become useful in many areas of American life.

B. Preparing for a test is always a challenge that gives me a special charge. I always enjoy the stimulus of preparing for a test. When I prepare for a test, I find that I always study with greater concentration. I always follow the same procedure in preparing for a test. It helps my concentration to have a routine. I have all my textbooks and class notes around me. I sit on my bed with a bowl of fruit for sustenance. Of course, I always go straight home from school on the afternoon before a test. I usually do not eat dinner with my family. They understand that I am "in training." I usually eat six apples and a few oranges by the time I am finished studying. I do not particularly like bananas. I have everything within easy reach. I quickly scan my textbook, looking for key terms from my notes. But first I read through my notes, since these include the points that my teacher thought most important. My notes also highlight the most significant matters covered in my class. I read more carefully what the textbook says about the various points brought up in my notes. Then I begin to make up possible test questions, trying to answer them. When I can practically recite what is on each page of my notes and my textbook, I know that I am ready for the test.

Writer's Choice

Writer's Choice #1

ASSIGNMENT Write a paragraph on a subject of your own choice, or use one of the following topic sentences:

Among the problems that concern people today are lack of money, fear of nuclear war, and the increase in crime.

Not many of us understand the difference between [courage and recklessness, hearing and listening, weather and climate.]

More TV programs deal with [news, family situations, educational topics, crime and violence, humor] than with any other subject.

LENGTH Six or seven sentences

AUDIENCE The students in your class

PURPOSE To introduce an expert who will speak to the class on the topic

PREWRITING Freewrite for at least five minutes.

WRITING Organize your paragraph according to cause and effect or comparison and contrast. Include details, facts, examples, or reasons as support.

REVISING Use the checklists.

Writer's Choice #2

ASSIGNMENT Write a paragraph on a topic of your own choice, or narrow down one of the following subjects to a topic that can be developed in one paragraph:

Leonardo Da Vinci
light year
responsibility
lunchtime

LENGTH Your choice

AUDIENCE Your choice

PURPOSE Your choice

OPTIONS Use the organization that is most suitable for developing your topic—chronological order, spatial order, cause and effect, or comparison and contrast.
Revise your support, development, and organization according to the checklist.

Revising the Paragraph

REVISING FOR PURPOSE AND AUDIENCE

REVISING THE TOPIC SENTENCE

REVISING SUPPORT, DEVELOPMENT, AND ORGANIZATION

REVISING FOR COHERENCE

REVISING WORD CHOICE

EDITING, PROOFREADING, AND PUBLISHING

Revising for Coherence

The sentences of a coherent paragraph are clearly and logically linked to one another. They create a sense of continuity.

As you revise, decide whether repeating words or using synonyms can improve the coherence of the paragraph. For example, study the following model. Notice that in the revised version the italicized synonyms and repeated words clearly link the second sentence to the first sentence, giving an impression of one continuous thought.

> In ancient Egypt, a pharaoh was not only a king. Akhenaton, Ramses II, and Thutmose III were also high priests, great builders, and sponsors of the arts.

> In ancient *Egypt a pharaoh* was *not only a king*. The *Egyptian rulers* Akhenaton, Ramses II, and Thutmose III were *not only kings* but also high priests, great builders, and patrons of the arts.

Using pronouns can help you give both coherence and conciseness to a paragraph. As you revise, make sure that your readers always know to what each pronoun refers.

> In ancient Egypt pharaohs were not only kings. Akhenaton, Ramses II, and Thutmose III were also "gods," high priests, great builders, and patrons of the arts.

> In ancient Egypt *pharaohs* were not only kings. *They* were also high priests, great builders, and patrons of the arts.

As you revise, you can use transitions to improve sentences by linking them together. The following model shows how you can use an example transition to increase coherence:

> In ancient Egypt pharaohs were not only kings. Akhenaton, Ramses II, and Thutmose III were also high priests, great builders, and patrons of the arts.

> In ancient Egypt pharaohs were not only kings. *For example,* Akhenaton, Ramses II, and Thutmose III were also high priests, great builders, and patrons of the arts.

Checklist for Revising for Coherence

1. Which words can I repeat and still give my sentences sufficient variety? What synonyms can I use?
2. Which pronouns can I use to achieve coherence?
3. What kinds of transitions can I add to the paragraph?

EXERCISE 4 **Revising for Coherence.** Rewrite the following paragraph, revising for coherence by using *repeated words* or *synonyms, pronoun references,* and *transitions.*

For years now, people have seen, or thought they have seen, a strange, huge creature swimming in Loch Ness, Scotland's deepest lake. Some of the people who have reported seeing the strange, huge creature describe the creature as a dragon or a monster. Other people who have reported seeing the strange, huge creature refer to the creature more affectionately as "Nessy." Scientists have used underwater cameras to discover the real identity of the strange, huge creature. The cameras took one picture of what appears to be a portion of an animal with a flipper. Scientists are unwilling to draw any conclusions about their investigations. Each year, thousands of people flock to Loch Ness hoping, or perhaps fearing, that they will catch a glimpse of the strange, huge creature.

Revising the Paragraph

REVISING FOR PURPOSE AND AUDIENCE
REVISING THE TOPIC SENTENCE
REVISING SUPPORT, DEVELOPMENT, AND ORGANIZATION
REVISING FOR COHERENCE
REVISING WORD CHOICE
EDITING, PROOFREADING, AND PUBLISHING

Revising Word Choice

The words you choose must be suitable to the *audience,* to the *occasion,* and to the *subject* of your writing. Unsuitable words in any of these areas will jar your readers and stand in the way of your *purpose.*

When you are revising, keep your audience constantly in mind. Will the words you have used be meaningful to them? To an audience of doctors, for example, you can use medical terms such as *cerebrospinal* and *lymphectomy.* However, if your readers are not familiar with medical terminology, you will have to use everyday words. If you decide you must use technical terms, you should define them.

Keep the occasion in mind as you revise. Are you writing a business letter or a note to a friend, a light article for the school paper, or a formal essay? Are the words you have used suitable for the occasion? For example, it would not be appropriate to use the following sentences in the answer to an easy question on a literature test: *Emily Dickinson is a neat writer. She really hits you where you live.*

As you continue to revise, do not lose sight of your subject. You should not use terms related to one subject to discuss another subject. For example, computer terminology, such as *interface* and *input,* is suitable for talking about the operations of a machine, but it is not at all suitable for talking about the activities of people.

The preceding examples show how jarring an inappropriate choice of words can be. In contrast, appropriate words will put your readers at ease. (You will have the opportunity to study more about word choice, or diction, in Chapter 5.)

Once you decide how formal or informal your words should be, you need to be consistent in using them. The words you use in your first sentences will create certain expectations in your readers, and if you fail to fulfill those expectations, you risk losing your readers. Unless you mean to create a shocking or humorous effect, avoid mixing formal and informal words. Study the examples below.

> Although Mortimer usually performs with a high degree of valor, he sure acted like a chicken that day.
>
> Although my mother enthusiastically endorsed the notion of a party, my good buddy threw that idea out the window.

Checklist for Revising Word Choice

1. Which words, if any, are not appropriate to the audience, to the occasion, to the subject? How should they be changed?
2. Which words or expressions, if any, are too formal or informal? How should they be changed?

EXERCISE 5 **Revising Word Choice.** Rewrite the following paragraph, paying special attention to appropriate and consistent diction. Assume that your audience is made up of the principal and faculty of your school. Your purpose is to persuade them to open a student recreational lounge.

As administrators and teachers, you should be aware that a student lounge would satisfy the unquestioned recreational needs of the young men and women who attend this school. I mean, you must have noticed us kids being totally exhausted after working our brains in classes all day. Furthermore, you've got the power to pull strings that we can't even locate. It wouldn't take much arm twisting to get the school board to fork over the moola it would cost to construct and equip a student lounge. Consider this last point: Such a lounge would improve student conduct, like you wouldn't have to spend so much time keeping us off the walls. After reading this request, you ladies and gentlemen, I am certain, will make all reasonable efforts to get this lounge thing moving real quick.

Revising the Paragraph

REVISING FOR PURPOSE AND AUDIENCE
REVISING THE TOPIC SENTENCE
REVISING SUPPORT, DEVELOPMENT, AND ORGANIZATION
REVISING FOR COHERENCE
REVISING WORD CHOICE
EDITING, PROOFREADING, AND PUBLISHING

Editing, Proofreading, and Publishing

In the final stage of revising, you check the grammar, usage, capitalization, punctuation, spelling, and overall appearance of your writing. This stage is not a tacked-on procedure. It is part of the writing process. It consists of making the refinements that give your writing the clean and correct appearance that is so important as you reach the goal of the writing process—presenting your writing to readers.

In general, **editing** means making changes in sentence structure and wording.

Use the following checklist to spot and correct possible errors in the drafts of your writing. The standard editing marks at the right of the chart provide a kind of shorthand for revising or commenting on any piece of writing.

CHECKLIST FOR EDITING

QUESTION	TYPICAL ERRORS	MARK
Do verbs and their subjects agree?	Paul ~~don't~~ ^doesn't live here. Each of the boys ~~are~~ ^is tall.	agree
Is every pronoun in the correct case?	Come with Doreen and ~~I~~ ^me. Invite ~~whoever~~ ^whomever you wish.	case
Is every pronoun reference correct and clear?	The doctor ^knew that ~~informed~~ the patient ~~that he~~ would feel much better after the operation ^and told him so.	ref
Are all double negatives avoided?	I don't want ~~no~~ ^any trouble.	neg
Is each verb tense correct and consistent?	We use^d to see Karen often. If you ~~would~~ ^had ~~have~~ practiced more, you would have won.	tense
Are all comparisons properly expressed?	That is the ~~most hugest~~ ^largest bear. A rose is more beautiful than any ^other flower.	adj
Are all clauses complete and properly joined?	~~A~~ ^Martha is a person who likes to help. Ken knows, ^but he won't tell.	frag run-on
Have all dangling or misplaced words been avoided?	~~Reaching~~ ^When I reached for the can of paint, the ladder moved. The priceless statue was smuggled out of the museum by a tall man in a briefcase.	dangling misplaced
Has all wordiness been avoided?	The innovations ~~and new methods~~ will ~~commence and~~ start on the first of the month.	redundancy wordiness

In general, **proofreading** means checking for errors in spelling, capitalization, and punctuation.

Use the following proofreading marks as you revise your own writing or comment on someone else's writing.

CHECKLIST FOR PROOFREADING

MEANING	EXAMPLE	MARK
punctuation	Have you visited Washington^?	punct.
delete	It is the nation's ~~national~~ capital.	(delete mark)
insert	It is a^n inspiring city to visit.	^
space	Many famous buildings are|in Washington. (#)	#
close up	We saw many of ⁐them.	⁐
capital	We toured the w͇hite h͇ouse first.	≡
lower case	Then W/e climbed the Washington monument.	/
spelling	Next we went to the Link^c oln Memorial.	sp
transpose	The building Capitol was the last stop.	∽
new paragraph	often in the future. ¶ When we left	¶
stet (let stand something marked for change)	Washington is truly every ~~patriotic~~ American's "home town."	. . . . .

When you have finished revising and you are ready to make a final copy of your work, follow these standard rules for preparing your manuscript. (Be sure to ask your teacher about any different or additional rules for your class.) Your work will then be ready for **publishing**—that is, any form of sharing your writing with an audience. You may, for example, publish your writing in a book, send a letter to a newspaper, or mail a business letter.

GUIDELINES FOR MANUSCRIPT PREPARATION

1. Use standard size paper (8 1/2 × 11 inches) and blue or black ink or a black typewriter or word processor ribbon or cartridge.
2. If you are handwriting your work, use only one side of each page. If you are typing, double space.
3. Maintain an even margin of 1 1/2 inches on the left and a margin of about 1 inch on the right.
4. Indent the first line of each paragraph five spaces.
5. If you are handwriting your work, be sure that every word is legible—readable—so that your audience does not have to strain.

The following model paragraph demonstrates how editing and proofreading can apply the finishing touches to a piece of writing.

DRAFT WITH EDITING AND PROOFREADING MARKS

¶When it becomes necessary in the coarse of human events for one single ¶/tr/sp
people to dissolve the political binds which has connected them with tr | tense
an other, and to assume among the powers of the Earth, the separate equal lc
situation or equivalent position to which the laws of nature andof #
nature's God shall entitle them, a decent respect to the opinions of
Mankind, requires that they should declare the causes which impels them lc
to the seperation. ¶We hold these truths to be self-evident That all men sp/¶/ /lc
are created equal, that they are endowed by their creator with certain cap
unalienables rights, that among these are life, liberty and the pursuit of adj.
happiness.

FINAL REVISED COPY

When in the course of human events it becomes necessary for one people to dissolve the political bonds which have connected them with another and to assume among the powers of the earth the separate and equal station to which the laws of nature and of nature's God entitle them, a decent respect to the opinion of mankind requires that they should declare the causes which impel them to the separation.

We hold these truths to be self-evident, that all men are created equal, that they are endowed by their Creator with certain unalienable rights, that among these are life, liberty, and the pursuit of happiness.

EXERCISE 6 **Editing and Proofreading.** Revise the following paragraph, editing and proofreading to correct all errors.

You should not feel ashamed if you are afraid of a dog, but perhaps you should feel ashamed if a dog is afraid of you. Some people cannot hold there own in equal competition with other people, they vented their frustration by abusing their dogs. This behavior is one of the most surest forms of an inferiority complex. According to psychologists. Psychologists also point out that a person's character may be judged by the kinds of books he or she reads, the subjects of his or her conversations, and the behavior of his or her dog. Perhaps a better statement would be: Books and conversations reveals a person's intelligents, a person's character is most clearly revealed by the behavior of his or her dog.

General Checklist for Revising

PURPOSE AND AUDIENCE

1. Which sentence or sentences, if any, do not directly fulfill the purpose of the paragraph?
2. What changes should be made to make every sentence understandable or enjoyable?

TOPIC SENTENCE

3. If the topic sentence circles around the main idea without ever stating it directly, how can I revise the topic sentence?
4. What revision would improve the direction or the placement of the topic sentence?

SUPPORT, DEVELOPMENT, AND ORGANIZATION

5. Which concrete details, facts, examples, or reasons form the strongest support for my main idea? Which sentence or sentences, if any, merely repeat the main idea?
6. Why is the method of organization used in the paragraph the best possible one?

COHERENCE

7. Which words can I repeat and still give my sentences sufficient variety? What synonyms can I use?
8. Which pronouns can I use to achieve coherence, conciseness, and a sense of continuity?
9. What kinds of transitions can I use?

WORD CHOICE

10. Which words, if any, are not appropriate to the audience, to the occasion, to the subject?
11. Which words, if any, are inconsistent with the others?

EDITING, PROOFREADING, AND PUBLISHING

12. Does every verb agree with its subject?
13. Is every pronoun in the correct case? Is every pronoun reference correct and clear?
14. Are all double negatives avoided?
15. Is each verb tense correct and consistent?
16. Are all comparisons properly expressed?
17. Are all clauses complete and properly joined?
18. Have all dangling or misplaced words been avoided?
19. Has all redundancy and wordiness been avoided?
20. Has all proofreading been done carefully?
21. Have the rules of manuscript preparation been followed?

Writer's Choice

Writer's Choice #1

ASSIGNMENT Write a paragraph on a topic of your own choice or on one of the following topics:
why I should be the first student to go to the moon
how computers are changing our lives
fast foods

LENGTH Seven sentences

AUDIENCE Your great-great-grandchildren

PURPOSE To provide one paragraph for a family time capsule, to inform your descendants about one aspect of your life

PREWRITING Freewrite for five minutes on your topic. Then identify your main idea, and list supporting ideas.

WRITING Write a clear topic sentence that states precisely your main idea. Then write five supporting sentences. End with a sentence that summarizes your position.

REVISING Refer to the preceding checklist, and make all the changes that are necessary.

Writer's Choice #2

ASSIGNMENT Write a paragraph on a topic of your own choice, or narrow down one of the following subjects:
education music the future

LENGTH Seven sentences

AUDIENCE Adult readers of your local newspaper

PURPOSE To present the viewpoint of people your age

OPTIONS Brainstorm for five minutes. Use examples and reasons for development, but also consider details and statistics. As you revise, refer to the checklist on pages 86–87.

Writer's Choice #3

ASSIGNMENT Write a paragraph on a topic of your own choice, or use one of the following topics, narrowing it as necessary:
the three best and worst movies I've seen
my grandfather's life and mine
If you prefer, look for a writing idea in the *Writer's Sourcebook,* pages 354–357.

OPTIONS Determine your own length, audience, and purpose. Consider comparison and contrast as your method of organization. As you revise, refer to the checklist.

Writers on Writing

Chris Kolkhorst wrote the following paragraph when he was a student at Midlothian High School in Midlothian, Virginia. An avid baseball fan, Chris plans to major in engineering or computer science.

THE FIRST DRAFT

Read his first draft, which he marked with numbers referring to his revising notes. Then take a look at his revising notes, and read his finished product.

> At last the time draws near[1] for my first real decision.[2] The first decision having an impact on the rest[3] of my life. The process of choosing a college is one to which I am very unaccustomed.[4] After numerous visits, I discover my mind often wandering during visits to colleges in which I am not particularly interested.[5] Each college has merits and faults, and this simple characteristic[6] is the factor which makes the decision so difficult. My views probably represent the views of many, but I look for three specific traits in a college.[7]

THE PROCESS

[1]better word choice; change *draws near* to *has come*
[2]combine sentences; . . . *decision, the first decision* . . .
[3]better word choice; change *rest* to *remainder*
[4]wordy; change to *very new to me*
[5]disoriented, not in sync with paragraph; delete sentence
[6]redundant; delete *simple characteristic*
[7]don't make your views sound trivial or unimportant; change to *When I visit a college, I look for three elements.*

THE FINISHED PRODUCT

> At last the time has come for my first real decision, the first decision with a major impact on the remainder of my life—choosing a college. The process of choosing a college is very new to me. Each college has merits and faults, and this is the factor which makes the decision so difficult. When I visit a college, I look for three basic elements.

YOUR TURN *Revising a Paragraph*

Write a paragraph on any topic you choose, or choose a first draft you have already written. Revise the paragraph using the skills you practiced in this chapter. Refer to the General Checklist for Revising.

Review

CHAPTERS 2–4 THE WRITING PROCESS

CHAPTER 2 PREWRITING

Generating and Exploring Ideas [pages 20–30] Read the following brainstorming notes, and then answer the questions.

accidents	work accidents
within the home	home accident avoidance
automobile accidents	home's danger spots

1. Which idea could be generated from these brainstorming notes?
   (a) national accident statistics (c) accidental fires
   (b) avoiding home accidents (d) first-aid programs
2. Which question(s) could be used to explore this idea?
   (a) What are the special danger spots in and around the home?
   (b) Why do home accidents happen? (c) What are my experiences with home accidents? (d) All of these

Topic, Purpose, and Audience [pages 30–35] Write the letter of the item that correctly answers the question.

3. Which of the following topics is the most focused?
   (a) burns (b) injuries (c) caring for burns
4. Which audience would be the most interested in this topic?
   (a) young children (b) teachers (c) nurses

Writing for Review Plan to write a paragraph about something useful that you have learned recently. Generate ideas through freewriting, and then explore your ideas with questions. Then list a purpose, audience, and main idea. Finally, express your main ideas in a sentence.

CHAPTER 3 WRITING THE PARAGRAPH

Answer the questions based on the following paragraph.

[1]The aardvark is a strange-looking animal. [2]The duckbill platypus is perhaps a bit more unusual in appearance. [3]For instance, the aardvark has a long snout like a pig's, drooping eyelids with long lashes, and pointed ears like a donkey's. [4]Its legs are short, but its body is very fat and covered with thick fur. [5]The animal has a long tapering tail, and from the tip of its tail to the tip of its snout, an aardvark measures about six feet in length. [6]When fully grown, this strange creature weighs about one hundred pounds.

Topic Sentences [pages 46–49]

1. Which sentence is the topic sentence of the paragraph?
   (a) sentence 1 (b) sentence 3 (c) sentence 5 (d) sentence 6

Developing a Topic Sentence [pages 49–54]

2. The topic sentence in this paragraph is developed with
   (a) facts (b) reasons (c) details

Unity, Coherence, and Organization [pages 56–65]

3. Which sentence is not directly related to the topic sentence?
   (a) sentence 2 (b) sentence 3 (c) sentence 4 (d) sentence 5
4. The order used to organize the paragraph is
   (a) chronological (b) spatial (c) comparison and contrast

Writing for Review Write a paragraph based on the prewriting notes you made in the Writing for Review for Chapter 2.

CHAPTER 4 REVISING THE PARAGRAPH

Read the following paragraph, and answer the questions based on it.

[1]The sinking of the *Titanic* was an important event. [2]It changed much about life at sea. [3]Prior to the sinking, ships did not have to carry enough lifeboats for all passengers. [4]After the sinking, space was provided. [5]People no longer took sea travel lightly. [6]Everyone understood the importance of a ship's lifeboat drills and safe operation.

Revising the Topic Sentence [pages 72–73]

1. Which of the following is the better revision of sentence 1?
   (a) The sinking of the *Titanic* was an interesting event.
   (b) The sinking of the *Titanic* was an important event that brought about needed change.
   (c) The sinking of the *Titanic* shocked the world.

Revising Support and Development [pages 75–77]

2. Which is the best revision of sentence 2?
   (a) It lead to increased safety for people at sea.
   (b) It changed many of the practices of the shipping companies.
   (c) It made people think about sea travel.

Revising for Coherence [pages 79–80]

3. To which sentence would you add the transition *consequently?*
   (a) sentence 3 (b) sentence 5 (c) sentence 6

Revising Word Choice [pages 80–81]

4. Which of the following is the best revision of sentence 4?
   (a) After the sinking, space became available.
   (b) After the sinking, lifeboats improved.
   (c) After the sinking, lifeboat space was provided for everyone.

Writing for Review Revise the paragraph that you wrote for Review 3.

The Development of a Personal Writing Style

Thinking About Thinking: Recognizing Alternatives

Style is a matter of making choices. Suppose you are going to a fancy party and you choose to wear jeans instead of formal clothes: You are making a choice and making a statement. The same is true of language. When you choose the word *unusual* rather than the word *spectacular* to describe a new musical group, you make a statement about the qualities you want to emphasize. As you develop your personal writing style, you make choices. You engage in the thinking process called decision making.

Defining the Skill

One specific thinking skill that is essential to decision making is **RECOGNIZING ALTERNATIVES.** In order to decide whether one word works better in a sentence than another word, you need to recognize the variety of possible words you have to choose from. Recognizing your options, seeing possibilities, will help you make better decisions.

Applying the Skill

Look at the photograph. Notice that it shows both a foreground and a background. In the foreground you see objects near to the camera; in the background you see distant objects. Write a paragraph about one part of the picture—foreground or background—while a partner writes about the other part. Compare your descriptions. Decide which paragraph comes closer to communicating the idea of the whole picture. What *other* alternative ways of looking at the picture can you suggest?

CHAPTER 5

Choosing Words

"When I use a word," Humpty Dumpty said, "it means just what I choose it to mean—neither more or less."

"The question is," said Alice, "whether you can make the words mean so many different things."

"The question is," said Humpty Dumpty, "which is to be the master—that's all."

—Lewis Carroll

Words are a writer's tools. Like other craftspeople, a writer must, in Lewis Carroll's words, "master" the tools of the trade. To achieve such mastery, serious writers spend a lifetime studying words. They are fascinated by words and their countless shades of meaning. They know that the ability to choose words well makes writing easier and more exact.

Skillful writers are not content just with knowing the meanings of countless words. They also want to know how words are categorized and labeled and when to use a given word. For example, is *sloppy* a slang word? Is it all right to use this word in formal writing?

In this chapter you will have many opportunities to practice skills that will help you make informed choices about words. These skills include:

writing precisely
writing concisely
writing with figurative language

Your goal in this chapter is to recognize that word choice, or diction, is a deliberate act. It is an act that you can "master" during prewriting, writing, and revising. Only *you* know what you want to say. Therefore, only *you* can choose the words that express your ideas precisely.

Writing Precisely

Connotation is the unspoken or unwritten meaning associated with a word beyond its exact, dictionary meaning, or **denotation.**

To express ideas precisely, you need to know the connotations and denotations of words. You can easily check a word's denotation by referring to a dictionary, but you will not find the word's connotations fully explained there. Nevertheless, you need not worry: You have already learned countless connotations from speaking and writing. Your long experience in using the English language has given you intuitions that help you to judge which word is right for a given situation. For example, the denotations of the words *slender* and *skinny* are similar. Both words denote an absence of excess flesh. You know, however, that the connotations of the two words are very different. The two words cannot really be used interchangeably. The word *slender* connotes a pleasing absence of excess flesh while *skinny* suggests an absence of flesh that borders upon undernourishment. Try to use each word to complete the following sentence. Use *slender* first. You should be able to see at once the different connotations of these two words.

Proper diet and exercise produce a __________ body.

EXERCISE 1 **Determining Denotations and Connotations.** Use the dictionary to find the denotation of each of the following words. Write the denotation. Then, calling on your knowledge of English, your imagination, and your life experiences, list at least three connotations you associate with each defined word.

SAMPLE crafty
DENOTATION skillfully clever; able to manage things to advantage; shrewd; sharp
CONNOTATIONS scheming; deceitful; dishonest

1. talkative
2. flag
3. unconventional
4. friend
5. daring

EXERCISE 2 **Selecting Words by Connotation.** The following quotations are by famous writers. Above each quotation are three words that might be used to complete the writer's thought. In fact, one of the three is the word that the writer actually used. Call on your knowledge of English and your intuitions to help you choose the word that best completes each quotation. Write one reason for each of your choices.

1. intelligence wisdom sense
   Authority without ________ is like a heavy axe without an edge,
   fitter to bruise than polish.

   —Anne Bradstreet

2. grasp understanding hold
   Ah, but a man's reach should exceed his ________,
   Or what's a heaven for?

   —Robert Browning

3. flowed dripped trickled
   His answer ________ through my head,
   like water through a sieve.

   —Lewis Carroll

4. enlightened activated inspired
   Mankind was never so happily ________ as when it made a cathedral.

   —Robert Louis Stevenson

5. stupid ignorant uneducated
   If a nation expects to be ________ and free, in a state of civilization, it expects what never was and never will be.

   —Thomas Jefferson

General and Specific Words

A **general** word is all-embracing, infinite, and broad in scope, while a **specific** word is explicit, definite, and narrower in scope.

GENERAL	SPECIFIC	MORE SPECIFIC
artist	writer	poet
creature	bird	peacock
move	walk	swagger

Use specific words in your writing as often as possible. Because specific words are narrower in scope, they are more informative than general words. They help your readers to understand your meaning more exactly. Notice, for example, how much more you can tell about Grandma's attic when the word *things* is replaced with specific words in the second sentence.

GENERAL Grandma's attic was crowded with all kinds of things.

SPECIFIC Grandma's attic was crowded with dusty trunks, broken picture frames, old lamps, piles of magazines, a few rickety chairs, and a huge bureau.

EXERCISE 3 **Ordering Words from General to Specific.** Arrange in a written list the words in each of the following groups, starting with the most general word and ending with the most specific.

1. pet, animal, Fifi, quadruped, poodle, dog
2. writer, biped, woman, Jade Snow Wong, human
3. game, checkers, activity, board game, entertainment
4. mammal, creature, dolphin, bottlenosed dolphin
5. jet, machine, 747, vehicle, airplane

Concrete and Abstract Words

Concrete words refer to a thing or a feature that you can see, touch, taste, smell, or hear. Words are **abstract** when they refer to ideas, qualities, and feelings.

CONCRETE rainbow, lemon, siren, sour, salty

ABSTRACT equality, grief, wisdom, delightful, intelligent

If you use concrete words, you will convey your precise meaning to your readers. When you write about such abstract ideas as liberty and tyranny, use concrete words to make your ideas definite. For example, you can convey a more exact meaning of the abstract word *courage* by adding details, as in the following sentence: "When faced with danger, some people show their courage by overcoming personal fear and performing some necessary action." The meaning of *courage* could be made even more definite, as in this sentence: "Although her legs were like jelly and her heart was pounding, Lucille summoned the courage to put herself between the child and the ferocious dog."

If you want to know whether or not a sentence contains concrete words, ask yourself questions about it that begin with *Who? What? When? Where? Why?* and *How?*—the five *W*s and *H* that were introduced in Chapter 2. If the sentence can answer one or more of these questions exactly and precisely, it probably does contain concrete words. Without such words, your writing will lack life and color.

EXERCISE 4 **Recognizing Concrete and Abstract Words.** As you read the following passage, decide which of the underlined words and phrases are abstract and which are concrete. On a separate sheet of paper, list each underlined item under the heading *abstract* or *concrete*. Then indicate which sense each concrete item is meant to stimulate. Some of the items may stimulate more than one of your five senses.

"Then we saw the lightning, and that was the guns; and then we heard the thunder, and that was the big guns; and then we heard the rain falling, and that was the drops of blood falling; and when we came to get in the crops, it was the dead men that we reaped." So the escaped slave, Harriet Tubman, described one of the battles of the [Civil War] in which she took part, for she was in the thick of the fighting. Before the War Harriet Tubman devoted her life to the cause of freedom, and after the War to the advancement of her people.

She was born in Maryland, a slave, one of eleven sons and daughters. No one kept a record of her birth, so the exact year is not known. . . . She was a homely child, morose, willful, wild, and constantly in rebellion against slavery. . . . As a little girl, on the very first day that she was sent to work in the Big House, her mistress whipped her four times. Once she ran away and hid in a pig sty for five days, eating the scraps thrown to the pigs. "There were good masters and mistresses, so I've heard tell," she once said, "but I didn't happen to come across any of them."

. . . One day when she was in her early teens, something happened that affected her whole life. It was evening, and a young slave had, without permission, gone to a country store. The overseer followed him to whip him. He ordered Harriet to help tie him up. As Harriet refused, the slave ran. The overseer picked up a heavy iron weight and threw it. But he did not hit the fellow. He struck Harriet's head, almost crushing her skull, and leaving a deep scar forever. . . .

—Langston Hughes, "Harriet Tubman: The Moses of Her People"

Levels of Diction

The three levels of diction are informal, middle, and formal. If you are aware of these levels while writing, you will probably choose the right words—words that are appropriate to your purpose and audience. Some purposes and audiences require a more formal treatment than others. The lists that follow present several examples of the three levels of diction.

INFORMAL	MIDDLE	FORMAL
bum	beggar	mendicant
chicken	cowardly	faint-hearted
skinny	thin	gaunt
bash	party	celebration

Informal diction includes words used in everyday conversations with friends.

Informal diction is too casual for most written schoolwork but is often perfect for dialogue in a story. For example, a character in one of your stories may say, "The new play at the Shubert is a big flop." Yet you probably would not use this sentence as the topic sentence of a formal paragraph in a review written for English class. Check the dictionary if you are uncertain about whether or not a word is informal. There you may find the word labeled as *informal, colloquial,* or *slang*—two other kinds of informal words.

Colloquial is a term that refers to words used in everyday conversation and in writing intended to give the feeling of actual speech. Words such as *brainy, gym,* and *A-OK* are common colloquialisms. **Slang** is a label given to extremely informal (or highly colloquial) words. Slang is composed mostly of new words or unusual uses of existing words. In both writing and speech slang creates a noticeable effect, such as humor or exaggeration. *Creep, hood, ticker* (for *heart*), *fink,* and *cop* are all familiar slang words. Neither slang nor colloquialisms are considered "incorrect" or "bad" English. As older people can tell you, some items that were considered slang twenty years ago have become quite respectable.

Middle diction falls between informal and formal diction.

Middle diction includes words most often used in newspaper and magazine writing and in television newscasts. Middle diction is the best level for your writing, whether in a school paper or a letter to a relative. The words are familiar both to you and to your audience, and they will let you express your ideas in a straightforward and down-to-earth way. For example, if you are writing a paragraph for English class, you might begin with this sentence: "In my opinion most people have the wrong attitude toward insects."

Formal diction is the language most often found in scholarly journals and books.

If you use formal words without being aware of their connotations and denotations, your writing will be judged unnatural and forced.

Avoid formal diction unless it is appropriate to your subject and audience. By doing so, you will eliminate mixed diction, an inconsistency that can confuse your readers. If you are writing a serious paper on insects in which you mix formal, middle, and informal diction, your readers may find your article confusing, or even humorous. Consider the problems in this sentence, for example: "Although a great many unthinking people express their abhorrence for insects, bugs do not bug me in the least."

EXERCISE 5 **Determining Level of Diction.** To which level of diction—informal, middle, or formal—does each of the following words belong? Make a heading for each level, and categorize the words. Use a dictionary if necessary. Provide a middle-level synonym for each word on your formal and informal lists. Remember, a middle-level synonym is a word that would be familiar to you and to most other people. It would be a word that is suitable for use in a school paper.

For example, if the word *buddy* appeared in the following list, you would include it on the list headed *informal*. You might note *friend* as a middle-level equivalent.

1. funny
2. firearms
3. criminal
4. blast (noun)
5. cinema
6. discipline
7. boss
8. insane
9. doodlebug
10. goldbricker

Writing Concisely

Inflated diction is unnatural, pretentious, imprecise, and overly formal language.

Do not use "big" words simply to impress your readers. If you do, your readers will be too busy translating the pretentious words into plain English to be impressed. You can avoid inflated diction by asking yourself two questions: How would I express this idea if I were speaking? Are my words specific and concrete enough to convey my meaning clearly?

If you should ever be tempted to use inflated diction in your writing, think of these words of H. L. Mencken, the American editor, critic, and writer: "If you think a flea is as large as a Newfoundland dog, as beautiful as the Queen of Sheba, and as dignified as the Archbishop of Canterbury, then say, 'A conflagration consumed the edifice'; otherwise say, 'The house burned down.' "

EXERCISE 6 **Deflating Inflated Diction.** Rewrite the following sentences, using middle-level diction. Asking yourself these questions will help eliminate inflated diction: How would I express this idea if I were speaking? Are the words specific and concrete enough to convey the meaning clearly?

SAMPLE Refrain from producing all that clamor.
REWRITE Stop making all that noise.

1. A feathered vertebrate is vocalizing a melody.
2. An unknown person is projecting portions of petrified matter.
3. Members of the human race are classified as bipedal.
4. Cleanse the digited extremities of your upper limbs in advance of consuming your repast.
5. The woman who filled the maternal role dispatched her male offspring to procure assistance.

Clichés

A **cliché** is an expression that has become trite through excessive use.

An expression that is now a cliché was at one time a vital, effective expression. After the expression was used over and over again, it lost its meaning and freshness. You might have to use a cliché in writing now and then, but your writing will be livelier if you invent your own expressions and use straightforward language. Writing that is full of clichés sounds flat and unimaginative. Consider these examples:

CLICHÉ The good news came out of the blue on Monday.
BETTER The good news came unexpectedly on Monday.

CLICHÉ Henry and his father are cut from the same bolt.
BETTER Henry and his father are very much alike.

Decide whether or not an expression is a cliché by reading the first few words of the expression. Then see if the last part automatically comes to mind. Try this approach with the following examples: *with bated . . . , so near and yet . . . , beat a hasty . . . .*

EXERCISE 7 **Replacing a Cliché with a Specific Word.** Substitute one specific, carefully chosen word or phrase for each cliché below.

1. old Sol
2. at death's door
3. bury the hatchet
4. diamond in the rough
5. goodly number
6. whisper sweet nothings
7. square shooter
8. walk on air
9. tried and true
10. leave no stone unturned

EXERCISE 8 **Eliminating Clichés.** Rewrite the following sentences, substituting more original words for the underlined clichés. Some sentences have more than one cliché.

1. Al is feeling in the pink and is eager to get rolling again.
2. Grandpa always tells me to make hay while the sun shines.
3. Gretchen has a mind like a steel trap.
4. I am glad you think the test was a piece of cake.
5. Pete always gets down in the dumps on rainy days.
6. Don't criticize Audrey until you have walked in her shoes for a while.
7. Mel gives everything the old college try.
8. It is never wise to have too many irons in the fire.
9. Dad always says that a bird in the hand is worth two in the bush.
10. Stop making mountains out of molehills.

Jargon

Jargon is the specialized vocabulary of a group or profession.

All groups have their own vocabulary and lawyers, doctors, computer programmers, and mechanics are no exceptions. Jargon is appropriate and acceptable when used by a specialist writing or speaking to other specialists in the same field. It is inappropriate in school writing when ordinary words will convey the meaning just as well. Jargon clouds the meaning of your writing, and, like inflated diction, jargon must often be translated into plain English to be understood. Study the following examples.

JARGON Get a breakdown of the promotional expenditures for the previous month's sales leaders a.s.a.p.

BETTER Get an analysis of the amount of money spent on advertising for last month's best-selling products as soon as possible.

JARGON Science professionals have verified and established that sunlight augments the food value of plants by photosynthesis.

BETTER Scientists have proven time and time again that sunlight builds up the food value of green plants.

EXERCISE 9 **Replacing Jargon.** Write a clearer word or phrase for each example of jargon in the following list. If necessary, use the dictionary to learn the exact meaning of each example.

1. update (verb)
2. pinpoint (verb)
3. median income
4. interface (verb)

Writing with Figurative Language

A **figure of speech,** or **figurative language,** is a word or phrase used in an imaginative, rather than literal, sense. **Literal language** is language that means exactly what it says, word for word.

By using figurative language, you can make your writing more vivid and lively. Two figures of speech that you can use when you write are simile and metaphor.

A **simile** is a figure of speech that directly compares two seemingly unlike things and uses a comparing word such as *like* or *as*.

The items compared in a simile are basically unalike, but they do share some characteristics. For example, consider the simile in these two lines of a poem by Sir John Suckling:

> Her feet beneath her petticoat,
> *Like* little mice, stole in and out.
>
> —"A Ballad upon a Wedding"

The poet sees the woman walking, and compares her feet darting in and out from her floor-length skirt to the darting movements of mice. In this model the word *like* signals that a simile is coming. *Like* does not always signal a simile, however; consider the following sentence, which compares two things that are actually alike: "Marita is like her father." The word *as* can also signal a simile as in these lines written by American poet Elinor Wylie:

> His arms were thick *as* hickory logs
> Whittled to little wrists:
> Strong *as* the teeth of terrier dogs
> Were the fingers of his fists.
>
> —"The Puritan's Ballad"

A **metaphor** is a figure of speech that makes an implied comparison between two seemingly unlike things.

Unlike a simile, a metaphor does not use the words *like* or *as:*

SIMILE She is like a feather in the wind.
METAPHOR She is a feather in the wind.

Metaphors make writing lively and exciting because they surprise readers by revealing similarities in objects not normally considered alike. Metaphors can lend great power to your writing. Consider these examples from a short story by American writer Eugenia Collier:

> Poverty was the cage in which we all were trapped, and our hatred of it was still the vague, undirected restlessness of the zoo-bred flamingo who knows that nature created him to fly.
>
> —"Marigolds"

EXERCISE 10 **Identifying Figurative Language.** Indicate in writing the kind of figurative language used in each of the following sentences. Then explain why the simile or metaphor is effective.

1. My life has been one great big joke,
   A dance that's walked
   A song that's spoke . . . —Maya Angelou, "When I Think About Myself"
2. Age, like distance, lends a double charm. —Oliver Wendell Holmes
3. I am a guitar string cutting through the Smog
   Vibrating and bringing in morning —Victor Hernandez Cruz, "Side 32"
4. The white mares of the moon rush along the sky Beating their golden hoofs upon the glass Heavens . . .

   —Amy Lowell, "Night Clouds"
5. My memories are as magical as golden wings, lifting me to heights, carrying me distances that even birds don't remember.

   —Trebor Srevart, "Mind Flights"

EXERCISE 11 **Writing Figurative Language.** Select five ideas from the list below. Write a sentence that expresses each idea through simile or metaphor. Use the figures of speech in Exercise 10 as models.

1. a fish jumping out of water
2. traffic at rush hour
3. an elephant walking
4. the face of an older person
5. a baby sleeping or playing
6. a cold drink on a hot day
7. a violent electrical storm
8. a favorite book

Checklist for Choosing Words

1. Are the denotations and connotations of my words precise?
2. Which of my general words can I replace with specific words?
3. Which of my abstract words can I replace with concrete words?
4. What level of diction have I used—informal, middle, or formal? Can I make my word choice more consistent?
5. Which clichés, inflated diction, or jargon should be changed?
6. What similes and metaphors would improve my writing?
7. Have I avoided figures of speech that are clichés, such as "cool as a cucumber," "happy as a lark," and "pretty as a picture"?
8. Have I avoided far-fetched, elaborate figures of speech, such as, "The weeping babe was a gentle spring shower nourishing the loving care in his mother's heart"?
9. Does my word choice suit my purpose and audience?

Writer's Choice

Writer's Choice #1

ASSIGNMENT To write a paragraph about a race you saw

LENGTH Up to ten sentences

AUDIENCE The readers of the sports section in a newspaper

PURPOSE To describe the race clearly and vividly.

PREWRITING Run an instant replay of the race in your mind. List five to ten things you see in the instant replay.

WRITING Begin by giving the results of the race. Tell when and where the race took place. Then in four or five sentences use precise and colorful words to explain how the race looks to you. End with a sentence about how you reacted to the outcome of the race.

REVISING Ask yourself the questions in the checklist on page 104. Then edit, proofread, and share your paragraph.

Writer's Choice #2

ASSIGNMENT To write a paragraph about smart shopping

LENGTH Six to seven sentences

AUDIENCE Shoppers in general

PURPOSE To point out the connotations of the names of products and of words used in advertising them

PREWRITING Make a list of five product names and their connotations. Then choose three names for your paragraph.

WRITING In your topic sentence tell why you are writing the paragraph. Then write four or five sentences to explain the connotations three product names have for you and how these connotations may influence shoppers. End with a sentence advising your audience to think about the connotations of the product names before they buy.

REVISING Ask yourself the questions in the checklist on page 104. Then edit, proofread, and share your paragraph.

Writer's Choice #3

ASSIGNMENT To revise a paragraph on any topic

LENGTH Your choice

AUDIENCE Your choice

PURPOSE To describe exactly what you see

OPTIONS You may wish to base your description on a photograph in the Writer's Sourcebook, pages 354–357.

REVISING Remember to prewrite and revise.

Writers on Writing

Born in Illinois, Carin Chabut attended Indian Hill High School in Cincinnati, Ohio. She spends her spare time listening to all types of music, watching James Bond films, and traveling as much as she can.

THE PRODUCT

A stream is a restful place. Nestled in a criblike valley, it stretches between two hills whose green foliage provides a blanket for the tiny stream. The fragrance of the surrounding land is soft and sweet. Sunshine glistens on the skin of the water, giving it a newborn, freshly scrubbed look. Water trickles over stones, making a soft, gurgling sound. All is quiet, and nothing disturbs the stream's slumber.

THE PROCESS

I am a writer who likes to revise, but I am also the kind of writer who sometimes cannot continue a project without the "perfect" word choice and word order. I usually do not have problems finding the right word (although occasionally I do get stuck and frustrated when a certain word does not suit my purpose). Instead, my problems in writing involve putting the words in the best order. Which adjective should come first? Which idea should come first in the sentence? Also, I tend to rely on adjectives a bit too often—they are possibly my specialty. I would like to concentrate more on nouns and verbs.

I enjoy descriptive writing because it gives me the chance to play around with colorful words and connotations, something I love. My style in this kind of writing usually involves colorful but simple words. I do not like to get caught up in elaborate words, because they can distract me from what I am trying to say.

I began this passage intending merely to write about a stream using descriptive words. The second sentence, however, gave me an idea—I decided to compare the stream to a baby. This new idea gave me a new direction in my paragraph, and then I had to be even more careful about word choice.

YOUR TURN *Writing Figuratively*

In her finished product Carin personified a stream, giving it the qualities of a baby. Write about a natural or urban scene of your own choice, and find something within your scene that you can personify.

CHAPTER 6

Writing and Combining Sentences

It is incumbent upon the person who wants to become a writer to learn the language, to have that language in such control that she can ball up a handful of words and throw them against the wall and make them bounce like a basketball, or that she can rearrange them to make people weep.

—Maya Angelou

How do you come to know the language so thoroughly that you can control your writing in this way? An old joke says, "How do you get to Carnegie Hall?" The answer: "Practice." If you practice—and *practice*—putting words together into sentences, you will find that your sentences will begin to bounce, slither, or soar at your command. They will also make your readers listen carefully to whatever you say.

Read the following paragraph. Does it hold your attention?

> The archaeologist hopped out of the jeep. She carried a long steel rod. She strode quickly toward a high mound of sand. The mound rose ten feet from the desert floor. She began to press the rod into the mound. Her face brightened suddenly. The rod had touched something inside the mound. She wondered what it could be. She hoped for an ancient artifact. She pulled out an old boot. It was not an ancient one, unfortunately.

If you nodded off about halfway through the paragraph, it is not surprising. The brief, repetitious sentences probably wore you down. Subject, verb, modifier or object—the words of every sentence are arranged in the same basic way. Now read this.

> Carrying a long steel rod, the archaeologist hopped out of the jeep and strode quickly toward a high mound of sand that rose ten feet from the desert floor. She began to press the rod into the mound. Suddenly her face brightened: The rod had touched something inside the mound. What could it be? She hoped for an ancient artifact; unfortunately, what she pulled out was an old—but not ancient—boot.

The second paragraph probably held your attention from beginning to end. As your eyes moved from sentence to sentence, the scene became clearer. The words in this paragraph are practically the same as those in the first paragraph. What then made you react differently to the second paragraph? If you are thinking something like "the way the words are arranged in the sentences," you are beginning to see the point of this chapter. By analyzing the sentences, you can see that the writer has joined some sentences, alternated short and long sentences, inverted normal word order in some sentences, and varied the beginnings of the sentences. As a result the paragraph is alive, it flows naturally, and it makes you want to keep reading.

In this chapter, you will practice these skills:

- expanding sentences with words and phrases
- combining sentences through coordination
- combining sentences through subordination
- combining sentences through coordination and subordination
- combining sentences by using other structures
- writing concise sentences and paragraphs
- creating variety in sentences
- using parallelism for effect

As you perfect these skills, you will be learning how to write truly effective sentences, sentences that "bounce" the way you want them to. What is more, you will write sentences that will make your audience listen carefully to what you have to say.

Expanding Sentences with Words and Phrases

Look or think back to the last piece of writing you did. Was it a collection of short, choppy sentences like those in the first model paragraph on page 107? Are the sentences you write usually like this? If so, you will find this section of the chapter helpful.

You can expand too-brief sentences by adding words and phrases that give more information about nouns and verbs.

A kumquat is a fruit.

A kumquat is a **small, subtropical**, fruit with **an edible skin.** [expanded with adjectives and a prepositional phrase that modify the noun *fruit*]

The women picked the kumquats.

Quickly and **skillfully** the women picked the kumquats **from the dwarf trees.** [expanded with adverbs and a prepositional phrase that modify the verb *picked*]

Where do you find information to add to choppy sentences? You can supply new details by asking such questions as *how many? what kind? when? how?* and *where?*

EXERCISE 1 **Expanding Sentences by Adding Details.** Expand the following sentences by adding appropriate words or phrases to each. The questions after each sentence suggest details you can add.

SAMPLE The archaeologist examined the mummy. (a) What was the archaeologist like? (b) How did he examine the mummy?

REVISION *The tall German* archaeologist examined the mummy *with great care.*

REVISION *With great care the tall German* archaeologist examined the mummy.

1. The astronauts worked.
   a. How many astronauts were there?
   b. On what did they work?
2. The president waved.
   a. Which president waved?
   b. To whom or what did the president wave?
3. The astronomers observed the comet.
   a. When did the astronomers observe the comet?
   b. Through what did they observe it?
4. The walls were crumbling.
   a. What kind of walls were crumbling?
   b. Where and how were the walls crumbling?
5. The lizard climbed.
   a. What was the size and color of the lizard?
   b. How and where did it climb?

Combining Sentences Through Coordination

In the process of learning to speak as a child, one of the "language tricks" you picked up from the speech of others was coordinating, or tying together, sentences or parts of sentences. You learned to do this by using coordinating conjunctions, such as *and, or, nor, but* and *for.* For example, study this pair of sentences:

> You should be careful when operating an electric saw. Using this tool carelessly can cause serious injury.

The two sentences present closely related ideas, ideas that are probably too closely related to be walled apart by a period. Instead, combine them in the same sentence by using the coordinator *for*, which indicates that you are giving a reason:

> You should be careful when operating an electric saw, **for** using this tool carelessly can cause serious injury.

If two sentences are closely related and almost equal in importance, stress their relatedness and equality by combining them through coordination.

It is up to you to choose when to combine sentences through coordination. You should, however, avoid writing many coordinated sentences one after the other, for it can make your writing repetitious and uninteresting. If you use coordination, be sure to select the most appropriate word or phrase to combine sentences. The following chart lists the most common of these words or phrases. Note the punctuation used with each.

COORDINATION CHART

PURPOSE	COORDINATOR	EXAMPLE
To show an alternative	or, nor, otherwise	Wear sunglasses, **or** you will hurt your eyes. Wear sunglasses; **otherwise** you will hurt your eyes.
To signal an addition	and, also, furthermore, in addition, similarly	Goldfish are easy to care for, **and** they are restful to watch. Goldfish are easy to care for; **in addition**, they are restful to watch.
To show a reason	for/because	Many people travel on jet planes, for they are fast and safe.
To signal contrast	but, yet, instead, nevertheless, still, however	Jet planes are safer than automobiles, **yet** some people are afraid to fly. Jet planes are safer than automobiles; **nevertheless**, some people are afraid to fly.
To signal an example	for example, for instance	Some diseases have been controlled; **for instance**, vaccines have made people immune to polio.
To show a result	as a result, thus, so, therefore	Writing poetry is a demanding task; **thus**, few people choose to become poets.
To show balance	*semicolon*	Alaska is the largest state; Rhode Island is the smallest.

EXERCISE 2 **Combining Complete Sentences Through Coordination.** Combine each of the following pairs of sentences. Use a coordinating word or phrase that indicates the relationship shown in parentheses. For help in choosing words and phrases and punctuating correctly, refer to the preceding coordination chart.

1. Some Presidents have served very briefly in office. William Henry Harrison was President for only one month. (example)
2. Several Presidents have served for two terms. Grover Cleveland was the only President to serve for two noncontinuous terms. (contrast)
3. Upon the death of President McKinley, Theodore Roosevelt became the youngest President of the United States. John F. Kennedy was the youngest candidate to be elected President. (balance)
4. Voters should exercise their right to vote in every election. They will have no right to complain about their public officials. (alternative)
5. The symbol of the Republican Party is the elephant. The symbol of the Democratice Party is the donkey. (balance)
6. Richard M. Nixon holds a unique position in American history. He is the only President to resign from office. (reason)
7. Franklin Roosevelt could not walk. His wife, Eleanor, often represented him in public appearances. (result)

EXERCISE 3 **Combining Sentences Through Coordination.** Rewrite the following paragraph, combining sentences through coordination. You may combine any number of sentences; you may also leave some sentences as they are. The paragraph now contains ten sentences. Your version should contain between five and eight.

In Britain the day before the beginning of Lent has several names. It is known as Shrove Tuesday and Pancake Day. The British people once celebrated this day by eating tall stacks of pancakes. Long ago during

Lent people did not eat milk or eggs. Pancake Day may have begun as a way of using up leftover dairy products. Shrove Tuesday merriment included pancake-flipping contests. The idea was to catch your pancakes in midair. You might have to retrieve them from the fire. Today most British people do not celebrate Shrove Tuesday in this way. They still eat many pancakes.

Combining Sentences Through Subordination

You can have too much of a good thing—even coordination. An uninterrupted string of coordinated sentences is repetitious and can be unappealing to readers. Consider this passage:

> The *Peanuts* comic strip is read avidly by millions, and it was created by cartoonist Charles Schulz. Of course, the cartoon characters make us laugh, but they still teach us something. Charlie Brown never stops trying, yet he fails at everything. Linus's blanket goes everywhere he goes, for it makes him feel secure. Readers do not always like to laugh at their own faults; however, they can still laugh at the faults of these delightful *Peanuts* characters.

In this passage the writer has written six coordinated sentences one after another, thus giving equal emphasis to every idea in the passage. The following revision of the passage is more lively because the sentences are varied. The revision also affects the meaning—it emphasizes some ideas and de-emphasizes others.

> The *Peanuts* comic strip, which is read avidly by millions, was created by cartoonist Charles Schulz. Although the cartoon characters make us chuckle, they also teach us something. Charlie Brown, who fails at everything, never stops trying. Linus's blanket goes everywhere he goes because it makes him feel secure. Readers who do not like to laugh at their own faults can still laugh at the faults of these delightful *Peanuts* characters.

As you can see, the revised passage has some coordination. The writer, however, has used a technique called *subordination* to call attention to some ideas and to put others in the background. *Subordination* refers to a method of placing one thing below another in rank and importance.

Subordinate a less important idea to a more important one.

The following pages will give you practice in using three different methods of subordination.

Subordinating Information About Nouns

Think about how you could combine these two sentences:

1. Neil Armstrong is an American hero.
2. Neil Armstrong was the first person to step on the moon.

You could combine the two sentences by using coordination, thus giving equal emphasis to the ideas in both.

3. Neil Armstrong is an American hero, for he was the first person to step on the moon.

Suppose, however, that you want to give the idea in one sentence more importance than the idea in the other. You could use subordination to combine the sentences:

VERSION A Neil Armstrong, **who is an American hero**, was the first person to step on the moon. [Sentence 1 has been subordinated to an adjective clause that tells more about the noun *Neil Armstrong*.]

VERSION B Neil Armstrong, **who was the first person to step on the moon**, is an American hero. [Sentence 2 has been subordinated to an adjective clause that modifies the noun *Neil Armstrong*.]

VERSION C Neil Armstrong is an American hero **who was the first person to step on the moon.** [Sentence 2 has been subordinated to an adjective clause that tells more about the noun *hero*.]

In version A the idea about Armstrong's status as an American hero is subordinated to the idea about his unique experience on the moon. In versions B and C the reverse is true: The idea about Armstrong's unique experience is subordinated to the idea about his status as a hero. As you can see, the subordinated idea in all three versions is introduced by the word *who* which replaces the proper noun *Neil Armstrong* in the original sentence.

Subordinate information in one sentence to modify a noun or pronoun in another sentence by using the words *who, whose, that,* and *which*.

A subordinated group of words that tells more about a noun is called a *relative clause,* or an *adjective clause*. The word that introduces the clause is called a *relative pronoun*.

Reread version A and B. In both versions the relative clause is separated by commas from the rest of the sentence. The clauses in the two sentences are set off this way because neither is essential to the meaning of the rest of the sentence. In each sentence, the relative clause gives additional information about a noun—*Neil Armstrong*—that is already clear to us. On the other hand, the relative clause in version C is essential to the meaning of the sentence; that is, it limits or restricts the meaning of the noun *hero*. You should not use commas to set off a relative clause that is essential to the meaning of a sentence.

To find more information about essential and nonessential relative clauses, refer to Chapter 20. More information about punctuating relative clauses is given in Chapter 27.

When you need help in using relative pronouns to subordinate information about nouns, you can consult the following chart:

SUBORDINATING INFORMATION ABOUT NOUNS

ORIGINAL SENTENCES	COMBINED THROUGH SUBORDINATION
Thomas Edison made many contributions to the world. He was called the "wizard of Menlo Park."	*Thomas Edison, who is called the "wizard of Menlo Park," made many contributions to the world.*
Edison is famous for many inventions. These inventions changed history.	*Edison is famous for many inventions that changed history.*
Edison's dictaphone was considered a marvel when it first appeared. The dictaphone was eventually replaced by better recording devices.	*Edison's dictaphone, which was eventually replaced by better recording devices, was considered a marvel when it first appeared.*
Edison was a skilled businessman. His inventions earned him millions of dollars.	*Edison was a skilled businessman whose inventions earned him millions of dollars.*
Edison was a great inventor. I admire him tremendously.	*Edison was a great inventor whom I admire tremendously.*

EXERCISE 4 **Subordinating Information About Nouns.** Rewrite each of the following pairs of sentences as a single sentence with subordinate information about a noun.

SAMPLE Chubby Checker became well known in the 1960s. He popularized a dance called the "twist."

REVISION Chubby Checker, *who popularized a dance called the "twist,"* became well known in the 1960s.

REVISION Chubby Checker, *who became well known in the 1960s,* popularized a dance called the "twist."

1. The game of soccer has been called the only international language. This game is played throughout the world.
2. The World Cup soccer match is the most widely viewed sports event on earth. It is held every four years.
3. Pele might well have been called the ambassador of world soccer. His daring playing style was admired by fans everywhere.
4. American sports fans became interested in soccer because of Pele. They knew very little about the sport.
5. Pele's skill earned him the respect of other players. His skill combined precision and artistry.
6. Rio de Janiero has a soccer stadium. This stadium seats 160,000.
7. Soccer fans often lose control of their emotions during a game. They are passionate rooters.
8. In one stadium a moat separates the playing field from the stands. It is meant to protect the players from excitable fans.
9. One Uruguayan player was knocked out by adoring fans. Their congratulations became dangerously enthusiastic.
10. To escape a mob one Greek referee had to disguise himself as a priest. The mob strongly disagreed with some of his calls.

Subordinating Information About Verbs

You can also combine two sentences by subordinating information in one sentence to modify a verb in the other. One sentence will thus be subordinated to tell *when, where, how, why, to what extent* or *under what conditions* the action of the verb in the other sentence is performed.

You can create several different sentences by combining the two that follow:

> People must conserve water. The weather is dry.

These are a few possibilities:

> People must conserve water **when the weather is dry.**
> People must conserve water **because the weather is dry.**
> People must conserve water **wherever the weather is dry.**

In each sentence, *People must conserve water* is the most important information. The subordinated, less important information tells *when, why,* or *where* people must conserve water. This subordinated information is presented in adverb clauses that modify the verb *must conserve.*

Subordinate one sentence to another in order to tell *when, where, how, why, to what extent,* or *under what conditions* the action of the other sentence was performed.

Many options are open to you when you write sentences using subordinates of this kind. First decide *which idea to subordinate:*

> Booker T. Washington was born a slave. He later became a college president.
>
> **Although he was born a slave**, Booker T. Washington later became a college president.
>
> **Although he later became a college president**, Booker T. Washington was born a slave.

A second option is to put the adverb clause in different positions within the sentence. A final option is to determine the relationship between the two ideas you want to highlight. The word you choose to introduce the subordinated idea will indicate this relationship. Notice the different relationships between the two ideas in the following sentences.

> We stay healthy **because** we take care of our bodies.
> We stay healthy **if** we take care of our bodies.
> We stay healthy **as long as** we take care of our bodies.

The words *because, if,* and *as long as* introduce the subordinate idea in each of the preceding sentences. The following list supplies you with other such words:

1. To introduce subordinate ideas that tell *when:*

after	as soon as	since	when	while
as	before	until	whenever	

2. To introduce subordinate ideas that tell *where:*

   where   wherever

3. To introduce subordinate ideas that tell *how:*

   as   as if   as though

4. To introduce subordinate ideas that tell *why:*

   as   because   in order that   since   so that

5. To introduce subordinate ideas that tell *to what extent:*

   as far as   as fast as   as long as   than

6. To introduce subordinate ideas that state *conditions:*

although	(even) if	so long as	whether (or not)
considering	in as much as	unless	while

For more information about adverb clauses, refer to Chapter 20. For guidance in punctuating adverb clauses, see Chapter 27.

EXERCISE 5 **Subordinating Information About Verbs.** Rewrite each of the following sentence pairs as a single sentence with a subordinate idea that tells more about the main verb. You will have to choose between several alternative ways of rewriting each pair of sentences.

SAMPLE Some species of whale may become extinct. Many countries refuse to ban whale hunting.

REVISION Some species of whale may become extinct *since many countries refuse to ban whale hunting.*

REVISION *So long as many countries refuse to ban whale hunting,* some species of whale may become extinct.

1. Trivial Pursuit is a game. Many people take it very seriously.
2. Members of Congress should not vote themselves a pay raise. The government is asking citizens to hold down wages.
3. Vitamin pills are not necessary. You eat well-balanced meals.
4. The students turned fifteen. They applied for Social Security cards.
5. Tornado funnel clouds whirl through an area. They cause staggering amounts of damage.
6. The thirteen colonies declared their independence from Great Britain. They became the United States.
7. Diana Ross was not known as an actress. She played singer Billie Holiday in *Lady Sings the Blues.*
8. Hikers put moleskin on their feet. They do not get blisters.
9. Shirley Temple used to sing "On the Good Ship Lollipop." She could not wait to sail on it.
10. An electronic calculator is useless without power. The abacus could be the calculator of the energy-conscious future.

Creating Noun Substitutes

Suppose that you wish to combine the following two sentences by subordinating the one that is underlined:

You want the money. The bank can lend you the money.

Study these options:

VERSION A The bank can lend you the money **that you want.** [information subordinated in a relative, or adjective, clause to tell more about the noun *money*]

VERSION B The bank can lend you the money **as soon as you want.** [information subordinated in an adverb clause to modify the verb *lend*]

VERSION C The bank can lend you **whatever you want.** [information subordinated in a noun clause which substitutes for the noun *money*]

If you use the subordination option presented in version A, you combine the two sentences in order to give more information about a *noun.* In choosing the option presented in version B, you subordinated one sentence to tell more about a *verb* in the other. The option presented in version C will let you subordinate one sentence and use it *as a substitute for a noun or pronoun* in the other. This is an effective option if you want to state a fact or include a question within another sentence. Consider the following examples:

> Why was the thief given such a light sentence? This mystified us.
> **Why the thief was given such a light sentence** mystified us.
>
> Broccoli has health benefits. Scientists are proving this.
> Scientists are proving **that broccoli has health benefits.**

The sentences in the first example were combined by placing the question of the first sentence before the information in the second. The sentences in the second example were combined by placing the statement of fact from the first sentence after the information given in the second.

When you want to state a fact or question within a sentence, subordinate the material, and use it as a noun or pronoun.

The following chart will help you find the correct word for introducing the subordinate clause. (For more information about noun substitutes, see Chapter 20.)

CREATING NOUN SUBSTITUTES

INTRODUCTORY WORD	ORIGINAL SENTENCES	COMBINED WITH SUBORDINATION
who, whoever, whomever, whose	Who had the idea for Busch Gardens in Florida? He or she deserves our thanks.	**Whoever had the idea for Busch Gardens in Florida** deserves our thanks.
what, whatever	What should I see at Busch Gardens? Please tell me.	Please tell me **what I should see at Busch Gardens.**
which, whichever	Which exhibits and rides have you already picked out? You will love them.	You will love **whichever exhibits and rides you have already picked out.**
how, that, when, why, where, if, whether (or not)	The prices there are low. I was delighted by this fact.	I was delighted **that the prices there were so low.**

EXERCISE 6 **Creating Noun Substitutes at the End of Sentences.** Rewrite the following pairs of sentences. Place the statement of fact or question in one sentence at the end of the information in the other. Use the preceding chart to find words to replace nouns or pronouns.

SAMPLE Who built the ancient, snakelike mounds in the Midwest? Scientists cannot tell us this.

REVISION Scientists cannot tell us who built the ancient, snakelike mounds in the Midwest.

1. Halley's Comet reappeared in 1986. Scientists estimated this.
2. What causes cancer? Medical researchers are making progress in discovering it.
3. Ancient people once constructed huge stone heads on Easter Island in the Pacific. Anthropologists can only wonder how.
4. Who will be our first woman President? Political experts have tried to predict the answer.

EXERCISE 7 **Creating Noun Substitutes at the Beginning of a Sentence.** Rewrite the following pairs of sentences. Place the statement of fact or question in one sentence at the beginning of the information in the other.

SAMPLE The Russian winter was causing deep suffering to his men. *It* made little difference to Napoleon.

REVISION *That* the Russian winter was causing deep suffering to his men made little difference to Napoleon.

1. What causes the strange happenings in the Bermuda Triangle? This remains an intriguing puzzle.
2. He was misunderstood by many Americans. That must have disheartened President Lincoln.
3. Why was Lee Harvey Oswald killed after he shot President Kennedy? This is an unanswered question of American history.
4. Where should the national capital be located? That was one of the many decisions George Washington had to make.

Combining Through Coordination and Subordination

Suppose you are revising the first paragraph of a social studies paper. When you come across the following three sentences, you decide that they should be combined into one:

1. The electric company never sends bills to the people of Sinks of Gandy.
2. Visitors never hear telephones ring there.
3. These visitors chance upon the small West Virginia village.

Here is how you finally combine the three sentences.

> The electric company never sends bills to the people of Sinks of Gandy, and visitors who chance upon this small West Virginia village never hear telephones ring there.

By using both coordination and subordination in the new sentence, you showed how all the ideas in the three original sentences are related. The ideas in sentences 1 and 2 become the major ones in the new sentence. You coordinated the two ideas with a comma and the word *and*. You use the word *who* to subordinate the information in sentence 3 to tell more about *visitors*.

You can use both **coordination** and **subordination** to join two or more equally important ideas with ideas that are less important.

When you use both coordination and subordination you must decide which ideas to emphasize and which to subordinate. You must also decide on the order in which you will present the ideas and on the words you can use to join them. You can always decide *not* to use both coordination and subordination in the same sentence. Long sentences like the one about Sinks of Gandy are useful only occasionally.

EXERCISE 8 **Revising a Paragraph.** Rewrite the following paragraph. Combine some of these short sentences, using techniques you have been practicing: (1) coordination, (2) subordination, and (3) coordination and subordination. The paragraph contains thirteen sentences; your version should contain between seven and nine.

Someone mentions Africa. We often call up images of thick tropical forests. Wild animals live in them. These forests are also home to scattered tribes of people in tiny villages. These images do not describe the whole continent. This fact may surprise you. Tropical forests grow on only one-fifth of Africa's surface. Deserts and grasslands cover the remaining four-fifths of the continent. Furthermore, not all Africans live in villages. Nairobi is the capital city of Kenya. It is a modern city of over half a million people. Casablanca, Dakar, Brazzaville, and Khartoum are only a few of the other large, modern cities. They dot the African landscape.

Combining Sentences by Using Other Structures

Coordination and subordination are not the only methods of combining ideas in sentences. More concise methods, such as the ones you will practice in the next few pages, may create the effect you want.

Combining with Appositives

To identify or describe a noun in a sentence, you do not always need to insert a whole statement into the sentence. As an alternative, you can use a word or phrase that will define or describe the noun more concisely. The word or phrase you use is an *appositive*. Take a look at how appositives can help you put information together into sentences:

In *Singin' in the Rain* Gene Kelly danced brilliantly. *Singin' in the Rain* is a movie made in 1952.

VERSION A In *Singin' in the Rain,* **which is a movie made in 1952**, Gene Kelly danced brilliantly.

VERSION B In *Singin' in the Rain,* **a 1952 movie**, Gene Kelly danced brilliantly.

If you are writing a paragraph and need a long sentence at some point, you might use version A. Version B is more concise; it eliminates the subject (*which*) and the verb, and gets right to the identification: *a 1952 musical.* This phrase is one example of an appositive. You would probably use version B if you needed a short sentence at some point in your paragraph. (If you need more information about appositives, refer to Chapter 19.)

When one statement identifies or briefly describes a noun, you can shorten that statement by making it an appositive.

An appositive often follows the noun it identifies or describes, as in version A. You can also put an appositive at the beginning of a sentence for greater emphasis, as in version B:

VERSION A Marie Curie, **an outstanding Polish scientist**, discovered radium.

VERSION B **An outstanding Polish scientist**, Marie Curie discovered radium.

You can also revise the sentence to make other words the appositive, as in the following example:

VERSION C Marie Curie, **the discoverer of radium**, was an outstanding Polish scientist.

EXERCISE 9 **Combining Sentences by Using Appositives.** Use an appositive to combine each of the following pairs of sentences. In some instances, you will have to decide which sentence to make the appositive and where to place it in the sentence.

SAMPLE The symbol for polonium is Po. Polonium is a radioactive element.

REVISION The symbol for polonium, a radioactive element, is Po.

1. The symbol for gold is Au. Gold was the most prized element in the ancient world.
2. Ag is the symbol for silver. It is a soft, malleable element.
3. Uranium is named after the planet Uranus. Uranium is the main component of nuclear fuels and weapons.
4. Uranus was discovered only a short time before uranium. Uranus is the third largest planet in the solar system.
5. Uranus was named after a Greek god. This Greek god was the mythical ruler of the universe.
6. Uranus was the father of the Titans. The Titans were giants once thought to rule the world.
7. Titanium is named for the Titans. Titanium is a light but strong element.
8. Prometheus was a Titan. Prometheus is the bringer of fire.
9. Prometheus has also given his name to an element. This element is promethium.
10. The connection between science and mythology is fascinating. Mythology is an early attempt to explain the world.

Combining with Participles and Participial Phrases

Suppose that you want to combine the following sentences to emphasize the action of the stunt pilot.

The stunt pilot zigzagged joyfully across the sky. She was suspended upside-down. She flipped her wing flaps.

You might consider this possibility:

The stunt pilot, who was suspended upside-down and who flipped her wing flaps, zigzagged joyfully across the sky.

This sentence is good as far as it goes. Here are two other possibilities that capture the pilot's actions more vividly:

VERSION A The stunt pilot, **suspended upside-down** and **flipping her wing flaps**, zigzagged joyfully across the sky.

VERSION B **Suspended upside-down**, the stunt pilot zigzagged joyfully across the sky, **flipping her wing flaps.**

These revisions condense the ideas about the action into two *participial phrases: suspended upside-down* and *flipping her wing flaps.*

You can use participles and participial phrases to signal simultaneous action.

The three sentences that follow tell about simultaneous actions—actions that take place at the same time:

SIMULTANEOUS ACTION 1 The comedian picked up the monkey.
SIMULTANEOUS ACTION 2 The comedian crossed his eyes.
SIMULTANEOUS ACTION 3 The comedian told a joke.

In the following versions the three sentences are combined to show the action happening simultaneously:

VERSION A Crossing his eyes and telling a joke, the comedian picked up the monkey.

VERSION B The comedian crossed his eyes, telling a joke and picking up the monkey.

Compare these two versions with the three sentences that show the simultaneous actions. Notice that version A was constructed by leaving action 1 as is, expressing action 2 as the participial phrase *crossing his eyes,* and changing action 3 to the participle *telling a joke.* Version B was formed by keeping action 2 and converting actions 1 and 3 into participial phrases. As you can see, whichever action is left in its original form stands out as the main action.

In both version A and version B, the writer carefully positioned the participle and participial phrases where they would make sense. Consider how the meaning of the sentence would have changed if the writer had not taken such care:

> The comedian picked up the monkey, telling a joke and crossing his eyes.

Notice that the sentence in this version suggests that the monkey, and not the comedian, is doing the joke-telling and eye-crossing. To avoid writing such misleading sentences, place participles and participial phrases as often as possible just before or just after the words they modify. (For more information, see Chapter 19.)

EXERCISE 10 **Combining Sentences by Using Participles and Participial Phrases.** Combine each of the following groups of sentences by forming at least two participles or participial phrases. You will need to choose one sentence as the main action.

SAMPLE The commuters rushed out of the train station. They were strained. They looked frequently at their watches or at the clocks outside.

REVISION *Strained and looking frequently at their watches or at the clocks outside,* the commuters rushed out of the train station.

REVISION The commuters were strained, *rushing out of the train station and looking frequently at their watches or at clocks outside.*

1. She spent weeks in the laboratory. She mixed chemicals. She carefully observed the reactions. She recorded her observations scrupulously in a black notebook.
2. The old horse heaved the heavy wagon. It tottered up the steep hill. It grunted and groaned plaintively.
3. The batter was carefully watching the pitcher. He dreamed of hitting a home run to save the game. He hoisted the bat up and down.
4. Kim was exhausted. She walked on heedlessly. She lost her way before long.
5. The noise came from outside the house. It shattered his rest. It caused him to rush to the window.
6. The racing car streaked down the straightaway. It hurtled toward the finish line. It was smoking hot.
7. The skater was looking determined. She coiled her body as tightly as a spring. She performed the difficult triple jump with ease.
8. The champion prepared himself for the crucial dive. He stretched his arms high above his head. He stood on tiptoe.
9. The soldier crouched behind the wall. He whirled the knobs of the radio. He was desperately attempting to warn headquarters of the enemy force.
10. Patricia was angered by the remark. She struggled to control herself. She refused to be provoked.

Writing Concisely

In revising your writing, you may have to change your sentences to make them more concise. Concise sentences do not overflow with unneeded words. They are uncluttered, compact, and direct.

You can make your writing concise by removing unnecessary or repetitious language and by simplifying long structures.

1. Eliminate unnecessary words and phrases, including:
   phrases such as "I think" or "in my opinion." Your reader knows that your writing is your opinion.
   words such as "probably" or "somewhat." Say what you mean.
   redundant, or excess, words and phrases.

UNNECESSARY WORDS SHADED — If you ask me, a schoolwide campaign against sloppy dress should immediately be launched at once, involving every person in this school. As an initial first step, of course, several full-length mirrors should perhaps be placed at strategic points and locations on each and every floor of this school. The mirrors would serve the purpose of letting people see and view how really sloppy and untidy they look to others.

CONCISE REVISION — A schoolwide campaign against sloppy dress should be launched at once. As an initial step, several full-length mirrors should be placed at strategic points on every floor of this school. The mirrors would let people know how sloppy they look to others.

2. Combine related sentences.

CHOPPY — In 1975 the *Apollo* and *Soyuz* locked together 138 miles above the earth. The *Apollo* and *Soyuz* were American and Russian spaceships. The crews of the two ships jointly conducted scientific experiments.

CONCISE — In 1975 the *Apollo* and *Soyuz*, American and Russian spaceships, locked together 138 miles above the earth, so that the crews of the two ships could jointly conduct scientific experiments.

3. Reduce clauses to words or phrases.

WORDY — Karen practiced her guitar, and Mo practiced his.
CONCISE — Karen and Mo practiced their guitars.
WORDY — Because the detectives were satisfied that no crime had been committed, they called off the investigation.
CONCISE — Satisfied that no crime had been committed, the detectives called off the investigation.
WORDY — Mrs. Wolocek is a woman who is always fair.
CONCISE — Mrs. Wolocek is always fair.

4. Break up rambling sentences into shorter sentences.

RAMBLING — The students charged out of the main doors of the school, and some were chattering excitedly, while others just stared wide-eyed and it was apparent that something had happened.

CONCISE — The students charged out of the main door of the school. Some were chattering excitedly, while others just stared wide-eyed. Apparently something had happened.

EXERCISE 11 **Writing Concisely.** Rewrite the following paragraph to make the sentences more concise. In some cases you will need to remove the repetitious language and shorten long sentences; in other cases, you will need to combine or break up sentences.

It is my considered opinion that the question of what to do with nuclear waste continues to remain an important question. Nuclear waste, I believe, is made up of leftover materials that keep their radioactivity for maybe hundreds of years. People who live near recommended storage sites object strongly to the possible potential dangers from radioactive materials. The number of plants that produce nuclear power sort of increases with the passing of time. The question of how to dispose of radioactive waste will become more and more crucial. A feasible and practical solution to this problem must be worked out. It must be worked out now.

Creating Variety in Sentences

As you have written your way to this point in the chapter, you have had the opportunity to practice a number of methods of combining sentences. In this section of the chapter, you will practice using these methods in paragraphs to make your writing more interesting and effective.

Varying Sentence Length and Structure

Like members of an acrobatic troupe, sentences create their effects by bouncing off one another. A short sentence snaps smartly into place after a longer one; a long sentence creates an easy, flowing rhythm when it follows a shorter one. However, sentences that look and sound the same—whether all short or all long—do not bounce or glide. They bore. Give your readers—and your own ideas—a break by mixing short and long, simple and complicated sentences.

Vary the length and structure of your sentences.

The following suggestions will help you to vary the length and structure of your sentences.

1. Find a sample of your own writing, and read it aloud, listening to your sentences. Are all the sentences the same length, or does the length vary? If you write only short sentences, combine them to make longer ones. If your sentences are mostly long and rambling, break them up.
2. Use coordinated structures for a series of items or for balancing and contrasting ideas.

3. Subordinated structures not only sound more sophisticated but are also quite versatile. They offer many possibilities for arranging and emphasizing ideas.
4. Use participles and appositives as shorthand ways of expressing information. Participles also create a sense of dynamic action.
5. One short sentence following several longer ones will emphasize a point, indicate a change of thought, or clinch a paragraph.

Here is an example of a paragraph containing sentences of varying lengths and structures. The notes in the margin point out the way in which these varied sentences work together effectively.

Participle conveys simultaneous action.

Adverb clause adds variety.

Short sentence contrasts with longer sentences, and clinches paragraph.

Chuckling, she watched the long line of penguins taking turns pushing each other off the edge of the ice floe. If only she could get this behavior on film, she could share her enjoyment of it with the readers of her magazine. She opened the bag and took out her camera. She worked quickly. The cold Antarctic air numbed her fingers as the latch on the camera stuck and, worst of all, the film turned brittle and threatened to break. At last she was ready to click off shot after shot of the clownish penguins. Prizewinners all, she thought happily.

EXERCISE 12 **Varying Sentence Length and Structure.** Rewrite the following paragraph, combining sentences and rearranging information to create sentences of varying lengths and structures.

It was the morning of July 13, 1959. The huge, four-engine jet had just taken off from San Francisco. It was headed for Honolulu, Hawaii. The airlines had only recently started to fly jet planes. The flight was enjoyable for the first fifteen minutes. The situation changed suddenly. The outer engine on the right caught fire. Flames crept along the wing. One of the passengers recalled the flight later. She looked out the window. She saw the end of the plane's right wing fall off. She was horrified. Her horror soon turned to icy calm. She remembered thinking, "Well, there goes the wing"—just like that. Fortunately, luck was with them. The pilot managed to turn the damaged jet around. It landed safely at San Francisco.

Varying Sentence Beginnings

In English a sentence usually begins with its subject. Your sentences will have greater impact if you begin them in different ways.

Try to vary the beginnings of successive sentences.

When you are writing consider these different ways to begin your sentences:

1. You can begin a sentence with a single word:

   Boisterously the fans greeted the victorious team.

2. You can begin a sentence with a phrase:

   Digging feverishly, Captain Forebush at last struck the top of a metal box.

3. You can begin a sentence with a subordinate idea:

   Wherever true justice is present, people are contented with their lives.

4. You can invert the order of a sentence from subject-verb-modifier to modifier-subject-verb.

   MODIFIER VERB SUBJECT
   Far below the ocean surface prowled a solitary submarine.

EXERCISE 13 **Varying Sentence Beginnings.** Rewrite the following paragraph, combining sentences and rearranging their structures to create a variety of sentence beginnings.

Alice Cunningham Fletcher began a career in anthropology. She began at the age of forty-three. She was a woman from Boston. She wanted to help others. She went to Nebraska. She worked with the Omaha Indians. Alice Cunningham Fletcher was soon trusted by the tribe. She consistently showed sensitivity to the rights and needs of the Omaha. The Omaha objected to government policies. So the woman from Boston went to Washington to speak for the tribe. Fletcher felt she had done all she could for the Omaha. This was after many years. She returned to Boston. She did this with reluctance. There she wrote informative books about the Omaha.

Varying Sentence Types

Read the following passage, which is made up solely of statements:

> Unadventurous people claim that they "hate" some kinds of food without ever tasting them. If they dared to try, say, rattlesnake meat, caribou steak, or chocolate-covered ants, they might actually enjoy the taste. They should take a chance. They should try a food they never ate before. Their taste buds deserve a change.

The following revision sprinkles the same passage with questions and commands, thus making it more direct, forceful, and vibrant.

> Do you lack a sense of adventure? Do you claim to "hate" some kinds of food without ever tasting them? If you dared to try, say, rattlesnake meat, caribou steak, or chocolate-covered ants, you might actually enjoy the taste. Take a chance. Try a food you never ate before. Don't your tastebuds deserve a change?

Vary your sentence types by using occasional questions and commands.

EXERCISE 14 **Varying Sentence Types.** Rewrite the following passage, combining the choppy sentences to create sentences of varying lengths, structures, and beginnings. Use at least one question and one command.

You may not know much about the various kinds of weird gadgets. Such gadgets have been invented over the years. If you read on, you will learn about a few. A dog-powered washing machine is one weird gadget. A tree-climbing bicycle and a winged bicycle are two more. A floor-waxing robot is also a weird gadget. So is an automatic spaghetti winder. Some weird gadgets do succeed. This is surprising. You should consider the Wright brothers' crazy flying machine. You may have a question about what to do with your own secret idea for a weird gadget. You should build a working model. You should try to sell it to a manufacturer. If you do these things, this could happen: You could wake up one morning and find yourself a millionaire.

Using Parallelism for Effect

> Ask not what your country can do for you; ask what you can do for your country.

Why do you think this statement by President Kennedy became instantly memorable? One reason is that the statement repeats a particular structure—verb, subordinate clause; verb, subordinate clause. You can connect related ideas by repeating similar structures within a sentence or a series of sentences. This technique is known as *parallelism*.

Use parallelism to emphasize the links between related ideas.

Because you have practiced writing varied sentences, you may be wondering if parallelism will make your writing sound monotonous. It will not, unless you overdo it. Usually two or three parallel structures in a row will be enough to create your effect.

If you decide to use parallelism, you must be sure that your structures are truly parallel, that they truly match.

NOT PARALLEL When you take a picture, you should **frame your shot** in the viewfinder, **hold the camera** steady, and **to press** the shutter release button firmly.

PARALLEL When you take a picture, **frame your shot** in the viewfinder, **hold the camera** steady, and **press the shutter release button** firmly.

You can use parallelism to present a series of related ideas:

NOT PARALLEL The critics were delighted with the clarity of the soprano's diction and with **what a great range her voice had.**

PARALLEL The critics were delighted with the clarity of the soprano's diction and with the **great range of her voice.**

You can also use parallelism to balance or contrast ideas:

NOT PARALLEL A penny saved is **like earning a penny.**

PARALLEL A penny saved is **a penny earned.**

NOT PARALLEL **Warm was the sun**, but the wind was cold.

PARALLEL **The sun was warm**, but the wind was cold.

EXERCISE 15 **Creating Parallelism Within Sentences.** Rewrite each of the following sentences to express related ideas in similar or parallel structures.

SAMPLE Linda is courageous in what she says and *her actions.*

REVISION Linda is courageous in what she says and *what she does.*

1. My parents expect us to be truthful, honest and have loyalty.
2. Boston has more clouds than it is sunny throughout the year.
3. Franklin Delano Roosevelt was a governor, a secretary of the Navy, and he became President.
4. Lucille can read and write Russian, but the language is hard to speak.
5. Antonia made the breads for the bake sale; the rolls were made by Charlie.
6. Isabella, the queen of Spain and who was the patron of Columbus, was a strong ruler.
7. People who work in banks and bakers should know a good deal about dough.
8. Globes, which have parallels and on which there are meridians, are useful locational tools.
9. Last winter was frigid, snowy, and there was wind.
10. Sheila locked her suitcase, checked her plane ticket, and a cab took her to the airport.

EXERCISE 16 **Creating Parallel Constructions.** Imagine that you are running for mayor in your town and are giving a short speech. Rewrite the speech here to do the following: (a) Correct faulty parallelism within sentences. (b) Combine sentences by creating new parallel structures to connect related ideas. Feel free to rearrange the words here.

Why should you vote for me? Who am I and you must be wondering what is it that I stand for. I am your neighbor. Now it is your mayor that I want to be. I have lived in this town all of my life. In this town I went to school. My wife I met in this town. Our children were raised here. This town is loved by me. Because of my love for this town, I hate to see the sidewalks needing repair. Another hated sight is that of streetlights that are broken. In addition, there are businesses that are closing down. The mayor tells you that everything is fine. You will be told by me in this campaign that fineness is something that much of our town falls short of. Listen to me. If you like what you are hearing, it would be a good idea to vote for me. Thank you.

Writer's Choice

Writer's Choice #1

ASSIGNMENT To imitate the sentences used by a professional writer

LENGTH A paragraph of five sentences

AUDIENCE Readers of fantasy

PURPOSE To portray an imaginary creature of your own choice

PREWRITING Read the following model, in which science fiction and fantasy author Ray Bradbury describes the appearance of an ancient sea monster. Then imagine a creature of your own, decide what it looks like, and list the features that you want to include in your passage.

WRITING Using sentence structures similar to those Bradbury uses, write about the creature you have imagined, and arrange your sentences in the same order.

REVISING Make sure that your sentences echo those of the model. When you are satisfied, check your grammar, usage, spelling, and punctuation.

MODEL And then, from the surface of the cold sea came a head, a large head, dark-colored, with immense eyes, and then a neck. . . . The head rose a full forty feet above the water on a slender and beautiful dark neck. Only then did the body, like a little island of black coral and shells and crayfish, drip up from the subterranean. There was a flicker of tail. In all, from head to tip of tail, I estimated the monster at ninety or a hundred feet.

—Ray Bradbury, "The Fog Horn"

Writer's Choice #2

ASSIGNMENT To write a speech

LENGTH Your choice

AUDIENCE Your choice

PURPOSE Your choice

OPTIONS: You may find an idea in the Writer's Sourcebook, pages 354–357.

Follow the prewriting, writing, and revising steps you practiced in Chapters 1–4.

As you revise, pay particular attention to your sentence structure. Find opportunities for using parallelism

Writers on Writing

Susan Maas plans to juggle her love of writing with a career in international law. At the time that she wrote the paragraph and commentary below, Susan was a student at North Allegheny Senior High School in Wexford, Pennsylvania.

THE PRODUCT

You may not have thought much about it: the word *fair*. It suggests equality, but how many times do you find that *fair* does not really mean *equal* at all? You might even conclude that anything that is good is not fair. Take life, for instance. It seems that someone or something is always out there just waiting to outdo each of us. In the struggle for money, power, happiness, there can be only a few winners, and many losers are left behind. Thus, one person's *fair* is another person's *unfair*.

THE PROCESS

When an artist first sketches a portrait, he or she may subsequently redo the nose or the ears. It is the same with writing. The sentences in my first drafts tend to ramble and appear fragmented. I always *plan* to begin and end sentences at logical places, but somehow what I write always sounds different when I read it aloud from the way it did when it passed through my thoughts. So I enjoy going through my writing and combining sentences, dropping, adding, and manipulating the parts.

I usually start with a thought seemingly out of nowhere, something abstract like my beginning "You have probably not thought much about it: the word *fair*." I also find that most of my writings end with a question or puzzle of some kind, such as "Thus, one person's *fair* is another person's *unfair*." Throughout the middle I try to vary my sentences, making some shorter, some longer, some simple, some complex. If most of the sentences in a passage are short and simple, the result will be unrefined and choppy. In my passage above, for example, I try to mix short, medium-length, and long sentences.

I think if you try to write a perfect sentence the first time, your results will be less than satisfactory. It is better to get your thoughts down on paper and *then* manipulate your sentences.

YOUR TURN *Commenting on Your Writing*

Take one of the paragraphs that you have already written and revised, and list three or four characteristics of your own style. Be sure to note the various lengths of your sentences, as Susan did.

Review

CHAPTERS 5–6 DEVELOPING A PERSONAL STYLE

CHAPTER 5 CHOOSING WORDS

Writing Precisely and Writing Concisely [pages 94–100 and 100–102] Read the following passage, and indicate the letter of the item that correctly answers each question.

[1]The fire fighters had been called to a common brush fire. [2]Just as they arrived, however, a brisk wind came up from the east. [3]Suddenly an ordinary fire became an intense incendiary conflagration. [4]Once verdant grass, moribund from winter's onslaught, combusted and was consumed in an instant. [5]Yet the fire fighters stood their ground. [6]They interfaced smoothly as they attacked the flames. [7]Before long, the fire gave up.

1. Which is a connotation of the word *common* in sentence 1?
   (a) unimportant (b) ordinary (c) shared
2. Choose a more specific term for *came up* in sentence 2:
   (a) arrived (b) started up (c) sprang up
3. Sentence 3 mixes which levels of diction?
   (a) middle/formal (b) informal/middle (c) informal/formal
4. How would you improve the diction in sentence 4?
   (a) The grass ignited.
   (b) The fire devoured the dry grass.
5. Which of the following is an example of jargon?
   (a) "arrived" (b) "combusted" (c) "attacked" (d) "interfaced"
6. Which sentence contains a cliché?
   (a) sentence 2 (b) sentence 4 (c) sentence 5 (d) sentence 6
7. Which would be more specific than *gave up* in sentence 7?
   (a) went out (b) surrendered (c) weakened

Writing Figuratively [pages 103–104] Indicate the letter of the item that correctly answers each question.

8. Which of the following is a simile?
   (a) The clouds are balls of cotton. (b) The clouds are like balls of cotton.
9. Which of the following is a metaphor for life?
   (a) Life is unpredictable. (c) Life is a voyage.
   (b) Life is like a dream. (d) Life is as mysterious as a riddle.
10. Which word would complete the following metaphor? "Dreams are ____________."
    (a) frightening (b) dreams (c) messengers (d) empty

Writing for Review Write a paragraph about your feelings and sensations just before you do something that you do not want to do. Use concrete words and at least one figure of speech. Revise your draft.

CHAPTER 6 WRITING AND COMBINING SENTENCES

Combining Sentences with Coordination, Subordination, and Participles [pages 109–124] Read the following passage and indicate the letter of the item that correctly answers each question.

[1]Amelia Earhart lived a brief but exciting life. [2]She was born in 1898 in Atchison, Kansas. [3]She served as a nurse in the Canadian Army during World War I. [4]The war ended in 1918. [5]She became a social worker in Boston. [6]She learned to fly in the early 1920s. [7]Her family opposed her flying. [8]She flew across the Atlantic Ocean as a passenger in 1928. [9]In 1932 she became the first woman to fly alone across the Atlantic. [10]She flew across the United States many times in 1933 and 1934. [11]She became the first woman to fly solo from Hawaii to California in 1935. [12]She died in 1937. [13]She was attempting to complete an around-the-world flight.

1. Which of these pairs of sentences would be better if combined?
   (a) 1 and 2 (b) 6 and 7 (c) 11 and 12
2. Which sentences could be combined with a participle?
   (a) 2 and 3 (b) 8 and 9 (c) 10 and 11
3. Which sentences should you combine through coordination?
   (a) 5 and 6 (b) 8 and 9 (c) 12 and 13

Writing Varied Sentences and Using Parallelism [pages 126–131] Read the following passage, and indicate the letter of the item that correctly answers each question.

[1]The male and female cuckoo are very lazy birds. [2]They work well together. [3]Because the female is too lazy to build a nest, she lays her eggs on the ground. [4]The male cuckoo then immediately finds a nest that sparrows have built. [5]He begins a confrontation and to fight with the sparrows, who chase him into another tree. [6]The male cuckoo then leads and conducts them even farther and more distant from their nest. [7]Finally, the female moves into the nest and claims it for her own.

4. Which sentence contains structures that should be parallel?
   (a) 3 (b) 4 (c) 5 (d) 7
5. Which word could be used to combine sentences 1 and 2?
   (a) because (b) while (c) although

Writing for Review Rewrite the paragraph that you did in the Writing for Review for Chapter 5. Vary sentence length and structure.

UNIT III

The Modes of Writing

Thinking About Thinking: Identifying Varying Perspectives

Writing in different modes requires you to look at a subject in different ways. In this unit you will learn about four major modes of writing—description, narration, exposition, and persuasion. All the modes of writing, however, involve one essential thinking process—critical analysis. Whether you are working on a short story or an essay, you need to analyze your topic, your organization, even your purpose and audience.

Defining the Skill

One specific thinking skill you use in analyzing a topic is **IDENTIFYING VARYING PERSPECTIVES** on the topic. Realizing that something can be looked at from different angles, different points of view, is a thinking skill that you can develop. In fact, as you develop this skill, you will find that it will free you to analyze anything—not only your writing—more effectively.

Applying the Skill

Look at the two photographs of the sculpture by Henry Moore. The photographs show the same sculpture from two different angles, two different positions of the camera's eye. Describe exactly what you see in each picture. What parts or qualities are emphasized by each picture? What do the different angles tell you about the sculpture? What can you see from one angle that you cannot see from the other? How can you tell that the two photos show the same sculpture?

CHAPTER 7

Descriptive Writing

There is only one trait that marks the writer. He is always watching. It's a kind of a tick of the mind and he is born with it.

—Morley Callaghan

After reading Morley Callaghan's words, you may have wondered, what does "watching" have to do with descriptive writing? To Callaghan watching is observing, an essential habit for writers. Through observation writers constantly gather and store impressions and ideas that they can call forth at a later time.

Observing is not just seeing; it is also hearing, smelling, tasting, and touching. How observant are you? For example, what color are the walls in your school cafeteria? What sounds do you hear most often in your neighborhood at night? How would you describe the taste of a green apple or the smell of raw cabbage? How does the skin of an orange feel? Answering questions like these forms the basis for this chapter on descriptive writing.

Above all, descriptive writing is concrete and detailed. Its concrete details stimulate a reader's senses. Descriptive writing is never vague, general, or abstract.

Descriptive writing creates a clear and vivid impression of a person, place, or thing.

In this chapter you will practice the following steps and various types of descriptive writing:

prewriting: purpose and audience
prewriting: sensory details
prewriting: overall impression
writing a description: organization and coherence
writing a description: descriptive language
writing a character sketch
writing a longer description
revising, **editing**, and **publishing** descriptive writing

As you write your way through this chapter, you will be describing people, places, and things. Your goal in writing each description will be to describe your subject so exactly that your readers will see, hear, smell, taste, or touch it.

Prewriting: Purpose and Audience

The purpose of descriptive writing, of course, is to describe. Before you begin to write a description, however, you should decide on a more specific purpose. Unless you have a clear idea of *why* you want to describe a particular person, place, or thing, you will probably not know how to put a description of a subject together. For example, if you were involved in a minor automobile accident, your description of it in an official police report would be different from your description of the accident in an informal letter.

While deciding on your purpose for writing a description, you should also be giving careful thought to your audience, the people who will be reading your description. Being aware of the audience you are writing for will help you determine the words, sentence structure, and organization you will use in your description. For example, if you were describing a painting to six-year-old children, you would use one approach; if you were preparing a description of a painting for people your own age, you would use another approach.

To define your purpose and audience, ask yourself the following questions:

1. Why do I want to write this description? To inform? To entertain? To influence thinking? Do I have another purpose or combination of purposes?
2. Who is going to read the description? How much do my readers already know about my subject? Will they need special information to understand any part of my subject?

EXERCISE 1 **Identifying Purposes for a Description.** For each of the following subjects, list two specific purposes that a writer could have in mind during the prewriting stage of descriptive writing. Study the following example.

SUBJECT OF DESCRIPTION	POSSIBLE PURPOSES OF DESCRIPTION
city noises	To entertain readers with the sound of the city
	To persuade readers to organize against noise pollution

1. a pair of shoes
2. crowd waiting for the presidential motorcade
3. a spoiled child

EXERCISE 2 **Selecting an Audience for a Description.** First select one of the following subjects for descriptive writing. Then in two or three sentences state whether you would prefer to write for an expert or a nonexpert audience, and explain your decision.

SUBJECT OF DESCRIPTION	EXPERT AUDIENCE	NONEXPERT AUDIENCE
a microwave oven	an engineer	a homeowner who has never used one
an oil painting	an artist	art students
an exciting goal scored in a hockey game	a group of hockey players	people who have never seen a hockey game

Prewriting: Sensory Details

Details are concrete, specific features of a person, object, place, or experience. **Sensory details** are details that appeal to the sensations of sight, sound, smell, taste, touch, and motion.

Everything you know about the people, places, and things of the world has come to you *and to your readers* through the senses. Since your readers are accustomed to perceiving the world through sensation, you can bring your descriptive writing to life for them by using as many sensory details as possible. When you describe a display of fireworks on a hot summer night, include sensory details that will make it possible for your readers to *see* the brilliant colors and varied design, *hear* the booming explosions and exclamations of the crowd, *smell* and *taste* the acrid smoke, and *feel* the sticky warmth of the night overcome by occasional cooling breezes.

Remember, however, that in order to stimulate your readers' senses with vivid sensory details, you must first use your own senses to observe what you wish to describe. In the following paragraph, Helen Keller—who was blind from infancy—gives some helpful recommendations on the most effective way to use your senses for observing.

> . . . Use your eyes as if tomorrow you would be stricken blind. And the same method can be applied to the other senses. Hear the music of voices, the song of a bird, the mighty strains of an orchestra, as if you would be stricken deaf tomorrow. Touch each object you want to touch as if tomorrow your tactile sense [sense of touch] would fail. Smell the perfume of flowers, taste with relish each morsel as if tomorrow you could never smell and taste again. Make the most of every sense; glory in all the facets of pleasure and beauty which the world reveals to you through the several means of contact which Nature provides.
>
> —Helen Keller, "Three Days to See"

In the following paragraph writer Eugenia Collier describes the setting of a childhood experience. Be aware of the author's use of sensory details and which senses they are meant to stimulate.

> Miss Lottie's marigolds were perhaps the strangest part of the picture. Certainly they did not fit in with the crumbling decay of the rest of her yard. Beyond the dusty brown yard, in front of the sorry gray house, rose suddenly and shockingly a dazzling strip of bright blossoms, clumped together in enormous mounds, warm and passionate and sun-golden. . . . For some perverse reason, we children hated those marigolds. They interfered with the perfect ugliness of the place. . . .
>
> —Eugenia Collier, "Marigolds"

The author's description stimulates the sense of sight with remarkable effect. The sensory details are essential to the picture the author wished her readers to visualize. Here is what the first part of the paragraph would read like if the sensory details were omitted:

> Miss Lottie's marigolds were perhaps the strangest part of the picture. Certainly they did not fit in with the rest of the yard. Beyond the yard, in front of the house, rose a strip of blossoms, in mounds.

Which version creates a more vivid picture of the author's childhood experience? The first version does, of course, because it evokes the sights of the experience, and it allows readers to share in the author's feelings about it. The whole experience, as the author remembers it, is lost in the second version because the sensory details are omitted.

EXERCISE 3 **Thinking About Sensory Details.** Read the following descriptive paragraph, and list the concrete sensory details that the author uses to describe his impressions of the East—the Orient. On your list note which of your senses each detail stimulates.

And this is how I see the East. I have seen its secret places and have looked into its very soul; but now I see it always from a small boat, a high outline of mountains, blue and afar in the morning; like a faint mist at noon; a jagged wall of purple at sunset. I have the feel of the oar in my hand, the vision of the scorching blue sea in my eyes. And I see a bay, a wide bay, smooth as glass and polished like ice shimmering in the dark. A red light burns far off upon the gloom of the land, and the night is soft and warm. We drag at the oars with aching arms, and suddenly a puff of wind, a puff faint and tepid and laden with strange odors of blossoms, or aromatic wood, comes out of the still night—the first sigh of the East on my face. That I can never forget. It was impalpable and enslaving, like a charm, like a whispered promise of mysterious delight.

—Joseph Conrad, "The East"

Collecting Sensory Details

In order to write effective description, you need to use your senses to observe and remember as many sensory details as you can. Sharpen your powers of observation and your memory with questions like these:

1. What does my subject look like? What is its color, size, shape?
2. What prominent or unusual features does it have?
3. What sounds can I associate with my subject?
4. What smells and tastes can I associate with it?
5. What does it feel like to the touch? Is it warm or cool, rough or smooth, hard or soft?
6. How would I know my subject if I were blindfolded?
7. How does my subject move?

You can collect the answers to these questions on an observation table like the one shown here. In this table details that describe a city bus are listed for each sense.

OBSERVATION TABLE

SUBJECT: *a city bus*			
SIGHTS	SOUNDS	SMELLS/ TASTES	TOUCH/ MOVEMENTS
• *names scratched on backs of seats* • *raindrops on windows* • *variety of things carried by passengers* • *backs of passengers' heads*	• *coins dropping in fare box* • *traffic noises outside* • *buzz of conversations* • *sound of bus brakes and doors opening and closing*	• *gas fumes* • *women's perfumes* • *wet clothing* • *garlic on passenger's breath*	• *people swaying on overhead handholds* • *cold air from ceiling fan* • *passengers lurching down aisle* • *bumpiness of bus*

You can use some of the details listed in a similar observation table when you write a description of your subject. When you are finished with your observation table, you may decide that certain details can be used more effectively than others.

EXERCISE 4 **Prewriting to Collect Sensory Details.** Choose one topic listed here or any other that you would like to describe. Think about your purpose and audience. Ask yourself questions from those listed earlier, and place the answers on an observation table. Fill in columns for three different senses. Save your table.

1. a good meal
2. an old photo
3. your street
4. a fish market
5. a work crew
6. a favorite chair

Prewriting: Overall Impression

The details in a description should add up to a single **overall impression** of the subject.

If you weave the sensory details of a description together to create a single, overall or dominant picture in the minds of your readers, your description will be successful. Consider the following list of sensory details that could be used to describe a house.

high ceilings	servants' quarters	tall windows
ten bedrooms	marble floors	wall murals
enormous rooms	crystal chandelier	winding staircase
rare woods	silk wallpaper	

All of these details could be used to support the overall impression expressed in the following topic sentence.

Everything about the abandoned house on Queen Street spoke of a past grandeur.

Notice how each of the details in the list work together in the following paragraph to create the single overall impression the topic sentence promises to the reader.

Everything about the abandoned house on Queen Street spoke of a past grandeur. The brilliant glow from the remains of a crystal chandelier must have spotlighted the elegant dress and glittering jewelry of guests going up and down, to and from the grand ballroom at the bottom of the graceful winding staircase. Royalty would have been at home in any of the other enormous rooms on the first floor with their high ceilings, tall windows, marble floors, and now-faded wall murals. Patches of silk wallpaper once matched the rare woods of paneling and doors in the ten second-floor bedrooms, each with its own bath and sitting room. The servants' quarters on the third floor, though spacious, had none of these luxuries. Passing through these quarters, one could not help but wonder what had happened to these servants and those they served.

The topic sentence is at the beginning of the preceding paragraph. As you learned in Chapter 3, however, in the paragraphs you write you may decide to present supporting details first and effectively tie them together with a topic sentence at the end.

In her original prewriting notes, the author of the preceding paragraph had listed the following details. You can see that they could not be used in the paragraph without shattering the overall impression of the past grandeur of the house.

broken windows	cracks in walls
cobwebs and dust	doors hanging on hinges
holes in ceilings	

As you write descriptive paragraphs in this chapter, remember to use only those details that contribute to the overall impression that you intend to convey to your readers.

EXERCISE 5 **Prewriting to Create an Overall Impression.** Look again at the observation table that lists sensory details about a city bus. On the basis of these details, decide on one overall impression of this scene that you could present to a general audience. Write a sentence that could serve as the topic sentence of a paragraph. Then list details that will develop the overall impression. You may add appropriate details of your own. Save your sentences and details for Exercise 8.

EXERCISE 6 **Prewriting to Create an Overall Impression.** Look back at the details that you listed in Exercise 4. Now write a sentence expressing one overall impression of the place you chose. List additional details to develop that impression. Save your notes for Writer's Choice #3 on page 148.

EXERCISE 7 **Maintaining an Overall Impression.** Read the following paragraph, and identify the overall impression it conveys. Then rewrite the paragraph to eliminate any details that undercut the overall impression. You may replace those details with others that are more appropriate.

Not so long after Labor Day, the beach was as lonely as a crater on the far side of the moon. Here and there, dented cans and crumpled wrappers, half-buried by the restless sands, were the sole reminders of the bronzed throngs of summer. A meandering line of jagged black rocks extended far into the water. The mourning wind and frantic surf no longer had to compete with the babble of happy voices. Even the footprints had been erased by the mindless coming and going of the eternal tides. Gray waves reached up to the gray skies. A solitary hungry gull at the fingertip of one wave searched in vain for the discarded bounty from summer picnic baskets. The colorful hulls of a fishing fleet shattered the straight line of the horizon.

Writing: Organization and Coherence

An effective description should be **organized** so that the details build on each other naturally and logically.

You must give some organization to the sensory details in a description. Depending on what subject you decide to describe, you may choose several methods of organization. In working through this section of the chapter, you will consider and make use of one method of organizing the sensory details in your description.

Grouping Similar Details

Grouping similar details is a method of organization that works quite well in descriptive writing. It is a natural way of linking up the sensory details of a description. If you were describing a person, for example, you might begin by zeroing in on the most striking impression the person makes on you, perhaps focusing on one physical detail such as height, hair color, or facial description. Then you might include other physical characteristics of the person—a way of walking or sitting, gestures, or the sound of the person's voice. After that, you might move on to interesting details of the person's clothing. Of course, you will want to give your description coherence by using appropriate transitions. (See Chapter 3.)

Notice how similar details are grouped together in the following descriptive paragraph.

> Even the quickest glance at the grim look on Alice's face lets you know that she was not on peaceful terms with the inhabitants of this planet and didn't want to be. Darting, suspicious eyes and an unsmiling mouth warned off even the friendliest souls. Alice did not walk past people approaching her on the sidewalk; she bulldozed through them. If those she cleared from her path attempted to protest, the resounding explosion of her words overcame their feeble sputterings. To those who knew how to interpret it, Alice's "mode" of dressing was another warning signal. Her coils of red-gray hair were held down—almost—with a limp bandana. Safety pins took the place of buttons on the man's tweed jacket she wore. To complete her ensemble, Alice squeezed her bare feet into a pair of silver sneakers, size 5.

Notice that the first two sentences group the writer's most striking details of Alice's physical appearance. The next two sentences group other details of Alice's physical characteristics—the way she walked and the way she talked. The remaining sentences group details that describe Alice's dress. The three groups of details combine to convey a single vivid picture of Alice.

EXERCISE 8 **Grouping Similar Details in a Description.** Use the topic sentence you wrote for Exercise 5 (about a city bus) and write a descriptive paragraph that develops this topic sentence. As you write, arrange similar details in groups. Be sure each detail supports your topic sentence. After you have finished your first draft, revise and edit it. Then make a neat copy, and proofread the final version.

Writing: Descriptive Language

Effective descriptive writing uses exact and vivid **language.**

If you want your readers to know how the subject you describe looks, sounds, smells, tastes, or feels, you will have to choose your words carefully and place them exactly. By exercising such care in choosing and placing words, you will make your description vivid. In addition, the precise words you choose will place your individual stamp on your writing.

When it comes time to choose between two similar words to use in a description, keep the following suggestions in mind. If you want to know more about any of these suggestions, refer to Chapter 5.

1. Always choose the most specific word.

GENERAL The *building* stood on the *place* like a silent sentinel.
SPECIFIC The *castle* stood on the *cliff* like a silent sentinel.

2. Avoid using a colorless word and a modifier when one strong word will convey the same meaning more vividly.

DULL "Fire!" she *said loudly* and *ran suddenly* out of the house.
VIVID "Fire!" she *shrieked* and *bolted* out of the house.

3. Make use of the connotations associated with words.

The police officer radioed for help when he spotted the *excited gathering* of people.
The police officer radioed for help when he spotted the *frantic mob*.

4. Use a figure of speech to give added punch to your description of a subject.

BLAND Jeff is *a valuable friend to have when you're in trouble.*
SPECIAL Jeff is *as valuable as a life preserver on a sinking ship.*

5. Use your own words. Avoid trite, overworked expressions.

CLICHÉ After the long hike, all of us were *hungry as wolves.*
ORIGINAL After the long hike, all of us were *as hungry as ants at a picnic.*

The English language is made up of a rich variety of words. You can find words to describe almost any sensory detail that occurs to you while writing a description. You may have to spend time looking for them, but if you do, you will find them. If necessary, you can use a thesaurus to help you locate exactly the words you need. (Information about the way to use a thesaurus can be found in Chapter 33.)

EXERCISE 9 **Using Descriptive Language.** Rewrite the following paragraph using using more exact and vivid language. Use figures of speech in at least one sentence. Feel free to combine any sentences as you see fit.

Paul stopped rowing to look at the sunset. It was as pretty as a picture. A group of birds moved just over the water one last time before going to their roosting places. Shadows of the trees were on the water of the lake. Behind the trees the sun looked beautiful. A shiny fish came out of the water near Paul's boat. It scared him. Everything was so quiet. When it got dark, Paul took the boat back to shore. He had a good feeling.

Writer's Choice

Writer's Choice #1

ASSIGNMENT To describe briefly a new building in your neighborhood

LENGTH A paragraph of six to eight sentences

PURPOSE To describe the building so that anyone can recognize it

AUDIENCE A neighbor who has moved away

PREWRITING Choose your building, and decide which sensory details to use in your description of it.

WRITING Begin by identifying the building and describing its single most noticeable feature. Organize the paragraph by grouping similar details.

REVISING Will your neighbor be able to visualize the subject from your writing? Make sure to edit and proofread carefully.

Writer's Choice #2

ASSIGNMENT To describe fans at a ball park just after their favorite player has hit a home run that wins the game

LENGTH A paragraph of seven to nine sentences

PURPOSE Either to show how the fans act as a unit or to focus on the behavior of individual fans

AUDIENCE Your choice

PREWRITING You might use an observation table to record sensory details. Decide on an overall impression of the group.

WRITING Begin by stating your overall impression in a topic sentence. Then group similar details. As often as possible, use vivid, exact language to capture the scene.

REVISING Does your paragraph truly support your topic sentence? Do you need to change the topic sentence or add details?

Writer's Choice #3

ASSIGNMENT To describe a subject of your choice

LENGTH Your choice

PURPOSE Your choice

AUDIENCE Your choice

OPTIONS You might describe the subject for which you did prewriting in Exercises 4 and 6.

Be sure to revise and edit your first draft. Then copy and proofread your final draft.

Writing a Character Sketch

A **character sketch** is a description that portrays an individual's psychological traits and physical appearance.

A description of a person is not simply a collection of sensory details of the person's physical appearance. A human being has a personality as well as physical characteristics. Therefore, a description of a human being must include both physical characteristics and at least some of the psychological traits that make up the personality. That is not all, however. In describing a person to readers, you will want to show how the outer person is related to the inner person, how your subject's physical appearance and behavior connect with his or her personality.

Physical appearance and behavior are frequently expressions of aspects of someone's personality. Read again the description of Alice on page 146. This description begins by calling attention to the most noticeable feature of Alice's physical appearance—the expression on her face. The writer of the description then moves to group other details of Alice's physical appearance—her behavior, her hair, and her clothing. Together, these details suggest certain aspects of her personality to readers: Alice is an eccentric and antisocial person.

The following character sketch was written by Eugenia Collier. As you read this sketch, watch for the author's grouping of details.

> Miss Lottie seemed to be at least a hundred years old. Her big frame still held traces of the tall, powerful woman she must have been in youth, although it was now bent and drawn. Her smooth skin was a dark reddish-brown, and her face had Indian-like features and the stern stoicism that one associates with Indian faces. Miss Lottie didn't like intruders either, especially children. She never left her yard, and nobody ever visited her. We never knew how she managed those necessities which depend on human interaction—how she ate, for example, or even whether she ate. When we were tiny children, we thought Miss Lottie was a witch and we made up tales, that we half-believed ourselves, about her exploits. We were far too sophisticated now, of course, to believe the witch-nonsense.
>
> —Eugenia Collier, "Marigolds"

You probably noticed that the author starts this character sketch by describing an outstanding feature of Miss Lottie's appearance—her look of great age. Then the author presents other physical details of the old woman—her body build, her skin, and her facial features. In the last few sentences, the author gives readers a glimpse of Miss Lottie's personality by revealing some of the woman's psychological traits—her dislike of intruders and her self-imposed isolation.

Before you begin to write a character sketch, ask yourself the following prewriting questions:

1. What overall impression of my subject's appearance and personality do I want to convey? Can I focus on one basic quality as a key to understanding this person?
2. What can I say about my subject's height, weight, hair color, complexion, face, and clothing? What is the first thing I notice about my subject?
3. What can I say about the way my subject speaks and moves? About my subject's facial expressions?
4. What can I say about the way my subject behaves toward other people? How do other people treat my subject?
5. What can I say about my subject's character traits, likes, dislikes, strengths, and problems?
6. What specific examples or anecdotes can I offer to show these character traits in action?

You may decide to organize your character sketch by grouping similar details. For example, you may start by presenting details of your subject's physical appearance. Then you may continue by presenting details describing psychological traits.

EXERCISE 10 **Writing a Character Sketch.** Plan a character sketch about someone you know. Prewrite by answering the preceding questions, listing as many physical and psychological details as you can. Decide on an overall impression. You may organize the details in your description by beginning with physical characteristics and continuing with some of your subject's psychological traits. Be sure to revise and edit your first draft. When you are satisfied, make a neat final copy, and proofread it.

Writing a Longer Description

An effective description of your subject may require **more than one paragraph.**

Not every description of a subject can fit neatly into the confines of a single paragraph. Often you will want to develop your description over the course of several paragraphs much as a composer develops a symphony over the course of several movements. In the following paragraphs from the novel *Great Expectations* by Charles Dickens, a young boy describes a strange room inhabited by an even stranger woman. As you read, notice the many vivid visual details that contribute to the overall impression of eerie decay.

> I entered, therefore, and found myself in a pretty large room, well lighted with wax candles. No glimpse of daylight was to be seen in it. It was a dressing-room, as I supposed from the furniture, though much of it was of forms and uses then quite unknown to me. But prominent in it was a draped table with a gilded looking-glass, and that I made out at first sight to be a fine lady's dressing-table.
>
> Whether I should have made out this object so soon if there had been no fine lady sitting at it, I cannot say. In an arm-chair, with an elbow resting on the table and her head leaning on that hand, sat the strangest lady I have ever seen, or shall ever see.
>
> She was dressed in rich materials—satins, and lace, and silks—all of white. Her shoes were white. And she had a long white veil dependent from her hair, and she had bridal flowers in her hair, but her hair was white. Some bright jewels sparkled on her neck and on her hands, and some other jewels lay sparkling on the table. Dresses less splendid than the dress she wore, and half-packed trunks, were scattered about. She had not quite finished dressing, for she had but one shoe on—the other was on the table near her hand—her veil was but half arranged, her watch and chain were not put on, and some lace for her bosom lay with those trinkets, and with her handkerchief, and gloves, and some flowers, and a prayer-book, all confusedly heaped about the looking-glass.
>
> It was not in the first few moments that I saw all these things, though I saw more of them in the first moments than might be supposed. But, I saw that everything within my view which ought to be white, had been white long ago, and had lost its lustre, and was faded and yellow. I saw that the bride within the bridal dress had withered like the dress, and like the flowers, and had no brightness left but the brightness of her sunken eyes. I saw that the dress had been put upon the rounded figure of a young woman, and that the figure upon which it now hung loose had shrunk to skin and bone. Once, I had been taken to see some ghastly waxwork at the fair, representing I know not what impossible personage lying in state. Once, I had been taken to one of our old marsh churches to see a skeleton in the ashes of a rich dress that had been dug out of a vault under the church pavement. Now, waxwork and skeleton seemed to have dark eyes that moved and looked at me. I should have cried out, if I could.
>
> —Charles Dickens, *Great Expectations*

Dickens needed more than one paragraph for this description because he is describing both a place and a character in particularly lavish detail. Dickens' purpose is to show us that the woman is as faded and worn out as the room she inhabits. Notice how Dickens accomplishes this purpose: In the first paragraph he gives us a general description of the room and then in the second paragraph he describes the woman. In the third paragraph the description becomes more focused as Dickens presents many specific details of the woman's clothing and physical appearance. The last paragraph associates the faded luster of the objects in the room with the "ghastly waxwork" that the woman herself has become. Dickens' method of organization allows us to experience the scene with ever-growing awareness and realization.

EXERCISE 11 **Writing a Longer Description.** Plan to write about a place, such as a park, that you can describe effectively in three or four paragraphs. After you have completed your planning, write, revise, and edit your first draft. When you are satisfied that your draft fulfills your plan, make a neat final copy, and proofread it.

Revising, Editing, and Publishing

In Chapter 4 you learned to ask certain questions to help you revise the first draft of a paragraph. These questions should be applied to revising descriptive writing too. Additional questions, however, should be asked about the first draft of a description—questions that will help you write a final copy that accomplishes your purpose and is geared to your audience.

Checklist for Revising Descriptive Writing

1. What sensory details have I used? Which work best? Which could I do without? Which should I add?
2. What single, overall impression have I created through my choice of details? Is the impression stated in a sentence? Does this impression reflect all the details I use? How should I change this impression, if at all, to create a truer picture of my subject?
3. In organizing my description have I grouped similar details?
4. Do I need transitions to add coherence to my description? Which ones should I use?
5. Which exact and vivid words will help the reader to picture my subject? What words could I add to make that picture even more precise? What figures of speech will bring my subject to life?
6. For a human subject, which details describe the person's physical characteristics? Which ones describe psychological traits? What overall impression have I created of this person? What additional details does my reader need in order to see the person as I do?
7. How many paragraphs do I need to describe my subject fully?

Writer's Choice

Writer's Choice #1

ASSIGNMENT To write a paragraph about a favorite object

LENGTH Six to eight sentences

PURPOSE To describe the object so that the reader can understand why it is a favorite of yours

AUDIENCE A younger person

PREWRITING List sensory details of the object. Try to connect a few of these details to happy memories. Then decide on the overall impression you want to convey.

WRITING As you write, address your reader directly. You might start by announcing why you want the reader to know about this object. Then describe your object in affectionate detail, pointing out the best memories that it calls up. Organize your description by grouping similar details.

REVISING Check to see if your feeling for the object comes across. Make sure to edit and proofread also.

Writer's Choice #2

ASSIGNMENT To write a character sketch based on a character in a suitable TV series. (You may prefer to base a sketch on a photograph in the Writer's Sourcebook, pages 358–359.)

LENGTH Your choice

PURPOSE To describe your subject in such a way that your audience will be either eager or reluctant to meet her or him

AUDIENCE Your choice

OPTIONS The psychological details you describe should grow logically from the physical details and behavior you include in the sketch.

Try making up your own prewriting questions.

Writer's Choice #3

ASSIGNMENT To describe a subject of your choice

LENGTH Your choice

PURPOSE Your choice

AUDIENCE Your choice

OPTIONS You can use materials in the Writer's Sourcebook to spark ideas for your description.

You can make an observation table to help you gather sensory details about your subject.

Writers on Writing

Paul Kalomeres has lived in Cincinnati, Ohio, all his life. He hopes to study biochemistry and eventually to become a physician specializing in sports medicine. He wrote the following descriptive paragraph and commentary when he was a student at Indian Hill High School in Cincinnati.

THE PRODUCT

Getting out of bed in the morning is like getting up from a boxer's knockout punch. Just as a fighter reacts with pain to a powerhouse punch, so a sleeper winces at the sound of the blaring alarm. As the fighter does, the sleeper replaces pain with a feeling of numbness. The prizefighter struggles to survive the ten count; in the same way the sleeper tries to stay awake. Slowly the fighter climbs to his knees, searching for the agility that had once been his. The sleeper, similarly, raises the body against the weariness that fills the blood. The fighter is up. The sleeper is up. They have found the old life that once surged through their bodies—the drive to keep going.

THE PROCESS

The subject of waking is one that puzzles me every school day of the year. Every morning I feel as if I know what a boxer must go through when he tries to recover from a monstrous blow. As I developed this parallel, I found more and more comparisons that I could carry through my writing—the feeling of numbness being the most important.

Since waking up is a universal experience, I think my comparison can be understood and appreciated by a wide audience. The combination of wide audience appeal and good personal understanding of the experience enabled me to write my description with considerable ease.

YOUR TURN *Describing a Common Experience*

As Paul did, choose a very common experience and describe it in vivid terms, concentrating on the sense of feeling. You may want to compare your experience to something else, as Paul compared waking up to getting up from a knockout punch.

CHAPTER 7 DESCRIPTIVE WRITING

Sensory Details [pages 140–143] Indicate which sense is called up in each sentence: (a) sight; (b) sound; (c) smell; (d) taste; (e) touch.

1. The old car idled, its engine banging, coughing, and screeching.
2. In the crimson rays of the setting sun, the river turned a deep purple, bordered by dark trees with gold-flecked tops.
3. My grandmother's kitchen is always filled with the sweet aroma of vanilla enlivened by the sharp scent of cinnamon.
4. Expecting the smooth and slimy, I reached out to touch the snake and was surprised by the rough, leathery texture of its skin.

Overall Impression and Descriptive Language [pages 143–145 and 146–147] Read the following paragraph, and indicate the letter of the item that correctly answers each question.

Buenos Aires, decked out for spring, was looking her best. The tall and elegant buildings seemed to gleam like icebergs in the sun, and the broad avenues were lined with jacaranda trees covered with a mist of navy blue flowers, or *palo barracho,* with their strange bottle-shaped trunks and their spindly branches starred with yellow and white flowers. The springlike atmosphere seemed to have infected the pedestrians, who fled across the road through the traffic with even less caution than usual, while the drivers of the trains, buses, and cars vied with each other in the time-honored Buenos Aires game of seeing how close they could get . . . at the maximum speed without actually crashing.

—Gerald Durrell, *The Whispering Land*

5. Which item states the overall impression of the passage?
   (a) Buenos Aires is a dangerous place.
   (b) Buenos Aires is beautiful and alive.
   (c) Spring in Buenos Aires creates problems.
   (d) Buenos Aires is strange and frightening.
6. "Mist" in line 3 is a good descriptive word because it suggests
   (a) delicacy. (c) grayness.
   (b) vagueness. (d) a watery nature.
7. Which of the following is a figure of speech?
   (a) "springlike atmosphere" (c) "spindly branches"
   (b) "tall and elegant buildings" (d) "gleams like icebergs"

Writing for Review Write a two-paragraph description that captures the mood of a room. After you write, underline at least four sensory details, three vivid words, and one figure of speech.

CHAPTER 8

Narrative Writing

And now it seems to me that what is real is what is happening. . . . I write then, out of that.

—*Alice Walker*

It was a moment I wanted to recapture and hold for myself.

—*Russell Baker*

Both Alice Walker and Russell Baker have won Pulitzer Prizes for telling stories, for narrating events. Walker won her prize for fiction; Baker, for nonfiction. Nevertheless, the quotations help us see that whenever we tell stories—fictional or nonfictional—we ground them in reality so that we can hold the attention of our readers.

Narration is the kind of writing that tells a story, real or imagined. A **nonfiction narrative** is factual prose writing that tells a true story. A **fiction narrative** is prose writing that is imagined.

Here is an excerpt from Russell Baker's autobiography. In it he recounts his first solo flight while training in the Navy during World War II.

> The takeoff wasn't too bad, although I nearly skidded off the runway before getting airborne. All I had to do was climb to 800 feet, turn 180 degrees, turn again, put the nose down, and land. It was exhilarating not having Jim [Baker's flight instructor] riding the controls, but I was surprised, too. The plane seemed to have acquired a mind of its own. It insisted on going all the way to 1,200 feet when I wanted to level off at 800, then when I tried to get back down it dived all the way to 600 feet before leveling off. It finally consented to circle the field, and I got the nose pointed toward the runway and headed for earth at a civilized speed. When the wheels touched down it looked as if I might survive, and, feeling solid runway underneath, I slammed on the brakes. The plane spun violently through a 180-degree ground loop and wound up fifty yards off the runway in the grass. Since my ground loop hadn't flipped the plane and destroyed a wing, the jury that weighed my case decided to give me a second chance instead of washing me out of the program.
>
> —Russell Baker, *Growing Up*

Baker went on to pass his flight test with rave reviews—and then later to get outstanding reviews as a newspaper columnist.

Most likely you yourself have been narrating incidents orally since you were very young. Think of the number of times you have begun a conversation with a friend or family member using words like these: "Do you know what I saw on the way to school?" or "You should hear what Pete told me about his trip to Florida" or "What a story I have for you!"

Of course you have also written narratives—in short stories, in compositions about personal experiences, in "newsy" letters to friends, in plot summaries of book reviews, and so forth. In writing narratives you use many of the skills you use in oral narration; for as British writer Beryl Bainbridge tells us, writing is "simply talking on paper."

In this chapter you will have the opportunity to build on your skills of oral narration as you practice these other skills:

prewriting: the elements of a narrative
prewriting: subject, purpose, and audience
prewriting: a narrative outline
writing a narrative
writing: using dialogue in a narrative
writing: using vivid verbs in a narrative
writing an anecdote
revising, **editing**, and **publishing** narrative writing

Prewriting: The Elements of a Narrative

Although a narrative can be either fiction or nonfiction, you will be writing only nonfiction narratives as you work your way through the chapter. Nevertheless, your narratives will sometimes contain elements of fiction used by writers of short stories. These elements include plot, setting, and point of view.

For example, in the preceding model Russell Baker built in a plot (the beginning of the flight, the middle of the flight, and the end of the flight); he definitely had a setting (the plane and its environs); he selected the obvious point of view for an autobiography (first person). He could have communicated the same basic facts in a single sentence such as "My first solo flight was exhilarating and frightening, but at least I survived it." However, by including details and filling out the plot, setting, and point of view, Baker made his narrative much more lively and enjoyable.

In the next few sections, you can take a closer look at these short story elements and consider how they can be used in writing a narrative. You will follow one student writer as she develops a subject for a short narrative.

The **plot** is the sequence of events that occurs in a narrative. Often at the center of a plot is a problem, or **conflict.** As a person in a narrative tries to solve the conflict, the plot builds to the point of highest interest, or the **climax.** The **resolution** brings the narrative to a satisfying and logical conclusion.

A plot is not an essential part of every nonfiction narrative. You can narrate an incident involved in a visit to the zoo without introducing a conflict or problem of any kind. As a reader yourself, though, you have probably discovered that a narrative with a conflict—however minor it may be—is frequently more interesting to read.

Plot in a successful narrative—even one as brief as the preceding model—includes a meaningful and sometimes suspenseful sequence of events. For example, the plot of the model begins with a problem: How can I get this plane to do what I have to do? The climax of this very brief plot is reached when Baker brings the plane to a stop. The resolution is simple: He learns that he can try it again.

The **setting** of a narrative is the time and place in which the narrative occurs.

The place in the setting may be a room in a house, one spot in the landscape, or an entire geographical area such as a country, a state, a city, or a town. The time in the setting may be a few minutes or a few hours, a day or several weeks or years, a season, or the whole of a historical period such as the Civil War era in the United States. Setting may also include the weather and the culture of the people of the country where the events of the narrative happen. A writer may describe a setting with many sensory details or simply sketch it with a detail or two. Baker suggests the setting by mentioning that the plane seemed to have a mind of its own: It could not have been too smooth a ride. He also talks about the *solid* runway.

Point of view represents the relationship of the narrator to the story.

The narrator is the one who relates the events of a narrative. A nonfiction narrative told from the *first-person point of view* is related by the author, who addresses the reader directly and uses first-person pronouns such as *I, me, my,* and *mine.* As you can see, the nonfiction story about the solo flight is a first-person narrative. In a narrative told from the *third-person point of view,* the narrator stands back from the events and uses such third-person pronouns as *he, she,* and *they* to refer to the characters. As a writer, it will be up to you to choose the point of view that will most effectively tell your story.

EXERCISE 1 **Recognizing the Elements of a Narrative.** Read the following narrative, and write your answers to each of the numbered questions.

I could see the road only in places—the walls were covered over most of their length, but the farm was visible all the way. I had gone about half a mile toward it when a sudden gust of wind blew up the surface snow into a cloud of fine particles. Just for a few seconds I found myself completely alone. The farm, the surrounding moor, everything disappeared, and I had an eerie sense of isolation till the veil cleared.

—James Herriot, *All Creatures Great and Small*

1. Briefly describe the plot of the narrative.
2. Where is the narrative set?
3. Is the story told from the first- or third-person point of view?

Prewriting: Subject, Purpose, and Audience

You can find a subject for a narrative among your common, everyday experiences, not only in exciting or dramatic events. Think about familiar people and events, and you may be surprised at the number of subjects you discover. For help in generating and exploring ideas, you will no doubt wish to use prewriting techniques you learned in Chapter 2—freewriting, brainstorming, and charting.

In the remaining pages of this chapter, you will follow one student through the prewriting and writing steps of creating a narrative. When assigned to write the narrative, this was the only restriction placed on the student: Be sure the incident you choose as a subject can be narrated in a single paragraph. This restriction will also apply to the narratives that you write for this chapter.

EXERCISE 2 **Prewriting for a Narrative.** Choose one of the subjects listed here or a subject of your own. Freewrite or brainstorm for a while. Then ask the questions *Who? What? When? Where? Why?* and *How?* Work for ten minutes to generate and explore ideas for a subject that you can deal with in a single paragraph. Save your notes for a narrative that you will write later.

1. making something
2. a small victory
3. discovering
4. a funny experience
5. taking a test
6. going to the dentist
7. a sunset (or sunrise)
8. an unexpected experience

Defining Purpose and Audience

Every narrative has a general or specific *purpose,* or goal. If you are not assigned a specific purpose, then it is up to you to choose one. The goal of a news narrative is to inform. A sports narrative may be meant to entertain. The purpose of an autobiographical narrative could be to share an insight about life. Sometimes a narrative may have a combination of purposes. Once you have identified your goal, you will want to plan your writing to accomplish it.

As in all kinds of writing, the purpose of a narrative and the audience for whom it is written are closely related. In prewriting for your narrative, you should give careful thought to your audience. Consider the type of experience and knowledge your reader is likely to have. Select details and events that will make your purpose for writing the narrative clear to them. And, perhaps most important, consider whether your approach will maintain the interest of your audience.

The student whose prewriting and writing activities you will follow made the prewriting notes below. The notes reveal the purpose and intended audience for a narrative about "orphan" bird eggs.

PREWRITING NOTES

1. *The purpose of the narrative is to make the point that people can sometimes give nature a helping hand.*
2. *My English teacher and students in the English class make up my audience. All of them have a basic knowledge of my subject—the hatching of bird eggs.*

EXERCISE 3 **Defining Purpose and Audience.** Choose one of the subjects for which you generated ideas in Exercise 2, or choose a different subject if you wish. Then state in writing the purpose and audience for the narrative you will write later.

Prewriting: A Narrative Outline

As you prewrite, you will choose the events you wish to include in your narrative. The following questions will help you to think about all the events related to the incident or experience you will narrate and direct you to zero in on the most essential ones. The answers in the second column were written during the prewriting step by the student who is planning the narrative on the "orphan" bird eggs.

QUESTIONS TO EXPLORE THE EVENTS OF A NARRATIVE	SAMPLE ANSWERS
1. In what way did the experience or incident begin?	*The experience began when my family moved into a new apartment and I saw a nest with eggs on the fire escape.*
2. What problem, or conflict, did I or another character involved in the experience or incident face?	*The eggs were apparently abandoned by the parent birds and would not hatch unless someone came to the rescue.*
3. What was my or another character's reaction to this problem?	*I decided I would try to find a way to hatch the eggs and raise the baby birds.*
4. In what way did I or another character solve the problem?	*After consulting a veterinarian on the phone, I used a heating pad to hatch the eggs.*
5. Did any obstacles prevent me or another character from solving this problem?	*One possible obstacle was a stray cat (Jaws, Jr.) who was just as eager as I was to have the eggs hatch but for a different reason. Placing a cardboard carton over the nest kept the cat away.*
6. What was my or another character's reaction to the solution?	*I was overjoyed when the baby birds finally pecked their way out of the eggs in about two weeks. Jaws, Jr., was glum because it couldn't get at the tasty baby birds.*
7. What was the final outcome?	*After feeding the baby birds with the advice of the veterinarian for about a month, I watched sadly one day when the last of them flew away from the fire escape.*

EXERCISE 4 **Choosing Events for a Narrative.** Use one of the narrative subjects you worked with in Exercises 2 and 3 or another of your own choosing. List the events of your narrative by writing an answer for each of the seven questions on the preceding chart. Add any other important events not covered by the questions. Save your notes for Exercise 5.

Eliminating Unnecessary Events

Eliminating unnecessary events and details is an essential step in planning a narrative, especially when the writer is restricted to one paragraph as you are. For example, the student planning the narrative on the "orphan" bird eggs made a list of events that might be included in the narrative. Reviewing the list later, the student recognized that some of the events were not directly related to the purpose and drew a line through them. As a result, she was then able to plan a much more focused narrative on her subject.

> I saw a bird nest with four eggs on the fire escape outside the kitchen of my apartment.
>
> I realized that the parent birds had abandoned the eggs.
>
> A cat on the fire escape presented a threat to the eggs.
>
> I decided I had to protect the eggs from the cat, hatch them if possible, and take care of the baby birds until they could fly.
>
> I called a veterinarian who suggested using a heating pad to hatch the birds.
>
> ~~It took me awhile to find the heating pad, since we had just moved and many things were still in boxes.~~
>
> I put a cardboard carton over the nest to prevent the cat from getting at the eggs.
>
> After about two weeks, the eggs hatched.
>
> Then I had to feed the baby birds (again I needed the veterinarian's advice), which turned out to be pigeons.
>
> I thought about how much I disliked pigeons.
>
> Nearly a month later, the young pigeons flew away and never returned, which made me sad.
>
> ~~When the pigeons had gone, I decided to try fireplace gardening next spring.~~

EXERCISE 5 **Eliminating Unnecessary Events.** Look at the list of events you made for your narrative in Exercise 4. Which events, if any, are unnecessary or unrelated to the purpose and focus of your narrative? Draw a line through each unnecessary event.

Collecting Narrative Details

Although the narrative you write will be only one paragraph, you should try to include some details about the setting and the people. In the narrative about the solo flight, Russell Baker gave some details about the movements of the plane; in the narrative by James Herriot, you will find details of the setting.

To generate details for your narrative, think how the people involved looked, sounded, and acted. Imagine the setting of the experience, and decide on sensory details that will describe the setting. To organize the details of your narrative, charts like the following may be useful.

PEOPLE AND ANIMALS IN A NARRATIVE

SUBJECT: *hatching bird eggs*			
PEOPLE/ ANIMALS	TRAITS	BEHAVIOR/ REACTION	WHAT WAS LEARNED
me	*sympathetic, intelligent, hopeful*	*worried, dedicated, delighted*	*Sometimes nature needs a helping hand*
Jaws, Jr.	*greedy, watchful, eager*	*sly, determined, disgruntled*	

SETTING FOR A NARRATIVE

SUBJECT: *hatching bird eggs*			
PLACE	TIME OF DAY/YEAR	WEATHER	DETAILS OF SETTING
Fire escape outside my apartment	*Early spring*	*Hovering between cold and warm*	*Rusty fire escape with a bird nest in the corner nearest my kitchen window*

EXERCISE 6 **Collecting Narrative Details.** Use the narrative subject you have worked with in preceding exercises or another of your own choice. Create two charts like the preceding ones. Modify the headings if necessary. Then fill in the information about the people and setting of your narrative. Save your charts for Exercise 7.

Filling in the Narrative Outline

Spread all your writing notes on a table or tape them on a wall so that you can refer to them easily. You will need your notes to complete the final prewriting step—making a writing plan, or outline, for your narrative. The outline that follows was prepared by the student planning the narrative on hatching bird eggs. As you can see, the outline begins by stating the purpose of the narrative. It continues with a list of the events in *chronological* order, the order in which the events actually happen, with each part of the outline leading clearly to the next. Notice that the outline also includes descriptions of characters and setting. To put it another way, the outline assembles in one place all the prewriting notes made to this point.

NARRATIVE OUTLINE FOR HATCHING BIRD EGGS

I. Beginning
   A. State the purpose of your narrative in an introductory sentence.
      Earlier this year, I learned that people can sometimes give nature a helping hand.
   B. Describe the setting.
      One day this spring my family moved into a new apartment with a rusty fire escape outside one of the kitchen windows.
   C. Give important background information.
      I am a city dweller who doesn't have much contact with nature.
   D. Begin to tell what happened.
      Looking out the window, I spotted in one corner of the fire escape a bird nest with four eggs. When I investigated, I found that the eggs were still warm, but the parent birds were nowhere to be seen.

II. Middle
   A. Introduce and describe the other characters involved.
      As I was examining the eggs, I became aware of motion in the other corner of the fire escape. Turning, I saw a hungry-looking cat peering at me and then greedily toward the eggs in the nest. I dubbed the cat Jaws, Jr.
   B. Show your reaction to the conflict with a direct statement.
      I had to do something to protect the eggs from sly old Jaws and, if possible, hatch them and take care of the baby birds until they could fly.
   C. Build toward a climax, the point of highest interest.
      Since I knew nothing about hatching eggs, I called a veterinarian who suggested using a heating pad to keep the eggs at the proper temperature. To prevent Jaws from feasting on the eggs, I simply placed a cardboard carton over the nest.

III. Ending
    A. Write a climax.
        After about two weeks, the baby birds, one after another, carefully pecked their way out of the eggs. Now, feeding the birds (with the advice of the veterinarian) would become my chief occupation. As the baby birds grew, I was disappointed to see that they were pigeons, but not Jaws, Jr. One meal was as tasty as another to that hungry cat.
    B. Write a resolution.
        Somehow, after nearly a month of mothering four young pigeons, the day came when they flew off the balcony and never returned. I was sorry to see them go and so was Jaws, but I'm sure he had different reasons.

EXERCISE 7 **Preparing a Narrative Outline.** Using the subject you developed in preceding exercises or another subject of your choice, make a narrative outline. Include as many of the categories in the model outline as possible, and save your outline.

Writing a Narrative

It is now time to begin the first draft of your narrative. You should have all your prewriting ideas arranged chronologically in outline form. As you follow the outline to write your narrative, you will need to use *transitions* to indicate the time order of the events. Some transitions used frequently in narrative writing follow:

after	finally	immediately	meanwhile	soon
always	first	last	now	then
before	following	later	sometimes	until

A MODEL NARRATIVE

The student whom you have been following in this chapter finally wrote a one-paragraph narrative based on all her prewriting notes:

> This past spring I learned that people can sometimes give nature a helping hand. The lesson began when my family moved into an apartment with a rusty fire escape outside the kitchen window. Looking out the window, I spotted four eggs in a bird nest in one corner of the fire escape. When I investigated, I found that the eggs were still warm, but the parent birds were nowhere to be seen. As I was examining the eggs, I encountered a hungry-looking cat peering at me and then greedily toward the eggs in the nest. I dubbed the cat—who might have been the reason that the parent birds had apparently abandoned the eggs—Jaws, Jr. I had to do something to protect the eggs from the sly, old cat and, if

them and care for the baby birds until they could fly.
nothing about hatching eggs, I called a veterinarian, who
sing a heating pad to keep the eggs at room temperature. To
aws from feasting on them, I simply placed a cardboard carton
e nest. After about two weeks, I was overjoyed to see the baby
, one after another, peck their way out of the eggs. My mission was
omplished. Well, at least partially. Now, feeding the birds (with the
dvice of the veterinarian) would become my chief occupation. As the baby birds grew, I was disappointed to see that they were pigeons, but not Jaws, Jr. One meal was as tasty as another to that hungry cat. Somehow, after nearly a month of mothering the four young pigeons, the day came when they flew off and never returned. I was sorry to see them go and so was Jaws, but I'm sure he had different reasons.

EXERCISE 8 **Writing from a Narrative Outline.** Write the first draft of a narrative using the outline that you prepared in Exercise 7. Present your narrative in chronological order, using transitions to help your reader follow the sequence of events. Limit your narrative to one paragraph. Review your draft to see what improvements you can make.

Writing: Using Dialogue

Dialogue is the conversation between individuals in a narrative, quoted word-for-word and enclosed in quotation marks.

Writers use dialogue in both fiction narratives and nonfiction narratives. The dialogue in a fiction narrative is made up, whereas in the dialogue of a nonfiction narrative the writer uses the exact words of real people. Read the following nonfiction narrative, and note how dialogue helps bring a historical event to life.

> When James Buchanan was a member of the U.S. Senate, many years before his rise to the presidency, he often tangled with Henry Clay. One day the debate centered on Buchanan's alleged disloyalty during the War of 1812. To prove his loyalty, Buchanan stated that he had entered a company of volunteers at the time of the Battle of North Point and marched to Baltimore. "True," he said, "I was not in any engagement, as the British had retreated before my company got there."
>
> "You marched to Baltimore, though?" Clay asked.
>
> "Yes, sir, I did," Buchanan shot back.
>
> "Armed and equipped?" Clay continued.
>
> "Yes," said Buchanan, "armed and equipped."
>
> "Will you be good enough to inform this Senate," demanded Clay, "whether the British retreated in consequence of your valiantly marching to the relief of Baltimore, or whether you marched to the relief of Baltimore in consequence of the British having already retreated?"
>
> That was too much for Buchanan and he was quiet for the remainder of the session.
>
> —John F. Parker, *The Fun and Laughter of Politics*

EXERCISE 9 **Changing Indirect Quotation to Dialogue.** The following passage was taken from a diary kept by a boy in Boston. The writer presents dialogue indirectly. Rewrite the passage, changing the indirect quotations to dialogue. Hint: Dialogue can be used six times in the passage. If you need to review the rules for punctuating dialogue, see Chapter 27.

This afternoon my brother Matt burst into the kitchen and shouted excitedly that my little sister Beverly was at the top of the apple tree in the backyard and couldn't get down. All of us tried to get out of the kitchen door at once in our desire to help poor Bev. Mother called to Beverly to come down at once and Dad mumbled that someone should call the fire department, the police, or *someone*. For the next several minutes we ran around the trunk of the apple tree bumping into each other and waving our arms in the air, but no one could think of any way to get a little girl out of a tree. While all of this was going on, Beverly seemed very unconcerned. She sat on her branch among the blossoms near the top of the tree and gazed at some distant vision. Our next-door neighbor leaned across the fence and touched Dad on the shoulder, explaining that she had called the police, the fire department, *and* the Society for the Prevention of Cruelty to Animals. As she was speaking, we could hear the din of sirens, bells and whistles of the approaching rescuers. In our eagerness to witness the arrival of what sounded like a medium-sized army, no one noticed that Beverly had somehow descended from her perch at the top of the apple tree. Matt was the first to see her and it was his shrieking of her name that caused all of us to turn in her direction. When Beverly saw all of us staring open-mouthed at her, her matter-of-fact comment was that you really couldn't see much of anything from up there.

Writing: Using Vivid Verbs

To convey action in a convincing way, use vivid, precise verbs in your narrative. Such verbs will evoke more realistic images in your readers. Compare the image evoked by each verb in the first column with the image evoked by each of the corresponding verbs in the second column:

LESS PRECISE VERBS	VIVID, PRECISE VERBS
jumped	sprang, catapulted
yelled	bellowed, thundered
moved	lunged, wriggled
walked	glided, waddled
wept	sobbed, blubbered

EXERCISE 10 **Using Vivid Verbs to Convey Action.** Below the following paragraph is a list of vivid verbs. Make the narrative more exciting by replacing the underlined verbs in the paragraph with verbs from the verb list.

Runner Joan Hanson [1]<u>had</u> a personal victory at the 1984 Summer Olympics in the 3,000-meter race. On the day of the race, she [2]<u>walked</u> nervously back and forth, waiting to be called to the starting line. The moment arrived. Joan [3]<u>bent</u> down tensely at her starting position. She [4]<u>listened</u> to hear the starter's pistol, and at last the pistol [5]<u>fired</u> sharply. She [6]<u>moved</u> through the first two and a half laps with ease. Then she stumbled and [7]<u>fell</u> to the ground, a bundle of flailing arms and legs.

Joan lay dazed on the track, fighting disappointment and discouragement as the distance between herself and the other runners [8]increased. Instead of giving in to her feelings, Joan [9]got to her feet and ran on to finish in eighth place. Joan's performance [10]got her no medals, but for her it proved a triumph of spirit over disappointment.

VIVID VERBS

achieved	paced
cracked	streaked
crashed	strained
crouched	widened
leaped	won

Writing an Anecdote as Part of a Longer Narrative

An **anecdote** is a short narrative that is often used to illustrate a point within a longer piece of writing.

An anecdote may be about a historical person or event or about an incident that happened to the writer. Unlike other short narratives, such as tall tales, whose primary purpose is to amuse, anecdotes are usually included to illustrate a point—though they are often amusing as well. Using an anecdote can be an effective strategy for presenting your ideas when your main purpose is to explain or to persuade. The following anecdote, for example, is taken from an expository essay. The author uses it to illustrate the point that important scientific discoveries are often the result of flashes of intuition rather than deliberate reasoned thought.

> The German physiologist Otto Loewi was working on the mechanism of nerve action, in particular, on the chemicals produced by nerve endings. He awoke at 3 A.M. one night in 1921 with a perfectly clear notion of the type of experiment he would have to run to settle a key point that was puzzling him. He wrote it down and went back to sleep. When he woke in the morning, he found he couldn't remember what his inspiration had been. He remembered he had written it down, but he couldn't read his writing.
>
> The next night, he woke again at 3 A.M. with the clear thought once more in mind. This time, he didn't fool around. He got up, dressed himself, went straight to the laboratory and began work. By 5 A.M. he had proved his point and the consequences of his findings became important enough in later years so that in 1936 he received a share in the Nobel prize in medicine and physiology.

> How very often this sort of thing must happen, and what a shame that scientists are so devoted to their belief in conscious thought that they so consistently obscure the actual methods by which they obtain their results.
>
> —Isaac Asimov, "The Eureka Phenomenon"

Notice that Asimov's anecdote has many of the elements of a narrative, such as a sequence of events, or plot, a character (Otto Loewi), and a setting (Loewi's bedroom and laboratory). Transitions, such as "at 3 A.M.," "in the morning," and "the next night," give the anecdote a definite chronological order and help move the plot forward. Note also that Asimov needed more than one paragraph to structure this particular anecdote effectively. In the first paragraph he tells about the first night and presents Loewi's problem. In the second paragraph Asimov relates the events of the second night and presents the climax (Loewi had "proved his point") and resolution ("he received a share in the Nobel prize"). In the third paragraph Asimov clearly states the point of the anecdote.

EXERCISE 11 **Analyzing an Anecdote.** Find an example of an anecdote that is part of a longer narrative. You may choose from either a fiction or nonfiction narrative. (Remember to identify the author and the work you are using.) Analyze the structure of the anecdote by discussing the following items: the sequence of events, plot, character or characters, and setting; specific transitions used by the author to give the anecdote definite chronological order; the climax and resolution; the point of the anecdote and how it relates to the purpose of the longer work.

EXERCISE 12 **Writing an Anecdote.** Write an anecdote of three paragraphs in which you relate a personal incident that taught you a valuable lesson about life. As part of your prewriting, state the point that your anecdote will illustrate, and prepare a narrative outline. Then draft your anecdote, being sure to use chronological order for coherence.

Revising, Editing, and Publishing

When you are revising the first draft of any paragraph, you ask the general questions that are given in Chapter 4. When you are revising a piece of narrative writing, you ask these same questions *plus* the questions that follow. You ask all these questions in order to revise your narrative so that it will accomplish your purpose and be suitable for your audience.

Checklist for Revising a Narrative

1. What makes my narrative a nonfiction narrative or a fiction narrative?
2. What is my purpose and who is my audience?
3. What questions have helped me to choose the events for my narrative?
4. Which events are not really necessary to include in my narrative?
5. What conflict, if any, does my narrative contain? How is the conflict resolved?
6. What narrative details have I included?
7. Have I checked my first draft against my narrative outline to be sure that the first draft is complete?
8. What transitional words and phrases give my narrative coherence? Have I used chronological order?
9. Where can I add dialogue to my narrative?
10. Where and how have I used vivid verbs to convey action?
11. Can I strengthen my narrative by adding an anecdote to illustrate the main point?
12. How many paragraphs do I need to fully tell my story?

Writer's Choice

Writer's Choice #1

ASSIGNMENT A historical narrative

LENGTH A paragraph of six to ten sentences

AUDIENCE A group of younger students

PURPOSE To narrate a significant event in your state, city, or town's history

PREWRITING List all the events involved in the incident. Use the exploring questions. Then eliminate those events that do not seem important. Make sure that the remaining events are in chronological order. Prepare charts for details of setting and descriptions of other characters. Then put all your notes into a narrative outline.

WRITING Write an introductory statement that describes the historical incident. Then narrate the events leading to the incident.

REVISING Be sure that you have developed your paragraph with specific details that present the incident accurately. If you presented a conflict in your paragraph, did you show how the conflict was resolved? Edit your work, checking in particular for transitions. Prepare a final version of your paragraph to share with your audience. Make sure you remember to proofread it.

Writer's Choice #2

ASSIGNMENT A sports narrative

LENGTH A paragraph of six to ten sentences

AUDIENCE Your classmates

PURPOSE To write a brief account of a real sports event in which you witnessed an obstacle overcome or a challenge met.

PREWRITING List the important events in chronological order. Use the exploring questions. Make a chart of narrative details. Fill in a narrative outline.

WRITING In your introductory statement provide background information about time and place. Then show how the narrative unfolded. End by telling how the plot is resolved.

REVISING Be sure that you have thoroughly explained the obstacle that was overcome or the challenge that was met. Edit your work, prepare a final version, and proofread it.

Writer's Choice #3

ASSIGNMENT A news narrative
LENGTH Your choice
AUDIENCE Your choice
PURPOSE To report a newsworthy incident that has occurred in your community within the past week
PREWRITING List the important details in order of importance, including people and setting.
WRITING In your opening sentence identify the time and place of the incident. Then narrate the most important details of the incident, using as many vivid verbs as possible.
REVISING Make sure that you have included only the details that your readers will need in order to understand the incident. Edit your work and proofread it.

Writer's Choice #4

ASSIGNMENT A personal narrative
LENGTH Your choice
AUDIENCE Your choice
PURPOSE To write a first-person account of one of the following topics or a topic of your own choosing.
a humorous incident
an unusual trip
meeting someone unexpectedly
eating your favorite meal
OPTIONS You may want to include dialogue.
You may want to concentrate on using vivid verbs.

Writer's Choice #5

ASSIGNMENT A narrative of any kind
LENGTH Your choice
AUDIENCE Your choice
PURPOSE Your choice
OPTIONS Write on any subject you choose.
You may want to try writing a narrative of more than one paragraph.
You may want to base your narrative on a photograph in the Writer's Sourcebook, pages 360–361.

Writers on Writing

Born in Philadelphia, Robert Nichols now lives in Cincinnati, Ohio. His interests include playing percussion and French horn and participating in basketball, baseball, and tennis. He wrote the following narrative and commentary as a student at Indian Hill High School in Cincinnati.

THE PRODUCT

It was an hour before dawn. The beach was cold and windy. Nothing to be seen but other fishermen in the distance, waiting to catch the one creature that was the talk of the town: the bluefish. Until this moment, the men's efforts had gone unrewarded. Not a single fish had been caught. Discouraged, some of the men began to pack up when, all of a sudden, one man's pole bent, and he tightened his grip. Yes, there was a bluefish on the line. It fought furiously. The pole was taking much stress, but the man refused to give up. You could see the fish in the distance struggling to free itself. At least twenty pounds. The battle continued. The fish was within five feet of the shore now and was fighting harder than ever. The fisherman tried to pull him in, but the fish would not give up. Still, it could not fight forever—it was tired. Eventually, it could not resist the man's strength, and it was pulled ashore. All the men on the beach stared at the magnificent fish for a minute. Its gills opened and closed as if it were exhausted from the fight. They weighed it: twenty-five pounds. Then the man who caught it said, "He's too beautiful to keep. Let him swim another day." And with that he threw the fish back into the ocean and watched it swim away.

THE PROCESS

First I had to find something to write about. I searched my mind for something I knew about that would be exciting for others to read. I considered some sports such as skiing, basketball, and mountain climbing, but I ruled those out because I didn't think most readers would find them interesting. I also thought about some of my hobbies, such as music and art, but those did not seem exciting enough either. Then in one of our family discussions, someone brought up the subject of the fish my brother had caught on vacation. I decided that this was the subject I wanted.

Before I began to write, I listed some of the things I would mention, such as the setting, the size of the fish, and the reaction of the fishermen. When I finally began writing, I did a first draft, covering all my ideas and writing as well as I could. After that I got out my trusty dictionary and thesaurus, changing errors and fixing repetitions. Next I read it out loud to see if the phrases fit together; if one phrase did not fit in, I used the thesaurus to find words that meant the same thing but sounded better. Once I had finished that, I was ready for the final draft.

In conclusion, my advice to you is always to write about subjects that you know and that are compatible with your style. Always use a dictionary and thesaurus when you need to. And, finally, believe in your writing. Most everyone has the ability to write well. Just use the correct procedure, and try to write what sounds best to you.

YOUR TURN *Writing A Narrative*

Write a narrative about an exciting experience that happened to someone you know. Use the prewriting steps that Robert mentions, as well as others that you have learned in this chapter. Set the scene with details, as Robert did in his story about the fish. Relate the sequence of events in a way that builds excitement. As Robert did, you may want to end with a surprising twist. Edit and revise your first draft, using the checklist on page 171. When you are satisfied with your narrative, make a neat final copy and proofread it.

Review

CHAPTER 8 NARRATIVE WRITING

Answer the questions based on the following narrative paragraph.

[1]Once Lindbergh and his *Spirit of St. Louis* reached the Massachusetts coast, the excitement of his takeoff from Long Island's Roosevelt Field had worn off. [2]He realized that between the Massachusetts coast and Nova Scotia he would have to face two hours of flight over open water. [3]As he thought about the next two hours, he suddenly realized how sleepy he felt. [4]His drowsiness was probably traceable to the fact that he had not slept in twenty-four hours and had already flown four hours. [5]His eyelids yearned to close. [6]He fought against sleep, realized that to yield to it would be fatal. [7]Then he noticed something that so angered him that he became instantly alert. [8]There on the wing was a bit of mud thrown up during his takeoff. [9]He had worked so hard to cut every ounce from his plane and was now forced to carry a tiny load of mud to Europe. [10]Whenever sleep beckoned, the thought of the mud passenger brought him instantly awake.

Narrative Elements [pages 157–159]

1. Which sentence identifies the setting?
   (a) sentence 1 (b) sentence 5 (c) sentence 7
2. From which point of view is the narrative told?
   (a) first-person point of view (b) third-person point of view
3. Which sentence identifies the conflict or central problem?
   (a) sentence 1 (b) sentence 3 (c) sentence 4 (d) sentence 7
4. Which sentence describes the climax of the narrative?
   (a) sentence 3 (b) sentence 5 (c) sentence 7 (d) sentence 10
5. Which sentence provides the resolution of the narrative?
   (a) sentence 7 (b) sentence 8 (c) sentence 9 (d) sentence 10

Narrative Details [page 163]

6. Which sentence contains details about the setting?
   (a) sentence 2 (b) sentence 3 (c) sentence 5 (d) sentence 7
7. Which contains significant details about the main character?
   (a) sentence 2 (b) sentence 4 (c) sentence 8 (d) sentence 9

Chronological Order, Coherence, and Vivid Verbs [pages 164–169]

8. Which sentence contains a transition that indicates time order?
   (a) sentence 5 (b) sentence 6 (c) sentence 7 (d) sentence 9
9. Which verb suggests the powerful attractiveness of sleep?
   (a) yearned (b) was traceable (c) tried (d) angered

Writing for Review Write a two-paragraph narrative that has a clear, definite climax.

CHAPTER 9

Expository Writing

If I am not clear, all my world crumbles to nothing.

—Stendahl

Expository writing is meant to inform the reader by presenting facts and explaining ideas.

The Latin root of the word *expository* means "to set forth" or "present." In expository writing you set forth or present information to your readers; you inform them with facts and ideas. Stendahl's words in the opening quotation apply to every type of writing, but they are especially applicable to expository writing.

In expository writing you can use certain strategies that will help you convey information clearly. The following list contains the thinking and writing strategies you will have the opportunity to practice:

determining purpose and audience
explaining a process: prewriting, writing, and revising
explaining cause and effects: prewriting, writing, and revising
dividing and classifying: prewriting, writing, and revising
defining: prewriting, writing, and revising
comparing and contrasting: prewriting, writing, and rewriting
combining strategies in a longer expository composition

As you practice these strategies, you will be using the basic skills of the writing process you learned in Unit I. You will begin each writing activity with raw information—facts and ideas. By the time you finish, however, you will have used the strategies to fashion the raw facts and ideas into a finished piece of expository writing that will help your readers to see the facts and ideas in a new and memorable way.

Purpose and Audience in Expository Writing

You can transform raw information into a finished piece of expository writing by using one of the strategies you see listed above. For some writing exercises that are assigned, you will be told which strategy to use; for others, you will make the choice. When the choice is up to you, thinking about your purpose for writing and the audience for your work will help you choose the most effective strategy.

For example, suppose your writing assignment is to inform your audience about one of the great cities of the world. Since no strategy has been suggested, you must decide which one will be most appropriate. To make this decision, you should first ask yourself what your purpose is. Do you want to explain why a particular city has become one of the world's leading urban centers? If so, you will most likely decide to write a *cause-and-effect* paragraph. Perhaps you prefer to inform your readers of how this city is unique, different from all the other great cities on Earth. In this case, you will probably decide to write a paragraph *contrasting* the features of the city with those of several others. Maybe your purpose is to give your readers information about how the people of your city choose their government leaders. Then you will no doubt decide on a strategy that will help you to explain the *process* in which the people make their choices. As you can see, different purposes require different strategies. The purpose and related strategy determine which raw facts and ideas you select to transform into a finished expository paragraph. Later in the chapter you will become familiar with the details of the preceding strategies.

Your choice of strategy depends not only on your purpose for writing but also on your audience's experience and knowledge. Readers who are already familiar with the reasons why great cities develop may not be interested in reading about these reasons again. Less informed readers, however, may be very interested.

EXERCISE 1 **Identifying Purposes for Expository Writing.** Think about each of the following subjects. Then list two specific purposes a writer might have in mind while prewriting for an expository paragraph. Study the example.

SUBJECT Tornadoes

POSSIBLE PURPOSES To explain the process by which a tornado develops
To contrast a tornado with a hurricane

1. television programs
2. your community
3. a musical instrument
4. a potential energy source

EXERCISE 2 **Selecting an Audience for Expository Writing.** First select one of the following subjects for expository writing. Then state in two or three sentences whether you would prefer to write for the expert audience or the nonexpert audience, and explain your preference.

SUBJECT OF EXPOSITION	EXPERT AUDIENCE	NONEXPERT AUDIENCE
1. taking good photographs	a professional photographer	some friends
2. a new book	a book reviewer	someone in your family
3. playing tennis	a tennis pro	a group of children
4. a rocket engine	an astronaut	your science class

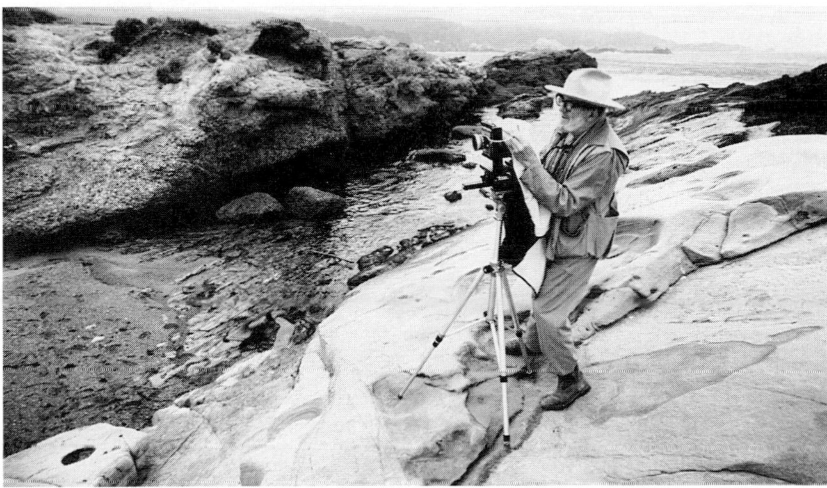

Explaining a Process

Explaining a process means showing how something works or how one accomplishes a particular task.

Suppose you had to write an expository paragraph on one of the following subjects: how a battery helps a car engine to start, how to write an outline, how to bathe a big dog that does not want to be bathed. For any of the three subjects, the paragraph you write would explain a process. The clearest way to explain any process is to take your readers through the process one step at a time. Before beginning to write the expository paragraph, think through each step. Keep in mind the knowledge and experience of your audience.

Prewriting

Start your prewriting by listing the steps of the process in chronological, or time, order. Then, to be sure you include all the essential information about the process, answer questions like those in the chart on page 180.

LISTING STEPS IN A PROCESS

PROCESS: *Getting a learner's permit to operate an automobile*

QUESTIONS	SAMPLE ANSWERS
1. For what audience am I writing?	*Beginning drivers, 16*
2. What are the steps in the process?	*a. Obtain an application from any office of the agency that issues permits and licenses.* *b. Present the completed application and required fee.* *c. Obtain an instruction manual from the same office.* *d. Answer every question on the application.* *e. Have your parents sign the parental consent portion of the application.* *f. Make an appointment to take an eye exam and a written exam.* *g. Study the manual to prepare for the written exam.* *h. Be punctual in reporting for the exams.* *i. Present your approved application and a birth certificate to the examiner.* *j. Take both exams.* *k. Wait until the permit is issued before operating an automobile.*
3. Should the order of any steps be changed?	*Place step b after step e.*
4. Can any steps be mentioned together?	*Steps a and c, d and e, and j and k could be combined.*
5. Does my audience need any more information to understand the process?	• *Indicate how long a permit is valid* • *Explain what to do if an applicant fails the eye exam or written exam.*

EXERCISE 3 **Listing the Steps in a Process.** From the following list, choose a process. If you prefer, substitute one of your own. Decide on an appropriate audience for an explanation of that process. Then complete a chart like the one shown earlier. Save the completed chart for a paragraph you will write later.

1. how to locate a library book
2. how to hit a baseball
3. how to start a car
4. how to dial long distance
5. how an elevator works
6. how citizens register to vote

Writing a First Draft

In writing an explanation of a process, use language that is suitable to your purpose and understandable to your audience. When explaining how to accomplish a task, it is permissible, even desirable, to address your readers as *you*. If your explanation tells how something works, remember to give the meanings of any unfamiliar technical terms.

Present in chronological order the steps of the process you are explaining. Make your explanation coherent by using transitions that indicate the order of the steps. The following transitions are among the ones you might use:

after	before	immediately	next	so that
always	finally	in order to	now	then
as soon as	first	last	second	until
at the same time	following	meanwhile	soon	

The following expository paragraph is based on the notes made in the chart shown earlier. Notice that the writer presents the steps in chronological order and ties them together with appropriate transitions.

> To get a learner's permit to operate an automobile, you must follow a certain procedure. First go to any office of the agency that issues drivers' permits and licenses in order to obtain an application and instruction manual. Next answer every question on the application, and have your parents sign the parental consent portion. When the application is complete, present it and the required fee at the office of the agency, and make an appointment to take an eye exam and a written exam. While waiting to take the exams, study the manual carefully. On the day the exams are scheduled, be punctual. As soon as you arrive, present your approved application and a birth certificate to the examiner. Then take the two exams as directed. If you should fail either or both of the exams, consult the examiner to find out what to do. Once you have passed the exams, wait until your permit is issued before you operate an automobile. The learner's permit you receive is valid for one year.

Revising, Editing, and Publishing

After you write the first draft of your explanation of a process, read it aloud, and use the following checklist to help you revise, edit, and proofread. Then publish the final copy of your explanation by sharing it with readers.

Checklist for Explaining a Process

1. Which steps in the process should be added to my explanation? Which ones can be omitted or grouped together?
2. Are the steps presented in the most logical order?
3. What can I do to make this process clearer to a reader who does not know anything about it? Have I adequately explained all unfamiliar technical terms?
4. What transitions would add to the coherence of my writing?
5. Is each sentence complete? Have I avoided errors in the use of verbs, pronouns, and modifiers?
6. Have I correctly capitalized and punctuated each sentence? Are all the words spelled correctly?
7. What might be a good way of presenting my writing to my intended audience? Reading it to them? Writing a letter?

EXERCISE 4 **Writing and Revising an Explanation of a Process.** Consult the chart that you prepared for Exercise 3. Then write an expository paragraph explaining the process you chose, including transitions for coherence. Finally, refer to the preceding checklist to help you revise, edit, proofread, and publish your expository paragraph.

Explaining a Cause-and-Effect Relationship

A **cause** is an event or condition that produces a result, which is known as an **effect.**

If you want to explain the reasons for a particular event or condition, or if you want to give the result of the event or condition, use a cause-and-effect writing strategy. You can use this strategy when you write about subjects like the following: why sunsets are colorful, what happened as a result of the Declaration of Independence, why people immigrate to the United States.

Prewriting

When planning to write about a cause-and-effect relationship, be certain that the events are related as causes and effects and not simply by time. In a chronological relationship, events simply occur one after another. In a true cause-and-effect relationship, however, one event actually *causes* another event to happen.

Study the following sentences. Which explains a true cause-and-effect relationship? Which presents a chronological relationship?

A. Last night it rained hard. This morning the sun is out.

B. Last night it rained hard. The carnival was postponed.

The events in item A are related by time alone: One thing happened, and then, later, another thing happened. The rain last night did not cause the sun to shine this morning. Item B expresses a cause-and-effect relationship: The rain most likely *did* cause a postponement.

Choose a topic and decide whether you are explaining causes, effects, or both. Then use brainstorming to discover the causes and effects.

When brainstorming for *causes*, consider the event or condition on which you are focusing and list the series of events that led up to it or made it happen. Your prewriting notes can take the form of a rough flow chart. Arrows can be drawn to show how one event in the series caused a second, how the second event caused a third event, and so on. If you are brainstorming for *effects*, place your event or condition on the chart and use arrows to show the results that branch out from it.

Suppose you are prewriting for an expository paragraph that will explain why trees, fish, and lake plants are being injured or killed in some parts of eastern Canada and the United States. You might make the following brainstorming notes:

BRAINSTORMING TO EXPLORE A CAUSE-AND-EFFECT RELATIONSHIP

TOPIC: *Why trees, fish, and lake plants are being damaged*

Factories burn high-sulfur coal to run machines.

↓

Smoke from burning coal is carried into the air by smokestacks.

↓

Smoke releases sulfur dioxide and nitrogen oxide into the air.

↓

Sulfur dioxide and nitrogen oxide mix with water in the clouds and form acids.

↓

Winds carry acid-filled clouds over land.

↓

Water in clouds condenses and falls as acid rain or snow.

↓

Acidic rainwater or melting snow sinks into soil and drains into lakes, injuring or killing trees, fish, and lake plants.

EXERCISE 5 **Identifying True Cause-and-Effect Relationships.** Write whether the relationship between the sentences in each item is a *chronological relationship* or a true *cause-and-effect relationship*.

1. Frank raised his bat. He swung at the ball and struck out.
2. Linda's car had been stolen. She went to the police station.
3. Snowfall was below average this winter. Ski resorts lost money.
4. Tuesday night, Sandy had a piercing toothache. Wednesday afternoon she went to see her dentist.
5. A large flock of migrating geese rested on the cables of the suspension bridge. Less than an hour later, the bridge collapsed.

EXERCISE 6 **Prewriting: Explaining Cause-and-Effect Relationships.** Choose a subject of your own, or use one of the following. Decide whether you want to explain the causes or effects of your subject. Make brainstorming notes in the form of an appropriate chart.

1. an iceberg
2. physical fitness
3. a current fad
4. success in school
5. laughter
6. an election result

Writing a First Draft

To write the first draft of your expository paragraph, go over your chart showing the causes or effects of your subject. Generate a topic sentence to express the main idea of your paragraph. Then select from your chart the points that will provide the strongest support for your main idea. When you have your topic sentence and supporting points, you will be ready to write your paragraph. As you write it, be sure to use appropriate transitions.

TO INDICATE CAUSES AND EFFECTS

as a result	consequently	is the effect of	so
because	if . . . then	leads to	therefore
causes	is due to	since	the reason for

TO INDICATE DEGREES OF CERTAINTY

possibly	likely	certainly	undoubtedly
maybe	probably	necessarily	unquestionably

The following paragraph presents a series of causes that result in destructive acid rain. The passage is based on the notes in the chart shown earlier.

The destructive acid rain that falls on parts of eastern Canada and the United States results from a number of related events, beginning with busy factories in the central United States and Canada. These factories burn high-sulfur coal to generate power to run machinery. Tall smokestacks carry smoke from the burning coal high into the air. Once in the air, sulfur dioxide and nitrogen oxide from the smoke mix with water in the clouds and form acids. Winds carry the acid-filled clouds eastward, and when the water in the clouds condenses it falls as acid rain or snow. On the ground the acidic rainwater or melting snow sinks into the soil and drains into lakes. The final result of these connected events is serious injury to trees, fish, and lake plants in the eastern parts of Canada and the United States.

Revising, Editing, and Publishing

After you complete your first draft, refer to the following checklist. For further help, refer to the checklist on page 182.

Checklist for Explaining a Cause-and-Effect Relationship

1. Where have I identified the causes and effects related to the event or condition on which I am focusing?
2. Am I presenting a true cause-and-effect relationship?
3. Which, if any, causes and effects should I add or omit?
4. What can I do to make clearer the connection between each cause and its effect? What transitions can I add?

EXERCISE 7 **Writing and Revising a Cause-and-Effect Paragraph.** Use the notes that you made for the chart in Exercise 6, and write a paragraph explaining a cause-and-effect relationship. Use appropriate transitions to clarify the relationship. Finally, use the preceding checklist to help you revise, edit, proofread, and publish your explanation.

Dividing and Classifying

Division breaks up an item into its main parts. **Classification** groups items together into categories.

In expository writing you can break up, or *divide,* practically anything into its important parts. You can divide the week into seven days. You can divide a baseball into its outer covering and inner parts. Division is an effective writing strategy if you want to explain a single, complex subject that consists of several individual parts—a car engine, a government, a rock group, or a play.

In expository writing you can also *classify* things, from dogs to dinosaurs to the dialects spoken in the United States. Classification is an appropriate strategy to use when you are writing about a large number of broadly related items that can be sorted into a few groups. For example, one discontented American publisher grouped people who read books into the following categories: those who buy books, those who borrow books, and those who beg for free copies from the author.

Keep in mind that division and classification are opposites. In division you take one item and write about its parts. In classification you take many items and group them into categories. Use the strategy that is most appropriate for your subject.

Prewriting: Division

What can you divide in expository writing? Choose an easy subject first—a zoo, perhaps. What are the parts that make up a zoo? You can divide a zoo into the different animal exhibits that it includes—the monkey house, the lion exhibit, the aviary, the reptile exhibit, and so forth. What would be the purpose of writing about these divisions? Maybe you want to inform people of the many different kinds of wildlife that can be viewed there. You can also divide the zoo into the part that is open to the public and the part that is involved in research, thus making the point that a zoo has several different functions.

Once you have decided on a subject, construct a chart like the one that follows. This chart explores several different methods of dividing a town into some of the parts that make it up.

PREWRITING CHART FOR DIVISION

SUBJECT FOR DIVISION: *a city*	
METHOD OF DIVIDING	PARTS
METHOD 1: *government*	1. *mayor* 2. *council* 3. *service agencies* 4. *citizen participation*
METHOD 2: *recreational facilities*	1. *parks* 2. *sport facilities* 3. *bike paths* 4. *entertainment opportunities*
METHOD 3: *cultural opportunities*	1. *theater* 2. *music* 3. *education* 4. *museums* 5. *libraries*

EXERCISE 8 **Prewriting: Division.** Decide on a subject of your own or choose one from the list that follows: Think of one method of dividing the subject. Then list the parts that make it up. Save your list to help you write a paragraph later.

SAMPLE library—divided on the basis of materials available: (1) number and kinds of circulating books, (2) reference materials, (3) audiovisual materials and equipment, (4) computer-loan information from other libraries.

1. a passenger jet
2. a mobile home
3. a flower
4. a club
5. a story
6. a typewriter
7. a house
8. a supermarket

Writing a First Draft: Division

When drafting an expository paragraph that divides a subject into its parts, choose a type of organization appropriate to both your subject and to the method you have used to divide it. For example, consider *spatial order* to explain to your readers the locations of the stores in a shopping mall and *chronological order* to show your readers how your school has changed during various periods of its history. In addition to choosing a type of organization, be sure to select transitions that fit the type of organization you have chosen and that will give your paragraph coherence.

The following expository paragraph divides a city according to its cultural features. As you read the passage, be aware that it is organized according to spatial order.

> In most ways Columbia, my city, is no better and no worse than other cities, but in the area of cultural opportunities, Columbia cannot be surpassed. Columbia is unique because of what we call the Cultural Cluster—one section of the city where all the cultural facilities are located. Little Broadway, the theater district (of course), is located in the southern end of the city. Here three theaters occupy a whole block. Two of the theaters feature plays from the *real* Broadway; the third theater is home to Columbia's own theater group. The two blocks north of Little Broadway are referred to as Brains Row. Within these two blocks are two colleges and one of the city's best high schools. Opposite the high school, you will find the Columbia Symphonic Orchestra, the Conservatory of Music, and the Civic Opera Company. Neighboring these musical attractions is the Columbia Central Library, noted throughout the country for its collection of manuscripts by American authors. Finally, on the block south of the library are Columbia's two museums. One is devoted solely to artifacts and documents of Columbia's history, and the other contains the works of outstanding American painters, sculptors, and photographers. So, if you ever feel a cultural gap opening up in your life, you can close it quickly with a visit to Columbia.

EXERCISE 9 **Writing and Revising: Division.** Look again at the list you wrote for Exercise 8 and the method you selected for dividing your subject. Write an expository paragraph using that method of division. Add appropriate transitions to show the relationship between the various parts of your subject. Then revise your paragraph, keeping in mind what you have learned so far.

Prewriting: Classification

Try classifying something familiar, such as horses. You can group horses by breed into draft horses, heavy-harness horses, light-harness horses, and ponies. You can also group them into the following weight categories: heavy horses, light horses, and ponies. You can also group horses by their coloring, the type of work they do, and even by the markings on their faces.

In classifying items, be sure to create meaningful categories—that is, categories that have the same basis and that do not overlap. You would not, for example, classify one book as a *novel* and another as a *narrative*. The category *novel* is based on the literary form of a book, whereas the category *narrative* is based on a technique of writing. The categories also overlap, since the category *narrative* includes the category *novel:* All novels are narratives.

When prewriting for an expository paragraph that classifies items, make a chart like the one shown here. Your chart will help you keep your categories meaningful. The following chart points out three different ways of classifying clothes:

PREWRITING CHART FOR CLASSIFICATION

SUBJECT FOR CLASSIFICATION: *clothes*	
METHOD OF CLASSIFYING	CATEGORIES
METHOD 1: *materials used*	1. *wool* 2. *cotton* 3. *synthetics*
METHOD 2: *occasions when worn*	1. *work (everyday) clothes* 2. *play clothes* 3. *clothes for special occasions*
METHOD 3: *historical styles*	1. *colonial dress* 2. *nineteenth-century dress* 3. *contemporary dress*

EXERCISE 10 **Prewriting: Classification.** Each numbered item contains a set of categories. Think about the categories. Then indicate in writing whether or not the categories are meaningful. Finally, write a sentence explaining your answer.

1. guard dogs, racing dogs, sheepherding dogs
2. pitchers, shortstops, baseball stars
3. haiku, ballad, free verse

EXERCISE 11 **Prewriting: Classification.** Choose one of the subjects listed here, and list three or four categories into which you can group its members. Be sure that you list meaningful categories.

1. athletes
2. animals
3. musicians
4. desserts
5. movies
6. governments
7. hobbies
8. works of art

Writing a First Draft: Classification

As you are writing the draft of a paragraph that categorizes items, you may decide to develop the paragraph by giving examples of the different categories. In the following expository paragraph, the writer has given a few examples of each clothing category.

> Not all of us own extensive wardrobes, but we do have clothing that we wear on different occasions. Work or everyday clothes are neat and clean, but they are not "Sunday best." A construction worker may wear overalls, a hard hat, and heavy-duty shoes. A salesperson in a store may wear a second-best dress, a smock, and a pair of old but comfortable shoes. Students may wear jeans and a favorite sweater, or perhaps a school uniform. A second category of clothing is play clothes—those that we don't mind getting dirty. Many people also have some clothing for special kinds of play—jogging suits and shoes, tennis shorts, sports uniforms, and swim suits. A third category of clothing is reserved for special occasions, such as parties, weddings, and so forth. On these occasions, a man may wear his best suit, a shirt, a tie, and a shiny pair of shoes. A woman may wear an elegant dress and equally elegant accessories. Come to think of it, maybe our wardrobes are more extensive than they first seem.

EXERCISE 12 **Writing and Revising: Classification.** Go over your notes for Exercise 11. Then write an expository paragraph creating the classes that you chose. Be certain that your categories are meaningful and that you use appropriate transitions to link your sentences. When you have finished your first draft, revise your paragraph, keeping in mind what you have learned so far about revising. For additional help with revising, refer to the checklist on page 190.

Revising, Editing, and Publishing

After completing your first draft of a division or a classification, refer to the following checklist to help you revise your work.

Checklist for Dividing and Classifying

1. *For division:* Into how many parts have I divided my subject? Are these enough? Too many? Are the divisions clear?
   For classification: Into how many categories have I grouped the members of my subject? Are these categories meaningful?
2. What can I do to clarify my reason for dividing or classifying my subject in this way?
3. How might I organize my writing more logically?

Defining

A **definition** explains the meaning of a term.

You can write a definition when you want to tell your audience what a *Tom Swiftie* is, what a *psychrometer* does, or how a *pettifogger* behaves. You can also write a definition when you want to explain the special meaning a generally known term has for you in particular. You may, for example, want to write your personal definition of *home*.

Perhaps when you read the word *definition* you think of something that resembles a dictionary entry. Although it is true that a paragraph whose purpose is to define shares some similarities with a dictionary entry, the explanation is usually much more complete. Moreover, your paragraph may express your own views about the item, whereas a dictionary definition should be strictly objective and impersonal.

Prewriting: Defining an Unfamiliar Term

To define an unfamiliar term, first identify the term as a member of a class of items that your audience will recognize. Next explain how the term differs from the other members of its class. Finally, give examples and make comparisons that will help your readers to understand clearly the meaning of the term.

When you are planning to define an unfamiliar term, ask questions like those in the following chart. The sample answers in the chart will help the writer to define the term *psychrometer*.

PREWRITING CHART FOR DEFINING AN UNFAMILIAR TERM

TERM TO BE DEFINED: *psychrometer*	
QUESTIONS	SAMPLE ANSWERS
1. In what class of items can I place the term?	*Scientific measuring instruments*
2. What distinguishes this item from the other members of its class?	*Its function—to measure the amount of water vapor, or humidity, in the air of a particular place.*
3. What examples or comparisons with other items would help my audience understand this term?	*Compare it to a thermometer?*

EXERCISE 13 **Prewriting to Define an Unfamiliar Term.** From your reading, school work, or a hobby, select a term that may be unfamiliar to others. For example, your recent reading about or experience with computers may have brought to your attention a new meaning of the term *bit.* Plan to define the term you choose by asking and answering questions like the ones in the preceding chart. Save your answers for use in a later exercise.

Writing a First Draft: Defining an Unfamiliar Term

The answers you wrote for the questions in your chart will guide you as you write an expository paragraph defining an unfamiliar term. Your topic sentence will name the class of items to which the unfamiliar object belongs. Study this example:

> A psychrometer is a scientific measuring instrument. It is made up of two thermometers mounted on a metal frame and a handle that is attached to the frame. One thermometer—the dry-bulb thermometer—is covered with a fabric. The other thermometer is called a wet-bulb thermometer. Meteorologists use the psychrometer to measure the water vapor, or humidity, in the air of a particular place. By grasping the handle and swinging the psychrometer at about ten miles per hour, the meteorologist is able to obtain different air temperature readings from the two thermometers. By computing the difference and finding it on a chart, the meteorologist can determine the humidity of the air.

Your paragraph may end with a comparison to help your nonexpert audience more clearly understand what your subject does:

> Like a thermometer, a psychrometer measures the heat in the air. That, however, is only one function of a psychrometer. Because the psychrometer records two different air temperatures, meteorologists can use the difference between the two measurements to determine a second measurement—the moisture in the air.

EXERCISE 14 **Writing and Revising a Definition of an Unfamiliar Term.** Using the answers you wrote in the chart you made for Exercise 13, write an expository paragraph defining the term you chose. After you have completed your first draft, revise your paragraph. If you need additional help with revising, refer to the checklists in this chapter.

Prewriting: Defining a Familiar Term

Why should you bother to define a term familiar to almost everyone? You may want to share your particular experiences of an abstract word, such as *loyalty* or *grief*. You may also want your readers to reconsider the meaning of such a term.

You can plan to define a familiar term by asking questions like those in the following chart:

PREWRITING CHART TO DEFINE A FAMILIAR TERM

TERM TO BE DEFINED: *courage*	
QUESTIONS	SAMPLE ANSWERS
1. What is the term's common meaning?	*Most people think courage is showy heroics—taking a chance or risking one's life—something done only once or twice in a lifetime.*
2. In what ways does my definition differ from the common one?	*To me, courage is quieter, less dramatic, something shown day by day.*
3. What incidents and examples might clarify my definition?	*Parents who stick with their responsibilities when money and hopes are low; disabled people with big smiles on their faces; little brothers and sisters who keep offering their love even after being ignored by those they look up to.*

EXERCISE 15 **Prewriting to Define a Familiar Term.** Select one of the following terms, or choose one of your own. Plan to write a personal definition of the term. Prewrite by asking and answering questions like those in the preceding chart.

1. wisdom
2. living
3. rebel
4. friend
5. fear
6. politeness
7. sleep
8. laughter
9. failure

Writing a First Draft: Defining a Familiar Term

Because your audience already knows the meaning of the term you are going to define, you have greater leeway in writing your personal definition. That is, you can start with what readers already know.

As you write the first draft of your definition, begin by presenting the commonly accepted definition of the term. Then offer your personal definition. Give your definition life and clarity by citing concrete examples. In the following paragraph the writer presents a personal definition of *courage*:

> A great many people I know seem to think of courage as showy heroics that have something to do with taking a chance or risking one's life, maybe once or twice in a lifetime. In some cases these people are right. To me, though, courage is a smaller, quieter trait that some people exhibit every day of their lives. Take my parents, for instance. When I see how they stick with their responsibilities steadily, day-by-day, even when finances and hopes are low and the going gets tougher and tougher, I think admiringly, "That's *courage!*" When I see that blind man walking fearlessly down the street, I think with awe, "That's *courage!*" When I have been really rotten to my little brother Tom and he still comes up to me and says, "Want to play ball?" I think with shame, "That's *courage!*" Unknown heroes like these brighten the dark moments of my life as stars brighten the night sky.

EXERCISE 16 **Writing and Revising a Definition of a Familiar Term.** Consult the questions and answers you wrote for Exercise 15. Then write an expository paragraph presenting your personal definition of the term you chose. Explain how your definition differs from the one most people accept. Try to make your definition clearer with examples, personal experiences, and figures of speech. After you have completed your first draft, revise your paragraph. For help with revising, refer to the following checklist.

Revising, Editing, and Publishing

Refer to the following checklist for help in revising your first draft. If you need more guidance in editing, proofreading and publishing the final copy of your paragraph, refer to the checklist for explaining a process.

Checklist for Defining

1. *For definitions of unfamiliar terms:* Have I indicated the class to which the term belongs? Have I explained what sets the term apart from others in its class?
2. *For definitions of familiar terms:* How can I make even clearer my reasons for defining this term? What specific details and incidents can I add to clarify what the term means to me?

Comparing and Contrasting

When you **compare** items, you point out their similarities. When you **contrast** items, you point out their differences.

Whether you plan to write about the similarities or differences, you must pick items with important things in common—for example, two writers, two kinds of airplanes, two members of the same family, or two geographical regions. It would make little sense to compare and contrast two items as different as a peanut and an elephant. Remember, too, that you compare and contrast for a purpose—to say something about each item. You may, for instance, want to make the point that one item is better in some way than the other. You may want to point out what makes each appealing.

Prewriting

Start your prewriting by listing *both* the similarities *and* the differences of the items you have chosen. Your list will help you decide whether to stress similarities or differences when you begin writing. The list will also help you organize facts and ideas.

When you are planning to compare and contrast two items, one helpful technique is a three-column *comparison frame*. Decide which aspects of the items you wish to compare. List these aspects, or bases for comparison, in the first column of the comparison frame. In the second and third columns tell if the items are similar or different for each aspect you listed in the first column.

The following comparison frame compares and contrasts two makers of popular comic films, Woody Allen and Mel Brooks.

COMPARISON FRAME

BASIS FOR COMPARISON	Woody Allen	Mel Brooks
professional history	*wrote for Your Show of Shows, then became a standup comedian*	*wrote for Your Show of Shows, then developed comic routines of his own*
personality	*shy*	*boisterous*
humor	*intellectual, witty*	*broad, slapstick*
range	*wide—makes both serious films and comic films*	*narrower—strictly comic films*
audience appeal	*wide*	*wide*

EXERCISE 17 **Prewriting: Making a Comparison Frame.** Choose one of the subjects from the following list. Identify two specific items you wish to compare and contrast. Decide on a purpose for comparing them. Then make a comparison frame for these items. In the frame, list four points on which the two items can be compared and contrasted, and indicate specific examples of their similarities and differences.

PARTIAL SAMPLE ANSWER Two vacation spots—New York City and Miami Beach
To decide which would be most enjoyable for my family and me

1. two career possibilities
2. two neighbors
3. two professional athletes
4. two kinds of boats
5. two types of homes
6. two actresses
7. two literary characters
8. two writing implements
9. two universities
10. two high schools

Writing a First Draft

When your comparison frame is finished, you will consider how to organize your presentation of the similarities and differences between the two items. One effective way to organize your presentation is to order your information *item by item*. For example, the writer comparing

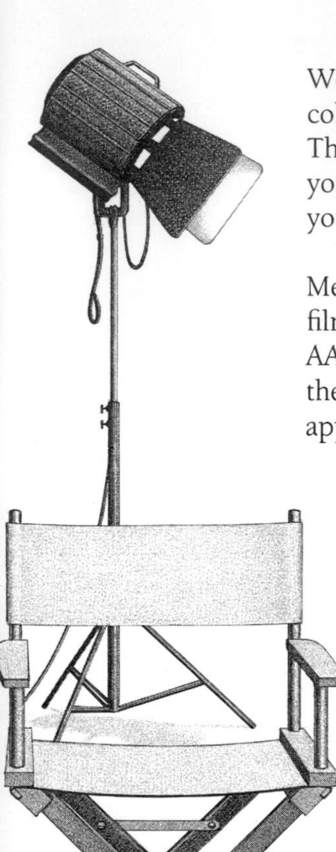

Woody Allen and Mel Brooks could discuss all the points listed in the column for Woody Allen and then all the points listed for Mel Brooks. This type of organization is known as AAABBB because you present all your information for item A (in this case, Woody Allen) and then all your information for item B (in this case, Mel Brooks).

The following paragraph compares and contrasts Woody Allen and Mel Brooks with the purpose of presenting each man's special gift as a filmmaker. As you read the paragraph, notice that the writer uses the AAABBB method of organization. Also note that the writer highlights the differences between the two men and achieves coherence by using appropriate transitions.

> Woody Allen and Mel Brooks share a great deal. They are the two outstanding American directors of comic films. They both began their careers by writing for the pioneer television comedy hour, *Your Show of Shows;* then they both branched out to become huge popular successes on their own. Both appeal to wide audiences, and many moviegoers are ardent fans of both. Yet the two men differ widely as people and as creators of screen comedy. Allen, a shy man, makes films in which the humor is sophisticated, verbal, and often based on literary references. Allen is also a very versatile filmmaker. Besides his comedies, he has made such serious films as *Interiors, Manhattan,* and *The Purple Rose of Cairo,* and most of his later films mix comedy and seriousness. Mel Brooks, on the other hand, is a boisterous, exuberant man famous for his use of broad slapstick sketches that depend on physical humor. Brooks specializes in making his audiences laugh as long and as hard as possible. His comedy is pure, unmixed with serious elements. Which one is funnier? That depends on your taste in comedy. Which is the better filmmaker? Woody Allen's skill in combining different kinds of films may give him an edge here. However, each in his own way is a wonderfully gifted director whose movies rank among the best in our time.

EXERCISE 18 **Writing a Comparison-Contrast Paragraph.** Use the information in the comparison frame you made for Exercise 17 to write a paragraph comparing and contrasting the items you chose. Follow AAABBB organization in writing your paragraph. Be sure to use appropriate transitions to give your work coherence.

Revising, Editing, and Publishing

After completing your first draft, read it aloud, and use the following checklist to help you revise your work. For additional guidance in editing, proofreading, and publishing your final version, see the checklist for explaining a process.

Checklist for Comparing and Contrasting

1. How can I make my comparison-contrast clearer?
2. Have I used the AAABBB type of organization correctly? Have I presented all the information about one item first and then presented all the same information about the other item? Have I presented the information in the same order in each case?

Combining Strategies in a Longer Expository Composition

Longer forms of expository writing may use **more than one strategy** for presenting facts and exploring ideas.

To treat certain subjects thoroughly in expository writing, you will often find that you will need to use more than one strategy. For example, you may want to devote one paragraph to defining and classifying your subject, another paragraph to presenting pertinent cause-and-effect relationships, and yet another to comparing or contrasting. The kinds of strategies you use will depend on your overall purpose. In the following excerpt from a chapter about the Great Pyramid of Egypt, the author uses several strategies to explain why that pyramid has long been considered one of the wonders of the world.

> In its present form the Great Pyramid has the raw power of hugeness, but when Herodotus [a Greek historian] saw it, it must also have been beautiful. In his time the Pyramid was covered with a casing of white limestone blocks, smooth and fine, which turned its sides into steeply sloping, perfectly flat surfaces. That must have been impressive to behold—especially when the bright Egyptian sunlight glistened on the gleaming stone. But the smooth white casing was peeled away about a thousand years ago by the Arabs, who used it in the bridges and houses of Cairo. Only a few small patches remain at the base, although the neighboring Pyramid of Khafre still has the topmost hundred feet of its casing.
>
> The accuracy with which the limestone blocks of casing were put in place is one of the reasons why the Great Pyramid was deemed a wonder of the world. The British archaeologist William Matthews Flinders Petrie, who examined the remaining casing at the base of the Great Pyramid in 1881, found that the stone blocks had been cut so carefully that the average distance between them was only one-fiftieth of an inch, and in places they were as close as one-five hundredth of an inch. The builders then had managed to fill the microscopic space between the stones with cement.

The placing of the Great Pyramid was equally perfect. Flinders Petrie called it "a triumph of skill; its errors, both in length and in angles, could be covered by placing one's thumb on them." Though lacking any of the instruments of a modern surveyor, the architects of Khufu's Pyramid laid it out so that its four sides were almost exactly lined up with true north, south, east, and west. The variations from mathematical perfection were so slight that they can be detected only by careful calculation. Each of the Pyramid's four corners is a nearly perfect right angle, also; the greatest variation from the proper ninety-degree angle is less than *one-twentieth of a degree*. How such accuracy was achieved is a baffling puzzle; the architects must have used the sun and the stars as their guides, but it is still not easy to understand how relatively primitive surveying methods produced such startling results.

—Robert Silverberg, *The Seven Wonders of the Ancient World*

Carefully study the preceding excerpt, and note how it fulfills the following plan.

EXPOSITORY PLAN USING SEVERAL STRATEGIES

SUBJECT	the Great Pyramid of Egypt
PURPOSE	to explain why the Great Pyramid is considered a wonder of the world
AUDIENCE	general readers
STRATEGIES	paragraph 1: *comparison and contrast* of the pyramid's appearance today with its beautiful appearance in ancient times paragraph 2: *presenting facts* to illustrate the accuracy with which the pyramid's blocks were placed paragraph 3: *presenting expert testimony and facts* to attest to the perfect placement of the pyramid as a whole

Despite the various strategies, each paragraph contributes to the single overall purpose by focusing on a different reason why the Great Pyramid is considered a wonder of the world.

EXERCISE 19 **Using Several Strategies in Expository Writing.** Prepare to write a short expository composition of three or four paragraphs. Begin by completing a plan like the one shown above. Choose a subject that will lend itself to a variety of strategies. After you write a first draft, use the appropriate checklists in this chapter for revising, editing, and publishing your work.

Writer's Choice

Writer's Choice #1

ASSIGNMENT To explain how to perform a simple task

LENGTH Two paragraphs, each approximatly five sentences long

AUDIENCE Paragraph 1—a visitor from a rural section of Africa; paragraph 2—a student in your English class

PURPOSE To explain how to start a car, cross a busy street in the city, or eat a pizza

PREWRITING Choose one task, and list the steps involved in performing it. Then think about your two different audiences, and modify the list for each audience, adding or combining steps as appropriate.

WRITING As you write each paragraph, use language appropriate for your audience.

REVISING As you revise each paragraph, put yourself in the place of your reader. Would a visitor from Africa understand the instructions you give in the first paragraph? Would a student in your English class find those given in the second paragraph useful?

Writer's Choice #2

ASSIGNMENT To explain a cause-effect relationship

LENGTH Two paragraphs, each approximately six sentences long

AUDIENCE Paragraph 1—an adult; paragraph 2—a small child

PURPOSE To write two answers to *one* of the following questions: Why does it thunder? Why is the ocean salty? What does an eclipse do? What happens when a volcano erupts? The first answer should be a logical, scientific explanation directed to an adult; the second should be a story that would satisfy a small child.

PREWRITING Choose your event, and make notes for your scientific explanation first. You may need to check an encyclopedia or science text. Then plan your storylike explanation; you may want to think of it as a kind of myth.

WRITING When your write your scientific explanation, be sure to lead logically from one event to the other and use transitions to make your writing coherent. When you write your more imaginative explanation, you could use the form of a magical tale.

REVISING Does each explanation work for its audience? Is the tone of your writing appropriate for each?

Writer's Choice #3

ASSIGNMENT To define a term

LENGTH Your choice

PURPOSE To create a term and write a definition of it

AUDIENCE Your choice

PREWRITING First create your word. You might make up a new word based on parts of actual words; for example, a *deskmobile* could be a desk you drive around the school; a *teacher-saver* could refer to a machine that cuts down on a teacher's work. Decide on the class of items to which your term belongs and the features that distinguish it from the other items in the class.

WRITING Follow the suggestions for writing a definition of an unfamiliar term. Include examples.

REVISING Does your definition create a good picture of the object that your created word names?

Writer's Choice #4

ASSIGNMENT To compare and contrast two young children

LENGTH Your choice

PURPOSE To show that you like both for different reasons

AUDIENCE Your choice

PREWRITING Decide on the children about whom you will write, and think of points that could serve as a basis for your comparison-contrast. Then make a comparison frame to highlight their similarities and differences.

WRITING Organize your comparison-contrast according to the AAABBB pattern, and use transitions to add to the coherence of your writing.

REVISING After reading your comparison-contrast, will someone who does not know you or the two children have a good picture of them and understand why you like each?

Writer's Choice #5

ASSIGNMENT To write a short expository paper on any subject

LENGTH Your choice

PURPOSE Your choice

AUDIENCE Your choice

OPTION You might base your writing on one or more of the items presented in the Writer's Sourcebook, pages 362–363.

Writers on Writing

A student at Nathan Hale School in West Allis, Wisconsin, Sharon Anich plans a career as a physical therapist. This interest prompted her to write the following expository piece and commentary.

THE PRODUCT

In the United States some thirty-five thousand physical therapists find job security, financial benefits, and personal satisfaction in careers devoted to helping others. Physical therapists will always be in demand. We live in a computer age in which many jobs have been taken over by machines. But computers cannot massage paralyzed limbs or make judgments about treatment. A physical therapist must design a special program of treatment for each patient, reflecting the patient's injury, build, and age. Besides job security, physical therapists enjoy financial benefits. Beginning salaries range between $16,000 and $22,000, depending on location, and experienced therapists can advance to even better paying positions. Best of all, physical therapists gain a great sense of satisfaction from their work. Patients feel good when they master a task, and that satisfaction carries over to the therapist; realizing how he or she has helped one patient makes a physical therapist work even harder on the next one. Therapists feel wonderful when their patients smile and thank them for making life a little easier.

THE PROCESS

I had few problems deciding on a topic for this composition. This past summer I spent part of my time volunteering at a local hospital. I was placed in the physical therapy department, where I performed odd jobs. The wide variety of patients and injuries allowed me to help in many different ways. Talking to professional, including speech and occupational therapists, exposed me to career possibilities that I had not previously thought of. I have now been accepted in a pre-physical therapy program at a state university. I hope that others who read my composition will realize that there are many more careers open to them.

YOUR TURN *Writing About a Possible Career*

Write an informative composition about career possibilities in a field in which you are interested. You might concentrate on the rewards of the work, as Sharon did, or on the training required. If possible, try to talk with some professionals in this field and see what new ideas they can give you. Your purpose is to make others consider a career in this area. Use the various checklists in this chapter to edit and revise your work. Prepare a final copy and proofread it.

Review

CHAPTER 9 EXPOSITORY WRITING

Explaining a Process [pages 179–182] Arrange the steps of cardiopulmonary resuscitation (CPR), *in order*. Write the number of each item, and next to it write *a* for the first step, *b* for the second step, and so on.

1. Take a deep breath, open your mouth, and blow into victim's mouth rapidly four times, expanding victim's lungs and chest.
2. Place victim on his or her back.
3. Lift neck with one hand, and tilt head back with other hand.
4. Pinch victim's nose closed.

Division and Classification [pages 185–190] Indicate the letter of the item that correctly answers the question.

5. Which item sorts dogs into meaningful classes?
   (a) terriers/hunting dogs (b) long hair/short hair (c) work dogs/miniatures

Definition [pages 190–194] Read the following parts of a definition. Then indicate the letter of the item that correctly answers each question. An awl (a) is an instrument (b) for piercing small holes.

6. Which phrase sets off the term from other members of its group?
7. Which phrase indicates the group to which the term belongs?

Comparison/Contrast [pages 194–197] Read the following passage. Indicate the letter of the correct answer for each question.

In 1898 a man named Morgan Robertson wrote a novel about an ocean liner named the *Titan*. In 1912 Britain's White Star Line christened its new liner the *Titanic*. Robertson's ship was of 70,000 tons displacement. The White Star ship displaced 66,000 tons. The fictional ship was 800 feet long. The real ship was 882.5 feet long. The fictional ship hit an iceberg and sank with great loss of life. The *Titanic* also hit an iceberg, and 1,503 people lost their lives.

8. What does the paragraph illustrate?
   (a) similarities (b) differences
9. Which would be a good topic sentence for this passage?
   (a) Some people can foresee events.
   (b) Fiction and truth can parallel each other.
   (c) Traveling on ocean liners was dangerous.

Writing for Review Write a paragraph presenting either causes or effects for one of the following: (1) the interest in solar energy (2) the increase in day care centers (3) the popularity of cable television.

CHAPTER 10

Critical Thinking and Persuasive Writing

To the vast majority of mankind nothing is more agreeable than to escape the need for mental exertion. . . . To most people nothing is more troublesome than the effort of thinking.

—James Bryce

These words of James Bryce, a British historian and diplomat, ought to make immediate sense to most people. Thinking can be difficult, and it always demands a real effort on the part of the thinker. Thinking, however, is an extraordinarily necessary activity, for we live in a world in which other people are continually trying to get us to think as they wish us to think. Much of the writing that we are exposed to daily—product advertisements, newspaper editorials, political statements—is deliberately designed to influence us to think and to act as the writer wishes. To deal with this floodtide of persuasive writing, we must be able to think intelligently and deliberately. We must make the "mental exertion" that thinking requires.

Persuasive writing is writing that tries to influence a reader to accept an idea, adopt a point of view, or perform an action.

The fundamental purpose of persuasive writing is to change the ideas or actions of the reader. Readers who do not recognize persuasive writing or do not know how to think critically about it run the risk of having their ideas and actions "engineered." They may be persuaded unconsciously to accept ideas, adopt points of view, and perform actions. To prevent being manipulated in this way, readers can apply critical thinking skills to all persuasive writing they encounter.

Critical thinking refers to analyzing and evaluating the information presented to you or that you plan to present to others in defense of an opinion.

The following advertisement is an example of persuasive writing. If you did not apply critical thinking skills to the advertisement, you might unconsciously be persuaded to buy Beam the next time you need toothpaste.

BUY THE BEST! BUY *BEAM!*

Here are the reasons you'll be glad you did:

1. *BEAM* is the creamiest, most delicious-tasting toothpaste on the market today.
2. *BEAM* comes in a streamlined, see-through plastic container specially designed by fashion great Pierre Piette.
3. You'll be welcomed into the BEAM-ers, a prestige group whose members include rock music favorite Tom-Tom Toomey.
4. *BEAM*-ers win more friends and influence more people.
5. Millions of Americans have become satisfied BEAM users. Shouldn't you be in their ranks?

When you apply critical thinking skills to this ad, you become aware of logical weaknesses in the "reasons" given for buying BEAM: (1) People should buy toothpaste because it cleans teeth, not because it is creamy or tastes delicious. (2) The package for a product has nothing to do with the quality of the product inside. (3) The claim that well-known people use a product does not guarantee its worth. (4) A person's ability to win friends depends on factors unrelated to the brand of toothpaste she or he uses. (5) Your decision to buy or not to buy a product should be based on the product's effectiveness, not on the number of people who use it.

The techniques in the BEAM ad have been exaggerated, of course. Nevertheless, every day you are bombarded with advertisements as well as newspaper editorials, political statements, and other forms of persuasive writing, each attempting to influence you to purchase a product, vote in a certain way, or adopt certain ideas. In order to think and act for yourself, you must learn to recognize persuasive writing and develop critical thinking skills that will help you to evaluate ideas and actions.

Like descriptive, narrative, and expository writing, the best persuasive writing results from following the steps of the writing process—prewriting, writing, and revising. The writing process applies to persuasive writing of any length, but in this chapter you will be applying it to paragraphs. You will concentrate on the following areas as you think critically and write persuasively:

prewriting: purpose and opinion
prewriting: audience
prewriting: support
writing an argument
revising, **editing**, and **publishing**: avoiding faulty persuasion

Prewriting: Purpose and Opinion

Your **purpose** in persuasive writing is to persuade readers to accept your opinion. If you keep your purpose and opinion clearly in mind, then you stand a good chance of convincing your readers to accept your opinion.

As you plan to write persuasively, be sure that (1) your opinion is worth defending and (2) your audience will be willing to accept your opinion if you support it with convincing evidence. Some opinions are not worth defending in persuasive writing. For example a personal opinion such as "Pink is the most beautiful color" is not an appropriate topic for a persuasive paragraph. On the other hand, a fact is not an appropriate topic for persuasion since no one needs to be persuaded to accept a fact.

In addition, when you are selecting a purpose, be sure you can accomplish it in the space available. For example, to try in a single paragraph to persuade lawmakers to change the specifics of our complicated tax laws would be impossible. Consider which of the following would be appropriate material for a persuasive paragraph:

1. An earthquake is a series of sudden and violent movements of parts of the earth's surface.
2. An earthquake is without doubt the most horrible kind of natural disaster.
3. People should petition the government to finance research into forecasting earthquakes.

The first sentence gives not an opinion, but a definition—a kind of factual information; people who have experienced a tornado, a volcanic eruption, or a hurricane would not be willing to accept the broad opinion expressed in sentence 2. Neither sentence expresses an appropriate topic for a persuasive paragraph. You could, however, use sentence 3. It expresses an opinion that is both specific and directed toward an action: You want to persuade people to petition the government.

EXERCISE 1 **Selecting Appropriate Topics.** Number your paper from 1 to 10. Write *appropriate* next to the number of each statement that is an appropriate one for a single persuasive paragraph. Write *inappropriate* next to the number of each topic that is inappropriate.

1. This school should provide more sports opportunities for girls.
2. Cigarette smoking is one of the most dangerous habits you can develop.
3. The duck-billed platypus is a strange Australian animal.

4. To save lives, car manufacturers should install inflatable airbags in the cars they produce.
5. Sunset is the most peaceful time of day.
6. The Greeks and Romans made many contributions to the world.
7. People should learn to recognize persuasive writing and to think critically.
8. Basketball is a more exciting game than hockey.
9. Lynn is certain to capture the diving championship next month.
10. The plays and sonnets of Shakespeare are the greatest literature ever written.

EXERCISE 2 **Selecting Suitable Topics.** Choose a general topic of your own or one from the following list. Then write one sentence in which you state an opinion that could be used as the basis of a single persuasive paragraph.

1. professional athletes
2. mathematics
3. Chinese food
4. grouchy people
5. cats as pets
6. weekends
7. painting
8. electronic calculators

Prewriting: Audience

Advertising agencies often conduct surveys to discover as much as possible about the people who will make up the audience for their ads. When you are planning a piece of persuasive writing, you should put together a mental picture, or profile, of the readers you wish to address. A **profile** is a brief sketch providing basic facts and relevant information. Such a profile will help you select the supporting details that are most likely to persuade your audience to accept your opinion.

When you make a profile of your intended readers, jot down their characteristics. As you do your prewriting, choose the points that are most relevant to your purpose. Questions like the following will help you start your audience profile:

Why are these readers likely to listen to me in the first place?
What supporting details will capture and hold their attention?
What attitudes are they most likely to have about this topic?
What experiences have they probably had that relate to the topic?
Would they respond better to plain or to elegant language?

In the prewriting stage, you must select the supporting details that will have the greatest influence on your audience. As you are writing your first draft, the decisions you make about your audience—combined with a clear purpose—will determine much of what you say.

If you know your readers well, you should also know whether or not you will be able to persuade them to accept your opinion. There would be no need to persuade your readers to accept an opinion they already hold. For example, it would be unnecessary to convince American citizens that freedom is valuable. If your intended readers are almost certain to reject your opinion, however convincingly you plan to support it, it will probably do no good to try to persuade them to accept it. For example, you would be almost sure to fail to persuade an audience of students to accept this opinion: The school week should be lengthened to include Saturday. On the other hand, you may be able to persuade them to agree with this opinion: The gym and library in this school should be available for students' use in the evenings during the week, on weekends, and on holidays.

EXERCISE 3 **Suiting Topic to Audience.** Number your paper from 1 to 5. For each audience and opinion listed, write the following:

a. if the opinion is appropriate for this audience
b. if it is not necessary to convince this audience of this opinion
c. if it is unlikely that you will convince this audience of this opinion

1. *Audience:* hockey fans. *Opinion:* Home games should no longer be carried on any of the local television stations.
2. *Audience:* hockey fans. *Opinion:* Fans who buy tickets to four consecutive home games should be given a free ticket to the fifth game.
3. *Audience:* high school students. *Opinion:* To make the best use of school buildings, students should attend school twelve months a year.
4. *Audience:* high school students. *Opinion:* Students should be part of a school committee that decides on appropriate disciplinary actions for major and minor infractions of school rules and school policies.
5. *Audience:* high school students. *Opinion:* Student recommendations should be taken into consideration when each week's cafeteria menu is being planned.

Prewriting: Support

Writers skilled in the techniques of persuasive writing are usually successful in persuading their readers because they show *why* readers should accept certain opinions, adopt certain attitudes, or act in certain ways. When you are writing a persuasive paragraph, you cannot simply state your opinion once and then restate it in several different versions if you want your readers to accept your opinion. Readers expect you to give evidence that supports your opinion so that they can decide intelligently whether or not to make your opinion their own.

In persuasive writing **evidence** refers to the reasons that directly support your opinion. Usually the most effective reasons are facts.

In a friendly argument with others, you might state an opinion about something. As soon as you do, one of the others might say, "Prove it." In much the same way, when your audience begins to read a persuasive paragraph you have written, they will mentally challenge you to prove that your opinion is worth accepting. To convince your audience, you can support your opinion with reliable evidence, evidence that is precise, accurate, and relevant.

As you are prewriting, use brainstorming, freewriting, and charting to gather as much evidence for your opinion as possible. Then determine the reliability of each bit of evidence by asking this question: *Is this a fact, or is it an opinion?*

A **fact** is something that is known to be true.

Here are some examples of statements of facts:

> Of all the water on earth, 97.3 percent is salty, and 2.7 percent is fresh.
>
> Howard University and Trinity College are located in Washington, D.C.
>
> The sun rises in the east and sets in the west.

Because it is impossible to disagree with facts, they are the most reliable evidence you can use to support an opinion. The accuracy of facts can be checked by calling on direct personal experience ("I know St. Louis is on the Mississippi River because I was there") or by consulting a generally recognized source of information (an encyclopedia or a primary source).

An **opinion** is a personal judgment based on what one person believes or feels to be true.

Although people cannot disagree about facts, they may, and often do, disagree about opinions. For example, compare the following statements of opinion with the preceding facts:

> Salt water is better for swimming than fresh water.
>
> Harvard University offers the best education available in the United States.
>
> Sunset is more beautiful than sunrise.

At times, certain types of opinions can be used as reliable evidence for the main opinion presented in a persuasive paragraph. These are referred to as sound opinions or authoritative opinions.

A **sound opinion** is one that is based on a sufficient number of precise and accurate facts. An **authoritative opinion** is one that comes from a reliable source, such as an eyewitness or a recognized expert.

Both sound opinions and authoritative opinions are based on facts. For this reason, they are almost as reliable for evidence as facts and sometimes can be used when facts cannot do the job. To understand how important sound opinions and authoritative opinions can be, decide which of the listed statements give the strongest support for this particular opinion: "The Gotham Symphony Orchestra is the best in the world."

1. The symphony has always attracted players who have graduated from Juilliard and other leading music schools.
2. The symphony has been in existence for 157 years.
3. I believe that the symphony is the best because it has received more awards and prizes for outstanding performance than any other symphony orchestra.
4. Musicians and music critics the world over have consistently acknowledged the superiority of the symphony.

The first statement gives a fact, but it does not supply enough information to support the opinion. The second statement also gives a fact, but it is not related specifically to the claim stated in the opinion. The third statement is a sound opinion because it is based on facts that are directly relevant to the opinion. The fourth statement is an authoritative opinion—the judgment of experts based on facts.

As you gather evidence to support an opinion, keep in mind that your readers are most likely to be persuaded by facts. They also can be persuaded by sound opinions and authoritative opinions, but these are only as reliable as the facts and sources on which they are based. Unsound opinions—that is, personal preferences not based on facts—are not persuasive.

EXERCISE 4 **Identifying Facts and Opinions.** Indicate in writing which of the following items are facts, unsound opinions, sound opinions, or authoritative opinions. Tell why the opinions are unsound, sound, or authoritative.

1. Newspapers of the early to middle 1940s show how deeply preoccupied Americans of the times were with World War II.
2. Since most American presidents came from Virginia, Virginians must make the best presidents.
3. Because the board of health has warned that town water may well contain dangerous chemicals, I believe our water may be unsafe.
4. The water supplies of some towns have been contaminated by industrial wastes.
5. I think our town water is unsafe because I got a stomach ache the last time I drank a glass of it.
6. Without sufficient water, people, animals, and plants would die.
7. I am reassured because government and private investigative teams have both judged the city water safe for all uses.
8. There are thirty-six pillars on the Lincoln Memorial; I counted them.
9. The latest edition of the *Earth Almanac* estimates that over 2,500,000 people visit the Lincoln Memorial each year.
10. I believe that the Lincoln Memorial is the most impressive building in Washington, D.C.

Writing an Argument

An **argument** is an ordered presentation of support for an opinion that you want others to accept.

An argument consists of these four parts: (1) an opening statement of opinion, (2) background information that your readers may need, (3) the evidence that supports your opinion, and (4) a concluding statement.

At the beginning of your argument, state your opinion clearly; do not distract readers with emotional outbursts. Then give your readers any background information they may need in order to understand your opinion—the meaning of a term, a name or date, or an example that demonstrates exactly what you mean.

Organize the evidence that supports your opinion in a clear and straightforward way. If, for example, you include three facts or sound opinions, present them one at a time in the order of their importance or in some other logical order. Always let your readers know whether you are stating a fact or someone else's opinion in support of your own.

Guide your readers from one sentence of your argument to another by using techniques for achieving coherence: repeated words, pronouns, and transitions. (These techniques are explained in detail in Chapter 3.) Transitions are extremely important in writing persuasively: You want your readers to follow each step of your argument so that by the time they finish reading, they will be ready to accept your opinion. The following transitions are especially useful in persuasive writing:

TO PRESENT EVIDENCE
first, second, third
most importantly
for example
for instance
the facts show that
according to

TO STATE YOUR OPINION
in my opinion
from my point of view
I believe that
in my experience

TO DEAL WITH CONFLICTING OPINIONS
although
conversely
in opposition to
even though
in contrast to
still

Never forget that in persuasive writing your strongest device for convincing others is evidence. You should not, however, omit personal feelings about your topic. On the contrary, you want your readers to realize how strongly you feel about your opinion. Without losing your control and resorting to unnecessary emotional outbursts, you can and should let your reader know the degree of your commitment to your opinion.

A good conclusion will bring the parts of your argument together in one statement and motivate the reader to take action. If you have not already done so elsewhere in the argument, you may mention the specific action you feel is called for by the case you have just presented. The conclusion of a persuasive paragraph may be only one sentence long.

The following annotated model demonstrates how each part of an argument works together with the other parts in a well-planned, clearly written argument.

Clear statement of opinion
Background information

Authoritative opinion labeled

Support clearly labeled, with transitions used

Most important point labeled

Concluding statement with call to action

We desperately need a traffic signal at the intersection of Lavinia Street and Fourth Avenue. At least three times in the last year and a half, residents of the nearby neighborhood have petitioned City Hall to install a traffic light, but each time the reasonable request has been ignored. Even former traffic commissioner Peter Moses agrees that there are several good reasons for the installation of a traffic light. First, there are frequent near-accidents at this dangerous intersection; as a result, the screeching and whining of brakes (not to mention angry verbal exchanges) create an annoying din at all hours of the day and night. Second, the number of actual accidents has increased by more than fifty percent over the last year. The final and most compelling reason is what happened to little Timmy Daly last night. This morning, Tim lies in a bed at Memorial Hospital. Timmy was hit by a fast-moving car whose driver swerved into him on the sidewalk while attempting to avoid a truck in the middle of this infamous intersection. It should be clear that if our elected officials are reluctant to install a light at Lavinia and Fourth, local citizens must take whatever steps are necessary to force the politicians to take this long-overdue action—*now!*

EXERCISE 5 **Writing an Argument.** Write a one-paragraph persuasive argument on one of the following topics, or choose a topic of your own. State your opinion clearly, and include any necessary background information. Use transitions to help present your support. State your conclusion in one sentence, and if you wish, make a statement moving the reader to action.

1. for or against keeping the voting age at 18
2. for or against cable TV
3. for or against a 10 P.M. curfew for teen-agers
4. for or against making smoking cigarettes a crime
5. for or against the federal 55-m.p.h. speed limit

Writing a Longer Argument

Sometimes the amount of evidence that you will want or need in order to present your argument adequately and compellingly will require that you write more than one paragraph. For example, note how each item of support in the preceding paragraph can be expanded with additional support to create a multiparagraph argument.

We desperately need a traffic signal at the intersection of Lavinia Street and Fourth Avenue. At least three times in the last year and a half, residents of the nearby neighborhood have petitioned City Hall to install a traffic light, but each time the reasonable request has been ignored. Even former traffic commissioner Peter Moses agrees that there are several good reasons for the installation of a traffic light at this dangerous intersection.

First, there are frequent near-accidents at this dangerous intersection; as a result, the screeching and whining of brakes (not to mention angry verbal exchanges) create an annoying din at all hours of the day and night. A neighborhood committee has documented the number of near-accidents during the last three months. The record shows that within the last ninety days there were eighty-seven near-accidents—almost one a day. Alarmingly, a majority of these incidents—fifty-seven—occurred in afternoon, when the number of pedestrians is greatest.

Second, the number of actual accidents has increased by more than fifty percent over the last year. According to police records, twelve vehicular accidents occurred at the intersection last year. This year, there have already been eighteen reported collisions, and the year is not over yet. Of the thirty-six drivers involved in these accidents, seven required hospitalization of some type.

The final and most compelling reason is what happened to little Timmy Daly last night. This morning, Tim lies in a bed at Memorial Hospital. Timmy was hit by a fast-moving car whose driver swerved into him on the sidewalk while attempting to avoid a truck in the middlé of this infamous intersection. Timmy is not an isolated example. In fact, Timmy is just one of eleven children who have been injured there during the last five years.

Must we wait for a fatality before a traffic signal is installed? We have been fortunate up to now, but it is just a matter of time before a pedestrian or driver or one of our children is killed. It should be clear that if our elected officials are reluctant to install a light at Lavinia and Fourth, local citizens must take whatever steps are necessary to force the politicians to take this long-overdue action—*now!*

EXERCISE 6 **Writing a Longer Argument.** Expand the paragraph that you wrote in Exercise 5 into a multiparagraph argument. Consider adding the following:

1. additional information to your opening statement
2. further background information
3. more evidence to strengthen each item of support
4. additional discussion about the main opposing points of view
5. an elaboration of your conclusion urging your readers to take some particular action.

Avoiding Faulty Methods of Persuasion

When you are writing a persuasive paragraph, you may be tempted to use any means available to achieve your purpose. As a result, some false or faulty methods of persuasion may weaken otherwise sound arguments. As you revise your persuasive paragraph, watch for these faulty methods in your own work, and of course be alert to them in anything you read.

When you have completed a final draft of your paragraph, revise, edit, and proofread it, using the skills you mastered in Chapter 4, "Revising the Paragraph," and the checklist on page 219. Then share your paragraph with your audience.

Emotionally Loaded Words

How would you react if someone referred to you as *slender?* What different reaction might you have to being called *scrawny?* As you can see, some words arouse deep emotions, some positive and others negative. For example, the writer of an ad for a new fad diet would want to arouse the positive feelings of readers and might include a sentence like the following:

> Our diet will uncover the *slender* person hidden deep within, the real you.

On the other hand, the editor of a health magazine who wants to arouse negative feelings toward dangerous fad diets might begin an editorial with this question:

> Who started the myth that a *scrawny* body is a beautiful body?

Slender and *scrawny* are examples of emotionally loaded words. Good persuasive writers recognize that such words can manipulate readers by appealing either to strong positive or strong negative feelings. The writer who is honest with readers tries to use words that are emotionally more neutral.

The following list contains some examples of emotionally loaded words with more neutral alternatives.

LOADED WORDS	EMOTIONAL EFFECT	MORE NEUTRAL ALTERNATIVE
lie	negative	mislead
miserly	negative	thrifty
cowardly	negative	cautious
heroic	positive	brave
mansion	positive	dwelling
majestic	positive	large

EXERCISE 7 **Recognizing Emotionally Loaded Words.** Number your paper from 1 to 5. Read each sentence. Find the emotionally loaded word, and write it beside the appropriate number. Then write a more neutral alternative for this word. Use a dictionary or thesaurus for help.

SAMPLE 1. Tom wears very gaudy clothes.
1. gaudy, colorful

1. That little brat threw her new doll on the floor.
2. A large mob of people gathered in the square.
3. A small group of men lurked in the dark doorway.
4. I wonder where Brian got that foolish hat.
5. Cynthia soon tired of Andy's chatter.

Bandwagon

The **bandwagon** method attempts to persuade someone to do something because "everyone else is doing it."

Years ago during political campaigns the various candidates held parades. Usually, the band was on a horse-drawn wagon, the bandwagon. Voters who supported a candidate would literally jump on the candidate's bandwagon as it passed in the parade, thus demonstrating that they were for the candidate. Today, *get on the bandwagon* is used figuratively to mean "join the crowd" or "do what everyone else is doing."

The bandwagon method of arguing in persuasive writing is faulty. The argument that "everyone else" believes, wants, or does something is usually not based on facts, for there are always at least some people who go their own way, refusing to join the crowd. The bandwagon method is also illogical, since logic tells us that it is not necessarily true that one person will believe, want, or do something simply because "everyone else" does. The ability to be swayed by the bandwagon method usually stems from insecurity; bandwagon-style persuasion often appeals to people who cannot or will not think independently and critically.

Testimonial

The **testimonial** is an attempt at persuasion that is based on the advice or testimony of a famous person.

This faulty method of persuasion is especially misleading because it implies that well-known and admired public figures are qualified to give good advice about almost anything, even subjects that have nothing to do with their own accomplishments, skills, and talents. Here is an example:

> Here's what famous screen star Lance Lantana has to say about presidential candidate Georgie Goodenough: "I know a good thing when I see it. That's why I'm voting for Georgie Goodenough—the best thing to hit American politics since Lincoln."

Lance Lantana is perhaps a top film actor; however, his skill in film acting in no way qualifies him as an expert judge of a political candidate's worth. Lantana's words are simply the opinion of one more voter. Yet the words are used in a way that subtly suggests that he is a political expert. Voters who think critically will recognize that actor Lantana is being cited because he is famous, not because of his knowledge of politics.

You should think critically about all testimonials you encounter. A question like the following will help you keep things straight in your mind: *What is the logical connection between this person and what she or he is trying to make me think or do?*

EXERCISE 8 **Avoiding Bandwagon Persuasion and Testimonials.** Identify the faulty method of persuasion in each of the following statements. Then rewrite each statement, changing whatever is necessary to make the statement genuinely persuasive.

1. Why be the last one in your neighborhood to benefit from the advantages of owning a personal computer? Don't waste another minute. Arrange for a free home demonstration and trial of the Computer Buddy system.
2. With all the traveling I do as relief pitcher for the Belmont Wildcats, I had little time to keep up with my bills, fan mail, and important records. That was before the Computer Buddy personal computer system came into my life. I saved time and aggravation with the Buddy. You can too. Contact a sales agent now at 1-800-555-5555.
3. Join the Dream Vacation Club while the rolls are still open. But you'd better hurry. Millions of vacation dreamers have already joined, and we have almost reached our maximum enrollment.
4. Every day more and more voters in this state decide to cast their votes for Stephanie Crane—the next governor of this state. The last opinion poll reveals that on election day 80 percent of your fellow citizens will elect this friend of the people. Why remain in the minority?

5. In my visits to the finest homes in Europe, I notice that the walls in most of them are graced by a coat of EZ-UP interior latex paint. A balanced mix of just the right ingredients assures the extra smoothness and durability that satisfied users of EZ-UP have come to expect. As reigning queen of the silver screen, I can have any brand of paint I want, but I will permit only EZ-UP when it comes time to redecorate my homes.

Red Herring

There is another faulty method of persuasion that involves distracting the reader. Writers sometimes throw a red herring into a piece of persuasive writing to hide the fact that they have a weak or nonexistent argument.

A **red herring** is a second issue thrown in to distract attention from the first one.

A red herring is a means of changing to another subject when a writer has nothing convincing to say about the subject under discussion. The term comes from the practice of dragging a red herring (a strong-smelling fish) along the trail of a fox to make hunting dogs lose the fox's trail and follow the strong scent of the herring. Here is an example of this faulty method of arguing:

> Presidential candidate Georgie Goodenough has been charged with illegal campaign practices, and this editorial will show how false that charge is. No one is a harder worker than candidate Goodenough. She is up with the birds seven days a week. All day every day she is on the go to the cities and towns of this great nation, making personal contact with the nation's backbone—its people. Despite this exhausting schedule, this admirable woman keeps in close and frequent touch with her husband, Knott, and their three children, Linda May, Betty, and Knott, Jr. What's more, Georgie never misses a Sunday church service, wherever her campaign may lead her.

The writer of the editorial obviously does not answer the charge that candidate Goodenough's campaign practices were illegal; instead, he distracts readers with a glowing picture of her. Unfortunately, all the examples of her hard work and good family relations do not constitute reasons that logically refute the original charge. Writers of persuasion often introduce distracting or confusing side issues when they feel they cannot convincingly argue the relevant issue or when they have no genuine argument to offer. Critical thinkers, writers, and readers will not be thrown off the real trail by a red herring.

Either-Or Thinking

The **either-or error** is an oversimplification that takes only two choices into account.

This faulty thinking method tries to persuade readers that someone is either completely good or completely bad, competent or incompetent, for something or against something. The either-or error falsely limits a situation to one extreme or another without considering any degrees or possibilities in between. In the following example, Georgie Goodenough's words are used:

> The newspapers, TV stations, and radio stations are not playing down the charge made against me. Therefore, they must want to see my opponent elected to the Oval Office.

Candidate Goodenough mistakenly thinks that the two choices she mentions are the only ones possible. According to her erroneous argument, the media would play down the charges against her if they were on her side; since they are not playing down the charges, they must be on the side of her opponent. The candidate does not consider any possibilities between the two extremes—that, for example, the media are doing their jobs by reporting an important news development.

To test an argument for an either-or error, always ask yourself if there may be other relevant alternatives between the two extremes given in the argument.

EXERCISE 9 **Avoiding the Red Herring Method and Either-Or Thinking.** Identify the error in thinking in each of the following statements. Then rewrite the statement to eliminate the error.

1. Bud and Ginny said they would be here at 9:30 if they were coming to the picnic. It is 9:45 and they are not here, so they must have decided not to come.
2. Since Paul is a geologist, he would not be interested in this tour of the great archaeological sites of the Middle East.
3. The theme of this book is at first not very apparent. The characters, however, are well-developed and quite realistic. The author is deservedly famous for his skill in portraying three-dimensional characters.
4. The people of Eastern Europe have not overthrown their communist governments. They must be enemies of the democratic way of life.
5. The world is made up of two varieties of people—those who love the Beatles' music and those who hate it.

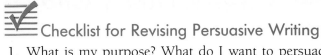

Checklist for Revising Persuasive Writing

1. What is my purpose? What do I want to persuade the reader to think or do?
2. Is my opinion worth defending? Can I persuade readers to accept it? Do I have to?
3. What qualities in my audience do I want to keep in mind as I write? What kinds of support are most likely to persuade them?
4. Which pieces of evidence are facts, which are sound opinions, and which are authoritative statements? Are there any unsound opinions?
5. What revisions are necessary to make sure that my opening statement is clear, specific, and directed toward my purpose?
6. What method of organization have I used to present my argument? Which transitions make my argument easy for readers to follow? Would another method of organization be preferable?
7. How clearly is my conclusion stated?
8. Have I used any faulty methods of persuasion—loaded words, bandwagon, testimonial, red herring, or the either-or error?

Writer's Choice

To practice writing persuasive paragraphs, choose from among these Writer's Choice assignments. Some are highly structured, with specific ideas on how to proceed. Others allow you to determine your own direction. Whichever assignment you choose, apply the skills you have learned in this chapter.

Writer's Choice #1

ASSIGNMENT A one-paragraph poster

LENGTH Six or seven sentences

AUDIENCE The residents of your neighborhood

PURPOSE To persuade the readers of the poster to plan and hold a block party on the next big holiday

PREWRITING Freewrite for five minutes on why you are proposing the block party. Then identify the points that would be most likely to persuade someone to become involved.

WRITING State your opinion in the opening sentence. In four or five sentences give your evidence: facts, statistics, examples, and, especially, your reasons. End with a sentence that will move the readers to action.

REVISING Apply all the questions on the checklist.

Writer's Choice #2

ASSIGNMENT An advertisement for a book you have enjoyed

LENGTH Your choice

AUDIENCE Your choice

PURPOSE To persuade the audience to buy and read the book

PREWRITING List all the good qualities of the book, and determine which qualities most appeal to your audience.

WRITING Whatever method of organization you choose, be sure to avoid faulty methods of persuasion.

REVISING Apply all the questions on the checklist.

Writer's Choice #3

ASSIGNMENT A persuasive paragraph on a topic of your own choice

OPTIONS Clearly identify your topic and your audience, and write a statement of your purpose. State your opinion in one sentence, and provide any necessary definitions or background information. Organize your facts and opinions in any logical way you choose, and use transitions to help present your support.

Writers on Writing

Brad Denton, a student at Rangeview High School in Aurora, Colorado, is interested in student government, journalism, running, and skiing. Brad plans to attend Brigham Young University. Brad thinks that he eventually would like to pursue a career in political science or international law.

THE PRODUCT

With the recently rekindled interest in the state of education in America's schools, many people are disputing the value of athletics in the education of today's youth. Contrary to the seemingly obvious view that any extracurricular activity must detract from study time, athletics are a great benefit to the high school student who participates in after-school sports.

The grades of athletes are strong evidence in themselves. For instance, the national grade point average of high school athletes is nearly half a point higher than that of nonathletes. In addition, athletes, who are required by eligibility rules to maintain respectable grades, have increased motivation to work for high marks.

Only a small minority of coaches and administrators demand victories at all costs. Most coaches stress fair play, responsible citizenship, and the growth of the individual through contribution to the team. In other words, extracurricular activities of all varieties are not "extras" that distract from a student's education but are fundamental parts of a person's development.

Today's schools should not have as their goal the discharging of academically literate but otherwise "uneducated" citizens. Schools should instead keep in mind that the ideal high school graduate has acquired, in addition to academic wealth, a variety of social skills—skills in dealing with himself or herself, with associates, and with society in general.

THE PROCESS

This persuasive paper grew out of one of my personal concerns. As a student athlete I have been concerned about the attitude that athletics are unimportant or even a detriment to students. I believe that athletics strengthen the character, and I decided that my purpose would be to support this main idea.

In my experience in cross-country running and track, I have learned to persevere, and I feel I have acquired a number of other positive character traits. As I reviewed my own experiences, they seemed very persuasive. I decided to use them, along with the evidence of athletes' grades, as the main part of my argument.

I also believe that no persuasive paper can be effective if it fails to address the questions and arguments posed by the opposing side. For this reason, I brought up the views of those who believe that athletics are an aim in themselves instead of being one aim of a student's education.

After putting these ideas down in a first draft, I wrote a conclusion which summarized and emphasized my ideas. After editing, changing inappropriate vocabulary and sentence structure, and proofreading, I finished my paper.

YOUR TURN *Writing Persuasively*

Write a persuasive paragraph on some issue in your school. Write out a statement of your purpose and audience. State your opinion clearly, and present your evidence in a logical fashion. Discuss the main opposing viewpoints and state reasons that allow you to refute these views. End with a strong concluding sentence, restating your main idea and, if you wish, moving your reader to action.

CHAPTER 10 CRITICAL THINKING AND PERSUASIVE WRITING

Selecting Appropriate Topics [pages 205–206]

1. Indicate which topic is appropriate for persuasive writing.
   (a) Commercial fishing demands hard work.
   (b) To protect resources, the government must regulate commercial fishing.
   (c) Commercial fishing is a livelihood for many.

Identifying Facts and Opinions [pages 207–210] Indicate whether each of the following items is (a) a fact, (b) an unsound opinion, (c) a sound opinion, or (d) an authoritative opinion.

2. California's most damaging earthquake struck San Francisco in 1906.
3. Some seismologists believe that earthquakes can be forecast.
4. I, a high school student, believe that no one can forecast an earthquake.

Faulty Methods of Persuasion [pages 214–218] Indicate whether each of the following statements demonstrates (a) bandwagon persuasion, (b) testimonial persuasion, (c) a red herring, (d) either-or thinking.

5. Everyone who knows anything vacations at Craven Point; you better make reservations now.
6. She vacations at the beach; obviously, she does not like the mountains.
7. Tom Velez, sportscaster, flies Karash Airways; you should too.
8. If Carla does not come to the meeting, she obviously must be opposed to our plan.
9. I agree that John did a wonderful job with the school fair, but we cannot really trust him with responsibilities: Look at the mess his friend made of the refreshments.
10. Buy your next vacuum cleaner from the manufacturer who has won over Lana Lenore, star of the silver screen.

Writing for Review Write a persuasive paragraph on a topic of your own choice. State your opinion clearly, organize and present your support in a logical way, and conclude with a statement that moves the reader to action.

UNIT IV

The Essay and the Research Report

Thinking About Thinking: Organizing Information

Research reports focus on facts; essays allow for personal expression. For example, a research report on lobsters might give statistics on the lobster industry. In an essay on lobsters you might tell how you eat them and whether or not you like them. Nevertheless, writing both research reports and essays requires you to engage in the thinking process called critical analysis.

Defining the Skill

One specific thinking skill that makes critical analysis possible is ORGANIZING INFORMATION. Organizing information involves examining information and arranging it in a reasonable order. Whether the information is a personal opinion or a group of facts, you need to put that information in order so that it makes sense to your reader.

Applying the Skill

Look at the photograph. The photo offers a great deal of information—a stadium, a field, spectators, individual players. However, the overall effect of the photo is its organization, its pattern. Write a paragraph in which you describe that pattern to someone. How is the photo organized? What shape or pattern does it form? How can you describe the shape so that you include all the available information? Does the shape have a center? What should you describe first?

CHAPTER 11

The Essay

Although the essay may deal with almost any subject, from coaches to cannibals, from wars to windows, from doors to dreams, there are certain large, persistent themes that essayists come back to again and again,—conversation, friendship, gardens, intolerance, courage, courtesy, reading, walking—and characters in life and literature.

—Houston Peterson

A newspaper reporter receives two assignments. The first is to write a news story about the rescue of seven people from a burning nursing home. The second is to write an editorial about the daring rescue. As an experienced writer, she knows that her approach to each assignment will be quite different. An editorial would express opinions about the incident and the heroic nurse. The news story, however, would report only the facts about the fire and the rescue. The editorial is a kind of essay, whereas the news story is not.

An **essay** is a personal statement that contains an introductory paragraph, a body of supporting paragraphs, and a concluding paragraph, all of which concentrate on one particular topic.

Of course, newspaper editorials are not the only kind of essay. The term **essay** may refer to answers to some test questions, to articles in magazines, to written passages required in college job applications, to movie reviews, and to newspaper opinion columns. All of these forms of writing can be called essays because they are all the authors' personal statements on various topics.

Essayists may express their views in very formal language, very informal language, or language of varying degrees of formality between these two styles. For example, consider the formality of this opening sentence of an essay about genius by the nineteenth-century English essayist Charles Lamb: "So far from the position holding true, that great wit (or genius, in our modern way of speaking) has a necessary alliance with insanity, the greatest wits, on the contrary, will ever be found to be the sanest writers." A student essay on the same topic begins: "You don't have to be crazy to be a genius." Both sentences express the writers' opinions; however, the styles and tones are completely different.

According to the preceding definition, an essay contains several paragraphs. Although they all must support the topic, they can be different kinds of paragraphs—descriptive paragraphs, narrative paragraphs, expository paragraphs, and persuasive paragraphs.

In this chapter you will apply the following steps of the writing process to the development of an essay:

prewriting: generating, exploring, and focusing ideas
prewriting: organizing an essay
writing a first draft
revising, **editing**, and **publishing** the essay

Prewriting: Generating, Exploring, and Focusing Ideas

The words of Houston Peterson that open this chapter imply that you can write an essay on just about any topic. At times an essay topic will be assigned to you, and you will have to mold the topic to put your personal stamp on it. At other times you will be given these instructions only: Write an essay on a topic of your choice. In either case the prewriting process you learned in Chapter 2 will help you. In this chapter, you will follow the steps of a student who was asked to choose a topic and who produced the essay that appears at the end of this chapter.

How do you get started when you may write your essay about anyone or anything you please? An experienced writer probably would suggest that you start by looking inside yourself. An essay is a personal statement so that it is logical to explore your own ideas and experiences when searching for a topic. The student you are following began his search with one of the prewriting techniques you first practiced in Chapter 2.

Freewriting

Freewriting means jotting down ideas as they occur to you during a specified, usually very brief, time period. Here is the freewriting the student produced.

> *Topic. Topic. My kingdom for a topic! A topic of my choice? Give me a break. I'm only human. I'm only human? I see red when I hear people use those words, or these: "It's only human." What's only about human? Why do I come unglued when I hear this said? A topic? Maybe yes. Maybe no. I could investigate reasons for my reaction. Would anyone be interested? I am, so maybe I can make my reasons interesting to others. I'll give it a whirl. If it doesn't click, I can think of another topic. I can, can't I?*

This writer is off and running—well, perhaps only walking fast. In any case, he has the beginnings of a topic for his essay.

EXERCISE 1 **Freewriting for an Essay Topic.** Spend five minutes freewriting in order to come up with a possible topic for a brief essay. If after five minutes you still have no ideas, do not worry. Just see if freewriting produces something worthwhile. Save your freewriting notes; you will need them in Exercise 2 and in later exercises.

Brainstorming

Brainstorming is a prewriting technique that involves free association of ideas.

> *"Only human"—Why do these words irritate me?*
>
> *"human"—something wonderful to me*
>
> *"Only human" suggests that not much can be expected of people.*
>
> *used mostly when speaking of a failure or shortcoming of a person or group; sometimes used as a reason for not really trying*
>
> *my use of "I'm only human" in freewriting almost automatic—a possible reason for giving up on trying to find a topic; effect of this attitude? negative influence on behavior? (If humans can't be expected to do this, why keep on trying?)*
>
> *real meaning of human? according to scientists? writers?*

This student's brainstorming session produced many questions; nevertheless he was able to clarify, at least to some extent, his reasons for getting upset when he hears the words "only human."

EXERCISE 2 **Brainstorming for an Essay Topic.** If your freewriting for Exercise 1 gave you an idea that you may want to pursue, brainstorm about it now. If you still have not come up with an idea, try one of these.

1. my feet
2. movies for teens
3. hall of fame of local characters
4. beards or mustaches

Save your notes for Exercise 3 and for later exercises.

Clustering

The writer you are following tried **clustering**—a third prewriting technique—in a further attempt to define his essay topic more precisely. He wrote one word—*human*—at the center of a piece of paper. Then he wrote other words and phrases suggested by *human* at different places around it. He connected related ideas with lines. This is called making a clustering diagram. The clustering diagram that this student made is shown at the top of page 229.

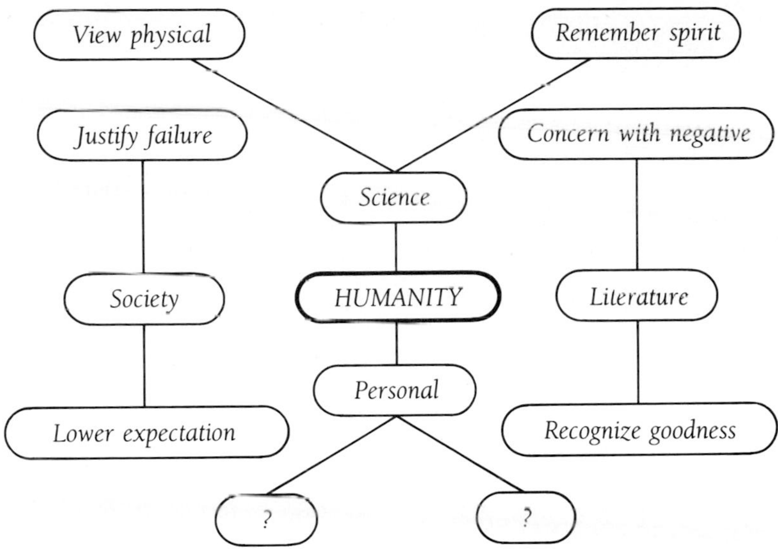

By clustering, this writer was able to add a few more details to his original ideas of *human*. He was also able to isolate four different views on the meaning of *human*. Notice that the details of one of these views will need additional thought.

EXERCISE 3 **Clustering for an Essay Topic.** Has one word emerged from Exercises 1 and 2 as a potential topic? If so, place it in the center of a page, and draw a circle around it. Then write down other words that this word suggests to you. You will have most success with this exercise if you work quickly and if you write down very specific, concrete words associated with the central word. Draw a circle around each new word, and use lines to show how one word leads to another. If you still have no idea to work with, put one of the following words in the center of a page, and build a cluster diagram around it:

1. meals
2. villains
3. sneezes
4. money

Exploring Subjects and Focusing Ideas

After you find a writing idea, either one you have generated yourself or one that has been assigned, the next step is to explore it in detail. One technique for exploring an idea is to ask questions about it. Study the answers to the questions in the following chart. The student planning the essay on the meaning of *human* wrote these answers.

PERSONAL QUESTIONS TO EXPLORE A SUBJECT	ANSWERS
1. Who or what is my subject?	*What's good about being human?*
2. What are my personal experiences with the subject?	*I often hear people putting down being human, talking about being "only human" as if humans are inferior in some way.*
3. What are my emotions during these experiences?	*I get mad because I think saying "I'm only human" suggests a wrong or incomplete picture of the human race. I think an expression like this is used as an excuse for not doing something difficult.*
4. What were my reactions to these experiences?	*I decided to investigate what being human really means. What do scientists have to say? How do writers portray human beings in literature? What is my own definition or view of human?*
5. What did I learn?	*My own thinking and observation revealed some negative things about being human (and this is what many people dwell on), but the positive side makes me proud to be human.*

By answering the questions, this student has begun to put the brainstorming and clustering details about his idea into a more definite form. Thus he is one step closer to writing his essay.

You must not say too little in an essay, but you should not attempt to say too much either. Your idea for an essay must be *focused*. For example, the student whose prewriting you have been following has focused the idea "human" so that it is limited to his personal viewpoint on what being human means.

EXERCISE 4 **Exploring a Topic for an Essay.** Make a chart containing questions to help you examine a topic from your work in Exercises 1–3. If you still have no topic, use one of the following:

1. problems with pets
2. a movie I wish I never saw
3. an unforgettable person
4. the future

Save your charts for use in Exercise 6 and later exercises.

EXERCISE 5 **Evaluating an Idea for an Essay.** Read each pair of ideas. Then say whether you would rather write an essay about *a* or *b*. Give reasons.

1. a. writing implements
   b. stubby pencils
2. a. the sport I play worst
   b. essential athletic skills
3. a. keeping fit
   b. bicycling for health
4. a. why I love literature
   b. my favorite poem
   (or story or novel or play)

EXERCISE 6 **Focusing an Idea for an Essay.** If you have successfully completed Exercises 1–4, state a focused topic that has emerged from all your prewriting activity. Save your response for Exercise 7.

Determining Your Purpose and Audience

After focusing your topic, you must identify the purpose of your essay. For example, you may want both to entertain your readers and to persuade them to accept your opinion on a certain issue. Here is the statement of purpose produced by the student you have been following:

> I want to explain what being human means to me.

When you are deciding the purpose of your essay, you must also think carefully about your audience. For example, the purpose of the essay about being human is to explain what being human means to the student writer. The student has selected as an audience readers his own age and older. His choice of audience will determine how he will write the essay—the vocabulary, the sentence structure, the examples he will use to illustrate ideas. If, however, the student has chosen fourth graders as an audience, he would have to keep vocabulary, sentence structure, and examples simple enough for children to understand.

EXERCISE 7 **Selecting a Purpose and an Audience.** *If you were able to state a focused topic in Exercise 6,* now is your chance to tell for whom you want to write and why. Identify in writing a purpose and an audience for the limited topic you stated in Exercise 6. *If you did not state a limited topic in Exercise 6,* look back to your answers for Exercise 5. Write a possible purpose and a possible audience for one of the topics you chose as an answer.

Prewriting: Organizing an Essay

After generating sufficient prewriting material, an experienced writer often organizes the material informally and immediately begins to write a first draft. Other writers prefer to take the time to organize the prewriting material they have collected into a formal outline before they begin to write a first draft. Writing an outline of your ideas will help you to clarify the nature and direction of your argument.

An **outline** is a writing plan that shows the main points you wish to make, the sequence in which they will be discussed, and their relation to one another.

Your teacher will help you decide whether you should develop a working outline or a formal outline before you start to write your first draft. The student whose work you have been observing followed this procedure: (1) he organized his prewriting material in a working outline; (2) he wrote and reviewed his first draft; (3) then he developed a formal outline as a map he could use to help him write the final copy of his essay.

The working outline was complete enough to help this writer at the first-draft stage. Making the outline permitted him to gather all his related prewriting notes in one place and to see which were main ideas and which were details that could be used to support the main idea. Notice that in this working outline the writer used a Roman numeral to indicate each main topic and a capital letter to show each detail that supports a main topic. Take particular notice of the fact that the student also included some new details that were not already in his prewriting notes.

WORKING OUTLINE

TOPIC: What it means to be human

I. Humanity in society
  A. Society's attitude
  B. My reaction

II. Humanity in science
  A. Scientists' attitude
  B. My reaction

III. Humanity in literature
  A. Writers' attitude
  B. My reaction

IV. My personal views
  A. Negative attitudes
  B. Positive attitudes

EXERCISE 8 **Writing a Working Outline.** *If your work from Exercises 1–4 has yielded many notes,* now is the time for you to go over them and organize them in a working outline. Decide what your main heads should be, and place details under each main head. You may discard some notes along the way. *If you still do not have enough notes for an outline,* apply the prewriting techniques of freewriting, brainstorming, clustering, and asking questions to one of the limited topics in Exercise 5 or to a writing idea of your own choosing. Either way, you should develop a working outline with at least three main heads. Save this working outline because you will be creating an essay based on it.

Writing a First Draft

With his working outline in front of him, the student began to write the first draft of his essay on being human. He recognized that a first draft is not supposed to be a piece of finished writing, and so he concentrated primarily on simply getting his ideas on paper in the sequence shown on the outline.

A thesis statement is frequently the first or last sentence of the introduction, or first paragraph, of an essay. In either position, readers are more likely to pay attention to it.

The **thesis statement** performs three important functions: (1) It states the main point of your essay. (2) It indicates your attitude toward the topic. (3) It suggests the organization that the essay will follow.

To develop an effective thesis statement, study your working outline, and keep in mind the purpose of your essay and the audience for whom you are writing it. Make your thesis statement a single sentence that suggests all of the main topics in your working outline. As you read the thesis statement for the essay on being human, notice that it covers the main topics in the writer's working outline and establishes the order in which these main ideas will be discussed in the essay.

> Although many people—including, to some extent, scientists and writers of literature—have an essentially negative attitude about what it means to be human, I am proud to be a member of the human race.

Besides stating the thesis of an essay, the introduction should be interesting enough to make your audience want to read more. To capture your readers' interest, you may want to try one of the following techniques in writing your introduction, or you may hit upon another technique for "hooking" your audience.

ASKING A QUESTION

The writer could have begun with a question like this: "How do you feel about being a member of the human race?"

ADDRESSING THE READER DIRECTLY

The opening sentence in the introduction of the essay might have been "If you are like many people, you may simply have acknowledged half consciously that you are a human being without giving much thought to what this idea means."

STATING AN INTERESTING FACT OR STATISTIC

The writer might have interested readers by beginning with a statistic: "In a recent poll fifty-seven percent of the students in our school felt that not enough is being done to improve the world we live in."

TELLING AN ANECDOTE

The writer might have begun with an amusing reference to his own life: "Smoke starts shooting out of both ears every time I hear people whine, 'I'm (He's, She's, They're, We're) *only* human.' "

QUOTING FROM A BOOK, POEM, OR SONG

Finally, the writer could have begun his introduction with a familiar quotation: "I'm with Nellie Forbush! She is the character in the musical *South Pacific* who sings these words in one part of the play:

'They say the human race
Is falling on its face,
And hasn't very far to go.
But every whippoorwill
Is selling me a bill,
Telling me it just ain't so.' "

In addition to stating the thesis, the introduction should also set the essay's **tone**—your attitude toward your topic and audience. Your tone may be formal or informal, humorous or serious, emotional or reflective, depending on your topic and your intended readers.

EXERCISE 9 **Evaluating Thesis Statements.** Read each pair of sentences. Then tell in writing which is the better thesis statement and why you think so.

1. a. Space exploration should be stopped for economic, social, and political reasons.
   b. Many Americans think space exploration is pointless.
2. a. The sports program in this school district leaves much to be desired, and something should be done about it.
   b. The lifeless sports program in this school district could be improved in its curriculum, facilities, and scheduling.
3. a. Readers admire Ernest Hemingway for his terse style and realistic portrayals of people.
   b. Ernest Hemingway is one of the most skilled American writers, as his devoted readers throughout the world will testify.

EXERCISE 10 **Stating a Thesis.** Referring to your working outline (Exercise 8), your statement of purpose, and your choice of audience (Exercise 7), write a thesis statement. Your sentence should make clear to your reader **(1)** what your main idea is, **(2)** what your attitude toward that idea is, and **(3)** how you will organize your essay. Save your thesis statement for Exercise 11.

EXERCISE 11 **Writing Introductory Paragraphs.** Write two different introductions for the essay for which you wrote a thesis statement in Exercise 10. State in writing which version you prefer and why you prefer it. Save the preferred version for Exercise 12.

The Body and the Conclusion

The paragraphs that make up the body of an essay develop, or support, the ideas of the thesis statement in the introduction. If you follow the order of your working outline, you will find it easier to write the paragraphs in the body. In most cases, you should write a paragraph for each main topic in the outline.

While writing the body paragraphs, think of the different modes of writing you can use to develop different parts of your writing outline—narration, description, exposition, and persuasion. If you need to review these modes, consult Chapters 7–10.

In an essay, each paragraph must be connected smoothly to the paragraph before and after it. The transitions discussed in Chapter 3 and 7–10 will help give your essay coherence, not only by bridging paragraphs but also by connecting sentences within paragraphs.

REPEATED WORDS AND SYNONYMS

If you use the same word near the end of one paragraph and at the beginning of the next paragraph, or if you use words with similar meanings at these spots, you will form a strong link between the paragraphs. Consider the following excerpt:

> Before we realize it, we have developed false *negative images* of ourselves. . . .
>
> Furthermore, this *negative* and potentially harmful *view* of humanity is harbored not only by society in general, but also, more specifically, by the scientific world.

TRANSITIONS

These words and phrases will give your writing coherence by making the connection between one paragraph and the next clear, smooth, and easy to follow. Transitions help your readers track your thinking and show them how you are progressing from one idea to the next. Here are some of the most frequently used transitions:

TIME	after	first	later	soon
	always	following	meanwhile	then
	before	immediately	now	until
	finally	last	sometimes	
PLACE	above	down	near	parallel
	ahead	far	next to	there
	around	here	opposite	under
	below	horizontally	outside	vertically
	beneath	inside	over	within
CAUSE-EFFECT	as a result	consequently	so that	
	because	so	therefore	
COMPARISON-CONTRAST	but	like	on the other hand	similarly
	however	likewise	on the contrary	unlike
EXAMPLES	for example	for instance	namely	that is

The last paragraph of your essay, the conclusion, closes and completes your work. A well-written conclusion can also strengthen your writing and increase its appeal to your readers. The following list suggests techniques for writing a conclusion.

1. Summarize the important points that you have presented.
2. Restate the thesis of the essay.
3. Describe your personal reaction to the topic.
4. Relate an anecdote that supports the topic.
5. Suggest a solution to a problem that you have discussed.
6. Ask a question that leads the reader to consider the topic.

EXERCISE 12 **Writing a First Draft.** With your working outline and your preferred introduction from Exercise 11 in front of you, write the first draft of your essay. If you have three main heads on your working outline, you will probably have three body paragraphs. Do not worry about sentence structure now. Just try to cover all the main points and the supporting details in your outline. Save your first draft. Your assignment in Writer's Choice #1 on page 242 will be to revise the draft.

Revising, Editing, and Publishing the Essay

When reviewing a composition, you review and rethink it. In reviewing your first draft, you may find that you need to develop some ideas further or eliminate others that do not support the topic. You may need to move a paragraph or strengthen your conclusion. The following checklist will be helpful in discovering specific problems in your first draft.

Checklist for Revising an Essay

1. What am I trying to tell my audience? Will my audience understand my attitude toward the topic?
2. How do the points I discuss support the thesis?
3. Which points are most important to me? Do they need to be developed more or introduced earlier?
4. Which points can I discard?
5. What is strong and what is weak about my organization?
6. How well or poorly do my ideas connect with one another?
7. How can my introduction and conclusion be improved?
8. What can I do to vary sentence structure and sentence length?
9. What adjustments should I make in grammar, usage, word choice, spelling, capitalization, and punctuation?

EXERCISE 13 **Revising a First Draft.** Begin your revision by asking yourself the questions on the Checklist for Revising an Essay on this page. Make notes on your first draft or on separate paper. These notes should indicate the kinds of changes you think you should make. Save your notes. You will write a formal outline and a revised version of your essay as Writer's Choice #1 on page 242.

The Formal Outline

You may recall that the student working on the essay about being human wrote his first draft from a working outline. When he reviewed the draft by asking the nine preceding questions, he realized that he wanted to make some changes. At this point he was also ready to complete the formal outline that follows. As you study it, you will see sections that differ from those on the outline on page 232. In addition, you will see that the formal outline is more detailed. Notice that the outline includes ideas just for the body paragraphs—not for the introduction and conclusion. If you or your teacher prefers, you may show the introduction and conclusion on your formal outline.

FORMAL OUTLINE

TOPIC: What it means to be human

I. Humanity in society
  A. Society's attitude
    1. Justifies failed attempts
    2. Excuses lack of attempt
  B. My reaction
    1. Accept negative self-image
    2. Lower expectations
    3. Diminish willingness to try
II. Humanity in science
  A. Scientists' attitude
    1. View physical side only
    2. Search for weakness
  B. My reaction
    1. Remember human spirit
    2. Recount human achievement
III. Humanity in literature
  A. Writers' attitude
    1. View whole person
    2. Concerned mainly with negative
  B. My reaction
    1. Recognize goodness
    2. Focus on positive

Compare this final outline with the writer's working outline to discover what changes and additions he has made. You will see that he dropped the whole of main topic IV with its subordinate ideas. Notice also the numbered details under the subordinate ideas. The notes on page 241 will show how he followed the outline while he was writing the final copy.

When you prepare your outline, consult the following guidelines:

1. Place your topic at the top of the outline.
2. For each main idea, write a main topic preceded by a Roman numeral. You must have a *II* if you have a *I*.
3. Under each main topic, list supporting subordinate ideas. Before each of these write a capital letter. You must have *B* if you have *A*.
4. Under each subordinate idea, list any supporting details that you want to mention. Before each of these write an Arabic numeral. You must have a *2* if you have a *1*.
5. Follow the indention that you see in the preceding model.
6. Begin the first word of each main topic, subordinate idea, and detail with a capital letter. If they are sentences, end each with a period. Most of the time you can use phrases instead of sentences.

When you read the final version of the essay, you will notice that the thesis statement differs somewhat from the thesis stated on page 233.

EXERCISE 14 **Preparing a Formal Outline.** Assume that you have written a first draft of an essay about the Alaskan tundra. Assume also that you are not satisfied with the first draft because it jumps from topic to topic. The working outline is weak. Now is the time for you to prepare a better formal outline. You realize after reading your first draft that the body of your essay should be organized into three main topics: *weather on the Alaskan tundra, animals on the Alaskan tundra,* and *outsiders on the Alaskan tundra.* Your task now is to organize all the subordinate ideas and details from your first draft under those three headings. Prepare a formal outline with three levels; use all the following notes:

Cold winter temperatures	Travel in packs	Poor vision
Dry air	Strong pack leader	Wolves
Minimal moisture	Military bases	Jeeps
"The Arctic desert"	Caribou	Electricity
Foxes	Grizzly bears	Civilian airports
	Hibernation	

The Title

The title of your essay should suggest some aspect of your thesis, and it should create audience interest. The title "On Being Human" would be too dull for the essay you have been tracing, and "Human Beings" would be too unfocused. Neither of these titles clearly suggests the thesis. However, the title "What's *Only* About *Human?*" arouses interest and gives some hint about the thesis.

Model of a Finished Essay

The final copy of the student writer's essay is printed on the following pages. As you read his essay, pay attention to the annotations below the model. They point out some of the ideas discussed in the chapter, and they show how the parts of the essay correspond to parts of the writer's formal outline on page 238.

What's Only About Human?

A Smoke and superheated steam come shooting out of both my ears when I hear people whine, "I'm only human" or "It's only human." I am, of course, exaggerating. Nevertheless, I do get upset when I hear expressions like these because they imply negative and false views of what it means to be human, views that differ in

B important ways from my own. For although society, science, and literature take an essentially negative attitude toward humanity, I am proud to be a human.

C First, let us consider the general attitude members of society hold regarding the concept of being human. People often offer the expression "I'm only human" as a justification for failure, as if human beings were inferior in some way and incapable of achieving great things. How many times have you heard someone make a remark such as, "All right, I made a mistake. I'm only human, you know!" In addition, many people may tend to use the words "only human" as an excuse for not even attempting something difficult. Gradually and unconsciously, this "only human" way of thinking leads to harmful results. We develop false negative images of ourselves. We lower our personal standards, and that diminishes our willingness to face new challenges.

D Furthermore, this negative and potentially harmful view of humanity is harbored not only by society in general, but also, more specifically, by the scientific world. Many scientists who deal with human beings--biologists and doctors for example--have a partial view--of human beings. As scientists, they see only the physical side of humanity, which is their chief concern. Most of the time, scientists search for what is wrong or weak or diseased. Viewing humanity in this somewhat negative way, they may convey their attitudes to the people they contact. To balance these attitudes, scientists should remember that the human spirit can overcome many afflictions. Likewise, the challenges presented by disease have motivated some of the greatest human achievements.

E In addition to its existence in society and in science, a negative attitude toward humanity abounds in the world of literature. I concede that, unlike scientists, writers of literature look at the whole person--the human mind and spirit as well as the human body. Nevertheless, many writers tend to be fascinated with the negative aspects of humanity--crime, violence, war, and dishonesty, for example. Unfortunately, this fascination makes their view of human beings unrealistically lopsided. Unconsciously, audiences may begin to accept this unbalanced view. However, life has its brightness, too. Many--maybe most--human beings <u>are</u> law-abiding, gentle, considerate, peaceful, and honest.

F I am firmly convinced that there are positive reasons to be proud as a member of the human race. My reply to negative attitudes about humanity is a foul and indignant cry, "Stop putting your humanity down!" Yes, at times we are all afraid to try something difficult, or we are reluctant to admit failure. "It's only human." However, isn't it also "only human' to accept a challenge and take the risks involved? Isn't it also "only human" to face up to wrongs for which we alone are responsible? If we are quick to acknowledge our weaknesses, shouldn't we be equally quick to acknowledge our strengths?

NOTES ABOUT THE MODEL STUDENT ESSAY

A The introduction of this essay begins with a brief anecdote.

B Notice the underlined thesis statement.

C This cause-and-effect paragraph follows part I of the formal outline.

D This paragraph corresponds to part II of the outline.

E This paragraph of comparison and contrast follows part III.

F In his concluding paragraph, the author restates the thesis. He also leaves the reader with questions.

Writer's Choice #1

ASSIGNMENT A final outline and a final copy of the essay you have planned and drafted in this chapter

LENGTH Five to seven paragraphs

AUDIENCE As you stated in Exercise 7 and Exercise 13

PURPOSE As you stated in Exercise 7 and Exercise 13

PREWRITING You have already finished this stage in Exercises 1–8.

WRITING You have already finished this stage in Exercise 12.

REVISING Use the checklist on page 237 to review and rethink your first draft. Prepare a formal outline indicating whatever changes and additions you want to make. Follow the guidelines on page 239 for a formal outline. Then use the outline and your first draft to write the final copy of your essay. Be sure to edit and proofread the essay.

Writer's Choice #2

ASSIGNMENT An essay on one of the following topics or another topic you choose:
What's *right* with America?
The world's greatest sport (or form of entertainment)
The most beautiful sights on earth

LENGTH Five to seven paragraphs

AUDIENCE The editors of a teen magazine

PURPOSE To describe, inform, or explain

PREWRITING Explore your subject by means of a series of informational or personal questions (see Chapter 2). Limit the topic, and organize the information, reasons, or opinions you wish to present into a working outline.

WRITING State your thesis clearly, and write a first draft.

REVISING Refer to the revising checklist, and then prepare a formal outline. Write your final version. Carefully edit, proofread, and share your work with readers.

Writer's Choice #3

ASSIGNMENT An essay on any topic you choose

OPTIONS Determine and state in writing the length, audience, and purpose of the essay. Use the prewriting technique that best fits the topic. Follow the writing stages: working outline, first draft, formal outline, final copy. Edit, proofread, and share your work.

Writers on Writing

Cesar Alvarez, a student at Lakewood High School in St. Petersburg, Florida, has lived in Florida for most of his life. Cesar works as an editor of the school newspaper, participates in student government, and enjoys playing soccer. He is drawn to the fields of journalism, law, and engineering.

THE PRODUCT

Cesar wrote the following essay about Angelus House while he was attending the Poynter Institute for Media Studies in St. Petersburg.

> Tucked away in a remote residential area of St. Petersburg is the home of the Angelus family. It is not important that this house is not very attractive on the outside, for its beauty is found within.
>
> The Angelus is a home for handicapped children, specifically those who are brain-damaged. In most cases, these children would have been placed in county institutions. Instead, this program allows them to be part of a happy family promising love and care.
>
> The Angelus was created in 1979 by Pauline Neri. Her project has since become the home of eleven handicapped children. The "mother" of this family, Linda Ferguson, has had years of experience in dealing with the handicapped. "This is a place for kids who have no place to go," she explains. "This is our home and we live here like one big family."
>
> For one afternoon I had the pleasure of becoming a part of this family. Mrs. Ferguson introduced me to the children, and soon I felt right at home. The eldest, Tracie, sat next to me in her wheelchair. She seemed very excited to tell me that the next day would be her seventeenth birthday. Pausing to think for a moment, she recalled her birthday list.
>
> "I want a pocketbook, a compact, and River Raid for my Atari!" she exclaimed.
>
> "Oh, girl, you're crazy!" shouted the two-year-old on the floor. A tiny girl with impish features bounced up and down, banging on a toy piano. Tara is the youngest member of the family. When she was little more than a few months old, she was the victim of crippling abuse. Her spirit and personality, however, haven't darkened at all, despite the events of her past.
>
> "She has a bright-light personality," said Michelle Muller. Michelle works at the Angelus helping to care for the children.
>
> "This is Missy," said Michelle, turning to the girl in the recliner chair. "You're sweet sixteen—have you ever been kissed?"
>
> Missy hid her face and began to blush in embarrassment. Realizing that her secret was out in the open, she recounted the story of her first kiss.
>
> Meanwhile, in the corner of the room, Dawn sat in silence on her rocking chair. She was very still, moving only to draw in an occasional

breath. Her dark-brown eyes stared blankly. The innocence that is visible in most of the other children has long since faded from her face. She lives in a solitary world, unable to speak or hear.

The dinner hour approached, and a procession of wheelchairs carried their hungry riders into the dining room. Shortly after, the chatter began. There at the end of the table sat Dawn, still deep in thought. Momentarily, she broke away from her fixed stare and peered up at me. Her pale, weak hand strained to reach out to me. Slowly, I took her hand. She put her arms around me and embraced me. Then I remembered what Linda had said: "Though their disease is incurable and there is no 'getting better,' there is one thing we can offer them . . . love."

THE PROCESS

This article is probably the most difficult piece I have ever written. Throughout the three weeks that it took to develop, I encountered several obstacles that had to be overcome.

I actually found it quite simple to do interviews and collect information. In fact, I ended up with much more information than I could possibly use. This presented a real problem. I had to sort through a mass of facts and choose only the most important ones. Pulling all of this information together became the most difficult part of the writing process.

Once I had decided which topics I would discuss, I began to organize my material. Drawing up a loose outline helped me put everything into perspective. The outline served as a guide that I could follow as I wrote.

After writing my first draft, I found it easier to see where my work was leading. I wanted to portray an emotion in words—I wanted the reader to feel the same things that I felt on that afternoon at Angelus House. The best way to accomplish this was to write about the things that made the biggest impression on me. I find that the emotions in my writing are more intense if I write about them while they are still vividly alive in me. I hope that I achieved this effect in writing about Angelus House.

YOUR TURN *Writing a Human Interest Essay*

As Cesar did, visit a local humanitarian organization, and write an essay presenting your impressions of the place. If possible, include quotations from authorities at the institution you visited.

CHAPTER 11 THE ESSAY

Topic [pages 227–231] Indicate the letter of the item that correctly answers the question.

1. Which of the following is the most focused essay topic?
   (a) brothers and sisters (b) what my sister taught me (c) sisters

Outline, Introduction, and Thesis [pages 232–235] Read the following working outline, and then indicate the letter of the item that correctly answers each question.

I. What my sister taught me about people
   A. Accepting people as you find them
   B. Getting along with a variety of personalities
II. What my sister taught me about family
   A. Understanding my brothers and sisters
   B. Being helpful around the house
   C. Being a cheerful family member
III. What my sister taught me about school
   A. Taking my student responsibilities seriously
   B. Going a bit beyond an assignment

2. Where in this outline would you place an example about reading another book to understand better a chapter in a history book?
   (a) in I under B (b) in III under A (c) in III under B
3. Which thesis statement best reflects this outline?
   (a) I have finally learned to be a good student.
   (b) My sister helped me understand my role in the family.
   (c) I cannot remember when I started listening to my sister, but I am glad I did.

Body [page 235] Indicate the letter of the correct item.

4. Which item would body paragraph II for the preceding outline be most likely to discuss?
   (a) meeting new people (c) a real friend
   (b) learning to listen in class (d) doing chores with a smile
5. The introductory paragraph of an essay based upon the preceding outline would most likely discuss (a) making friends (b) how I decided to listen to my sister (c) problems as a student.

Writing for Review Write an essay about a topic with which you have some direct experience. Begin with a paragraph that engages your readers' interest and leads up to your thesis statement. Be sure that the paragraphs in the body discuss all the points raised in your thesis.

CHAPTER 12

The Research Report

Find a subject you care about and which you in your heart feel others should care about.

—Kurt Vonnegut, Jr.

Writing a research report involves (1) investigating a subject through the use of available sources of information and (2) writing the results of this research in your own words, using a set format and observing established writing conventions.

A **research report** deals with a limited topic and is based on information from print sources, such as books and magazines, or from nonprint sources, such as filmstrips, phonograph records, computer software, cassettes, and personal interviews with experts.

The research report you write in this chapter will be based on information you gather from at least five sources. It will be approximately one thousand words long (about four typewritten pages), unless your teacher suggests a different length.

Writing a research report can be very rewarding. Not only will you increase your knowledge, but you will develop personal opinions based on your new knowledge. You may even become something of an expert yourself.

To write your research report, you will be using many skills that you practiced in the preceding chapters—prewriting, writing, and revising; writing topic sentences; and writing unified and coherent paragraphs, among others. To express your ideas, you will use one or more of the modes of writing that you have studied: description, narration, exposition, and persuasion. This chapter will also give you practice in the following skills:

prewriting: selecting and limiting a topic
prewriting: beginning your research
prewriting: purpose, audience, and controlling idea
prewriting: preparing a working outline
prewriting: gathering sources and preparing a working bibliography
prewriting: taking notes
prewriting: preparing a formal outline
writing the first draft
revising the first draft
publishing the final draft

Prewriting: Selecting and Limiting a Topic

If a specific topic for your research report is not assigned, your first step in prewriting will be to choose a subject and then narrow it to a manageable topic. Ideally, when you look for a subject, you should follow the advice of American writer Kurt Vonnegut, Jr., quoted at the beginning of this chapter. As you look, use the prewriting techniques you know—freewriting, brainstorming, charting, and asking questions. If you need to review any of these techniques, refer to Chapter 2.

Be certain that the topic you select is not too general to deal with in a report that is only four pages long. One student, Betsy Thomassen, decided that her research report would be about eyesight. Realizing that she could not write about such a broad topic in a report of one thousand words, she decided to focus on a more limited aspect of eyesight. She narrowed her original topic in the following way:

GENERAL	Eyesight
LESS GENERAL	Sight Problems
LESS GENERAL	Correcting Sight Problems
LIMITED	Contact Lenses Today

Choosing a topic that is too limited may present more difficulties than choosing a topic that is too general. As you have seen, Betsy was able to limit her general topic without much trouble. However, suppose she had chosen a more limited topic, such as how to insert contact lenses. She would soon discover that she could not write about much more than the steps of the process.

When you think you have an appropriate topic for your report, make a preliminary check at the library to be certain that you will be able to find enough sources of information. Check the Subject Index of the library card catalog for books on your topic. Check reference books such as *The Readers' Guide to Periodical Literature* for magazine articles on your topic, and find out which of the magazines are carried by your library. Also consider newspaper articles and pamphlets in your library's vertical file. (See Chapter 34.)

For a report of a thousand words (about four typed pages), you will need to use at least five sources in addition to any encyclopedias you may consult. However, some of the sources you identify in this preliminary check will prove unsuitable for your research later. It is therefore a good idea to identify more sources now than the five you will be required to use.

Library sources are not the only sources of information, however. A **source** is anyone or anything that provides information on a topic. For example, watching a TV documentary or personally interviewing an expert in the field will provide valuable information on some topics. In addition, you may be able to obtain pamphlets and other printed material directly from businesses or government agencies.

Betsy Thomassen found that the library had an encyclopedia article, some books, and some magazine and newspaper articles about contact lenses. She also phoned her eye doctor and learned that his office could provide one or two pamphlets about contact lenses. She therefore decided that she could find enough information to proceed.

EXERCISE 1 **Limiting a Topic.** For five of the following general topics, suggest a limited topic that can be handled in a thousand-word report (about four typewritten pages). Then choose one of the limited topics (or another limited topic that interests you) for a thousand-word research report of your own.

GENERAL TOPIC Aviation
LIMITED TOPIC Pros and Cons of the *Concorde*

1. Your State
2. Medical Research
3. Composers and Songwriters
4. Mexico
5. American Poets
6. The Space Age

EXERCISE 2 **Checking the Library for Sources.** Go to the library, and find out how much material is available on the limited topic you selected in Exercise 1. At this point identify at least ten sources with information on your topic, since some of them may prove unsuitable later. If you cannot identify at least ten sources, choose another topic.

Prewriting: Beginning Your Research

You can start researching your limited topic by reading one or two encyclopedia articles about it. These articles will give you an overview of the basic facts and may contain a list of books on the topic.

The encyclopedias you consult may have a separate article about your topic. You may find, however, that you have to use the encyclopedia index to locate the information in one or more articles. For example, the index may indicate that to locate information on the Aztec god Quetzalcoatl, you should consult encyclopedia articles under the titles "Aztec," "Mexico," and "Mythology."

Betsy Thomassen consulted an encyclopedia, where she found an article under the title "Contact Lens." She read this article and made a list of the most important points. She would later use this list to help her prepare a working outline and to take notes from other sources.

Checklist for Selecting a Topic and Beginning Research

1. Why do I want to write about this topic?
2. Is my topic too limited to discuss in the number of pages or words specified?
3. Can I cover all the important aspects of my topic in the length specified, or is my topic too general?
4. What books and articles about the topic are available?
5. Are enough sources available to supply me with the information I need for my report? In addition to library materials, have I considered sources such as interviews with experts or pamphlets from large companies, local businesses, and government offices?

EXERCISE 3 **Finding General Information on a Topic.** Read one or two encyclopedia articles to learn general information about the report topic for which you compiled your list of sources in Exercise 2. (If you are unable to find encyclopedia articles about your topic, locate and read at least one magazine article that you identified in Exercise 2.) As you read the encyclopedia or magazine articles, jot down at least five important points about your topic.

Prewriting: Purpose, Audience, and Controlling Idea

So far, you have selected and limited your report topic, checked the library for sources, and learned some general information about your topic. Now it is time to define your **purpose** for writing the report. For example, your purpose in writing about the works of Johann Sebastian Bach might be to persuade readers to listen to and appreciate his music. Your purpose in writing a report on Quetzalcoatl might be to inform readers about one aspect of the rich culture of Mexico's ancient Aztec people. You should be able to state your purpose in one sentence

While you are considering your purpose, you should also think about the **audience** for whom you will be writing. Consider how much knowledge, if any, your audience might already have. For example, you might write a report on Bach's works for classmates who know little about classical music; the audience for a report on Quetzalcoatl might be the teacher and students in your history class. Choosing a specific audience for your report will help you determine the kind and amount of information to include. If you were to write the report on Bach's works for classmates unfamiliar with classical music, you might include less technical information than you would for an audience of classical music lovers. Instead, you might spend more time trying to convince your audience of Bach's greatness.

After determining your purpose and audience, the next prewriting task is to state the controlling idea. The **controlling idea** is the central thought you intend to develop in the report. Stating the controlling idea accomplishes three important objectives: (1) It states the main point of the report; (2) it lets your audience know your attitude toward your topic; and (3) it suggests the path that your report will follow. Here is Betsy Thomassen's statement of the controlling idea of her report: "Contact lenses are one fascinating recent example of the way human beings are always trying to improve their lives."

PREWRITING CHART

TOPIC ____________________

PURPOSE ____________________

____

____

AUDIENCE ____________________

____

____

CONTROLLING IDEA ____________________

____

____

EXERCISE 4 **Determining Your Purpose, Audience, and Controlling Idea.** Write the purpose, define your audience, and state the controlling idea of the research report you have been planning. Use a chart like the one above.

Prewriting: Preparing a Working Outline

A **working outline** is a preliminary outline that will guide you in your research and note taking.

Now that you have an overview of your topic, you can decide which points you will discuss in your research report and how you want to organize them. You are ready to make a working outline to help you take notes on information you find in your sources. As you take notes, you will probably change your outline by adding subheadings, deciding on new major headings, or dropping some headings entirely.

To get started on your working outline, look at the important points you listed for your topic in Exercise 3. Ask yourself specific questions about these main points. These questions will often lead you to the headings in your working outline. Here are some of the questions Betsy Thomassen asked after completing her initial research:

1. When were contact lenses first invented, and how have they developed?
2. Are there different kinds of contact lenses and, if so, what are they like?
3. What are the latest developments regarding contact lenses?

Using these questions as a guide, Betsy then constructed this working outline to help her take notes on her sources:

BREAKTHROUGHS IN CONTACT LENSES

I. History of contact lenses
II. Kinds of contact lenses
  A. Hard lenses
  B. Soft lenses
  C. Extended-wear lenses
III. Recent developments in contact lenses

EXERCISE 5 **Preparing a Working Outline.** Write down specific questions about the important aspects of your report topic. Then construct a working outline, using the one above as a model.

Prewriting: Gathering Sources and Preparing a Working Bibliography

When you complete your working outline, you are ready to gather your sources of information. Begin by obtaining copies of the books, magazine articles, and other sources that you identified when you first checked the library (Exercise 2). You will not always be able to obtain all the information sources you listed. In addition, not every source you obtain will be suitable for your research. For example, a magazine article may prove far shorter than you expected, or it may duplicate information that you have already found elsewhere.

A **working bibliography** is a list of books and other source materials that you will consult in researching your topic.

After you have found a book or another printed source of information, skim it to decide whether it contains data you may be able to use in your report. If it does, make it part of your working bibliography by writing the following information about the source on a **bibliography card**, a three-by-five-inch index card.

FOR A BOOK

1. the author(s) (or editor, labeled *ed.*, if no author is identified)
2. the complete title (put any subtitle after a colon)
3. the publisher
4. the place of publication (for large cities, only the city is needed)
5. the edition, if one is specified in the book (use abbreviations such as *rev. ed., 2nd ed., 3rd ed., 4th ed.*, and so on)
6. the copyright date (or most recent copyright date)

FOR A SECTION OF A BOOK, include the same information plus

1. the author of the section (if different from the main author or editor)
2. the title of the section (if no title is specified, use a descriptive label such as *introduction* or *essay*)
3. the page number(s) of the section

FOR AN ARTICLE IN A MAGAZINE, NEWSPAPER, OR ENCYCLOPEDIA

1. the author(s) of the article (if identified in the source)
2. the title of the article
3. the title of the source in which the article appears
4. the source's date of publication
5. the source's volume number (not needed for newspapers)
6. the page number(s) of the article (for newspapers, include any section letters that precede page numbers)

FOR A PAMPHLET OR A BROCHURE

1. the author(s) or editor(s), if identified
2. the title
3. the company or organization that published the work
4. the location of the company or organization
5. the date of publication

Write a different number in the left corner of each bibliography card. This number system is a simple way of identifying each source later.

Here are some of the bibliography cards that Betsy prepared.

BIBLIOGRAPHY CARD FOR A BOOK

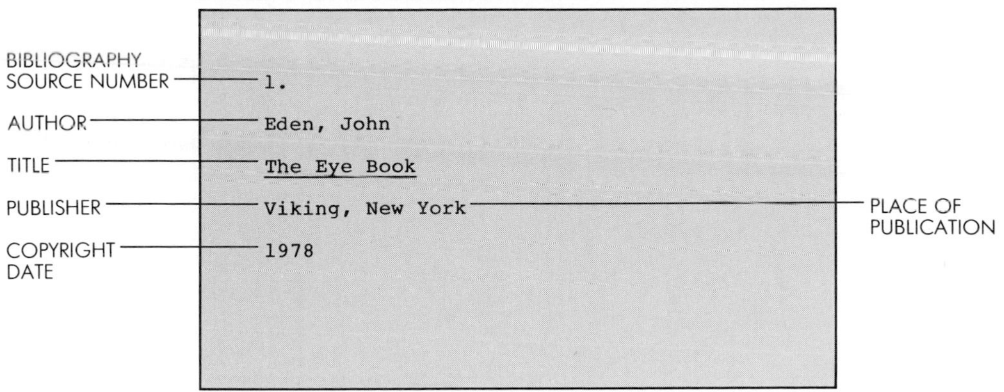

BIBLIOGRAPHY CARD FOR A BOOK WITH TWO AUTHORS (book is also a second edition)

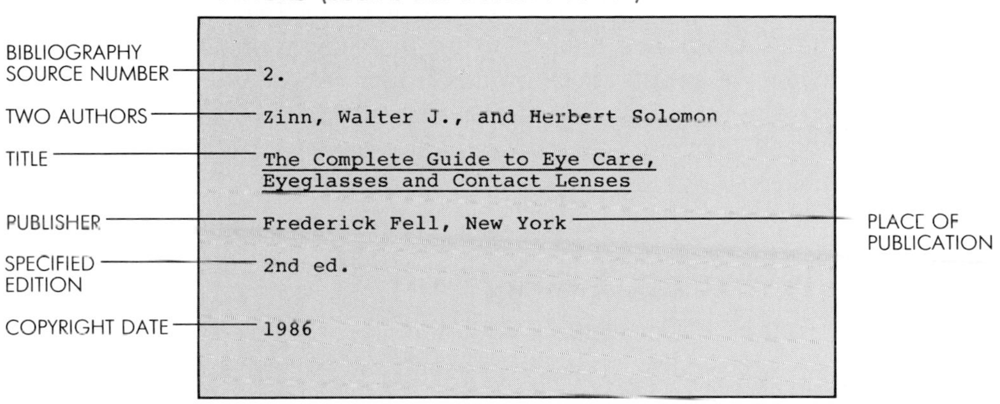

BIBLIOGRAPHY CARD FOR A SECTION OF A BOOK

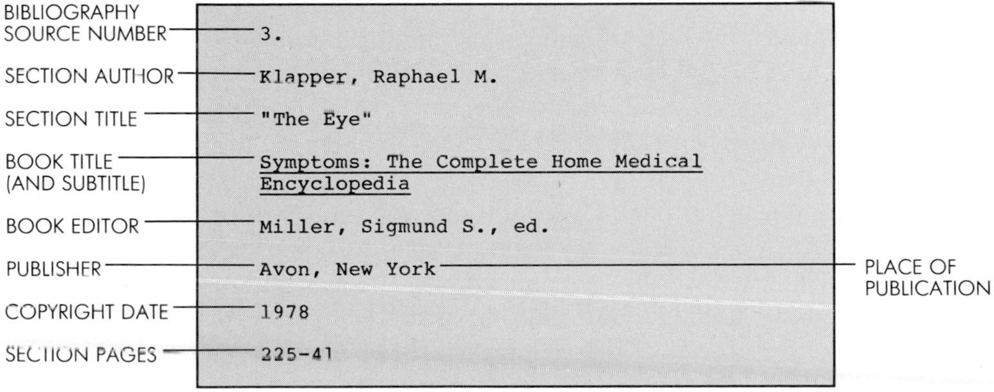

BIBLIOGRAPHY CARD FOR A MAGAZINE ARTICLE

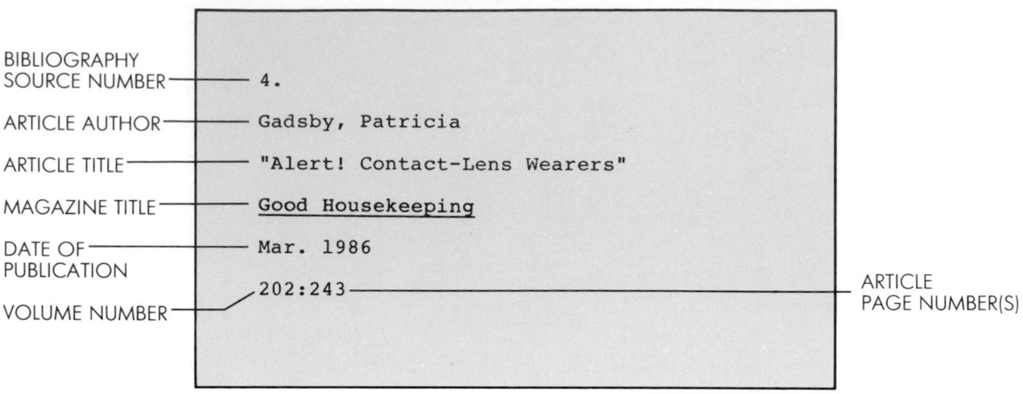

EXERCISE 6 **Gathering Sources and Preparing a Working Bibliography.** Find the sources you identified in Exercise 2, or as many of those sources as you can. Skim the sources, and then write bibliography cards for those that you plan to use. In writing your bibliography cards, follow the formats shown in this chapter. Also be sure to write bibliography cards for any encyclopedias or other sources that you consulted in Exercise 3, since those sources should also appear in your final bibliography.

Prewriting: Taking Notes

You have your working outline and your source material, and you have prepared your working bibliography. Now you can begin serious reading and taking notes. If you keep your outline in front of you as you read, you will be able to focus on the points on which you want to take notes.

As you read, do not attempt to absorb all the information your sources provide. Instead, focus only on information related to your topic. For full-length books, study the tables of contents and indexes to find pages with information that relates to the headings in your working outline. Then skim the pages looking only for the related information.

When you find information that you think will be useful, there are three ways of taking notes on that information: paraphrasing, summarizing, and writing direct quotations. You may find that different methods are useful for different purposes. Each method is covered in detail in the subsections that follow. Whichever method you use, be sure you can read and understand your notes later.

Paraphrasing

Paraphrasing is restating an author's ideas in your own words.

You should read the source several times and then write your own version of the ideas. Here is a passage from one of Betsy Thomassen's sources:

> The oldest of the contact lenses now available are hard contacts. They were originally made of glass but are now commonly made of a plastic called polymethyl methacrylate. . . . They do not bend easily and can still be used if they accidentally dry out.
>
> Soft lenses, in contrast, are made from a material that looks like thick cellophane but is mostly water. They bend and stretch, and if left in the air away from water or tears for even a short time, they become brittle and unusable.

Here is an example of a paraphrase of the preceding passage:

> Hard lenses are the oldest type. Once glass, they are now usually polymethyl methacrylate (a plastic) and are not very pliant. However, if they dry out by accident, they can still be used. Soft lenses are made of a water-based cellophane-like material and are very pliant. However, if they dry out even briefly, they break easily and cannot be used.

If you use paraphrased material in your report, you will need to give credit to the author whose ideas you are restating. Presenting someone else's words or ideas as your own is known as **plagiarism** and is illegal. (Later in this chapter you will learn the different means by which you can give credit to authors for their words or ideas.)

EXERCISE 7 **Practicing Paraphrasing.** Restate each of the following passages in your own words. If a passage contains an unfamiliar word, look up the meaning of the word in a dictionary.

1. What might be called science fiction began with *Somnium* (1634) by Johannes Kepler. Kepler was a great pioneer astronomer who first established the mathematical principles to explain the orbits of the planets. . . . As the title indicates, this story takes place in a dream, where a spirit carries Kepler to the moon and planets.

   —Lester del Rey, *The World of Science Fiction*

2. Ghana's judicial system had both a lower court and a court of appeal. But the king was more or less the supreme court of the land. There was no question as to whether he could make his decisions stick, since the king was also commander-in-chief of one of the biggest armies in the world.

   —Daniel Chu and Elliot Skinner, *A Glorious Age in Africa*

3. For the first twelve years of the Academy Awards, the final results of the balloting were released to the press prior to the ceremony to accommodate newspaper deadlines, but when one paper broke the pledge not to print the winners' names until after the ceremony, the practice of advance notice ended. With the 1940 awards came sealed envelopes and secrecy.

—Richard Schale, *Academy Awards,* 2nd ed.

4. Virtually the oldest mountain range in the world, the Ozarks reach heights of only 2250 feet after ages of weathering. Nonetheless, the eighteenth- and nineteenth-century American settlers and the Native Americans centuries before them found the terrain rough and treacherous.

—Paul J. Psychas, ed., *Let's Go: The Budget Guide to the USA, 1986*

5. **Georgette** Whether she invented it or not isn't known, but the finespun fabric georgette renders honor to Madame Georgette de la Plante, a celebrated Parisian dressmaker . . . of the late nineteenth century. The formerly trademarked sheer silk crepe is used primarily for blouses and gowns.

—Robert Hendrickson, *The Dictionary of Eponyms: Names That Became Words*

Summarizing

Summarizing is restating only the main points and important supporting details of a passage.

The following example summarizes the same passage that was paraphrased on page 255. Notice that, unlike the paraphrase, this summary includes only the main points and details.

Made of plastic, hard lenses are not as pliant as the newer, water-based soft lenses. However, unlike soft lenses, they can be reused if they dry out.

Summarizing requires a bit more thought than paraphrasing, since you must decide which points are important enough to include in your summary. However, because it requires far less writing, summarizing can save you a great deal of time. For this reason, you will probably find summarizing to be the most useful way of taking notes, particularly for a lengthy article or a long section of a book.

EXERCISE 8 **Practicing Summarizing.** Restate only the main points and most important details in each of the following passages. If a passage contains an unfamiliar word, look up the meaning of the word in a dictionary.

1. George Gershwin was almost unique among famous songwriters in that his ambition, talent, and search for ever larger forms resulted in a double career: popular songwriter and formal composer. Though well launched on a songwriting career, . . . he began experimenting with larger musical forms.

   —Alec Wilder, *American Popular Song: The Great Innovators, 1900–1950*

2. The origin of chess has been the subject of innumerable legends and fanciful histories. The earliest description of a game unmistakably chess comes from the eighth century, not from an Egyptian papyrus of 4000 B.C., as was once asserted. There is little doubt, however, that chess developed from simpler board games of remote times. It probably developed in India, whence it spread to Persia and Arabia and entered Europe through Spain and Italy. The present form of the game as now played in most of the world was reached about four hundred years ago. From India the game also spread eastward and in Japan developed a form markedly different from the Western game.

   —Albert H. Morehead and Geoffrey Mott-Smith, eds., *Hoyle's Rules of Games,* 2nd rev. ed.

3. The alligator, decreed rare and endangered only nineteen years ago, has come back with a vengeance across the South, from the brackish coastal lowlands of the Carolinas to the swamps of southeast Texas. . . . The problem is, the number of people in the region has also been growing, especially in the coastal areas favored by alligators. Collisions are inevitable.

   —William E. Schmidt, "Once-Rare Alligators Lumber Across Dixie"

4. The fur trade was significantly different from the Santa Fe trade. Fur traders dealt in one commodity—pelts—with beaver pelts the most prized. . . . While some Santa Fe traders dealt in pelts, especially beaver, most concentrated on general merchandise. They bought and sold goods and carried on their business between two principal areas, Missouri and New Mexico. The fur traders, however, were suppliers, and they roamed the length and width of the American West seeking beaver wherever they could find them.

   —David Dary, *Entrepreneurs of the Old West*

5. Higher. Faster. Scarier. Those are the bywords of America's brand new generation of gut-wrenching amusement park rides. . . . Today's breed of hi-tech, exotic scream machines are taking the old-fashioned roller coaster to new heights. Equipped with computerized fail-safe systems, they feature sheer drops, dizzying loops, and convolutions that would give a contortionist cramps.

   —Steve Birnbaum, "Beyond Rollercoasters"

Direct Quotations

A **direct quotation** presents the exact words from a source.

In examining your sources, you may occasionally come across a particularly relevant or powerful phrase, sentence, or passage that you may want to quote in your report. If so, copy it carefully into your notes, and enclose it within quotation marks. Remember that if you use a quotation in your report, you will need to give credit to the author; otherwise, you will be guilty of plagiarism.

Preparing Note Cards

Whether your note consists of a paraphrase, a summary, or a direct quotation, you need some way of recording it. Many people find that large (four-by-six-inch) index cards are convenient for taking notes, organizing them, and rearranging them. In the upper left corner of the **note card**, write the number that you assigned to the source of the note when you prepared your working bibliography. That number will quickly refer you to the information you listed on your bibliography card for the source. To the right of this bibliography source number, write a heading that identifies the information in your note. This will usually be one of the headings from your working outline. In the upper right corner of each card, write a number to identify the note card. In the center of the card, write the note itself—your paraphrase, your summary, or the direct quotation. Finally, at the bottom of the note card, briefly restate the source of the note, and write the number of the page on which the information appeared.

Here is an example of one of Betsy Thomassen's note cards for her report on contact lenses. This particular note card is for a direct quotation, as indicated by the quotation marks; however, the same format would be used for a paraphrase or a summary.

SAMPLE NOTE CARD

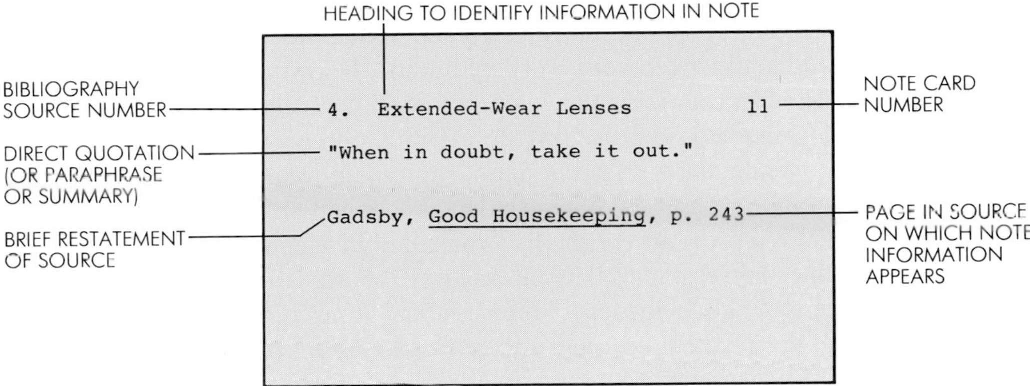

EXERCISE 9 **Taking Notes.** From the sources you listed in your working bibliography in Exercise 6, take notes on the information that you think will be useful in writing your report. Use four-by-six-inch note cards, and model your notes on Betsy Thomassen's note card shown above. Paraphrase or summarize most of the information; however, when you come across a passage that you may want to quote in your report, record it exactly.

Prewriting: Preparing a Formal Outline

A **formal outline** is the final outline that will guide you in writing your first draft.

As you read and take notes, you will probably find that your working outline will need some changes. The revised outline that you construct will be your formal outline. To prepare your formal outline, read over your note cards carefully and group them in stacks, one stack for each important point about your topic. If some note cards do not seem relevant, set them aside. Then compare your stacks of note cards with your working outline by asking yourself the following questions:

1. How do the headings of the piles of note cards correspond to the headings in my working outline? What other main headings should be added to the outline? Have I discovered any information that would change the controlling idea?
2. What other information do I need in order to cover all the main headings in my working outline? Where can I find the information? Should I consider eliminating headings?
3. What logical subdivisions can I introduce for the main headings?
4. What is the best order for presenting my ideas?

Using these questions as a guide, make the appropriate changes in and additions to your working outline. Draw up a formal outline that presents your ideas in a logical order. If you need help, see Chapter 11 for instructions on setting up a formal outline.

While doing research, Betsy Thomassen found information about a number of aspects of contact lenses that had not been discussed in the encyclopedia article she had consulted in preparing her working outline. For example, Betsy learned of the availability of bifocal contact lenses. She decided to add the heading "Kinds of Bifocal Lenses," as well as several other headings and subheadings, to her formal outline, which is shown here:

BREAKTHROUGHS IN CONTACT LENSES

I. Definition and history of contact lenses
II. Kinds of lenses
    A. Hard Lenses
        1. Advantages
        2. Disadvantages
    B. Soft lenses
        1. Advantages
        2. Disadvantages
III. Kinds of bifocal lenses
    A. Nonrotational lenses
    B. Rotational lenses
IV. Recent developments in contact lenses
    A. Extended-wear lenses
        1. Benefits
        2. Problems
    B. Rigid gas-permeable lenses

EXERCISE 10 **Writing a Formal Outline.** Using your stacks of note cards, your working outline, and the questions at the top of this page, construct a formal outline for your research report. Follow the outline style shown above.

Writing the First Draft

Set aside two to three uninterrupted hours to write the first draft of your research report. It will be easier for you to write your first draft if you first arrange your note cards so that they follow the order of the headings in your formal outline. Read over your note cards once again before writing each section of your paper, and refer to them as needed when you write. Every time you include information from a note card, also include the number of the note card right after the information. By doing so, you will be able to credit the source of the information quickly later.

Write your first draft on every other line so that you will later have plenty of room to make revisions and insertions.

As you write your first draft, devote most of your time and effort to putting your ideas on paper in a logical sequence. Do not spend a great deal of time choosing exact words or ideal sentences to express your ideas. You can take care of such matters when you revise. For the moment, concentrate on moving from one point of your formal outline to the next, and remember to link the sections of the report with effective transitions.

Most important of all, write as much of the first draft as possible using your own words and ideas. View each section of your report as a whole before you begin to write it; decide exactly what you want each section to tell your audience. Use quotations and other examples from your sources as support for your own ideas.

Your research report will need both an **introduction** and a **conclusion,** although neither of these needs to be listed on your formal outline. Your introduction should identify your topic and explain your controlling idea (see Exercise 4). The introduction should also capture the interest of your audience. Your concluding paragraph should restate and tie together the main ideas of your report. The conclusion should convince the reader that your research was worthwhile.

Make no attempt to revise your first draft immediately. Put it aside for several hours or an entire day, and then come back to it. By that time you should be able to evaluate your first writing attempts more objectively.

EXERCISE 11 **Writing the First Draft.** Write the first draft of your report on the topic you have been researching. Follow your formal outline, and keep in mind the purpose, audience, and controlling idea that you identified in Exercise 4. Be sure to include an introduction and a conclusion.

Revising the First Draft

When you return to your first draft after setting it aside for a while, you will be able to look at it with a fresh and critical eye. To decide what revisions you need to make, read through the draft carefully and objectively. Use the following questions to guide your thinking.

1. How effective is my introduction? Does it clearly state my topic and controlling idea?
2. Does my report follow my outline? Did I leave anything out?
3. Are my ideas clearly and logically presented? Do I need better transitions between ideas?
4. How can I make my sentences clearer and easier to understand? Have I used precise terms and clear definitions?
5. What details and examples have I included to support general statements? Are they effective? Should I add other examples?
6. Have I kept my audience in mind throughout? Where would a different approach, such as more persuasion or more narration, help me in reaching my audience?
7. How can I improve my language or vary sentence structures to make reading my report more interesting?
8. Is my purpose clear? Are there sections that stray from the purpose and need to be rewritten or deleted?
9. Is my conclusion effective? Does it sum up the main points of my report?
10. Is all my information accurate? Is my report free from errors in spelling, punctuation, capitalization, grammar, and usage?

EXERCISE 12 **Revising the First Draft.** After setting aside your report for a few hours or overnight, revise it with a fresh eye. Use the preceding list of questions to guide you.

Crediting Sources: Footnotes or Endnotes and a Bibliography

To avoid plagiarism, your report must give credit to any ideas or direct quotations borrowed from other sources. In addition, providing the sources of your information helps your reader to evaluate its validity. For example, suppose you are writing a report about cancer research and include statistics from an American Cancer Society publication. When your readers see the source of those statistics, they will recognize that your data comes from a respected authority on cancer research.

One method of crediting sources in your report is to use footnotes or endnotes and a bibliography.

A **footnote** is a note at the bottom of a page. It gives additional information, including source data, about a statement that occurs on that page.

Footnotes are numbered sequentially throughout a report—that is, the first footnote is 1, the next is 2, and so on. Within the body of a report, a raised footnote number called a **superscript** appears at the end of a sentence containing a quotation or a borrowed idea. The same raised number appears at the beginning of the footnote that gives credit to the source of the quotation or idea.

The following example shows part of a report containing two footnotes.

Soft contact lenses are made of a pliable, water-absorbing plastic. Because they are flexible and conform to the contours of the eye, they can be worn for as long as eighteen hours.[1] However, "because the soft lens is malleable, a slight bending tends to occur every time you blink. This results in waves in the surface of the soft lens that create an optical distortion that does not occur with hard lenses."[2]

[1]Wendy Murphy, "Remedies for Eye Complaints," Touch, Taste, Smell, Sight and Hearing (Alexandria, VA: Time-Life Books, 1982) 80.

[2]John Eden, The Eye Book (New York: Viking, 1978) 55-56.

If you have written and organized your note cards and bibliography cards carefully, the process of providing footnotes for your report will not be difficult. When you wrote the first draft, you included a note card number after each quotation or borrowed idea. Now you will replace the note card numbers with superscripts in numerical order. For each superscript number that you insert, you will write a footnote with the same number. That footnote will give the page number for the quotation or borrowed idea, which you get from your note card. The footnote will also include other source information, which you get from your bibliography card for the source.

The Style Chart for Footnotes and Endnotes, which follows, shows you the specific information that should be included in footnotes for different kinds of sources. It also shows you proper punctuation for footnotes. Note that when a footnote credits the same source for a second time—like footnote 2 on the Style Chart—you need to provide only the author's last name and the page number (since readers can consult the earlier footnote for the rest of the information). However, if two works by the same author are credited in the footnotes, a repeated footnote for one of the works—like footnote 3 on the Style Chart—must include a short form of the title.

STYLE CHART FOR FOOTNOTES AND ENDNOTES

FOR A BOOK *(use a colon before a subtitle)*

[1]Barry Weissman, A Contact Lens Primer: A Manual (Philadelphia: Lea & Febiger, 1984) 57.

TO CREDIT THE SAME WORK AGAIN

When no other works by author appear in footnotes or endnotes, use only author's last name and page number(s):

[2]Weissman 15.

When other works by author appear, include short form of title:

[3]Weissman, Contact Lens Primer 15.

FOR A BOOK WITH TWO AUTHORS; FOR A SPECIFIED EDITION

[4]Walter J. Zinn and Herbert Solomon, The Complete Guide to Eye Care, Eyeglasses and Contact Lenses, 2nd ed. (New York: Frederick Fell, 1986) 95–96.

FOR A BOOK WITH AN EDITOR AND NO SPECIFIED AUTHOR

[5]Gordon Gebert, ed., Health-Care (Elmsford, NY: Pergamon, 1981) 91.

FOR A SECTION BY AN AUTHOR IN A BOOK WITH AN EDITOR

[6]Raphael M. Klapper, "The Eye," Symptoms: The Complete Home Medical Encyclopedia, ed. Sigmund S. Miller (New York: Avon, 1978) 226.

FOR A MAGAZINE ARTICLE

[7]Patricia Gadsby, "Alert! Contact-Lens Wearers," Good Housekeeping Mar. 1986: 243.

FOR A NEWSPAPER ARTICLE

[8]Lisa Belkin, "Buying Contact Lenses: New World of Choices," New York Times 5 Jan. 1985: A44.

FOR AN UNSIGNED ARTICLE

[9]"Eye Infections Linked to Long-Wear Lenses," New York Times 9 Nov. 1985: A34.

FOR A PAMPHLET WITH NO SPECIFIED AUTHOR

[10]"Live the Soft Life" (Woodbury, NY: American Hydron, 1985) 2.

FOR AN ENCYCLOPEDIA ARTICLE

[11]John R. McWilliams, "Contact Lens," World Book Encyclopedia, 1984 ed.: 800.

Endnotes are just like footnotes, except that they are grouped together at the end of a report under the heading "Notes" instead of being placed at the bottom of each page.

Endnotes are arranged in numerical order, with numbers that again correspond to the superscripts in the body of the report. They use the same style as footnotes, except that they are double-spaced when you type them. (If you wish to see an example of endnotes occurring in a "Notes" section at the end of a report, examine the final draft of Betsy Thomassen's report on contact lenses, which starts on page 273.

EXERCISE 13 **Practicing Footnote or Endnote Style.** Write footnotes based on the information provided in each numbered item. Use the number of the item as the number of the footnote.

1. You are crediting information that appeared on page 201 of the book *City Women,* subtitled *Works, Jobs, Occupations, Careers,* by Helena Z. Lopata, published in New York in 1984 by Praeger.
2. You are crediting information from the magazine article "Here Comes Oprah" by Joan Barthel, which appeared on page 40 of the August 1986 edition of *Ms.*
3. You are crediting a quotation from "The New Woman and the Old" by Anne Warner. The selection appeared on pages 115–28 of *The Experience of the American Woman,* edited by Barbara H. Solomon and published in New York in 1978 by New American Library. The quotation appeared on page 128.
4. You are crediting information that appeared on page 26 of the second edition of *The Assertive Woman* by Stanlee Phelps and Nancy Austin, published in San Luis Obispo, CA, in 1985 by Impact.
5. You are crediting for a second time the same source you credited in item 1, this time for information on page 68. You have also credited *another* book by Helena Z. Lopata in your footnotes.

Whether you use footnotes or endnotes, you must also include a bibliography at the end of your report.

A **bibliography** is an alphabetical list of all the sources consulted in preparing a report.

To prepare your bibliography, you need only your bibliography cards. The Style Chart for Bibliography Entries, which begins on this page, shows the specific information that should be included in bibliography entries for different kinds of sources. It also shows proper punctuation and indentation for bibliography entries. Bibliography entries are arranged alphabetically by the first word to appear in each entry, excluding *a, an,* or *the.*

The first word to appear in each bibliography entry is usually an author's or editor's last name. However, if no author or editor is identified, the first word will be part of a title. If more than one work by the same author is listed, first group all entries for that author alphabetically by the author's last name; then, within the grouping, alphabetize the entries by the first words of titles, excluding *a, an,* or *the.* Instead of repeating the author's name, use a long dash, as in the second example in the Style Chart below.

STYLE CHART FOR BIBLIOGRAPHY ENTRIES

FOR A BOOK *(use a colon before a subtitle)*

Weissman, Barry. A Contact Lens Primer: A Manual. Philadelphia: Lea & Febiger, 1984.

FOR TWO BOOKS BY THE SAME AUTHOR

Ruben, Montagu. Soft Contact Lenses. New York: John Wiley, 1978.

————. Understanding Contact Lenses. Philadelphia: International Ideas, 1976.

FOR A BOOK WITH TWO AUTHORS; FOR A SPECIFIED EDITION

Zinn, Walter J., and Herbert Solomon. The Complete Guide to Eye Care, Eyeglasses and Contact Lenses. 2nd ed. New York: Frederick Fell, 1986.

FOR A BOOK WITH AN EDITOR AND NO SPECIFIED AUTHOR

Gebert, Gordon, ed. Health-Care. Elmsford, NY: Pergamon, 1981.

FOR A SECTION BY AN AUTHOR IN A BOOK WITH AN EDITOR

Klapper, Raphael M. "The Eye." Symptoms: The Complete Home Medical Encyclopedia. Ed. Sigmund S. Miller. New York: Avon, 1978. 225–41.

FOR A MAGAZINE ARTICLE

Gadsby, Patricia. "Alert! Contact-Lens Wearers." Good Housekeeping Mar. 1986: 243.

FOR A NEWSPAPER ARTICLE

Belkin, Lisa. "Buying Contact Lenses: New World of Choices." New York Times 5 Jan. 1985: A44.

FOR AN UNSIGNED ARTICLE

"Eye Infections Linked to Long-Wear Lenses." New York Times 9 Nov. 1985: A34.

FOR A PAMPHLET WITH NO SPECIFIED AUTHOR

"Live the Soft Life." Woodbury, NY: American Hydron, 1985.

FOR AN ENCYCLOPEDIA ARTICLE

McWilliams, John R. "Contact Lens." World Book Encyclopedia. 1984 ed.

EXERCISE 14 **Practicing Bibliography Style.** Write a bibliography that lists the sources in items 1–4 of Exercise 13 plus the following source: the book *Occupation: Housewife* by Helena Z. Lopata, published in Westport, CT, in 1980 by Greenwood.

Crediting Sources: Parenthetical Documentation

Rather than using footnotes or endnotes, many students are using parenthetical documentation to credit specific quotations and borrowed ideas within the body of their reports.

Parenthetical documentation provides brief source information in parentheses within the body of a report.

For more complete source information, readers consult the alphabetized **bibliography** at the back of the report. The bibliography uses exactly the same style as a bibliography that accompanies footnotes or endnotes; however, if all the works it lists have parenthetical documentation in the report, the bibliography is sometimes called "Works Cited."

Parenthetical documentation may be as brief as possible, as long as it does two things: (1) It must clearly identify only one source listed in the bibliography, and (2) it must indicate from what page or pages of that source the borrowed idea or quotation comes. You should become familiar with the conventions in the subsections that follow.

FOR AN AUTHOR LISTED ONLY ONCE IN THE BIBLIOGRAPHY

Suppose a report includes an idea borrowed from page 61 of *The Eye Book* by John Eden, listed in the bibliography as follows:

> Eden, John. The Eye Book. New York: Viking, 1978.

If no other works by John Eden are listed in the bibliography, the parenthetical documentation needs only the author's last name and the page number. In the body of the report, it would look like this:

> Bifocal contact lenses do not correct vision as well as other contact lenses do (Eden 61).

If the sentence containing the borrowed idea makes the author's name clear, the parenthetical documentation needs only the page number.

> John Eden reports that bifocal contact lenses do not correct vision as well as other contact lenses do (61).

Parenthetical documentation uses the same style for any author listed just once in the bibliography—whether the author wrote a book, a magazine article, a newspaper article, an encyclopedia article, or a section of a book. For example, suppose a report borrows an idea from pages 110–11 of a magazine article listed in the bibliography as:

> Stuller, Jay. "What's New in Contact Lenses?" Reader's Digest July 1985: 109–12.

If no other works by Jay Stuller appear in the bibliography, the parenthetical documentation would again require only the author's name and the pages from which the idea was borrowed (Stuller 110–11). In the body of the report, it would look like this:

> Gas-permeable contact lenses provide the same crisp vision as regular hard lenses (Stuller 110–11).

Again, if the wording in the body of the report makes the author's name clear, the parenthetical documentation needs only the page numbers:

> Jay Stuller reports that gas-permeable contact lenses provide the same crisp vision as regular hard lenses (110–11).

FOR A WORK WITH TWO AUTHORS

If a work has two authors, both authors' names should be used in the parenthetical documentation. For example, suppose a report borrows an idea from page 99 of a work listed in the bibliography as follows:

> Zinn, Walter J., and Herbert Solomon. The Complete Guide to Eye Care, Eyeglasses and Contact Lenses. 2nd ed. New York: Frederick Fell, 1986.

If no other works by Zinn and Solomon are listed in the bibliography, the parenthetical documentation might look like this:

> A soft contact lens absorbs from 20 to 80 percent of the eye's tears (Zinn and Solomon 99).

or it might look like this:

> According to Zinn and Solomon, a soft contact lens absorbs from 20 to 80 percent of the eye's tears (99).

FOR A WORK WITH NO SPECIFIED AUTHOR

If a work has an editor but no specified author, use the editor's last name (without the *ed.* abbreviation) in the parenthetical documentation. If a work has no specified author or editor, use a short form of the title in the parenthetical documentation. For example, suppose a report borrows an idea from the unsigned newspaper article listed in the bibliography as:

> "Eye Infections Linked to Long-Wear Lenses." New York Times 9 Nov. 1985: A34.

The parenthetical documentation might look like this:

> Because of the risk of eye infections, the University of Minnesota is no longer prescribing extended-wear contact lenses for cosmetic purposes ("Eye Infections" A34).

If the wording in the body of the report makes the article's title clear, then you need to use only the page number in the parenthetical documentation:

> The New York Times article "Eye Infections Linked to Long-Wear Lenses" reported that the University of Minnesota is no longer prescribing extended-wear contact lenses for cosmetic purposes (A34).

FOR AN AUTHOR LISTED MORE THAN ONCE IN THE BIBLIOGRAPHY

If a report's bibliography lists two or more works by the same author, the parenthetical documentation must include a short form of the work's title. Otherwise, readers would not know to which of the author's works the parenthetical documentation refers. For example, suppose *The Eye Book* is not the only work by John Eden listed in the bibliography. To credit page 61 of *The Eye Book,* the parenthetical documentation has to include a short form of the work's title (separated from the author's name with a comma):

> Bifocal contect lenses do not correct vision as well as other contact lenses do (Eden, Eye Book 61).

If the wording in the body of the report makes the author's name clear, the parenthetical documentation requires only the title and the page:

> John Eden reports that bifocal contact lenses do not correct vision as well as other contact lenses do (Eye Book 61).

If the wording in the body of the report makes both the author's name and the title clear, the parenthetical documentation requires only the page:

> In The Eye Book, John Eden reports that bifocal contact lenses do not correct vision as well as other contact lenses do (61).

PLACEMENT OF PARENTHETICAL DOCUMENTATION

When you use parenthetical documentation, you have to maintain a consistent style in placing the parenthetical information. Place the parenthetical documentation where a pause would naturally occur, preferably at the end of the sentence. Follow these guidelines:

1. Place the parentheses before the punctuation mark that concludes the sentence (or clause or phrase) that contains the material you are crediting.

   > Gas-permeable contact lenses provide the same crisp vision as regular hard lenses (Stuller 110–11).
   >
   > Gas-permeable contact lenses provide the same crisp vision as regular hard lenses (Stuller 110–11), and the gas-permeable lenses are more comfortable.

2. If the credited material is a direct quotation in quotation marks, close the quotation *before* the parenthetical documentation, and put the punctuation mark that concludes the sentence *after* the parenthetical documentation.

   > Good advice regarding an extended-wear contact lens is "when in doubt, take it out" (Gadsby 243).

EXERCISE 15 **Practicing Parenthetical Documentation.** Rewrite the following report passages to include parenthetical documentation. Obtain the information for your parenthetical documentation from the source data provided below each passage.

1. About fifty miles from Glen Canyon Dam in Utah is Rainbow Natural Bridge, the world's largest natural bridge.
   source: Information is from page 106 of *Let's Go: The Budget Guide to the USA, 1986,* edited by Paul J. Psychas, published in New York in 1986 by St. Martin's. No other work by Psychas is listed in your bibliography.

2. Smaller microwaves have now become available. "Low price and small size have turned the microwave oven into a commonplace convenience."
   source: Quotation is from page 708 of the article "Compact Microwave Ovens: How Do You Find One That Fits Your Kitchen and Your Life?" The article appeared in the November 1986 edition of *Consumer Reports*. The article had no specified author.
3. Jean Johnson reports that most writers find parenthetical documentation easier to use than footnotes or endnotes.
   source: Information is from page 213 of *The Bedford Guide to the Research Process* by Jean Johnson, published in New York in 1987 by St. Martin's. No other work by Johnson appears in your bibliography.
4. Adventurous fur traders traveled all over the old West.
   source: Information *in the first clause* is from pages 43–44 of *Entrepreneurs of the Old West* by David Dary, published in New York in 1986 by Alfred A. Knopf. One other book by Dary appears in your bibliography.

EXERCISE 16 **Crediting Sources.** Now that you have learned how to credit sources, go back to the report you have been preparing and provide credits where necessary. The note card numbers that you included after each borrowed idea or quotation in your report will remind you where you need to cite a specific source. The note card numbers will also refer you to the note cards and bibliography cards that contain the source information you need to include in your credits. After you provide each credit, delete the number from your report.

Also write a bibliography that lists all the works you consulted in preparing your report. Use the style that you learned for bibliography entries, and remember to list the entries in alphabetical order.

Publishing the Final Draft

To prepare the final draft of your report for publication, you may use a word processor, a typewriter, or a pen. If your teacher has no specific instructions on the following points, use these guidelines:

1. The **title page** is the first page of your report. It should contain the title, your name, your teacher's name, the name or number of the course, and the date. The report title and your name should be centered in the middle of the page. The other information should be listed in the lower right corner of the page.

2. The report **body** should have one-inch margins all around. If you type the report, double space everything except set-off quotations and footnotes. Indent the beginning of each paragraph five spaces.
3. **Quotations** of under four lines should usually be placed within quotation marks and run into the body of your report. For a longer quotation, instead of using quotation marks, set off the quotation from the body of the report with one space above and below it and *two*-inch margins on the left and right.
4. **Footnotes** should be single-spaced. Indent the first line of each footnote, and follow the Style Chart on pages 264–265. Remember to leave space for footnotes when you first type your report.
5. If you are using **parenthetical documentation** instead of footnotes or endnotes, follow the guidelines on page 270.
6. Put **endnotes** on a separate page after the body of the report, under the centered heading "Notes." Endnotes follow the same style as footnotes, except that they are double-spaced.
7. List your **bibliography** entries on the last page of your report under the centered heading "Bibliography." Begin each entry at the left margin; when an entry runs longer than on line, indent the additional line or lines. Follow the Style Chart for Bibliography Entries on pages 266–267, and alphabetize the entries.
8. **Number** each page of your report except the title page. Place an Arabic number (1, 2, 3, and so on) in the upper right corner of each page; do *not* precede the number with a *p*. However, it is a good idea to precede each page number with your last name, in case a page of your report goes astray.
9. **Proofread** your final draft at least twice for errors in typing, spelling, capitalization, grammar, punctuation, and style. Make necessary corrections neatly.

EXERCISE 17 **Publishing the Final Draft.** Prepare the final draft of the thousand-word report on which you have been working. Use the method of crediting sources that you used in Exercise 16, and follow Betsy Thomassen's model on pages 273–278 and the guidelines above (unless your teacher instructs you to follow another style).

The following model report is the final draft of Betsy Thomassen's report on contact lenses, which you have been tracking throughout this chapter. Notice the lettered annotations, which point out some of the important features of the report. Notice, too, that Betsy Thomassen chose to use endnotes to credit sources of specific information.

TITLE PAGE

A

B Breakthroughs in Contact Lenses

C Betsy Thomassen

English
D Mrs. Comba
May 26, 19--

Thomassen 2

E Human beings are always trying to better themselves. Through science, they constantly work to find causes and cures for defects in the human body. One of the more recent and fascinating developments in medical technology is the contact lens, a thin shell of glass or plastic that, unlike eyeglasses, is placed directly over the cornea, the transparent front part of the eye. Though many people wear contact lenses for cosmetic reasons, contact lenses are also used to treat eye ailments that eyeglasses cannot correct. In addition, unlike eyeglasses, contact lenses do not limit peripheral vision, the ability to
F view objects just outside the line of direct sight.[1] This is one reason why people who switch from eyeglasses to contact lenses feel they can see better.

Real development of the contact lens began in 1888, when scientists in Switzerland and France started making glass contact lenses.[2] In the 1940s the development of a transparent plastic and a molding technique allowed production of contact lenses in quantity.[3] Today an estimated 18 million people wear contact lenses, with that figure expected to double[4] in the next five years.

NOTES ABOUT THE SAMPLE REPORT

A The title page is not given a page number.

B The title is centered but not underlined or put in quotation marks.

C The author's name—your name—is also centered.

D The course name, teacher's name, and date of submission are listed in the lower right corner.

E The first paragraph is an introduction that states the topic and focus of the paper. Betsy includes a definition of her topic, contact lenses.

F Betsy uses superscript numbers and endnotes to credit sources.

Many kinds of contact lenses are on the market, and many more are still in development. The two kinds used most frequently are hard contact lenses and soft contact lenses.

G

Hard lenses, which have been worn since the 1950s, are made of clear, hard plastic. Both nearsighted and farsighted persons can wear hard lenses because they provide good all-around clarity. Even those with astigmatism, an irregularity in the shape of the cornea, can wear hard contact lenses because the hard surface of the lens compensates for the condition. Hard lenses are more durable and less expensive than soft contact lenses.

There are, however, certain disadvantages to hard contact lenses. They can be a little difficult to center on the eye and occasionally slip off the iris onto the white of the eye. They can also block the flow of oxygen to the eye and thereby cause swelling and eye irritation. Furthermore, because they are rigid, they tends to be less comfortable than soft contact lenses. In addition, they are harder to adjust to.

It takes anywhere from eleven days to four weeks for most wearers to adjust to hard contact lenses. If people should stop wearing the hard contacts for several days, they must once again gradually build up tolerance to the lenses.

Soft contact lenses, on the other hand, are much easier to get used to. Usually a person wearing soft contacts needs only about a week to build tolerance to maximum daily wear. Soft contacts are made of pliable, water-absorbing plastic. Because they are flexible and conform easily to the contours of the eye, they are more comfortable than hard lenses and can be worn for as long as eighteen hours.[5] Soft lenses are also very unlikely to pop off the eye, and so they are good for people who engage in sports.

One serious drawback to soft lenses is that they correct fewer vision problems than hard lenses do.

H

> Because the soft lens is malleable, a slight bending tends to occur every time you blink. This results in waves in the surface of the soft lens that can create an optical distortion that does not occur with hard lenses, which retain their shape at all times.[6]

Persons with astigmatism are among those who generally cannot wear soft contacts.

Soft contact lenses are also about twice as expensive as hard contact lenses. In addition, they take longer to clean

Thomassen 3

each day, and the chemicals that many soft-contact-lens wearers use to clean their lenses tend to cost more than the chemicals used in cleaning hard lenses.

Besides developing both hard and soft contact lenses, scientists have made breakthroughs with bifocal contact lenses. Benjamin Franklin made a brilliant contribution to the world of optics when, in 1784, he invented bifocal eyeglasses. These double spectacles contain two powers of lenses in the same pair of eyeglasses, enabling wearers to see at a distance and close up without changing glasses. There are two kinds of bifocal contact lenses: nonrotational and rotational contacts.

Normally, as the eye blinks, the contact lens rotates upon the cornea. A nonrotational contact lens, however, does not rotate because it is weighted to keep it in place. Nonrotational contacts have the distance lens power on the upper half, and the near lens power on the lower half, as in bifocal spectacles.

On the other hand, a rotational lens is made with the distance lens power in the center and the near lens power completely surrounding it. As the eye blinks and the lens rotates, the near prescription is always on the bottom, enabling the wearer to read with ease.[7]

An even newer kind of bifocal lens called rotational bifocal aspheric eliminates the "jump" that occurs when shifting from distance power to near power in regular bifocal contacts. This new lens is specially ground so that the switch is gradual, from central (distance) power to the outer (near) power.[8]

I Dr. John Eden, an ophthalmologist in New York City, says that in his experience bifocal contacts "do not work terribly well."[9] Dr. Eden has a unique solution: He fits one eye with a lens for seeing close up and fits the other eye with a lens for seeing far away. Dr. Eden says that this system "allows one eye

NOTES ABOUT THE SAMPLE REPORT

G Notice that Betsy's report closely follows her formal outline. After defining contact lenses and briefly discussing their history, she moves into a discussion of their advantages and disadvantages.

H A quotation of more than three lines is set off from the body of the report.

I Quotation marks are used for short quotations run into the body of the report.

to see well at the distance but not sharply in the distance."[10] The brain uses both images to create a clear view, and the wearer can see clearly close up and far away.

In 1981 wearing contact lenses became even easier with the increased availability of extended-wear soft lenses, which can be kept in the eyes for several weeks at a time -- even during sleep.[11] For people who have difficulty in inserting or removing contact lenses due to motor difficulties or other medical complications, these lenses offer a distinct advantage over other contact lenses, which must be removed and cleaned daily.

However, recently some eye doctors have reported severe vision impairment--even blindness--caused by bacterial eye infections in a few patients who use extended-wear lenses. It seems that because extended-wear lenses are not removed during sleeping hours, they are more likely to permit the growth of harmful bacteria in the eye.[12] Though cases of blindness are rare, some doctors have stopped prescribing extended-wear lenses for cosmetic purposes only.[13] Doctors also advise patients to follow carefully guidelines for cleaning all contact lenses and to remove lenses immediately if they experience any itching, swelling, or pain. A slogan often repeated is "when in doubt, take it out."[14]

One of the most promising recent developments in contact lenses is the rigid gas-permeable lens. This lens is actually a type of hard lens, but it is made of silicone or other gas-permeable plastics that allow more oxygen to reach the eye. The flow of oxygen cuts down on the swelling and irritation often associated with hard-lens wear, while the rigidity of the lenses results in better visual accuracy than soft lenses usually provide.[15]

J In the past thirty years contact lenses have developed from a revolutionary new optical aid to one that is increasingly commonplace. New kinds of lenses are constantly being researched and developed. Perhaps the day will come when contact lenses are worn by everyone who needs vision corrections and eyeglasses become curiosities and antiques.

NOTES ABOUT THE SAMPLE REPORT

J The final paragraph is a conclusion that sums up the report's main points.

Thomassen 5

Notes

[1]Robert J. Morrison, *The Contact Lens Book* (Cornwall-on-Hudson, NY: HRL, 1976) 4.

[2]Wendy Murphy, "Remedies for Eye Complaints," *Touch, Taste, Smell, Sight and Hearing* (Alexandria, VA: Time-Life Books, 1982) 80.

[3]Walter J. Zinn and Herbert Solomon, *The Complete Guide to Eye Care, Eyeglasses and Contact Lenses*, 2nd ed. (New York: Frederick Fell, 1986) 96.

[4]Lisa Belkin, "Buying Contact Lenses: New World of Choices, " *New York Times* 5 Jan. 1985: A 44.

[5]Murphy 80.

[6]John Eden, *The Eye Book* (New York: Viking, 1978) 55-56.

[7]Nadine Brozan, "Bifocal Contact Lenses," *New York Times* 22 Mar. 1986: A52.

[8]Brozan A 52.

[9]Eden 61.

[10]Eden 61.

[11]John R. McWilliams, "Contact Lens," *World Book Encyclopedia*, 1984 ed.: 800.

[12]Patricia Gadsby, "Alert! Contact-Lens Wearers," *Good Housekeeping* Mar. 1986: 243.

[13]"Eye Infections Linked to Long-Wear Lenses," *New York Times* 9 Nov. 1985: A34.

[14]Gadsby 243.

[15]Jay Stuller, "What's New in Contact Lenses?" *Reader's Digest* July 1985: 111.

Thomassen 6

Bibliography

Belkin, Lisa, "Buying Contact Lenses: New World of Choices." New York Times 5 Jan. 1985: A44.

Brozan, Nadine. "Bifocal Contact Lenses." New York Times 22 Mar. 1986: A52.

Eden, John. The Eye Book. New York: Viking, 1978.

"Eye Infections Linked to Long-Wear Lenses." New York Times 9 Nov. 1985: A34.

Gadsby, Patricia. "Alert! Contact-Lens Wearers." Good Housekeeping Mar. 1986: 243.

Klapper, Raphael M. "The Eye." Symptoms: The Complete Home Medical Encyclopedia. Ed. Sigmund S. Miller, New York: Avon, 1978. 225-41.

"Live the Soft Life." Woodbury, NY: American Hydron, 1985.

McWilliams, John R. "Contact Lens." World Book Encyclopedia. 1984 ed.

Morrison, Robert J. The Contact Lens Book. Cornwall-on-Hudson, NY: HRL, 1976.

Murphy, Wendy. "Remedies for Eye Complaints." Touch, Taste, Smell, Sight and Hearing. Alexandria, VA: Time-Life Books, 1982.

Stuller, Jay. "What's New in Contact Lenses?" Reader's Digest July 1985: 109-12.

Zinn, Walter J., and Herbert Solomon. The Complete Guide to Eye Care, Eyeglasses and Contact Lenses. 2nd ed. New York: Frederick Fell, 1986.

CHAPTER 12 THE RESEARCH REPORT

Limiting a Topic and Beginning Research [pages 247–249]

1. Which is probably the best topic for a research report?
   (a) why I want to join the U.S. Coast Guard (b) the U.S. Coast Guard (c) the U.S. Coast Guard and safety at sea
2. Which controlling statement would best guide research?
   (a) The U.S. Coast Guard has countless responsibilities.
   (b) Coast Guard careers appeal to many.
   (c) The Coast Guard has a tradition of working for safety at sea.
3. Which of these sources is more relevant to this topic?
   (a) a book about the Coast Guard's sea rescue function
   (b) Coast Guard recruitment pamphlet

Gathering Information [pages 251–259] Read this notecard:

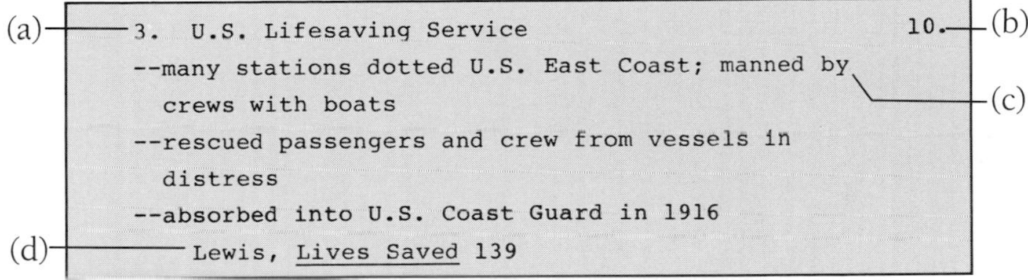
(a) 3. U.S. Lifesaving Service (b) 10.

--many stations dotted U.S. East Coast; manned by (c)
crews with boats

--rescued passengers and crew from vessels in
distress

--absorbed into U.S. Coast Guard in 1916

(d) Lewis, Lives Saved 139

4. Which item identifies the number of the note card?
5. Which item presents information in the notetaker's own words?
6. Which item locates the information within the source?
7. Which item categorizes the information noted on the card?

Footnotes and Bibliography [pages 262–267]

8. Which item represents the correct footnote form for crediting the same work a second time?
   (a) [5]Tute, Warren, p. 94. (b) [5]Tute 94. (c) [5]Warren Tute, p. 94.
9. Which form is correct for a bibliography citation?
   (a) Bowen, Frank. A Century of Atlantic Travel, 1830–1930. Boston: Little, Brown, and Company, 1930.
   (b) A Century of Atlantic Travel, 1830–1930, by Frank Bowen. Little, Brown, and Company, Boston, 1930.
10. In your bibliography how would you list a periodical article?
    (a) title of article first (b) author first

Writing for Review Choose a topic that you are interested in and one that you can research. Focus your topic, and find one source related to it. Then take notes from that source on two notecards.

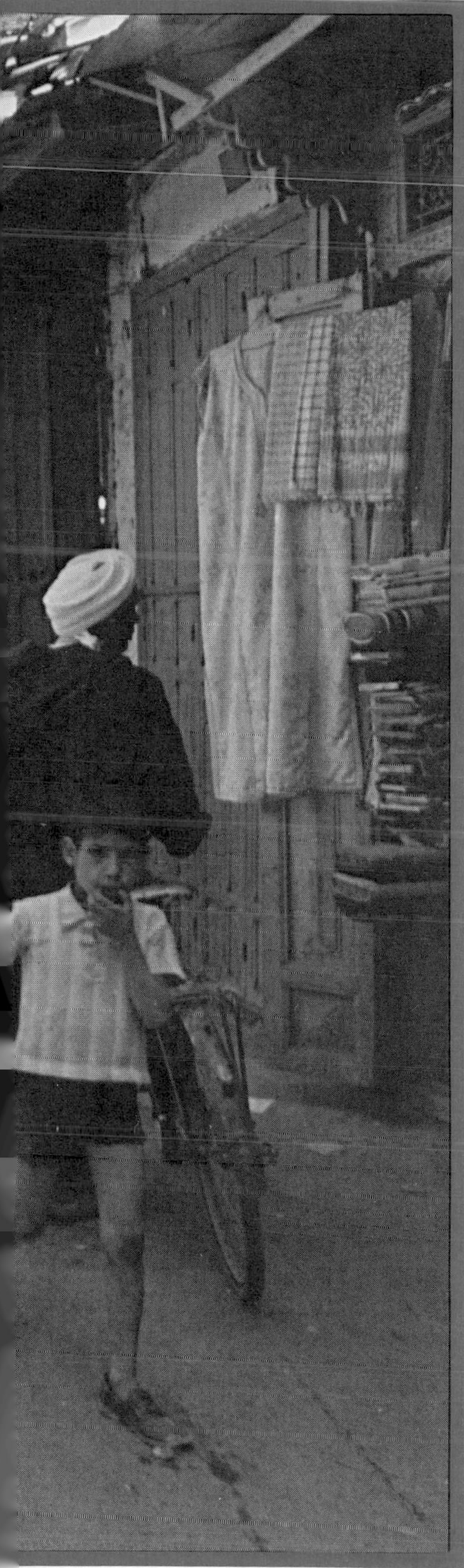

Writing Across the Curriculum

Thinking About Thinking: Generating Ideas About a Topic

In this unit you will discover ways to apply the writing process when you are writing about social studies, science, and literature. Especially when you are prewriting, you engage in the thinking process called invention, no matter what your topic. When you write about social studies, science, or literature, you are called upon to invent ideas related to one specific subject area.

Defining the Skill

Freewriting lets you discover ideas that you did not know you had. When you freewrite on a specific topic, you discover ideas about that topic. Focused freewriting on a specific topic will help you to develop the thinking skill called GENERATING IDEAS ABOUT A TOPIC.

Applying the Skill

Look at the photograph of the marketplace. Discuss the photograph in groups of four students. What familiar items do you see? What looks strange or unusual to you? What connections can you make with your own experience? Then freewrite for three minutes about the photograph. Direct your freewriting by starting with this sentence: This is what I can tell or imagine about the culture by looking at this photograph.

CHAPTER 13

Writing About Social Studies

Liberty cannot be preserved without a general knowledge among the people. . . . Let us dare to read, think, speak, and write.

—John Adams

As a student of **social studies**, you learn about people living in groups and the cultures, or ways of life, that they have developed. Social studies involves you in many subject areas—history, geography, civics, economics, and sociology. Some authorities say that, since social studies concerns people and their cultures, it includes anything related to human beings.

In social studies you may be called upon to write *narratives* of historical incidents, *descriptions* of places and individuals, *expository* essays and research papers on any number of subjects, and *persuasive* responses to test questions. It does not matter whether you are writing about a historical person or event, a culture, an economic development, a geographical location, or a function of your state government: You will need to adapt thinking and writing skills you have learned to your social studies writing. Here are the skills you will put to work as you think and write throughout this chapter:

prewriting: topic, audience, and purpose
prewriting: evidence, sources, and documentation
prewriting: making generalizations
writing objectively
writing chronologically
writing about causes and effects
writing with comparison and contrast
revising, **editing**, and **publishing**

Prewriting: Topic, Audience, and Purpose

The writing topics in this chapter are related to civics. Civics is the social studies subject that deals with the organization and function of local, state, and national governments, as well as the rights and responsibilities of citizens. The Adams quotation that opens this chapter calls attention to one of our civic responsibilities—to keep informed, to have "general knowledge." To express your "general knowledge" you must practice skills that help you "speak" and "write."

When you write about civics or any other subject, you must focus your topic with care. You can focus a civics topic by asking the following questions about it: *Who? What? When? Where? How? Why?* Suppose you were prewriting for an essay about the House of Representatives. This subject is so large that, unless you brought it into focus, your essay would be vague and rambling. By investigating the *what, when,* and *who* of the subject, you can narrow it to a focused topic:

What? The House of Representatives
↓
When? The House of Representatives in the 1980s
↓
Who? Leaders of the House of Representatives in the 1980s

As you write about civics topics in this chapter, your audience will be your teacher and the other students in your class. Nevertheless, during prewriting you will ask yourself the same two questions you would ask yourself for any other audience:

1. What does the audience need to know? (Think about any basic information your readers need in order to understand you, including any terms you need to define.)
2. What is the audience's point of view—biased in favor, biased against, or neutral? (Think about what level of diction will be most appealing to your readers.)

As part of prewriting, you should also clearly identify your purpose. Clarifying your purpose will not only make the writing more understandable to your audience, it may also make the writing somewhat easier for you. Fix your purpose in your mind by putting it in writing: Do you intend to inform, explain, persuade, entertain, narrate, or describe? Do you have a combination of purposes, such as to describe something in order to explain it?

EXERCISE 1 **Focusing a Topic in Social Studies.** Write the questions the writer asked to arrive at the following focused topic.

Levels of Government
↓
Levels of Government in the United States
↓
State governments since 1950
↓
The role of the modern governor
↓
Ceremonial duties of a modern governor

EXERCISE 2 **Focusing a Topic in Social Studies.** Think of a social studies topic of your own, or select one of those that follow. Ask yourself *who? what? when? where? how?* and *why?* to focus the topic so that you can write a three-paragraph paper about it.

political conventions
making laws
the United States Constitution
the rights of citizenship
the responsibilities of citizenship
American local government
the Federal budget
minorities and government
the Federal court system

Prewriting: Evidence, Sources, and Documentation

At certain times in its history, the United States Supreme Court has declared laws passed by Congress null and void. Historians accept the preceding statement because *evidence* can be cited to support it. When you write about civics and the other social studies, you should be sure you can support your writing with evidence.

A **fact** is a statement about an event that actually happened. Some facts are common knowledge: For example, the center of national government in the United States is Washington, D.C., or two senators represent each state in Congress. No evidence needs to be offered to support facts that are common knowledge. On the other hand, if a fact is not generally known—for example, the names of the senators who voted for and against a bill recently passed by Congress—*sources* of information containing evidence that supports the fact must be provided to the reader.

Sources of information are of two types. A **primary source** states the words of someone actually involved in the event. Documents, diaries, letters, and autobiographies are all primary sources. A **secondary source** states the words of someone like a political scientist or historian who has examined a primary source and commented on it. For example, Thomas Jefferson wrote the Declaration of Independence almost single-handedly. You can find references to this fact in Jefferson's own letters and other writing by him—primary sources. You can also find references to this fact in secondary sources, such as biographies and other books about Jefferson. A primary source usually carries greater authority because it is closer to the event.

You must provide documentation for the sources you use in civics papers. In general, **documentation** is the information your readers will need to find these sources (author, title, publication, publication date).

In this way, readers can decide for themselves what importance to attach to the evidence you have taken from your sources. To review the proper form of footnotes and endnotes, refer to Chapter 12, "The Research Report."

EXERCISE 3 **Evaluating Evidence.** Indicate whether each of the following items is a statement of fact, an opinion, a part of a primary source, or a part of a secondary source.

1. a chapter from *The Living U.S. Constitution* by Saul K. Padover
2. a passage from a speech by Abraham Lincoln
3. The first ten amendments are known as the Bill of Rights.
4. Lincoln was by far the best President the United States ever had.

Prewriting: Making Generalizations

When you write about civics and the other social studies, you often begin with facts and lead toward generalizations. A **generalization** is a broad statement that is based on facts and may or may not be true. You make generalizations by examining and synthesizing factual details and then formulating a broad statement about them. The generalization highlights the common elements you have discovered in the factual details.

During prewriting you can form a generalization by studying the factual details you have gathered and asking yourself, What elements do all of these factual details have in common? Consider these factual statements, for example:

> Representatives of labor unions attempt to persuade Congress to enact legislation favorable to unions.
>
> Farmers hire spokespersons to try to persuade state legislators to pass laws that will benefit agriculture.
>
> Business associations hire lobbyists to promote business interests among senators in Washington.
>
> Individual citizens also try to influence their city, state, and national legislators to enact favorable legislation.

When you first study these statements, you might form this generalization: *Special-interest groups attempt to persuade lawmakers at all levels of government to pass laws favorable to them.* A second look at the factual details indicates that your generalization does not account for the last detail. This detail reveals that special-interest groups are not the *only* ones who try to persuade lawmakers. Since your generalization is too broad, you might revise it to something like the following: *Special-interest groups as well as individual citizens attempt to persuade lawmakers at all levels of government to pass laws favorable to them.*

Notice that the scope of the generalization was changed by adding *as well as*—a qualifying phrase that defines a statement more precisely and makes it conform more closely to all the facts. In writing about civics and the other social studies, qualifying words and phrases are extremely important because they take exceptions into account, and in a field as wide and varied as social studies there are many exceptions. In all your social studies writing avoid absolute, or all-inclusive, statements; instead, as often as possible, use qualifying words and phrases such as *one of the, some of the, many of the, in most cases, usually, often, some,* and *sometimes.*

EXERCISE 4 **Making Generalizations.** Assume that during prewriting you have gathered the following factual details on the subject of amendments to the Constitution. Form a generalization from the details, and use appropriate qualifying words or phrases.

The first amendment to the Constitution guarantees people the right to freedom of religion, speech, and press.

The right to bear arms is guaranteed by the second amendment.

The fifth amendment recognizes the right of accused persons to remain silent so they will not give self-incriminating evidence.

Congress is given the power to levy and collect taxes on personal incomes.

The twenty-second amendment limits a President to two terms.

Writing Objectively

On July 1, 1776, the leaders of the American colonies proclaimed the Declaration of Independence. Supposing you uncovered three primary sources whose writers comment on this event, in which each is deeply involved. Each writer interprets what actually happened in a different way.

> Samual Adams, an American revolutionary: "a justifiable act"
>
> Abigail Dinsmore, a colonist loyal to Great Britain: "a regrettable step that will lead to tragic consequences"
>
> George III, King of England: "treason"

Each of these primary sources provides important insights into people of the time. However, none of them is *objective.*

Objective writing, unlike that in the three statements above, is writing that contains no bias or prejudice. When you write about a topic in civics or one of the other social studies, be on the lookout for biases or prejudices in the sources you use. The following guidelines will help you to keep your social studies writing objective:

1. Present facts and events in clear, straightforward language.
2. When you quote someone, use that person's *exact* words. Do not omit, add, or change words for any reason whatsoever.
3. If you include an opinion, your own or someone else's, be sure your readers will recognize it as an opinion.

EXERCISE 5 **Writing Objectively.** Imagine that the following paragraph appeared in a news story the day after a presidential election. Rewrite the paragraph, rewording statements as necessary to make the paragraph an objective account.

By this time, every citizen in the United States has heard the tragic results of yesterday's election. James Martin will be our President beginning in January of next year. That Inauguration Day will begin the bleakest period in our national history; this President-elect has none of the qualifications that are expected of even the most ineffective national leader. Martin's defeated opponent, Lorinda Elsworthy, made a concession speech and congratulated the victor. If we add only a few words to her speech, her real meaning becomes clear: "The American people made their choice and now they will have to face the consequences." The victorious candidate could not be reached at his hotel suite this morning. Undoubtedly, the victory celebrations that lasted until dawn left him in an unfit condition to face the microphones, cameras, and notebooks of the news media.

Writing Chronologically

In many of the papers you write for civics and the other social studies, you will present events or processes in **chronological**, or time, **order.** It is important for your readers to know whether one event happens before or after another, since they will not be able to understand the events fully unless you present them in their proper *order*. For example, if readers are to have a complete or correct idea of how a bill becomes a national law, it is important for them to know that the bill must be approved by a committee in one house of Congress *before* it can come up for debate.

If you wish to review what you have already learned about chronological order, refer to Chapter 3, "Writing the Paragraph," and Chapter 8, "Narrative Writing." As you write about topics in civics or one of the other social studies, use transitions that signal the time order of events. Among such transitions are *before, after, then,* and *at the same time.*

EXERCISE 6 **Writing Chronologically.** Write a paragraph based on the chart in the Writer's Sourcebook (page 368). Describe some of the events of a city's growth in chronological order. Be sure that you have appropriate transitions.

Writing About Causes and Effects

Identifying and relating the causes and effects of events provides another focus for the writing you do in civics and the other social studies. Social studies writers state *what happened* and then must often answer the question *Why did it happen?*

When you write a science paper on the freezing of liquids, you can state certainly that one event causes another: *The temperature went below 32 degrees Fahrenheit, and therefore the liquid froze*. When you write about a social studies topic, however, you must remember that you are dealing with *people* in action. Where people are involved, events frequently have a number of causes and a number of effects. For example, it would not be enough to write *Franklin Delano Roosevelt was a popular American President because he was a strong leader*. In order to give a complete explanation, you would have to consider other possible causes—the role he played in ending the Depression, his accomplishments during World War II, his magnetic personality, his sense of humor, and so forth.

As you are writing about causes and effects, look at your topic from different viewpoints, and ask yourself whether you have considered all the possible causes and effects. The following questions may help you:

PERSONAL Who was directly responsible? Who was directly affected? A single person? A group of persons? Was someone behind the scenes also responsible?

SOCIAL What general beliefs or attitudes of the society made the event possible? In what way did the event change people's beliefs or attitudes? What system of government made the event possible? How did the event change the system of government?

ECONOMIC What economic factors made the event possible? Who profited or lost because of the event?

Consider this final point: Causes and effects can be either short-term or long-term. A short-term, or immediate, cause or effect is most often a specific event that can be pinpointed. A long-term cause or effect is frequently more difficult to pinpoint, but it is more important to a greater number of people in the long run.

EXERCISE 7 **Writing About Causes and Effects.** Write a paragraph about the causes or effects of a cultural or historical event. Choose an event of your own, or use one of the following. Be sure to consider the wide variety of possible causes or effects. Think carefully about what your audience needs to know.

1. taxes paid to governments
2. the election of the most recent President
3. corrupt government officials
4. well-informed citizens

Writing with Comparison and Contrast

Writing that involves comparison and contrast is useful in civics and other social studies. **Comparison** is writing that describes similarities; **contrast** is writing that describes differences. The events that you deal with in social studies writing do not happen independently of each other. When you compare and contrast people, historical events, governments, and cultures, you give your readers the opportunity to view them in a larger context and appreciate their significance more fully.

If you decide during prewriting which points of your subject you wish to compare and contrast, your writing task will be easier for you.

More important, your comparisons and contrasts will be clearer to your readers (see Chapter 9, "Expository Writing"). To help you with this prewriting activity, you can make a chart like the following to identify the similarities and differences between two subjects:

CONGRESS OF THE UNITED STATES	PRESIDENT OF THE UNITED STATES
SIMILARITIES	
• elected by the people • many Constitutional powers	
DIFFERENCES	
• legislative branch of Federal government makes laws • can refuse to ratify treaties • can reject presidential appointees • can impeach President	• head of executive branch of Federal government • can veto laws • makes treaties with foreign countries • appoints federal officials

Begin writing by introducing your subjects to your readers and stating that you are going to compare or contrast them. Organize your writing in this way: *AAABBB,* in which all the *A*s are statements about one subject and all the *B*s are statements about the other subject. Be careful to make clear the points you are comparing in the two subjects. You may wish to conclude your writing with a summary statement that unites all your points of comparison or contrast. A chart like the preceding one might result in the following civics paragraph:

> The Congress and the President of the United States—the legislative and the executive branches of our government—are alike in certain basic ways: They are both elected by the people, and both have their powers spelled out in the Constitution. However, the differences between them reveal a great deal about the nature of our government and the way it functions. For example, Congress has the power to create laws. It has the authority to ratify, or not to ratify, treaties made by the President. Congress can also reject presidential appointees; in fact, Congress can even impeach and remove the President. On the other hand, the President has the power to veto laws passed by the Congress. The President has the authority to sign, or not to sign, treaties with foreign countries and to appoint federal officials. Contrasting their powers in this way reveals that the Congress and the President not only have the authority to carry out their own legislative or executive functions; they also check and balance one another.

EXERCISE 8 **Writing with Comparison and Contrast.** Write a paragraph contrasting two forms of government. If you wish, use the information given in the following chart.

HOW A TOTALITARIAN STATE DIFFERS FROM A DEMOCRACY

	TOTALITARIAN STATE	DEMOCRACY
POWER	Power is in the hands of one person or a small group.	Power originates with the people and is delegated to leaders.
CITIZENS	Citizens have little or no say.	Citizens decide how they will lead their lives.
POLITICS	The government directs elections.	Free elections are held often.

Revising, Editing, and Publishing

To revise a paragraph, essay, or research paper in civics or one of the other social studies, use all the basic revising skills you learned in Chapter 4, "Revising the Paragraph." In addition, as you are revising, you will also want to keep in mind the particular social studies writing skills you learned in this chapter. After editing the first draft of your writing, prepare a final copy and proofread it. Then share your work.

Checklist for Revising a Social Studies Report

1. Which of these can I apply to the social studies topic to define and focus it: *who? what? when? where? how? why?*
2. What basic social studies facts or definitions does the audience need? What statements or word choices, if any, are inappropriate to the audience? What is the purpose of this report?
3. Is any source, primary or secondary, incorrectly or insufficiently identified? Is the proper format for documentation always used?
4. What words should be used to qualify any generalizations?
5. Which statements are not as objective as possible? Which, if any, use unclear language, inexact quotations, or unlabeled opinions?
6. Which transitions that show time can be used to make chronological writing absolutely clear?
7. Which personal, social, or economic causes and effects need to be reconsidered and expanded?
8. Are any points of comparison or contrast unclear? Should any changes be made in the organization so that the *AAABBB* comparison or contrast will be easier for the reader to follow?

Writer's Choice

Writer's Choice #1

ASSIGNMENT Answer this civics examination question: Which of the ten amendments that make up the Bill of Rights do you think has had the greatest effect on freedom in the United States, and why?

LENGTH One paragraph

AUDIENCE Your teacher

PURPOSE To inform and explain

PREWRITING Make a list of the long-term effects of the amendment and a list of reasons for your opinon.

WRITING Begin by identifying your choice. Then give the long-term effects. End your paragraph with a general statement about the amendment.

REVISING Refer to the checklist on page 291 to revise your paragraph. Edit your first draft, prepare a final copy, and proofread it.

Writer's Choice #2

ASSIGNMENT Write a letter to the editor or an opinion column in which you compare or contrast the strengths and weaknesses of two political candidates, real or imaginary.

LENGTH Your choice

AUDIENCE Your choice

PURPOSE To inform and explain

PREWRITING Make a chart of the similarities or the differences between the two candidates.

WRITING Order your paragraph according to the *AAABBB* structure. End with a general statement about the two candidates. Use appropriate qualifying words.

REVISING Refer to the checklist on page 291.

Writer's Choice #3

ASSIGNMENT A paragraph or brief essay about a topic that is related to civics

OPTIONS Determine your own length, audience, and purpose. Write on any civics topic you wish. You may want to refer to the Writer's Sourcebook (pages 365–369) for an idea. Limit and focus your topic during prewriting, and clearly identify it at the beginning of your paragraph or essay. Use the checklist on page 291 to revise what you have written.

Writers on Writing

As a student at Yorktown High School in Yorktown Heights, New York, James O'Brien wrote the following paper about American foreign policy after the Revolutionary War. Jim enjoys debating and was a member of the Yorktown High School Mock Congress. He hopes to pursue a career in science or medicine.

THE PRODUCT

As America has grown and prospered, many historians have noted marked periods of particular types of foreign policy. This general sequence reflects the country's development and its needs at each stage in its growth.

In the early years after dissolving its bonds with England, America followed a policy termed the "Protection of National Independence." This period, typical of new nations, lasted roughly from 1776 to 1823. The chief example of American interaction with other countries after the Revolution was the War of 1812 with England. At this point in its history, America's only goal was to remain free and establish a sound government. By forming an alliance with France, Congress also became involved in the rivalry between that country and England.

The War of 1812 was so consistent with the idea of a nation freeing itself from a colonial power that it is often referred to as "the Second Revolutionary War." Despite the fact that the results of the war did not affect the rest of the world and that the conflict remained largely unresolved with no definite victor, the United States felt that it had proved itself capable of protecting its own needs. Therefore, the alliance with France—the first such pact with another country since the Revolution—and the War of 1812 represented one pattern of foreign policy in U.S. history. A necessary stage in the development of a new country, this period reflected the basic need of the American people to convince themselves that they were indeed a free nation.

THE PROCESS

Social studies essays are different from literary essays not only in their topics but also in their style and format. When I write papers on subjects such as American history (as in the excerpt above), there are two basic principles that I keep in mind constantly. These key rules are organization and objectivity.

First of all, a social studies essay is in some ways more restricted than a free-flowing literary paper. It places more emphasis on fact than on interpretation. When I write a social studies paper, I create an outline that divides the topic into several subsets that will develop it. Within each section, then, I plan to present the details that support my ideas.

For example, in the excerpt above, the broad opening paragraph deals with key time periods in America's growth as a nation. The first time period after the Revolution seemed the logical choice for the first subset. Calling this period the "Protection of National Independence," I went on in the next two paragraphs to use major events from the period as supporting items—in this case, the alliance with France and the War of 1812.

However, there is more to a social studies essay than organization. Just as a literary essay is based on a text, so a social studies paper must also be based on history and actual events. When you write about social studies, remember that your essay must develop its topic with facts. Do not stray from the subject by including your own extraneous ideas and views. Above all, DON'T MOLD HISTORY TO SUIT YOUR NEEDS! Many of us have a tendency to taint events with our own theories (which may not be correct), and then we end up twisting the truth to fit those ideas. For example, the excerpt above deals with a subject for which we all hold a bias—our own country. But however righteous one might think the colonies were in their actions, one cannot simply state that feeling as fact in a paper.

One might argue that the social studies essay is not art, because of its tight format. I maintain that treating any subject properly, no matter how strict the format, is an art in itself.

YOUR TURN *Writing a Commentary*

As Jim did, choose an essay that you wrote for a social studies class, and offer pointers to your fellow students about the best way to write such an essay. Include examples from your original social studies essay. (You can work either with an in-class essay that you wrote as an answer to a test question or with an essay written outside of class.)

CHAPTER 14

Writing About Science and Technology

A writer's problem does not change. He himself changes and the world he lives in changes, but his problem remains the same. It is always how to write truly and, having found out what is true, to project it in such a way that it becomes a part of the experience of the person who reads it.

—Ernest Hemingway

Scientific and technical writing involves finding out through research "what is true" about our rapidly changing world and then writing about these findings in a clear, organized, and readable way. As you work your way through this chapter, your goal will be to learn to present scientific or technical information in such a way that "it becomes a part of the experience of the person who reads it."

Scientific or technical reports follow a set format to present clearly, accurately, and concisely factual information based on research.

In this chapter, you will consider the accepted conventions for scientific and technical reports in terms of the writing process:

prewriting: exploring scientific and technical writing
prewriting: finding a suitable topic
prewriting: purpose and audience
prewriting: gathering information
writing a scientific or technical report
revising, editing, and publishing a scientific or technical report

Perfecting these skills will improve your reports for science classes. You will benefit in the long run, too, for scientific and technical writing is becoming increasingly important in our times.

Prewriting: Exploring Scientific and Technical Writing

Read the following excerpt from a scientific paper on cells:

> A cell is the essential element of every type of life. Every single cell has the same basic and simple structure. The thin outer covering of a cell encloses a jellylike liquid known as cytoplasm. Near the center of the cell is a nucleus that directs nearly all of the cell's activities according to a

"master plan," a chemical substance known as DNA (deoxyribonucleic acid).

Notice that this paragraph has a serious and objective tone. The writer has included no sentences that express personal feelings or opinions about cells. All of the sentences deal with facts drawn from the writer's research. Note the inclusion of scientific terms such as *cytoplasm, nucleus,* and *DNA*. The scientific writing you do in this chapter will have the same objective tone and factual content.

Prewriting: Finding a Suitable Topic

Study the following examples of suitable and unsuitable topics for a scientific paper or technical report:

SUITABLE	UNSUITABLE
1. the noise levels of supersonic jets	listening to audio tapes at 35,000 feet
2. noise pollution and human health	my thoughts about what noise does

In this chapter you will follow a high school student who is planning to write a paper with the title "Noise Pollution: A Study of Its Effects on People." The student began with an interest in the general topic of environmental pollution. Then, by applying various prewriting techniques, she narrowed this topic to the effects of noise pollution.

EXERCISE 1 **Evaluating the Suitability of Topics.** Read the following list of topics. On your paper write *Suitable* for each topic that is suitable for a scientific or technical report. Write *Unsuitable* for each topic that is unsuitable, and explain why it is not suitable.

1. the use of technology in the training of athletes
2. high-tech versus traditional methods of training athletes
3. my experience with high-tech athletic training
4. ten reasons why athletes should use high-tech training methods
5. a personal opinion about using computers in training athletes

EXERCISE 2 **Selecting a Topic.** From the following list of broad topics, select one, and begin to generate and explore ideas about it. (See Chapter 2.) If you wish, select another general topic. The purpose of this exercise is to help you find a topic for the scientific or technical report that you will write for Writer's Choice #1 on page 308.

1. organ transplants
2. old and new astronomy equipment
3. science and police work
4. extinct animals

Prewriting: Purpose and Audience

The general purpose of scientific or technical writing is to inform. The specific purpose may be one of the following.

1. *to explain a process:* for example, to show how a machine operates or to describe the steps in a scientific procedure
2. *to analyze causes and effects:* for example, to predict the long-term effects of a human activity
3. *to divide and classify items:* for example, to divide a problem into its logical parts and relate the problem to a larger problem or to a general scientific or technical concern
4. *to define terms:* for example, to explain technical terminology
5. *to compare and contrast items:* for example, to point out similarities and differences among operations

Once you have decided on a purpose, you must then decide what audience you will address. Ask yourself the following questions:

1. Who will be my audience?
2. How much will my readers already know about my topic? Could they be considered experts—people who have an above-average knowledge of the topic? Should I consider them nonexperts—people who have little or no knowledge about the topic?
3. Will this topic interest my intended audience? If not, what can I do to arouse their interest? Should I select another topic?

EXERCISE 3 **Determining a Purpose.** State your specific purpose for writing about the topic that you selected in Exercise 2. Think about the five kinds of purposes listed previously. Write your purpose in a single sentence. Save this sentence for Writer's Choice #1 on page 308.

EXERCISE 4 **Matching Audience and Writing.** Read each of the short paragraphs that follow. On your paper write *Expert* if you think the paragraph is suitable for an audience of experts. Write *Nonexpert* if you think it more suitable for readers without specialized knowledge. Use specific examples from each paragraph to explain.

1. This report analyzes three alternative strategies to adjust the economy of Brazil to the oil shocks of 1974 and 1979. The basic objective of the three strategies is to shift Brazil's energy dependence from foreign sources to less costly domestic sources.
2. This report considers three different plans to help the economy of Brazil to recover from the oil shortages of 1974 and 1979. All three plans aim to make Brazil less dependent on expensive foreign oil.

EXERCISE 5 **Identifying Your Audience.** Decide what audience you think will read the report you have been considering in Exercises 2 and 3. Write a sentence or two describing this audience, indicating whether it is expert or nonexpert. Tell how much your intended readers know about your topic. Save your comments for Writer's Choice #1.

Prewriting: Gathering Information

Prepare a chart similar to the one that follows. The answers you write will help you to decide what information you will need to include in your report and the kind and amount of research you will have to do.

QUESTIONS TO GATHER INFORMATION	SAMPLE ANSWERS
1. What problem or idea do I want to discuss?	*The effects of noise pollution on human beings*
2. What is the best way to present this information?	*Perhaps to focus on causes and effects of noise pollution?*
3. Who is my audience? What does my audience need to know?	*Nonexpert audience—so include basic information giving examples of noise pollution and explaining its effects. Define technical terms.*
4. What questions about my topic do I need to answer?	*What is noise pollution? What causes it? How does it affect people? What can be done about it?*
5. Where can I find answers to these questions?	*Begin with general sources—encyclopedias. They will refer me to more specific sources. Check magazine articles. Try to interview acoustical engineers and other experts.*
6. How do my ideas relate to/ build on previous research?	*I will summarize previous research, but I will not go beyond it for a nonexpert audience.*

Your next step will be to consult a general reference book to find some basic information about your topic. You might begin with an encyclopedia that deals only with scientific and technological topics, such as the *McGraw-Hill Encyclopedia of Science and Technology* or *Van Nostrand's Scientific Encyclopedia.*

After consulting a general reference book, find a reference book that deals specifically with your topic. For example:

Aviation and Space Dictionary
Encyclopedia of Computer Science, edited by Anthony Ralston
McGraw-Hill Encyclopedia of Oceanography by Rhodes W. Fairbridge
The Encyclopedia of the Biological Sciences, by George L. Clark
Words of Science and the History Behind Them and *More Words of Science,* by Isaac Asimov

When you have consulted your general and specific reference works, you will be ready to prepare a *working outline* that will serve as a guide for the rest of your research. (See Chapter 12 for more information on preparing a working outline for a research report.) Here is the working outline by the student writing the report on noise pollution:

NOISE POLLUTION: A STUDY OF ITS EFFECTS ON PEOPLE

I. What noise pollution is
II. Sources of noise pollution
III. Effects of noise pollution on people
IV. What is being done about noise pollution
V. Conclusions

Use the library card catalog and indexes to periodicals to find other books and articles with additional details about your topic. Look for books or articles published very recently, since knowledge in science and technology changes daily.

Fill out a bibliography card for each potentially useful source. Read the sources with care, using your working outline as a guide. Take notes on information that relates to each main topic of your outline. Then use appropriate notes as subtopics and details in a final outline.

The student planning the report on noise pollution consulted the *Readers' Guide to Periodical Literature.* This index lists articles in magazines such as *Scientific American* and *Science.* She also checked articles listed in the *Applied Science and Technology Index.* Finally, she consulted people such as science teachers for more details.

EXERCISE 6 **Gathering Information.** Follow the steps indicated here as you begin to research the topic you wish to develop into a report.

1. Ask general questions to guide your early research.
2. Check a general reference work for background information.
3. Prepare a working outline.
4. Locate specific sources, and begin reading and taking notes.
5. Decide whether your report would benefit from interviews.
6. Use your notes to prepare a final outline.

Writing a Scientific or Technical Report

Writers of scientific or technical reports should use precise language and include relevant scientific or technical terms to develop their topics in an accurate, logical, and unbiased manner. They should also use third-person pronouns rather than first-person pronouns such as *I* or *me*, which are more suitable in personal writing.

APPROPRIATE Sounds audible to the human ear range from 15 to 140 decibels.

INAPPROPRIATE I'll explain that we can hear things that are both soft and loud.

All carefully planned writing has a distinct beginning, middle, and end. Scientific and technical reports usually label each of these three parts to help readers know where they are at all times. Labeling is one of the conventions of scientific or technical writing. Study the following description of the three parts.

INTRODUCTION

The purpose of the introduction is to explain to the reader what general problem or idea you intend to discuss. Here you can present background information about the issue, in addition to clearly stating your specific purpose.

DISCUSSION OR BODY

The discussion (or body) is the major section of the report and contains the most important information from your research. It focuses on facts, their relationships, and their importance.

CONCLUSIONS

In this final part of your report, you state the conclusions that you have reached regarding your topic. Your findings must agree with the facts you included in the introduction and discussion.

Scientific and technical reports include other unique features. These are some of the other conventions that such writing follows:

TITLE PAGE

This page includes the following information: the title of the report, your name, your teacher's name, and the date.

TABLE OF CONTENTS

The table of contents lists in sequence all the parts of the report, including the introduction, discussion, conclusions, and bibliography, along with the page number on which each part begins.

BIBLIOGRAPHY

Put the bibliography on a separate page with its own heading. Use the formats presented in Chapter 12.

In all writing **mechanics** refers to the use of punctuation, capital letters, and abbreviations. In a scientific or technical report, you pay special attention to mechanics in order to express your thoughts more precisely.

ABBREVIATIONS

Writers may use abbreviations in scientific or technical reports, especially abbreviations of words that name units of measurement (for example, *ft, lb, km*). Always write the full word (*kilometer*) the first time you use it, and follow with its abbreviation (*km*) in parentheses. In the rest of the report, use the abbreviation only.

NUMBERS

Study this list of conventions relating to the use of numbers in scientific and technical writing:

1. Spell out numbers from one to ten (*six reference books*) except when writing small numbers in a mathematical expression (*9 minus 2*).
2. Use Arabic numerals for all numbers above ten (*12 pages*).
3. Use numerals to express fractions, percentages, decimals, page numbers, figures, monetary units, and exact measurements.
4. Never begin a sentence with a number written as a numeral.

DOCUMENTATION

Unlike other research reports, scientific or technical reports do not have footnotes or endnotes. Instead, you use an author–date–page-number system to cite your sources. In this system you write in parentheses the author's last name, the year of publication, and the page reference when citing the source for the first time as in this example: (*Clark, 1985, p. 13*). If you cite the same reference more than once, omit the date after the first citation. Remember to list these sources in the bibliography.

ILLUSTRATIONS

Many scientific or technical reports include sketches, tables, and diagrams to clarify or take the place of complicated explanations. Number each sketch, table, and diagram, and refer to it by number in the body of the paper, as in this example: (*see Figure 1*). Place each different sketch, table, and diagram on a separate page, and identify it: *Figure 1: Structure of a Capillary*.

EXERCISE 7 **Analyzing a Scientific or Technical Report.** In order to see how the preceding advice can be followed, examine the sample report beginning on page 303, and answer the following:

1. How does the introduction differ from the discussion? How does the conclusion differ from the discussion?
2. How does the first citation of the Trainor source in the introduction differ from the second citation of that source?
3. What is the purpose of Figure 1?

Revising, Editing, and Publishing

All the general questions you ask when you revise your writing (see Chapter 4) apply to scientific or technical writing. In addition, there are special questions to ask about the first draft of a scientific or technical report—questions that will help you revise your report so that it will accomplish your purpose and be appropriate for your audience.

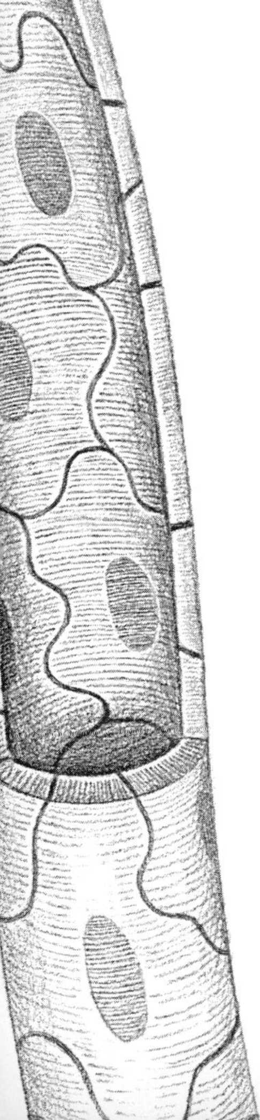

Checklist for Revising a Scientific or Technical Report

1. Is there anything that distracts from the serious, objective tone of my report? Have I removed any references to personal experiences or opinions? Have I used third-person pronouns?
2. What background information does the introduction provide? How well does the introduction state my purpose?
3. What, if anything, can I do to present my findings more concisely and objectively in the discussion?
4. What conclusions have I stated? Are the conclusions consistent with the facts presented earlier?
5. What corrections, if any, do I need to make on the title page, in the table of contents, and in the bibliography? Are all elements of mechanics correct?
6. How can I increase the precision of my language?
7. What other editing should I do on a sentence-by-sentence basis?
8. How carefully have I proofread the final version?

Once you have revised your report, you are ready to share it with your audience. Whether your audience is your class, your teacher, the readers of a science club publication, or a community group, you will be presenting a report that should give your readers new insights into your topic.

Model of the Finished Report

Noise Pollution:
A Study of Its Effects on People

Maureen Egan

Mr. Koffler
April 30, 19__

Table of Contents

Introduction

Living in a highly technological age brings many benefits to people. Scientific and technological advances also bring many problems, among them various types of environmental pollution. Most people are well aware of the problems associated with water and air pollution; however, fewer people recognize noise pollution as a threat to human health and well-being.

Noise is measured in decibels. A decibel (db) is "a unit used in expressing the loudness of sounds" (American Heritage School Dictionary, 1977, p. 240)--the louder or more intense a sound, the greater the number of decibels. The intensity of sounds heard by the human ear ranges from 0 db, the threshold of audibility, through 120 db, the threshold of feeling or pain, to 140 db.

Noise pollution is defined in terms of decibels. According to the Federal government, noise becomes a pollutant at 90 db (Trainor, 1985, p. 137). Others say that noise pollution first occurs at the threshold of feeling (120 db), "the point at which noise begins to hurt" (Trainor, p. 139).

The general purpose of this paper is to demonstrate the effects of noise pollution. The following are the more specific purposes of the paper:

1. To identify various sources of noise pollution
2. To examine the effects noise pollution has on people
3. To suggest what is being done about noise pollution

Discussion

The majority of unwanted sounds that make up noise pollution have many sources, all of them the results of scientific and technical advances made within the last century. Residents of neighborhoods near airports are exposed to the din of arriving and departing jet airplanes. People who live and work in cities are exposed daily to an unpleasing symphony of loud noises: "the horns and motors of cars, trucks, buses, trains, and motorcycles moving in and out of the city competing with the sounds of construction equipment at the sites of new buildings" (Birch, 1983, p. 74). Workers in industrial plants must shout to make themselves heard above the whirring and roaring of the machinery they operate. Explosions, gunblasts, backfires, even natural sounds such as thunder add to the clamor that pollutes the environment.

Heading the list of polluting decibel producers are the screaming engines of jet planes heard at close range. They produce sounds measured at 140 db. Next among the noise polluters is highly amplified music, such as that produced by rock bands. This music at its loudest can measure 135 db, not much less than powerful jet engines (Lipscomb, 1982, p. 343). Such music produces the same volume whether it is heard in a concert hall or through earphones connected to a stereo set or radio (Trainor, p. 202). (See Figure 1.)

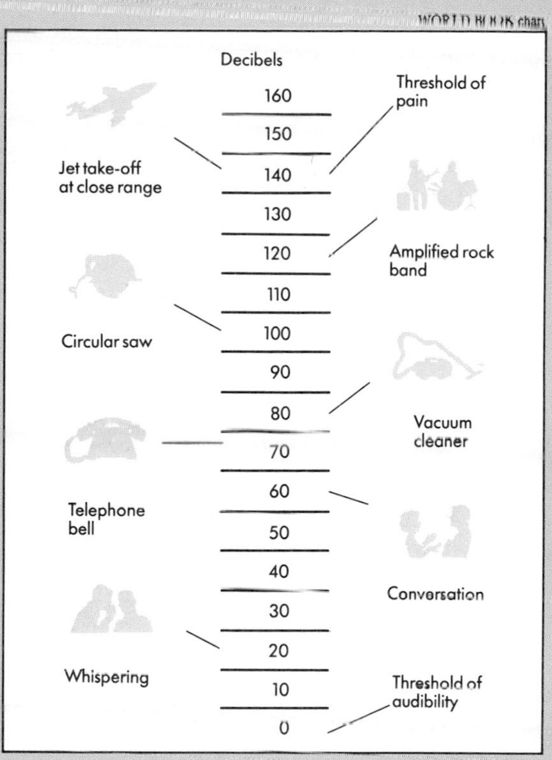

Figure 1. Intensity of Some Common Sounds.
Source: "Sound," World Book, 1984.

The loud noises that pollute the environment can produce serious negative effects on the people who are exposed to them. Doctors have traced temporary high blood pressure in some of their patients to noise pollution (Birch, p. 76). Psychiatrists point to muscle tension caused by prolonged exposure to loud noises as the reason for fatigue and irritability in some of the people they treat (Trainor, p. 142). In both cases, when the patients were removed from the noise-polluted environment, their symptoms disappeared within days or even hours.

Diminishment of hearing and sometimes deafness can be another serious negative effect of noise pollution. As David Lipscomb points out in his Science Year article, "On rare occasions, sudden intense noises can hurt the eardrum and break apart the _malleus_ . . . , _incus_ . . . and _stapes_ . . . ,the connected bones in the middle ear, causing hearing impairment." Another author asserted that continued exposure to less intense noise can cause temporary loss of hearing because such exposure may destroy cells in the cochlea of the ear, the cells that perform the vital function of transmitting sound impulses to the brain (Trainor, p. 165). The worst effect of noise pollution, however, is permanent and total deafness. Construction workers, factory workers, printers, and especially those airport workers whose jobs require that they be close to screaming jet engines run the serious risk of injuring their ears and going completely deaf.

The preceding negative effects of noise pollution can be eliminated or lessened significantly in three general ways. First, the source of the unwanted noise can be eliminated. For example, a factory or an airport can be relocated. Second, the movement of the unwanted noise from one place to another can be blocked in some way. For example, thick doors or walls can be constructed to keep the noise out of homes and offices. Third, special materials and equipment can be used to absorb the unwanted noise. Factory workers, for example, can wear sound-absorbent earplugs or earmuffs; sound-absorbent materials can be used in the walls, ceilings, and floors of busy offices and noisy industrial plants (Birch, p. 83).

The United States Government has taken steps recently to deal with the threat of noise pollution. The Federal Aviation Administration has set strict limits for the amount of noise that will be tolerated at airports. In the Airports and Airways Development Act of 1970, Congress stipulated that Federal funds would be granted to the developers of new airports only if the plans provided for effective ways of minimizing noise pollution. In 1972 Congress established the Office of Technology Assessment, which is responsible for evaluating the possible negative effects (including noise pollution) that new technologies may have.

Individuals can avoid the possible negative effects of noise pollution by avoiding the following situations in which dangerous noise levels may cause a diminishing or total and permanent loss of hearing (Lipscomb, p.343):

> If you have to shout directly into someone's ear to talk in the presence of high-level sound, there is a great risk that the sound will cause hearing loss.
>
> If your ears ring after leaving a noisy area, you have been exposed to dangerous sound levels.

If you experience "dullness" of hearing after being exposed to high-level sound, your hearing sensitivity has probably been diminished. This effect is usually temporary, and normal hearing should return. However, constant repetition can do permanent damage.

Conclusions

This study of the effects of noise pollution shows that intense noises can seriously damage people's health and well-being, especially their hearing. Dangerous noise pollution is a part of life in this technological age. Yet the negative effects of intense noise can be lessened or overcome completely. People who are aware of noise pollution and take the proper steps are less likely to have their health and well-being harmed by it.

Bibliography

American Heritage School Dictionary. Boston: Houghton Mifflin Company, 1977.

Beyer, Robert T. "Sound." The World Book Encyclopedia, 1981 ed.

Birch, Justin, and Priscilla Monte. Block Your Ears: An Analysis of Harmful Noises in the Environment. London: Friends of the Earth, Inc., 1983.

Lipscomb, David M. "Killing Your Ears with the Sound of Music," Science Year. Chicago: World Book-Childcraft International Inc., 1982 ed.

Trainor, June E. Surviving in Our Technological World. San Jose: Green World Press, 1985.

Writer's Choice

Writer's Choice #1

ASSIGNMENT A scientific or technical report based on your work in Exercises 2, 3, 5, and 6

LENGTH 500 to 1,000 words

AUDIENCE As you stated in Exercise 5

PURPOSE As you stated in Exercise 3

PREWRITING You finished this stage by completing Exercises 2, 3, 5, and 6.

WRITING Prepare a first draft. Begin with the discussion, which should follow your formal outline. Then prepare an introduction and conclusion. Add illustrations if needed. Prepare the other parts of the paper: title page, table of contents, and bibliography.

REVISING Use the checklist for revising to make sure that you have followed the conventions of scientific and technical writing. Be sure to consider large issues, such as organization, as well as matters of editing and proofreading. When your final draft is ready, share it with your audience.

Writer's Choice #2

ASSIGNMENT To write about an environmental problem in your locality

LENGTH Two or three pages for discussion

AUDIENCE The citizens of your town, city, or state

PURPOSE To present all sides of an environmental problem and to suggest a solution

PREWRITING Use prewriting techniques from Chapter 2 to develop and explore a specific problem. You may get an idea by looking at the illustrations in the Writer's Sourcebook on pages 353–383. Do general reading, and prepare a working outline. Then locate sources for more detailed reading, and take notes. Prepare a final outline from your notes.

WRITING Write a first draft. Begin with the discussion, following your final outline. Add illustrations if helpful. Draft an introduction and conclusion. Prepare a title page, a table of contents, and a bibliography.

REVISING Use the checklist for revising. Be sure to consider large issues as well as matters of editing and proofreading. Finally, write your final copy and share it with others.

CHAPTER 15

Writing About Literature

In a very real sense, people who have read good literature have lived more than people who cannot or will not read. . . . It is not true that we have only one life to live; if we can read, we can live as many more lives and as many kinds of lives as we wish.

—S. I. Hayakawa

In the quotation that opens this chapter, the American expert on language S. I. Hayakawa makes clear the value of literature. The same idea has been expressed eloquently by many others, including the English novelist and literary critic Aldous Huxley, who put it this way: "Every man who knows how to read has it in his power to magnify himself, to multiply the ways in which he exists, to make his life full, significant, and interesting."

As you work your way through this chapter, you will be writing about three forms of literature—a short story by Anton Chekhov; a scene from the drama, or play, *Romeo and Juliet* by William Shakespeare; and a poem by E. E. Cummings. As you write about each of these literary works, you will be addressing an audience of readers who know the works. Your task will be to explain what each of the works means and what techniques the writer used to communicate that meaning. You will see that writing about literature is in some ways similar to and in some ways different from other writing you have done.

In order to write intelligently about these three literary works, you must, of course, understand the ideas that they contain. Understanding these ideas involves more than simply interpreting the author's words, however. It also involves the ability to recognize the various techniques the writers have used to put their ideas into words, sentences, paragraphs, and lines of poetry that communicate these ideas to you, the reader.

Many students feel that Hayakawa's "good literature" is too lofty for them. They picture short-story writers, playwrights, and poets as mysterious creatures who write about their "high-flying" insights into people and life. Writers *do* deal in "high-flying" ideas about people and life. That is why, by reading their works, "we can live as many more lives and as many kinds of lives as we wish" and why their stories, plays, and poems make our lives "full, significant, and interesting."

Students who shy away from literature because of its "high-flying" ideas should remember that there is also a nitty-gritty side to the writing of great stories, plays, and poems. This is where a writer's knowledge of writing techniques comes in. For writers are as much craftspeople as cabinet-makers, tailors, and weavers are. Like all craftspeople, writers must be skillful in using the particular techniques that will create useful, beautiful, and enduring works.

As you prepare to write about the three literary works in this chapter, you will be considering the writers' ideas and their skillful use of the writing techniques associated with their craft. Moreover, you will benefit from analyzing the three works of literature in all the ways Hayakawa and Huxley described.

The following pages will give you practice in these general areas:

writing about a short story
writing about a dramatic scene
writing about poetry

Writing About a Short Story

Think of a story you have particularly enjoyed. Did you ever ask yourself: What was it about this story that made it so enjoyable? You can answer this question by analyzing the story—discovering what the story says and how the parts of the story work together to say it. You can analyze a story by using the following suggestions. Then you will be ready to begin to write about your analysis.

Prewriting: First Responses to a Story

Begin your analysis by reading the story through once. As you read it the first time, think mostly about the characters and action. Then freewrite or brainstorm about your first reaction to the story. The freewriting that follows was done after the writer read "The Slander," a short story by the nineteenth-century Russian author Anton Chekhov. Before you look at the freewriting, read "A Slander" beginning on page 374 of the Writer's Sourcebook.

> *Title: What was the slander? Who was the slanderer? First impressions of Ahineyev, the main character—a shallow, silly, vain man. Not much action of the jumping-up-and-down, running-around kind—much conversation between characters. The only ones really doing anything are the servants. First reaction? I liked the story, especially what it says about stuffed shirts like the main character Ahineyev.*

Prewriting: Exploring a Story

After you write your first reaction to the story, read the story again and begin to analyze the *reason* for your reaction and what the author meant to say by writing the story. This brief review of the main elements of short stories will help you.

1. The **plot** is the sequence of events in a story. The plot develops out of a **conflict**—a problem or struggle of some kind faced by the main character. The plot builds to a **climax**, or high point. After the climax the conflict is resolved.
2. We understand the **characters** in a story by carefully observing their actions and words, the comments and actions of other characters, and the direct statements of the narrator, or storyteller.
3. The **setting** is the time and place—the when and where—of the story's action. The setting often creates an atmosphere, or mood, that colors the whole story.
4. The relationship between the narrator and a story is called the **point of view** of the story. Some stories are told from a **first-person point of view**, through the eyes of a character—the "I" in such stories. Other stories are told from a **third-person point of view**, by a narrator who observes, describes, and comments on the story's characters and their actions. A third-person narrator is usually not a character in the story.
5. The **theme** of the story is the underlying idea about life or the impression of life conveyed by the story's events, characters, setting, and point of view. The themes of most stories are implied, or revealed indirectly, by the authors.

You can analyze a short story by asking questions like those that follow about each of its elements. The sample answers to the questions are based on "A Slander."

QUESTIONS TO EXPLORE A STORY	SAMPLE ANSWERS FOR "A SLANDER"
1. What is the main conflict in the story?	*Ahineyev, the main character, feels he must protect his reputation against a slander he imagines Vankin has made against him.*
2. What is the climax?	*Ahineyev confronts Vankin after being reprimanded by his principal and accused by his wife.*
3. How is the conflict resolved?	*Because of Ahineyev's inability to see that he himself, not Vankin, has spread the slander, the conflict is not resolved. After accepting Vankin's denial of guilt, Ahineyev still wonders who* did *slander him.*
4. How would I describe the main character or characters? Are they sympathetic? Why or why not?	*The main character, Ahineyev, is a shallow, nervous, humorless, and vain man. He is definitely not sympathetic.*
5. Describe the story's setting and atmosphere, or mood.	*The story takes place at an indefinite time in a small community—a ballroom, a school, Ahineyev's home, and Vankin's home. The setting does not really matter. The mood changes from the happiness of the wedding party to anxiety when Ahineyev worries that his reputation will be ruined, then to confusion when Ahineyev cannot figure out "who else" but Vankin could have slandered him.*
6. From what point of view is the story told?	*The story is told from the third-person point of view by a narrator who observes and reports the actions of the characters.*
7. How would I state the theme, or underlying idea, of the story?	*Something like: By foolishly attempting to protect your reputation, you can unknowingly damage it. Or: Vanity can lead to foolish behavior.*

Prewriting: Main Idea and Support

Once you have answered exploratory questions, you are ready to think about a thesis statement that expresses the main idea that you will present. You should state the story's theme and name the elements that most clearly convey the theme, as in this example:

> By skillfully weaving together the words and actions that reveal Ahineyev's character with the events of the plot, Chekhov shows how humorlessness and vanity can make people act foolishly and harm themselves.

EXERCISE 1 **Prewriting for an Essay About a Short Story.** Plan an essay about a short story of your own choosing. Begin by reading the story and then try freewriting or brainstorming about your first reaction to the story. Read the story again, and then write your answers to exploratory questions like those shown earlier. Finally, use your answers to help you write a thesis statement for an essay.

Writing About a Story: Structure

An essay that analyzes a short story (or any other literary work) will be divided into several paragraphs. Under the next four headings, you will find what information each of these paragraphs should contain.

INTRODUCTION AND THESIS STATEMENT

The introductory paragraph should include your thesis statement, which expresses the main idea of your essay. When you write about a story, your thesis statement should give your interpretation of the story's theme and point out the techniques you think the author has used to suggest that theme.

BODY

The body of your essay will consist of several paragraphs that focus on the story elements that, in your judgment, most clearly suggest the story's theme. Each paragraph should discuss a single element and should begin with a topic sentence stating the main idea of that paragraph. Each paragraph should also have unity, a clear organization, and coherence. Transitions such as *however, in addition, therefore, similarly,* and *as a result* will give coherence to the paragraphs.

QUOTATIONS

Use quotations from the story to support your interpretations. Quotations of less than five lines can be included within a paragraph. Enclose these quotations in quotation marks. Quotations of five or more lines should be set off from paragraphs by skipping a line and indenting from the left margin. (If you are typing your essay double-spaced, you should single-space such quotations.) No quotation marks are needed for quotations set off in this way.

CONCLUSION

End your essay with a concluding paragraph that repeats your thesis statement in different words. Try to make the last sentence of this paragraph a clincher that expresses your overall response to the story in an original and memorable way.

You can adapt the preceding suggestions to a story analysis that is limited to one paragraph. Begin with a strong topic sentence. Make sure that each of the following sentences develops and supports one aspect of the topic sentence.

Model of a Paper About a Short Story

The following paper discusses "A Slander." Note how the writer's freewriting, the answers to exploratory questions, and the main idea expressed in a thesis statement have contributed to the development of this analysis.

"A Slander"

A Chekhov's "A Slander" is an amusing, yet sad, comment on human behavior--specifically on the behavior of Sergei Kapitonich Ahineyev, the main character in the story. By skillfully interweaving the words and actions that reveal Ahineyev's character with the events of the plot, Chekhov shows how humorlessness and vanity can make people act foolishly and harm themselves.

B At a wedding party for his daughter, Ahineyev goes into the kitchen and smacks his lips. Vankin, an assistant teacher at the school where Ahineyev teaches, is outside the door of the kitchen and hears the smacking sound. He enters the kitchen and jokingly accuses Ahineyev of kissing Marfa, the cook. Although he denies the charge, Ahineyev fears that Vankin will spread stories about him. Therefore, he defends himself to everyone at the party. Nevertheless, stories about Ahineyev and Marfa do circulate. As a result, Ahineyev is reprimanded by his principal and slapped by his wife for his unbecoming conduct. After these incidents Ahineyev confronts Vankin and accuses him of spreading untrue gossip. When Vankin convinces him he is wrong, Ahineyev is perplexed. "Who else?" he asks, sincerely unable to recognize that it was he who damaged his own reputation by trying to protect it.

C By revealing Ahineyev's character traits through his words and actions, Chekhov prepares readers for the ending of the story. Ahineyev has no sense of humor. He does does not understand that Vankin is just teasing him about kissing Marfa. Chekhov reveals Ahineyev's humorlessness in the following words: "'Not at all, I am not kissing her,' said Ahineyev with embarrassment. 'Who told you that, you fool? I just . . . smacked my lips because of . . . my pleasure . . . at the sight of the fish.'" What is more, Ahineyev is a shallow man. Chekhov tells us that he fears being "put to shame before the whole town." To prevent this development, Ahineyev does what he thinks Vankin will do--he nervously tells what happened in the kitchen to the guests at the wedding party. Chekhov lets Ahineyev's words reveal his vanity as he defends himself to the guests. Why should a man like him want to kiss Marfa who "looks like a beast"? He protests that he would "rather kiss a stray dog" or "a turkey than Marfa." Whatever sympathy readers might have had for Ahineyev quickly disappears.

D If Ahineyev had been a different kind of man, this story would have ended with his laughter at Vankin's teasing accusation in the kitchen. It should be obvious to the reader of Chekhov's story that vanity often ends up losing the face that a little humor could have saved.

NOTES ABOUT MODEL PAPER ON A SHORT STORY

A The thesis statement expresses the main idea and identifies two story elements: character and plot.

B Body paragraph 1 discusses plot. Notice the transitions that give coherence to the paragraph.

C Body paragraph 2 discusses Ahineyev's character traits. Note the format for short prose quotations.

D The concluding paragraph restates the main idea in a clincher sentence.

Revising, Editing, and Publishing

Put the first draft of your essay aside for a while. Then revise it, edit it, and proofread it, using the following questions:

1. Which sentence in the introduction is my thesis statement? In what way can it state the story's theme more clearly? On which story elements does my thesis statement focus?
2. Are the ideas expressed in my thesis statement taken up in the following paragraphs of the essay? Does each paragraph have a topic sentence?
3. Each time I discuss one of the story's elements, what details from the story do I use? According to my essay, how does each element contribute to the theme?
4. What transitions and other writing techniques do I use to create effective, clear movement among sentences and from paragraph to paragraph?
5. How might I rewrite the ending of the essay in a more original and memorable way?
6. Is each sentence a complete sentence? Have I avoided errors in the use of verbs, pronouns, and modifiers?
7. Is the final draft of my essay neatly copied? Are all the sentences correctly capitalized and punctuated? Are all the words correctly spelled?

EXERCISE 2 **Writing and Revising an Essay About a Short Story.** Using the work that you did for Exercise 1, write an essay about the story you have chosen. In the introductory paragraph, include a thesis statement giving your interpretation of the story's theme and identifying the elements that you think the author has used to suggest that theme. Be sure to discuss each element that you mention in your thesis statement. Also, do not forget to tie your writing together with transitions. End the concluding paragraph by restating the main idea of your essay in a memorable way.

Writing About a Dramatic Scene

A playwright composes a drama, or play, to be performed by actors before an audience. One way of interpreting a play is to analyze a single scene in it. When you write your essay about the scene, your purpose will be to show how the scene works as a part of the play: how it moves the action forward, reveals the traits of the characters, and relates to the themes developed by the play as a whole.

Prewriting: First Responses to a Dramatic Scene

In order to analyze a dramatic scene effectively, you should first become familiar with the play from which it comes. After familiarizing yourself with the whole play, read your scene aloud to get a feeling for the characters and action. Then think about how the scene fits into the play.

Now you are ready to freewrite or brainstorm about your first reaction to the scene. The following freewriting was based on Act II, Scene ii, of William Shakespeare's *Romeo and Juliet,* which begins on page 376 of the Writer's Sourcebook. The play as a whole portrays the romance of Romeo and Juliet and the bloody feud between their families. Eventually, the feud brings about the deaths of the two young lovers.

> *What a difference between the tender quietness of this scene and the action, violence, and hatred in much of the rest of the play! It really emphasizes the problem that Romeo and Juliet face—their love for each other* vs. *the hatred between their families. The scene reveals something about the two lovers' character traits, too—Romeo's eagerness and enthusiasm; his bravery in risking discovery by his enemies to be with Juliet; Juliet's love for Romeo conflicting with her loyalty to her family; her concern for Romeo's safety.*

Prewriting: Exploring a Dramatic Scene

Now you can explore what is going on in the scene and what the scene contributes to the whole play. The following review of the basic elements of drama will help you explore the characters and action in your scene.

1. A play is made up of **dialogue**—the speeches of the characters—and **stage directions**—the playwright's instructions about stage sets, scenery, lighting, and characters' costumes, tone of voice, movements, and gestures.
2. Like a story, a play presents a **plot**, or series of events, that grows out of a conflict faced by the main characters. Each scene presents one or more events in the plot.
3. We understand the **characters** in a drama through their own words and behavior and through other characters' words about them and behavior toward them.
4. Some **conflict** between the characters or within one character is revealed in each scene in a play. Each character in a scene wants to achieve a particular goal; the conflict comes from the fact that the characters pursue different goals or that one character wants to achieve opposing goals.

5. The **setting** is the time and place of the scene; setting influences the scene's characters and action.
6. Several **themes**, or ideas about life, are usually presented in a play. One scene may develop one or more of these themes.

To explore a dramatic scene you can ask questions like those that follow. The answers are based on one person's reading of Act II, Scene ii, of *Romeo and Juliet.*

QUESTIONS TO EXPLORE A SCENE	SAMPLE ANSWER FOR *ROMEO AND JULIET*
1. What happens in the scene?	*Romeo (a Montague) and Juliet (a Capulet, blood enemies of the Montagues) meet and express their love.*
2. What is each character like? What is the goal of each?	*Romeo is rash (brave?), emotional, and poetic. Juliet is practical, concerned for Romeo's safety, and torn between her love for Romeo and loyalty to her family. Both share the same goal—to announce their love publicly and marry.*
3. What conflict occurs between characters? How is it resolved? Does conflict occur within a character?	*Within themselves, as this scene shows, both young people face the same conflict: How can they, as members of warring families, love each other and marry?*
4. What is the scene's setting? How might the setting affect the characters?	*It is night in the orchard of Juliet's family home. Juliet is afraid that someone in her family will find out that Romeo is there and harm him. Romeo is (or pretends to be) unconcerned about being discovered by Juliet's family. The moonlit setting adds to the romantic mood.*
5. Does the scene develop any of the themes of the whole play?	*The play is a study of love and hatred—the destructiveness and waste of hatred; the power of love over hatred. The theme evolves in Romeo's words in this scene, ". . . stony limits (walls) cannot hold love out."*

Prewriting: Main Idea and Support

Once the preceding exploratory questions have been answered, you are ready to think about the main idea that you will express in the thesis statement in your essay on the dramatic scene. You will be stating how the scene contributes to the play as a whole, as in this example:

> Act II, Scene ii, of *Romeo and Juliet* is important for what it reveals about the conflict the two main characters must resolve, the central conflict in the play.

EXERCISE 3 **Prewriting for an Essay About a Dramatic Scene.** Plan to write a short paper about another scene from *Romeo and Juliet* or about a scene from a play of your own choosing. Begin by reading the whole work; then read the scene aloud. Freewrite or brainstorm about your first reaction to the scene. Then write answers to the exploratory questions like the preceding ones. Finally, use your answers to help you write a thesis statement expressing your main ideas.

Writing About a Dramatic Scene: Structure

The introductory paragraph of an essay that analyzes a dramatic scene should identify the scene and the play in which it appears. The last sentence should be a thesis statement indicating why the scene is important and how it relates to the play as a whole.

Growing out of your thesis statement, the first paragraph in the body of your essay should summarize the action of the scene and briefly describe the characters. In the second paragraph of the body, you should focus on the most important character in the scene, pointing out any statements or actions that reveal the character's traits, goals, conflicts, and so forth.

If you are quoting the speech of one character, you can include the quotation within a paragraph. If the quotation is in prose, follow the format illustrated on pages 314–315. If the quotation is in verse, follow the format illustrated on pages 320–321. If you are quoting dialogue involving two or more characters, however, set the quoted material off from a paragraph, as shown here:

> The following dialogue between Juliet and Romeo takes place after Juliet discovers that Romeo is in the orchard below her balcony.
>
> JULIET. I would not for the world they saw thee here.
> ROMEO. I have night's cloak to hide me from their eyes;
> And but thou love me, let them find me here.
> My life were better ended by their hate
> Than death proroguèd, wanting of thy love.

End your essay with a concluding paragraph that ties the scene to the rest of the play. In the last sentence you might state your opinion of the scene's most important contribution to the play.

Model of an Essay About a Dramatic Scene

The following essay discusses Act II, Scene ii, of *Romeo and Juliet.* Notice how the writer used freewriting, answers to exploratory questions, and his main idea in writing this essay.

<u>Romeo and Juliet,</u> Act II, Scene ii

A William Shakespeare's <u>Romeo and Juliet</u> portrays a bloody feud between the family of Romeo (the Montagues) and the family of Juliet (the Capulets), a feud that eventually leads to the death of the two young lovers. The play is a study of love and hatred--the destructiveness and waste of hatred; the eventual victory of love over hatred. Act II, Scene ii, of <u>Romeo and Juliet</u> is important for what it reveals about the conflict the two main characters must resolve, the central conflict of the play.

B The scene opens in the orchard next to the home of the Capulets. Romeo earlier had been an uninvited guest at a feast given by the Capulets. There he saw Juliet and fell in love with her. He has come to the orchard, hoping to see Juliet. She has come out onto a balcony, not realizing that Romeo is in the orchard below. She speaks to the night about her newly discovered love for
C Romeo: "O Romeo, Romeo! Wherefore art thou Romeo!/Deny thy father and refuse thy name;/Or if thou wilt not, be but sworn my love, /And I'll no longer be a Capulet." Besides expressing her love for Romeo, Juliet's words reveal the conflict between her love for Romeo and loyalty to her family. After Romeo reveals his presence to Juliet, he too expresses a similar feeling of conflict:

JULIET. What man art thou, that, thus
bescreened in night,
So stumblest on my counsel?
ROMEO. By a name
I know not how to tell thee who I am.
My name, dear saint, is hateful to myself
Because it is an enemy to thee.
Had I it written, I would tear the word.
JULIET. . . . Art thou not Romeo and a
Montague?
ROMEO. Neither, fair maid, if either thee
dislike.

D The scene provides some insight into the characters of both Romeo and Juliet. By coming to the Capulets' orchard, a dangerous place for a Montague, Romeo shows a certain rashness or even courage. His expressions of love for Juliet indicate that he is capable of deep emotion and is more than a little poetic. Juliet is practical. Her practicality expresses itself in concern about Romeo's rashness in coming to the Capulet's orchard: ". . . the place [is] death, considering who thou art,/If any of my kinsmen find thee here."

E Because of a series of unlucky circumstances, Romeo and Juliet do not happily resolve the conflict they face. Although they are both dead by the end of the play, their love triumphs over the hatred of their families. The Montagues and Capulets, grief-stricken over the deaths of their children, end their feud--but at what a cost!

NOTES ABOUT MODEL ESSAY ON A DRAMATIC SCENE

A The introductory paragraph explains how the scene fits into the play. The thesis statement explains why the scene is important.

B Body paragraph 1 summarizes the scene and briefly describes the characters.

C Notice the format for quoting the words of one character and the format for quoting the dialogue of two characters.

D Body paragraph 2 examines the two characters in some detail.

E The concluding paragraph ties the scene to the rest of the play and ends with a "clincher" sentence.

Revising, Editing, and Publishing

The questions that follow will help you revise your essay about a dramatic scene. Also see questions listed on page 318.

1. Where do I identify the scene and the play?
2. Where do I mention the scene's contribution to the play as a whole? How can I state this idea more clearly?
3. How can I summarize the action of the scene more clearly?
4. What examples do I give of a character's speech and behavior?

EXERCISE 4 **Writing and Revising an Essay About a Dramatic Scene.** Refer to the prewriting you did in Exercise 3. Use the ideas to write a short essay analyzing the scene you chose from *Romeo and Juliet* or from another play. In the introductory paragraph be sure to include a thesis statement that expresses your idea about how the scene fits into the play. In the paragraphs of the body, summarize the action in the scene and discuss the characters, quoting statements that reveal their traits. In the concluding paragraph, restate your main idea.

Writing About a Poem

According to British author W. Somerset Maugham, "The crown of literature is poetry. It is its end and aim. It is the sublimest activity of the human mind. It is the achievement of beauty and delicacy. The writer of prose can only step aside when the poet passes." Emily Dickinson, the American poet, said it another way: "If I feel physically as if the top of my head were taken off, I know that is poetry."

As both these writers acknowledge, poems are special. They have a wondrous quality. Considering this, analyzing a poem may seem like tearing a rainbow into pieces. How can you write an analysis of a poem without destroying the wonder of it? The answer is that analyzing a poem does not destroy the wonder; rather, it helps you to discover the sources of the wonder—the ideas and techniques of the poet.

Prewriting: First Responses to a Poem

After reading a poem several times, out loud, you should begin to think about its meaning. To get your mind moving, freewrite or brainstorm about the poem. Here is a sample of freewriting about E. E. Cummings's poem "maggie and milly and molly and may." Before you read the freewriting sample, study the poem itself, which is on page 379 in the Writer's Sourcebook.

> *At the beach. Four girls (women? Does it make a difference?) find four different objects in the sand—a seashell, a starfish, a "horrible thing blowing bubbles," and a smooth round stone. Think about what each object might reveal about the one who finds it. The girls' names—Maggie, Milly, Molly, May—all begin with the letter m. Does this mean anything or is it just for the sound? Second-last line of poem begins with a capital f, the only capital letter in the poem. Why? The sea must be meant to represent something. What?*

Prewriting: Exploring a Poem

After writing down your first ideas about the poem's meaning, you can think about the techniques that the poet used to convey this meaning and to stir a response in you. Use this brief review of poetic techniques to help you think about the poem's meaning and your responses:

1. The **speaker** of the poem is the voice we "hear" in the poem. Sometimes the speaker is the poet; sometimes the speaker is a character created by the poet.
2. The poet may use any number of **sound effects**, including the **repetition** of certain words or phrases; **rhyme**—the repetition of similar sounds; **rhythm**—the pattern of stressed and unstressed syllables; **onomatopoeia**—the use of a word or phrase that imitates a sound; and **alliteration**—the repetition of initial consonant sounds.
3. A poet creates **images** through the use of concrete sensory details. The images help to communicate the poet's meaning.
4. A poet may also create meaning with **figures of speech** that embroider or exaggerate the facts. A **simile** compares two unlike items using the words *like* or *as*. A **metaphor** compares two unlike things without using *like* or *as*. **Personification** gives human traits to an animal or object.

To analyze a poem, ask questions like those that follow. The answers are based on one person's reading of the poem "maggie and milly and molly and may." They show how the reader analyzed the poet's use of various techniques to create meaning.

QUESTIONS TO EXPLORE A POEM	SAMPLE ANSWERS FOR "MAGGIE AND MILLY AND MOLLY AND MAY"
1. Who is the speaker in the poem? What is the speaker doing?	*The speaker is an unidentified third-person narrator who describes what the girls find on the beach and comments on the significance of their findings.*
2. What words or phrases are repeated? What ideas or feelings does the poet emphasize with this repetition?	*Besides the names of the four girls, the word <u>and</u> is repeated at the beginning and end of the second and fourth verses. The repetition of <u>and</u> in these positions connects the actions of the girls.*
3. What rhymes do I notice? What effects do these rhymes have?	*The words at the end of the lines of the first, fifth, and last verses rhyme. Also <u>troubles, and</u> and <u>bubbles and</u> rhyme (unusual). Words that almost rhyme: <u>sang</u> (second verse) and <u>thing</u> (fourth verse); <u>star</u> and <u>were</u> (third verse). The unusual rhymes hold the reader's attention.*
4. How can I describe the rhythm? What effect does it create?	*The first line of the poem has four stressed syllables. The other lines in the poem repeat this pattern, suggesting a playful mood.*
5. What other sound devices do I notice? What do these add to the poem's meaning?	*Alliteration (repeating <u>m</u> sounds) gives a musical quality to the first line. The alliteration is used for the joy of the sound.*
6. What do the poem's images make me see, hear, smell, taste, touch? What do the images add to the meaning?	*<u>See</u>: the starfish, the motion of the "horrible" crab, the round stone; <u>hear</u>: the singing of the shell; <u>feel</u>: the smoothness of the stone. The images carry the meaning of the poem which is stated in the last verse. The capital <u>f</u> at the beginning of the last verse—the only capital in the poem—signifies the importance of the verse.*

QUESTIONS TO EXPLORE A POEM	SAMPLE ANSWERS FOR "MAGGIE AND MILLY AND MOLLY AND MAY"
7. What figures of speech do I notice? What might they mean?	*Personification (second verse)—the shell is said to sing; metaphor (third verse)—implied comparison between rays of a starfish and fingers of a hand; similes (fifth verse)—smallness of stone compared to a world, largeness of stone compared to being alone.*

Prewriting: Main Idea and Support

Now that you have answered the exploratory questions, you are ready to think about a thesis statement. The thesis statement will point out that the poet used various poetic techniques to create the poem's meaning. For example:

> In "maggie and milly and molly and may" E. E. Cummings uses a series of images to say that people's perceptions of the outside world reveal their inner natures.

EXERCISE 5 **Prewriting for an Essay About a Poem.** Choose a poem, and plan to write about it. Begin by reading the poem, out loud, several times. Freewrite or brainstorm about your first response to the poem. Then write answers to exploratory questions like the ones shown earlier. Finally, write a thesis statement about the poem's meaning.

Writing About a Poem: Structure

The introductory paragraph of your essay should present your thesis statement, which expresses your interpretation of the poem. The thesis statement should also single out the poetic techniques that, in your opinion, contribute most to that meaning. The paragraphs in the body of your paper should discuss each of the techniques.

If you quote from a poem, quote exactly, and pay attention to the poet's original capitalization and line breaks. You can include quotations of three lines or less within your paragraph, enclosing these short quotations in quotation marks. Mark the ends of lines with a slash as in this example: "may came home with a smooth round stone/as small as a world and as large as alone." Set off quotations of four or more lines from a paragraph by skipping a line, indenting, and (if you type) single-spacing the quotation. You do not need to use quotation marks.

In the concluding paragraph of your essay, refer again to your thesis. The last sentence of this paragraph could convey your overall feeling about the poem.

Model of an Essay About a Poem

The following essay analyzes "maggie and milly and molly and may." Note how ideas from the writer's freewriting, answers to exploratory questions, and thesis statement have been used in writing this essay.

"maggie and milly and molly and may"

A E. E. Cummings's poem "maggie and milly and molly and may" appears on first reading to be a light-hearted poem about a day spent at the beach by four girls. Actually, a closer reading reveals a deeper meaning. The poet uses a series of images to say that what we see in the external world reveals what we are.

B The second verse calls up an image of maggie holding a seashell to her ear. The song the shell sings to her is so sweet "she couldn't remember her troubles."Listening to the music of the shell, maggie rediscovers in herself the ability to appreciate beautiful things.

The words *befriended,* *stranded,* and *languid* in the third verse suggest a picture of milly putting a beached, nearly dead starfish back into the water. By this action, milly reveals a kindness and sympathy within herself.

C Picture molly in the fourth verse: With a horrified look on her face, she is trying frantically to escape from the clutches of "a horrible thing/which raced sideways while blowing bubbles"--a crab. Through this experience, molly finds in herself a fertile imagination or perhaps a fear of the unfamiliar.

The words of the fifth verse help us to see a rather small girl gazing with wonder at "a smooth round stone/as small as a world and as large as alone" which she holds in the palm of her hand. With her discovery of this stone on the beach, may finds in herself a capacity to see the marvelous in even the ordinary things of the world.

D Thus, in a string of "word pictures" E. E. Cummings conveys the underlying meaning, or theme, of his poem. The poet states his meaning directly in the last verse: "For whatever we lose (like a you or a me)/it's always ourselves we find in the sea." In other words, whatever we forget who we are, all we need to do is to respond to the world around us (in this case, the sea), and we will find ourselves again.

NOTES ABOUT A MODEL ESSAY ON A POEM

A The thesis statement expresses the central idea.

B Body paragraphs 1–4 discuss the imagery of the poem and relate it to the theme.

C Notice the format for quotations of three lines or less.

D The concluding paragraph repeats the thesis statement in different words and ends with a "clincher" sentence.

Revising, Editing, and Publishing

These questions are meant to help you revise an essay about a poem. For further help in revising, see page 316.

1. Where do I state my idea about the poem's meaning?
2. What specific poetic techniques do I discuss? According to my essay, how does each technique contribute to the poem?
3. Do I write the poem's words and lines exactly as the poet did?

EXERCISE 6 **Writing and Revising an Essay About a Poem.** Refer to the prewriting you did for Exercise 5. Use the ideas to write a short essay about the poem you chose. In the introductory paragraph include a thesis statement. In the body of the essay, include one paragraph for each technique. In the concluding paragraph restate your main idea in an interesting way.

Writer's Choice

Writer's Choice #1

ASSIGNMENT To write an essay about a short story, dramatic scene, or poem

LENGTH Your choice

AUDIENCE The readers of a school magazine

PURPOSE To share your enjoyment of the work, explaining how you interpreted its meaning

PREWRITING Freewrite or brainstorm about the work and ask exploratory questions about it.

WRITING Write your interpretation of the work, and end by urging your audience to read it.

REVISING Be sure that your interpretation will make sense to your audience and that you have made no mistakes in grammar, usage, spelling, or punctuation.

Writer's Choice #2

ASSIGNMENT To write a letter about a story, dramatic scene, or poem that younger students would enjoy

LENGTH Your choice

AUDIENCE A textbook publisher

PURPOSE To persuade the publisher to include the work in a reading textbook

OPTIONS You may wish to write about a work you enjoyed reading when you were younger. You may prefer to write about a work you yourself have written.

Be sure that your persuasive letter expresses your interpretation of the work and mentions why you think younger students would benefit from reading it.

Writer's Choice #3

ASSIGNMENT To compare two stories, dramatic scenes, or poems

LENGTH Your choice

AUDIENCE Your choice

PURPOSE Your choice

OPTIONS Choose a work and compare it with one of the works you have read or written about in this chapter.

Be sure to choose two works that have something in common. For example, you might compare "A Slander" with another story in which the flaw in a character gets her or him into trouble.

Writers on Writing

Pamela Dulcin was a student at Casa Roble Fundamental High School in Sacramento, California, at the time that she wrote a paper about the stories of Edgar Allan Poe. Pamela, whose interests include cheerleading and the National Honor Society, plans to pursue a career in civil engineering.

THE PRODUCT

This is the introduction to Pamela's paper about Poe.

> The tales of Edgar Allan Poe often reflect a character's, or, more accurately, the author's, obsession with the fear of death. However, because Poe's main purpose was to entertain his readers, he rarely stressed the serious themes of his works. Instead, he wished to excite and shock his readers. Poe achieved this goal through his use of elaborate and exotic language that, when used to describe a scene or situation, could easily send a chill through the spine.

THE PROCESS

> Deciding on a subject was fairly easy in that the stories of Edgar Allan Poe have always intrigued me. After I chose my topic, I wrote a brief outline of what I wanted to include in the body paragraphs of the paper. In collecting information on my subject, I used notecards and labeled them according to my paragraphs. In this way I was able to organize the ideas I wanted to present, instead of having everything scattered around—which tends to confuse me more than I am already. From there on, everything else is a snap. All that is left for me to do is to write the actual sentences and to revise until I have found the right words for what I am trying to say.

YOUR TURN *Writing About a Favorite Author*

Pam wrote about Edgar Allan Poe because he "intrigued" her. Choose an author whom you find intriguing, and write a brief essay explaining what appeals to you most about that author's writing.

CHAPTER 16

Creative Writing

Inspiration is another name for knowing your job and getting down to it.

—*Joyce Cary*

Some people picture creative writers as special mortals who receive inspiration for their work from the sparkling wands of hovering, white-robed beings. If your image of a creative writer is similar to this one, the words of British novelist Joyce Cary in the opening quotation will surprise you. Since Cary is an outstanding writer himself, you can take his word for what is involved in the process known as creative writing. Teaching you to "know your job" as a creative writer is the purpose of this chapter. "Getting down to it" is up to you.

Creative writing is writing in which an author invents characters, situations, images, and emotions and puts these inventions into stories, novels, plays, and poems.

In this chapter you will apply the writing process to the following types of creative writing:

prewriting, writing, and revising a short story
prewriting, writing, and revising a dramatic scene
prewriting, writing, and revising a poem

In practicing the appropriate writing skills to create a short story, a scene from a play, and a poem, you probably will discover that you are less and less dependent on "inspiration" to get your imagination working. The more creative writing you do, the less mysterious the process will seem. You may even begin to think, with Joyce Cary, that writing creatively is in large part "knowing your job and getting down to it."

Writing a Short Story

"Getting down to" writing a short story means diving into your own imagination and seeing what ideas float around in it. You might spot an idea for a memorable character or place. You might recall a moment in your life—a small achievement, a friend's kindness, a private joke—worth expanding into a story.

No matter how you start, your story will involve elements that are present in all stories.

1. a **plot**—a sequence of events that build to a **climax**, or high point. Your plot will grow out of a **conflict**, or problem. Conflict may occur between an individual and an outside force such as nature or society, between two people, or within one individual.
2. one or more **characters**, who will have believable personalities and clear motives for their actions
3. a **setting**—a specific time and place in which the story occurs
4. a **narrator** through whom you tell your story. A **first person narrator** is a character in the story; a **third-person narrator** relates the story's events and the actions, words, and thoughts of its characters.
5. a **theme**—an idea about life or an impression of life suggested by the specific situation, people, and environment of the story

Prewriting: Generating Ideas for a Story

Begin to write your story by generating story ideas. You might get underway by constructing a chart like the one that follows. Use such a chart to record ideas for several possible situations/problems, characters, and settings.

CHART OF STORY IDEAS

SITUATION/PROBLEM	CHARACTER(S)	SETTING
Getting lost in the fog	*A brother and sister returning from a party*	*A highway late at night*
A swimming meet	*Two competitors who are also friends*	*A high school pool*
Using a telephone for the first time	*A person from the distant past*	*My house*
A mysterious old trunk	*Two teen-agers*	*Grandparents' attic*
A ride on the roller coaster	*A small boy*	*The front seat of the roller coaster*
Meeting a space ship from Mars	*Four astronauts*	*A U.S. space ship on the way to Mars*
An argument about baseball	*Two fans*	*The bleachers in a ball park*

EXERCISE 1 **Prewriting: Generating Ideas for a Story.** Generate ideas for a story by making the kind of chart shown above. You can use the Writer's Sourcebook (pages 380–383) as one source of ideas.

Prewriting: Exploring Ideas for a Story

Now you can explore one of the ideas you generated. Imagine the appearance and behavior of the characters. Picture the setting in which the story unfolds. Use questions like those that follow to guide your exploration of the story idea you select. Note that the writer used these questions to explore the first idea in the preceding chart.

STORY IDEA: *Getting lost in the fog*	
QUESTIONS TO EXPLORE A STORY IDEA	SAMPLE ANSWERS
1. Why would I like to explore this idea?	*Something like it happened to me; humorous as it turned out*
2. What is the *conflict?*	*A brother and sister driving back to college late at night after a party get caught in thick fog. The situation brings out tensions.*
3. Who are the main *characters?* How old are they?	*Martie, 21, and her brother Steve, 17*
4. What do they look like—height, weight, coloring, features, clothing?	*Martie: tall, slender, long red hair, sophisticated clothes* *Steve: tall, thin, red hair, glasses*
5. What are their personalities like? How do they speak and act?	*Martie: witty, cautious, affectionate scorn for her "baby brother"* *Steve: eccentric, funny, immature, overconfident*
6. How do they react to the conflict?	*Steve wants to drive on through the fog; Martie doesn't. They argue about the party, where Steve had insisted on playing his tapes.*
7. What is the *setting*—locale, season, weather?	*A mountain highway, deserted except for the car Martie is driving; a foggy autumn night*
8. What *narrator* would work well for this story—first person or third person?	*Try a third-person narrator.*
9. What *theme* might this story express? How?	*The story could show that the ties between brother and sister can survive occasional "bad weather."*

Prewriting: Developing a Story Outline

You might find it helpful to work out your plot in an outline. The writer planning the story about Martie and Steve made this outline:

I. Beginning
   A. Introduce the main characters.
      The third-person narrator introduces Martie and Steve through dialogue and descriptions of their behavior.
   B. Describe the setting.
      A lonely stretch of mountain highway; about 11:30 P.M. on a Saturday night, fog is rolling in quickly.
   C. Establish the basic situation.
      Steve and Martie are on their way back to college after a party where Steve's behavior irritated Martie; fog can stop them.

II. Middle
   A. Introduce the conflict or problem.
      The fog becomes so thick that Martie insists they stop and wait. Steve objects but has to give in (it's her car).
   B. Show the characters reacting to the problem.
      Time passes, and the fog thickens. Increasingly worried about the weather and the mountain road, they begin to argue about Steve's antics at the party: He had repeatedly played his tapes and assumed that Martie's friends found him irresistible.
   C. Lead up to the climax.
      Appealing to Martie's good nature, Steve plays his most notorious tape at full volume "to cheer us up."

III. End
   A. Present the climax.
      They see a group of car lights approaching them from the fog. Mysterious figures emerge from the cars. Steve suddenly becomes protective of his sister.
   B. Wind down the action.
      The figures turn out to be police officers, phoned by a resident of the area who had been frightened by yowls on Steve's tape and thought a wild animal was loose. Martie takes responsibility for the tape.
   C. Present the final outcome.
      The police laugh at the tape and then guide the car down the mountain road. Steve, subdued for a change, confesses that he had been "a little scared." Martie kisses and thanks him for trying to protect her.

EXERCISE 2 **Prewriting: Exploring and Outlining a Story Idea.** Choose one story idea from the chart you made in Exercise 1. Decide on the audience. Explore your story idea by asking questions like those shown on page 332. Then outline the main events in the plot.

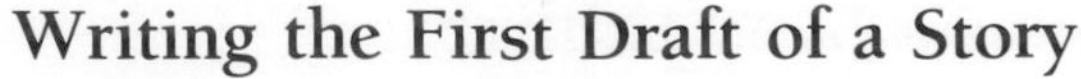

Writing the First Draft of a Story

The following suggestions will help you write the first draft of your short story.

BEGINNING

Make your narrator introduce the characters and describe the setting in a way that captures your reader's interest immediately. If you have decided on a first-person narrator, use first-person pronouns (*I, me*) throughout the story. If you have chosen a third-person narrator to tell your story, use third-person pronouns (*he, she, it, them*).

In the following passage, the writer planning the story about Martie and Steve uses a third-person narrator to launch the story in an attention-getting way.

> The fog was so thick that Martie began to wonder if they were high enough up the mountain to be driving through a cloud. She shook her head to clear it of such silly ideas. Driving herself and the tall person she insisted on thinking of as her baby brother safely back would take all her concentration. The baby brother, or *Steve,* as he thought of himself (or better yet, Mr. Cool), seemed to be in a world of his own, tapping rhythm to a song she did not hear. He was seventeen, four years younger than she, with a skinny, Howdy-Doody version of her pretty, serious face, crowned by an electric variation on her smooth red hair.
>
> If the fog didn't clear, they would have to stop. Steve would protest, she knew. It would be just like him.

CHARACTERIZATION AND DIALOGUE

Make your characters come alive by letting their words and actions reveal their personalities. Rather than writing "Steve was overconfident," for example, the writer of this story will let Steve say and do things that reveal his surplus confidence.

Make **dialogue**, or conversation between characters, an important part of your story. Dialogue adds realism and excitement to a short story. In writing dialogue, keep the following points in mind:

Place all words spoken by characters within quotation marks. A direct quotation can come at the beginning or end of a sentence.

Begin a direct quotation with a capital letter. If you interrupt a quoted sentence in the middle, begin the second part with a small letter.

Begin a new paragraph each time the speaker changes.

Set off direct quotations with commas.

Notice how these points have been applied here:

> Steve broke his silence. "That was one great party. I'm pretty sure Gina likes me," he confided, "but I'm going to play hard to get."

Martie sighed. She thought of sophisticated Gina, tactfully listening to one of Steve's monologues. At least a little *sister* wouldn't start believing she was Burt Reynolds. "Steve—"

But he was on a roll. "They *loved* my tapes. I'm going to splice a whole new tape with amazingly weird sound effects. I could do—let's see, I could do a bat on the space shuttle. Or, hey!—this is terrific—a wolf in a laundromat! *Magnifico,* eh?"

"Steve," she assumed the Voice of Responsibility, "I think we're going to have to stop for a while."

"Hey, no, why? It's *great* driving here, I love it!"

SUSPENSE, CLIMAX, AND RESOLUTION

As you develop the conflict toward the point of highest interest, create **suspense**, or tension, in your readers. Then present the climax, the high point of the plot:

> The fog had grown even thicker, if that was possible. Steve challenged her. "If you're so terrified of going on, why don't you just let *me* drive?"
>
> Martie gave him a withering look; her temper finally snapped. "You don't even have your license yet. Steve, you have been totally obnoxious all night—"
>
> "What? *What???* I was fan*tastic*, I was the *life* of that party. What are you talking about?"
>
> "Oh, Steven, you kept playing those ridiculous tapes over and over when everyone else just wanted to dance!"
>
> "They're *great* tapes. They are incredible tapes. What do you mean? Everyone loved them! Listen—"
>
> Before she could stop him, he had slipped his favorite sound-effects cassette into the tape deck. She groaned, but he began to cajole: "Come on, Marthie" (her old nickname), "it'll cheer us up."
>
> The tape began to play. Steve's eyes grew rapt as the speakers emitted a series of blood-curdling animal yowls. Riled as she was, Martie could not rob her brother of this odd pleasure. Irrationally, she remembered him at the age of four watching water drip from a leaky faucet. This is ridiculous, she thought.
>
> After a few minutes, they realized that they were no longer alone. Cars seemed to be gathering nearby; shadowy figures approached them. Steve grabbed his sister's hand. "It's OK, Marthie," he whispered hoarsely. "I've been studying karate."
>
> A man in uniform loomed out of the fog waving a flashlight, and then two more appeared. Policemen.

After the climax, wind down the action by showing how the conflict is resolved. You might briefly show what the characters have learned. For example, look at the paragraphs on the next page.

The police officers explained that a woman living just above them on the mountain had mistaken the sound-effects tape for the cry of a real and terrifying animal. Martie assured them that the tape was hers and that she would never, ever play it again within a fifty-mile radius of that mountain.

As the police guided them out of the fog and toward the main highway, a subdued Steve glanced at Martie. "To tell the truth, I was just a *little* bit nervous back there, you know, before we knew who they were. Just a little." He paused. "What about you?"

"A bit." He looked *so* young. With a sudden pang of love for him, she leaned over and kissed the freckled cheek. "Thanks for the offer of the karate." She added in a comical monotone, "I only hope that I can return the favor sometime, little lady" (her John Wayne impression always broke him up). They both had a good long laugh as she drove the car out of the fog into the clear night air.

TITLE

Give your story a title that will attract readers. Your title can reflect an important event, character, or place in the story. If possible, the title should suggest the story's theme. The writer of the story about Martie and Steve decided to call the story "Fogbound."

Revising, Editing, and Publishing

After completing your first draft, your next task is to revise your story until you are satisfied that it is as good as you can make it. Begin by reading your story aloud. Answer the questions in the following checklist as you revise, edit, proofread, and finally publish your story:

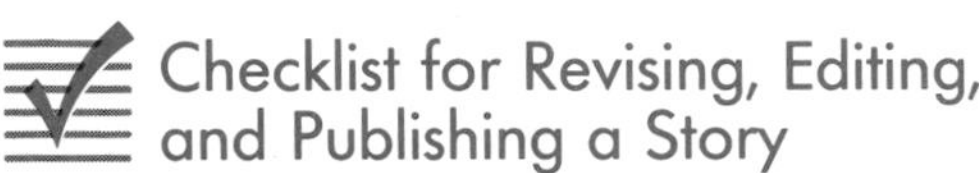

1. What details describe the setting?
2. What details depict the physical traits of the characters? What personality traits do the characters display, and what words and actions convey these traits? What motives lie behind each character's actions?
3. What kind of narrator relates the events of the story? Does the story stay within the point of view of the narrator?
4. What conflict does the story introduce, develop, and resolve?
5. How is each event connected to what happens before and after it?
6. Where do I use dialogue? How can I make it sound more true to life? Do I use the correct format for each quotation?

7. At what moment does the climax of the story occur? How is the conflict resolved?
8. Is the language concrete and vivid throughout the story?
9. Is each sentence complete? Have I avoided errors in the use of verbs, pronouns, and modifiers?
10. Have I correctly capitalized and punctuated each sentence? Are all words correctly spelled?
11. What might be a good way to "publish" or share my story—letting friends and teachers read it? Entering it in a contest?

EXERCISE 3 **Writing, Revising, and Sharing a Story.** Use the notes and outline that you created for Exercise 2 to write a short story. Then use the preceding checklist to revise and edit your first draft. Make a final copy of your story, proofread that copy, and present it to an audience of your choice.

Writing a Dramatic Scene

In this section of the chapter, you will be "getting down to" writing a dramatic scene—that is, a scene for a play. A **dramatic scene** consists entirely of dialogue and stage directions.

Although the format of a scene differs greatly from that of a short story, both contain most of the same elements:

1. The **plot** of a scene grows out of a **conflict** of some kind, most often a conflict between characters. As the characters work through their conflict, the scene builds to a **climax**, or high point.
2. At least two **characters** are needed for a scene, although there may be more. The characters reveal themselves entirely through their dialogue and behavior. **Stage directions** describe the characters' actions and sometimes their motives.
3. The **setting** of the scene is also described in the stage directions. Stage directions provide detailed information about the scenery, the lighting, and the **props**, items used by the characters during the scene.

Prewriting: Generating Ideas for a Scene

Keep in mind that you must have at least two characters in a dramatic scene. Imagine characters who have contrasting personality traits, backgrounds, interests, and goals. Throw an interesting mix of characters into the scene, and then think of conflicts that might be caused by their interactions. Record your ideas in a chart like the following:

CHART OF SCENE IDEAS

FIRST CHARACTER	SECOND CHARACTER	CONFLICT
New toy	*Old toy*	*How to get along with your owner*
American teen-ager	*Russian teen-ager*	*Why can't we be friends?*
Basketball player	*Ballet dancer*	*What have we got in common?*
Rock musician	*Classical musician*	*My music is better.*
Father	*Son*	*Short hair or long hair?*
Juliet Capulet	*William Shakespeare*	*A different ending for Romeo and Juliet*
English teacher	*High school student*	*Is writing well really important?*

EXERCISE 4 **Prewriting: Generating Ideas for a Scene.** Generate ideas for a scene by making the kind of chart shown above. The Writer's Sourcebook (pages 380–383) might be a source of ideas.

Prewriting: Exploring Ideas for a Scene

Select the characters and conflict that you think might lead to the most interesting scene. Explore ideas for the scene by answering questions like the ones that appear in the chart on the following page.

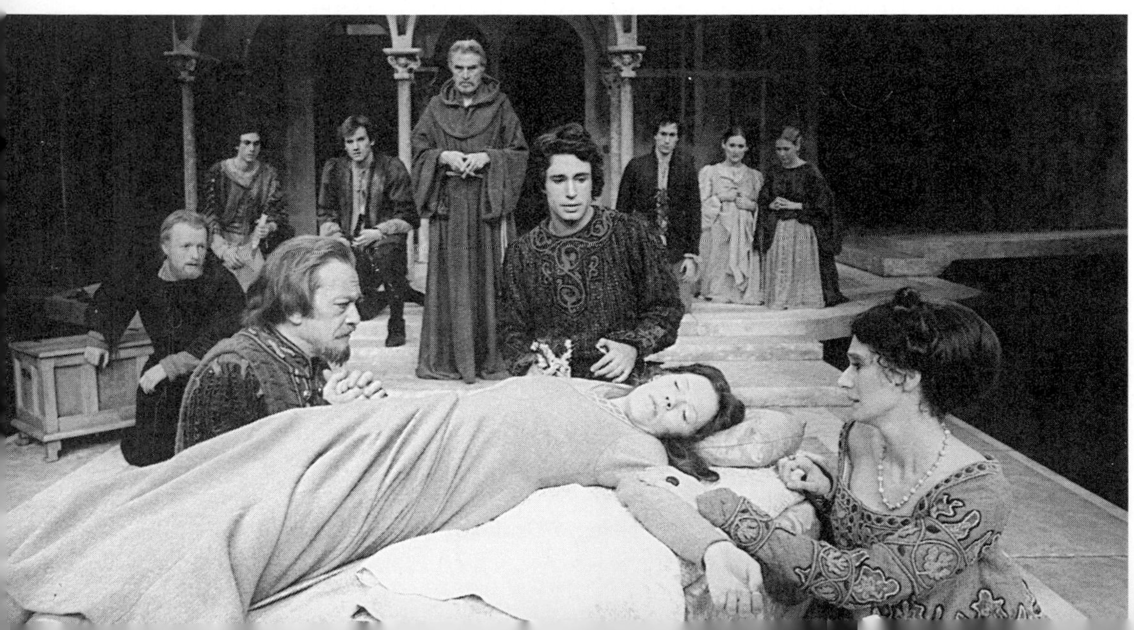

SCENE IDEA: *Juliet asks Shakespeare to rewrite Romeo and Juliet.*	
QUESTIONS TO EXPLORE A SCENE IDEA	SAMPLE ANSWERS
1. Who are the characters? How old are they?	*William Shakespeare: seventeenth-century English dramatist; 40's* *Juliet Capulet: a character he once created; a young teen-ager*
2. What do they look like—height, weight, coloring, features, clothing?	*Shakespeare: handsome, medium height, graying hair; wears a simple white shirt and leather knee breeches* *Juliet: small, with long dark hair; a beautiful, intelligent face; wears a simple red wool gown*
3. What are their personalities like?	*Shakespeare: eloquent, kind* *Juliet: gentle but tenacious*
4. How do they speak and act?	*Shakespeare: speaks forcefully; moves with the confidence of success* *Juliet: speaks softly but firmly; makes quick, darting movements*
5. What does each want in the scene?	*Shakespeare: not to change play* *Juliet: to persuade him to write a happier ending for Romeo and Juliet*
6. When and where does the scene take place? How is it lit? What props do the characters use?	*The scene occurs fifteen years after the first performance of Romeo and Juliet. It takes place in Shakespeare's study, a simple room with two chairs and a table. It is lit softly by candlelight. Shakespeare uses a quill pen and parchment.*

Prewriting: Developing a Scene Outline

You can organize your scene by outlining its main actions. On the following page is the outline developed by the writer planning the scene about Shakespeare and Juliet.

I. Beginning
   A. Establish your characters' identities and their relationship.
      Fifteen years after Shakespeare wrote Romeo and Juliet, Juliet appears mysteriously in Shakespeare's study as he is trying to write a new play. She introduces herself.
   B. Introduce the problem or conflict.
      Juliet explains that she wants Shakespeare to rewrite Romeo and Juliet to give it a happy ending.

II. Middle
   A. Present the characters' reactions to the conflict.
      Shakespeare gently argues that he had his own reasons for writing the tragic ending and that the play is now well established.
   B. Build toward the climax, the point of highest tension.
      Juliet argues that as the play stands, good triumphs only at the cost of innocent lives. She also wishes that she could have grown into a woman.

III. End
   A. Reach the point of highest interest.
      Shakespeare is moved by her plea but is still unwilling to change Romeo and Juliet. Then he gets the idea to write a new play about an innocent, lovely woman (a grown Juliet) who comes back from death.
   B. Show the characters' reactions at the climax.
      Juliet is overjoyed; Shakespeare is excited about his new idea.
   C. Present the final outcome.
      Juliet leaves as mysteriously as she came. Shakespeare wonders if the encounter had been a dream. He begins to write The Winter's Tale (one of his very last plays).

EXERCISE 5 **Prewriting: Exploring and Outlining a Scene Idea.** Choose one of the scene ideas that you generated in Exercise 4, and think of an audience to whom the scene might appeal. Then explore your idea with questions like those shown on page 339. After exploring your idea, outline the scene's main actions.

Writing the First Draft

The suggestions below will help you to write your first draft.

CAST OF CHARACTERS

At the beginning of your scene, list the characters in the order in which they appear. Include some identification of each.

WILLIAM SHAKESPEARE seventeenth-century English writer
JULIET CAPULET the heroine of Shakespeare's *Romeo and Juliet*

SETTING THE STAGE

Following the cast of characters, write stage directions describing the scenery, furniture, and lighting that the audience will see on stage at the beginning of the scene. Then describe the characters who are on stage at the opening of the scene. Enclose these stage directions in brackets, as shown here:

> [*Shakespeare's study, fifteen years after the writing of* Romeo and Juliet. *It is a small room lit by candles. It contains two plain wooden chairs and a table littered with parchment. William Shakespeare sits here, trying to write but apparently not succeeding, since he is surrounded by crumpled pages. He is a handsome man in his mid-forties with graying hair. He wears a plain white shirt and leather knee breeches. As he stares at one wall, he suddenly sees Juliet emerge from the shadows. She is a beautiful young girl; small, with long dark hair, wearing a red dress.*]

DIALOGUE AND ACTION

On the first line after the stage directions, write the name of the first character to speak, along with that character's first speech. Include stage directions to describe how the character speaks and moves. Then on a new line write the words spoken by the second character. Remember that your characters come alive as their personalities are revealed through dialogue and action. Study the following example:

> WILL. [*He jumps to his feet, startled.*] Soft, who comes?
>
> JULIET. Master Will Shakespeare?
>
> WILL. [*He smiles.*] The lady seems strangely familiar.
>
> JULIET. And so should she, for she is your Juliet.
>
> WILL. [Laughing.] My Juliet? But I know no Juliet!
>
> JULIET. The Juliet you wrote of in your play. I am your Juliet, Romeo's Juliet, Juliet Capulet.
>
> WILL. [*Stunned. To himself.*] A dream come to life? I'll not believe it. Yet she looks, now that I remember, as I once thought Juliet would look. I'll question her further. [*To her.*] Why do you come here?
>
> JULIET. I came to ask but one thing, Will Shakespeare. Undo your play's tragic end. Let Romeo and Juliet live!

CONFLICT AND CLIMAX

Following your outline, introduce the scene's conflict through dialogue and action. Create suspense about the outcome as you bring the scene to its climax, or high point:

> WILL. [*Shaking his head.*] I cannot change the play. It is too well known. Of all my works it is the one they come to see most.
>
> JULIET. It is our *love* they come to see, and not our death.

WILL. [*Weakening, then firm.*] Nay, I *will not* change the play. The warring families must suffer the deaths of these two innocents so that peace can spring from their woe.

JULIET. But must the innocents suffer too? Oh, how I have longed to grow from girlhood, to grow to womanhood, to grow old! [*Pleading.*] My father, let me grow old with my Romeo!

WILL. [*To himself, almost relenting.*] I cannot refuse her, and yet I must. [*Looks at the parchment on his writing table. His eyes flash with a sudden idea. He speaks excitedly.*] Look you, Juliet, I have begun a new play. There could be in this play a gentle lady like yourself, but older, grown to womanhood. She will seem to die, as you did. But she will come back to life and be restored to her dear love. I cannot change what I have writ, but I can write anew. Will it please you, my lady?

[*Juliet says nothing but nods, her eyes shining with joy.*]

RESOLUTION

Show how the characters react to the climax. Then wind down the action and write a brief ending.

WILL. [*Bustling with energy.*] What shall I call the play, my Juliet?

JULIET. [*Touching the gray in Will's hair. Smiling.*] Call it "The Winter's Tale."

[*He smiles and begins to sort out the parchment. She withdraws to the shadows and disappears. Will, working at his writing table, does not notice at first.*]

WILL. "The Winter's Tale." [*He looks up.*] Juliet? [*He rubs his eyes.*] Was it a dream, after all? [*He shakes his head to clear it, and a petal from a red rose drops into his hand. He touches it to his lips and then begins to write.*] "The Winter's Tale."

TITLE

Create an interest-arousing title for your scene. Your title might echo the conflict, the setting, an aspect of one or more characters, or even a single line of dialogue. The writer of the scene about Shakespeare and Juliet entitled it "The Happy Ending."

Revising, Editing, and Publishing

If you know your job as a writer of scenes, you know that your next task involves revising, editing, and publishing your work. Read your scene aloud or, better still, do a dramatic reading with one or more friends. Decide what changes are needed to make your scene as good as it can be. Use the following checklist to revise and edit your work before you publish it.

Checklist for Revising, Editing, and Publishing a Scene

1. At the beginning of the scene, have I clearly identified each character? What more do I need to say about the scenery?
2. What personality traits does each character display in word and action? How can the dialogue and stage directions convey these traits more clearly?
3. Out of what conflict does the action of the scene grow? How have I developed and resolved the conflict?
4. At what moment does the climax of the scene happen? How is the conflict resolved?
5. Have I used the correct form for dialogue and stage directions?
6. In what way can I present my scene to an audience—an informal reading? A full staging with costumes?

EXERCISE 6 **Writing, Revising, and Publishing a Scene.** Write a scene using the notes and outline that you created for Exercise 5. Then use the preceding checklist to revise and edit your first draft. Make a final copy of your scene, and proofread that copy. Publish the scene in a reading or a performance.

Writing a Poem

What would you say a poem is? Even if you cannot give a scholarly answer to this question, more than likely you recognize a poem when you see one, and you know that poetry is very different from prose. You can identify poems without much difficulty because poetry has its own special characteristics:

1. A poet communicates meaning in a poem largely through the use of **images**—mental pictures made up of details that appeal to the senses of sight, hearing, smell, taste, and touch.
2. A poet can also use **figures of speech** to go beyond the literal facts. In a **simile** a poet compares two seemingly unlike items by using the words *like* or *as*. In a **metaphor** the poet links two unlike things without using such words. In **personification** the poet gives human qualities to animals, objects, or ideas.
3. A poet often puts together special **sound effects** in a poem. Not every poet uses all of these sound effects, but most poets use at least some of them. Sound effects that poets frequently use are

repetition, **rhyme**, and **rhythm**. Among other sound effects are **onomatopoeia**, the imitation of a sound by a word; **alliteration**, the repetition of initial consonant sounds.

4. Every poem has an overall pattern, or **form**. Some poems are divided into **stanzas**, or groups of lines.

Prewriting: Generating Ideas for a Poem

In this section of the chapter, you will experiment with imagery, figurative language, and sound effects to help you generate ideas for a poem.

IMAGERY

Images are mental pictures called up by concrete details we perceive through our senses. You can practice creating concrete, vivid images by making a chart like the one that follows.

ITEM	SENSE	IMAGE
A potato chip	• *sight* • *sound* • *smell* • *taste* • *touch*	• *a wavy wafer, a crisp amoeba* • *munch, crunch, crackle* • *appetizing, fresh* • *salty, oily* • *bumpy, oily*

EXERCISE 7 **Generating Ideas for a Poem by Practicing with Imagery.** Choose one of the following items or an item of your own. Make a chart like the preceding one, listing images to describe your item. Appeal to at least three different senses. Save your notes.

1. an apple
2. a waterfall
3. cooked fish
4. spaghetti
5. a snake
6. a store

FIGURATIVE LANGUAGE

Poets use figurative language to capture real things in vivid and memorable images. Notice how the following figures of speech produce images in your mind.

SIMILE The stars are like millions of cats' eyes peering out of darkness.

METAPHOR Stars are blazing islands in the night.

PERSONIFICATION The stars gaze down on us, seeing neither good nor evil.

EXERCISE 8 **Practicing with Figurative Language to Generate Ideas.** Choose one of the following numbered sets of items, or invent a set of your own. Write a simile for the item in the left-hand column and a metaphor using the middle item. Then personify the item in the right-hand column. Save your notes.

1. an old man's face	an old man's hair	a rocking chair
2. the circus	sports fans	a football
3. a playful breeze	a newspaper blowing	a row of buildings

SOUND EFFECTS: ALLITERATION AND ONOMATOPOEIA

One device poets can use to produce sound effects in their work is alliteration—the placing together of words that begin with the same consonant sound. Read the following example aloud:

> *B*art *b*ounced the *b*attered *b*asketball *b*etter than *B*en.

Poets also use onomatopoeia to produce sound effects. Onomatopoeia is the use of words that imitate the sounds of the things they name: *bong, buzz, crash, ping, slurp, whoosh.*

EXERCISE 9 **Practicing with Onomatopoeia and Alliteration.** Choose two of the following items, or think of two items of your own. Then write a sentence about each. Use either onomatopoeia or alliteration in the sentence. Save your sentences for use in a poem.

1. an old car	3. a playground	5. a rainstorm
2. the circus	4. a pencil sharpener	6. a mountain

CHARTING TO GENERATE IDEAS FOR A POEM

To help you find a subject for a poem, you can make a chart like the one that follows.

CHART OF IDEAS FOR A POEM

GENERAL CATEGORY	SPECIFIC SUBJECT FOR A POEM
A person (you, a relative, a celebrity)	*Aunty Al*
An animal (real or imagined)	*The flecked flopperdiddget*
An object (natural or artificial)	*An artificial satellite*
A scene (actual or invented)	*The planet Radura*
An event (real or imagined)	*A volcano erupting*
An emotion	*Relief; anger*

EXERCISE 10 **Charting to Generate Ideas for a Poem.** Make a chart like the preceding one. For each general category, fill in one specific item about which you could write a poem. You might find ideas in the Writer's Sourcebook (pages 380–383). Save your chart.

EXERCISE 11 **Compiling Your Ideas for a Poem.** Review the notes you created in Exercises 7–10. Star six ideas for use in a poem.

Prewriting: Exploring Ideas for a Poem

Think of a subject for a poem. Then explore your subject by answering questions like the ones in the following chart:

POEM IDEA: *The feeling of anger*	
QUESTIONS TO EXPLORE AN IDEA FOR A POEM	SAMPLE ANSWERS
1. What do I see, hear, taste, and touch when I think about this idea?	*See—flames, ashes, darkness; hear—exploding words; taste—bitterness; touch—heat, sharp edges*
2. What emotions does this idea evoke in me?	*Sadness at the wastefulness of anger*
3. What figure of speech could I use?	*A string of metaphors comparing anger to birds, flames, and other things perceived by the senses*
4. How can I use alliteration or onomatopoeia?	*Alliteration—flame/flash, onomatopoeia—sizzling*

EXERCISE 12 **Exploring an Idea for a Poem.** Plan to write a poem of any length. You may use rhyme or not. You can work with one of the ideas that you starred in Exercise 11 or a new idea. Think about the audience. Explore your idea using questions like those above.

Writing the First Draft of a Poem

In your first lines, introduce your subject, using concrete language. Choose words that work well together, as in this sample stanza.

Anger!
A flock of words
Like frantic birds
That scatter

In the stanzas that follow your opening stanza, include ideas, images, figures of speech, sound effects, and patterns that you noted as you generated and explored ideas for your poem

Anger!
A flame that burns,
A flash that turns
To ashes
A sizzling night.
All heat, no light
To guide you.

Present your most striking images and ideas in the last stanza so that they will remain with your readers.

A heart that's shut,
A love that's not
But could be.

After completing your first draft, create a title that does justice to your poem. The writer of the preceding poem decided on the simple title "Images of Anger."

Revising, Editing, and Publishing

Read your poem aloud, and then decide how to revise it by asking yourself the following questions:

Checklist for Revising, Editing, and Publishing a Poem

1. To what senses do the images in my poem appeal? Which images can I sharpen or intensify?
2. What figures of speech have I used?
3. Have I used alliteration or onomatopoeia? Is each appropriate?
4. What would be a good way of presenting my poem to my intended audience—compiling a student anthology?

EXERCISE 13 **Writing, Revising, and Publishing a Poem.** From the notes that you created in Exercise 11, write a poem. When you have written your first draft, read your poem aloud, and revise it by asking yourself the questions shown on this page. When you are satisfied with your poem, write a neat final copy and proofread it. Finally, present your poem to your audience.

Writer's Choice #1

ASSIGNMENT To write a short story or dramatic scene
LENGTH Your choice
PURPOSE To re-create a real experience, altering that experience as you please
AUDIENCE Your choice
PREWRITING Choose an experience either from your life or from history. Decide whether you want to convert it into a story or scene. Then follow the relevant prewriting suggestions presented in this chapter. As you develop your plot outline, decide how you will alter the real experience.
WRITING Follow the suggestions for writing a story or a scene.
REVISING Have you altered the real experience? Does your story or scene stand on its own? Proofread your final copy. Then share your finished work with the audience you chose.

Writer's Choice #2

ASSIGNMENT To write a poem of two to four stanzas
LENGTH Your choice
PURPOSE To express a positive or negative feeling
AUDIENCE Your choice
PREWRITING Decide on the feeling that you want to express and the images, figures of speech, and sound effects you will use.
WRITING Write your poem, following the suggestions on page 346.
REVISING Read your poem aloud. Does it evoke the feeling you had in mind? Do the words and images of your poem work well together? Be sure to proofread your final copy; then present it to the audience you chose.

Writer's Choice #3

ASSIGNMENT To write a story, scene, or poem
LENGTH Your choice
PURPOSE Your choice
AUDIENCE Your choice
OPTIONS You might use a story, scene, or poem idea that you generated but did not explore in this chapter. You might also use the Writer's Sourcebook (pages 380–383) as a source of material.
Whatever you write, follow the prewriting, writing, and revising steps related to that type of writing.

Writers on Writing

Most of Michelle Calentine's activities center on her interest in dance. She hopes to study modern dance in college. When she was a student at Eastwood High School in El Paso, Texas, she wrote the following poem, entitled "The Silent Dancer," and the commentary that follows it.

THE PRODUCT

Protective curtains vanish;
Staring spotlights appear.
Posture; so gracefully supporting
The human cathedral of muscles
Trained to obey on cue.
Head held high, focusing over the
Crowd and on the dream,
Achieved solely through determination.
Rhythm is tuned to her body,
As the dance becomes her heart
And the music provides the blood
To keep it beating.

THE PROCESS

Since dance is a very significant part of my life, I wanted to portray a dancer through writing. I didn't want the dancer to be an ordinary person. I wanted to show the deep inner motion and feeling that combine to make the dancer appear flawless.

With these things in mind, I placed myself on a stage, alone. There I felt the security of the curtains suddenly interrupted by spotlights and people's faces. I mentally moved myself from the stage into the auditorium to view the dancer with a dancer's eye. I then returned to the stage and expressed the dancer's inner closeness with the music.

YOUR TURN *Writing a Poem About Motion*

Write a short, unrhymed poem about a series of actions performed by a professional person, just as Michelle wrote about a dancer. You might write about an athlete, an actor, a factory worker, a hairdresser—anyone who is an expert in some kind of movement.

Writers on Writing

Ghia Euskirchen believes that being an exchange student in Switzerland improved her writing by helping her reflect objectively on her community and country. As a student at Indian Hill High School in Cincinnati, Ohio, Ghia wrote the following story excerpt and commentary.

THE PRODUCT

Polly Ethylene was unaware of the change in her body as she climbed out of bed. When she washed her face, however, the soap and water just slid off her skin, which had an artificial, bubble-gum-pink tinge to it. Polly poked herself, leaving an indentation. Her skin felt smooth and cold. It had turned to plastic! Amazing—skin that was pliable, like dough. Now she could smooth out that bump on her nose and the dimple in her chin.

Really, the change should not have surprised her. After all, the year was 2025, and they were already twenty-five years into the Plastic Age. Virtually everything natural had been replaced by plastic long ago. Grass had been replaced by Astroturf; furniture was made from simulated wood. Food was synthesized in a laboratory.

Polly dressed herself in a pair of candy-colored sandals and a "leather" dress that was made of vinyl. Her stomach rumbled, and she stumbled down the stairs for breakfast. Her joints felt stiff.

THE PROCESS

This excerpt comes from "Doubletake," a short story I wrote about a girl who finds one morning that she and everyone else have turned to plastic. She seeks aid from people who should help her: her parents and a plastic surgeon. Instead, these people are cold and indifferent because they have taken on the characteristics of their heartless plastic bodies.

The description of the setting was important for the story. I tried to relate 2025 to our time by bringing in some common elements from the 1980s, such as Astroturf, simulated wood, and food full of artificial colors, flavors, and preservatives. I also tried to choose appropriate names, such as Polly Ethylene (her surgeon is named Dr. Saran). I feel that good description is especially important when a story covers unfamiliar ground—for instance, when it takes place, as "Doubletake" does, in the future.

YOUR TURN *Writing a Story About the Future*

Try writing a short story that is set far in the future. You may find it helpful to bring in certain details from our own time.

CHAPTERS 13–16 WRITING ACROSS THE CURRICULUM

CHAPTER 13 WRITING ABOUT SOCIAL STUDIES

Focusing a Topic [pages 282–284]

1. Which of the following topics is most narrowly focused?
   (a) Baltic states (b) Lithuania (c) the importance of Lithuania in medieval Europe

Evidence and Sources [pages 284–285] Which item is (a) a primary source, (b) a secondary source, (c) a fact, or (d) an opinion?

2. A biography of Czar Alexander II of Russia
3. Czar Alexander II had absolutely no understanding of the peasants.
4. Three pages from a diary kept by Czar Alexander II
5. Czar Alexander II abolished slavery in Russia in 1861.

Making Generalizations [pages 285–286]

6. Which of the following statements is properly qualified?
   (a) Michaelangelo was a towering figure of Renaissance art.
   (b) All painters after Michaelangelo imitated his style.
   (c) Michaelangelo was the only worthwhile Renaissance painter.

Organization [pages 288–291] Which statement demonstrates (a) chronological order, (b) cause and effect, (c) comparison, or (d) contrast?

7. Napoleon's popularity made it easy for him to become Emperor.
8. Napoleon had himself proclaimed emperor in May of 1804, and in December of that year he was crowned.
9. The Russian winter destroyed Napoleon's army just as it would destroy the German army during World War II.
10. Unlike many military leaders, Napoleon always had the love and respect of his soldiers.

Writing for Review. Write a paragraph about a social studies topic of your own choice. Follow the complete writing process.

CHAPTER 14 WRITING ABOUT SCIENCE AND TECHNOLOGY

Topic and Purpose. [pages 296–298] Indicate the letter of the item that correctly answers each question.

1. Which topic is more suitable for a scientific or technical report?
   (a) early peoples' reactions to meteors
   (b) meteors and meteorites in the 1980s
2. Which purpose would probably suit this topic best?
   (a) to contrast
   (b) to explain a process

Structure [pages 300–302] Match each part of a scientific or technical report in the left column with the phrase in the right column most likely to be found in that part.

3. Introduction	(a) This paper will demonstrate . . .
4. Bibliography entry	(b) (Holmes, 1963, p. 131)
5. Conclusion	(c) This report suggests . . .
6. Discussion	(d) Tornadoes, for example . . .
7. Internal source citation	(e) Battan, Louis J. The Thunderstorm . . .

Style, Tone, and Mechanics [pages 300–302] Read the following passage. Items 8, 9, and 10 are presented in two forms. Indicate which form is correct for each item—the *a* form or the *b* form.

Raindrops (*always*, *I notice*) vary in diameter from about (½, *one half*) to (5½ *mm*, *five and one-half millimeters*).
8.(a) 8.(b) 9.(a) 9.(b) 10.(a) 10.(b)

Writing for Review Write an introductory paragraph for a paper about a scientific or technical subject of your own choosing. Be sure to follow the writing process.

CHAPTER 15 WRITING ABOUT LITERATURE

Writing About a Story and Scene [pages 309–322]. Indicate the letter of the item that correctly answers each question.

1. Which is the best topic for a paper about "A Slander"?
   (a) Chekhov's life (b) Ahineyev's self-destruction (c) dullness of Russian stories (d) the importance of the setting
2. If you were writing a paper about "A Slander," what term would you use to describe Ahineyev?
   (a) humble (b) dynamic (c) truthful (d) humorless
3. If you were planning a paper about Act II, Scene ii, of *Romeo and Juliet,* which question would you ask about Juliet?
   (a) Why does she fear for Romeo? (b) How old is Juliet?

Writing for Review Write a short essay about a story or poem of your own choosing. Follow the writing process.

CHAPTER 16 CREATIVE WRITING

Writing for Review Write a poem, a story, or a scene from a play that shows a conflict between two characters or between one character and an external force, such as nature. If you choose to write a story or dramatic scene, decide on your setting and characters, and outline your plot. If you choose to write a poem, decide on the poetic techniques that your poem will use. Then write and revise your work.

WRITER'S SOURCEBOOK

The Writer's Sourcebook is a collection of illustrations and assignments that correspond to many of the chapters in Part 1: Composition. For example, as shown in the contents below, the Writer's Sourcebook opens with a section called "The Writing Process and Style," which presents paintings, photographs, and assignments coordinated with the first two units of the book.

Using the Writer's Sourcebook

You may work with the Writer's Sourcebook in a variety of ways:

Just looking through the Writer's Sourcebook may help you generate ideas for writing.

You may respond to specific material in the Writer's Sourcebook by completing the assignment suggested for each illustration.

Illustrations from the Writer's Sourcebook will help you to complete certain Writer's Choice assignments, which appear regularly throughout Part 1: Composition.

For instance, in responding to Writer's Choice #5 in the chapter on narrative writing, you may choose the option that refers you to the photographs headed "Narrative Writing" in the Writer's Sourcebook. You may then write a narrative based on the action you see in the photographs.

Writer's Sourcebook Contents

THE WRITING PROCESS AND STYLE

1

Detail, anonymous, *Running before the Storm,* c. 1877. Oil on canvas. H. 24 in. W. 36 ¼ in. Museum of Fine Arts, Boston.

2

William Morris Hunt (1824–1879). *Girl with Cat.* Oil on canvas. Museum of Fine Arts, Boston.

3

4

5

ASSIGNMENTS

Generating and Exploring Ideas in Prewriting *(pages 21–30).* Choose three illustrations on pages 354–357, and use various techniques of prewriting to generate at least two writing ideas for each. Then decide on your most promising idea, and explore it using either informational questions (pages 27–28) or personal questions (page 29). Narrow your thinking to a topic that you can cover in one paragraph.

Writing a Variety of Topic Sentences *(pages 46–47).* Choose a new topic or use one based on the writing ideas that you developed in the assignment above, and write two different topic sentences for a paragraph.

Using Spatial Order *(pages 62–63).* Write a paragraph about painting 1 using spatial order to organize your writing. Use spatial transitions to increase the coherence of your writing.

The illustrations on these two pages complement the instruction in Chapters 1–6.

DESCRIPTIVE WRITING

1

Frederic Remington, *Howl of the Weather.* Frederic Remington Art Museum

2

Andrew Wyeth, *Nicolas Wyeth.* Anonymous lender

ASSIGNMENTS

Using Descriptive Language *(pages 146–147)* Use exact and vivid language to write a paragraph that describes painting 3. First ask yourself any appropriate questions from page 142. Then make an observation table (page 142), and fill in columns for at least three different senses. Bring your subject to life by including a variety of concrete sensory details and figures of speech.

Creating an Overall Impression *(pages 143–145).* Write a paragraph about the impression created in painting 1. Freewrite for one minute. Then write a topic sentence stating the overall impression, and develop the paragraph by discussing specific supporting details. Use vivid and precise language to portray the scene.

3

4

Uncle Sam Whirligig, New England c. 1850–1900. ©Museum of American Folk Art.

Describing a Person *(pages 149–150).* Write a character sketch of the person in painting 2. Begin with a topic sentence in which you express an overall impression. Then describe the individual's physical traits. Finally, discuss the psychological traits that the picture suggests. Try to show a connection between the inner and the outer person.

Organizing a Description *(pages 145–146).* Write a descriptive paragraph about illustration 4, a whirligig, which is set into motion by the wind. Begin with a topic sentence, and then choose one way of ordering the details that support your topic sentence. Be sure to use appropriate transitions.

The illustrations on these two pages complement the instruction in Chapter 7.

NARRATIVE WRITING

1

2

ASSIGNMENTS

Prewriting for a Narrative *(pages 157–160).* Study illustrations 1 and 2 on pages 360–361. Then ask the questions *who? what? when? where? why?* and *how?* to generate ideas for a nonfiction narrative about one of the illustrations.

Preparing a Narrative Outline *(pages 161–165).* Write a narrative outline for illustration 1 or 2 on pages 360–361. First state the purpose of the narrative. Then list the events in chronological order. Include descriptions of characters and setting.

Writing a Narrative in Chronological Order *(pages 164–166).* Write a narrative about illustration 1 or 2 on pages 360–361. Include all the elements of a narrative, as well as specific details presented with descriptive language. Write your narrative in chronological order.

Using Vivid Verbs and Narrative Details to Convey Action *(pages 163, 168–169).* Revise the narrative you wrote for the assignment above. First, replace any weak verbs with vivid, precise verbs. Then add details to make your narrative richer and more informative.

The illustrations on these two pages complement the instruction in Chapter 8.

EXPOSITORY WRITING

1

Jefferson Gauntt (1806*1864). *Two Children,* 1843. Oil on canvas. H. 50 in. W. 40 in. Museum of fine Arts, Boston.

3

4

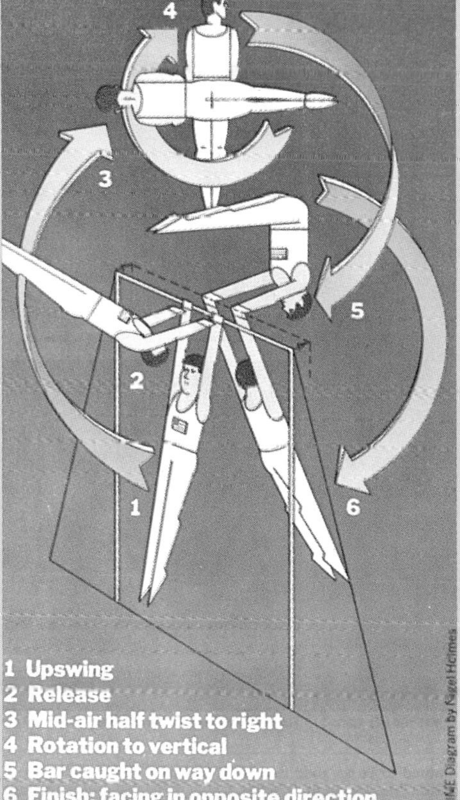

5

ASSIGNMENTS

Dividing Items *(pages 185–188).* Use spatial order to explain in a paragraph how the quilt in illustration 4 may be divided into a number of different parts. Use appropriate transitions to show the relationships between the parts.

Explaining a Cause-and-Effect Relationship *(pages 182–185).* Write a paragraph about the causes and effects shown in the dust storm in illustration 1. Use transitions to clarify the relationship that you are presenting.

Explaining a Process *(pages 179–182).* Examine the process shown in illustration 5. Fill out a chart listing the steps in the process (page 180). Then write a paragraph about the process. Use appropriate transitions, and add any information that you think your audience needs.

Comparing and Contrasting Items *(pages 194–197).* Using a comparison frame (page 195), write a comparison-contrast based on painting 2 and illustration 3. Consider using item-by-item organization.

The illustrations on these two pages complement the instruction in Chapter 9.

CRITICAL THINKING AND PERSUASIVE WRITING

1

2

3

4

ASSIGNMENTS

Selecting a Topic and Suiting Topic to Audience *(pages 205–207).* Study the photographs on pages 364–365, and write down an opinion to use as the basis for a persuasive paragraph. Next, determine your audience by responding to the profile questions on page 206.

Identifying Facts and Opinions *(pages 207–210).* Gather evidence about the topic you selected above. Then make a list of facts and a list of opinions that directly support your opinion about physical fitness. Eliminate any inadequate and unreliable evidence.

Writing an Argument *(pages 210–213).* Write an argument based on your work in the assignments above. First state your position clearly. Then give your audience any necessary background information. Organize the evidence that supports your opinion in a clear and straightforward way. Use transitions to help your readers follow each step you take. End your argument with a strong concluding statement.

The illustrations on these two pages complement the instruction in Chapter 10.

WRITING ABOUT SOCIAL STUDIES

Headline: briefly indicates the subject of the story

By-line: tells who wrote the story

Dateline: shows when and where the story was written

Lead: the first paragraph, which generally answers the questions *who? what? when? where? why? and how?*

Subhead: alerts the reader about upcoming information and breaks up long columns of type

ASTRONAUTS STOW GEAR AS THEY HEAD FOR COAST LANDING

MISSION TERMED SUCCESS

Weight of Spacelab in Cargo Bay Is a Factor in Shifting Touchdown to Mojave

By RICHARD D. LYONS

Special to The New York Times

EDWARDS AIR FORCE BASE, Calif., May 5 — The seven astronauts aboard the space shuttle Challenger ended experiments today and stowed equipment in preparation for their scheduled landing here Monday at the end of what has been hailed as a highly successful seven-day mission.

The Challenger is due to swoop in from the South Pacific, rake Los Angeles with a sonic boom from 90,000 feet and alight on the dry lake bed of the Mojave Desert here shortly after 9 A.M. (noon, Eastern daylight time).

The landing was originally scheduled to take place at Cape Canaveral, Fla., but the hard landing of the Discovery spacecraft there last month, which damaged that shuttle's brakes, blew one of its four main tires and seriously frayed the other three, led officials of the National Aeronautics and Space Administration to switch sites as a precaution.

Reason for Switching Sites

With the Spacelab scientific laboratory nestled in its cargo bay, the Challenger is 12 tons heavier than the Discovery, and the almost endless dry lake beds here provide more flexibility in case of trouble.

2

3

ASSIGNMENTS

Writing With Comparison and Contrast *(pages 289–291)*. Photographs often offer clues about a place's surface features, climate, and natural vegetation. They may also present clues about people and how they live. Study the photographs in illustrations 2 and 3. The top photograph shows a village in southern Italy. The photograph below is of a village in the Swiss Alps.

Write a paragraph that compares and contrasts the two photographs. As prewriting, fill out a chart like the one on page 290. You may want to consider the following as you work on your chart: (1) the time of year the photographs were taken, (2) predominant surface features of the area, (3) uses of the land and its surroundings, and (4) types of houses. You may want to use an AAABBB organization (page 290) in your paragraph.

Using Definition in an Expository Paragraph *(pages 190–194)*. Based on the information in illustration 1, write a paragraph that explains the main parts of a newspaper story. As prewriting, list the parts of the story, and define them in your own words. Then find an example of each definition from the story in illustration 1.

Write a first draft, incorporating your prewriting notes. Add transitions to show the relationship between the various parts of your subject. When you have finished your first draft, revise your paragraph. Check to be sure that all your divisions are clear and that your paragraph is organized as logically as possible.

The illustrations on these two pages complement the instruction in Chapter 13.

ASSIGNMENTS

Writing About Causes and Effects *(pages 288–289).* Study illustration 1 above, and ask yourself why the typical American city develops according to the pattern shown. As preparation for writing a paragraph in answer to this question, briefly describe the pattern of development presented in illustration 1. Then decide whether your paragraph will be explaining causes, effects, or both. Use brainstorming to discover the causes and effects related to your topic, and, with the help of the personal, social, and economic questions on page 289, examine your topic from different viewpoints. Finally, decide whether or not your causes and effects are short-term or long-term (page 289).

Write a first draft of your paragraph based on your prewriting notes. Begin with a topic sentence that expresses your main idea. As you write, be sure to use transitions both to indicate causes and effects and to indicate degrees of certainty. When you have finished your first draft, revise your paragraph. Think carefully about what you would like your audience to learn from your writing about causes and effects.

1

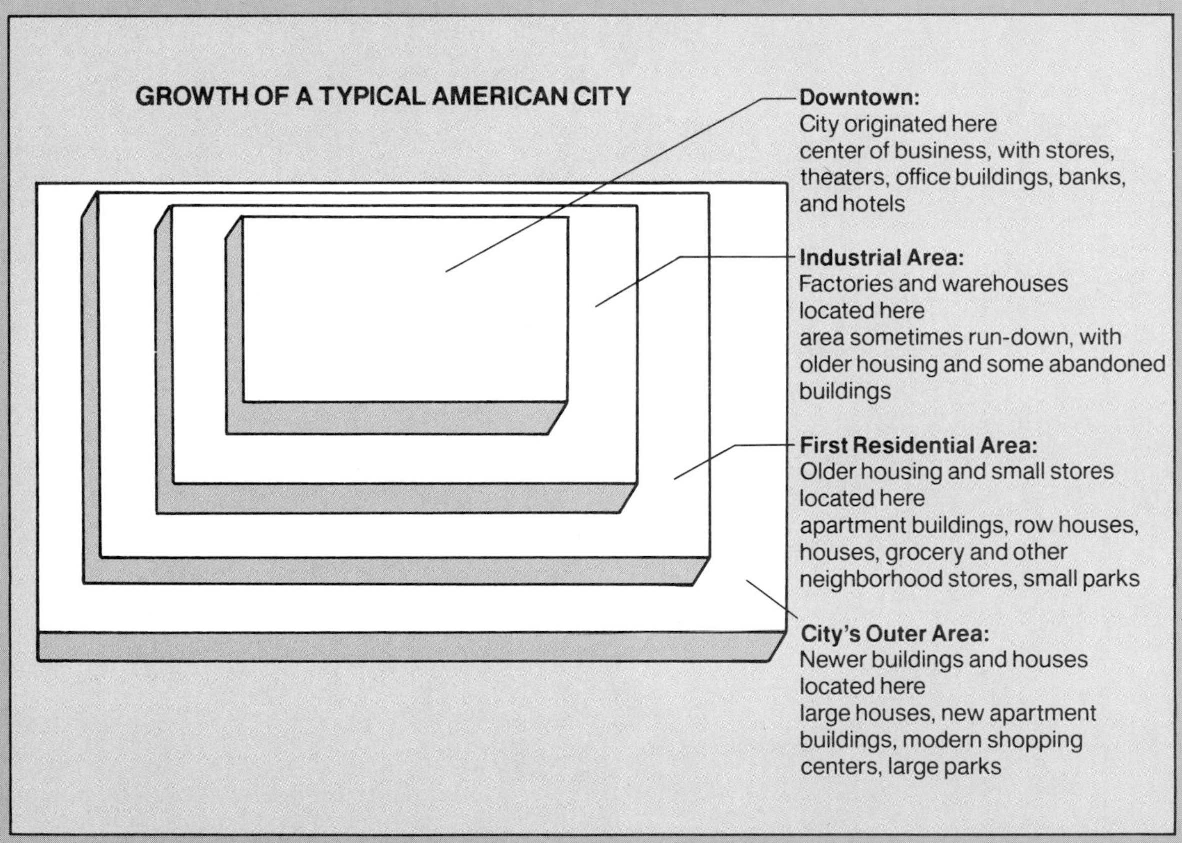

2

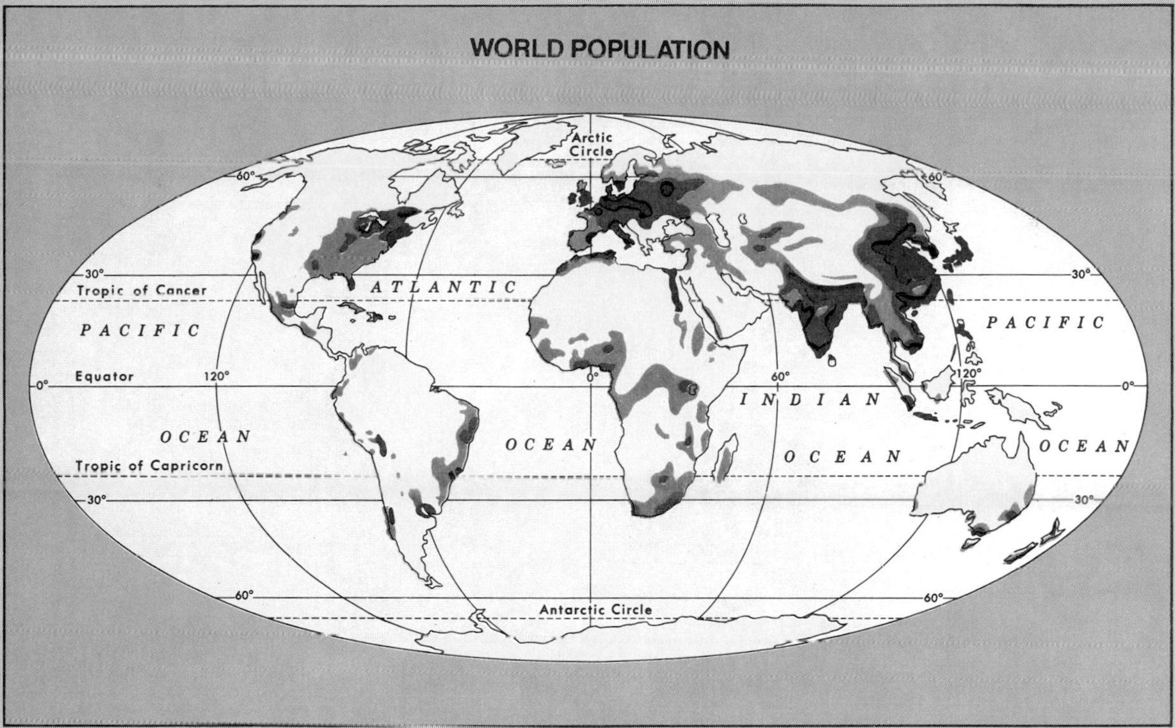

WORLD POPULATION

Arctic Circle
Tropic of Cancer
Equator
Tropic of Capricorn
Antarctic Circle
PACIFIC OCEAN
ATLANTIC OCEAN
INDIAN OCEAN
PACIFIC OCEAN

Writing with Comparison and Contrast *(pages 289–291).* The map in illustration 2 shows the difference in world population density, or the number of persons per square kilometer or square mile. Each color on the map stands for a different number of people per square kilometer or square mile.

Write a paragraph that compares and contrasts the area where you live with at least three other areas. As prewriting, first decide in which kind of area you live. Is it densely populated (black), sparsely populated (yellow), or moderately populated (orange and red)? Then choose three different areas with which to compare your area, and make notes on the population density of each. Finally, write your paragraph based on your prewriting notes. Follow AAABBB organization (page 290).

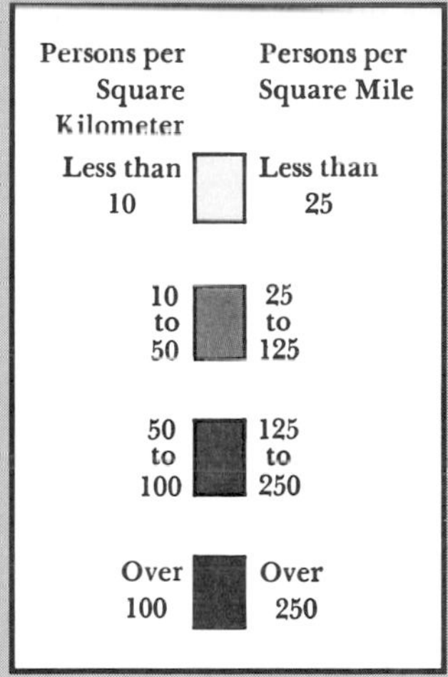

The illustrations on these two pages complement the instruction in Chapter 13.

WRITING ABOUT SCIENCE AND TECHNOLOGY

1

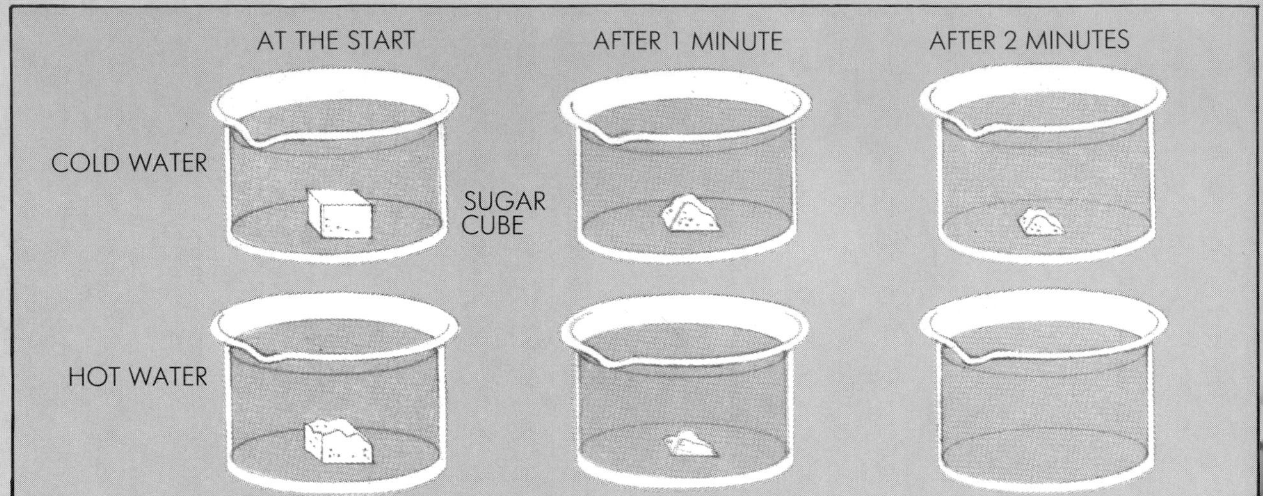

ASSIGNMENTS

Explaining a Process for a Scientific Report *(page 297).* Illustration 2 shows the process of digestion. Write a paragraph about this process. Assume that the process begins just after you have taken a bite of a sandwich, which contains proteins, starches, and fats. As prewriting, do research to find a definition of *digestion*. Make a chart showing the substances digested by the different parts of the body. Then list the steps of the process in chronological order, and decide on an appropriate audience for your paragraph.

Using your prewriting notes, write a first draft of your paragraph. Present the steps of the process in a logical order, and include transitions to add coherence to your writing.

Writing a Description for a Scientific Report *(page 297).* Write a description of the experiment shown in illustration 1. Assume that you are writing a report on scientific experiments suitable for young children. As prewriting, first decide on the *objective,* or purpose of the experiment. Then list the materials used, and the steps to be followed in the experiment. What *data,* or information, is obtained as a result of performing the experiment? Finally, draw a conclusion on the basis of the data you have obtained. A *conclusion* is often a statement of the truth or falsity of the objective.

Write a first draft based on your prewriting notes. Choose precise language, and include relevant scientific terms to develop your paragraph. Use third-person pronouns rather than first-person pronouns such as *I* or *me*. Revise your paragraph when you have finished your first draft. Ask yourself whether or not you can present your findings more concisely and your conclusion more consistently with facts presented earlier.

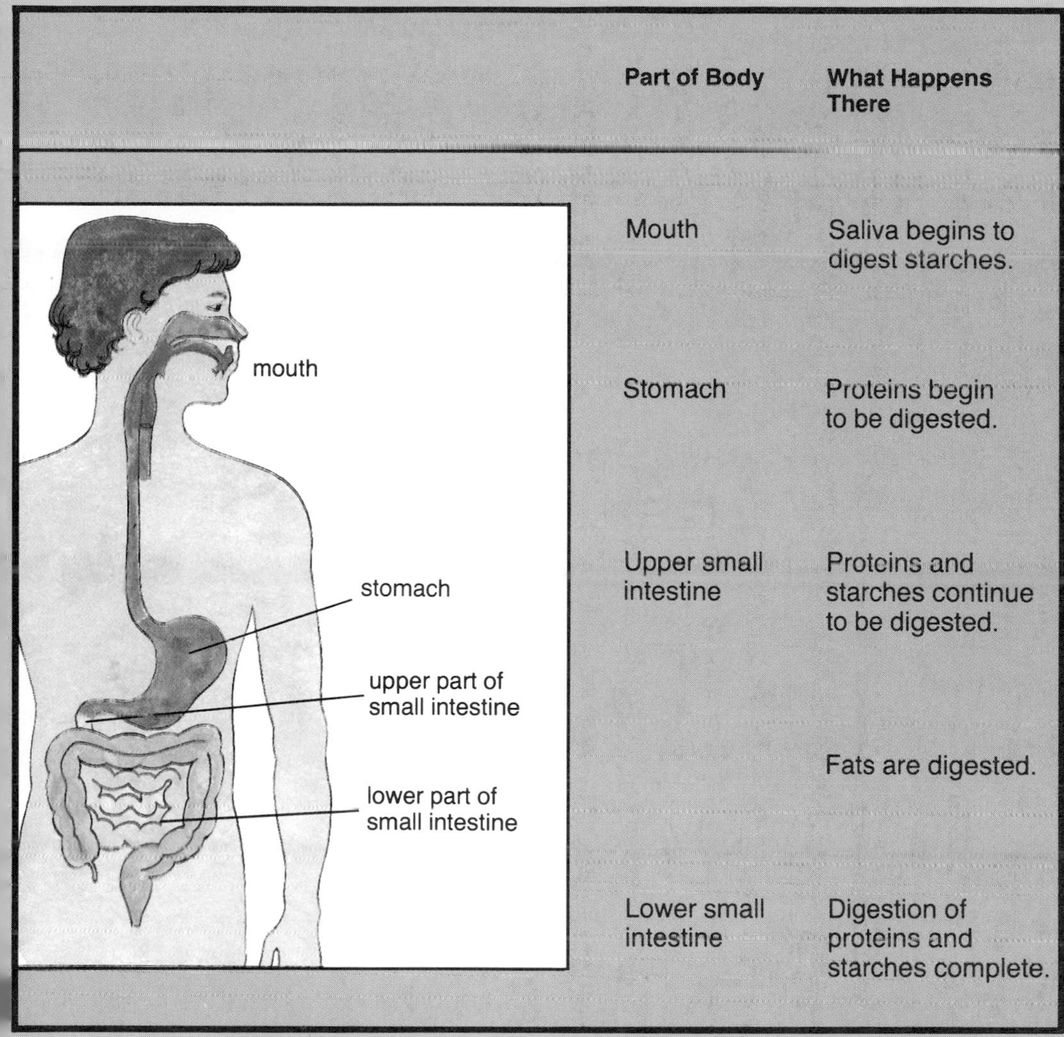

Part of Body	What Happens There
Mouth	Saliva begins to digest starches.
Stomach	Proteins begin to be digested.
Upper small intestine	Proteins and starches continue to be digested.
	Fats are digested.
Lower small intestine	Digestion of proteins and starches complete.

The illustrations on these two pages complement the instruction in Chapter 14.

1

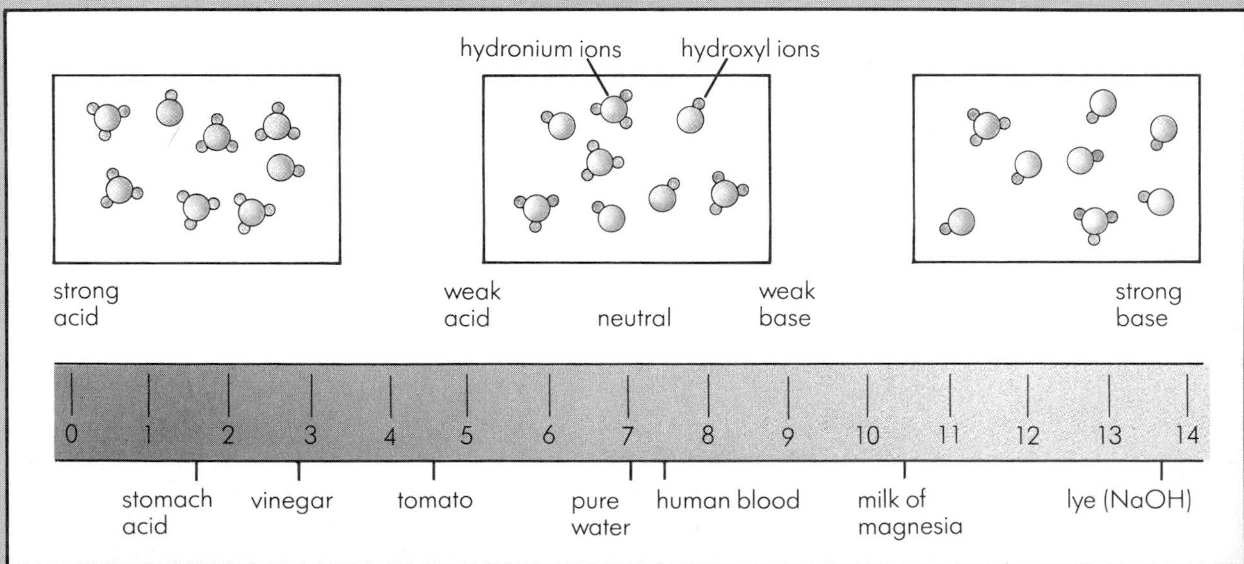

hydronium ions
hydroxyl ions
strong acid
weak acid
neutral
weak base
strong base
0
1
2
3
4
5
6
7
8
9
10
11
12
13
14
stomach acid
vinegar
tomato
pure water
human blood
milk of magnesia
lye (NaOH)

2

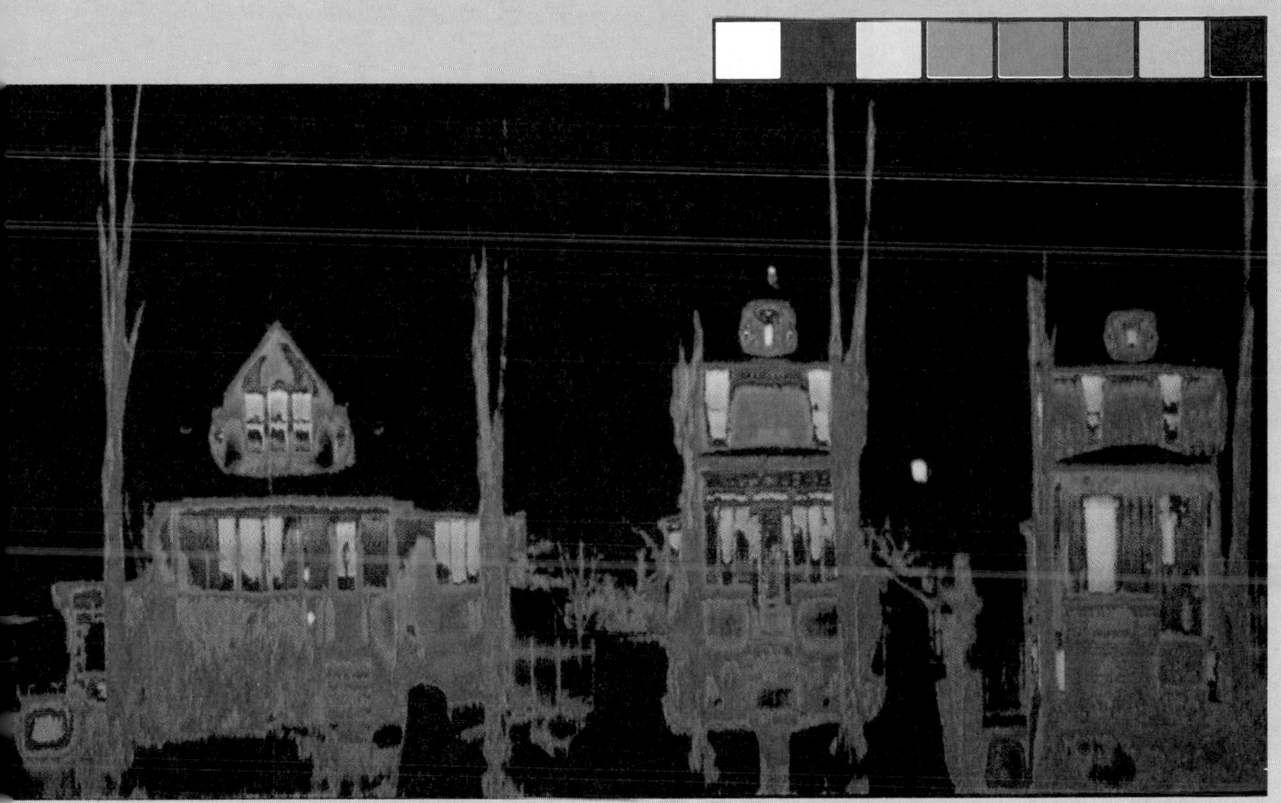

ASSIGNMENTS

Classifying Items *(page 297)*. Illustration 2 shows a pH scale, which expresses the strengths of acids and bases. The strength of an acid depends on the number of hydronium ions it produces in a solution.

Use the pH scale in illustration 2 to classify the substances shown there. As prewriting, decide under which categories to group the items. Then write a paragraph, using transitions to link your sentences.

Dividing Items *(page 297)*. Some cameras can take pictures with film sensitive to infrared radiation. Illustration 1 shows prints, or thermograms, made from heat-sensitive film. From the color scale, you can see that some parts of each house are warmer than others. Thermograms help people to tell what parts of their homes need better insulation.

Write a paragraph in which you advise the home owners on this block as to which parts of their homes need insulation. As prewriting, make a list of the colors on the chart, and record the parts of the buildings you see in each color. Then write an expository paragraph about your findings.

The illustrations on these two pages complement the instruction in Chapter 14.

WRITING ABOUT LITERATURE

Anton Chekhov

A Slander

The penmanship teacher Sergei Kapitonich Ahineyev[1] was marrying his daughter Natalia to the history and geography teacher. The wedding gaiety was at its height. People sang, played, and danced in the ballroom. Hired waiters, dressed in black tails and dirty white ties, scurried back and forth like madmen. Noise filled the air. The mathematics teacher, the French teacher, and the tax assessor, sitting side by side on the sofa, talked hurriedly, interrupting each other to tell the guests about cases of people buried alive, and expressing their opinions of spiritualism.[2] None of the three believed in spiritualism, but all admitted that there are many things in this world which a human mind will never understand. In the next room the literature teacher was explaining the cases in which a sentry has the right to shoot at passers-by. As you can see, the conversations were terrifying but highly pleasant. From the yard, people whose social standing did not give them the right to enter looked through the windows.

Exactly at midnight, Ahineyev, the host, walked into the kitchen to see whether everything was ready for supper. The kitchen was full of fumes from the goose and duck, mixed with many other smells. Appetizers and drinks were spread in artistic disorder on two tables. Marfa, the cook, a red-faced woman whose figure was like a balloon with a belt around it, bustled near the tables.

"Show me the sturgeon,[3] Marfa," said Ahineyev, rubbing his hands and licking his lips. "What an aroma! I could eat up the whole kitchen. Now then, show me the sturgeon!"

Marfa went to a bench and carefully lifted a greasy newspaper. Under the paper, on an enormous platter, rested a big jellied sturgeon, dazzling with olives and carrots. Ahineyev looked at the sturgeon and gasped. His face beamed, his eyes rolled up. He bent over and made a sound like an ungreased wheel. After a while he snapped his fingers with pleasure and smacked his lips once more.

"Oh, the sound of a passionate kiss! . . . Who are you kissing in there, little Marfa?" asked a voice from the next room, and Vankin, an assistant teacher, stuck his cropped head through the door. "Who are you with? Ah, ah, ah . . . very nice! With Sergei Kapitonich! You're a fine grandfather, alone here with a woman!"

"Not at all, I am not kissing her," said Ahineyev with embarrassment. "Who told you that, you fool? I just . . . smacked my lips because of . . . my pleasure . . . at the sight of the fish."

"Tell me another one!" Vankin's head smiled broadly and disappeared behind the door. Ahineyev blushed.

---

1. **Sergei Kapitonich Ahineyev** [ser gā′ kä pē tō′ nēch akh ē nā′yef]
2. **spiritualism**: belief that the dead can communicate with the living.
3. **sturgeon** [stur′jən]: large fish.

"What now?" he thought. "The scoundrel will go now and gossip. He will put me to shame before the whole town, the beast. . ."

Ahineyev timidly entered the ballroom and looked around: where was Vankin? Vankin was standing at the piano and dashingly bent over to whisper something to the laughing sister-in-law of the inspector.

"It is about me," thought Ahineyev, "about me. He should be torn apart! And she believes . . . believes! She's laughing. I can't let this go on . . . no . . . I must arrange it so that no one will believe him . . . I will talk to everybody and show what a fool and gossip he is."

Ahineyev scratched himself and, still embarrassed, approached the French teacher.

"I was just in the kitchen, arranging the supper," he told the Frenchman. "I know you love fish and I have a sturgeon, old chap. Two yards long. Ha, ha, ha . . . oh, yes, I almost forgot . . . In the kitchen now, with the sturgeon . . . it was a real joke! I went to the kitchen and wanted to examine the food . . . I looked at the sturgeon and from the pleasure, the aroma of it, I smacked my lips! But at this moment suddenly this fool Vankin came in and said . . . ha, ha, ha . . . and said . . . 'Ah, are you kissing in here?' Kissing Marfa, the cook! He made it all up, the fool. The woman looks like a beast, such a face, such skin . . . and he . . . kissing! Funny man!"

"Who is funny?" asked the mathematics teacher, coming over.

"That one there, Vankin! I came into the kitchen . . . " and he told the story of Vankin. "He made me laugh, he's so funny! I think I'd rather kiss a stray dog than Marfa," added Ahineyev, turning around and seeing the tax assessor behind him.

"We are talking about Vankin," said he. "Such a funny man! He came in the kitchen, saw me near Marfa . . . well, he started to invent all kinds of stories. 'Why,' he says, 'are you kissing?' He was drunk and made it up. And I said, 'I would rather kiss a turkey than Marfa. I have a wife,' I told him, 'you are such a fool.' He made me laugh."

"Who made you laugh?" asked the priest who taught Scripture in the school, coming to Ahineyev.

"Vankin. I was, you know, standing in the kitchen and looking at the sturgeon . . . "

And so forth. In half an hour all the guests knew the story of the sturgeon and Vankin.

"Let him tell the stories now!" thought Ahineyev, rubbing his hands. "Let him! He'll start telling stories, and everyone will say right away: 'Stop talking nonsense, you fool! We know all about it.' "

And Ahineyev was so reassured that he drank four glasses too much from joy. After supper he saw the newlyweds to their room, went home, and slept like an innocent child, and the next day he had already forgotten the story of the sturgeon. But, alas! Man supposes, but God disposes.[4] Wicked tongues will wag, and Ahineyev's cunning did not help him. Exactly a week later, after the third lesson on Wednesday, when Ahineyev was standing in the staff room discussing the evil ways of one of his students, the principal came to him and called him aside.

"Well, Sergei Kapitonich," said the principal, "excuse me . . . it's not my business, but still I must explain . . . my duty. You see, there is talk that you have kissed this . . .

The literary works presented here complement the instruction in Chapter 15.

4. Man...disposes: A proverb. No matter how much man may plan, God can cause unexpected events.

cook. It is not my business, but . . . kiss her . . . anything you want but, please, not so publicly. Please! Don't forget, you are a teacher."

Ahineyev got chilly and faint. He felt as if he had been stung by a swarm of bees and scalded in boiling water. As he walked home, it seemed to him that the whole town was looking at him as if he were smeared with tar. New trouble awaited him at home.

"Why don't you eat anything?" his wife asked him during dinner. "What are you thinking about? Your love life? Lonesome without Little Marfa? I know all about it, Mohammedan![5] Good people opened my eyes! O-o-oh, barbarian!"

And she slapped him on the cheek. He left the table in a daze, without his hat and coat, and wandered to Vankin. Vankin was home.

"You scoundrel!" Ahineyev addressed Vankin. "Why did you smear me with mud before the entire world? Why did you slander me?"

"What slander? What are you inventing?"

"Who gossiped that I kissed Marfa? Not you? Not you, robber?"

Vankin blinked and winked with all his worn face, raised his eyes to the icon,[6] and said, "Let God punish me! Let my eyes burst, let me die, if I ever said one word about you! Bad luck to me! Cholera[7] is not enough!"

The sincerity of Vankin could not be doubted. Evidently he had not gossiped.

"But who? Who?" thought Ahineyev, turning over in his mind all his acquaintances and beating his breast. "Who else?"

"Who else?" we will also ask the reader . . .

---

5. **Mohammedan** [mō ham′id en]: Moslem. Ahineyev's wife implies that Moslem men have more than one wife.
6. **icon** [ī′kon]: painting of a holy person or saint.
7. **Cholera** [kol′ər a]: infectious disease of the intestines.

The literary works presented here complement the instruction in Chapter 15.

William Shakespeare

from Romeo and Juliet

from Act II, Scene ii. Late at night, CAPULET'*s orchard, Verona, Italy. The fourteenth century.*

[ROMEO MONTAGUE *is in the orchard outside the home of his father's enemy,* LORD CAPULET. ROMEO *wishes to remain near* JULIET, CAPULET'*s daughter, whom he met and fell in love with at a party given by* CAPULET *earlier that evening.* ROMEO *was able to attend the party because he wore a mask to conceal his identity.* JULIET *enters at a window above and stands on a balcony. She does not know that* ROMEO *is nearby.]*

ROMEO. But soft! What light through yonder window breaks?
It is the East, and Juliet is the sun!
Arise, fair sun, and kill the envious moon,
Who is already sick and pale with grief
That thou her maid art far more fair than she.
Be not her maid, since she is envious.
Her vestal livery[1] is but sick and green,
And none but fools do wear it. Cast it off.
It is my lady! O, it is my love!
O, that she knew she were!
She speaks, yet she says nothing. What of that?
Her eye discourses;[2] I will answer it.
I am too bold; 'tis not to me she speaks.
Two of the fairest stars in all the heaven,
Having some business, do entreat her eyes
To twinkle in their spheres[3] till they return.
What if her eyes were there, they in her head?
The brightness of her cheek would shame those stars
As daylight doth a lamp; her eyes in heaven
Would through the airy region stream so bright
That birds would sing and think it were not night.
See how she leans her cheek upon her hand!
O, that I were a glove upon the hand,
That I might touch that cheek! . . .

JULIET. O Romeo, Romeo! Wherefore art thou Romeo?[4]
Deny thy father and refuse thy name;
Or, if thou will not, be but sworn my love,
And I'll no longer be a Capulet.

ROMEO. *[Aside]* Shall I hear more, or shall I speak at this?

JULIET. 'Tis but thy name that is my enemy.
Thou art thyself, though not[5] a Montague.
What's a Montague? It is nor[6] hand, nor foot,
Nor arm, nor face. O, be some other name
Belonging to a man.
What's in a name? That which we call a rose
By any other word would smell as sweet.
So Romeo would, were he not Romeo called,
Retain that dear perfection which he owes[7]
Without that title. Romeo, doff[8] thy name;
And for thy name, which is no part of thee,
Take all myself.

[ROMEO *speaks aloud so that* JULIET *can hear him for the first time.]*

ROMEO. I take thee at thy word.
Call me but love, and I'll be new baptized;
Henceforth I never will be Romeo.

---

1. **Her vestal livery:** the moon's white dress. The moon becomes pale beside Juliet, the sun.
2. **discourses:** speaks.
3. **spheres:** orbits.
4. **Wherefore...Romeo:** Why are you called *Romeo* (a Montague)
5. **though not:** even if you were not.
6. **nor:** neither.
7. **owes:** owns.
8. **doff:** remove.

The literary works presented here complement the instruction in Chapter 15.

JULIET. What man art thou, that, thus bescreened[9] in night,
So stumbles on my counsel?[10]

ROMEO. By a name
I know not how to tell thee who I am.
My name, dear saint, is hateful to myself
Because it is an enemy to thee.
Had I it written, I would tear the word.

JULIET. My ears have yet not drunk a hundred words
Of thy tongue's uttering, yet I know the sound.
Art thou not Romeo, and a Montague?

ROMEO. Neither, fair maid, if either thee dislike.

JULIET. How camest thou hither, tell me, and wherefore?
The orchard walls are high and hard to climb,
And the place death, considering who thou art,
If any of my kinsmen find thee here.

ROMEO. With love's light wings did I o'erperch[11] these walls;
For stony limits cannot hold love out,
And what love can do, that dares love attempt.
Therefore thy kinsmen are no stop to me.

JULIET. If they do see thee, they will murder thee.

ROMEO. Alack, there lies more peril in thine eye
Than twenty of their swords! Look thou but sweet,
And I am proof[12] against their enmity.

JULIET. I would not for the world they saw thee here.

ROMEO. I have night's cloak to hide me from their eyes;
And but[13] thou love me, let them find me here.
My life were better ended by their hate
Than death proroguèd,[14] wanting of[15] thy love.

---

9. **bescreened:** hidden.
10. **counsel:** secret thoughts.
11. **o'erperch:** fly over.
12. **proof:** protected.
13. **And but:** unless.
14. **proroguèd:** postponed.
15. **wanting of:** lacking.

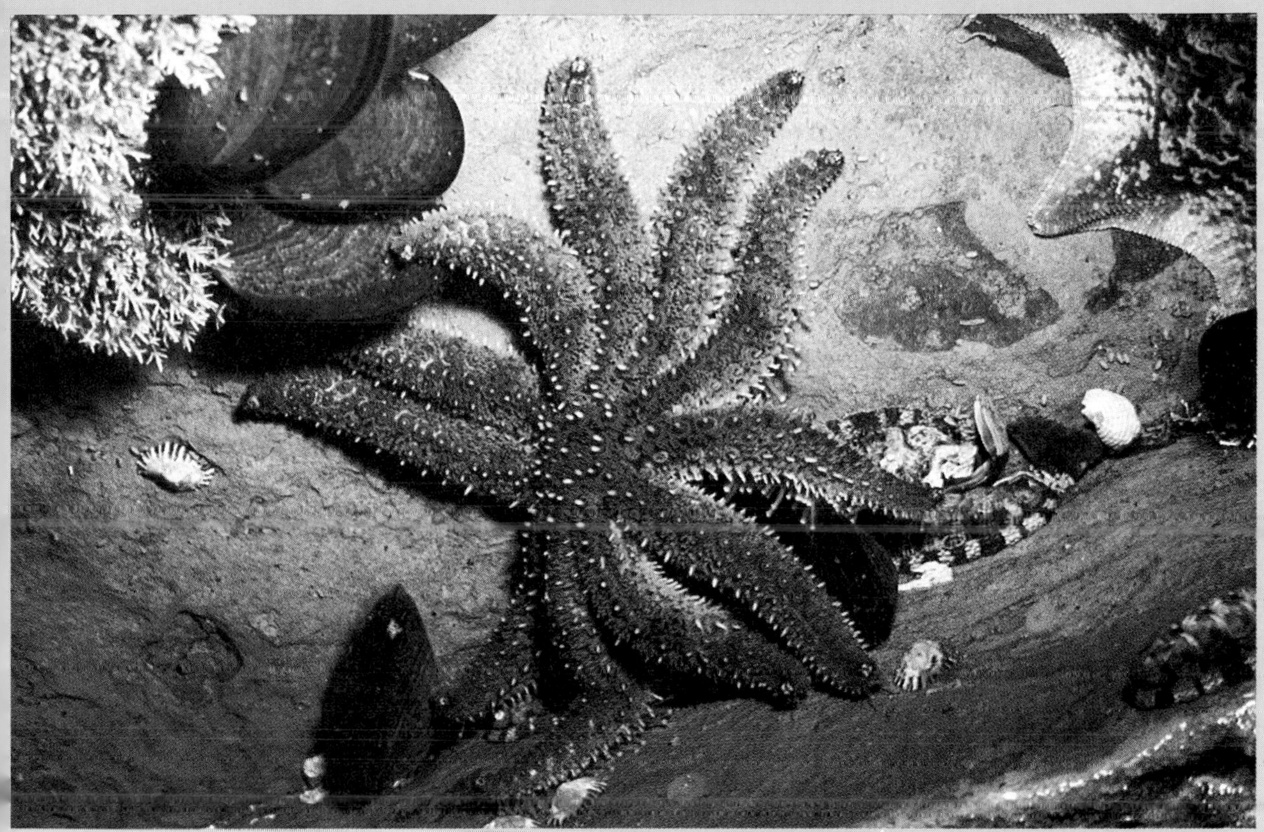

E.E. Cummings

maggie and milly and molly and may

maggie and milly and molly and may
went down to the beach(to play one day)

and maggie discovered a shell that sang
so sweetly she couldn't remember her troubles,and

milly befriended a stranded star
whose rays five languid fingers were;

and molly was chased by a horrible thing
which raced sideways while blowing bubbles:and

may came home with a smooth round stone
as small as a world and as large as alone.

For whatever we lose(like a you or a me)
it's always ourselves we find in the sea

CREATIVE WRITING

1

2

3

4

ASSIGNMENTS

Exploring and Outlining a Story Idea *(pages 332–333).* Select a photograph from pages 380–383, and use it to answer the questions for exploring a story idea (page 332). Decide on an audience that might enjoy a story based on this idea. Then write an outline of the events in the story's plot.

Writing a Story *(pages 334–337).* Write a story based on your work for the assignment above. Your story should include the following elements: beginning, characterization and dialogue, suspense, climax, resolution, and a title. Use the checklist on pages 336–337 to revise your story.

Generating Ideas for a Scene *(pages 337–338).* Complete a chart of scene ideas (page 338) using three photographs from pages 380–383. Keep in mind that you must have at least two characters in a dramatic scene. Imagine characters who have contrasting personality traits, backgrounds, interests, and goals.

The illustrations on these two pages complement the instruction in chapter 16.

1

2

3

4

ASSIGNMENTS

Exploring and Outlining a Scene Idea *(pages 338–340).* Look over the chart you made for the previous assignment, and choose the idea that you like best. Explore your idea with questions like those on page 339. After exploring your idea, outline the scene's action.

Writing a Dramatic Scene *(pages 340–343).* Write a dramatic scene based on your work for the assignment above. Your scene should include setting, dialogue and action, conflict and climax, resolution, and a title.

Exploring Ideas for a Poem *(page 346).* Select a photograph on pages 380–383, and use it to answer the questions for exploring ideas for a poem (page 346). Your poem need not rhyme.

Writing a Poem *(pages 346–347).* Write a poem of any form and any length from the notes you created for the assignment above.

The illustrations on these two pages complement the instruction in Chapter 16.

Identification of Writer's Sourcebook Illustrations

Pages 354–355—The Writing Process and Style: 1. Detail, anonymous, *Running Before the Storm,* c. 1877. Museum of Fine Arts, Boston. **2.** Street scene. **3.** Monument Valley, Utah. **4.** Dog with glasses in car, Sweden. **5.** Nature scene. **Pages 356–357—The Writing Process and Style (continued): 1.** Anonymous, *Running Before the Storm,* c. 1877. Museum of Fine Arts, Boston. **2.** Passengers boarding aircraft. **3.** Statue of Liberty, New York. **4.** William Morris Hunt (1824–1879), *Girl with Cat.* Museum of Fine Arts, Boston. **5.** Young people in costumes. **Pages 358–359—Descriptive Writing: 1.** Frederick Remington, *Howl of the Weather.* Frederick Remington Art Museum, Ogdensburg, New York. **2.** Andrew Wyeth, *Nicolas Wyeth.* Private collection. **3.** Scene of country fair. **4.** Uncle Sam Whirligig, New England, c. 1850–1900. Museum of American Folk Art, New York. **Pages 360–361—Narrative Writing: 1.** Royal wedding sequence, left to right: Prince Charles and Lady Diana Spencer walk up the aisle of St. Paul's Cathedral, passing, from right to left in row one, Queen Elizabeth, Prince Philip, and the Queen Mother; in row two, Princess Anne; her husband, Captain Mark Phillips; Princess Margaret; and Prince Andrew. The couple then walk back down the aisle, stand on the steps of the cathedral, and finally ride in a carriage to Buckingham Palace. **2.** Whitewater kayaking. **Pages 362–363—Expository Writing: 1.** Dust and wind storm, Michigan. **2.** Jefferson Gauntt (1806–1864), *Two Children,* 1843. Museum of Fine Arts, Boston. **3.** Photograph of contemporary girl and boy. **4.** Pieced quilt in pinwheel pattern. New York, c. 1870. **5.** Diagram of gymnastic move by U.S. athlete in 1984 Los Angeles Olympics. **Pages 364–365—Critical Thinking and Persuasive Writing: 1.** Fruit and vegetable stand. **2.** Girl and dog running. **3.** Couple folk dancing. **4.** Wheelchair race. **Pages 366–367—Writing About Social Studies: 1.** *New York Times* clipping. **2.** Beach and town. Paired with town in mountains. **Pages 368–369—Writing About Social Studies (continued): 1.** Graph—Growth of a Typical American City. **2.** Map: World Population. **Pages 370–371—Writing About Science and Technology: 1.** Illustration of experiment on dissolving solids. **2.** Human digestive system. **Pages 372–373—Writing About Science and Technology (continued): 1.** Prints of houses photographed with heat-sensitive film. **2.** Illustration of pH scale. **Pages 374–379—Writing About Literature:** Selected pieces of literature. **Pages 380–381—Creative Writing: 1.** Lion and cubs. **2.** Orchid. **3.** Young person hiking. **4.** Ice-covered spider web. **Pages 382–383—Creative Writing (continued): 1.** Dog sled on the Yukon Trail, Canada. **2.** Three girls with schoolbooks. **3.** "Invasion" of zucchini. **4.** Robots.

Grammar, Usage, and Mechanics

PART

2

Using English: letters and numerals in lead type

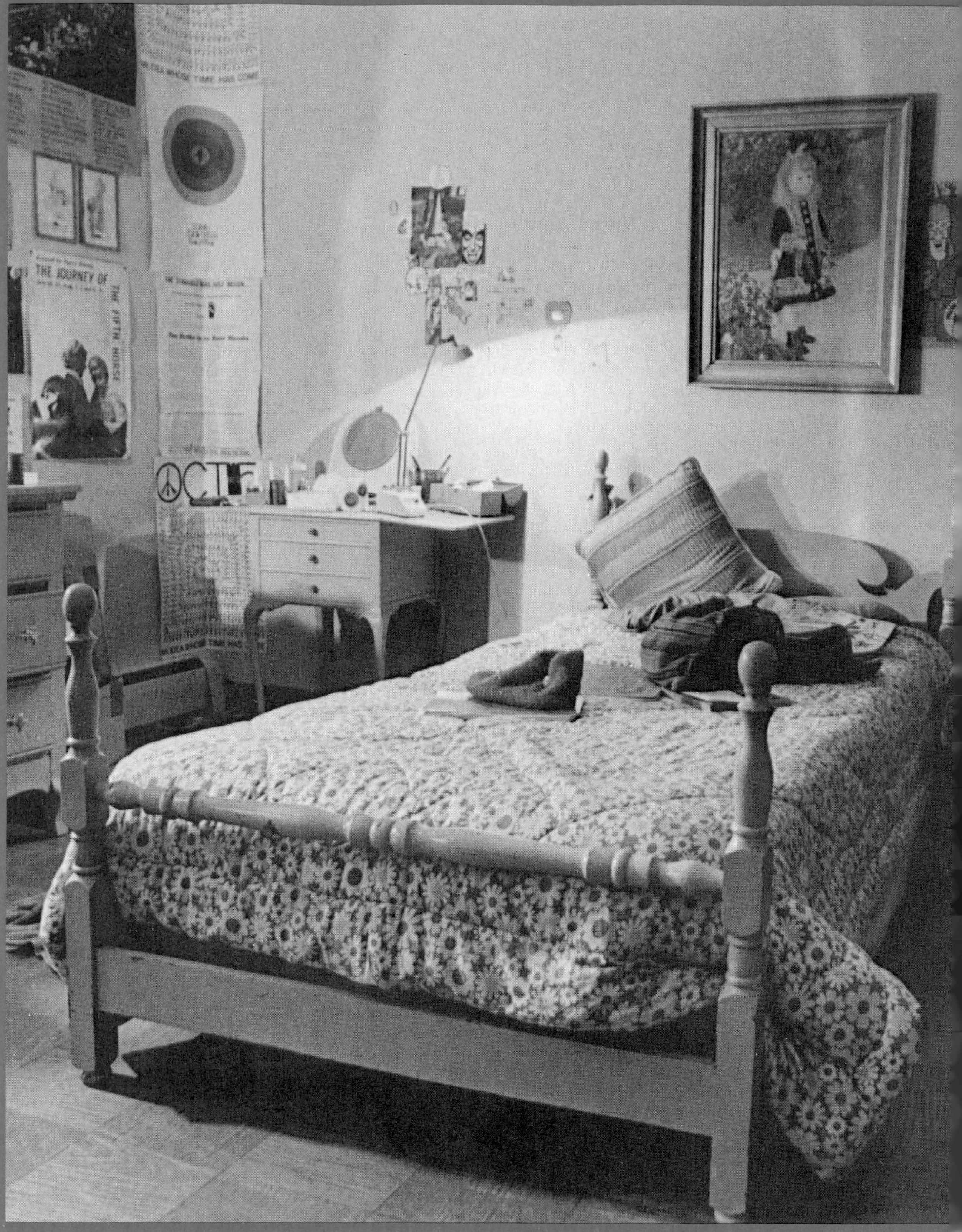

THE JOURNEY OF
THE FIFTH HORSE

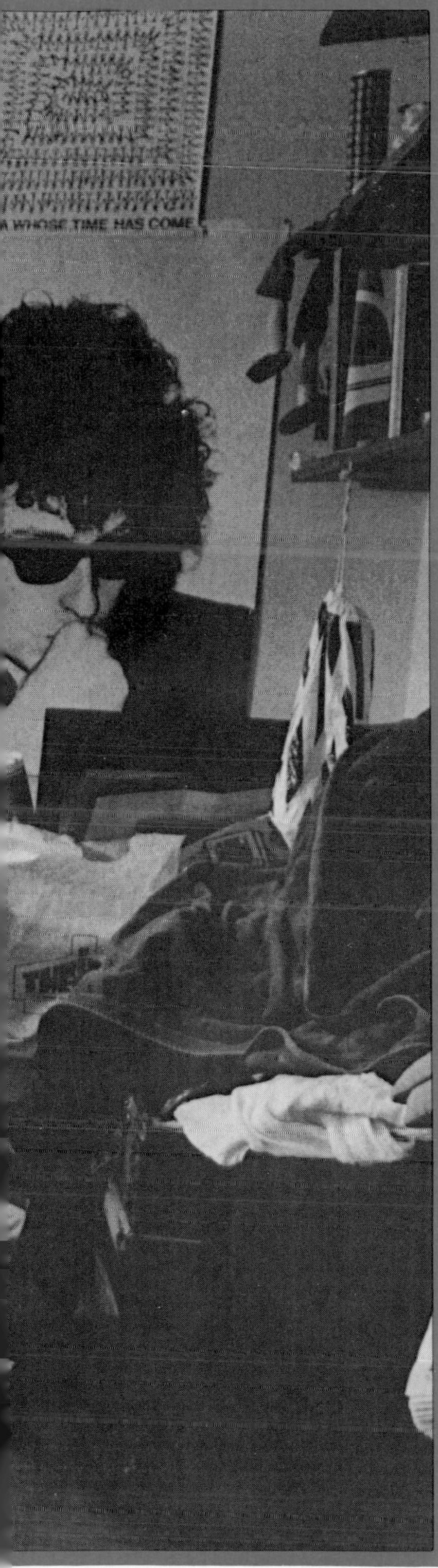

Grammar

Thinking About Thinking: Categorizing Information

When you reason logically about two or more pieces of information, you come to a conclusion about them. For example, you may look at a group of words and see that some words share certain qualities and others share different qualities. You may then say that therefore it would be logical to divide the words into different groups. As this unit shows, grammar provides a framework for this kind of orderly thinking about words.

Defining the Skill

CATEGORIZING INFORMATION is a specific thinking skill. Suppose that while walking on a seashore you collected a pile of natural objects. If you then separated these objects according to the qualities they have in common, you might have three piles: a pile of stones, a pile of driftwood, and a pile of shells. Then you might separate each pile again according to color or size or shape. Grammar does the same thing in our language. It organizes into categories, or "piles," the words we use. Those piles are called parts of speech.

Applying the Skill

Look at the photograph and make a list of everything you see in the picture. Combine your list with a partner's list to make sure you have not missed anything. Then, with your partner, group everything on your list into categories, making sure every item has been included.

CHAPTER 17

Parts of Speech

Nouns

A **noun** is a word that names a person, a place, a thing, or an idea.

A noun can name a person, place, or thing (living or nonliving) that occupies space.

PERSON	teacher, uncle, niece, nephew
PLACE	star, garage, city, park
LIVING THING	carrot, paw, shrub, giraffe
NONLIVING THING	bicycle, book, sock, envelope

A noun can also name something that does not occupy space. Not only can we say, "We know about that *museum*," but we can also say, "We know about *sorrow*." In other words, some nouns allow us to take an aspect of experience—such as feeling sorry—and talk about it as though it were a thing to which we could actually point. Here are some other examples of nouns that do not occupy space:

Thanksgiving is a **holiday**.
Biology is my favorite **subject**.
The final **outcome** of the **game** was a **tie**.

Recognizing Nouns

As you have just seen, you can classify a word as a noun if it names something. In addition, you can identify a word as a noun if it satisfies one of the following tests.

1. A word is a noun if it makes sense in one of the blanks in the following sentences.

   I have a(n) ____________.
   We know about (the) ____________.
   (The) ____________ is (are) interesting.

2. The following suffixes almost always signal that a word is a noun: *-acy, -age, -cy, -dom, -ee, -ence, -ency, -er, -ery, -ess, -et, -ette, -hood, -ian, -ics, -ion, -ism, -ite, -ity, -let, -ment, -ness, -or, -ship, -tion.*

heritage	booklet
donor	urgency
kingdom	union
childhood	cleanliness
referee	argument

Nouns can be singular or plural, depending on whether they name *one* person, place, thing, or idea, or *more than one.*

SINGULAR boy, body, watch, hoof, ox
PLURAL boys, bodies, watches, hooves, oxen

(For rules on making the plural forms of nouns, see Chapter 30.)

Nouns have a form to show possession, ownership, or the relationship between two nouns.

SINGULAR	PLURAL
the **car's** hood	the **cars'** hoods
a **baby's** bottle	the **babies'** bottles
an **ox's** tail	the **oxen's** tails
the **fish's** mouth	the **fishes'** mouths

EXERCISE 1 **Identifying Nouns.** On your paper list the twenty nouns that appear in the following passage. Identify the nouns by finding the words that name something, by testing the words to see whether they make sense in any of the blanks in the sentences on page 388, and by noticing the suffixes on the words.

[1]The painter studied the works of her elders and carefully analyzed their methods. [2]The techniques were then applied in the creation of portraits and pictures of contemporary events. [3]Using bold lines and brilliant tints, she made her canvases glow with emotion and excitement. [4]Children romping with pets and workers engaged in ordinary tasks showed equally clearly the individuality of her vision.

EXERCISE 2 **Completing Sentences with Nouns.** On your paper complete each sentence by filling the blanks with nouns. Be sure that your completed sentences make sense.

Suggested answers appear in the blanks.

1. The __________ galloped by on her __________.
2. Two of her __________ waved their red __________.
3. The other __________ of her __________ cheered.
4. Her yellow __________ blew off her __________.
5. The __________ made her __________ fly wildly.

Proper and Common Nouns

A **proper noun** is the name of a particular person, place, thing, or idea.

A **common noun** is the general—not the particular—name of a person, place, thing, or idea.

The word *proper* comes from the Latin word *proprius,* which means "one's own." Therefore, a word that is "one's own"—such as a person's name—is considered *proper*. Proper nouns are usually capitalized. (For rules on capitalizing proper nouns, see Chapter 26.)

	PROPER NOUNS
PERSON	Raul Julia, Uncle Peter, Emily Dickinson
PLACE	Mexico, Lake George, the Grand Canyon
THING	the Statue of Liberty, *The Pearl,* Adidas shoes
IDEA	Islam, Romanticism, the Renaissance

EXERCISE 3 **Matching Proper Nouns with Common Nouns.** On your paper match the numbered proper nouns on the left with the lettered common nouns on the right.

1. Middle Ages	a. ocean
2. *Romeo and Juliet*	b. mountains
3. Cuba	c. building complex
4. *Moby Dick*	d. team
5. Renoir	e. painter
6. the Rockies	f. play
7. Chicago Cubs	g. river
8. the Pacific	h. island
9. the Nile	i. historical era
10. Houston Space Center	j. book

Collective Nouns

A **collective noun** names a group.

family	(the) police
band	(the) senate
(the) press	(an) audience
(a) gaggle (of geese)	(the) board (of directors)

A collective noun may be considered either singular or plural. You consider a collective noun singular when you talk about a group as a whole. You consider a collective noun plural when you talk about the individual members of a group. (For help with subject-verb agreement with collective nouns, see Chapter 22.)

SINGULAR The **audience** shouts its approval.
PLURAL The **audience** have arrived in small groups.

EXERCISE 4 **Identifying Collective Nouns.** On your paper list the five collective nouns in each of the following paragraphs.

A. [1]The 1985 production of George Gershwin's *Porgy and Bess* had a chorus of seventy voices. [2]The cast included such noted opera stars as Grace Bumbry and Simon Estes. [3]The Metropolitan's orchestra was conducted by James Levine. [4]The audience had bought their tickets well in advance for all sixteen performances. [5]The huge stage was massed with over a hundred people representing the population of Catfish Row.

B. [1]In Africa a team of zoologists can observe many kinds of wild animals. [2]In a western forest one might see a family of chimpanzees. [3]In the eastern grasslands quiet watchers might spy a herd of roaming zebras. [4]In the northern desert a flock of ostriches is not an uncommon sight. [5]The African continent is home to a rich collection of wildlife.

Compound Nouns

A **compound noun** is a noun made up of more than one word.

homework	apple butter	sister-in-law
keystone	night light	actor-director
doorknob	motion picture	vice-chancellor
airport	ice cream	X-ray

Sometimes two words are written as one word to form a compound noun; sometimes a compound noun is written as two separate words, and sometimes it is written with hyphens. Check a dictionary if you are not sure of the way a compound noun should be written.

Proper nouns that name particular people or places may be compound: George Bush, Daisy Mae, Great Britain.

EXERCISE 5 **Forming Compound Nouns.** Match the nouns in column 1 with the nouns in column 2 to form as many compound nouns as you can. (At least twenty-two possibilities exist.)

1	2
foot	board
half	light(s)
head	line
sea	note
side	step
sky	way(s)

Concrete and Abstract Nouns

A **concrete noun** names an object that occupies space or can be recognized by any of the senses.

petal smoke cough orange nook

An **abstract noun** names an idea, a quality, or a characteristic.

motion humor quantity tact rudeness

EXERCISE 6 **Supplying Abstract and Concrete Nouns.** For each concrete noun in item 1, write an abstract noun that names an idea with which the concrete noun can be associated. For each abstract noun in item 2, write a concrete noun that has the quality of the abstract noun.

SAMPLE ANSWERS 1. mechanic—deftness
2. taste—salt

1. bicycle, laughter, itch, home run, snow
2. haste, warmth, poverty, reward, weather

SENTENCE WRITING **Creating Sentences with Nouns.** Write five sentences about a shop in your town or neighborhood. Rely especially on concrete nouns to convey a vivid picture of the place.

REVIEW EXERCISE **Nouns.** On your paper complete each sentence by filling the blanks with the kinds of nouns specified in italics. Be sure that your completed sentences make sense.

1. The *abstract* of the Thanksgiving *concrete* scented the *concrete*.
2. *proper, compound* told the *common* of the *proper*.
3. All of the *collective* listened.
4. Set with our best *compound*, the table held serving dishes filled with *common* and *compound*.
5. On the *compound* we watched *proper, compound*.
6. For *common*, each of us had a generous *common* of *compound*.
7. Sitting by the blazing *concrete*, *proper, compound* told us that President Lincoln first proclaimed a national Thanksgiving Day.
8. Later that *common*, we agreed that the festivities had given us so much *abstract* that we could not wait for *proper*.

Revising Your Writing

In the following sentence from *Time and Again,* Jack Finney uses nouns to convey mystery and surprise.

> The patch of snow lay just within the circle of pale light from a street lamp, and at the edge of the patch, sharply and clearly impressed in the snow, was a replica in miniature of the tombstone whose photograph Kate had shown me over the grave of Andrew Carmody outside Gillis, Montana.

Study the passage above closely, and try to apply some of Finney's techniques when you write and revise your own work.

1. Try to choose nouns for the effect of their sound as well as for their meaning. For example, notice the *p* sounds in Finney's "the patch, sharply and clearly impressed."
2. Try to replace general words with precise concrete nouns. Notice that Finney does not merely say that the street lamp lighted the spot. Instead, he helps you visualize the circle of pale light on the patch of snow.
3. Try to expand single nouns into longer word groups that are more specific and detailed. Finney expands the concrete noun *replica* into "a replica in miniature of the tombstone."

Practice these techniques by revising the following passage on your paper. Pay particular attention to the italicized words.

> By seven o'clock on that snowy morning, the park was a *scene* of great activity. A *bunch* of *dogs* was racing across the *clearing* putting *birds* to flight. Squirrels flicked their *tails* and scampered to *safety*. Along the *pathway*, the dog owners stamped their *feet* in the snow and chatted about *things*.

Pronouns

A **pronoun** is a word that takes the place of a noun, a group of nouns, or another pronoun.

Pronouns allow you to avoid unnecessary repetitions when you speak or write. The word or group of words that a pronoun replaces is called its *antecedent.*

> When James Baldwin was fourteen, **he** became a preacher. [The pronoun *he* takes the place of the proper noun *James Baldwin.*]
>
> When Georgia O'Keeffe and Alfred Stieglitz were married in 1924, **they** were **both** already famous artists. [The pronouns *they* and *both* take the place of the nouns *Georgia O'Keeffe* and *Alfred Stieglitz.*]
>
> Although Georgia O'Keeffe **herself** was a painter, **her** husband was a photographer. [The pronouns *herself* and *her* take the place of the noun *Georgia O'Keeffe.*]

English has about seventy-five pronouns, which fall into one or more of the following categories: personal pronouns, reflexive and intensive pronouns, demonstrative pronouns, interrogative pronouns, relative pronouns, and indefinite pronouns.

Personal Pronouns

A **personal pronoun** refers to a specific person or thing by indicating the person speaking (the first person), the person being addressed (the second person), or any other person or thing being discussed (the third person). Personal pronouns also express *number;* they are singular or plural.

	SINGULAR	PLURAL
FIRST PERSON	I, me	we, us
SECOND PERSON	you	you
THIRD PERSON	he, him she, her it	they, them

FIRST PERSON **I** kept the dog. [*I* refers to the person speaking.]

SECOND PERSON The dog was afraid of **you.** [*You* refers to the person being addressed.]

THIRD PERSON **It** ran away from **them.** [*It* refers to the dog in the previous sentence. *Them* refers to the persons being discussed.]

Third-person pronouns express *gender*. *He* and *him* are masculine; *she* and *her* are feminine; *it* is neuter—it is neither masculine nor feminine.

The personal pronouns include several forms that indicate possession or ownership. These *possessive pronouns* take the place of the possessive forms of nouns.

	SINGULAR	PLURAL
FIRST PERSON	my, mine	our, ours
SECOND PERSON	your, yours	your, yours
THIRD PERSON	his	their, theirs
	her, hers	
	its	

Some possessive forms are used before nouns. Other possessive forms can be used by themselves.

USED BEFORE NOUN	Bring **your** bathing suit.
USED ALONE	That bathing suit is **yours.**

EXERCISE 7 **Using Personal and Possessive Pronouns.** Improve the following paragraphs by replacing the underlined words or groups of words with personal or possessive pronouns. Write your answers on your paper.

A. [1]Born in February, the bear cubs were not seen by the bear cubs' mother until the cubs were two months old. [2]The cubs were born in a cave the mother bear had dug. [3]All winter, snow drifts covered the opening of the cave except for the tiny hole formed by the mother bear's breath. [4]When the snow melted, the mother bear stumbled out of the winter den followed by the mother bear's cubs. [5]The cubs were using the cubs' legs for the first time. [6]The reader of this passage could learn more about young animals by reading Sally Carrighar's book *Wild Heritage*. [7]Sally Carrighar wrote *Wild Heritage* in 1965. [8]Sally Carrighar said Sally Carrighar wrote *Wild Heritage* to show how much human beings can discover about themselves from animals.

B. [1]At age thirty Robert Peary led an expedition to Greenland to study Arctic conditions. [2]Peary returned to Greenland five times before Peary's first attempt to reach the North Pole in 1898. [3]Though this attempt failed, Peary learned about the difficulties of the Arctic. [4]In 1905 a new ship was built for Peary according to Peary's own specifications. [5]The vessel, designed to force the vessel's way through ice fields, took Peary to within 174 miles of the pole before food ran out. [6]In 1908 Peary and his crew set off with 19 sleds and 133 dogs. [7]As the men neared the Arctic Circle, the men realized that if some of the men turned back, the others could stretch supplies. [8]The men's efforts insured that Peary would successfully gain the North Pole on April 9, 1909.

Reflexive and Intensive Pronouns*

Reflexive and intensive pronouns are formed by adding *-self* or *-selves* to certain of the personal pronouns, as shown below.

	SINGULAR	PLURAL
FIRST PERSON	myself	ourselves
SECOND PERSON	yourself	yourselves
THIRD PERSON	himself	themselves
	herself	
	itself	

A **reflexive pronoun** refers to a noun or another pronoun and indicates that the same person or thing is involved.

You outdid **yourself** when you wrote that song.

She always timed **herself** when jogging.

In dancing class we watch **ourselves** in the mirror.

An **intensive pronoun** adds emphasis to another noun or pronoun.

The team **itself** chose the captain.

Tricia **herself** opened the door.

George and Pedro planned the party **themselves.**

EXERCISE 8 **Using Reflexive and Intensive Pronouns.** Supply the appropriate reflexive or intensive pronoun for each blank. Write your answers on your paper.

1. She carried the big bass viol __________.
2. He reminded __________ to watch the conductor's baton.
3. The string, woodwind, brass, and percussion sections had prepared __________ during rehearsals.
4. Even the conductor, Sarah Caldwell __________, seemed nervous at first.
5. The air __________ seemed motionless in expectation.
6. We positioned __________ for the opening note.
7. Throughout the piece you found __________ listening anxiously for your cues.
8. We were so inspired by the occasion that our instruments seemed to play __________.
9. The audience applauded so enthusiastically that we all felt very proud of __________.
10. The orchestra members __________ joined in the applause.

*Reflexive and intensive pronouns are also called *compound pronouns.*

Demonstrative Pronouns

A **demonstrative pronoun** points out specific persons, places, things, or ideas.

SINGULAR	this	that
PLURAL	these	those

This is your homeroom.
These are your classmates.
That will be your seat.
The first books you will read are **those**.

EXERCISE 9 **Identifying Demonstrative Pronouns.** On your paper write the demonstrative pronoun in each sentence.

1. That looks like a hard climb.
2. I hope this is the shortest way.
3. Those are rougher trails.
4. My friend marked these as the most scenic trails.
5. This is a great way to spend a weekend.
6. That is one of the best national parks for hiking.
7. The guidebook says those are the largest national forests in the West.
8. "Take these," she said, "a map, a compass, and a first-aid kit."
9. That is an easy trail to hike, compared to the one we hiked last summer.
10. A cap, a T-shirt, shorts, and strong boots—those are the clothes to wear on a hike.

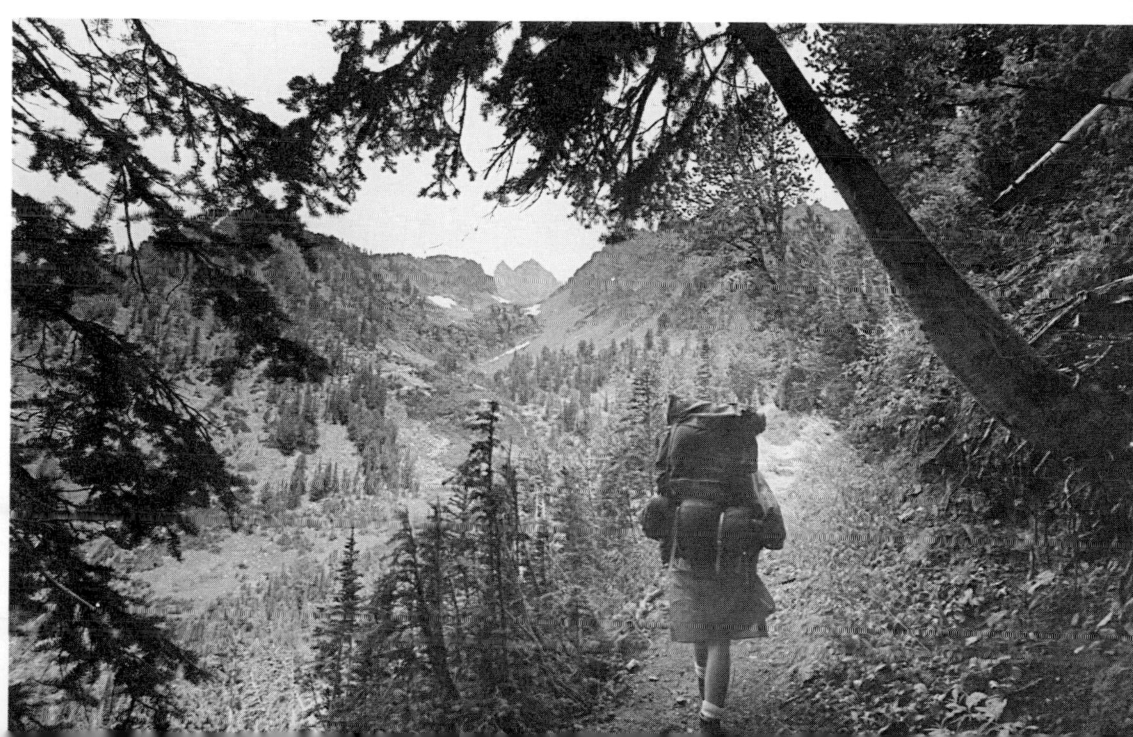

Interrogative and Relative Pronouns

An **interrogative pronoun** is used to form questions.

These are the interrogative pronouns:

who?	what?	which?
whom?		
whose?		

Who will lead the way?
Whose is the lightest pack?
Which of these paths is easiest?
Whom would you choose?
What makes a good leader?

A **relative pronoun** is used to begin a special subject-verb word group called a subordinate clause (see Chapter 20).

These are the relative pronouns:

who	which	that
whom		
whose		

The people **who** invented Trivial Pursuit were surprised by its success. [The relative pronoun *who* begins the subordinate clause *who invented Trivial Pursuit.*]

Dominoes is a game **that** many Texans play. [The relative pronoun *that* begins the subordinate clause *that many Texans play.*]

One chess player **whose** strategy is studied is Robert J. Fischer. [The relative pronoun *whose* begins the subordinate clause *whose strategy is studied.*]

Note that all the relative pronouns except *that* can also be used as interrogative pronouns to ask questions.

EXERCISE 10 **Distinguishing Between Interrogative and Relative Pronouns.** On your paper list the interrogative or relative pronoun in each sentence. Indicate whether it is used as a relative or an interrogative pronoun.

1. Lady Mary Stewart, who wrote four Arthurian novels, also wrote three children's books.
2. The teacher asked, "Which of Stewart's novels won the Frederick Niven Prize?"
3. She wrote *The Hollow Hills*, which tells the story of Merlin.
4. Whose is the most romantic Arthurian novel?
5. Lady Mary, whose husband is a geologist, lives in Scotland.
6. Which of the Arthurian legends was printed in 1485?
7. Do you know the name of the book that Sir Thomas Malory wrote?

8. The title is *Le Morte d'Arthur,* which is French for "The Death of Arthur."
9. Malory tells the adventures of Arthur, Guinevere, Lancelot, and other legendary characters whom you may know.
10. What is the source of Lerner and Loewe's musical, *Camelot*?

Indefinite Pronouns

An **indefinite pronoun** refers to persons, places, or things in a more general way than a noun does.

Some indefinite pronouns do not have identifiable antecedents.

Everyone needs food. [The indefinite pronoun *everyone* refers to people in general.]

Did you get **enough** to eat? [The indefinite pronoun *enough* does not indicate to what it specifically refers.]

Other indefinite pronouns often have specific antecedents.

After two hamburgers, he did not want **another.** [The indefinite pronoun *another* has the antecedent *hamburger.*]

Some indefinite pronouns are listed in the following chart.

all	either	most	other
another	enough	much	others
any	everybody	neither	plenty
anybody	everyone	nobody	several
anyone	everything	none	some
anything	few	no one	somebody
both	many	nothing	someone
each	more	one	something

EXERCISE 11 **Identifying Indefinite Pronouns.** On your paper list the ten indefinite pronouns in the following paragraph.

[1]Each of the fifteen thousand lakes in Minnesota covers at least ten acres. [2]Lake parties are given on lashed-together pontoon boats, with one for dancing and another for talking. [3]Anyone can easily understand why water skiing was born in Minnesota. [4]Few will deny the pleasures of eating the fish from Minnesota's lakes. [5]Many of the walleyed pike caught here are packed in lake ice cut during the cold winters. [6]Some of the people who play ice hockey on the frozen lakes are only six years old; others are over seventy. [7]In winter nothing is more thrilling than a snowmobile race across a frozen lake. [8]Somebody who enjoys canoeing would like a vacation in the Boundary Waters Canoe Area.

SENTENCE WRITING **Following Models.** Each of the following quotations contains pronouns. Using each quotation as a model, write your own version of it with the same pronouns in the same positions. A sample response is provided for each item.

1. They who cross the sea change their skies but not their natures.

—Horace, Latin poet

SAMPLE ANSWER They who repeat gossip gain listeners but not admirers.

2. No one can make you feel inferior without your consent.

—Anna Eleanor Roosevelt, American humanitarian

SAMPLE ANSWER No one will take you dancing without your shoes.

3. He knows all about art, but he doesn't know what he likes.

—James Thurber, American humorist

SAMPLE ANSWER He writes all about the game, but he does not know how to play.

4. If you have to ask what jazz is, you'll never know.

—Louis Armstrong, American musician

SAMPLE ANSWER If you have to ask what a thing costs, then you cannot afford it.

REVIEW EXERCISE **Pronouns.** (a) On your paper list in order the twenty-five pronouns contained in the following paragraph. (b) Identify each pronoun as personal, possessive, reflexive or intensive, demonstrative, interrogative, relative, or indefinite.

[1]Harry Houdini, a great magician who was born Ehrich Weiss, used a stage name borrowed from an earlier French magician called Houdin. [2]While many of Houdin's illusions were optical ones, those that made Harry Houdini famous were daring escapes from complex traps—most of them designed by Houdini himself. [3]The most famous escape of all was the water torture trick, in which Houdini, whose hands and feet were bound, was locked in a water-filled tank, only to emerge safe and free a moment later. [4]Audiences would ask themselves: What does Houdini do to free himself? [5]Wouldn't you wonder about this yourself? [6]Actually Houdini created much of his magic by practicing yoga techniques, learning to survive on less oxygen than others of us need. [7]Whose name is synonymous with magic? [8]Now that is a question everyone can answer: It is the name of Harry Houdini (born Ehrich Weiss).

Verbs

A **verb** is a word that expresses action or a state of being and is necessary to make a statement.

The verb is the part of speech that is essential to the formation of a sentence. The nouns and pronouns in sentences name people, places, or things, and the verbs tell what those people, places, or things *do* or *are*.

The violins **begin.**
A flutist **entered** late.
Rehearsals **are** important.
The conductor **seems** enthusiastic.

Recognizing Verbs

1. You can test whether a word is a verb by seeing if it makes sense in one of the blanks in the following sentences:

   The members __________.
   It __________ in the street.
   We __________ them here.
   They __________ it to him.
   The apple __________ sweet.

2. Certain suffixes signal that a word is a verb. These suffixes include *-ate, -en, -esce, -fly* and *-ize.*

operate	coalesce	idolize
widen	beautify	

The primary characteristic of a verb is its ability to express time—present, past, and future. Verbs express time by means of *tense* forms. (For rules on forming and using verb tenses, see pages 497–502.)

PRESENT TENSE They **walk** home together.
PAST TENSE They **walked** home together.
FUTURE TENSE They **will walk** home together.

EXERCISE 12 **Adding Verbs to Make Sentences.** On your paper write ten complete sentences by supplying a verb for each of the blanks in the items below.

1. Many people in the Northeast __________ vacations at Cape Cod, Massachusetts.
2. The fine beaches and lovely scenery __________ visitors to the area.
3. Summer __________ the most popular season on the Cape.

4. Some people __________ the less crowded times of year, however.
5. The ocean and landscape __________ strikingly different in the winter.
6. The fall is a pleasant season, especially if you __________ a bicycle.
7. The air __________ mild and refreshing through October.
8. The cape __________ many interesting clothing, book, and antique stores.
9. The magnificent beaches with their high dunes __________ among the most beautiful anywhere.
10. Visitors also __________ to Cape Cod for the great seafood.

Action Verbs

An **action verb** tells what someone or something does.

Some action verbs express physical action; others express mental action.

PHYSICAL ACTION In baseball the catcher often **signals** instructions to the pitcher.

MENTAL ACTION A good catcher **understands** the technique of each batter.

EXERCISE 13 **Identifying Action Verbs.** On your paper write the action verb in each of the following sentences.

1. Many Americans today enjoy Chinese food.
2. Some people even cook Chinese food at home.
3. They usually use a wok, a large, round skillet with high sides.
4. Chinese dishes frequently contain fresh vegetables.
5. Cooks sometimes mix various vegetables and spices with meat, fish, or poultry.
6. Chinese cooks generally cut the food into bite-sized pieces.
7. Then they stir the ingredients quickly in a very hot wok.
8. This step requires very little time.
9. Many people choose chopsticks instead of forks for Chinese food.
10. They prefer the authenticity of the chopsticks.

SENTENCE WRITING **Creating Sentences with Action Verbs.** Choose five of the action verbs that you identified in Exercise 13. For each verb write one sentence.

Transitive and Intransitive Verbs

A **transitive verb** is an action verb that is followed by a word or words that answer the question *what?* or *whom?*

The word that answers the question *what?* or *whom?* after the action verb is called the *direct object,* or *object of the verb.* (For more information about direct objects, see page 447.)

Dogs **obey** people. [The verb *obey* is followed by the direct object *people,* which answers the question *obey whom?*]

Cats **see** their prey in the dark. [The action verb *see* is followed by the direct object *prey,* which answers the question *see what?*]

Many action verbs are not transitive. That is, they are not followed by words that answer the question *what?* or *whom?*

An **intransitive verb** is an action verb without a direct object.

Intransitive verbs simply tell what someone or something does, or they are followed by words that tell only *when, where,* or *how* an action occurs.

Dogs **obey.** [The action verb works alone.]

Cats **see** well in the dark. [The action verb is followed by words that tell *how* and *when.*]

Many action verbs can be transitive or intransitive, as you can see by comparing the two preceding sets of examples. Some action verbs, however, are either always transitive or always intransitive. That is, some action verbs make sense only with a direct object, and some make sense only without a direct object.

ALWAYS TRANSITIVE
Wolves almost never **harm** people.
These wild animals **avoid** human contact if possible.

ALWAYS INTRANSITIVE
Threats to the wolves' safety **occur** frequently.
Wolf packs **react** like family groups.

EXERCISE 14 **Recognizing Transitive and Intransitive Verbs.** Write on your paper the action verb in each of the following sentences. Indicate whether each action verb is used as a transitive or an intransitive verb.

1. Animals react in many different ways to danger.
2. Lions and tigers fight with their claws and teeth.
3. Bees, wasps, and jellyfish sting attackers.
4. Ostriches as well as horses kick their enemies.
5. Opossums simply lie on the ground as if dead.
6. The chameleon and other lizards change colors for protection.
7. When in danger, skunks release a highly unpleasant odor.
8. Certain snakes poison attackers with their venomous bites.
9. Some octopuses squirt "ink" around themselves as a screen.
10. Rabbits run from danger as fast as possible.

SENTENCE WRITING **Creating Sentences with Transitive and Intransitive Verbs.** For each of the following action verbs, write two sentences. First use the word as a transitive verb. Then use it as an intransitive verb.

1. followed 2. dropped 3. performed 4. studied 5. flew

Linking Verbs

A **linking verb** links, or joins, a noun or pronoun (the subject of a sentence) with a word or expression that identifies or describes that noun or pronoun.

Be in all its forms—*am, is, are, was, were, will be, has been, was being*—is the most commonly used linking verb.*

I **am** an athlete.
Squash **is** an indoor sport.
The players **are** fast.
They **were** hockey fans.

Several other verbs besides the forms of *be* can act as linking verbs:

look	remain	sound	stay
grow	appear	become	smell
feel	seem	taste	

*Sometimes rather than acting as a linking verb, the forms of *be* are used to state *where* something exists (*horses are in the barn*) or *when* something happened (*the game is on Friday*). These uses of the verb *be* are usually considered intransitive constructions.

EXERCISE 15 **Identifying Action and Linking Verbs.** On your paper make a list of the ten verbs in the following paragraph. Identify each verb as either action or linking.

[1]In 1884 France presented the United States with a gift as a dramatic gesture of friendship. [2]This spectacular gift was in the form of a huge copper statue. [3]Its official name is *Liberty Enlightening the World.* [4]Most people, however, know it simply as the Statue of Liberty. [5]The pieces of the statue arrived in the United States in 214 cases. [6]The French people donated the money for the construction of the statue. [7]Grateful, the people of the United States collected the funds for the massive granite and concrete pedestal. [8]This impressive monument found a permanent home on Liberty Island in New York harbor. [9]At 151 feet and 1 inch high, it remains one of the largest statues in the world. [10]The monumental lady with the torch quickly became a symbol of American democracy.

Linking Verb or Action Verb?

Except for the forms of *be* and *seem*, all the words listed as linking verbs on page 404 can also be action verbs. Each of the following sentence pairs shows a word first used as a linking verb and then as an action verb.

LINKING Solar heaters on roofs **look** strange at first.
ACTION Scientists **look** for new energy resources.

LINKING Most people **grow** hungry before lunch.
ACTION Californians **grow** avocados.

LINKING German shepherds **appear** highly intelligent.
ACTION Animals occasionally **appear** on television shows.

LINKING Some Mexican dishes **taste** spicy.
ACTION Good cooks **taste** their food.

If you are unsure of whether a word is a linking verb, substitute the word *seem* in the sentence. If the sentence still makes sense, the word in question is probably a linking verb.

Some cheeses **smell** [seem] quite strong. [Here *smell* is a linking verb.]

Cheese lovers **smell** the odor happily. [Here *smell* is not a linking verb. *Seem* cannot be substituted for *smell.*]

The passengers **looked** [seemed] very comfortable. [Here *looked* is used as a linking verb.]

The passenger **looked** at the timetables carefully. [Here *looked* is not a linking verb. *Seemed* cannot be substituted for *looked.*]

EXERCISE 16 **Distinguishing Between Action Verbs and Linking Verbs.** For each of the following sentences, write the verb. Then indicate whether it is an action verb or a linking verb.

1. To many people crocodiles look like alligators.
2. Both kinds of ferocious reptiles look eagerly for their unsuspecting prey.
3. Sensible people stay away from the crocodile.
4. Crocodiles, though smaller, remain much more vicious than alligators.
5. Because of the shape of the skull, the eyes and nostrils of both reptiles remain above the water at all times.
6. Crocodiles' snouts appear pointier than the snouts of alligators.
7. Crocodiles appear in tropical countries throughout the world.
8. The skins, or hides, of both reptiles feel rough.
9. Female alligators and crocodiles grow quite protective of their young.
10. The babies grow about one foot a year, to a length of between nine and twelve feet.

SENTENCE WRITING **Changing Linking Verbs to Action Verbs.** Look again at the words in the preceding exercise that you identified as linking verbs. For each one write an original sentence using the word as an action verb.

Verb Phrases

The verb in a sentence may consist of more than one word. The words that accompany the main verb are called **auxiliary,** or helping, **verbs.**

A **verb phrase** consists of a main verb and all its auxiliary, or helping, verbs.

A main verb may have as many as three auxiliary verbs coming before it. The most common auxiliary verbs are the forms of *be* and of *have*.

BE am, is, are, was, were, be, being, been
HAVE have, has, had

These auxiliary verbs help the main verb to express the various tenses. (For more information about using auxiliary verbs to form tenses, see Chapter 21.)

We **are working.** We **have worked.** We **had been working.**

The following auxiliary verbs are used for other purposes besides expressing time. They are called modal auxiliaries.

do, does, did	would	will
may, might	should	shall
can, could	must	

All of the auxiliary verbs on the preceding list, with the exception of the forms of *do,* can be used with the forms of *be* and *have* and the main verb.

They **must have walked.** He **could have finished.**
I **should be leaving.** She **may be waiting.**

EXERCISE 17 **Identifying Verb Phrases.** On your paper write the verb phrase in each of the following sentences. Put parentheses around the auxiliary verbs in each phrase. (Words that interrupt a verb phrase are not considered part of the verb phrase.)

1. The development of airplanes has led to the development of parachutes.
2. A person with a parachute will fall to earth at the rate of eighteen feet per second.
3. Passenger planes may carry parachutes as safety devices.
4. Passengers would use the parachutes in an emergency.
5. Not everyone can jump out of an airplane, even with a parachute.
6. Researchers have experimented with parachute design.
7. Parachutes should be folded into small, lightweight packages.
8. A badly packed parachute could cause a fatal accident.
9. The parachute should open like an umbrella.
10. On the ground the harness must detach easily.
11. The drag-off method of parachuting is rarely used anymore.
12. A parachutist must climb far out on an airplane's wing.
13. At precisely the right moment the ripcord must be tugged.
14. The air will drag both parachute and flier off the wing.
15. The parachute, though, might be dragged into the plane's tail
16. The free-fall method has provided more safety and excitement.
17. A parachutist should dive from the plane's door into the air.
18. Clear of the plane, the parachutist may pull the ripcord.
19. Forest rangers have been utilizing parachutes for years.
20. The term "paratrooper" was coined during World War II.

SENTENCE WRITING **Creating Sentences with Vivid Verbs.** Write five sentences about one of your favorite sports. Choose very specific action verbs to convey a vivid sense of the sport.

REVIEW EXERCISE **Verbs.** On your paper complete each sentence in the following paragraph by supplying the underlined kinds of verbs. Be sure that your completed sentences make sense.

The massive World Trade Center in New York City [1]*linking verb* a city within a city. About fifty thousand people [2]*action verb (intransitive)* in its stores and offices, and another eighty thousand or so [3]*action verb (intransitive)* in and out each day. The center [4]*action verb (transitive)* 110 stories in its twin towers, and another six levels [5]*action verb (intransitive)* underground. Its dozens of stores, from florists to drugstores, [6]*linking verb* attractive and busy. The stores often [7]*action verb (transitive)* special services to their customers. Clients of the cleaners, for example, [8]*verb phrase* their clothes in large bags for protection on the subway. The enormous kitchens of the center [9]*verb phrase* as many as thirty thousand people each day. More than twenty restaurants [10]*action verb (intransitive)* inside the buildings. The vast complex even [11]*action verb (transitive)* its own police station, with a force of thirty-nine officers. The manager's office [12]*linking verb* busy all the time. In fact it [13]*action verb (transitive)* over two hundred calls for assistance each day. Some people [14]*linking verb* too hot and [15]*action verb (transitive)* a lower temperature. Others [16]*verb phrase* themselves out of their offices and [17]*action verb (transitive)* spare keys. An ambulance [18]*verb phrase* outside the complex at all times in case of an emergency, and paramedics, with the latest in life-support equipment, [19]*verb phrase* the life of a seriously ill or injured person. With its impressive population and variety of services, the World Trade Center [20]*linking verb* a small city in the middle of New York City.

Revising Your Writing

Here are guidelines for using verbs to crystallize poetic images.

1. Try to reduce a group of words to one action verb. For example, instead of writing "And let your hair fall loosely around your face," W. B. Yeats wrote "And tumble out your hair."
2. Instead of beginning sentences with "there is" or "there were," begin with a noun and follow up with a colorful action verb. Alfred, Lord Tennyson, for example, used the following image:

   > "The long light shakes across the lake." How flat the picture would have been had Tennyson stated, "There was a long light shining across the lake."

3. Whenever possible, use action verbs rather than linking verbs. Christina Rossetti begins a poem with the question "Does the road wind uphill all the way?" The action verb *wind* is stronger than any linking verb. Compare the effect of Rossetti's line with "Is the road uphill all the way?"
4. Try to replace general verbs with more precise action verbs. For example, Dylan Thomas, instead of writing "Old age should protest at close of day," wrote "Old age should burn and rave at close of day." *Burn* and *rave* convey exactly how the poet felt a person who has led a long life should react to the approach of death.

Practice these techniques by revising the following passage. Pay particular attention to the italicized words.

> Today *there was* a changed world. At some point very early in the morning, winter *went* and spring *was here*. When I *got up*, sunlight *was coming* through my window. My room *was light*, and my mood *became bright* to match it. I threw open the window and *gave the new season a greeting*. In response the mellow air *came in* and *made the room warm*.

Adjectives

An **adjective** is a word that modifies a noun or pronoun, by limiting its meaning.

Adjectives modify, or change, the meaning of a noun or pronoun by making it more specific. As the following examples show, adjectives can modify nouns and pronouns in any of four ways. The arrows point to the modified words.

1. Some adjectives *describe;* they answer the question *what is it like?*

   a **round** window She seems **happy**. a **romantic** story

2. Some adjectives *classify;* they answer the question *what kind is it?*

   adult cat **Scottish** wool **federal** law

3. Some adjectives *quantify;* they answer the question *how much* or *how many?*

   a basket **six** oranges **many** ideas **no** money

4. Some adjectives *identify;* they answer the question *which one?*

   that hat **these** books **my** report **their** opinion*

Adjectives that identify or quantify nouns or pronouns are sometimes called determiners.

Recognizing Adjectives

The vast majority of adjectives can be used either before a noun or after a noun and linking verb. That is, the vast majority of adjectives can logically fit in both blanks in the following sentences:

The ____________ book is ____________.
The ____________ athlete seems ____________.
The ____________ decision is ____________.
The ____________ puppy was ____________.

Certain suffixes signal that a word is an adjective. These suffixes include *-able* and *-ible, -al, -esque, -ful, -ic, -ish, -less,* and *-ous.*

usable	cheerful	foolish
brutal	scenic	humorous
helpless	audible	picturesque

*Possessive pronouns, such as *our* and *his,* can be considered adjectives because they modify nouns in addition to their usual function as pronouns. Similarly, possessive nouns can be considered adjectives: Julia's dream.

Many adjectives have different forms to indicate *degree of comparison*. (For rules on forming and using degrees of comparison, see Chapter 24.)

POSITIVE	COMPARATIVE	SUPERLATIVE
light	lighter	lightest
funny	funnier	funniest
practical	more practical	most practical

Adjectives may be used in various positions in relation to the words they modify.

How **obedient** the poodle is!
That **obedient** poodle belongs to her.
The poodle is **obedient.**
The judges considered the poodle **obedient.**
The poodle, always **obedient**, waited by the door.

EXERCISE 18 **Finding Adjectives.** On your paper list the twenty adjectives in the following passage, which describes a scene on a British heath during the last century. Count possessive pronouns as adjectives in this exercise, but do not count the words *a, an,* and *the*.

Before him stretched the long, laborious road, dry, empty, and white. It was quite open to the heath on each side, and bisected that vast, dark surface. . . . The old man frequently stretched his eyes ahead to gaze over the tract that he had yet to traverse. At length he discerned, a long distance in front of him, a moving spot. . . . Its rate of advance was slow. . . . When he drew nearer he perceived it to be a . . . van, ordinary in shape, but singular in color. . . . The driver walked beside it; and, like his van, he was completely red. —Thomas Hardy

EXERCISE 19 **Completing Sentences with Adjectives.** On your paper complete the following sentences by replacing each blank with the kind of adjective given in the parentheses.

1. The drum is the oldest __________ instrument. (classifying)
2. Kettledrums are __________ because they are the only drums that can be tuned to a definite pitch. (describing)
3. The playing surface of __________ drums is made of calfskin, which is loosened and tightened to change the pitch. (identifying)
4. Generally, a kettledrum produces a __________ tone when the player strikes the drumhead with a mallet. (describing)
5. Modern orchestras usually include a pair of kettledrums, and the __________ instruments are tuned to different pitches. (quantifying)

Articles

Articles are the adjectives *a, an,* and *the*. *A* and *an* are called indefinite articles. *The* is called a definite article.

INDEFINITE	She found **a** ring.	They spotted **an** iceberg.
DEFINITE	She found **the** ring.	They spotted **the** iceberg.

The definite and indefinite articles show how much you think the person that you are speaking to or writing to knows about whatever you are discussing. If Lisa says to her father, "I found *the* dog," the definite article *the* shows that she thinks her father knows which dog she is talking about. If she does not think he can identify the dog, she will use the indefinite article and say, "I found *a* dog."

EXERCISE 20 **Identifying Articles.** Find the articles in the following pairs of sentences. On your paper explain the differences in meaning between each pair.

1. Was Jason wearing a tie?
   Was Jason wearing the tie?
2. The elephant trumpeted his greeting.
   An elephant trumpeted his greeting.
3. I had a salad for lunch.
   I had the salad for lunch.
4. The book is interesting.
   A book is interesting.
5. A poet is a writer.
   The poet is the writer.

Proper Adjectives

A **proper adjective** is formed from a proper noun and begins with a capital letter.

Proper adjectives classify; they answer the question *what kind is it?*

Rembrandt was a **Dutch** painter.
The **French** Revolution began in 1789.

The following suffixes are often used to create proper adjectives: *-an, -ian, -n, -se,* and *-ish.*

PROPER NOUNS	PROPER ADJECTIVES
Canada	Canadian
Queen Victoria	Victorian
Vietnam	Vietnamese
Denmark	Danish

EXERCISE 21 **Forming Proper Adjectives.** Write a proper adjective formed from each of the following proper nouns. Consult a dictionary if you need help.

1. Africa
2. China
3. Britain
4. King Edward VII
5. Rome
6. Wales
7. Shakespeare
8. Greece
9. Mars
10. France

SENTENCE WRITING **Creating Sentences with Adjectives.** Write five sentences about someone you know and can picture clearly. In your description include details about the person's appearance, voice, behavior, and personality. Choose adjectives that are especially descriptive to convey a vivid image of the person.

REVIEW EXERCISE **Adjectives.** On your paper write the twenty adjectives, including articles, that appear in the following paragraph.

[1]Recent discoveries have revealed new facts about the Maya. [2]These people formed one of the oldest societies in Central America. [3]By A.D. 1000 they had already made impressive and original advancements in art and science. [4]Recently at a site in northern Belize, fortunate archaeologists unearthed the unmistakable remains of an early civilization. [5]This discovery was remarkable and significant, for it pushed back the origins of Mayan culture to 2400 B.C.

Revising Your Writing

Examine the following description of an important encounter in Charles Dickens' *Great Expectations*. Notice especially the effect of the italicized adjectives.

> Mr. Jaggers' room was lighted by a skylight only, and was a most *dismal* place; the skylight, eccentrically *patched* like a *broken* head, and the *distorted adjoining* houses looking as if they had twisted themselves to peep down at me through it. There were not so *many* papers about, as I should have expected to see; and there were some *odd* objects about, that I should not have expected to see—such as an *old rusty* pistol, a sword in a scabbard, *several strange-looking* boxes and packages, and *two dreadful* casts on a shelf, of faces peculiarly *swollen*, and *twitchy* about the nose. Mr. Jaggers' *own high-backed* chair was of *deadly black* horsehair, with rows of *brass* nails round it, like a coffin. . . .

Here are some of Dickens' techniques that you can apply when you write and revise your work:

1. Try to use adjectives that will make nouns more specific. Dickens makes his nouns more specific by using adjectives that describe color *(rusty, black)*, shape or position *(distorted, adjoining, swollen, high-backed)*, and other visual characteristics *(dismal, patched, broken, many, several, brass)*. These adjectives appeal to our senses.
2. Try to use adjectives that convey a consistent mood. Dickens describes the room as *dismal* and adds many other adjectives that fill out the dismal picture: *broken, distorted, old, rusty, strange-looking, dreadful, swollen, twitchy, deadly, black.*

3. Try to determine where adjectives are helpful and where they are not needed. For example, Dickens does not offer visual details about the shelf itself. He may not have wanted to distract attention from the well-described faces that sat on the shelf. Do not feel that every noun you write needs an adjective.

Here is a section that comes after the description above, but without some of Dickens' adjectives. Revise the passage adding your own adjectives in the places indicated by the carets (‸).

> I wondered what was the history of all the‸litter about the room, and how it came there. I wondered whether the‸faces were of Mr. Jaggers' family, and, if he were so unfortunate as to have had a pair of such‸relations, why he stuck them on that‸perch. . . . My spirits may have been oppressed by the‸air. . . .

Adverbs

An **adverb** is a word that modifies a verb, an adjective, or another adverb by making its meaning more specific.

Like adjectives, adverbs are modifiers. Adjectives modify nouns and pronouns; adverbs modify verbs, adjectives, and other adverbs. Adverbs modify by answering the questions *when? where? how?* and *to what degree?* The following sentence illustrates the use of adverbs to modify an adjective *(odd)*, a verb *(become)*, and an adverb *(surprisingly)*.

> **Extremely** odd styles **sometimes** become **rather** surprisingly popular.

Recognizing Adverbs

You can test whether a word is an adverb by seeing if it makes sense in one of the following sentences:

They did it ___________.	I am feeling ___________ sad.
We have ___________ done it.	You did it ___________ well.

Certain suffixes signal that a word is an adverb. By far the most widely used is *-ly* when it is added to an adjective. Other suffixes include *-ward* and *-wise*.

quick**ly**	home**ward**	length**wise**
immediate**ly**	back**ward**	clock**wise**

Like adjectives, some adverbs have different forms to indicate degree of comparison. (For rules on forming them, see Chapter 24.)

POSITIVE	COMPARATIVE	SUPERLATIVE
runs **fast**	runs **faster**	runs **fastest**
works **carefully**	works **more carefully**	works **most carefully**
sees **well**	sees **better**	sees **best**

When an adverb modifies a verb, it may be placed in various positions in relation to the verb. When an adverb modifies an adjective or another adverb, it immediately precedes the modified word.

MODIFYING A VERB	**Finally** the storm is ending.
	The storm **finally** is ending.
	The storm is **finally** ending.
	The storm is ending **finally**.
MODIFYING AN ADJECTIVE	The snow was **quite** heavy.
MODIFYING AN ADVERB	It **almost** never snows this heavily.

EXERCISE 22 **Identifying Adverbs.** Write the adverb in each sentence below. Then write the word or words each adverb modifies.

1. Bessie Smith is often considered a great blues singers.
2. She grew up in an extremely poor family in Chattanooga, Tennessee.
3. By the age of fourteen, she was already touring with Ma Rainey and her Rabbit Foot Minstrels.
4. Bessie Smith sang songs dramatically.
5. Jazz writers have called her style rhythmically adventurous.
6. In 1923 she began to make commercially successful records.
7. Louis Armstrong was one very famous jazz musician with whom she sang.
8. Probably her greatest fame came in the years 1923 to 1928.
9. Her record *Nobody's Blues but Mine,* which covers the period from 1925 to 1927, remains popular today.
10. Bessie Smith died tragically in a car accident in 1937.

EXERCISE 23 **Completing Sentences with Adverbs.** On your paper complete the following sentences by replacing each blank with the kind of adverb named in parentheses.

1. Pearls are *(to what degree)* unusual gems because they are found *(where)* rather than underground like other gems.
2. When a mollusk's body is irritated by something like a grain of sand, it begins to build up a layer of pearl that *(when)* surrounds the sand *(how)*.
3. In the past pearl-making was left to chance, but *(when)* there are *(to what degree)* sophisticated methods for producing pearls.
4. Pearls are "planted" when a mollusk's shell is opened *(how)* and a small mother-of-pearl bead is placed *(where)*.
5. Black pearls are *(to what degree)* rare and *(when)* valuable.
6. A pearl with *(to what degree)* one blemish is *(to what degree)* acceptable, because it can be drilled for stringing or mounting at the point of the flaw.
7. Pearls from abalone are *(when)* *(to what degree)* round.
8. The surface of a pearl is *(to what degree)* soft and *(how)* scratched.
9. *(How)* trained workers remove blemishes that are not *(to what degree)* deep.
10. Natural pearls must be *(to what degree)* matched in color, size, and shape to make a *(to what extent)* beautiful necklace.

EXERCISE 24 **Positioning Adverbs.** (a) On your paper add an appropriate verb-modifying adverb to each of the following sentences. (b) Rewrite each sentence, placing the adverb in a different position.

SAMPLE Track and field star Carl Lewis accepted his fourth gold medal.

ANSWER (a) Track and field star Carl Lewis proudly accepted his fourth gold medal.
(b) Proudly, track and field star Carl Lewis accepted his fourth gold medal.

1. The Olympic runners waited for their signal.
2. They took their positions on the track.
3. The huge crowd was roaring its support.
4. The starting shot rang out.
5. The race had begun.
6. The crowd's favorite began to lag.
7. Another runner pulled ahead of her.
8. They charged toward the finish line.
9. The favorite lost the gold medal.
10. She accepted the silver medal.

Kinds of Adverbs

An **adverb of time** tells *when.*

Some adverbs of time tell about a particular point in time *(tomorrow).* Some tell about duration *(temporarily).* Some tell about frequency *(often).*

I will call **tomorrow.** His phone rings **often.**
Their phone is disconnected **temporarily.**

An **adverb of place** tells *where.*

Some adverbs of place tell about position *(here).* Some tell about direction *(backward).*

The speaker will stand **here.**
The car rolled **backward.**

An **adverb of degree** tells *to what degree or to what extent.*

When adverbs of degree are used with adjectives or other adverbs, they are sometimes called *intensifiers* because they indicate the degree of intensity of the adjective or other adverb.

Extremely hot weather can make people **very** uncomfortable. [The adverbs tell the degree of heat and discomfort.]

The rain **almost** ruined the picnic. [The adverb tells the degree of ruin.]

The storm was **somewhat** sudden. [The adverb tells the degree of suddenness.]

An **adverb of manner** tells *how or the means by which* an action is performed.

Adverbs of manner generally answer the question *how?* or *by which means?* Sometimes adverbs of manner modify adjectives.

HOW	treated **badly**
	worked **efficiently**
	carefully polished
BY WHICH MEANS	treated **surgically**
	mechanically polished
MODIFYING AN ADJECTIVE	**sincerely** happy
	truly sorry

Most, but not all, adverbs of manner end in *-ly* (for example, *thoroughly, sadly*). The *-ly* is added to an adjective to form an adverb of manner. Be aware of other common words that do not end in *-ly* but are also adverbs of manner (for example, *together* or *alone,* as in *worked together* or *studied alone*).

NEGATIVE WORDS AS ADVERBS

The word *not* and the contraction *n't* are considered adverbs. Other negative words can function as adverbs of time and place.

The plane has **not** landed. They have **hardly** boarded.
The plane is **nowhere** in sight. I have **never** flown.

EXERCISE 25 **Classifying Adverbs.** Label each italicized adverb in the sentences below as: (a) an adverb of time, (b) an adverb of place, (c) an adverb of degree, (d) an adverb of manner, or (e) a negative adverb.

1. People may believe that North Americans and the British can *always* understand each other.
2. That is *not entirely* true.
3. While American English and British English are *almost* identical, certain words and expressions are used *quite differently*.
4. An American parent *proudly* wheels a child in a baby carriage, while a British parent strolls *outdoors* with a pram.
5. What we enjoy as corn *here* is called maize in England.
6. Londoners *never* put cars in a parking lot but *always* use a car park.
7. While American children may play *together* with a jump rope, British children *happily* use a skipping rope.
8. *Nowhere* can you find an orchestra seat in a London theater, but you can *easily* find a stall *there*.
9. At bus stops in England, people wait *patiently* in *rather* long queues.
10. Americans may be *quite* surprised to learn that they are *not* playing tick-tack-toe; they are playing naughts and crosses.

SENTENCE WRITING **Creating Sentences with Adverbs.** Select five of the adverbs that you identified for Exercise 25. Write one original sentence for each adverb.

REVIEW EXERCISE **Adverbs.** On your paper write each of the twenty adverbs in the following paragraph. Then write the word or words that each adverb modifies.

[1]Hurricanes are severe storms with extremely strong winds. [2]Storms with this name are always limited to the northern Atlantic Ocean. [3]The same storm in the western Pacific Ocean is not called a hurricane; it is a typhoon. [4]In the Indian Ocean such a storm generally is known as a cyclone. [5]A hurricane is defined officially as a storm with winds of at least seventy-five miles an hour. [6]Such storms usually start in the North Atlantic and move westward. [7]Sometimes they progress northeastward from the Mexican coast. [8]In the beginning they move at approximately ten miles an hour and gradually gain speed. [9]A fully mature hurricane is almost circular. [10]Air pressure in its center, or eye, can be extremely low. [11]In the eye the air barely moves, the atmosphere seems strangely calm, and the sky often looks blue. [12]Clouds that swirl rapidly outside quickly bring violent winds and rain.

SENTENCE WRITING **Following Models.** A "Tom Swifty" is a sentence in which an adverb comments in a humorous way on an action or object mentioned in a quotation. Note the relationship between each adverb and quotation in the following examples:

> "Will you hang up these wet clothes?" asked Ben dryly.
>
> "I've never seen such flat land," said the farmer plainly.

(a) Write each of the following Tom Swifties on your paper, completing each with an adverb that comments in a humorous way on the quotation. (b) Write five Tom Swifties of your own, using the adverbs provided. Consult a dictionary if necessary.

1. "Please turn on the light," asked Sara. ___________ .
2. "I need the sandpaper," said the carpenter ___________ .
3. "The temperature is rising," said the weather forecaster ___________ .
4. "Be careful with that knife!" warned Michael ___________ .
5. "My arm is aching," complained the pitcher ___________ .
6. coldly
7. heavily
8. sourly
9. snappily
10. sunnily

Revising Your Writing

Notice the italicized adverbs in the following sentences from Stephen Crane's story "The Open Boat."

> The birds sat *comfortably* in groups, and they were envied by some in the dinghy. . . . *Often* they came *very* close . . . and the men hooted *angrily* at them. . . . [One] bird flew parallel to the boat. His black eyes were *wistfully* fixed upon the captain's head.

Try reading the excerpt without the adverbs, and you will see how important they are to Crane's meaning. For example, if the birds were merely *sitting*, the uncomfortable men in the boat would not envy them so. Keep in mind the following techniques when you write:

1. Use adverbs to complete a picture, to justify the feeling or the mood. In Crane's sentences, for example, *comfortably* helps to explain the men's envy; *often* helps to explain their anger. *Wistfully* enhances the characterization of the bird and helps the reader see things from the men's point of view.
2. Use adverbs to emphasize and clarify a point. Crane uses *very* to stress how irritating the birds were. He adds *angrily* to underscore the men's feelings and clarify the effect of *hooted*.

Apply these techniques by revising the following passage. Add adverbs in the places indicated by carets (∧).

> His interview with the personnel manager was ∧ dreadful. While Ms. Evans sat ∧ in her padded armchair, he was forced ∧ to hunch ∧ in a flimsy straight-backed chair. Her questions were ∧ sharp and ∧ difficult, and she ∧ looked over his head as he ∧ tried to answer them.

Prepositions

A **preposition** is a word that shows the relationship of a noun or pronoun to some other word in a sentence.

Prepositions exist to help express space, time, and other relationships among words.

The silverware is **inside** the cabinet. [*Inside* shows the spatial relationship of the silverware and the cabinet.]

All the guests arrived **before** dinner. [*Before* tells the time relationship between the guests' arrival and dinner.]

He brought a gift **for** the host. [*For* does not cover a spatial or time relationship, but it does relate *gift* and *host*.]

She had lunch **after** the meeting. [*After* tells the time relationship between lunch and the meeting.]

As with pronouns, there are only a limited number of prepositions in English. The list below presents some of the most commonly used prepositions in our language.

aboard	beneath	in	since
about	beside	inside	through
above	besides	into	throughout
across	between	like	to
after	beyond	near	toward
against	but*	of	under
along	by	off	underneath
among	concerning	on	until
around	down	onto	up
at	during	outside	upon
before	except	over	with
behind	for	past	within
below	from	regarding	without

A **compound preposition** is a preposition that is made up of more than one word. Here are some common ones.

according to	in front of
ahead of	in spite of
along with	instead of
apart from	next to
aside from	on account of
because of	on top of
by means of	out of
in addition to	

*meaning "except"

Recognizing Prepositions

You can test whether a word is a preposition by seeing if it makes sense in one of the following sentences:

Everyone spoke ____________ her.
He placed it ____________ the box.
The dog barked ____________ the morning.

Prepositions begin phrases that generally end with a noun or pronoun, called the **object of the preposition.**

He drank a glass **of milk.**
She stood **in front of us.**
I ate some bread **with cheese.**

(For more about prepositional phrases, see Chapter 19.)

Unlike nouns, pronouns, verbs, adjectives, and adverbs, prepositions never undergo spelling changes. Every preposition has just one form.

The word *preposition* means "placed before." In general, a preposition comes before the noun or pronoun that ends the phrase.

EXERCISE 26 **Identifying Prepositions.** On your paper list the prepositions in each of the following sentences. Remember that some prepositions are made up of more than one word. (The numeral in parentheses at the end of each item indicates the number of prepositions in that sentence.)

1. The great jazz musician Sonny Rollins was born in New York in 1920 to musical parents. (3)
2. Instead of the usual piano or violin, Rollins chose the tenor saxophone for his instrument. (2)
3. Like many jazz musicians, he often improvised on themes within the music. (3)
4. His album *Moving Out* put him at the top of his profession. (2)
5. During the late fifties and into the sixties, his work became notable for its energy and daring. (3)
6. Rollins took music out of its usual locations and went beyond the usual limits of the saxophone. (3)
7. Sometimes he would play his saxophone outdoors instead of indoors. (1)
8. Another of his experiments involved making the sound from his saxophone bounce off walls and ceilings. (3)
9. Rollins continued experiments with music throughout the nineteen sixties. (2)
10. In addition to his experimental work, Rollins played the music for the movie *Alfie.* (2)

SENTENCE WRITING **Creating Sentences with Prepositions.** Choose five prepositions from the lists on page 423. Use each one in a sentence. Add adjectives and adverbs wherever necessary.

Conjunctions

A **conjunction** is a word that joins single words or groups of words.

Conjunctions are very important because they clarify the relationship between parts of a sentence. English has four kinds of conjunctions: *coordinating conjunctions, correlative conjunctions, subordinating conjunctions,* and *conjunctive adverbs.*

Here we will study the first two in detail and cover the second two briefly. Subordinating conjunctions will come up again in Chapter 20 and conjunctive adverbs in Chapter 27.

Coordinating Conjunctions

A **coordinating conjunction** joins words or groups of words that have equal grammatical weight in a sentence.

The coordinating conjunctions are *and, but, or, nor, for,* and *yet.* All the coordinating conjunctions, except *for,* can join words, phrases, or clauses. *For* joins only clauses and nothing else.

> Two **and** two are four. [joins words]
> She is good at algebra **but** not at arithmetic. [joins phrases]
> We must leave now, **or** we will be late. [joins clauses]
> The bell rang, **yet** everyone remained seated. [joins clauses]

EXERCISE 27 **Identifying Coordinating Conjunctions.** Write the coordinating conjunction in each of the following sentences.

1. Most museums house works of art, scientific exhibits, or historical collections.
2. The Cooper-Hewitt Museum in New York City is different, for it is a museum of design.
3. Textile designers and interior decorators make constant use of its unusual collections.
4. Peter Cooper had already established Cooper Union, a free adult school, but he also envisioned a museum for the decorative arts.
5. His daughter and three granddaughters, all named Hewitt, founded this museum in 1897, fourteen years after his death.
6. The Hewitts were somewhat eccentric, yet they had fine taste.

7. They traveled through Europe and bought whatever they liked.
8. Their purchases were not limited to textiles but included everything related to the decorative arts.
9. When they saw well-designed furniture, lace, buttons, clocks, china, cutlery, keys, locks, or jewelry, they would buy it.
10. Thanks to the Hewitts, you need not wonder how fork design developed, for you can go to the Cooper-Hewitt and find out.
11. The Cooper-Hewitt is located on the Upper East Side of Manhattan and is housed in the Andrew Carnegie mansion.
12. The museum is now part of the Smithsonian Institution but maintains its focus on decorative arts.
13. The exhibits are usually on a small scale, yet they well chosen.
14. In recent years, you may have seen the fine exhibit of illustrations for children's books or the superb show on wallpaper design.
15. Membership in the Cooper-Hewitt has risen in recent years, for the public appreciates this unique museum's special offerings.

Correlative Conjunctions

Correlative conjunctions work in pairs to join words and groups of words of equal weight in a sentence.

both . . . and	not only . . . but (also)
either . . . or	though . . . yet
just as . . . so	whether . . . or
neither . . . nor	

You use the first part of the correlative conjunction before one word or group of words and the second part before the related word or group of words. Correlative conjunctions make the relationship between words or groups of words a little clearer than do coordinating conjunctions.

COORDINATING CONJUNCTIONS	CORRELATIVE CONJUNCTIONS
She **and** I were there.	**Both** she **and** I were there. [*She* and *I* are of equal value: they are related words. The correlative conjunction *both . . . and* makes the relationship clearer and stronger than the coordinating conjunction *and*.]
She **or** I can go.	**Either** she **or** I can go. **Neither** she **nor** I can go.
I met Jean **and** Ed.	I met **not only** Jean **but also** Ed.

EXERCISE 28 **Identifying Correlative Conjunctions.** On your paper write both parts of the correlative conjunctions in the following sentences.

1. Just as people are interested in the weather forecast today, so people thousands of years ago tried to predict weather conditions.
2. Methods of predicting the weather have grown not only more complicated but also more accurate.
3. Both modern and ancient cultures have looked to the sky for weather signs.
4. The predictions of the ancients, whether correct or incorrect, were based on very different methods from those of today.
5. Neither the seemingly essential thermometer nor the equally useful barometer was invented until a few hundred years ago.
6. Both the modern telegraph and the even more recent satellite have made it possible to exchange weather information more rapidly.
7. Satellites are used for early spotting not only of hurricanes but also of cyclones and typhoons.
8. Though high-speed computers and other advanced equipment have taught us a lot about the weather, yet there is much to be learned before predictions become more reliable.
9. The National Oceanic and Atmospheric Administration is responsible for both studying the weather and forecasting it.
10. Weather forecasting is an activity not only of government agencies but also of private companies.

EXERCISE 29 **Completing Sentences with Coordinating and Correlative Conjunctions.** On your paper supply the coordinating or correlative conjunctions that make the most sense in each sentence.

1. There have always been female acrobats, trapeze artists, ___________ horseback riders in the circus.
2. In most of the circus's daring displays, the performers might be ___________ male ___________ female.
3. ___________ women have long appeared in various circus acts, ___________ "The Greatest Show on Earth" did not have a female clown until 1970.
4. Peggy Williams started out not as a clown ___________ as a speech therapist.
5. She planned to work in a clinic ___________ hospital, helping people with speech defects.
6. She attended the Ringling Brothers Clown College in 1969, ___________ as a future speech therapist, not as a clown.
7. At the Clown College she planned to concentrate on forms of nonverbal communication, such as pantomime, for the other subjects were ___________ related ___________ helpful to her chosen field.
8. Once there, however, she became interested ___________ in pantomime, ___________ in juggling, acrobatics, costuming, and other performing skills.
9. By graduation time she knew that she must choose between being an unhappy speech therapist ___________ a happy clown.
10. She auditioned for the Ringling Brothers Barnum and Bailey Circus ___________ in January 1970 took her first professional pratfalls as part of the largest circus in the world.

Subordinating Conjunctions

A **subordinating conjunction** joins two clauses, or ideas, in such a way as to make one grammatically dependent upon the other.

The idea, or clause, that a subordinating conjunction introduces is said to be "subordinate," or dependent, because it cannot stand by itself as a complete sentence. You will learn more about these conjunctions when you study adverb clauses on page 479. Here are examples of subordinating conjunctions in use:

We raked the leaves **because** so many had fallen.
We raked the leaves **before** we had lunch.
Wherever the leaves had fallen, we raked them into piles.
When more leaves fall, we will rake again.

Here is a list of common subordinating conjunctions.

after	as soon as	inasmuch as	unless
although	as though	in order that	until
as	because	since	when
as far as	before	so long as	whenever
as if	considering (that)	so that	where
as long as	if	than	while

EXERCISE 30 **Identifying Subordinating Conjunctions.** Write the subordinating conjunction in each sentence below. Remember that some subordinating conjunctions are made up of more than one word.

1. As far as most people are concerned, Timbuktu is an imaginary place.
2. People use the name whenever they want to express the idea of a faraway place.
3. Although many do not realize it, Timbuktu actually exists.
4. Inasmuch as about ten thousand people call it home, it is real.
5. It is a trading center because it lies at the crossroads of North Africa and West Africa.
6. Nomadic peoples go there when they want to trade.
7. The Taureg people founded Timbuktu in the eleventh century so that they would have a seasonal camp.
8. As it had a thriving gold trade, Timbuktu had become known in Europe by the fourteenth century.
9. Timbuktu was a center for education and Muslim culture while it was part of the Songhoi Empire from 1469 to 1591.
10. Timbuktu declined gradually until it was occupied by the French in 1893 and 1894.

Conjunctive Adverbs

A **conjunctive adverb** is used to clarify the relationship between clauses of equal weight in a sentence.

Conjunctive adverbs are usually stronger and more precise than coordinating conjunctions. Consider the difference in emphasis between the following two sentences.

COORDINATING CONJUNCTION Most people think of deserts as very hot places, **but** desert nights can be quite cool.

CONJUNCTIVE ADVERB Most people think of deserts as very hot places; **however**, desert nights can be quite cool.

Note that a semicolon comes before the conjunctive adverb, and the adverb is usually followed by a comma.

There are many conjunctive adverbs, and they have several uses, as the following examples show:

TO REPLACE *AND*	also, besides, furthermore, moreover
TO REPLACE *BUT*	however, nevertheless, still, though
TO STATE A RESULT	consequently, therefore, so, thus
TO STATE EQUALITY	equally, likewise, similarly

EXERCISE 31 **Identifying Conjunctive Adverbs.** Each of the following sentences has one conjunctive adverb. Write it on your paper.

1. The Toltec civilization of ancient Mexico was advanced in arts and architecture; moreover, it produced impressive stonework.
2. The Toltec religion at one time centered on Quetzalcoatl; consequently, this plumed serpent appeared in many legends and images.
3. Quetzalcoatl was the name of a deity; furthermore, it was the name of a legendary ruler.
4. Quetzalcoatl was the god of civilization; thus, he was the force of good.
5. Quetzalcoatl was the god of books, writing, and learning; so, he was worshiped in schools.
6. Quetzalcoatl was the inventor of the Toltec calendar; also, he was seen as the protector of all craftspeople.
7. Quetzalcoatl was identified with the morning star; however, as a symbol of the evening star, he was associated with death.
8. Quetzalcoatl was identified with the planet Venus; likewise, he was associated with the wind.
9. Usually Quetzalcoatl was represented as a plumed serpent; however, he was often shown as the wind god.
10. The people wished to please Quetzalcoatl; therefore, they built circular temples, which presented no sharp obstacles to the wind.
11. The religious ceremonies consisted of different rituals; moreover, they played a sacred ball game called *tlatchi.*
12. The Toltec civilization expanded southward during the tenth century; therefore, the Toltecs dominated the Mayas of the Yucatan.
13. Other nomadic Mexican tribes conquered the Toltec empire in the thirteenth century; thus, the Toltec civilization declined.
14. The Aztecs soon built their own empire; consequently, art and science continued to flourish in Mexico.
15. Aztec civilization grew strong; nevertheless, it too met its end.

SENTENCE WRITING **Following Models.** Each of the following quotations has conjunctions in it. Using each quotation as a model, write your own version with the same conjunctions in the same position. A possible sample response is provided for each of the following items.

1. If we cannot end now our differences, at least we can help make the world safe for diversity. —John F. Kennedy

   SAMPLE ANSWER If we cannot give an apple to everyone, at least we can give everyone some applesauce.

2. Just know your lines, and don't bump into the furniture. —Spencer Tracy, actor

   SAMPLE ANSWER Just keep your eye on the ball, and don't stop swinging.

3. Between the amateur and the professional . . . there is a difference not only in degree but in kind. —Bernard De Voto, writer

   SAMPLE ANSWER Among the children in the family there was a pride not only in one another but in themselves.

4. I never forget a face, but in your case I'll make an exception. —Groucho Marx, comedian

   SAMPLE ANSWER I never forget an insult, but in this case I will forget it entirely.

REVIEW EXERCISE **Conjunctions.** On your paper replace the blank or blanks in each of the following sentences with a conjunction that makes sense. The kind of conjunction to use is stated in parentheses at the end of each sentence. Be sure to use all commas and semicolons correctly.

1. Modern tunnel building is a complicated process; __________, it is a very costly process, involving millions of dollars. (conjunctive adverb)
2. __________ a tunnel under a river costs considerably more than a bridge, it may have certain advantages. (subordinating conjunction)
3. __________ does it allow the unhindered passage of ships, __________ it is less vulnerable. (correlative conjunction)
4. A tunnel is a marvelous construction, __________ building it is extremely hazardous. (coordinating conjunction)
5. There are basically three ways to build a tunnel; __________, tunnels may be divided into three types. (conjunctive adverb)
6. A "true" tunnel is dug horizontally through earth __________ rock. (coordinating conjunction)

7. For the cut-and-cover tunnel, a large ditch is dug, a tube is built in the ditch, __________ the tube is covered over. (coordinating conjunction)
8. __________ the first subway in the world, in London, __________ the first on the European continent, in Budapest, were built in this way. (correlative conjunction)
9. The trench tunnel involves a kind of cut-and-cover method used __________ the tunnel is dug underwater. (subordinating conjunction)
10. __________ a route is chosen for any tunnel, a careful geological study is made of the type of earth and rock along the way. (subordinating conjunction)

Revising Your Writing

Revise the paragraph below by replacing some of the coordinating conjunctions with more precise connectives. Use the following guidelines to help you:

1. Try to improve your writing by stressing the relationship between words with correlative conjunctions instead of relying on coordinating conjunctions.

   not only / but also

   SAMPLE They rehearsed ^ on weeknights ^ and on weekends.

2. Try to replace coordinating conjunctions with conjunctive adverbs to state a result or to state equality.

   however,

   SAMPLE The curtain fell; but the audience kept applauding.

3. Try to make the relationship between two ideas clearer by replacing coordinating conjunctions with subordinating conjunctions.

   Although

   SAMPLE ^ The curtain fell, but the audience kept applauding.

As you revise, pay particular attention to the italicized words and the places marked by carets (^).

> I have been trying to draw a picture of my cat, Blanche, ^ *but* she refuses to pose for me. ^ I have tried ^ explaining my purpose *and* bribing her with some cheese, *but* nothing has worked so far. ^ I place her in an interesting position, *and* she ^ rearranges herself *and* falls asleep. Obviously ^ I want a drawing of a cat, ^ *and so* I will have to buy one.

Interjections

An **interjection** is a word or phrase that expresses emotion or exclamation. An interjection has no grammatical connection to other words.

An interjection can be part of a sentence, or it can stand alone.

Oh, I didn't know that. **Whew**, it's hot.
Ouch! That hurts! **Why**, Stanley!

Interjections are used more frequently in informal speech than in writing.

EXERCISE 32 **Using Interjections.** On your paper fill the blank in each sentence below with an appropriate interjection from the list.

help	wow	oops	ssh	ah
well	whew	psst	yipes	alas

1. ____________ That was an amazing catch!
2. ____________ I dropped the plate.
3. ____________ you are here at last.
4. ____________ The dog got away!
5. ____________ the concert is beginning.
6. ____________ that was pretty close!
7. ____________ it is finally over.
8. ____________ come here a second, but do not let anyone see you.
9. ____________ that is the wildest thing I have ever heard!
10. ____________ It is pouring, and I forgot to shut the windows.

Words as More Than One Part of Speech

A word's part of speech is directly related to how the word is used in a sentence.

Many words can be more than one part of speech. Notice, for example, how the word *down* is a different part of speech in each of the following sentences:

NOUN The jacket is filled with **down.**
VERB She can **down** her milk in three swallows.
ADJECTIVE I sleep under a **down** blanket.
ADVERB The runner fell **down.**
PREPOSITION The dog ran **down** the stairs.

The following sections will explain how words normally considered one part of speech may often act as another part of speech.

Noun or Adjective?

Many words commonly listed as nouns in a dictionary may act as adjectives by modifying other nouns.

NOUNS She auditioned for the play at **school.**
I rode by **bicycle** to the stadium.
ADJECTIVES She auditioned for the **school** play.
The **bicycle** rider stopped to rest.

Some combinations of nouns that modify other nouns become so common that they are often thought of, to varying extents, as compound nouns (see page 391).

lawn mower
state legislature
chicken soup

EXERCISE 33 **Using Nouns as Adjectives.** On your paper use each of the following nouns as an adjective by adding another noun that the given word may modify.

SAMPLE garage
ANSWER garage door

1. bathroom
2. coat
3. ocean
4. summer
5. book
6. table
7. cat
8. cheese
9. tire
10. television

Pronoun or Adjective?

Many pronouns may be used like adjectives. Possessive pronouns, demonstrative pronouns, interrogative pronouns, and indefinite pronouns can all be used as adjectives when they modify a noun.

The following possessive pronouns by their very nature modify nouns by answering the question *which one?: my, your, his, her, its, our, their.*

POSSESSIVE PRONOUN The gloves are **his.**
POSSESSIVE ADJECTIVE **His** gloves are red.

This and *that* may modify singular nouns. *These* and *those* may modify plural nouns.

DEMONSTRATIVE PRONOUN **That** is a friendly dog.
DEMONSTRATIVE ADJECTIVE **That** dog is friendly.
DEMONSTRATIVE PRONOUN **These** are big dogs.
DEMONSTRATIVE ADJECTIVE **These** dogs are big.

The interrogative pronouns *whose, what,* and *which* may be used as adjectives.

INTERROGATIVE PRONOUN **Which** is their car?
DEMONSTRATIVE ADJECTIVE **Which** car is theirs?

Many of the words listed on page 399 as indefinite pronouns often function in sentences as adjectives.

INDEFINITE PRONOUNS **Many** left early.
They gave **some** away.
INDEFINITE ADJECTIVES **Many** guests left early.
They gave **some** books away.

EXERCISE 34 **Distinguishing Between Pronouns and Adjectives.** List on your paper the twenty-five italicized words from the following sentences. Then indicate whether each word is used here as a pronoun or an adjective.

1*What* animal is more familiar to humans than the dog? Probably 2*none* is. Dogs are unusual for 3*several* reasons. First, they inhabit 4*all* parts of 5*our* world. 6*Some* live in the tropics, and 7*a few* have adapted to the frozen north. 8*Theirs* may seem like a difficult life, but 9*this* may not be true for the animals. 10*Another* feature of dogs is the variation in 11*their* size. 12*Several* are as much as three feet high at the shoulder. 13*These* include the giant Irish wolfhound and the Great Dane. 14*Other* dogs are only six inches high. 15*Which* is the smallest dog of 16*all?* 17*That* is the tiny Chihuahua. 18*Most* dogs fall between 19*these* extremes, of course. For 20*many* centuries humans have bred and trained the dog to meet 21*their* needs, which included hunting, guarding, retrieving, herding, running, and sled pulling. For 22*most* people in 23*our* society, however, dogs meet 24*one* need in particular. 25*That* is the need for affection.

Preposition or Adverb?

Many of the words listed as prepositions on page 423 can, in some sentences, be adverbs. If the word stands alone and answers a question such as *where?* or *when?* and if it does not connect a noun or pronoun to the rest of the sentence, consider the word an adverb. Otherwise, consider it a preposition.

ADVERB Please wait **outside**. [answers the question *where?*]

PREPOSITION Please wait **outside** the door. [connects the noun *door* to the rest of the sentence]

EXERCISE 35 **Distinguishing Between Prepositions and Adverbs.** Decide whether the italicized word in each sentence is a preposition or an adverb. Write the answer on your paper.

1. It is four minutes and ten seconds *before* six o'clock.
2. Everyone present has witnessed the scene many times *before*.
3. Reporters and technicians are standing *around* and talking.
4. Two women and a man are seated *around* a large desk.
5. *Behind* them are three large screens.
6. Preparations are running ten seconds *behind*, and the stage manager issues a general warning about the time.
7. His voice can barely be heard *above* the din.
8. Some bright lights flicker *above* and then glow steadily.
9. More and more lights are turned *on* as the countdown begins.
10. Finally the six o'clock news is *on* the air.
11. Turn the radio *off*.
12. Be careful when you get *off* the bus.
13. The nails are *in* the jar.
14. My sister let the cat *in*.
15. I was happy to put the heavy package *down*.

Preposition or Conjunction?

The words *after, before, since, as* and *until* can function in sentences as either prepositions or subordinating conjunctions. As prepositions these words connect a noun or pronoun to the rest of the sentence. As subordinating conjunctions they will be followed by a word group that without the conjunction could stand alone as a sentence.

PREPOSITIONS Finish your homework **before** dinner.
Work **until** dinnertime.

SUBORDINATING CONJUNCTIONS Finish your work **before** you eat dinner.
Work **until** dinnertime arrives.

EXERCISE 36 **Distinguishing Between Prepositions and Conjunctions.** List on your paper the ten italicized words from the following sentences. Identify each word as a preposition or a conjunction.

[1]*As* you may know, the popular musical *The King and I* is based on actual people. Anna Leonowens, a British teacher, traveled to faraway Siam [2]*after* her husband died in order to teach the children of the king. Despite profound cultural differences, she grew fond of the king and remained in Siam [3]*until* he passed away. The king portrayed in the show actually ruled Siam [4]*as* Rama IV, fourth in the dynasty that has been in power [5]*since* the year 1782. [6]*After* the ascent of Rama IV to the throne in 1851, the country became known as Siam. This remained its name [7]*until* 1938, when it was renamed Thailand. [8]*Since* Rama IV, or King Mongkut, wished to avoid becoming part of the expanding British or French empires, he signed trade agreements and opened his country to modernization. He did not tremble [9]*before* the powerful European nations. Instead he wisely decided to insist on internal reforms [10]*before* the Europeans could try to take advantage of any discontent within Siam. Today Siam, or Thailand, remains the only country in Southeast Asia that has never been ruled by a European power.

SENTENCE WRITING **Using Words as Various Parts of Speech.** Write a sentence for each of the following words, using it as the part of speech indicated.

1. picture (noun)
2. picture (adjective)
3. that (pronoun)
4. that (adjective)
5. left (noun)
6. left (adjective)
7. around (preposition)
8. around (adverb)
9. after (preposition)
10. after (conjunction)

CHAPTER 17 PARTS OF SPEECH

Nouns [pages 388–392] Identify each of the ten underlined nouns as (a) proper, (b) common and concrete, (c) common and abstract, (d) collective, or (e) common and compound.

The first [1]people to cultivate the potato lived in the highlands of [2]Peru more than three thousand years ago. Potatoes grow in that [3]land in such amazing [4]variety that an occasional [5]group of scientists will still travel high into the [6]Andes to collect specimens. A single farmer may grow as many as forty-five different kinds of potato on tiny [7]plots scattered over the [8]hillsides. This popular vegetable was unknown to [9]Europeans until the [10]1530s.

Pronouns [pages 394–400] Indicate whether the underlined pronoun is (a) personal or possessive, (b) reflexive or intensive, (c) demonstrative, (d) relative or interrogative, or (e) indefinite.

11. He himself found the solution to his problem.
12. He himself found the solution to his problem.
13. That is not the answer to the problem.
14. Who helped them find the answer?
15. Who helped them find the answer?
16. The cat watched the sparrows that came to the bird feeder.
17. The cat washed itself after eating.
18. Nobody taught it to do that.
19. Is it your cat or your cousin's?
20. She fed both of the cats.

Verbs [pages 401–408] Indicate whether each of the ten underlined verbs is (a) a transitive action verb, (b) an intransitive action verb, (c) a linking verb, (d) an auxiliary, or (e) a verb phrase.

From 1911 to 1967, the newsreel [21]was a part of every visit to the movies. Most theaters [22]showed these ten-minute summaries of current events between feature films. Consequently, movie patrons [23]could watch an "illustrated magazine on film" decades before television [24]existed. In fact, newsreels actually [25]covered the news photographically before newspapers and magazines did. Old newsreels [26]look primitive to our eyes, but they [27]became the direct ancestors of TV news. While yesterday's moviegoer was pleased to see events only days after they [28]occurred, today's TV watcher [29]can witness important stories as they [30]are happening.

Adjectives [pages 410–413] Match the underlined adjective in the left column with the correct identification in the right column.

31. He is learning a second language.	(a) comparative degree
32. His aunt speaks the language.	(b) superlative degree
33. They study French verbs together.	(c) definite article
34. She lent him the best book.	(d) indefinite article
35. It is clearer than his.	(e) proper adjective

Adverbs [pages 416–421] Match the underlined adverb in the left column with the correct identification in the right column.

36. Read the instructions carefully.	(a) adverb of time
37. Do not skip anything.	(b) adverb of place
38. It should be completely clear.	(c) adverb of degree
39. Put the instructions away.	(d) adverb of manner
40. Then you may begin.	(e) negative adverb

Prepositions, Conjunctions, and Interjections [pages 423–434] Indicate whether each of the ten underlined words as used here is (a) a preposition, (b) a coordinating conjunction, (c) part of a correlative conjunction, (d) a subordinating conjunction, or (e) an interjection.

The Gulf Stream is a current that runs [41]along the eastern coast of North America. Presumably it was named the Gulf Stream [42]because it comes from the Gulf of Mexico. Early mariners must have known about the current, [43]but many seemed to ignore it. [44]Well, many ships wasted weeks sailing against the current [45]on voyages to the New World. For example, [46]when ships from England traveled [47]to New York rather than to Rhode Island, the trip took weeks longer. [48]Neither distance nor climate could explain this unreasonable delay. It was Benjamin Franklin, [49]both curious and conscientious as always, who first charted the current in 1769 [50]and discovered that its waters were significantly warmer than the waters around it.

Writing for Review Write one paragraph on any subject you choose. Underline and identify in your paragraph at least one example of each of the following parts of speech: noun, pronoun, verb, adjective, adverb, preposition, and conjunction.

CHAPTER 18

Parts of the Sentence

Simple Subjects and Simple Predicates

A **sentence** is a group of words that expresses a complete thought.

Every sentence has two basic parts, a *subject* and a *predicate*.

The **simple subject** is the principal noun or pronoun that tells what a sentence is about. The **simple predicate** is the verb or verb phrase that tells something about the subject.

SIMPLE SUBJECT	SIMPLE PREDICATE
Horses	gallop.
Dionne Warwick	will perform.
Trees	are swaying.
Roads	were paved.
Rickey Henderson	ran.

The simple subject is found by asking *who?* or *what?* about the verb. For example, in the first sentence above, the noun *horses* answers the question *what gallop?*

Complete Subjects and Complete Predicates

In most sentences the meaning of the simple subject and the simple predicate is expanded or modified by the addition of other words and phrases.

The **complete subject** consists of the simple subject and all the words that modify it.

The **complete predicate** consists of the simple predicate and all the words that modify it or complete its meaning.

COMPLETE SUBJECT	COMPLETE PREDICATE
Wild horses	gallop thunderously along.
Talented Dionne Warwick	will perform her hits.
The lovely birch trees	are swaying slightly in the wind.
The old dirt roads	soon were paved.
The speedy Rickey Henderson	ran all the way home from first base on a double.

EXERCISE 1 **Identifying Subjects and Predicates.** Copy each of the following sentences, and indicate with a vertical line the division between the complete subject and the complete predicate. Then underline the simple subject once and the simple predicate twice.

SAMPLE ANSWER At one time American roads | were very different from the roads of today.

1. Many present American roads were once old pioneer trails.
2. Some pioneer trails run through the American West.
3. Pioneer trails are scenic and historic.
4. Some interesting Native American museums are found along pioneer trails.
5. Pioneers traveled slowly.
6. The pioneer trails in the Rocky Mountains were steep, rocky, and often icy.
7. The first pioneers explored bravely.
8. The trail through Death Valley was a sun-baked road.
9. The Pecos Trail in Texas now winds among oil fields.
10. The Cheyenne-Deadwood Trail led to gold fields.

Compound Subjects

A **compound subject** is made up of two or more simple subjects that are joined by a conjunction and have the same verb.

> **Tomatoes** and **carrots** are good vegetables.
> Neither the **tomato** nor the **pepper** grows underground.
> **Tomatoes, carrots,** and **peppers** are healthful.

EXERCISE 2 **Identifying Compound Subjects.** Write on your paper the compound subject in each of the following sentences.

SAMPLE John Updike and Denise Levertov live near Boston.
ANSWER John Updike, Denise Levertov

1. The lives and the works of many American writers are associated with the city of Boston.
2. Henry David Thoreau and E. E. Cummings are among Boston's best-known writers.
3. Henry Wadsworth Longfellow and Nathaniel Hawthorne also lived in the Boston area.
4. The city of Boston and several nearby towns are important in American literary history.
5. Cambridge, Concord, and Salem all gave America good writers.

6. Emerson, Thoreau, and Hawthorne are buried in Concord's Sleepy Hollow Cemetery.
7. *The Scarlet Letter* and *The House of the Seven Gables* were both set in Salem.
8. The Customs House and the house with seven gables are still standing in Salem today.
9. Ralph Waldo Emerson, from Concord, and James Russell Lowell, of Cambridge, played important roles in American literature in the 1800s.
10. Emerson's *Nature* and Thoreau's *Walden* both present back to nature ideas.

Compound Predicates

A **compound predicate** or **compound verb**, is made up of two or more verbs or verb phrases that are joined by a conjunction and have the same subject.

> Horses **gallop** and **charge.**
>
> Seagulls **will glide** or **swoop** down to the ocean.
>
> Mary Ellen **inserted** the film, **looked** through the viewfinder, and **snapped** the first photograph.

A sentence may have both a compound subject and a compound predicate. The terms *compound subject* and *compound verb* or *compound predicate* refer to a compound *simple* subject and a compound *simple* predicate.

> S S P P
> **Butterflies** and **hummingbirds** **dart** and **dip** in the air.

EXERCISE 3 **Identifying Compound Predicates.** Write on your paper the compound predicate in each of the following sentences.

1. Volcanoes are and always will be a source of fear to humans.
2. For hundreds of years, volcanoes have erupted and have spilled lava over many lands.
3. The earth's crust moves and shifts during these many eruptions.
4. Unseen forces within the earth build, expand, and explode through the volcano's vent, or opening.
5. An early eruption of the volcano called Mount Vesuvius overwhelmed and buried two cities in A.D. 79.
6. Some eruptions are accompanied by earthquakes or are followed by darkness.
7. Millions of years ago volcanoes erupted in North America and formed the western mountains from Canada to Mexico.
8. Crater Lake, Oregon, occupies the site of an old volcano but is not active.
9. The Hawaiian Islands were created by volcanic activity and still contain several active volcanoes.
10. Volcanoes have created several islands, destroyed cities, and built mountains.

EXERCISE 4 **Identifying Subjects and Predicates.** On your paper copy the following sentences. Then for each sentence underline the simple subject once and the simple predicate twice. Note that some subjects and predicates are compound.

1. People design and make beautiful patchwork quilts from scraps of fabric.
2. A cover or a blanket can be created with small pieces of cloth.
3. Calicoes or brocades look and work well in patchwork.
4. People design the pieces and cut them into geometric shapes.
5. Then the little squares, triangles, and rectangles are sewed together.
6. Traditional patterns and some modern patterns have names.
7. Ninepatch, grandma's flower garden, and the log cabin are popular patterns.
8. Antique quilts and handmade coverlets command high prices today.
9. Quilting exhibitions often come to museums.
10. New York's Museum of Modern Art presents shows featuring antique quilts.

SENTENCE WRITING **Expanding Subjects and Predicates.** (a) Write five sentences, each with one subject and one predicate. (b) Make the subject and predicate of each sentence compound.

SAMPLE ANSWER (a) Gene Kelly danced in movies in the 1940s.
(b) Gene Kelly and Frank Sinatra sang and danced in movies in the 1940s.

Order of Subject and Predicate

In most sentences in English, the subject comes before the verb. There are exceptions, however, to this normal word order.

1. In the case of commands or requests, the subject *you* is not expressed; it is "understood."

   [You] Run! [You] Give it to me. [You] Please be careful.

2. At times a sentence is written in inverted order—that is, with the predicate before the subject. This reversal of the usual order is made to add emphasis. In the following examples the simple predicates and the simple subjects are in bold type.

PREDICATE	SUBJECT
Across the field **galloped**	the three **horses.**
In the distance **ran**	a **river.**

3. The words *there* and *here* are sometimes used as expletives. An *expletive* is a word used to introduce or fill out a sentence. In sentences with expletives, the subject generally comes after the predicate. Often the expletive is followed by a form of the verb *be*.

PREDICATE	SUBJECT
There **is**	a **chill** in the air.
Here **are**	my **thoughts** on the subject.

EXERCISE 5 **Recognizing Word Order.** Copy each of the following sentences, and draw a vertical line between the complete subject and the complete predicate in each sentence. Then underline each simple subject once and each simple predicate twice.

SAMPLE ANSWER Here is | a discussion about left-handed people.

1. Life can be difficult for left-handed people.
2. Doorknobs are often a problem.
3. All American children once wrote with their right hands.
4. Some countries even have a taboo against eating with the left hand.

5. Special scissors are necessary for left-handed people.
6. Fountain pens may cause messy smears.
7. There is a store for left-handed people.
8. The store sells a bumper sticker with the slogan "Left On!"
9. There have been many famous left-handed people.
10. Among them are Leonardo da Vinci, Charlie Chaplin, Paul McCartney, Judy Garland, and Babe Ruth.

EXERCISE 6 **Writing Inverted Sentences.** Rewrite each sentence below as an inverted sentence, that is, with the predicate first.

1. The stranger wandered through the driving, swirling snow.
2. The sound of a dog howling came through the heavy rain.
3. A lean man on horseback appeared under the blazing sun.
4. The brave sailors fought against the extreme winds.
5. The lone wind-surfer glided over the ocean.
6. The determined climbers inched up the steep mountain slope.
7. The marathon runners charged over the roller-coasterlike terrain for several hours.
8. The magnificent hawk hovered in the vast, bright, silent sky.
9. Strange and beautiful fish swim in the dark cold depths of the ocean.
10. Forest firefighters, called "smoke jumpers," parachuted from helicopters and airplanes.

Complements

A **complement** is a word or group of words that completes the meaning of a verb.

A complement is anything that helps to make something else complete. A painting, for example, can be complemented by a frame. Similarly, a subject and a verb often need a *complement* in order for the meaning of a sentence to be complete. Note that the following sentences sound incomplete even though they include a subject and a verb:

Marcus built ____________.
That dress seems ____________.

What complements would help complete the meaning of each of the preceding items?

The next four sections will discuss four kinds of complements that can be used to complete sentences: *direct objects, indirect objects, object complements,* and *subject complements.*

Direct Objects

A **direct object** answers the question *what?* or *whom?* after an action verb.

The subject of a sentence usually performs the action indicated by the verb. That action may be directed toward or may be received by someone or something—the direct object. Nouns, pronouns, or words acting as nouns may serve as direct objects. Only transitive verbs have direct objects.

Stanley served **dinner**. [Stanley served *what?*]

Eleanor admires **him** deeply. [Eleanor admires *whom?*]

The children contributed their **savings**. [The children contributed *what?*]

Like other sentence parts, direct objects may be *compound:*

Stanley served **dinner** and **dessert**. [Stanley served *what?*]

EXERCISE 7 **Identifying Direct Objects.** On your paper write the action verb in each of the following sentences. Then list any direct objects. (One sentence has a compound object.)

1. Scuba divers seek adventure in the ocean.
2. Divers use special breathing equipment for staying underwater.
3. Besides masks and fins they wear air-filled tanks.
4. Scuba divers sometimes find spectacular corals.
5. In some areas divers discover lost treasure.
6. Many scuba divers observe tropical fish, such as parrotfish, yellowtail snappers, and angelfish.
7. Other divers conduct studies of the ocean.
8. Jacques Cousteau has studied it for many years.
9. Some professional scuba divers repair bridges.
10. Divers also inspect dams and pipelines.

EXERCISE 8 **Adding Direct Objects.** On your paper complete the following subjects and verbs by adding a direct object. You may also add any additional words that you may need to make a sentence that makes sense.

1. Architects build ____________________.
2. Composers write ____________________.
3. Dancers perform ____________________.
4. Sculptors produce ____________________.
5. Comedians provide ____________________.

6. Athletes display ______________________________.
7. Poets express ______________________________.
8. Actors create ______________________________.
9. Musicians play ______________________________.
10. Filmmakers invent ______________________________.

SENTENCE WRITING **Creating Sentences with Direct Objects.** Write five sentences describing how to make or do something. Use action verbs. Identify the subjects, verbs, and direct objects in these sentences.

Indirect Objects

An **indirect object** answers the question *to whom? for whom? to what?* or *for what?* after an action verb.

A sentence may have an indirect object only if it has a direct object. The indirect object will always come between the verb and the direct object, never after a preposition. Indirect objects are usually nouns or pronouns.

Stanley served his **sisters** dinner. [Stanley served dinner *to whom?*]

Eleanor saved **him** a seat. [Eleanor saved a seat *for whom?*]

The children gave the **charity** all their savings. [The children gave all their savings *to what?*]

Indirect objects may be *compound.*

Eleanor saved **David** and **Laura** seats. [Eleanor saved seats *for whom?*]

EXERCISE 9 **Identifying Indirect Objects.** First write on your paper the direct objects in each of the following sentences. Then list any indirect objects. (Not all sentences have an indirect object.)

1. Professional sports offer young people many interesting careers.
2. Television or radio sportscasters broadcast sporting events.
3. A good sports announcer gives fans play-by-play descriptions.
4. The announcer tells them interesting anecdotes.
5. Writers and photographers also cover athletic competitions.
6. Newspapers in particular give sports much coverage.
7. Teaching a sport may give a person much satisfaction.
8. Managers, coaches, and trainers all bring teams success.
9. Sports also give referees, umpires, and doctors jobs.
10. Athletic events even give hot-dog and peanut vendors work.

Object Complements

An **object complement** answers the question *what?* after a direct object. That is, it *completes* the meaning of the direct object by identifying or describing it.

Object complements occur only in sentences with direct objects and only in those sentences with action verbs like the following:

appoint	elect	render	consider	name
choose	make	call	find	think

An object complement usually follows a direct object. It may be an adjective, a noun, or a pronoun.

Residents find the park **peaceful**. [adjective]
Critics call him a **genius**. [noun]
My grandmother considers the property **hers**. [pronoun]
Katie appointed me **assistant**, **treasurer**, and **cook**. [nouns]

Object complements may be *compound*, as in the last example.

EXERCISE 10 **Identifying Object Complements.** Write the object complement (or complements) that appears in each of the following.

1. Diana finds chocolate preferable.
2. Mary chooses the color blue.
3. Diana names Mozart her favorite.
4. Mary considers Bach stupendous.
5. Both Mary and Diana make music a priority.
6. Mark calls Verdi a great composer and a musical genius.
7. Mary finds opera silly.
8. Diana considers opera sublime.
9. She names Marilyn Horne her favorite.
10. Mark finds the whole subject highly stimulating.

Subject Complements

A **subject complement** follows a subject and a linking verb and identifies or describes the subject.

A linking verb almost always needs one or more additional words in the predicate to complete its meaning. After all, a linking verb *links* a subject to something else. The something else is the subject complement. There are two kinds of subject complements: *predicate nominatives* and *predicate adjectives.*

A **predicate nominative** is a noun or pronoun that follows a linking verb and points back to the subject to identify it further.

Sopranos are **singers.**

The soprano in this opera is **she.**

Predicate nominatives are usually found in sentences that contain forms of the linking verb **be.** Often these are sentences that classify things. A few other linking verbs (for example, *become* and *remain*) can be followed by a predicate nominative.

A tenor is a **singer.**
Rome is a **city.**
Would you become the **star** of this show?
That experience remains a cherished **memory** for me.

Like other sentence parts, predicate nominatives may also be *compound.*

Arnie is a **teacher** and a **friend.**
Julia became both a **musician** and an **actress.**
The winners are **Robert** and **Julia.**

A **predicate adjective** follows a linking verb and points back to the subject and further describes it.

Ballerinas are **graceful.**

Ballerinas must be very **dedicated.**

Predicate adjectives may follow any linking verb and may also be *compound.*

The runners had become very **tired.**
I felt completely **drained.**
Only a few marathoners appeared **fresh** even now.
The cups of water seemed **delicious.**
My friend Amy looked **exhausted** but **happy.**

EXERCISE 11 **Identifying Subject Complements.** On your paper write all the subject complements in the following sentences. Identify each as a predicate nominative or a predicate adjective. (One sentence has more than one subject complement.)

1. The history of the modern tomato is unusual and colorful.
2. According to scientists the tomato is actually a fruit.
3. Wild tomatoes were common in Mexico before the time of the Spanish conquest.
4. The tomato became a curiosity in Europe in the 1500s.
5. Tomatoes were poisonous, according to most Europeans and Americans in the sixteenth century.
6. Thomas Jefferson was a fan of tomatoes.
7. The tomato became a crop at his farm.
8. Today the tomato has become a common food.
9. Beefsteak tomatoes are large.
10. The original tomato remains tasty.

SENTENCE WRITING **Writing Sentences with Complements.** Write four sentences about a natural phenomenon, such as an eclipse, a thunderstorm, or a sunset. In each sentence use at least one of the four kinds of complements: direct object, indirect object, object complement, and subject complement. Label the complements.

REVIEW EXERCISE **Complements.** On your paper write the complements that appear in the following sentences. Next to each complement write what kind of complement it is: direct object, indirect object, object complement, predicate nominative, or predicate adjective. (Some sentences have a compound complement.)

1. Davenport, Iowa, was the home of jazz musician Leon Bix Beiderbecke, who lived from 1903 to 1931.
2. Mississippi riverboats floating past Davenport gave Bix Beiderbecke the opportunity to hear jazz.
3. Bix Beiderbecke played the cornet and the piano.
4. The cornet's sound is mellow and rich.
5. Bix Beiderbecke carried his cornet in a brown paper bag.
6. Louis Armstrong once met young Bix on a Mississippi riverboat.
7. Beiderbecke's parents were conservative, wealthy midwesterners.
8. They did not give Bix any financial assistance.
9. Beiderbecke's reputation is high in musical circles today.
10. In fact, many consider him a true American classic.

Basic Sentence Patterns

You regularly combine the parts of the sentence in ways that produce recurring patterns. You can express these patterns in a kind of shorthand using capital letters. Most sentences fall into one of the following patterns:

1. Subject + Action Verb (Intransitive)

   S AV(I)
   Horses gallop.

2. Subject + Action Verb (Transitive) + Direct Object

   S AV(T) DO
   Horses carry riders.

3. Subject + Action Verb (Transitive) + Indirect Object + Direct Object

   S AV(T) IO DO
   Riders can teach horses tricks

4. Subject + Action Verb (Transitive) + Direct Object + Object Complement

   S AV(T) DO OC
   My grandfather found horses beautiful.

5. Subject + Linking Verb + Subject Complement (Predicate Nominative)

   S LV SC(PN)
   Horses are runners.

6. Subject + Linking Verb + Subject Complement (Predicate Adjective)

   S LV SC(PA)
   Horses are majestic.

You may expand each of these basic patterns by adding modifiers, such as adjectives and adverbs:

S AV(I)
Those strong wild horses normally gallop freely over the plain.

Another common method of expand basic sentence patterns is by compounding. Sentences may have various combinations of compound subjects, verbs, and complements.

S S AV(T) DO
Neither the hippopotamus nor the elephant can outrun the horse or
AV(T) DO
match its beauty.

EXERCISE 12 **Identifying Sentence Patterns.** On your paper write the basic sentence pattern of each sentence.

1. Loch Ness is a famous lake in Scotland.
2. A giant sea creature may inhabit Loch Ness.
3. People call this legendary creature Nessie.
4. Many doubt its existence.
5. Nessie has flippers, humps, and a long neck.
6. In the 1930s several people photographed Nessie.
7. In 1960 Tim Dinsdale filmed a dark shape in Loch Ness.
8. Scientists have explored the Loch Ness waters.
9. They have used sound waves to detect objects underwater.
10. Yet Nessie remains elusive.

SENTENCE WRITING **Creating Sentences with Various Patterns.** Write one sentence for each of the following sentence patterns. To make your sentences clear, you may need to add modifiers to your subjects, verbs, and complements.

1. S + S + AV(T) + DO
2. S + AV(T) + DO + OC
3. S + LV + SC(PA)
4. S + AV(I) + AV(I)
5. S + AV(T) + IO + DO

Diagraming Basic Sentence Patterns

Diagramming is a method of showing the relationship of various words and parts of a sentence to the sentence as a whole.

The following examples show the traditional method of diagraming the six basic sentence patterns summarized in the preceding section. The examples also show how to diagram modifiers, such as adjectives and adverbs, and how to represent compound sentence parts, such as compound subjects and predicates.

You begin to diagram a sentence by finding the simple subject, keeping in mind that a sentence may have a compound subject. After you have found the subject, find the action or linking verb that goes with it. Write the subject and the verb on a horizontal line. Separate them with a vertical line that bisects the horizontal line to indicate the division between the complete subject and the complete predicate.

Additional sentence elements are added in the following:

1. Subject + Action Verb (Intransitive)
   Athletes train.

subject | action verb   Athletes | train

2. Subject + Action Verb (Intransitive), with adjectives and adverbs
   Very good athletes train extremely hard.

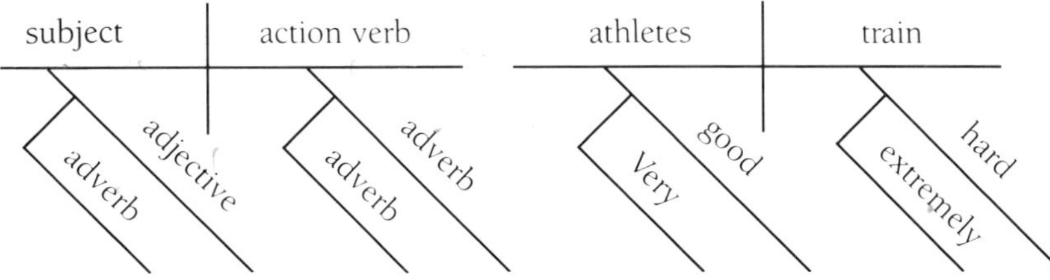

3. Subject + Action Verb (Transitive) + Indirect Object + Direct Object
   Athletes give schools spirit.

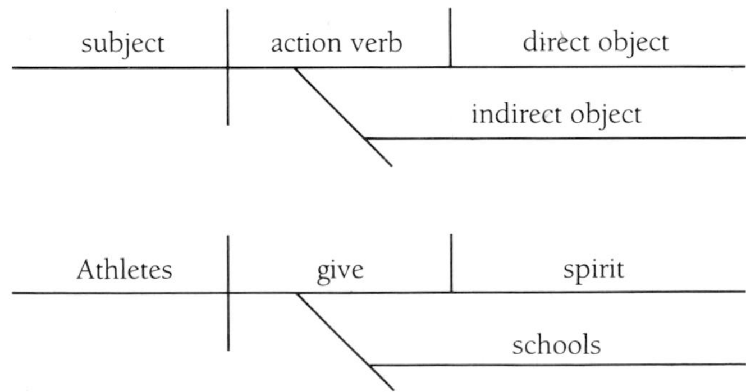

4. Compound Subject + Action Verb (Transitive) + Direct Object + Object Complement

Coaches and players consider practice essential.

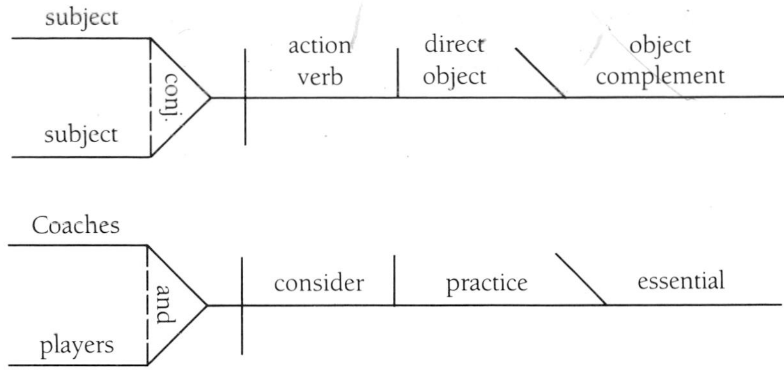

5. Subject + Linking Verb + Subject Complement (Predicate Nominative)

Swimmers are athletes.

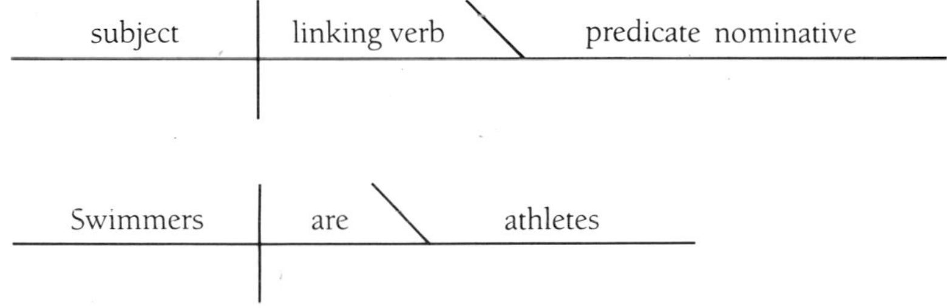

6. Subject + Compound Linking Verb + Subject Complement (Predicate Adjective)

Gymnasts are strong and must be coordinated.

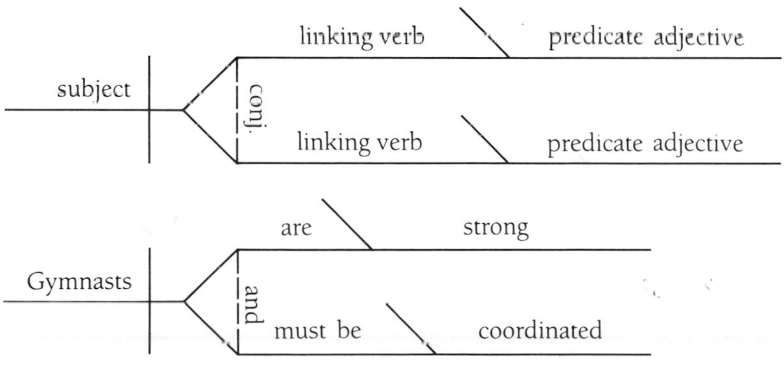

EXERCISE 13 **Diagraming Basic Sentence Patterns.** Use the preceding models as you diagram the following sentences.

1. The game was starting.
2. The muddy soccer field was drying slowly.
3. A coach gave the players instructions.
4. The players and the coach considered the game critical.
5. It was the championship game.
6. The players were ready but felt nervous.
7. Loyal fans cheered enthusiastically.
8. A watchful goalie made a spectacular block.
9. The right wing was quick but looked weary.
10. Everyone found the game sensational.

Revising Your Writing

In this passage from *The Call of the Wild,* Jack London uses a variety of sentence patterns to create a lively, engaging prose rhythm.

> Buck's first day on the Dyea beach was like a nightmare. Every hour was filled with shock and surprise. He had been suddenly jerked from the heart of civilization and flung into the heart of things primordial. No lazy, sun-kissed life was this, with nothing to do but loaf and be bored. Here was neither peace, nor rest, nor a moment's safety.

Try to use London's techniques when you write and revise your work.

1. Avoid monotony by varying the lengths of your sentences. In the passage above, London uses a compound predicate in the third sentence (" had been jerked," "flung") and a compound subject in the last sentence ("peace," "rest," "safety").
2. Achieve sentence variety by occasionally varying word order. In the fourth sentence London wrote "No lazy, sun-kissed life was this" rather than "This was no lazy, sun-kissed life." Moreover, note in the last sentence that London uses the expletive "here" so that the linking verb "was" precedes the compound subject.

Revise the following passage adapted from *The Call of the Wild,* using compounding to expand basic sentence patterns. Decide which sentence would be most effective in inverted order.

> Then an old wolf, gaunt and battle-scarred, came forward. Buck writhed his lips into the preliminary of a snarl. He sniffed noses with him. Whereupon the old wolf sat down. He pointed nose at the moon. He broke out the long wolf howl. The others sat down. They howled. And now the call came to Buck in unmistakable accents. He, too, sat down. He howled. . . . And the story of Buck may well end here.

Review

CHAPTER 18 PARTS OF THE SENTENCE

Subjects and Predicates [pages 441–446] For each of the following sentences, identify the underlined word or words as **(a)** a complete subject, **(b)** a complete predicate, **(c)** a simple subject, **(d)** a simple predicate, or **(e)** a compound subject.

1. A more accurate name for the planet Earth <u>would be</u> Water.
2. Most of our planet <u>is covered not by land but by water</u>.
3. <u>The oceans and seas</u> account for 72 percent of its surface.
4. Most <u>people</u> think of the world as huge land masses divided by bodies of water.
5. Actually, <u>the continents</u> are islands in a single, vast ocean.

Complements [pages 446–451] For each of the following sentences, identify the underlined word or words as **(a)** a direct object, **(b)** an indirect object, **(c)** an object complement, **(d)** a predicate nominative, or **(e)** a predicate adjective.

6. In the seventeenth century, the British were exploring the <u>oceans</u> yet knew little about them.
7. Despite advances in exploration and knowledge, most people considered the ocean a vast and frightening <u>mystery</u>.
8. Britain was an island <u>nation</u> with a growing empire.
9. Increased knowledge of the ocean became extremely <u>important</u>.
10. In 1660 British scientists founded the <u>Royal Society of London for Improving Natural Knowledge</u>.
11. One of the first activities of the society was <u>study</u> of the ocean.
12. The Royal Society gave <u>sailors</u> lists of suggestions for research.
13. Because the members could not go to sea themselves, they made the sailors <u>scientists</u>.
14. Soon sea captains were sending the <u>society</u> measurements.
15. The society's techniques may have been <u>primitive</u>, but they marked the beginning of serious ocean research.

Basic Sentence Patterns [pages 452–453] Match the sentence in the left column with the sentence pattern in the right column. *Code:* S = subject, AV = action verb, LV = linking verb, IO = indirect object, DO = direct object, OC = object complement, and SC = subject complement

16. Ivan IV was the first czar of Russia.	(a) S+AV+DO
17. He lived from 1530 to 1584.	(b) S+AV+IO+DO

18. Ivan IV made Moscow the capital.
19. His crafty policies strengthened Russia.
20. People gave him the name of Ivan the Terrible.

(c) S+AV+DO+OC
(d) S+LV+SC
(e) S+AV

Diagraming Basic Sentence Patterns [pages 453–456] Indicate the letter of the position of each numbered word in the following sentence should occupy in the diagram below.

<u>Ivan IV</u> and his <u>policies</u> <u>gave</u> <u>Russia</u> more <u>power</u>.

21 (Ivan IV) 22 (policies) 23 (gave) 24 (Russia) 25 (power)

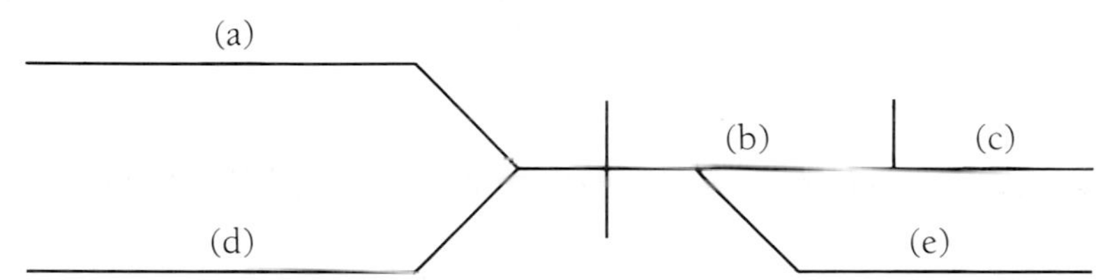

Writing For Review Write a paragraph on a topic of your choice. Demonstrate your knowledge of sentence parts by using a variety of sentence patterns. Underline and identify in your paragraph at least five of the following: simple subject, simple predicate, direct object, indirect object, object complement, predicate nominative, predicate adjective.

CHAPTER 19

Phrases

A **phrase** is a group of words that acts in a sentence as a single part of speech.

You have already learned about verb phrases (Chapter 17). In this chapter you will learn about three other kinds of phrases: *prepositional phrases, appositive phrases,* and *verbal phrases.*

Prepositional Phrases

A **prepositional phrase** is a group of words that begins with a preposition and usually ends with a noun or a pronoun, called the **object of the preposition.**

The stairs led **to the attic.** [*Attic* is the object of the preposition *to.*]

The staircase is too steep **for her.** [*Her* is the object of the preposition *for.*]

(For lists of common prepositions, see page 423.)

Adjectives and other modifiers may be placed between the preposition and its object. Also, a preposition may have more than one object.

The staircase leads **to the crowded, dusty attic.** [adjectives added]

That staircase leads **to the attic and the roof.** [two objects]

A prepositional phrase normally acts in a sentence in the same way that an adjective or an adverb does. Used as an adjective, a prepositional phrase is called an *adjectival phrase;* it modifies a noun or a pronoun. Used as an adverb, it is called an *adverbial phrase;* it modifies a verb, an adjective, or an adverb.

They used the staircase **on the left.** [adjectival phrase modifying the noun *staircase*]

Which **of the staircases** leads downstairs? [adjectival phrase modifying the pronoun *which*]

At midnight you can come downstairs **to the kitchen.** [adverbial phrases modifying the verb phrase *can come*]

Those midnight snacks were healthful **for us.** [adverbial phrase modifying the adjective *healthful*]

She walks very quickly **for a young baby.** [adverbial phrase modifying the adverb *quickly*]

EXERCISE 1 **Identifying Prepositional Phrases.** Copy the following sentences. Then underline each prepositional phrase.

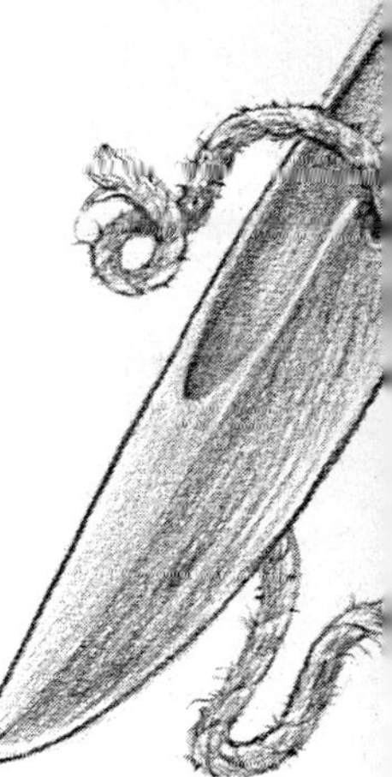

1. A tapestry of great beauty can be hand-woven.
2. First wrap string vertically around a frame (called the warp).
3. Then weave colored thread or wool horizontally between the warp strings (this is called the weft).
4. Alternately weave two light-colored strands and two dark-colored strands for a wavy design.
5. With one dark and one light strand you can create vertical stripes.
6. You can also weave grasses, twigs, or flowers of many colors.
7. Knots in the weft threads create a rough and nubby effect.
8. When you have finished, tie all the loose threads at the back.
9. Cut a fringe at the bottom.
10. Attach a stick to the top, and hang your finished tapestry.

EXERCISE 2 **Identifying Adjectival and Adverbial Phrases.** Write the word each prepositional phrase in Exercise 1 modifies. Indicate whether each phrase is *adjectival* or *adverbial*.

SENTENCE WRITING **Expanding Sentences with Prepositional Phrases.** Expand the following sentences by adding at least one adjectival phrase and one adverbial phrase to each.

1. The candle flame flickers.
2. Someone should have asked me.
3. The comedian performed.
4. The gardener pulled up the weeds
5. The children brought flowers.

Appositives and Appositive Phrases

An **appositive** is a noun or pronoun that is placed next to another noun or pronoun to identify or give additional information about it.

An **appositive phrase** is an appositive plus any words that modify the appositive.

> My friend **Paul** sends me long letters from France. [The appositive *Paul* identifies the noun *friend*.]
>
> He is living and working in Paris, **the famous capital city of France.** [The appositive phrase, in bold type, identifies *Paris*.]

(For rules about using commas, see Chapter 27.)

EXERCISE 3 **Identifying Appositives and Appositive Phrases.** Write the appositive or the appositive phrase in each sentence.

1. Pablo Picasso, the great Spanish painter, lived in France for years.
2. The dancer Agnes De Mille choreographed *Oklahoma!*
3. One of the most popular singers of the twentieth century is Frank Sinatra, an accomplished actor as well.
4. The filmmaker Orson Welles is best known for *Citizen Kane*.
5. *The Heart is a Lonely Hunter* is a novel by the American writer Carson McCullers.
6. The jazz singer Billie Holiday usually wore a gardenia in her hair.
7. Isak Dinesen, the author of *Seven Gothic Tales*, owned and managed a coffee plantation in East Africa from 1914 to 1931.
8. Mike Nichols, the celebrated director, originally was part of a comedy team with Elaine May.
9. The Guggenheim Museum in New York was one of the last projects of Frank Lloyd Wright, America's greatest modern architect.
10. Georgia O'Keeffe, one of the most influential modern American painters, lived in New Mexico from 1949 to 1986.

EXERCISE 4 **Adding Appositive Phrases to Sentences.** Each of the sentences below is followed by a group of words in parentheses. Rewrite each sentence, incorporating the group of words in parentheses into the sentence as an appositive phrase. Use a comma or commas to set off the appositive phrase from the rest of the sentence.

SAMPLE The White House is an important building in Washington, D.C. (the home of the President of the United States)

ANSWER The White House, the home of the President of the United States, is an important building in Washington, D.C.

1. The Statue of Liberty stands near Manhattan. (a great symbol of American freedom)
2. You can ride an elevator up the inside of the Eiffel Tower. (the most familiar sight in Paris)
3. The Pyramids are located in Egypt. (an astonishing feat of construction)
4. The Parthenon is situated on the Acropolis in Athens. (a magnificent ancient Greek temple)
5. The Leaning Tower of Pisa took about two hundred years to build and is made entirely of marble. (one of the seven wonders of the modern world)

SENTENCE WRITING **Writing Sentences with Appositive Phrases.** On your paper expand the following sentences by adding an appositive phrase to each. Be sure to use commas where necessary

SAMPLE Vitus Bering was the first European to land in Alaska.
ANSWER Vitus Bering, a Danish explorer, was the first European to land in Alaska.

1. The film was nominated for an Academy Award.
2. The local newspaper printed my letter on its editorial page.
3. Robert Frost wrote the poem.
4. Alaska entered the Union in 1959.
5. Every year New Orleans celebrates Mardi Gras.

Verbals and Verbal Phrases

A **verbal** is a form of a verb that works in a sentence as a noun, an adjective, or an adverb.

While working in sentences as nouns, adjectives, and adverbs, verbals retain some of the qualities of verbs. For example, verbals can show action and can have complements and modifiers.

A **verbal phrase** is a verbal plus any complements and modifiers.

There are three kinds of verbals: *participles*, *gerunds*, and *infinitives*. All three types of verbals can be expanded into phrases.

Participles and Participial Phrases

A **participle** is a form of a verb that works as an adjective.

Present participles end in *-ing*. *Past participles* often end in *-ed*, but they can also take other forms. Many of the adjectives that you commonly use in sentences are actually participles.

No one would eat the **burned** toast.

We were warned to watch out for **falling** rocks.

The **fallen** tree blocked the **winding** road.

When a participle is part of a verb phrase in the predicate of a sentence, it is not acting as an adjective.

PARTICIPLE AS ADJECTIVE The **growing** child was curious.
PARTICIPLE IN VERB PHRASE His parents saw that he **was growing** stronger.

(For more information about forming present and past participles, see Chapter 21.)

A **participial phrase** contains a participle plus any complements and modifiers.

A participial phrase can contain a present or a past participle. Participial phrases act as adjectives and can be placed in various positions.

We watched the best teams **playing baseball.**

Smiling confidently, the first batter stepped to the plate.

The **badly defeated** team accepted their fate with grace.

(For practice in avoiding misplaced or dangling participles, see Chapter 24.)

EXERCISE 5 **Identifying Participles and Participial Phrases.** Write the participle or the participial phrase in each of the following sentences. Then identify the word each modifies.

1. The Northwest Coast of North America, extending from southern Alaska to northern California, was the home of many tribes.
2. The dense forests inhabited by these tribes have a temperate climate with plentiful rainfall.
3. Salmon caught in streams was an important source of food.
4. Knowing the woodlands well, the tribes gathered wild fruit.
5. The Northwest tribes ordinarily lived in houses built of wood.
6. Dressed for battle, they wore armor and helmets.
7. Some of the tribes had totem poles decorated with carvings.
8. Displaying great artistic skill, the Northwest tribes produced baskets, rattles, and masks.
9. The Northwest tribes had a distinctive, established culture.
10. Determined Europeans who sought furs and natural resources finally came to the area in the late 1700s.

Gerunds and Gerund Phrases

A **gerund** is a form of a verb that ends in *-ing* and is used in the same ways a noun is used.

Eating is something I enjoy. [gerund as subject]

My grandfather likes **strolling.** [gerund as direct object]

Diana gives **cooking** her best effort. [gerund as indirect object]

How much enthusiasm do you feel for **bowling?** [gerund as object of preposition]

Her first love is **painting.** [gerund as predicate nominative]

My hobbies, **writing** and **reading**, are quiet activities. [gerunds as appositives]

A **gerund phrase** is a gerund plus any complements and modifiers.

A gerund phrase can vary in length, depending on how many complements and modifiers are added to the gerund.

> **Fred Astaire's marvelous dancing** will always be exciting.
> **Dancing the tango** is not as easy as it looks.
> **Dancing gracefully** is the goal of every ballerina.

The difference between a present participle and a gerund, both of which end in *-ing*, is that a present participle is used as an adjective and a gerund is used as a noun.

> **Running** around the track, Mary felt exhilarated. [present participle]
> **Running** gives Mary a sense of well-being. [gerund]

EXERCISE 6 **Identifying Gerunds and Gerund Phrases.** List on your paper the gerunds and gerund phrases in the following sentences. The number of gerunds or gerund phrases is given in parentheses.

1. In the late 1970s skating suddenly became a national craze. (1)
2. Replacing noisy metal wheels with new plastic wheels made the sport quieter and more pleasant. (1)
3. In city parks skating replaced jogging and bicycling. (3)
4. Skaters also tried dancing. (1)
5. Learning fundamental skills is important for the beginner. (1)
6. A difficulty at first is balancing. (1)
7. Another problem is stopping, which for many beginners means falling down gracefully. (2)
8. Skating downhill requires particular skill and good balance. (1)
9. The possibility of crashing does not discourage skaters. (1)
10. Coasting on skates is much more thrilling than walking or even running. (3)

EXERCISE 7 **Identifying the Uses of Gerunds.** Look again at your answers for sentences 4, 5, 6, and 9 in Exercise 6. On your paper identify the way in which each gerund or gerund phrase is used: as subject, direct object, or object of a preposition.

SAMPLE skating (in sentence 1)
ANSWER subject

SENTENCE WRITING **Writing Sentences with Gerunds.** Select five of the gerunds that you identified in Exercise 6, and write an original sentence for each. Make sure that you use the *-ing* word as a gerund, not as a present participle or as part of a verb phrase.

Infinitives and Infinitive Phrases

An **infinitive** is a form of a verb that is usually preceded by the word *to* and is used as a noun, an adjective, or an adverb.

When you use the word *to* before a verb, the *to* is not a preposition but part of the infinitive form of the verb. Infinitives can be used in the same ways as nouns, adjectives, and adverbs.

> **To stand** can be uncomfortable. [infinitive as subject]
> Infants first learn **to crawl.** [infinitive as direct object]
> Her aim is **to walk.** [infinitive as predicate nominative]
> Birds have an instinct **to fly.** [infinitive as adjective]
> I am determined **to run.** [infinitive as adverb]

An **infinitive phrase** contains an infinitive plus any complements and modifiers.

> We decided **to sail across the lake.**
> They wanted **to drive slowly around the park.**
> I hope **to run in a marathon someday.**

EXERCISE 8 **Identifying Infinitives and Infinitive Phrases.** Write the infinitive or infinitive phrase in each of the following sentences.

1. Mary Cassatt was one of the foremost American artists to paint in the Impressionist style.
2. Cassatt grew up in Philadelphia and decided to study at the Pennsylvania Academy of the Fine Arts.
3. In 1868 she went to live and to study in Paris, France.
4. The great French painter Edgar Degas began to influence her work.
5. Degas helped to develop Cassatt's precise and delicate style.
6. Cassatt often chose to paint portraits of mothers and children.
7. Degas invited her to exhibit paintings with other Impressionists.
8. Cassatt encouraged American relatives and friends to purchase the paintings of the French Impressionists.
9. In so doing Cassatt helped to influence American taste in art.
10. Today art lovers are able to appreciate Cassatt's own work.

EXERCISE 9 **Identifying the Uses of Infinitives.** Look again at your answers to the first five items in Exercise 8. Indicate in writing how each infinitive phrase is used: as a noun, an adjective, or an adverb.

SENTENCE WRITING **Using Infinitives.** Jot down five action verbs. Then use each in an infinitive phrase in an original sentence. Underline the infinitive phrases.

REVIEW EXERCISE **Verbal Phrases.** On your paper write each of the verbal phrases in the following sentences. Tell whether each is a participial phrase, a gerund phrase, or an infinitive phrase.

1. Elephants have the distinction of being the largest land mammals.
2. Living in the tropical regions of Asia and Africa, they may reach a height of thirteen feet.
3. Their tusks, weighing up to two hundred pounds each, can be more than ten feet long.
4. Their ears are huge, measuring up to forty-two inches wide.
5. They use their fingerlike trunks to pick up objects.
6. Elephants browse all day, feeding on leaves, shoots, and tall grasses.
7. Elephants can learn to carry logs and to perform in circuses.
8. Training young elephants takes great skill.
9. It can be difficult to handle them, too.
10. Hunted for food and for ivory, elephants now must struggle for their survival.

Diagraming Phrases

This section is a continuation of Diagraming Basic Sentence Patterns at the end of Chapter 18. Review the diagrams in that section before proceeding.

7. Prepositional Phrase

Place the preposition on a slanted line that comes down from the word modified by the prepositional phrase. Then draw a horizontal line from the slanted line. Place the object of the preposition on the horizontal line.

Athletes of today set new records at every opportunity during a season.

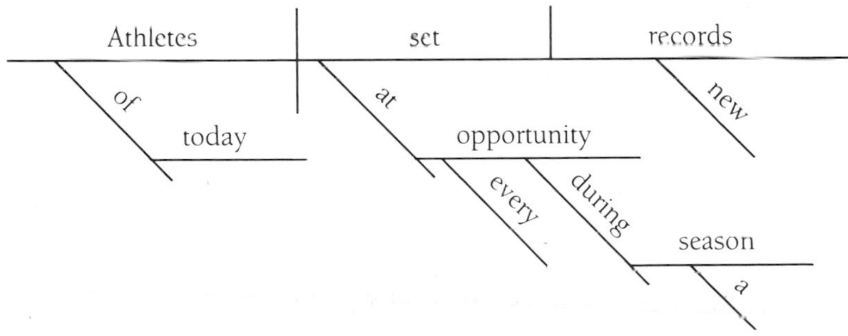

8. Appositives and Appositive Phrases

Place the appositive in parentheses after the noun or pronoun it identifies. Add any words that modify the appositive beneath it.

The coach, a graduate of the school, teaches us team spirit, an important ingredient.

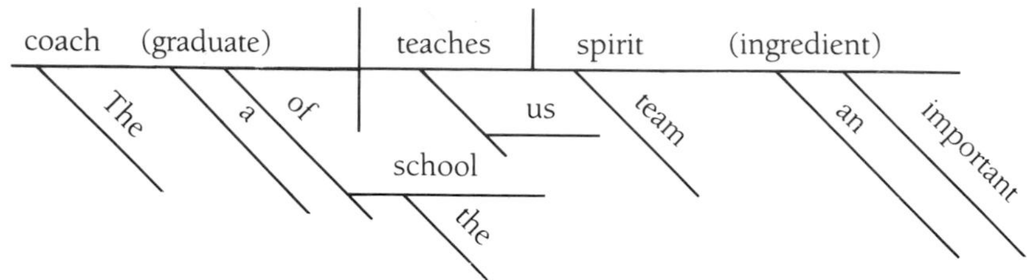

9. Participles and Participial Phrases

Curve the participle as shown below. Add modifiers and complements in the usual way.

Recovering his balance, the quarterback completed the pass.

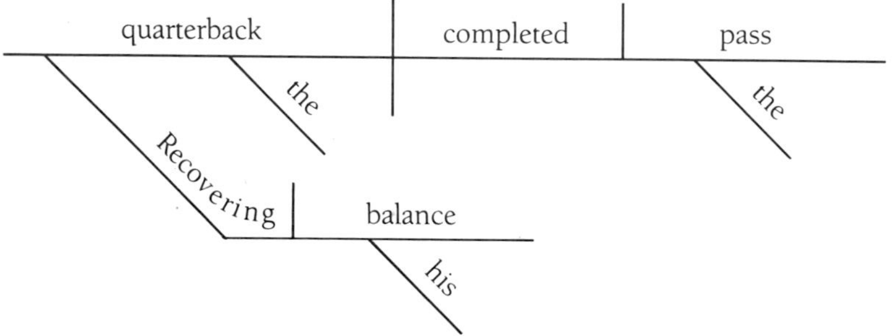

10. Gerunds and Gerund Phrases

Place the gerund on a step as shown below. The phrase in the subject or complement position is placed on a "stilt" so that it will fit.

Winning every game is one way of gaining confidence.

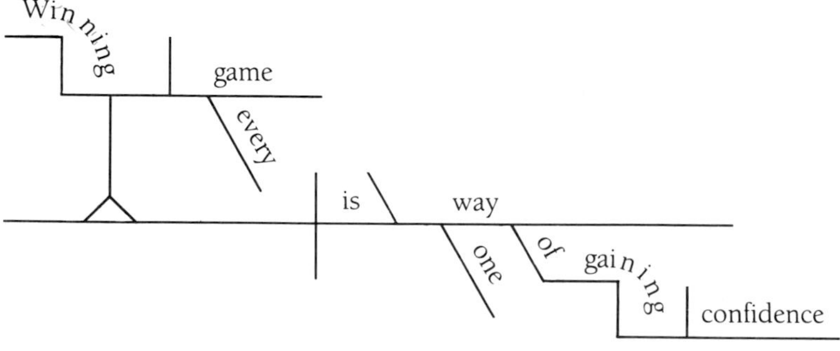

11. Infinitives and Infinitive Phrases Used as Adjectives or Adverbs

These infinitives are diagramed like prepositional phrases (see Diagram 7).

Athletes are going to travel far.

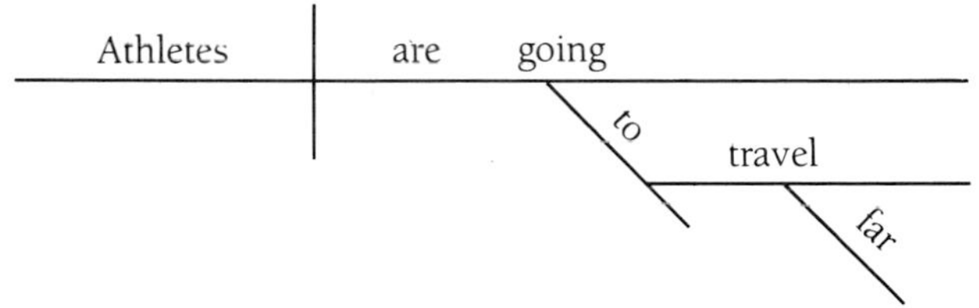

12. Infinitives and Infinitive Phrases Used as Nouns

Here you have to use stilts again.

To be a champion is to taste glory.

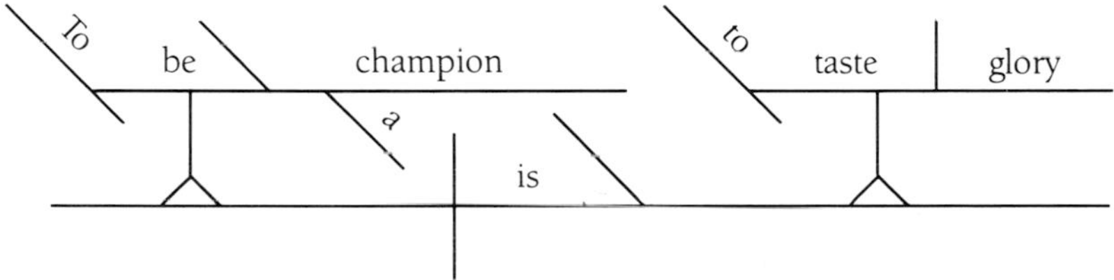

EXERCISE 10 **Diagraming Prepositional Phrases.** Using Diagram 7 as a model, diagram the five example sentences preceding Exercise 1 of this chapter.

EXERCISE 11 **Diagraming Appositives and Appositive Phrases.** Using Diagram 8 as a model, diagram sentences 1 and 5 in Exercise 3 of this chapter.

EXERCISE 12 **Diagraming Participles and Participial Phrases.** Using Diagram 9 as a model, diagram the three example sentences preceding Exercise 5 of this chapter.

EXERCISE 13 **Diagraming Gerunds and Gerund Phrases.** Using Diagram 10 as a model, diagram sentences 1, 5, 6, and 9 in Exercise 6 of this chapter.

EXERCISE 14 **Diagraming Infinitives and Infinitive Phrases.** Using Diagrams 11 and 12 as models, diagram sentences 4, 5, 6 and 10 in Exercise 8.

Revising Your Writing

Phrases can act as nouns, adjectives, or adverbs. This versatility allows writers to expand basic sentence patterns by adding precise description and detail. In addition, the placement of phrases in the sentence often allows writers to control the rhythm of their prose. Keep in mind the following techniques when you revise your writing.

1. Use prepositional phrases to add precise description and detail to your sentences. Notice that the underlined prepositional phrases in the following sentence from "Of Dry Goods and Black Bow Ties" by Yoshiko Uchida help the author's meaning come alive.

   > My father was impressed <u>with these modest words</u> <u>from a man of such success</u>. He accepted them <u>with a sense of mission</u> and <u>from that day</u> was committed to <u>white shirts and black bow ties</u>, and treated every customer, no matter how humble, <u>with respect and courtesy</u>.

   Without the prepositional phrases, Uchida's sentences would have been imprecise and flat. Try replacing "with respect and courtesy" with the adverb *well* to see how effective Uchida's phrase is.

2. When you revise, see if adding participial, infinitive, or appositive phrases improves the flow of your sentences or creates an appropriate pause. For example, in the following sentence from *Barrio Boy,* Ernesto Galarza uses the underlined appositive phrase to create a slight pause in the rhythm of the sentence, thus heightening the sense of tension and fright.

   > We stepped down into a frightening scene, <u>a huge barn filled with smoke and noise and the smell of burnt oil</u>.

   Notice how less dramatic the effect would be if "a frightening scene" were moved to the end of the sentence.

Apply these techniques in revising the following passage adapted from "The Most Dangerous Game," by Richard Connell. Follow the directions below.

> He leaped upon the rail and balanced himself there. His pipe was knocked away.

1. Add the phrase "to get greater elevation" to the first sentence.
2. Replace "away" with a more descriptive prepositional phrase.
3. Add the verbal phrase "striking a rope" to the second sentence.

CHAPTER 19 PHRASES

Identifying Phrases [pages 460–467] Tell whether the underlined phrase is (a) a prepositional phrase, (b) an appositive phrase, (c) a participial phrase, (d) a gerund phrase, or (e) an infinitive phrase.

1. Ivory is a hard white substance that comes from animal tusks.
2. The material is used to make piano keys and decorative objects.
3. Carving ivory is an ancient art.
4. Prehistoric carvings were found in Dordogne, an area in southern France.
5. Using layers of ivory, Greek sculptors created faces and hands.

Prepositional Phrases [pages 460–461] In each sentence, tell whether the prepositional phrase is (a) adjectival or (b) adverbial.

6. Elephants in India have relatively small tusks.
7. The larger tusks of African elephants provide the best ivory.
8. These animals have long been hunted for their valuable tusks.
9. Today it is forbidden by law to hunt most elephants.
10. Imitation ivory is available from certain South American palm trees.

Gerund Phrases [pages 464–465] Tell whether the gerund phrase is used as (a) a subject, (b) a direct object, (c) an object of a preposition, (d) a predicate nominative, or (e) an appositive.

11. Changing identity is common practice for a young insect.
12. Its goal becomes transforming itself into a different creature.
13. Metamorphosis, assuming a new form, is a dramatic process.
14. A butterfly begins crawling around as a fuzzy caterpillar.
15. After hiding, a changed creature emerges from a cocoon.

Infinitive Phrases [pages 466–467] Tell whether the infinitive phrase is used as (a) a noun, (b) an adjective, or (c) an adverb.

16. Indians were the first people to inhabit the Americas.
17. The Vikings began to send ships to North America in 1000.
18. Columbus, however, was the first European to establish permanent settlements.
19. He was unable to find his real destination, India.
20. To call the American natives "Indians" was actually an error.

Writing for Review Write a paragraph on any subject you choose. Include and underline at least one example of each kind of phrase—prepositional, appositive, participial, gerund, and infinitive.

CHAPTER 20

Clauses and Sentence Structure

A **clause** is a group of words that has a subject and a predicate and that is used as a part of a sentence.

There are two kinds of clauses: *main clauses,* also called *independent clauses,* and *subordinate clauses,* also called *dependent clauses.*

Main Clauses

A **main clause** has a subject and a predicate and can stand alone as a sentence.

Every sentence must have at least one main clause. A sentence may have more than one main clause. Both of the clauses in the following example are main clauses because both can stand alone as a sentence.

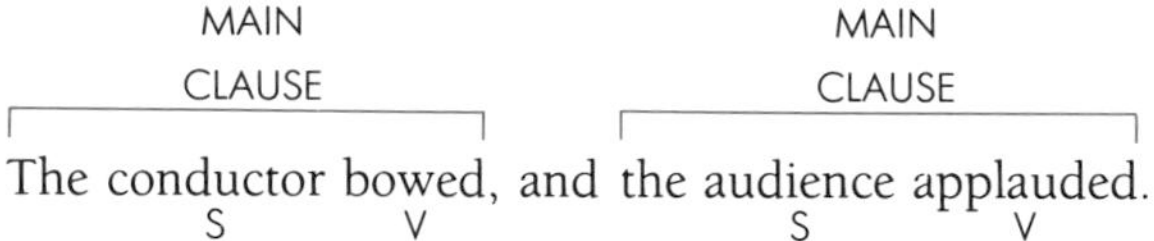
MAIN CLAUSE
MAIN CLAUSE
The conductor bowed, and the audience applauded.
S V S V

Subordinate Clauses

A **subordinate clause** has a subject and a predicate, but it cannot stand alone as a sentence.

A subordinate clause must be attached to a main clause in order for it to make sense. Subordinate clauses frequently begin with subordinating conjunctions (see page 425) or relative pronouns (see page 398).

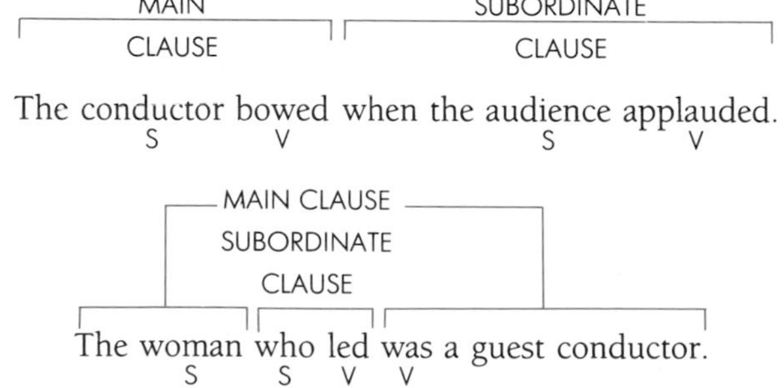
MAIN CLAUSE
SUBORDINATE CLAUSE
The conductor bowed when the audience applauded.
S V S V
MAIN CLAUSE
SUBORDINATE CLAUSE
The woman who led was a guest conductor.
S S V V

In the first example the subordinating conjunction *when* placed before *the audience applauded* creates a word group—*when the audience applauded*—that cannot stand alone as a main clause. Although the clause has a subject and a predicate, it does not express a complete thought.

In the second example the relative pronoun *who* begins a subordinate clause that comes between the subject and the verb of the main clause. *Who* also serves as the subject of the subordinate clause in the second example.

In the following pages you will see how various combinations of main clauses and subordinate clauses form the four kinds of sentence structures: *simple sentences, compound sentences, complex sentences,* and *compound-complex sentences.* You will also see how subordinate clauses act in sentences as adverbs, adjectives, and nouns. You also will learn rules for using clauses correctly.

EXERCISE 1 **Identifying Main and Subordinate Clauses.** In each of the following sentences, the first clause appears in italics. On your paper indicate whether it is a main clause or a subordinate clause. (Remember that a subordinate clause cannot stand alone as a sentence.)

1. *The bobcat and the lynx are two remarkably similar animals* that belong to the cat family.
2. *Because it can adapt to a wide variety of conditions,* the bobcat lives in swampy areas and in deserts.
3. *The lynx lives at the higher elevations,* where snow is on the ground during much of the year.
4. *The lynx can travel easily in deep snow* because its feet are large and padded with fur.
5. *Because a bobcat's paws are about half the size of a lynx's,* the bobcat cannot travel as well in snow.
6. *Although both animals look like big house cats,* they can be fierce fighters.
7. *When they are confronted by humans,* they will usually quickly disappear from sight.
8. *The bobcat is considered the fiercer of the two cats* because it must fight for survival.
9. *Because the lynx is so well suited to life in snowy areas,* it has no reason to fear other animals.
10. *The lynx lives in parts of Africa, Asia, Europe, and North America (particularly Canada and Alaska),* while the bobcat is native only to North America.

Simple and Compound Sentences

Two kinds of sentences are made up of main clauses only: *simple sentences* and *compound sentences.*

A **simple sentence** has only one main clause and no subordinate clauses.

A simple sentence may have a compound subject or a compound predicate or both (see Chapter 18). The simple subject and the simple predicate may also be expanded in many other ways. Adjectives, adverbs, prepositional phrases, appositives, and verbal phrases may make some simple sentences seem anything but simple. Yet as long as the sentence has only one main clause, it remains a simple sentence.

> Bobcats stalk. [simple sentence]
>
> Bobcats and lynxes stalk. [simple sentence with compound subject]
>
> Bobcats stalk and pounce. [simple sentence; compound predicate]
>
> Bobcats and lynxes stalk and pounce. [simple sentence with compound subject and compound predicate]
>
> Bobcats silently stalk their prey. [simple sentence expanded]

A **compound sentence** has two or more main clauses.

As the following examples show, each main clause of a compound sentence has its own subject and predicate. Notice that the main clauses of a compound sentence are usually joined by a comma and a coordinating conjunction, such as *and, but, or, nor, yet,* or *for.*

MAIN CLAUSE 1 [Bobcats stalk], and MAIN CLAUSE 2 [lynxes pursue].
(Bobcats = S, stalk = V; lynxes = S, pursue = V)

MAIN CLAUSE 1 [Bobcats stalk], and MAIN CLAUSE 2 [lynxes pursue], but MAIN CLAUSE 3 [house cats slink].
(Bobcats = S, stalk = V; lynxes = S, pursue = V; cats = S, slink = V)

Two main clauses may also be joined by a semicolon to form a compound sentence (see Chapter 27).

MAIN CLAUSE 1 [The rabbit ran]; MAIN CLAUSE 2 [the lynx followed].

EXERCISE 2 **Identifying Simple and Compound Sentences.** Indicate whether each item is a simple or a compound sentence.

1. Sir Edmund Hillary, a New Zealand mountain climber, and his Sherpa guide Tenzing Norgay were the first to climb Mount Everest.
2. Hillary took photographs of Norgay at the summit, but none of Hillary were taken.
3. Norgay was already a well-known mountaineer, but Hillary's experience was climbing in ice and snow in New Zealand.
4. Hillary and the other members of the expedition looked for the easiest route to the top of Mount Everest.
5. Today climbers look for greater challenges and choose the more difficult routes.
6. Hillary once traveled overland to the South Pole and also followed the Ganges River to its source.
7. The public and the media had shown interest in Hillary.
8. Fame came with Hillary's successful ascent of Mount Everest, and he raised money for the Sherpa people of Nepal.
9. They had helped Hillary, and in return he helped them.
10. Hillary gave lectures and raised funds for schools, hospitals, clinics, bridges, water pipelines, and airstrips in Nepal.

Complex and Compound-Complex Sentences

When subordinate clauses are added to simple sentences and compound sentences, they form complex sentences and compound-complex sentences.

A **complex sentence** has one main clause and one or more subordinate clauses.

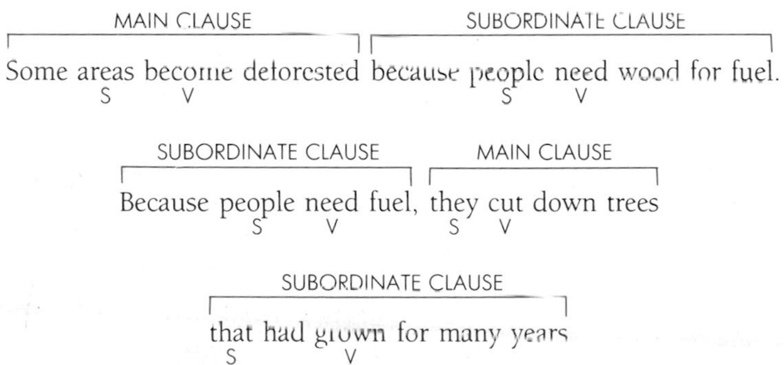
MAIN CLAUSE
SUBORDINATE CLAUSE
Some areas become deforested because people need wood for fuel.
S V S V
SUBORDINATE CLAUSE
MAIN CLAUSE
Because people need fuel, they cut down trees
S V S V
SUBORDINATE CLAUSE
that had grown for many years
S V

A **compound-complex sentence** has more than one main clause and at least one subordinate clause.

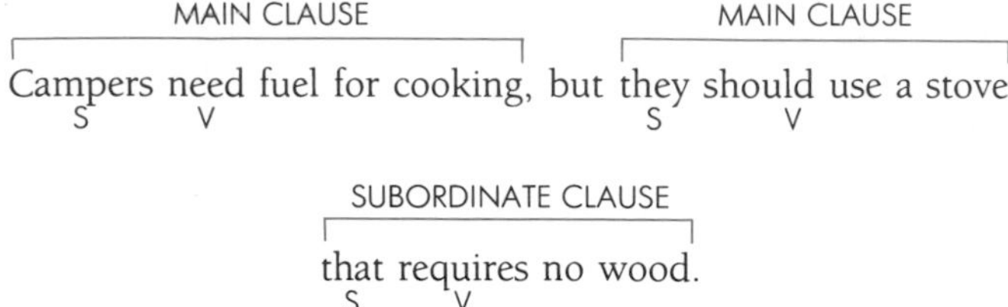

MAIN CLAUSE
MAIN CLAUSE
Campers need fuel for cooking, but they should use a stove
S
V
S
V

SUBORDINATE CLAUSE

that requires no wood.
S V

EXERCISE 3 **Identifying Complex and Compound-Complex Sentences.** Write on your paper the subordinate clause in each of the following sentences. Indicate whether each sentence is a complex sentence or a compound-complex sentence.

1. Because millions of energy-consuming devices are in use every day, energy conservation is of great importance.
2. When builders construct homes, they should use solar power and energy-saving appliances.
3. Although energy-efficient appliances cost more, their use results in savings for the owner, and the environment benefits too.
4. Because legislators have enacted certain laws, all new cars must soon be energy efficient.
5. When cars use less gas, the air is cleaner, and fewer people have trouble breathing.
6. While sulfur pollution is a threat to human health, it also damages lakes, wildlife, and buildings.
7. Although water power can generate electricity, hydroelectric dams may cause floods on farmland, in forest, and in wildlife areas.
8. We must find ways of producing more goods, while the devices must use less energy.
9. Conservation and solar power are the keys to a safe future, and so we must cautiously use the devices that cool, heat, and transport us.
10. Because our natural resources cannot last forever, we must plan better ways of conserving energy.

SENTENCE WRITING **Creating Sentences with Various Structures.** Write a simple sentence. Then rework it, making it a compound sentence. Rework it again, but now make it part of a complex sentence. Finally, take your compound sentence and rework it into a compound-complex sentence.

Adjective Clauses

An **adjective clause** is a subordinate clause that modifies a noun or a pronoun.

An adjective clause normally follows the word it modifies.

The hikers **who reached the peak** were overjoyed.
I forgot about the blisters **that covered my feet.**
The hiker **whom we appreciated most** carried the food.

In addition to relative pronouns (*who, whom, whose, that,* and *which*), the adverbs *where* and *when* may introduce adjective clauses.

I will always remember the time **when I hiked to the top of Mount Washington.**

That is the spot **where we set up camp.**

An adjective clause is sometimes essential to a sentence; that is, it is needed to make the meaning of the sentence clear. This kind of adjective clause is called an *essential clause,* or a *restrictive clause.* Without the essential adjective clause, the sentence would not make complete sense.

The one aspect **that most American Indians had in common** was their love of dancing. [essential clause]

The dance was often the way **that they reached out to the spirits.** [essential clause]

In the first example the meaning of the sentence would not make sense without the essential clause *that most American Indians had in common.* The adjective clause makes clear *which* aspect is being discussed. In the second example the adjective clause is needed because the sentence seems incomplete without it. The essential adjective clause *that they reached out to the spirits* limits, or restricts, the meaning of the noun *way* and helps the reader to recognize *which* way is being discussed.

An adjective clause that is *not* needed to make the meaning of a sentence clear is called a *nonessential clause,* or a *nonrestrictive clause.* It may add information to a sentence, but the sentence would be perfectly logical without it. Try reading the examples below to yourself, omitting the words in boldface type. You will see that the sentences are still meaningful, even without the adjective clauses.

The Iroquois people of the East, **who were farmers,** thanked the spirits for the gift of food. [nonessential clause]

In the Southwest, **where water is scarce,** the Pueblo people performed rain dances. [nonessential clause]

You can use either *that* or *which* to introduce an essential clause, but you must always use *which* to begin a nonessential clause. Never use *that* before a nonessential clause.

The Plains Indians hunted buffalo, **which supplied them with meat and skins for clothing and shelter.** [nonessential clause]

The animal **that was most important to the Plains Indian** was the buffalo. [essential clause]

(For rules about punctuating essential and nonessential clauses, see Chapter 27.)

EXERCISE 4 **Identifying Adjective Clauses.** On your paper write the adjective clause in each of the following sentences. Then write the word that the clause modifies.

1. The Pueblo rain dancers wore outfits with symbols that represented lightning, thunder, clouds, and rainbows.
2. In the eagle dance the dancers' movements are like those of the eagle, which swoops and dives for its food.
3. Chinese schoolchildren learn dances that require difficult head, wrist, and foot movements.
4. The Chinese ribbon dance, which has been performed for thousands of years, is often danced with red ribbons.
5. Red, which signifies happiness and good fortune in China, is the favorite ribbon color.
6. A dance that is popular everywhere is the square dance.
7. The Virginia reel, which became popular in George Washington's time, is probably the best-known square dance.
8. A dance that began in Spain is the flamenco.
9. Gypsies, who introduced the flamenco, perform this dance to the music of a guitar.
10. The folk dances of many regions require steps that are difficult to learn.

EXERCISE 5 **Recognizing Essential and Nonessential Clauses.** Here are five pairs of sentences. For each pair write the adjective clause, and then identify it as an essential (or restrictive) clause or a nonessential (or nonrestrictive) clause.

1. (a) Sacajuwea Hunter, who lost her legs at a very early age, competed in the 1984 Olympics.
   (b) One young athlete who competed in the 1984 Olympics lost her legs at a very early age.

2. (a) She was one of eight disabled women who competed in the 800-meter wheelchair exhibition race.
   (b) Sacajuwea Hunter, who competed in the 1984 Olympics, was one of eight disabled women in the 800-meter wheelchair exhibition race.
3. (a) Nearly 100,000 people watched the 800-meter wheelchair exhibition race, which was the first such event in Olympic history.
   (b) The race that was the first such event in Olympic history was the 800-meter wheelchair exhibition race.
4. (a) Bill Greene, who was Sacajuwea Hunter's special-education counselor, urged her to race.
   (b) The man who was Sacajuwea Hunter's special-education counselor urged her to race.
5. (a) Sacajuwea Hunter, who at fourteen was the youngest American in the 1984 Olympics, finished in fourth place overall.
   (b) Sacajuwea Hunter was the youngest American athlete who competed in the 1984 Olympics.

Adverb Clauses

An **adverb clause** is a subordinate clause that modifies a verb, an adjective, or an adverb. It tells *when, where, how, why, to what extent,* or *under what condition.*

> **Whenever it rains,** the river rises. [The adverb clause modifies the verb *rises.* It tells *when.*]
>
> The canoe is safe **as long as you remain seated.** [The adverb clause modifies the adjective *safe.* It tells *under what condition.*]
>
> You are paddling harder **than I am paddling.** [The adverb clause modifies the adverb *harder.* It tells *to what extent.*]

Subordinating conjunctions such as those listed on page 429 introduce adverb clauses. Being familiar with those conjunctions will help you recognize adverb clauses. Remember also that an adverb clause may come either before or after the main clause. Notice that the first example might have been written in this way:

> The river rises **whenever it rains.**

Occasionally words may be left out of an adverb clause. The omitted words can easily be supplied because they are understood, or implied. Such adverb clauses are described as *elliptical.*

> You are paddling harder **than I [am paddling].**
> Paddling made me more tired **than [it made] him [tired].**

EXERCISE 6 **Identifying Adverb Clauses.** On your paper write the adverb clauses in the following sentences. (Two sentences have more than one adverb clause.)

1. The ostrich cannot fly because it is so large.
2. Although the ostrich may look awkward, it can run with surprising speed.
3. Whenever it cannot outrun its enemies, the ostrich kicks with its powerful legs.
4. Ostriches feed on plants as they roam the grasslands and deserts of Africa.
5. When it is resting or hiding, the ostrich stretches its long neck along the ground so that it cannot be seen easily.
6. An ostrich never buries its head in the sand when it is hiding.
7. When ostriches have their young, several females will lay eggs in the same nest.
8. Because several females share one nest, the nest may hold sixty eggs.
9. It takes about a year before an ostrich chick is fully grown.
10. If you made an omelet with just one ostrich egg, you could feed a dozen people, since one ostrich egg equals about two dozen chicken eggs.

Noun Clauses

A **noun clause** is a subordinate clause used as a noun.

You can use a noun clause as a subject, a direct object, an object of a preposition, or a predicate nominative.

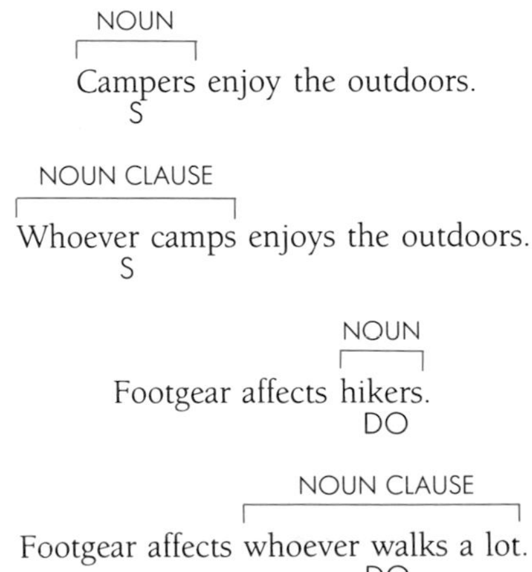

NOUN
Campers enjoy the outdoors.
S
NOUN CLAUSE
Whoever camps enjoys the outdoors.
S
NOUN
Footgear affects hikers.
DO
NOUN CLAUSE
Footgear affects whoever walks a lot.
DO

In the preceding examples notice that each noun clause is an inseparable part of the sentence's main clause. In the second sentence, for example, the noun clause is the subject of the main clause. In the last sentence the noun clause is the direct object of the main clause. Notice also that the examples with the nouns are simple sentences because each contains only one subject and one predicate. The examples with the noun clauses are complex sentences because each has a main clause (the entire sentence) and a subordinate clause (the noun clause).

Here are some of the words that can be used to introduce noun clauses.

how	when	who, whom
that	where	whoever
what	which	whose
whatever	whichever	why

Here are additional examples of noun clauses.

I do not know **where my hiking boots are.** [as a direct object]

That is **why I did not join the others.** [as a predicate nominative]

We will make do with **whatever camping equipment we can borrow.** [as an object of a preposition]

EXERCISE 7 **Identifying Noun Clauses.** On your paper write the noun clauses in each of the following sentences. (Three of the sentences have two noun clauses each.)

1. Everyone knows that dogs have a keen sense of smell.
2. What makes their sense of smell of great value is that people can train dogs to sniff out explosives.
3. Where a bomb may be is where specially trained dogs are sent.
4. What the dog finds may cause the saving of many lives.
5. That police dogs are valuable is well known.
6. Whoever works with a police dog is trained along with the dog.
7. What many police officers say is that police dogs make good partners.
8. That police dogs are vicious is not true.
9. That these dogs become aggressive upon command is true.
10. Police officers are appreciative of whatever help these dogs provide.

SENTENCE WRITING **Using Subordinate Clauses in Sentences.** Write four original sentences. In the first use an adverb clause. In the second use an adjective clause. In the third use a noun clause as a subject. In the fourth use a noun clause as a direct object.

REVIEW EXERCISE **Clauses.** On your paper write the subordinate clause in each sentence. Then indicate whether the subordinate clause is (a) an adverb clause, (b) an adjective clause, or (c) a noun clause.

1. Great gray owls are seldom seen because they live in secluded areas.
2. When a great gray owl has been sighted, bird watchers usually rush to the area.
3. British explorers who came to North America during the fur-trade era discovered the great gray owl.
4. Andrew Graham, who was a Hudson Bay Company agent and naturalist, gathered the first information about the bird in 1772.
5. That it took more than fifty years to find a great gray owl's nest is not really surprising.
6. Since the discovery of the first nest in 1826, two hundred great gray owls' nests have been discovered in various parts of North America.
7. The great gray owl, which builds no nest of its own, sometimes nests in a hollowed-out tree trunk.
8. No one knows where all the great owls live.
9. Because the great gray owl's range is so wide, it is a difficult bird to study.
10. That scientists will learn more about this bird is now possible through the use of radio tags.

Four Kinds of Sentences

Sentences may be classified according to their purpose. The four types of sentences are *declarative, imperative, interrogative,* and *exclamatory*.

A **declarative sentence** makes a statement.

An owl is hooting. I cannot see it.

A declarative sentence normally ends with a period. It is the type of sentence used most frequently in speaking and writing.

An **imperative sentence** gives a command or makes a request.

Look at that bird.
Please tell me what it is.

An imperative sentence usually ends with a period. The subject "you" is understood (see page 445).

An **interrogative sentence** asks a question.

What kind of bird is that?
Is the hawk hunting for prey?

An interrogative sentence ends with a question mark. It often begins with an interrogative pronoun (see page 398) or with an auxiliary verb.

An **exclamatory sentence** expresses strong emotion.

How fast that hawk swoops!
Look at that hawk!
How can it do that!

An exclamatory sentence is a declarative, imperative, or interrogative sentence expressed with strong emotion. The exclamation point at the end of the sentence conveys the strong emotion to the readers.

EXERCISE 8 **Identifying Kinds of Sentences.** On your paper indicate whether each of the following sentences is (a) declarative, (b) imperative, (c) interrogative, or (d) exclamatory.

1. Have you ever seen a blue rose?
2. Come home with me after school today.
3. I have grown a blue rose in my backyard.
4. The plant has two-inch blue flowers.
5. It has been blooming for weeks now.
6. Would you like to grow a blue rose, too?
7. Please tell me how to grow a blue rose.
8. The blue rose can be grown in a window box.
9. How unusual the blue rose is!
10. What a truly unusual rose it is!

SENTENCE WRITING **Creating Four Kinds of Sentences.** Write four sentences about a recent school event. Use one declarative, one imperative, one interrogative, and one exclamatory sentence.

Sentence Completeness

Unless you are mimicking conversation in your writing, your sentences should be complete. They should have at least one subject and one predicate and express a complete thought (see Chapter 18). Incomplete sentences, or sentence fragments, are considered a serious error because they confuse readers. Another kind of sentence error occurs when two or more sentences run on in such a way that readers cannot tell where one ends and the next begins.

Sentence Fragments

In general, avoid **sentence fragments** in your writing. Check that each sentence you write has a subject and a predicate and expresses a complete thought.

Sentence fragments are usually phrases or subordinate clauses that have mistakenly been capitalized and punctuated as if they were complete sentences. Often you can correct a sentence fragment by joining it to an idea that comes before or after the fragment. Sometimes, however, you may need to add missing words to form a complete sentence.

FRAGMENT	Hot-air ballooning must be exciting. **And very scary.**
COMPLETE SENTENCE	Hot-air ballooning must be exciting and very scary.
FRAGMENT	In 1983 people everywhere celebrated. **The two-hundredth anniversary of the first balloon flight by humans.**
COMPLETE SENTENCE	In 1983 people everywhere celebrated the two-hundredth anniversary of the first balloon flight by humans.
FRAGMENT	**Sometimes watched hot-air balloons travel. Over the mountains.**
COMPLETE SENTENCE	Sometimes I have watched hot-air balloons travel over the mountains.

EXERCISE 9 **Identifying Sentence Fragments.** Indicate on your paper whether each of the following numbered items is a complete sentence or a sentence fragment.

[1]A whale sometimes leaps completely out of the water. [2]And lands with a loud splash. [3]Whale watchers can identify individual whales. [4]By noting each whale's natural body marks and distinctive color patterns on the flukes. [5]Charles Jurasz, a researcher in Alaska's Glacier Bay National Monument. [6]Jurasz devised this means of whale identification. [7]Researchers take photographs of the whales and compare the photos. [8]With photos already on file. [9]In this way researchers can track the whereabouts of each whale. [10]And determine the whale's companions and pattern of behavior.

SENTENCE WRITING **Correcting Sentence Fragments.** Revise the preceding paragraph by correcting each fragment. Whenever possible, combine the fragments with other sentences in the paragraph.

Run-on Sentences

Avoid run-on sentences in your writing. A **run-on sentence** occurs when main clauses are run together without proper punctuation. Do not use a comma alone to separate two main clauses.

Run-on sentences are also called *comma splices* or *comma faults*.

RUN-ON Jellyfish live in oceans, they can give swimmers a painful sting.

You may correct run-on sentences like the preceding example in any of four ways.

1. with a comma and a coordinating conjunction

   Jellyfish live in oceans, **and** they can give swimmers a painful sting.

2. with a semicolon

   Jellyfish live in oceans; they can give swimmers a painful sting.

3. with a period and a capital letter

   Jellyfish live in oceans. **T**hey can give swimmers a painful sting.

4. by turning one of the main clauses into a subordinate clause

   Jellyfish live in oceans, **where they can give swimmers a painful sting.**

EXERCISE 10 **Correcting Run-on Sentences.** Rewrite each of the following run-on sentences. Use each of the four methods for correcting run-on sentences at least once in this exercise.

1. Zoo facilities are limited, zoo keepers cannot have every animal on display year-round.
2. In the winter in colder climates, most birds must be brought indoors, zoo keepers cannot always keep each bird on view for the public.
3. Many visitors are surprised to see that some animals remain outside all year, penguins, polar bears, bison, and timber wolves are happy outdoors in wintertime.
4. Some animals are always indoors in northern areas, reptiles and small desert animals always have indoor displays.
5. Zoo keepers must provide indoor shelters for large animals such as elephants and giraffes, how large those shelters must be!
6. Today zoologists understand much more about animal behavior, zoos are being designed that are very similar to the animals' natural habitats.

7. Visitors can closely observe animals at animal parks, animals roam free as if they were in the wild.
8. Zoo kitchens keep a wide variety of foods and food supplements, these are used to prepare meals that meet each animal's nutritional needs.
9. The earliest known zoo was established in Egypt around 1500 B.C., a half century later, a Chinese emperor built a zoo that covered about 1,500 acres.
10. Zoos contribute to wildlife conservation, they breed species that are in danger of becoming extinct.

REVIEW EXERCISE **Sentence Completeness.** Rewrite the following paragraph, correcting all sentence fragments and run-on sentences.

[1]A desert can change from a land of withered shrubs and sand to an expanse of green pasture. [2]The difference between wet season and dry season and the amount of annual rainfall. [3]Drought and overgrazing also can cause the water table to drop, the soil blows away, more desert land is created. [4]Proper land management practices can keep more fertile land from becoming a wasteland. [5]If a desert area is left unfarmed and ungrazed for perhaps as long as ten years. [6]The land can recover, the desert will bloom again.

Diagraming Clauses

This section is a continuation of Diagraming Basic Sentence Patterns (Chapter 18) and Diagraming Phrases (Chapter 19). Review the diagrams in those sections before proceeding.

13. Compound Sentences

Place each main clause in a diagram of its own. If the main clauses are connected by a semicolon, use a vertical dotted line to connect the verbs of each main clause. If the main clauses of the sentence are connected by a conjunction, then place the conjunction on a solid horizontal line.

Athletes like to win, but they must also learn to lose.

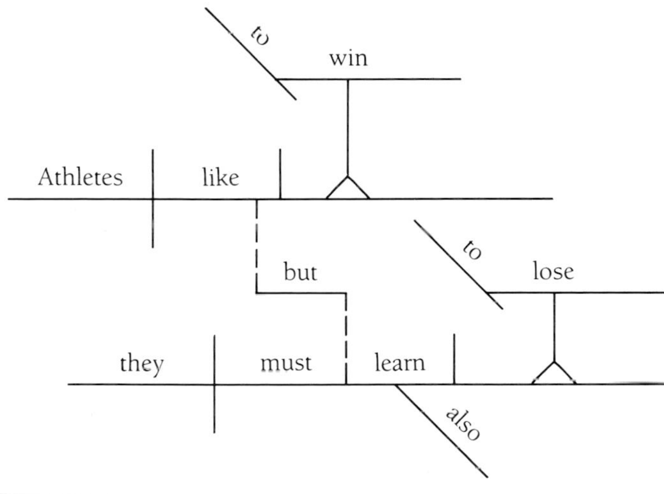

14. Complex Sentences: Adjective Clauses

Place the main clause of the sentence in one diagram and the adjective clause beneath it in another diagram. Use a dotted line to connect the relative pronoun or other introductory word that appears in the adjective clause to the modified noun or pronoun that occurs in the other clause.

The coach whom you like won games that were close.

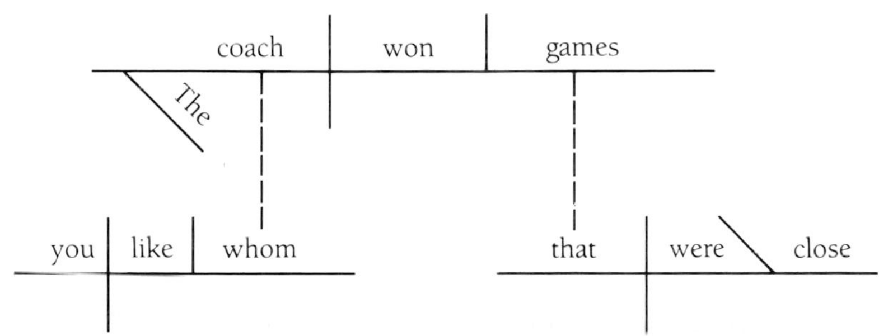

15. **Complex Sentences: Adverb Clauses**

Place the main clause in one diagram and the adverb clause beneath it in another diagram. Place the subordinating conjunction on a diagonal dotted line connecting the verb of the adverb clause to the modified verb, adjective, or adverb of the other clause.

Before a game begins, the coach gives encouragement.

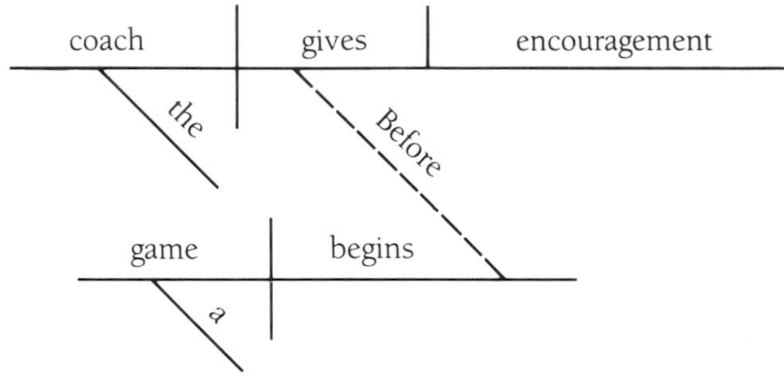

16. **Complex Sentences: Noun Clauses**

To diagram a sentence with a noun clause, first decide what role the noun clause plays within the main clause: subject, direct object, predicate nominative, or object of preposition. Then diagram the main clause with the noun clause on a stilt rising out of the appropriate position. Place the introductory word of the clause as the subject, object, or predicate nominative within the noun clause itself. If the introductory word merely begins the noun clause, simply place it on a line of its own.

AS DIRECT OBJECT
The coach knows that the rival may win.

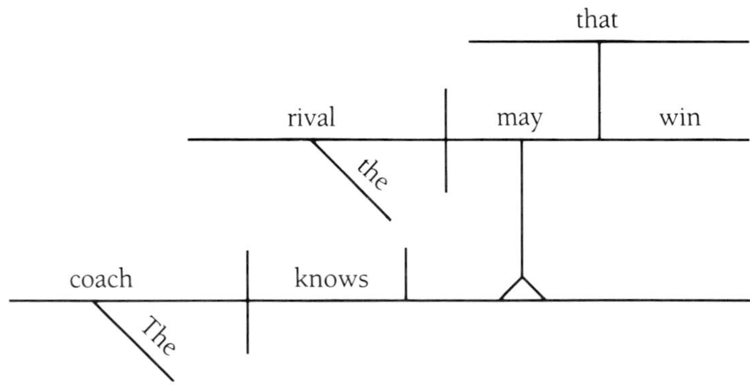

AS SUBJECT
What the coach says is important.

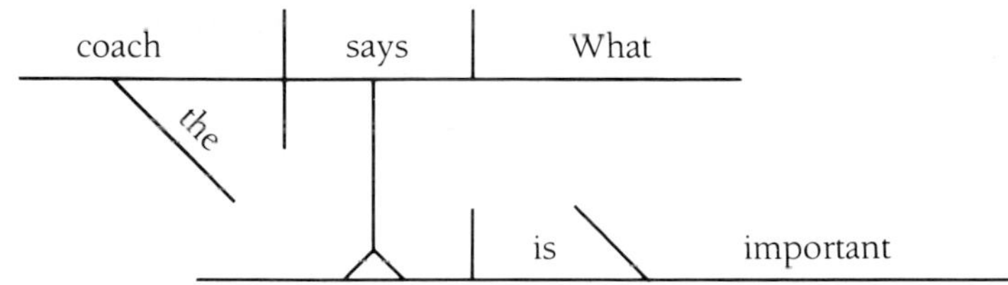

EXERCISE 11 **Diagraming Compound Sentences.** Using Diagram 13 as a model, diagram sentences 2, 3, 8, and 9 in Exercise 2 in this chapter.

EXERCISE 12 **Diagraming Adjective Clauses.** Using Diagram 14 as a model, diagram sentences 1, 4, 8, and 10 in Exercise 4 in this chapter.

EXERCISE 13 **Diagraming Adverb Clauses.** Using Diagram 15 as a model, diagram sentences 1, 2, 3, 8, and 9 in Exercise 6 in this chapter.

EXERCISE 14 **Diagraming Noun Clauses.** Using Diagram 16 as a model, diagram the second and fourth examples under "Noun Clauses" on page 480.

Revising Your Writing

In the following paragraph from "A Day's Pleasure," Hamlin Garland uses a variety of sentence patterns not only to capture reader interest but also to develop a pleasing rhythm and an appropriate mood of relaxation.

> They went into the little sitting room, so dainty and lovely to the farmer's wife, and as she sank into the easy chair she was faint and drowsy with the pleasure of it. She submitted to being brushed. She gave the baby into the hands of the Swedish girl, who washed its face and hands and sang it to sleep, while its mother sipped some tea. Through it all she lay back in her easy chair, not speaking a word, while the ache passed out of her back, and her hot, swollen head ceased to throb.

Notice how the structure of each of Garland's four sentences varies: compound-complex, simple, complex, compound-complex. Try to apply some of Garland's techniques when you write and revise your work.

1. Avoid using the same sentence structure repeatedly. A string of choppy, simple sentences can be as monotonous as a series of compound-complex sentences.
2. Use subordination not only to call attention to some ideas and to downplay others but also to control the rhythm of your sentences. Garland, for example, subordinates many of the wife's actions ("as she sank . . ."; "while its mother sipped . . ."; "while the ache passed") and calls attention to her feelings and responses ("she was faint and drowsy . . ."; "she submitted . . ."; she lay back . . ."). Also, the alternation between main clauses and subordinate clauses gives the paragraph an appropriate mood of ease and tranquility.

Apply these techniques in revising the following series of simple sentences adapted from "A Day's Pleasure." Decide which ideas should be subordinated, and try to use a variety of sentence structures.

> It grew warmer. They went on. A strong south wind arose. The dust settled upon the woman's shawl and hat. Her hair loosened and blew unkemptly about her face. The road led across the high, level prairie. It was quite smooth and dry, but still jolted her. The pain in her back increased.

CHAPTER 20 CLAUSES AND SENTENCE STRUCTURE

Clauses and the Sentences They Form [pages 472–476] Indicate whether each of the following sentences is (a) simple, (b) compound, (c) complex, or (d) compound–complex.

1. Fifteenth-century England had two kinds of timepieces, and their names remain with us.
2. Large clocks sat in towers or homes and struck the hour.
3. The word *clock* comes from Latin *clocca,* which meant "bell."
4. Watches were smaller timepieces than clocks, and they had only hands and dials that indicated the hour.
5. Because a watch had no bell, one had to *watch* for the time.

Kinds of Clauses [pages 477–482] Identify the underlined clause in each of the following sentences as (a) a main clause, (b) an adjective clause, (c) an adverb clause, or (d) a noun clause.

6. Until the nineteenth century, <u>only the wealthy owned timepieces</u>.
7. Most of those <u>who needed to know the time</u> used sundials.
8. People assumed <u>that their stomachs would alert them to mealtime</u>.
9. When clocks were placed on public buildings in the 1770s, they <u>announced the hour to the cities and towns of North America</u>.
10. <u>After cuckoo clocks arrived from Germany</u>, they became popular.

Kinds of Sentences [pages 482–483] For each sentence, write (a) declarative, (b) imperative, (c) interrogative, or (d) exclamatory.

11. Clockmakers began to mass-produce clocks in the 1800s.
12. What an important step forward that was!
13. As cities and businesses grew, punctuality became a fact of life.
14. Think about the importance of the following idea.
15. What time is it?

Sentence Completeness [pages 483–486] Identify each of the following items as (a) a fragment, (b) a run-on, or (c) a complete sentence.

16. The growing importance of clocks and punctuality in the 1840s.
17. People used the expression *on time,* and alarm clocks appeared.
18. Because grandfather clocks had become popular in the 1870s.
19. Time clocks appeared, the term *clock watcher* was coined.
20. The wristwatch appeared, soon the pocket watch disappeared.

Writing for Review Write a paragraph on a topic of your choice. Use at least one of each sentence type and a variety of clauses.

UNIT VII
Usage

Thinking About Thinking: Identifying Context

Grammar and usage go hand in hand. Grammar describes the way the language is organized. Usage shows the way people have decided to make the language work. In fact, usage is the result of an untold number of decisions about language that people made as they used words in an almost infinite number of situations. We all still engage in the thinking process called decision making whenever we use words.

Defining the Skill

To help you make decisions about words, you need to use the specific thinking skill called **IDENTIFYING CONTEXT**. Context is simply a situation. For example, a formal speech creates a different context for words than, say, a comic book. They are different situations, different "word events." Words and arrangements of words that might be appropriate in one context might be inappropriate in another. As you become more and more comfortable with English usage, you will be developing the thinking skill of identifying context.

Applying the Skill

Many situations give clues about the events that might take place in them. For example, you can figure out the purpose of a place by looking at the objects in it. Look at the picture. Name at least three activities that would be appropriate in the *context* of this room.

CHAPTER 21

Verb Tenses and Voice

Principal Parts of Verbs

All verbs have four **principal parts**—a *basic form,* a *present participle,* a *simple past form,* and a *past participle.* All the verb tenses are formed from these principal parts.

BASIC FORM	PRESENT PARTICIPLE	PAST FORM	PAST PARTICIPLE
nail	nailing	nailed	nailed
roar	roaring	roared	roared
talk	talking	talked	talked
ring	ringing	rang	rung
be	being	was, were	been
sit	sitting	sat	sat

The basic form is sometimes called the *present form* because it is the principal part used to form the present tense. The basic form is also called the *infinitive form* because it is the form that is used with *to.* The present participle is always formed by adding *-ing* to the basic form of the verb.

The basic form and the past form can be used by themselves as main verbs. To function as the simple predicate in a sentence, the present participle and the past participle must always be used with one or more auxiliary verbs.

Lions **roar.** [basic or present form]

Lions **roared.** [past form]

Lions **are roaring.** [present participle with auxiliary verb *are*]

Lions **have roared.** [past participle with auxiliary verb *have*]

Regular and Irregular Verbs

Verbs are regular or irregular depending on how their past form and their past participle are formed.

A **regular verb** forms its past and past participle by adding *-ed* to the basic form.

BASIC FORM	PAST FORM	PAST PARTICIPLE
roar	roared	roared
talk	talked	talked

Some regular verbs undergo spelling changes when a suffix beginning with a vowel is added.

concentrate + **-ed** = concentrat**ed**
ruffle + **ed** = ruffl**ed**
spy + **-ed** = sp**ied**
flop + **-ed** = flo**pped**

An **irregular verb** forms its past and past participle in some way other than by adding *-ed* to the basic form.

Some of the oldest and most common verbs in English are irregular. Study the list below and refer to it whenever you are unsure of a particular form.

BASIC FORM	PAST FORM	PAST PARTICIPLE
be	was, were	been
bear	bore	borne
beat	beat	beaten *or* beat
become	became	become
begin	began	begun
bite	bit	bitten
blow	blew	blown
break	broke	broken
bring	brought	brought
burst	burst	burst
cast	cast	cast
catch	caught	caught
choose	chose	chosen
come	came	come
creep	crept	crept
dive	dived *or* dove	dived
do, does	did	done
draw	drew	drawn
drink	drank	drunk
drive	drove	driven
eat	ate	eaten
fall	fell	fallen
feel	felt	felt
find	found	found
fling	flung	flung
fly	flew	flown
freeze	froze	frozen
get	got	got *or* gotten
give	gave	given
go	went	gone
grow	grew	grown

BASIC FORM	PAST FORM	PAST PARTICIPLE
hang	hanged *or* hung	hanged *or* hung
have, has	had	had
know	knew	known
lay*	laid	laid
lead	led	led
lend	lent	lent
lie*	lay	lain
lose	lost	lost
put	put	put
ride	rode	ridden
ring	rang	rung
rise*	rose	risen
run	ran	run
say	said	said
see	saw	seen
set*	set	set
shake	shook	shaken
shine	shone *or* shined†	shone *or* shined
shrink	shrank *or* shrunk	shrunk *or* shrunken
sing	sang	sung
sink	sank *or* sunk	sunk
sit*	sat	sat
slay	slew	slain
speak	spoke	spoken
spring	sprang *or* sprung	sprung
steal	stole	stolen
sting	stung	stung
swear	swore	sworn
swim	swam	swum
swing	swung	swung
take	took	taken
tear	tore	torn
tell	told	told
think	thought	thought
throw	threw	thrown
wear	wore	worn
win	won	won
write	wrote	written

---

*For more detailed instruction on *lay* versus *lie*, *raise* versus *rise*, and *sit* versus *set*, see Chapter 25.

†*Shone* is intransitive. (the sun *shone*.) *Shined* is transitive. (I *shined* the silverware.)

EXERCISE 1 **Supplying the Correct Principal Part.** Complete the following sentences with the principal part indicated in parentheses.

1. Maps are both fascinating and useful, and people have been ________ them for centuries. (present participle of *read*)
2. Over the centuries, maps have ________ from being merely simple navigational tools to being complex instruments conveying varied information. (past participle of *grow*)
3. Mapmakers over the centuries often have ________ that maps are as beautiful as many paintings. (past participle of *feel*)
4. Some artists even ________ to create maplike paintings as serious works of art. (past form of *begin*)
5. We often hear that the world has ________ because it is so much easier to get from one place to another these days. (past participle of *shrink*)
6. New and more sophisticated maps certainly ________ a part in creating this impression. (past form of *play*)
7. In the beginning of travel by automobile, people ________ without much help from maps. (past form of *drive*)
8. Good road maps later ________ a sense of security and independence to automobile drivers. (past form of *bring*)
9. Detailed road maps have ________ right along with the building of highways. (past participle of *develop*)
10. Maps have ________ travel out of the dark ages and into the modern world of transportation. (past participle of *take*)

Tense of Verbs

The **tenses** of a verb are the forms that help to show time.

Depending on which principal part of a verb you use and which, if any, auxiliary verbs you put before the principal part, you can show *when* the action or condition you are describing occurred.

There are six tenses in English: *present, past,* and *future* and *present perfect, past perfect,* and *future perfect.*

The Present Tense

The present tense of any action verb and of every linking verb other than *be* is the same as the verb's basic form. The following is a *conjugation,* or list of forms, for the present tense of *stay:*

	SINGULAR	PLURAL
FIRST PERSON	**I stay.**	We **stay.**
SECOND PERSON	You **stay.**	You **stay.**
THIRD PERSON	She, he, or it **stays.**	They **stay.**
	Bonnie **stays.**	The children **stay.**

Note that in the present-tense forms of the third-person singular, an -*s* is added to the basic form. In the following conjugation note that the present tense of *be* has three forms:

	SINGULAR	PLURAL
FIRST PERSON	**I am** sad.	We **are** sad.
SECOND PERSON	You **are** sad.	You **are** sad.
THIRD PERSON	She, he, or it **is** sad.	They **are** sad.

The **present tense** expresses a constant, repeated, or habitual action or condition. It can also express a general truth.

The garden **grows** well in the summer. [not just this summer but every summer—a repeated action]

Helena **bakes** bread well. [always—a habitual action]

Gold **is** valuable. [a condition that is always true]

The **present tense** can also express an action or condition that exists only now.

Jenny **feels** happy. [not always but just now]
I **see** a fly on the ceiling. [at this very moment]

The **present tense** is sometimes used in historical writing to express past events and, more often, in poetry, fiction, and reporting (especially sports) to convey to the reader a sense of "being there."

In the stadium the crowds suddenly **rise** to their feet with a roar.

The exhausted quarterback **tries** to get away from the other team, but he **is** finally **tackled.**

EXERCISE 2 **Using the Present Tense.** Write your answer to each question in a complete sentence, beginning with *Yes.*

SAMPLE Does the wholesaler supply goods?
ANSWER Yes, the wholesaler supplies goods.

1. Does a young lawyer need many skills?
2. Does a good lawyer always verify the clients' statements?
3. Does the law attempt to treat all people fairly?
4. Does a lawyer face many difficulties in defending clients?
5. Does the court open every weekday at nine o'clock?
6. Does the court reporter keep records of all that happens in court?
7. Does a defendant assist in his own defense?
8. Does a defense lawyer present evidence to help the client?
9. Does a defense lawyer have an important responsibility to the accused?
10. Does law hold many attractions for young people?

SENTENCE WRITING **Expressing the Present Tense in Sentences.** Write a sentence using each of the following verb forms. Make the content of your sentence express the kind of present time indicated in parentheses.

SAMPLE does (now and always)
ANSWER He does his housecleaning on Saturday.

1. sleeps (now and always)
2. feel (just now)
3. is (always true)
4. hopes (at this moment)
5. takes (always)

The Past Tense

Use the **past tense** to express an action or condition that was started and completed in the past.

The orchestra **performed** well.
The musicians **seemed** pleased.

All regular and irregular verbs—except *be*—have just one past-tense form, such as *soared or began*. When you use *be*, you must choose *was* or *were* depending on whether the person or thing you are talking about is first, second, or third person, singular or plural.

PAST TENSE OF *BE*

I **was** sad.	We **were** sad.
You **were** sad.	You **were** sad.
She, he, or it **was** sad.	They **were** sad.

EXERCISE 3 **Using the Past Tense.** Complete each sentence by writing the correct past-tense form of the verb in parentheses.

1. There was a time when nobody ________ about what type of food they were eating. (worry)
2. People unknowingly ________ foods that were too rich or that did not have enough nutritional value. (eat)
3. They did not know that food ________ to particular food groups such as fats and proteins (belong)
4. Eventually people ________ to care about the nutritional value of their food. (learn)
5. They ________ ways of preparing foods that increased their nutritional value. (find)

6. Health-conscious people __________ to include the four food groups in their diets. (try)
7. Nutrition handbooks __________ the nutritional value of particular foods. (define)
8. Researchers __________ good substitutes for foods like milk, salt, and sugar. (develop)
9. It __________ general knowledge that vegetables provide very important vitamins. (become)
10. People __________ to munch on raw vegetables. (begin)

The Future Tense

You form the future tense of any verb by using *shall* or *will* with the basic form: *I shall study, you will go.*

Use the **future tense** to express an action or condition that will occur in the future.

> Suzanne **will send** the telegram.
> I **shall practice** the piano tonight.

The following are other ways to express future time besides using *shall* or *will*.

1. Use *going to* with the present tense of *be* and the basic form of a verb.

   > Suzanne **is going to send** the telegram.

2. Use *about to* with the present tense of *be* and the basic form of the verb.

   > Suzanne **is about to send** the telegram.

3. Use the present tense with an adverb or an adverbial phrase that shows future time.

   > Suzanne **leaves tomorrow.**
   > Suzanne **arrives in the middle of next week.**

EXERCISE 4 **Identifying Expressions of Future Time.** Write the words that express future time in the following sentences.

SAMPLE Next spring we paint the house.
ANSWER Next spring, paint.

1. The people on my block are going to create a vegetable garden.
2. It will take a lot of hard work and care.
3. Everyone on the block will weed the garden.
4. I am going to take special care of the broccoli.

5. Broccoli will be the best vegetable in the garden.
6. Next week, we plant the seeds.
7. However, not everyone will want to help with this project.
8. I am about to ask all my friends to take part.
9. Not even a hot summer will prevent us from having a good time.
10. We shall celebrate our beautiful garden with a harvest party in the late summer.

SENTENCE WRITING **Expressing Future Time in Sentences.** Write five statements or predictions about the future. Your sentences can be as realistic or as imaginary as you wish. Try to use at least two other ways of expressing future time in addition to *shall* or *will.*

SAMPLE ANSWER Compact discs are going to become more popular than records.

The Perfect Tenses

In this section you will learn how to form and use the three perfect tenses—the *present perfect tense,* the *past perfect tense,* and the *future perfect tense.* The term *perfect* comes from the Latin word *perfectus,* meaning "completed," and all of these tenses refer to actions or conditions that are or will be completed.

To make the perfect tenses, you must use a form of the auxiliary verb *have* with the past participle of the main verb.

Present Perfect Tense

You form the present perfect tense by using *has* or *have* with the past participle of a verb: *has stopped, have waited.**

Use the **present perfect tense** to express an action or condition that occurred at some *indefinite* time in the past.

She **has caught** the flu.
They **have brought** a present for us.

The present perfect can refer to completed action in past time only in an indefinite way. Adverbs such as *yesterday* cannot be added to make the time more specific.

She **has completed** her project. [indefinite past]

*Do not be confused by the term *present perfect;* this tense expresses *past* time. *Present* refers to the tense of the auxiliary verb *has* or *have.*

To be specific about completed past time, you would normally use the simple past tense.

She **completed** her project yesterday.

The present perfect can also be used to communicate the idea that an action or a condition *began* in the past and *continues* into the present. This use normally involves adverbs of time or adverbial phrases.

He **has worked every day** on his new book.
The museum **has displayed** the exhibit **for months.**
We **have kept** the dogs indoors **for a week.**

Past Perfect Tense

You form the past perfect tense by using *had* with the past participle of a verb: *had loved, had written.*

Use the **past perfect tense** to indicate that one past action or condition began *and* ended before another past action started.

PAST PERFECT ... PAST
She **had been** the captain of the team before I **became** captain. [She was the captain; she stopped being captain; I became captain.]

PAST ... PAST PERFECT
Before I **slipped**, many other pedestrians **had slipped** in the same place. [They slipped; they finished slipping; I slipped.]

Future Perfect Tense

You form the future perfect tense by using *will have* or *shall have* with the past participle of a verb: *will have walked, shall have walked.*

Use the **future perfect tense** to express one future action or condition that will begin *and* end before another future event starts.

By summertime I **will have lived** here four months. [The four months will be over by the time another future event, the coming of summertime, occurs.]

By the time the astronauts reach Jupiter, they **will have practiced** the maneuver many times.

EXERCISE 5 **Identifying the Perfect Tenses.** On your paper write the tense of the italicized verbs in each of the following sentences.

1. Perhaps you *have thought* that making furniture is simple.
2. Maybe you *have felt* that a chair or desk would be easy to make.
3. Beautifully made furniture, however, *has taken* the carpenter many hours to complete.

4. Before wearing out, a handmade chair *will have given* its owner years of pleasure.
5. I *had bought* only machine-made pieces before I learned about the durability of handmade furniture.
6. Since then I *have found* a carpenter to do work for me.
7. Unfortunately I already *had bought* some new furniture before I saw her work.
8. Her skill is so great that she *has chosen* carpentry as her career.
9. I *had planned* to hire a professional decorator but I *have changed* my mind.
10. When I tell people what beautiful work my carpenter *has done*, they all want to hire her.

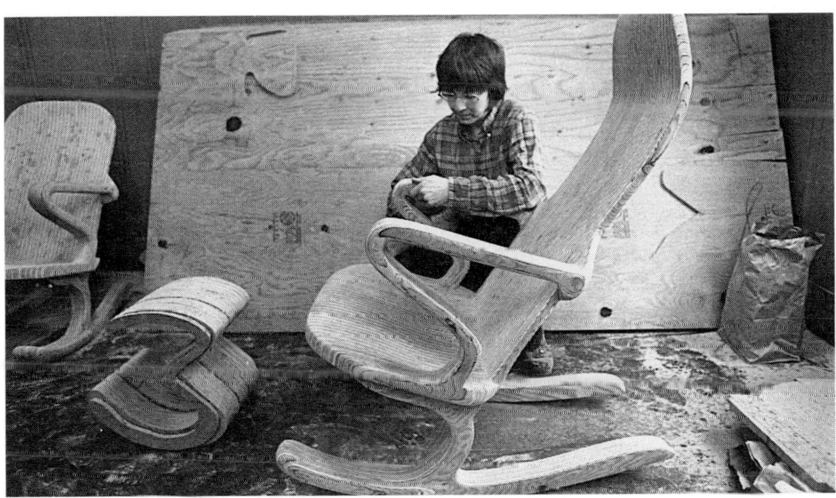

SENTENCE WRITING **Expressing the Present Perfect Tense in Sentences.** (a) Rewrite each of the following sentences, changing the tense of the verb from past to present perfect. (b) Add appropriate adverbs or adverbial phrases to each of your new sentences to communicate the idea that an action or condition began in the past and continues into the present.

SAMPLE We wanted to go to Paris.
ANSWER (a) We have wanted to go to Paris.
(b) We have wanted to go to Paris for two years.

1. She gave piano lessons.
2. My parents owned two dogs.
3. The trees were in bloom.
4. My friend wrote poetry.
5. The team played with determination.

The Progressive and Emphatic Forms

Each of the six tenses has a **progressive** form that expresses a continuing action.

You make the progressive forms by using the appropriate tense of the verb *be* with the present participle of the main verb.

PRESENT PROGRESSIVE	They ***are* reading.**
PAST PROGRESSIVE	They ***were* reading.**
FUTURE PROGRESSIVE	They ***will be* reading.**
PRESENT PERFECT PROGRESSIVE	They ***have been* reading.**
PAST PERFECT PROGRESSIVE	They ***had been* reading.**
FUTURE PERFECT PROGRESSIVE	They ***will have been* reading.**

The present and past tenses have additional forms, called **emphatic,** that add special force or emphasis to the verb.

You make the emphatic forms by using *do* or *did* with the basic form of the verb.

PRESENT EMPHATIC I **do read.** PAST EMPHATIC I **did read.**

EXERCISE 6 **Using the Present Progressive.** For each of the following sentences, write the present progressive form of the verb that appears in parentheses.

1. Today over seventy-five million Americans (use) bicycles.
2. Bicycle riding (become) a popular form of exercise.
3. Numerous organizations (work) to promote long-distance trips.
4. The bicycle also (provide) efficient transportation to and from work.
5. Many people (ride) bicycles in metropolitan areas.
6. Safety rules (grow) increasingly important for this reason.
7. Bicyclists (find) it difficult to ride on very busy streets.
8. Some (try) to get laws passed that will protect bicyclists.
9. Many cities (create) special lanes called *bikeways*.
10. At the same time new traffic laws (require) bicyclists to ride more carefully.

EXERCISE 7 **Using the Past Progressive.** For each of the following sentences, write the past progressive form of the verb in parentheses.

1. As long ago as the Stone Age, people (eat) the honey of bees.
2. Stone Age people already (make) rough beehives out of logs.
3. In the Middle Ages farmers in Europe (build) straw *skeps* that looked like upturned baskets.

4. By the seventeenth century American colonists (bring) honeybees with them from England.
5. Swarms of these bees (escape) from their hives and building new nests in the woods.
6. In the nineteenth century farmers (use) bees to pollinate many crops.
7. In the 1880's commercial beekeeping, called *apiculture,* (come) into vogue.
8. Beekeepers (sell) honey and beeswax.
9. At that time people (learn) to manage large colonies of bees.
10. Commercial beekeeping (become) a suitable means of livelihood for some people.

REVIEW EXERCISE **Verb Forms.** On your paper complete the following sentences by filling the blank with the verb form indicated in parentheses.

1. The telegraph __________ the first method used to send messages by electricity. (past tense of *be*)
2. Telegraph circuits __________ around the world by the beginning of the twentieth century. (past progressive of *stretch*)
3. The telegraph __________ the dots and dashes of the Morse code into electrical impulses that could send messages instantaneously over long distances. (past perfect tense of *change*)
4. Today the telephone and other sophisticated methods of communication __________ the telegraph for some purposes. (present progressive of *replace*)
5. However, businesses still __________ the telegraph to get in touch quickly and inexpensively with customers around the world. (present tense of *use*)
6. Nowadays scientists __________ on better means of communication. (present progressive of *work*)
7. Scientists __________ much more about communication systems by the twenty-first century. (future perfect tense of *learn*)
8. In the last century a messenger who __________ to deliver important news quickly might not have been able to keep that promise. (past tense of *promise*)
9. Soon people __________ how to solve many communications problems. (future tense of *know*)
10. We __________ the capacity to solve some of these problems right now. (present emphatic of *have*)

SENTENCE WRITING **Expressing Past Time in a Paragraph.** Write a paragraph of at least five sentences about an important event in your past. Underline five verbs or verb phrases that you have used, and identify the tense of each underlined item. (Remember that the perfect tenses as well as the past tense can be used to express past actions.)

Compatibility of Tenses

The various verb tenses enable you to show whether two or more events occur at the same time and whether one event precedes or follows another.

Do not shift, or change, tenses needlessly when two or more events occur at the same time.

INCORRECT During the concert the pianist **forgot** the notes, and she **stops** in the middle of the piece. [The tense needlessly shifts from the past to the present.]

CORRECT During the concert the pianist **forgot** the notes, and she **stopped** in the middle of the piece. [Now it is clear that both events happened at nearly the same time in the past.]

Shift tenses only to show that one event precedes or follows another.

INCORRECT By the time we **arrived,** they **ate** dinner. [The two past-tense verbs give the mistaken impression that both events happened at the same time.]

CORRECT By the time we **arrived,** they **had eaten** dinner. [The shift from the past tense *(arrived)* to the past perfect tense *(had eaten)* clearly indicates that the eating of dinner happened before the arriving.]

INCORRECT Since they **found** the old umbrella, it **rained** every day. [It is not clear which event came first.]

CORRECT Since they **found** the old umbrella, it **has rained** every day. [The past tense *(found)* indicates a completed action. The present perfect *(has rained)* indicates an action that has started in the past and continues into the present.]

EXERCISE 8 **Making Tenses Compatible.** First find the two verbs in each of the following sentences. Then rewrite each sentence, making the second verb compatible with the first verb.

1. As soon as we arrived, we want to see the new school.
2. The school was empty when we first see it.
3. Drawings were in the windows, and the colors look very bright.

4. Since the front door was standing ajar, we walk inside.
5. Everything appeared clean, and we feel a sense of newness.
6. A teacher spotted us and was showing us some classrooms.
7. He took us around, and we are listening to his comments about the new facilities.
8. He introduced us to another teacher, who leads us through the new gymnasium.
9. By the time we left, we saw the whole school.
10. We felt very glad that we are moving to this neighborhood.

REVIEW EXERCISE **Tense.** On your paper explain the difference in meaning between the sentences in each of the following pairs. (The sentences are all correct and are labeled for time and tense.)

1. (a) They lived in the town for two years. (past)
   (b) They have lived in the town for two years. (present perfect)
2. (a) What happened last year when they left town? (past; past)
   (b) What had happened last year when they left town? (past perfect; past)
3. (a) They have looked for a new place to live. (present perfect)
   (b) They looked for a new place to live. (past)
4. (a) They will have seen many new places in a year. (future perfect)
   (b) They will see many new places in a year. (future)
5. (a) Have the girls found a place to live? (present perfect)
   (b) Had the girls found a place to live? (past perfect)

Voice of Verbs

An action verb is in the **active voice** when the subject of the sentence performs the action.

The dog **pleased** the child.

An action verb is in the **passive voice** when its action is performed on the subject.

The child **was pleased** by the dog.

In the first sentence the *dog* (the subject of the sentence) performs the action. In the second sentence the *child* (now the subject of the sentence) takes center stage, and the dog is reduced to an *agent.*

As a writer you often have a choice between using a verb in the active or passive voice. It is often a question of whom you want to place in center stage—the dog or the child, for example.

Generally the active voice is stronger, but there are times when the passive voice is preferred or, in fact, necessary. If you do not want to call attention to the performer, or if you do not know the performer, use the passive voice, as in the following examples:

> The dinner **was ruined.** [You may not want to identify the culprit.]
>
> The manuscript **was stolen.** [You may not know who the culprit is.]

You form the passive voice by using a form of the auxiliary verb *be* with the past participle of the verb. The tense of a passive verb is determined by the tense of the auxiliary verb.

> The child **is pleased** by the dog. [present tense, passive voice]
>
> The child **was pleased.** [past tense, passive voice]
>
> The child **will be pleased** by the dog. [future tense, passive voice]

When a verb is in the passive voice, the performer of the action may be stated as the object of the preposition *by*.

> Robots are designed by **engineers.**

EXERCISE 9 **Changing the Voice of Verbs.** In each of the following sentences, change the active voice to the passive or the passive voice to the active.

1. The explorer robot has been brought to us by new technology.
2. Human beings operate some of these robots.
3. Areas that are dangerous to humans have been explored by these robots.
4. NASA can test some of these robots.
5. Marine biologists expect these robots to do underwater research.
6. Superior endurance to that of humans is offered by explorer robots.
7. Therefore, these robots can maintain underwater equipment.
8. Pictures of Mars were relayed to Earth by planetary explorer robots.
9. Engineers have designed some explorer robots to help the handicapped.
10. Scientists predict a great future for explorer robots.

Revising Your Writing

Good writers carefully avoid any unnecessary use of the passive voice. If Saki had relied too heavily on the passive voice in his short story "The Interlopers," he might have written this sentence:

> The skin of his face *had been slashed* by the descending twigs, and some drops of blood from his eyelashes *had to be winked away* by him before a general view of the disaster *could be taken in*.

Notice how flat this is in comparison with Saki's actual sentence.

> The descending twigs *had slashed* the skin of his face, and he *had to wink away* some drops of blood from his eyelashes before he *could take in* a general view of the disaster.

The active voice allows Saki to maintain strict chronology in his narrative. We readers see the descending twigs *before* we picture the slashed skin. In addition, the active voice clearly identifies *who* is doing the winking and the taking in of the general view. Finally, the version in the active voice is less wordy, by about 10 percent.

Apply these techniques in revising the following passage from "The Interlopers," which has been rewritten in the passive voice.

> The useless struggle to free themselves from the mass of wood by which they were held down had now been given up by both; Ulrich's endeavors were limited by him to an effort to have his one partially free arm brought near enough to his outer pocket to have his wine flask drawn out. Even when that operation had been accomplished, it was long before the unscrewing of the stopper could be managed or any of the liquid gotten down his throat.

CHAPTER 22

Subject-Verb Agreement

In this chapter, you will study how to use verbs correctly in sentences. The agreement of the verb with the subject is the central concern of the chapter. You will study examples of how intervening words or phrases, inverted word order, or special types of nouns may confuse you if you are not careful.

A verb must agree with its subject in person and number.

With most verbs the only change in form to indicate agreement occurs in the present tense. An *-s* (or *-es*) is added to the basic verb when its subject is third-person singular. The linking verb *be* changes in both the present and the past tense.

SINGULAR	PLURAL
She **speaks.**	They **speak.**
He **is** there.	They **are** there.
It **was** sweet.	They **were** sweet.

In verb phrases the auxiliary verbs *be, have,* and *do* change in form to show agreement with third-person subjects.

SINGULAR	PLURAL
She **is speaking.**	They **are speaking.**
She **has seen** a movie.	They **have seen** a movie.
Does he **stay** here?	**Do** they **stay** here?

Making a verb agree with its subject involves not only correctly identifying subjects and verbs but also telling whether a subject is singular or plural.

Intervening Prepositional Phrases

Do not mistake a prepositional phrase for the subject of a verb.

The simple subject is never within a prepositional phrase. Make sure the verb agrees with the actual subject and not with the object of a preposition.

The ***taste*** of the cherries **surprises** us. [The subject *taste* is singular; *of the cherries* is a prepositional phrase; therefore, the verb *surprises* is singular.]

The ***spices*** in the food **are** interesting. [The subject *spices* is plural; *in the food* is a prepositional phrase; therefore, the verb *are* is plural.]

EXERCISE 1 **Making Subjects and Verbs Agree When Prepositional Phrases Intervene.** First find the simple subject in each of the following sentences. Then write on your paper the verb in parentheses that agrees with the subject of each sentence.

1. Experiments with plant life (show/shows) that some flowers turn from loud music.
2. The sound of loud noises (seem/seems) to affect carnations in particular.
3. The stems of carnations gradually (lean/leans) away from the source of loud music.
4. The response of cyclamens (seem/seems) similar to the response of carnations.
5. The vibrations of loud stereo music (cause/causes) similar responses in the lily.
6. The arrangement of flowers (remain/remains) a vital decorative art in our culture.
7. The cultures of Egypt, Greece, and Rome (offers/offer) early examples of flower arranging.
8. Still, the floral arrangements of the Japanese (stands/stand) supreme.
9. The beauty of Japanese floral arrangements (lie/lies) in their serene and delicate naturalness.
10. The leaves in every floral arrangement (play/plays) a major part in the design.

Agreement with Linking Verbs

Do not be confused by a predicate nominative that is different in number from the subject. Only the subject affects the number of the linking verb.

> The lowest ***temperature* was** forty degrees below zero. [The singular verb *was* agrees with the singular subject *temperature,* not with the predicate nominative *degrees.*]
>
> The lightest ***crate* is** two tons. [The singular verb *is* agrees with the singular subject *crate,* not with the predicate nominative *tons.*]
>
> ***Poems*** about nature **were** the subject of the lecture. [The plural verb *were* agrees with the plural subject *poems,* not with the predicate nominative *subject.*]
>
> Recent ***studies*** on the behavior of wild animals ***are*** his topic for the day. [The plural verb *are* agrees with the plural subject *studies,* not with the predicate nominative *topic.*]

EXERCISE 2 **Making Linking Verbs Agree with Their Subjects.** First find the simple subject or subjects in each of the following sentences. Then write on your paper the verb in parentheses that agrees with the subject of each sentence.

1. The growing threats to wildlife (is/are) a national problem.
2. Wild animals (remain/remains) a part of the wonder of nature.
3. Research on plant and animal life (is/are) the means of much scientific discovery.
4. Not long ago our forest land (was/were) millions of acres larger.
5. By the 1980s the result of the loss (were/was) lists of endangered species.
6. The cost of deforestation (is/are) years of floods and damaging soil erosion.
7. Uncontrolled hunting and fishing (was/were) an additional problem with serious consequences.
8. The destructive results (are/is) a disturbance of nature's balance.
9. Protected lands (seem/seems) the only refuge left to some wildlife.
10. Joint government and private efforts (seems/seem) the solution.

Agreement in Inverted Sentences

When a subject follows its verb, carefully locate the simple subject and make sure that the verb agrees with the subject.

Inverted sentences are those in which the subject follows the verb. Inverted sentences often begin with prepositional phrases. Do not mistake the object of the preposition for the subject. Study the examples on the following page.

V S
SINGULAR In the jungle **roars** the ***lion.***

V
PLURAL In the jungle **roar** the ***lions.***

In inverted sentences beginning with the expletive *there* or *here,* look for the subject after the verb. An expletive is never the subject of a sentence.

V S
SINGULAR There **is** a ***lion*** in the jungle.

V S
Here **goes** the ***ambulance.***

V S
PLURAL There **are** ***lions*** in the jungle.

V S
Here **go** the two ***ambulances.***

In questions an auxiliary verb may come before the subject. Look for the subject between the auxiliary verb and the main verb.

V S V
SINGULAR **Does** that ***lion*** **live** in the jungle?

V S V
PLURAL **Do** those ***jungles*** **contain** lions?

EXERCISE 3 **Making Subjects and Verbs Agree in Inverted Sentences.** First find the simple subject in each of the following sentences. Then write on your paper the verb in parentheses that agrees with the subject of each sentence.

1. There (is/are) three excellent and unusual restaurants in my neighborhood.
2. In the window of one of the restaurants (hang/hangs) an interesting menu.
3. Over the door of another (swing/swings) an old and elaborate sign.
4. Outside the third (stand/stands) two statues representing a waiter and waitresss.
5. (Do/Does) the owners of the restaurants ever do any of the cooking and baking?
6. (Is/Are) expert chefs brought in to create mouthwatering specialties to please the demanding clientele?
7. There (are/is) a colorful, pleasant decor in all three restaurants.
8. Into the restaurants (crowd/crowds) the hungry customers.
9. Here (come/comes) the people who want to eat early.
10. There (gather/gathers) the people waiting to be seated.

Agreement with Special Subjects

Some subjects require careful attention when you select a verb to agree with them.

Collective Nouns

A **collective noun** names a group. Consider a collective noun singular when it refers to a group as a whole. Consider a collective noun plural when it refers to each member of a group individually.

SINGULAR	PLURAL
His ***family*** **arrives.**	His ***family*** **are** well.
The ***audience*** **applauds.**	The ***audience*** **leave** during intermission.
The ***committee*** **decides.**	The ***committee*** **sign** their names.

Special Nouns

Certain nouns that end in *s*, such as *mumps, measles,* and *mathematics,* take singular verbs.

SINGULAR ***Mumps*** **is** a disease.

Certain other nouns that end in *s*, such as *scissors, pants, binoculars,* and *eyeglasses,* take plural verbs.

PLURAL The ***scissors*** **were** sharp.
Your ***eyeglasses*** **need** cleaning.

Many nouns that end in *ics* may be singular or plural depending on meaning.

SINGULAR ***Statistics*** **is** an interesting subject. [one subject of interest]
PLURAL ***Statistics*** **show** that women live longer than men. [more than one application of this particular field of study]

Nouns of Amount

When the noun refers to a total considered as one unit, it is singular. When the noun refers to a number of individual units, it is plural.

SINGULAR Three ***dollars*** **is** not too much for that book. [one amount]
PLURAL Three ***dollars*** **are** on the table. [three individual bills]

SINGULAR Ten ***years*** **is** a decade. [one unit of time]
PLURAL Ten ***years*** **have passed.** [ten individual periods of time]

Titles

A title is always singular even if a noun within the title is plural.

SINGULAR ***Star Wars*** **was** one of the most popular films in motion picture history.

The Number, A Number

The number is considered singular. *A number* (meaning "some") is considered plural.

SINGULAR **The number** of swans in the lake **is** surprising.
PLURAL **A number** of swans **are** flying. [meaning "some" swans]

EXERCISE 4 **Making Verbs Agree with Special Subjects.** Find the subject in each sentence and write the verb in parentheses that agrees with the subject.

1. Three months (is/are) the time it takes to complete the first-aid course at the local high school.
2. If the group (is/are) working well with one another, the time can be cut almost in half.
3. A number of people (has/have) expressed interest in the course.
4. Special equipment (is/are) used to demonstrate various techniques.
5. Five minutes (is/are) the record time for saving someone from drowning.
6. Her entire family (has/have) joined the class.
7. The class (is/are) sharing their experiences with one another.
8. Usually, two weeks (is/are) the length of time required to learn the fundamentals of first aid.
9. *Helping to Save Lives* (was/were) written by one of the teachers.
10. The number of people interested in the class (is/are) impressive.

Agreement with Compound Subjects

When the subject of a sentence is compound, note the conjunction that joins the compound parts and the meaning of the entire subject to determine which verb form agrees with the compound subject.

1. Compound subjects joined by *and*

Compound subjects joined by *and* or by *both . . . and* are plural except when the parts of the compound subject are parts of one unit or when they refer to the same person or thing.

PLURAL The ***lion*** *and* the ***tiger*** **are roaring.**
Both ***skiing*** *and* ***skating*** **are** fun.
SINGULAR ***Peanut butter*** *and* ***jelly*** **is** a favorite combination. [Compound subject is one unit.]
Law and order **is** important to maintain. [Compound subject is one unit.]
His ***friend*** *and* ***companion*** **accompanies** him. [One person is both friend and companion.]

2. Compound subjects joined by *or* or *nor*

With compound subjects joined by *or* or *nor* (or by *either . . . or* or *neither . . . nor*), always make the verb agree with the subject nearer the verb.

PLURAL *Neither* the **lion** *nor* the **tigers are roaring.**
SINGULAR *Either* the **lion** *or* the **tiger is roaring.**
Neither the **lions** *nor* the **tiger roars.**

3. *Many a, every,* and *each* with compound subjects

When *many a, every,* or *each* precedes a compound subject, the subject is considered singular.

SINGULAR *Many a* ***giraffe*** and ***elephant*** **lives** in the preserve.
Every ***chair, bench,*** and ***table*** **was taken.**
Each **lion** and ***tiger*** **is roaring.**

Intervening Expressions

Certain expressions, such as *accompanied by, as well as, in addition to, plus,* and *together with,* introduce phrases that modify the subject but do not change its number. Although their meaning is similar to that of *and,* these expressions do not create compound subjects.

If a singular subject is linked to another noun by an intervening expression, such as "accompanied by," then the subject is still considered singular.

SINGULAR The ***pianist,*** as well as the lead singer, **is** late.
Sleet, in addition to snow, **is expected** tomorrow.

EXERCISE 5 **Making Verbs Agree with Their Subjects.** On your paper write the appropriate form of the verb in parentheses.

1. Fabric remnants and scraps (makes/make) colorful patchwork quilts.
2. Many a comforter or bedspread (has been created/have been created) with small pieces of cloth.
3. Either calico or pieces of brocade (work/works) well in patchwork.
4. First, the pieces of cloth (is cut/are cut) into geometric shapes.
5. Then, every square, triangle, and rectangle (is sewed/are sewed) together.
6. The patchwork top plus batting and backing (is quilted/are quilted) on a large frame.

7. Traditional and modern patterns (has/have) a name.
8. The ninepatch, the grandma's flower garden, and the log cabin (is/are) popular patterns.
9. A quilting party, as well as similar gatherings, (was/were) very common many years ago.
10. Many a pillowcase and blanket (is/are) pretty enough to frame.

SENTENCE WRITING **Creating Sentences with Compound Subjects.** Write sentences using each of the following compound subjects. Make the compound subject agree with a present-tense verb.

1. bread and butter
2. neither the coach nor the players
3. both the climate and the geography of the South
4. Aunt Susan or Uncle Harold
5. many a cat and dog

Indefinite Pronouns as Subjects

A verb must agree in number with an indefinite pronoun subject.

Indefinite pronouns (see Chapter 17) can be divided into the following three groups: those that are always singular; those that are always plural; and those that can be either singular or plural, depending upon the nouns to which they refer.

The following are the indefinite pronouns that are always singular:

each	everyone	nobody	anything
either	everybody	nothing	someone
neither	everything	anyone	somebody
one	no one	anybody	something

These are the indefinite pronouns that are always plural:

several few both many

These indefinite pronouns may be singular or plural:

some all any most none

The verb that you use with an indefinite pronoun from the third group often shows whether you are assigning the pronoun a singular or a plural meaning.

SINGULAR When I checked the puppies' cage, ***all* was** quiet. [*All* is used here in the sense of "everything," which is singular.]

PLURAL ***All*** in my neighborhood **tend** the community garden. [*All* is used here to refer to *people*, which is plural.]

SENTENCE WRITING **Making Verbs Agree with Indefinite Pronoun Subjects.** Write a sentence using each of the following indefinite pronouns as the subject. Use present-tense verbs that agree with each subject.

SAMPLE One
ANSWER One of my friends owns a ten-speed bike.

1. each
2. many
3. anybody
4. some
5. both
6. neither

SENTENCE WRITING **Creating Sentences with Indefinite Pronoun Subjects.** Write two sentences, using each of the following indefinite pronouns as the subject of both sentences. Write the first sentence of each pair with a singular present-tense verb and the second sentence with a plural present-tense verb.

SAMPLE Some
ANSWER Some of the work is not finished.
Some of the books are on the shelf.

1. none
2. any
3. most
4. all
5. some
6. none

Agreement in Adjective Clauses

The verb in an adjective clause must agree with its subject, which is often a relative pronoun. (See Chapter 20.) The number of the relative pronoun subject depends on the number of its antecedent in the main clause.

> The chimpanzee is one of the ***animals*** **that are being studied** by a team of zoologists at the San Diego Zoo. [The antecedent of *that* is *animals,* a plural noun.]

> The chimpanzee is the only ***one*** of the animals in the zoo **that makes** me laugh. [The antecedent of *that* is *one,* a third-person singular pronoun.]

If the expression "one of" appears in the main clause, you must take care to determine if the antecedent is "one," as in the second example above, or the noun that follows it, such as "animals" in the first example. (The word *the* before *one* indicates that *one* is the antecedent.)

The verb in an adjective clause with a relative pronoun subject must agree with the antecedent to which the relative pronoun refers.

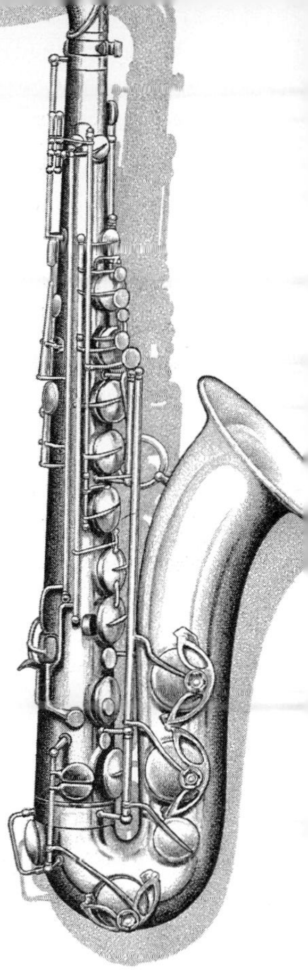

EXERCISE 6 **Making Subjects and Verbs Agree in Adjective Clauses.** On your paper complete the following sentences by choosing the correct form of the verb in parentheses. Study the example given below.

SAMPLE Chris Evert Lloyd is one of the tennis players who (has/have) won many tournaments.

ANSWER have won

1. The drum was probably the only one of the early instruments that (was/were) used to send messages over long distances.
2. The violin is one of the instruments that (has/have) evolved from the lute.
3. Historical records seem to indicate that the harp is the only one of the musical instruments that (was/were) played almost exclusively by women.
4. Hollowing out a piece of bamboo was one of the methods that (was/were) used to create the first flutes.
5. The piano is one of the instruments that (is/are) often used to teach music to young children.
6. The saxophone is one of the most popular instruments that (is/are) used to play jazz.
7. The xylophone is an example of a percussion instrument that (are/is) struck to produce different notes.
8. The trombone is the only one of the basic brass instruments that (has/have) a slide for controlling the pitch.
9. Pressing large foot pedals is one of the methods that (is/are) used to play the pipe organ.
10. The synthesizer is only one of the complex electronic instruments that (is/are) played nowadays.

REVIEW EXERCISE **Subject-Verb Agreement.** The paragraph on the following page contains ten errors in subject-verb agreement. Locate the sentences with errors, and rewrite those sentences with the correct verb form that agrees with the subject. (Some of the sentences will have more than one subject-verb combination.)

[1]In the beautiful old concert hall are a large stage with chairs for the musicians. [2]The audience purchases their tickets, and soon most of the seats are filled. [3]The concert hall, as well as several small rehearsal rooms, are in an old turn-of-the-century building that has been the center of controversy for many years. [4]A number of people wants to tear it down to make way for new high-rise apartments. [5]However, because the building is one of the few left in the city that has not been replaced by new construction, many of the citizens considers it worth preserving. [6]Of course, neither the musicians nor their conductor wish to see the building destroyed, for there is no other available concert halls. [7]Several thousand dollars are the amount needed to renovate the building, and the orchestra plan to hold a number of plans benefit performances to raise some of the necessary money.

Revising Your Writing

Many of the decisions that you face when revising your writing involve stylistic choices. Many other items in need of revision, however, will not be matters of style but of usage. For example, readers expect writers to adhere to the rules of subject-verb agreement. Writers who ignore these rules quickly lose the respect of their readers.

Keep the following guidelines in mind as you revise your work.

1. Be alert to prepositional phrases and other expressions that fall between a subject and its verb. Mentally block them out when you check for agreement.

   > "Young woman," she said, "do you deny that all this **nonsense** with eggs and telephone calls **is** an attempt to entangle my nephew into matrimony?" —Shirley Jackson, "About Two Nice People"

2. Be careful when you check for agreement in inverted sentences. Remember that the subject will follow the verb.

   > Couched in his kennel, like a log,
   > With paws of silver **sleeps** the **dog**. . . .
   >
   > —Walter de la Mare, "Silver"

Apply these techniques in revising the following excerpt adapted from May Swenson's poem "Water Picture." Imagine that the excerpt is a near-final draft. Correct any errors in agreement.

> The arched stone bridge
> is an eye, with underlid
> in the water. In its lens
> dips crinkled heads with hats
> that don't fall off. Dogs go by,
> barking on their backs.
> A baby, taken to feed the
> ducks, dangle upside-down,
> a pink balloon for a buoy.

CHAPTER 23

Using Pronouns Correctly

Several pronouns change their form depending on how they function in a sentence. Consider, for example, the following sentences:

Joyce knows Vicky. She knows her.

Notice that the nouns in the first sentence can be reversed *(Vicky knows Joyce)* but that the pronouns in the second sentence cannot. *Her knows she* is simply not normal English. This chapter will explain why pronouns such as *she* and *her* can fill only certain functions in sentences and not others. The last part of this chapter will discuss the relationship between pronouns and their antecedents and will give you guidelines for making them agree.

Case of Personal Pronouns

Pronouns that are used to refer to persons or things are called **personal** pronouns. Personal pronouns have three **cases,** or forms. The case of a personal pronoun depends on the pronoun's function in a sentence (whether it be a subject, object, etc.). The three cases are called **nominative, objective,** and **possessive.**

The following chart lists the case forms of personal pronouns according to the pronouns' function in sentences:

	SINGULAR	PLURAL	
NOMINATIVE	I, you, she, he, it	we, you, they	subject or predicate nominative
OBJECTIVE	me, you, her, him, it	us, you, them	direct object or indirect object or object of preposition
POSSESSIVE	my, mine, your, yours, her, hers, his, its	our, ours, your, yours, their, theirs	replacement for possessive noun(s)

You and *it* rarely cause usage problems because they have the same form in both the nominative and the objective case. You can learn to recognize the forms and functions of the other pronouns by carefully studying their case.

You can avoid errors involving the case of personal pronouns if you keep the following rules in mind:

1. Be sure to use the nominative case for a personal pronoun in a compound subject.

    Tony and **I** play the guitar. [not me play]
    He and his sister sing well. [not Him and his sister sing]
    She and **I** sing duets. [not Her and me sing]

2. Be sure to use the objective case for a personal pronoun in a compound object.

    Tony's sister accompanies Tony and **her.** [not Tony and she]
    This is between you and **me.** [not between you and I]
    I shall take Judy and them to the movies. [not Judy and they]

    When you have to choose the correct pronoun in a sentence with a compound subject or object, it is helpful to say the sentence to yourself without the conjunction and the other noun or pronoun subject.

3. In general, use the nominative case of a personal pronoun after a form of the linking verb *be.*

    The best guitar player is **he.** [not is him]
    The best singer in the show was **she.** [not was her]
    I hope a future star will be **I.** [not will be me]

    In informal speaking, people often use the objective case after a form of the linking verb *be:* they say "*It's me,*" and "*It was him.*" In writing, however, you should always use the nominative case after the linking verb *be.*

4. Be careful not to spell possessive pronouns with apostrophes.*

    This sheet music is **hers.** [not her's]
    The instruments are **theirs.** [not their's]

    It's is a contraction for *it is.* Do not confuse it with the possessive pronoun *its.*

5. Be sure to use possessive pronouns before gerunds (*-ing* forms used as nouns).

    Your dancing bothers me. [not You dancing bothers me]

    He wasn't pleased by **my** complaining to him. [not by me complaining to him]

**My, your, his, her, its, our,* and *their* are sometimes called possessive adjectives because they modify nouns: *This is her record,* for example.

EXERCISE 1 **Choosing the Correct Case Form.** In each of the following sentences, write the personal pronoun or pronouns that correctly complete the sentence.

1. My sister and (I/me) collect coins.
2. Our neighbor gave my sister and (I/me) a book on coins.
3. (Its/It's) section on how to start a coin collection is very helpful.
4. (You/Your) helping us sort the pennies saved us a great deal of time.
5. The Jefferson nickel is my favorite coin. What is (yours/your's)?
6. Our parents give their coins to Lila and (I/me) so that we can search for collectors' items.
7. These are plans for the display that Lila and (I/me) are making.
8. (She/Her) and I will trade some of our duplicate coins.
9. We welcome (you/your) suggesting ways for us to improve our coin collection.
10. Maybe someday Lila and (I/me) will have a complete collection of Lincoln pennies.

Pronouns in Appositive Phrases

Pronouns often appear with nouns in appositive phrases that follow other nouns or pronouns. (See Chapter 19.)

> The best musicians, **Marguerite and he**, should compete. [The pronoun *he* is part of a phrase that is in apposition to the noun *musicians.*]

Use the nominative case for a pronoun that is in apposition to a subject or predicate nominative.

> The judges, **she and Mrs. Hawkins**, will have a difficult task. [*Judges* is the subject.]

> The winners were the pianists, **Lindsay and he.** [*Pianists* is the predicate nominative.]

Use the objective case for a pronoun that is in apposition to a direct object, indirect object, or object of a preposition.

> The audience cheered their favorite performers, **Darnell and her.** [*Performers* is a direct object.]

> The director gave the stage crew, **Lee and him,** special thanks. [*Stage crew* is an indirect object.]

> The judges explained the rules to both groups, **them and us.** [*Groups* is the object of the preposition *to.*]

In appositive phrases with *we* and *us*, such as *we violinists* or *us musicians*, choose the case of the pronoun on the usual basis of its function in the sentence.

> **We violinists** hope one day to play in a concert hall. [*We* is the correct form because *we* is the subject of the sentence.]
>
> The music teacher handed the scores to **us musicians**. [*Us* is the correct form because *us* is the object of the preposition *to*.]

It is often helpful in choosing the correct pronoun to say the sentence without the noun.

EXERCISE 2 **Choosing the Correct Pronoun in Appositive Phrases.** In each of the following sentences, write the personal pronoun or pronouns that correctly complete the sentence.

1. The speakers taught (us/we) students how to evaluate television programs.
2. The speakers, an educator and (he/him), gave some interesting statistics about the viewing habits of teen-agers.
3. (Us/We) viewers should calculate how many hours of television we watch each week.
4. The most avid viewers are my friends (Julie and he/Julie and him).
5. The speaker gave (us/we) students guidelines for rating shows.

EXERCISE 3 **Supplying Pronouns in Appositive Phrases.** Complete the following paragraph by choosing the correct pronoun.

[1]The writing team, Lawrence Kasdan and (she/her) was always willing to make revisions in the script. [2]The director worked well with the male and female leads, Harrison Ford and (her/she). [3]The two cinematographers, Gordon Willis and (him/he), managed to work both efficiently and creatively. [4](We/Us) young actors were very lucky to work with such a fine team. [5]There is no question that working on this film had a positive effect on (we/us) beginners.

Pronouns After *Than* and *As*

In elliptical adverb clauses using *than* and *as* (see Chapter 20), choose the case of the pronoun that you would use if the missing words were fully expressed.

> You use a brush more skillfully than **I** (use a brush). [The nominative pronoun *I* is the subject of the adverb clause *than I use a brush*.]
>
> The logic of the problem puzzled Jennifer as much as (it puzzled) **me**. [The objective pronoun *me* is the direct object of the adverb clause *as much as it puzzled me*.]

SENTENCE WRITING **Using Pronouns After *Than* and *As*.** Expand each of the following expressions into a complex sentence containing an elliptical adverb clause. End each sentence with a personal pronoun other than *you* or *it*.

SAMPLE more interested than
ANSWER No one at the museum was more interested than I.

1. frightened than
2. as pleased as
3. more curious than
4. less than
5. as much as

Who and *Whom* in Questions and Subordinate Clauses

The pronoun *who* can function as an interrogative or a relative pronoun. (See Chapter 17.) It has these case forms:

NOMINATIVE who
OBJECTIVE whom
POSSESSIVE whose

When *who* is used as a relative pronoun to introduce a subordinate clause, its case is determined by its function in the subordinate clause.

Use the nominative pronoun *who* for subjects.

Who did you say won the contest? [*Who* is the subject of the verb *won.*]

Tell me **who** is in your class. [*Who* is the subject of the noun clause *who is in your class.*]

In questions, like the first example, with an interrupting expression such as "did you say" or "do you think," it is often helpful to drop the interrupting phrase to determine whether to use *who* or *whom*.

Who [do you think] will emcee the show?

Use the objective pronoun *whom* for the direct or indirect object of a verb or verbal or for the object of a preposition.

Whom are you introducing first? [*Whom* is the direct object of the verb *are introducing.*]

They told him **whom** he could invite to the show. [*Whom* is the direct object of the verb *could invite* in the noun clause *whom he could invite to the show.*]

Teddy Roosevelt is a President about **whom** I have read quite a bit. [*Whom* is the object of the preposition *about* in the adjective clause *about whom I have read quite a bit.*]

In informal speech, people generally use *who* in place of *whom* in sentences like this one: *Who did you tell?* In writing and in formal speaking situations, however, people are expected to make the distinctions between *who* and *whom*.

EXERCISE 4 **Choosing *Who* or *Whom*.** Write on your paper the appropriate form of the pronoun in each set of parentheses.

1. (Who/Whom) did you say gave you the passes to the Museum of Holography?
2. Setsuko Ishii is the holographic artist about (who/whom) I've been reading.
3. Setsuko Ishii, (who/whom) is Japan's top holographic artist, has put together an exhibit at the museum.
4. The director of the museum, (who/whom) our teacher knows, will show us a twenty-minute film on holography.
5. The director introduced us to several artists (who/whom) he said would be represented in future exhibitions.

EXERCISE 5 **Using *Who* or *Whom* in Sentences.** On your paper complete the following paragraph by filling each blank with *who* or *whom*.

[1]Mary Cassatt, __________ was one of the best nineteenth-century American painters, spent much of her career in France. [2]Her friends there included some of the great French Impressionists, among __________ was Edgar Degas. [3]Degas, __________ is famous for his paintings of ballerinas, greatly influenced Cassatt. [4]Cassatt also encouraged American collectors to purchase the art of the Impressionists, __________ she considered very important. [5]__________ are some other American artists influenced by the European Impressionists?

Pronoun-Antecedent Agreement

An **antecedent** is the word or group of words to which a pronoun refers or which a pronoun replaces. All pronouns must agree with their antecedents in number, gender, and person.

Agreement in Number and Gender

A pronoun must agree with its antecedent in number (singular or plural) and gender (masculine, feminine, or neuter).

A pronoun's antecedent may be a noun, another pronoun, or a phrase or clause acting as a noun. In the following examples the pronouns appear in bold type and their antecedents in bold italic type. Notice how they agree in both number and gender.

Helen Keller did not let blindness and deafness prevent **her** from graduating *cum laude* from Radcliffe College. [singular, feminine pronoun]

Helen Keller and ***Robert Smithdas*** overcame double handicaps to earn **their** college degrees. [plural pronoun]

Thomas Woodrow Wilson was one of the greatest statesmen of **his** era. [singular, masculine pronoun]

Walt Whitman and ***Emily Dickinson*** are known for **their** poetry. [plural pronoun]

The horseshoe ***crab,*** despite its name, is not a true crab but is related to spiders. [singular, neuter pronoun]

Oysters and ***clams*** are becoming endangered because of oil spills near **their** breeding grounds. [plural pronoun]

Traditionally, a masculine pronoun is used when the gender of the antecedent is not known or may be either masculine or feminine.

An ***author*** must capture **his** readers' interest.

If you do not wish to use a masculine pronoun when the antecedent may be feminine, you can frequently reword the sentence so that the pronoun is plural or eliminated entirely.

Authors must capture **their** readers' interest.
Authors must capture readers' interest. [no pronoun]

EXERCISE 6 **Making Pronouns and Antecedents Agree.** On your paper complete the following sentences by filling the blank with an appropriate possessive pronoun. Also write the antecedent for each pronoun that you supply.

1. Humanity has always had questions about __________ own surroundings.
2. We continue to wonder about __________ universe.

3. Space travel is one way that people have attempted to answer ________ questions.
4. In 1962 John H. Glenn, Jr. became the first American to pilot ________ spaceship around the earth.
5. On July 20, 1969, astronaut Neil A. Armstrong put ________ left foot on the lunar surface.
6. On April 12, 1981, the first space shuttle blazed ________ way into space.
7. Sally K. Ride made ________ first shuttle flight in 1983.
8. Of course, any spacecraft with a human crew is useless without ________ life-support systems.
9. Astronauts must be able to breathe, eat, drink, and take ________ exercise.
10. We hope that space flight will continue to help us understand more about ________ universe.

Agreement in Person

Personal pronouns must agree with their antecedents in person. Pronouns are in the first, second, and third person. (See Chapter 17.)

Do not use the second-person pronoun *you* to refer to an antecedent in the third person. Either change *you* to an appropriate third-person pronoun, or replace it with a suitable noun.

POOR Pam and Frank are going to visit the Everglades, where you can see storks and alligators.

BETTER Pam and Frank are going to visit the Everglades, where **they** can see storks and alligators.

BETTER Pam and Frank are going to visit the Everglades, where **tourists** can see storks and alligators.

EXERCISE 7 **Making Pronouns and Antecedents Agree in Person.** Rewrite each of the following, eliminating the inappropriate use of *you* by substituting a third-person pronoun or a suitable noun.

1. Contestants in the early Greek Olympics were required to take an oath. You had to promise to train for a ten-month period.
2. My friends are going to Henry Cowell State Park, where you can see redwoods that are several hundred years old.
3. My friends and I like to sit in the first or the last seat in the roller coaster, where you can get a greater thrill on the inclines.
4. Sportscasters have a language of their own. You use ordinary words in extraordinary ways.
5. My family and I enjoy driving through the country in autumn, when you can see the fall foliage.

Agreement with Indefinite Pronoun Antecedents

In general, use a singular personal pronoun when its antecedent is a singular indefinite pronoun, and use a plural personal pronoun when the antecedent is a plural indefinite pronoun. (See page 399 for a list of singular and plural indefinite pronouns.)

Each of the boys must buy his **own** uniform.
Each of the women has **her** own diving equipment.
Many of the students bring **their** lunch to school.

Notice that the plural nouns in the prepositional phrases—*of the boys, of the women*—do not affect the number of the personal pronouns. *His* and *her* are singular because *each,* their antecedent, is singular. In speaking, however, people often use the plural pronoun *their.*

INFORMAL ***Neither*** of the boys bought **their** own uniforms.

Writers traditionally make a masculine pronoun agree with an indefinite antecedent when no gender is specified.

Everyone must buy **his** own uniform.

If you do not want to use a masculine pronoun when the indefinite pronoun may refer to a female, try rewording your sentence. You might substitute a plural indefinite pronoun for the singular one or eliminate the personal pronoun entirely. Although some people use two pronouns, many writers consider such wording awkward.

All must buy **their** own uniforms.
Everyone must buy uniforms. [no pronoun]

EXERCISE 8 **Making Pronouns Agree with Indefinite Pronoun Antecedents.** On your paper supply the missing possessive personal pronoun in each of the following sentences. Then write the antecedent of each pronoun that you supply.

1. Everything in the world is an element or is made up of ______ own unique combination of chemical elements.
2. Each of the elements has ______ own symbol; for instance, H is the symbol for hydrogen, and O is the symbol for oxygen.
3. Both of these elements unite ______ components to form water, or H_2O.
4. Neither the element aluminum nor antimony has as ______ symbol the letter *A.*
5. Several of the elements, such as sulfur and gold, are ancient, and ______ discovery was made centuries ago.

6. Most of the elements are formed naturally, and ____________ presence may be detected in every natural substance on earth.
7. Some of the elements are manufactured by humans, and ____ composition is always radioactive.
8. Many of the elements are metals, and ____________ names include copper, nickel, iron, and tin.
9. One of the elements—radium—owes ____________ discovery to Marie and Pierre Curie.
10. All the students have completed ____________ reports on elements.

Clear Pronoun Reference

Make sure that the antecedent of a pronoun is clear and that a pronoun cannot possibly refer to more than one antecedent.

To correct unclear pronoun reference, either reword the sentence to make the antecedent clear or eliminate the pronoun.

UNCLEAR ANTECEDENT When the tickets slipped between the reports, **they** were lost. [Which word is the antecedent of *they*? Were the tickets or the reports lost?]

CLEAR ANTECEDENT The tickets were lost when **they** slipped between the reports.

NO PRONOUN When the tickets slipped between the reports, the tickets were lost.

NO PRONOUN The lost tickets were beneath the reports.

Do not use the relative pronoun *which* without a clearly stated antecedent.

NO ANTECEDENT Last week our garage burned, **which** started from a kerosene heater. [What started from a kerosene heater? A fire started, but *fire* is not mentioned.]

CLEAR ANTECEDENT Last week a fire, **which** started from a kerosene heater, burned our garage.

EXERCISE 9 **Making Pronoun Reference Clear.** On your paper rewrite each of the following sentences, making sure that all pronoun references are clearly stated.

1. The governor told the mayor that she would win by a landslide.
2. When the mayor thanked the governor, she was happy.
3. When the voters went to the polls, they were noisy.

4. Some citizens charged that the elections had been fixed, which angered the officials.
5. Many judges lost their seats, which was caused by a scandal.
6. The newspapers criticized the judges before they fully understood what had happened.
7. Bill's father was mayor of the city, which gave him considerable social status.
8. When the mayor's name was suddenly tarnished, it led to a loss of prestige.
9. Before the election the local anchor man told the mayor that he was not clear about the issues.
10. The election results pleased the senator, which had been predicted.

REVIEW EXERCISE **Pronoun Usage.** Rewrite each of the following sentences by eliminating any mistakes in the use of pronouns. Each sentence has one error.

1. Sportscasters and us use sports jargon in our everyday speech.
2. Many of our ordinary words change when its meanings are applied to sports.
3. The word *ace* is used in golf, which refers to a hole-in-one.
4. Another one of its' uses refers to a well-placed tennis serve.
5. In baseball, a beanball is a pitch thrown so near a batter's head that your head is in danger of being hit.
6. The pitcher may be removed from the game if the umpire determines that it was intentional.
7. My friends and me are familiar with the word *eagle*.
8. No one was more surprised than me to learn that in golf the word *eagle* means "two strokes under par."
9. Manuel's brother is a tennis pro, which gives him many fans.
10. I know sports, but it was her who first made me especially aware of sports jargon.

Revising Your Writing

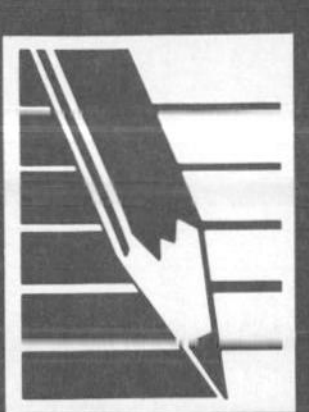

In the following excerpt from *Great Expectations* by Charles Dickens, the narrator, Pip, is discussing two other characters, Mr. Jaggers and Mr. Pocket. Note the many masculine pronouns, and try to discover how Dickens avoids unclear pronoun references.

> My guardian took me into *his* room, and while *he* lunched, standing, from a sandwich-box and a pocket flask of sherry (*he* seemed to bully *his* very sandwich as *he* ate it), informed me what arrangements *he* had made for me. I was to go to "Barnard's Inn," to young Mr. Pocket's rooms, where a bed had been sent in for my accommodation; I was to remain with young Mr. Pocket until Monday; on Monday I was to go with *him* to *his* father's house on a visit, that I might try how I liked it.

If Dickens had written "I was to remain with *him*" instead of "I was to remain with young *Mr. Pocket*," readers might have wondered whether Pip was to remain with his guardian or with Mr. Pocket. Dickens avoided confusion and kept the pronoun references clear by simply referring to Mr. Pocket by name in the middle of the second sentence. When you revise sentences containing many pronouns, pause to make sure that each pronoun has a clear antecedent. If some references are confusing, rephrase the sentence or replace some pronouns with the nouns to which they refer.

Apply these techniques in revising the following passage adapted from *Great Expectations*. Eliminate the confusion by making the unclear pronoun reference clear.

> I found Miss Havisham and Estella; she [was] seated on a settee near the fire, and the other on a cushion at her feet. She was knitting, and Miss Havisham was looking on.

CHAPTER 24

Using Modifiers Correctly

This chapter will discuss how adjectives and adverbs are used to make comparisons. In addition, it will show you how to avoid certain errors in making comparisons and how to correct misplaced and dangling modifiers.

The Three Degrees of Comparison

Most adjectives and adverbs have three degrees: the positive, or base, form; the comparative form; and the superlative form. A modifier in the **positive** degree is the form used as the entry word in the dictionary; it does not make a comparison. A modifier that shows two things being compared is called **comparative.** One that shows three or more things being compared is called **superlative.**

POSITIVE	My cousin is **tall.**
	The cat ran **swiftly.**
COMPARATIVE	My cousin is **taller** than I am.
	My dog ran **more swiftly** than the cat.
SUPERLATIVE	Of the three cousins, Sherry is **tallest.**
	I ran **most swiftly** of all.

The following are rules to guide you in forming the comparative and superlative degrees of adjectives and adverbs.

1. In general, add *-er* to form the comparative and *-est* to form the superlative of modifiers with one syllable.

   green, green**er**, green**est**
   The neighbor's grass always looks **greener.**
   loud, loud**er**, loud**est**
   That sonic boom is the **loudest** noise I've ever heard.

In some cases, there will be spelling changes when you add *-er* and *-est.* (See Chapter 29.)

big, bi**gger**, bi**ggest**   easy, eas**ier**, eas**iest**   true, tru**er**, tru**est**

Sometimes it may sound more natural to use *more* and *most* with some one-syllable modifiers.

just, **more just**, **most** just
Of the three, that judge's ruling was the **most just** of all.

2. Add *-er* to form the comparative and *-est* to form the superlative of most two-syllable adjectives.

ugly, ugl**ier**, ugl**iest**
Your mask is **uglier** than mine.
pretty, prett**ier**, prett**iest**
I think the daisy is the **prettiest** flower of all.

If *-er* and *-est* sound awkward with a two-syllable adjective, use *more* and *most.*

afraid, **more** afraid, **most** afraid
No one is **more afraid** of spiders than I am.

3. Always use *more* and *most* to form the comparative and superlative degrees of adverbs ending in *-ly.*

clearly, **more** clearly, **most** clearly
Max gives directions **more clearly** than most people.
rapidly, **more** rapidly, **most** rapidly
The express bus travels **most rapidly** of all.

4. Always use *more* and *most* to form the comparative and superlative degrees of modifiers of three or more syllables.

attractive, **more** attractive, **most** attractive
I think red looks **more attractive** on you than on me.

5. *Less* and *least,* the opposite of *more* and *most,* can also be used with most modifiers to show comparison.

Are prepared foods **less economical** than fresh foods?
I think cabbage is the **least appetizing** of the vegetables.

Irregular Comparison

A few modifiers form their comparative and superlative degrees irregularly. It is most helpful simply to memorize their forms.

POSITIVE	COMPARATIVE	SUPERLATIVE
good	better	(the) best
well	better	(the) best
bad	worse	(the) worst
badly	worse	(the) worst
ill	worse	(the) worst
far	farther	(the) farthest
far	further	(the) furthest
little (amount)	less	(the) least
many	more	(the) most
much	more	(the) most

EXERCISE 1 **Identifying Degrees of Comparison.** Write the degree of comparison of the italicized modifier in each sentence.

SAMPLE Which planet is *nearest* to the sun?
ANSWER superlative

1. Our solar system is only a *tiny* part of the Milky Way.
2. The planets are *larger* than any other objects, except the sun.
3. Jupiter is the *biggest* planet in our solar system.
4. Venus is *closer* to Earth than Mars is.
5. The *farthest* planet from the sun is Pluto.
6. Mercury is a *small* planet.
7. The early astronomer Kepler gave the *most accurate* description of the motion of the planets.
8. The *most minute* objects in our solar system are drifting particles called "interplanetary dust."
9. Some asteroids—small, planetlike objects—have diameters *greater* than 120 miles.
10. A comet, with its bright head and glowing tail, is one of the *most dazzling* sights you will ever see.

EXERCISE 2 **Making Correct Comparisons.** Complete each sentence with the correct form of the modifier in parentheses.

SAMPLE Attending a concert is ________ than watching one on television. (exciting)
ANSWER more exciting

1. Sue has attended ________ concerts than anyone else. (many)
2. None of my friends can agree as to the ________ group of all. (good)
3. No one group seems to be ________ than any other one. (outstanding)
4. Some groups rise to fame ________ than others. (quickly)
5. Groups that have recorded hit albums go ________ than those who make singles. (far)
6. Of all singing groups the Beatles will probably be remembered as the ________. (successful)
7. Which of the many Beatles' albums was the ________ hit? (big)
8. Several ________ groups have been formed by members of our high school band. (fine)
9. I wish I could learn to play the guitar ________ than the average player. (skillfully)
10. I wonder what it takes to be the ________ group around. (hot)

SENTENCE WRITING **Creating Sentences That Make Comparisons.** Select five of the irregular modifiers from the list on page 535. Write a sentence for each, using the positive and comparative degrees of the modifier. Underline your modifiers.

SAMPLE little

ANSWER Add just a <u>little</u> salt to the water, even <u>less</u> than a teaspoonful.

Double Comparisons

Do not make a double comparison by using both *-er* or *-est* and *more* or *most*.

INCORRECT A redwood grows more taller than an oak.

CORRECT A redwood grows taller than an oak.

EXERCISE 3 **Correcting Double Comparisons.** Rewrite each of the following sentences, correcting the double comparison.

1. Thomas Alva Edison was the world's most best inventors.
2. Some consider him even more greater than Leonardo da Vinci.
3. The phonograph and the electric light are probably his most usefulest creations.
4. Edison was most happiest with his phonograph.
5. But he was most proudest of his work on the electric light.
6. Electric light is certainly more safer than candlelight.
7. Edison also took others' inventions such as the telephone and the typewriter, and made them more better.
8. As a boy Edison was more curiouser than other children.
9. He worked more harder and longer than his peers.
10. Historians agree that Edison was one of the most fruitfulest inventors of modern times.

Incomplete Comparisons

Do not make an incomplete or unclear comparison by omitting *other* or *else* when you compare one member of a group to the other.

UNCLEAR Mercury is closer to the sun than any planet.
CLEAR Mercury is closer to the sun than any **other** planet.

UNCLEAR My aunt has more pets than anyone.
CLEAR My aunt has more pets than anyone **else.**

UNCLEAR The hummingbird beats its wings faster than all birds.
CLEAR The hummingbird beats its wings faster than all other birds.

Be sure your comparisons are between like things.

UNCLEAR The horsepower of a motorcycle is greater than a moped. [The horsepower of one vehicle is being compared illogically to a whole vehicle.]
CLEAR The horsepower of a motorcycle is greater than a **moped's.** [The word *horsepower* is understood after *moped's.*]
CLEAR The horsepower of a motorcycle is greater than **that of a moped.**

UNCLEAR The grace of a basketball player is more obvious than a baseball player. [The grace of a basketball player is being compared illogically to everything about a baseball player.]
CLEAR The grace of a basketball player is more obvious than a **baseball player's.**
CLEAR The grace of a basketball player is more obvious than **that of a baseball player.**

EXERCISE 4 **Making Complete Comparisons.** Rewrite each of the following sentences to correct the incomplete comparison.

1. The blue whale is larger than any animal in the world.
2. A stork's legs are considerably longer than a robin.
3. The song of a wood thrush is prettier than any other bird.
4. When we were vacationing at the beach, I saw more seals than anyone.
5. The bee hummingbird is smaller than any bird.
6. The ear of the African elephant is larger than any other animal.
7. The Australian cassowary, with its powerful legs and knifelike claws, is more dangerous than any bird.
8. The life span of the sturgeon—fifty years—is much longer than a minnow.
9. The cheetah runs faster than any land animal.
10. The speed of the duck hawk in flight, however, is nearly three times the cheetah.

Good or *Well*; *Bad* or *Badly*

Always use *good* as an adjective. *Well* may be used as an adverb of manner telling how ably something was done or as an adjective meaning "in good health."

Blue is a **good** color for you. [adjective]

You look **good** in blue. [adjective after linking verb]

You dress **well**. [adverb of manner]

Aren't you feeling **well?** [adjective meaning "in good health"]

Always use *bad* as an adjective. Therefore, *bad* is used after linking verbs. Use *badly* as an adverb. *Badly* almost always follows action verbs.

That was a **bad** idea. [adjective]

The milk tasted **bad.** [adjective following linking verb]

I feel **bad** about your moving to another state. [adjective following linking verb]

The faucet is leaking **badly**. [adverb following action verb]

EXERCISE 5 **Choosing the Correct Modifier.** On your paper complete the following sentences correctly by filling the blank with either *good, well, bad,* or *badly*.

1. No one can hike ____________ without comfortable hiking shoes.
2. Improper equipment can make a hiker or camper feel ____________.
3. ____________ planning is a very important part of a long hike.
4. A hike that is ____________ planned will not be enjoyable and may be unpleasant.
5. A ____________ trail is just as important as good planning for a successful hike.
6. A hiker who is not feeling ____________ can become a serious problem on the trail.
7. Hikers feel ____________ if they cannot keep up with their companions.
8. If a hike begins ____________, the hikers may become discouraged and decide to turn back.
9. Hikers can get a ____________ view from many places along the Appalachian Trail.
10. Hikers should know ____________ their capabilities before they start off on an ambitious hike.

Double Negatives

In general do not use a **double negative,** two negative words in the same clause. Use only one negative word to express a negative idea.

INCORRECT I don't have no stereo equipment.
CORRECT I do**n't** have **any** stereo equipment.

INCORRECT We haven't seen no concerts this year.
CORRECT We have**n't** seen **any** concerts this year.
CORRECT We have seen **no** concerts this year.

INCORRECT My parrot never says nothing.
CORRECT My parrot **never** says **anything.**
CORRECT My parrot says **nothing.**

EXERCISE 6 **Avoiding Double Negatives.** On your paper rewrite each of the following sentences, eliminating the double negative.

1. Most hikers and campers never have to worry about no dangerous bears.
2. Under normal circumstances bears will not attack no person who is hiking.
3. Never approach no mother bear that is with her cubs.
4. Park rangers do not want to discourage no backpackers from hiking into wilderness areas.
5. Campers can avoid attracting bears by never leaving no food lying around their campsite.
6. On a camping trip, children should never handle no axes or knives.
7. Campers should not touch no poison ivy, poison oak, or poison sumac.
8. In the event of lightning, don't stand under no tall trees.
9. If you get lost at night, you shouldn't do nothing until dawn.
10. Noisy campers do not have no respect for animals.

Misplaced and Dangling Modifiers

Place modifiers as close as possible to the words they modify in order to make the meaning of the sentence clear.

Misplaced modifiers modify the wrong word or seem to modify more than one word in a sentence. To correct a sentence with a misplaced modifier, move the modifier as close as possible to the word it modifies. Study the examples on the following page.

MISPLACED I took a photograph **in flight** of a rare ivory-billed woodpecker. [prepositional phrase]

CLEAR I took a photograph of a rare ivory-billed woodpecker **in flight.**

MISPLACED I took this photograph of a woodpecker **using high-speed film.** [participial phrase]

CLEAR **Using high-speed film**, I took this photograph of a woodpecker.

Dangling modifiers seem to modify no word at all. To correct a sentence with a dangling modifier, you must supply a word the dangling phrase can sensibly modify.

DANGLING **Working all night long**, the warehouse fire was extinguished. [participial phrase]

CLEAR **Working all night long**, fire fighters extinguished the warehouse fire.

DANGLING Sleeping soundly, the raucous alarm startled me into consciousness. [participial phrase]

CLEAR Sleeping soundly, I sprang into consciousness at the sound of the raucous alarm.

Be sure to place the modifier *only* close to the word you wish it to modify, or the meaning of your sentence may be unclear.

UNCLEAR Mike **only** has art on Wednesday. [Does he have only one class on Wednesday or no class on any day but Wednesday? Or is Mike the only person (in a group) who has one class on Wednesday?]

CLEAR Mike has **only** art on Wednesday. [not any other class]

CLEAR Mike has art **only** on Wednesday. [not on any other day]

EXERCISE 7 **Correcting Misplaced and Dangling Modifiers.** On your paper rewrite the following sentences, correcting the misplaced or dangling modifiers.

1. Walking along the shore, a shell cut my foot.
2. Driving very slowly, a deer suddenly appeared in the road.
3. We ran to the door laughing loudly.
4. Alison only runs two miles in the morning.
5. In the crystal vase, I rearranged the tulips.
6. Howling at the moon, we saw a dog.
7. Smiling into the mirror, his clothes looked wonderful.
8. The secretary ignored the telephone being busy.
9. Sleeping too late, the school bus had already left.
10. Walking out of the theater, the glare blinded her.

REVIEW EXERCISE **Modifiers.** The following paragraph contains ten errors in the use of modifiers. Rewrite the paragraph to correct these errors.

[1]Ted Williams is considered one of the most finest baseball players of all time. [2]At the age of seventeen, the San Diego Padres was the team he joined. [3]By 1939 he was playing good enough to start with the Boston Red Sox. [4]From that time until his retirement in 1960, Ted Williams only played baseball with the Red Sox; he never played for no other team. [5]Williams was one of baseball's all-time most greatest hitters. [6]His batting average was higher than most other players. [7]He hit especially good in 1941, when he had a .406 batting average. [8]Williams did not do so bad in 1942 either. [9]In both 1941 and 1942, he hit more home runs than any player in the league.

Revising Your Writing

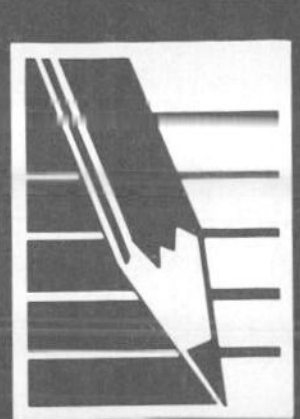

In the following sentence from "The Monkey's Paw" by W. W. Jacobs, notice the position of the participial phrase that modifies the subject *husband*. Is the modifier misplaced?

> But her husband was on his hands and knees *groping wildly on the floor in search of the paw.*

Although the participial phrase is positioned next to "knees," the meaning is clear. It is clear that the husband is groping. In fact, moving the modifier closer to "husband" drains the sentence of much drama.

> But her husband, *groping wildly on the floor in search of the paw*, was on his hands and knees.

Notice that the order of events in this second version is illogical: The husband could not begin groping until he was on his hands and knees. When you write and revise, keep these guidelines in mind.

1. Check to see if moving a participial phrase to another part of the sentence will make your meaning clearer. You may find that you sometimes have more than one option.
2. Remember that participles used as verbals not only modify but also convey action. Do not obscure the order of events in a sentence by positioning a participle or participial phrase awkwardly.

Revise the following sentences adapted from "The Monkey's Paw." They have been rearranged so that a participial phrase is misplaced or positioned illogically. Find the best position for each modifier.

1. He took the paw and suddenly threw it upon the fire, dangling it between his front finger and thumb.
2. Placing chairs, Mr. White dropped [the paw] back into his pocket and motioned his friend to the table.

CHAPTER 25

Glossary of Specific Usage Items

The glossary that follows presents some particularly troublesome matters of preferred usage. The glossary will give you guidance, for example, in choosing between two words that are often confused. It will also make you aware of certain words and expressions that you should avoid when speaking or writing for school or business purposes.

a, an Use the article *a* when the word that follows begins with a consonant sound, including a sounded *h: a poem, a house*. Use *an* when the word that follows begins with a vowel sound or an unsounded *h: an apple, an heirloom*. Use *a* before a word that begins with the "yew" sound: *a European, a unit.*

a lot, alot This expression is always written as two words and means "a large amount." Some authorities suggest avoiding it altogether in formal English.

> **A lot** of snow fell last night.

a while, awhile *A while* is made up of an article and a noun. *In* and *for* often come before *a while,* forming a prepositional phrase. *Awhile* is an adverb.

> We'll stop in **a while**.
> We'll stop for **a while**.
> We'll stop **awhile** before hiking to the top.

accept, except *Accept* is a verb that means "to receive" or "to agree to." *Except* is a preposition or a verb. As a preposition it means "but."

> Eric will **accept** the trophy for the team.
> Everyone will be at the ceremony **except** the captain.

affect, effect Although *affect* and *effect* sound nearly the same, they should not be confused. *Affect* is a verb that means "to cause a change in, to influence." *Effect* may be a noun or a verb. As a noun it means "result." As a verb it means "to bring about or accomplish."

> The mayor's policies have **affected** every city agency.
>
> The mayor's policies have had a good **effect** on every agency. [noun meaning "result"]
>
> The mayor has been able to **effect** his efficiency goals in every city agency. [verb meaning "bring about"]

ain't *Ain't* is unacceptable in speaking and in writing unless you are quoting somebody's exact words. Instead use *I am not, she is not, he is not,* and so on.

all ready, already The two words *all ready* should not be confused with the adverb *already. All ready* means "completely ready." *Already* means "before or by this time."

> The band was **all ready** to play its last number, but the fans were **already** leaving the stadium.

all right, alright Write this expression as two words. Although often seen in print as one word, most authorities prefer *all right.*

> She was sick yesterday, but today she feels **all right.**

all the farther, all the faster These are regional expressions. Use *as far as* and *as fast as* in writing.

> Many jets can travel **as fast as** the speed of sound.
> We drove **as far as** western Illinois.

all together, altogether Use *all together* to mean "in a group." Use the adverb *altogether* to mean "completely" or "on the whole."

> For the holidays, our family will be **all together** at my grandmother's house.
>
> My grandmother is **altogether** delighted to have us with her.

EXERCISE 1 **Making Usage Choices.** For each of the following sentences, identify and write the correct choice of the two expressions in parentheses.

1. San Francisco is in the heart of (a/an) section of California known as the Bay Area.
2. There are (a lot/alot) of people of Chinese ancestry in San Francisco.
3. At first the Chinese who came to San Francisco lived (all together/altogether) in one section of the city, called Chinatown.
4. There (ain't/is not) another Chinese community outside Asia as large as San Francisco's Chinatown.
5. When gold was discovered in California in 1848, miners seeking their fortunes traveled there (all the faster/as fast as) possible.
6. Although most of these miners found no gold, some of them discovered that living in a mild climate as ranchers or farmers was quite (all right/alright).
7. In 1850 Congress voted to (accept/except) California as the country's thirty-first state.

8. The earthquake and fire of 1906 had a disastrous (affect/effect) on San Francisco.
9. The city recovered quickly, however, and by 1916 San Francisco was (all ready/already) for a major exposition.
10. Visitors to San Francisco often rest (a while/awhile) on Telegraph Hill, enjoying the view of the city and the bay.

amount, number *Amount* and *number* both refer to quantity. Use *amount* when referring to nouns that cannot be counted. Use *number* when referring to nouns that can be counted.

Fort Knox contains a vast **amount** of gold.
Fort Knox contains a large **number** of gold bars.

bad, badly See Chapter 24.

being as, being that These expressions are sometimes used instead of *because* or *since* in informal conversation. In formal speaking and writing always use *because* or *since.*

Because their car broke down, they could not get here.
Since they did not call, we assumed they were not coming.

beside, besides These are different words, so use each of them carefully. *Beside* means "at the side of." *Besides* means "in addition to."

Melanie sat **beside** her mother at the table.
Besides yogurt and fruit, they had homemade muffins.

between, among Use *between* with two persons or things, or use it to compare one person or thing to other persons or things. *Between* may also be used with more than two persons or things when they are considered in a close relationship.

What is the difference **between** Seattle and Portland?
What was the difference **between** Pavlova and other ballet dancers?
The treaty **between** the four nations was signed.

Use *among* with groups of three or more.

The committee members were arguing **among** themselves.
This anthropologist has lived **among** the Quechua Indians.

borrow, lend, loan *Borrow* and *lend* have opposite meanings. *Borrow* is a verb meaning "to take something with the understanding that it must be returned." *Lend* is a verb meaning "to give something with the understanding that it will be returned." *Loan* is a noun. It may be used as a verb, but most authorities prefer *lend.*

May I **borrow** ten dollars till payday? [verb]
Will you **lend** me some money? [verb]
Did the bank give you a **loan?** [noun]

bring, take Use *bring* to mean "to carry to" or "to come with." Use *take* to mean "to carry with" or "to go with." *Bring* is related to *come* as *take* is to *go*.

Will you **bring** me some perfume when you come back from Paris?

Don't forget to **take** your passport when you go to Europe.

can, may *Can* indicates the ability to do something. *May* expresses permission to do something.

You **may** have a cup of hot chocolate before going to sleep.

You **can** make hot chocolate by dissolving cocoa and sugar in warm milk.

can't hardly, can't scarcely These terms are considered double negatives because *hardly* and *scarcely* by themselves have a negative meaning. Therefore, avoid using *hardly* and *scarcely* with *not* or *n't*.

Jim **can hardly** tell the twins apart.

The driver **can scarcely** see through the dense fog.

could of, might of, must of, should of, would of After *could, might, must, should,* or *would,* you need another verb form, not the preposition *of*. Use the helping verb *have* after *could, might, must, should,* or *would*.

Some historians say that the United States **could have** prevented the stock market crash of 1929.

The country **might have** avoided the Great Depression that followed.

EXERCISE 2 **Making Usage Choices.** For each of the following sentences, identify and write the correct choice of the two expressions in parentheses.

1. The Missouri River flows (between/among) Kansas City, Missouri, and Kansas City, Kansas.
2. If you look at a map, you (can/may) see that the Missouri River forms part of the boundary between Kansas and Missouri.
3. (Being as/Because) it is located on a river, Kansas City began as an important trading center for fur trappers.
4. A large (amount/number) of pioneers set out from Kansas City on the Oregon or Santa Fe trails.
5. In those days, a visitor to Kansas City (could of/could have) met Native Americans of several different tribes.
6. Today many towns in the area have names (borrowed/loaned) from Native American languages.
7. Be sure to (bring/take) a camera if you visit Old Shawnee, a fascinating replica of a Native American town near Kansas City.

8. One (can scarcely/can't scarcely) exaggerate the importance of Kansas City to the economy of the Midwest.
9. (Beside/Besides) being an important industrial area, Kansas City has huge grain elevators that store large quantities of wheat.
10. In recent years, Kansas City has carried out a large urban renewal program to rebuild areas that were run down (bad/badly).

different from Use *different from* before a noun or a pronoun.

Cross-country skiing is very **different from** downhill skiing.

doesn't, don't These are different contractions. *Doesn't* is a shorter form of *does not,* which is used with *he, she, it,* and singular nouns. *Don't* is a shorter form of *do not,* which is used with *I, you, we, they,* and plural nouns. Authorities usually discourage the use of contractions in formal writing situations.

The United States **doesn't** allow people to leave school before the age of sixteen.

Some foreign countries **don't** require their citizens to attend school.

emigrate, immigrate Use *emigrate* to mean "to go from one country to another to live." Use *immigrate* to mean "to come to a country to settle there." Use *from* with *emigrate* and *to* or *into* with *immigrate*.

Mr. Oh **emigrated** from South Korea.
He **immigrated** to the United States.

farther, further *Farther* should be used in reference to physical distance. *Further* should be used in reference to degree or time.

San Antonio is **farther** south than Dallas.
She did not question him **further.**

fewer, less Use *fewer* when referring to nouns that can be counted. Use *less* when referring to nouns that cannot be counted. *Less* may also be used with figures that are seen as a single amount or quantity.

Fewer students have enrolled in physics this year.

This year, there is **less** interest in physics among the students.

We traveled from Philadelphia to New York City in **less** than two hours. [Two is treated as a single period of time, not as individual hours.]

It cost **less** than twenty dollars to go by train. [The money is treated as a single sum, not as individual dollars.]

good, well See Chapter 24.

had of Do not use *of* between *had* and a past participle.

I wish **I had received** this information earlier.

hanged, hung *Hanged* and *hung* are the past-tense and past-participle forms of the verb *hang*. Use *hanged* when you mean "to put to death by hanging." Use *hung* in all other instances.

The teacher **hung** the bulletin board above her desk.

The State of New Hampshire **hanged** three convicts between 1900 and 1950.

in, into Use *in* to mean "inside" or "within" and *into* to indicate movement or direction from the outside to a point within. The preposition *in* suggests a fixed location within a particular area or place. The preposition *into* suggests movement within or between locations.

Jeanine was sitting outdoors **in** a lawn chair.
When it got too hot, she went **into** the house.

irregardless, regardless Use *regardless*. The prefix *ir-* and the suffix *-less* both have negative meanings. When used together, they produce a double negative, which is incorrect.

Regardless of what the critics said, I like the movie.

EXERCISE 3 **Making Usage Choices.** For each of the following sentences, identify and write the correct choice of the two expressions in parentheses.

1. During its early history, San Antonio, Texas, was under the control of no (fewer/less) than six different countries.
2. Many people who first settled in San Antonio (emigrated/immigrated) from Spain.
3. The beautiful spanish Mission San José in San Antonio still looks (good/well) after many years.
4. Today visitors to San Antonio (don't/doesn't) want to miss seeing the low, gray walls of the Alamo.
5. To see the Alamo, the site of the famous battle between Texas and Mexico, you must go (in/into) the center of San Antonio.
6. Perhaps if the Texas garrison (had/had of) been larger, it could have withstood the Mexican attack.
7. (Irregardless/Regardless) of their defeat at the Alamo, the Texans went on to win the war against Mexico.
8. The flag of the Independent Republic of Texas (hanged/hung) in buildings in San Antonio from 1836 to 1845.
9. During the 1800s, pioneers flocked to Texas, pushing the frontier (farther/further) west.
10. The modern city of San Antonio is quite different (from/than) the Spanish settlement of years ago.

this kind, these kinds *Kind* is singular. Therefore the singular form *this* or *that* modifies *kind. This* and *that* should also be used with *sort* and *type* (*this type, that type, this sort, that sort*). *Kinds* is plural. Therefore the plural form *these* or *those* modifies *kinds*. Use *these* and *those* with the plural nouns *sorts* and *types*.

> **This kind** of bulb should be used in your lamp.
> **These kinds** of lamps are very attractive.
> **This sort** of food is found in many different cultures.
> **These sorts** of foods are very nutritious.

lay, lie People often confuse these two words in both writing and speaking. *Lay* means "to put" or "to place"; it takes a direct object. *Lie* means "to recline" or "to be positioned"; it never takes an object.

> **Lay** your coat on the bed.
> I am going to **lie** in the sun now.

Problems arise particularly in using the principal parts of these verbs. Notice, for example, that the past tense of *lie* is *lay*.

BASIC FORM	lay	lie
PRESENT PARTICIPLE	laying	lying
PAST FORM	laid	lay
PAST PARTICIPLE	laid	lain

> She **laid** her coat on the bed.
> I **lay** in the sun too long and got sunburned.

learn, teach These words have different meanings. *Learn* means "to receive knowledge," and *teach* means "to give knowledge."

> Jon **learned** to play the piano at age ten.
> Mrs. Carlson **teaches** us American history.

leave, let *Leave* means "to go away," and *let* means "to allow" or "to permit." Some people use the expressions *leave alone* and *let alone* to mean the same thing, but they have different meanings. *Leave alone* means "to go away from," and *let alone* means "to permit to be alone" or "to refrain from disturbing."

> Please **let** me use your dictionary.
> Lisa and Gina were careful not to **leave** the baby alone.
> Kim will not finish her work if you don't **let** her alone!

like, as *Like* is a preposition and introduces a prepositional phrase. *As* is a subordinating conjunction and introduces a subordinate clause. Many authorities say that it is incorrect to use *like* before a clause.

> Phil plays baseball **like** a professional.
> Carol is confident, **as** I am, that everything will go well.

loose, lose Use *loose* to mean "free," "not firmly attached," or "not fitting tightly." Use the verb *lose* when you mean "to have no longer," "to misplace," or "to fail to win."

That ring is so **loose** that you are sure to **lose** it.

passed, past *Passed* is the past-tense and the past participle form of the verb *to pass*. *Past* may be an adjective, a preposition, an adverb, or a noun.

We **passed** your house on the way to school. [verb]

Chris had a cold this **past** week. [adjective]

We drove **past** your house last Sunday. [preposition]

What time did you drive **past**? [adverb]

Rosana's grandmother always tells wonderful stories about her **past**. [noun]

precede, proceed *Precede* means "to go or come before." *Proceed* means "to continue" or "to move along."

Our car **preceded** the parade, as the parade **proceeded** through town.

raise, rise The verb *raise* means "to cause to move upward"; it always takes an object. The verb *rise* means "to go up"; it is an intransitive verb and does not take an object.

Raise your hand if you know the answer.
The rocket will **rise** from the launching pad at 9:01 A.M.

reason is because *Because* means "for the reason that." Therefore do not use *because* after *reason is*. *Reason is because* is repetitive. Use *that* after *reason is,* or simply use *because* alone.

The **reason** I am tired is **that** I did not sleep last night.
I am tired **because** I did not sleep last night.

EXERCISE 4 **Making Usage Choices.** For each of the following sentences, identify and write the correct choice of the two expressions in parentheses.

1. Charleston, the second largest city in South Carolina, (lays/lies) on a peninsula on the Atlantic coast.
2. During colonial days, Charleston was a prosperous city, exporting products (as/like) cotton, indigo, and rice.
3. (This kind/These kinds) of profitable exports made Charleston one of the wealthiest cities in the South.
4. The destruction brought about by the Civil War caused Charleston to (loose/lose) its flourishing export business.

5. After the Civil War, Charleston (preceded/proceeded) to build new factories.
6. Today, tourists visit the historic waterfront to see buildings and other artifacts from the (passed/past).
7. During the annual Festival of Old Homes, residents (leave/let) visitors tour the elegant mansions.
8. Visitors to the Charleston Museum (learn/teach) much about life in colonial America.
9. One reason that many people enjoy Charleston is (because/that) it has a mild climate.
10. The temperature (raises/rises) to an average of 81°F. (27°C.) in summer and falls only to an average of 51°F. (50°C.) in winter.

respectfully, respectively Use these two words carefully. *Respectfully* means "with respect." *Respectively* means "in the order named."

> The audience listened **respectfully** as the poet spoke.
> Phoenix and Phoenixville are, **respectively**, in Arizona and Pennsylvania.

says, said *Says* is the third-person singular of the verb *say*. *Said* is the past tense of *say*. Be careful not to use *says* for *said*.

> At dinner last night Nelson **said** that he wasn't hungry.
> He always **says** that, but he eats everything anyway.

sit, set *Sit* means "to place oneself in a sitting position." *Sit* rarely takes an object. *Set* means "to place" or "to put" and usually takes an object. *Set* may also be an intransitive verb when it is used with *sun* to mean the sun is "going down" or "sinking out of sight." When *set* is used in this way, it does not take an object.

> Grandpa likes to **sit** on the porch.
> Judy **set** the pots on the stove after the sun **set.**

than, then *Than* is a conjunction used to introduce the second element in a comparison; it also shows exception.

> Kay is taller **than** Louise
> Our visitor was none other **than** Uncle Al!

Then is an adverb that means "at that time," "soon afterward," "the time mentioned," "at another time," or "for that reason," "in that case," and "besides."

> My grandmother was a young girl **then.**
> Joanne finished the book and **then** turned out the light.
> By **then**, the party was almost over.
> If it rains, **then** we cannot go.
> I like yogurt, and **then** it's healthier than ice cream.

this here, that there Avoid using *here* and *there* after *this* and *that*. Use only *this* and *that*.

All of us want to read **this** magazine. Have you heard **that** story?

where at Do not use *at* after *where*. **Where** is Valley Forge?

who, whom See Chapter 23.

EXERCISE 5 **Making Usage Choices.** For each of the following sentences, write the correct choice of the two expressions in parentheses.

1. Santa Fe, New Mexico, has more sites of historic interest (than/then) most American cities.
2. Tourists in Santa Fe can explore the narrow, winding streets and (than/then) visit museums that show Native American crafts.
3. In summer, audiences (set/sit) in the open-air theater of the Santa Fe Opera.
4. (This/This here) opera house is one of the most famous in the world.
5. Audiences listen (respectfully/respectively) as some of the world's greatest opera singers perform.
6. Pueblo Indians and Spanish colonists were, (respectfully/respectively), the first groups to reside in the Santa Fe area.
7. Many of the Spaniards (who/whom) first came to this area were searching for fabulous riches.
8. These early Spaniards had heard of a man who (said/says) he had seen seven cities of gold in the area.
9. Santa Fe is the place (where the historic Santa Fe Trail ended/where the historic Santa Fe Trail ended at).
10. (This/This here) trail was used by pioneers traveling west during the 1800s.

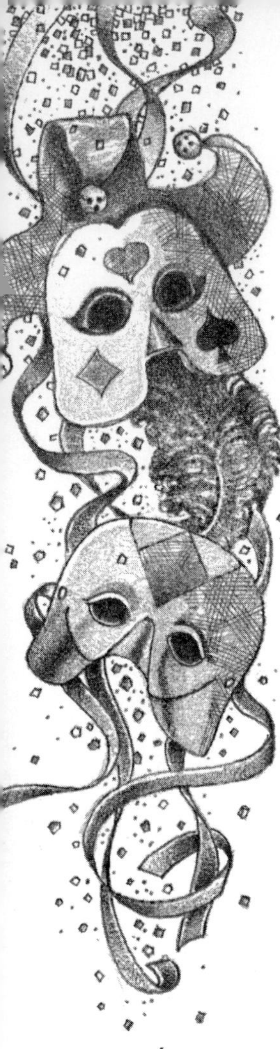

REVIEW EXERCISE **Usage (Part 1).** For each of the following sentences, write the correct choice of the two expressions in parentheses.

1. New Orleans, Louisiana, has (a/an) average elevation of one foot above sea level.
2. (A lot/Alot) of levees were constructed along the banks of the Mississippi River to prevent flooding.
3. The Mississippi River flows through Baton Rouge and then (precedes/proceeds) southeast to New Orleans, where it empties into the Gulf of Mexico.
4. New Orleans (ain't/is not) only a leading shipping center but also a popular city with tourists.
5. (Being that/Because) New Orleans is very picturesque, many people enjoy vacationing there.
6. The temperature in New Orleans (doesn't/don't) drop below freezing very often.
7. French and Spañish colonists (preceded/proceeded) Americans in New Orleans.
8. Many people from Italy (emigrated/immigrated) to New Orleans.
9. In New Orleans restaurants, customers can choose (among/between) French and Creole dishes.
10. Most visitors enjoy strolling through the streets of the historic French Quarter for quite (a while/awhile), taking in the beautiful architecture.
11. No skyscrapers (raise/rise) above the low skyline of the French Quarter.
12. Visitors need walk no (farther/further) than Basin and Bourbon streets to hear jazz.
13. A large (number/amount) of visitors attend concerts at music halls like the famous Preservation Hall.
14. Visitors crowd (in/into) this small hall whenever jazz is being played.
15. In Preservation Hall, fans (set/sit) on wooden benches or stand along the back wall of the room.
16. Here musicians play jazz (like/as) it was played in the early 1900s.
17. This style of jazz is quite different (from/than) modern jazz.
18. By February of each year, the citizens of New Orleans are (all ready/already) to hold their famous Mardi Gras festival.
19. During Mardi Gras the city (can scarcely/can't scarcely) accommodate its many visitors.
20. During this celebration, it is (all right/alright) to dress in elaborate costumes and take part in carnivals and parades.

REVIEW EXERCISE **Usage (Part 2).** For each of the following sentences, write the correct choice of the two expressions in parentheses.

1. Boston is an (all together/altogether) special place.
2. Boston (might have/might of) been the nation's capital if it had been more centrally located.
3. New York City and Philadelphia were, (respectively/respectfully), the first and second capitals of the United States.
4. In 1773, Bostonians, who would not (accept/except) King George III's taxes, dumped many pounds of tea into Boston Harbor.
5. They wanted independence from British taxation (bad/badly).
6. They (set/sit) an example that other colonists soon followed.
7. The city of Boston has (hanged/hung) plaques at historic sites.
8. Beacon Hill, more (than/then) any other area in Boston, is known for its beauty and historic importance.
9. Boston is a very accessible city. The reason is (because/that) it has an efficient transit system.
10. It had the first rapid transit system (in/into) the United States.
11. Several excellent universities (bring/take) many students to Boston.
12. A visitor can tour the Boston Museum of Fine Arts and (then/than) visit the Metropolitan Boston Arts Center.
13. Boston abounds in (this kind/these kinds) of cultural centers.
14. After the Charles River has (passed/past) through Boston, it empties into Boston Harbor.
15. People can picnic in parks (beside/besides) the Charles River.

REVIEW EXERCISE **Usage (Part 3).** For each of the following sentences, write the correct choice of the two expressions in parentheses.

1. Recently, a report (said/says) that Seattle, Washington, is one of America's most attractive cities.
2. (Irregardless/Regardless) of whether or not people choose to live in Seattle, most agree it is a beautiful place.
3. Many tourists (who/whom) the Century 21 Exposition attracted in 1962 later returned to Seattle to live.
4. Seattle is known as the Emerald City, a name (borrowed/loaned) from *The Wizard of Oz*.
5. The city of Seattle (lays/lies) near the Pacific Ocean.
6. (This/This here) location made Seattle a gateway to the Far East.
7. (Between/Among) Seattle's early settlers were Japanese.
8. Other early settlers (emigrated/immigrated) from Scandinavia.
9. The Cascade Mountains (raise/rise) to the east of Seattle.
10. This is the mountain range (where Mount St. Helens is located/where Mount St. Helens is located at).

Review

CHAPTERS 21–25 USAGE

CHAPTER 21 VERB TENSES AND VOICE

Principal Parts of Verbs [pages 494–497]

1. Which of the following items uses the underlined participle correctly to form a complete sentence?
   (a) The steamboat traveling down the Mississippi River.
   (b) The passengers been on the deck for hours.
   (c) Steamboats were docking at Hannibal when Mark Twain was a boy.

Regular and Irregular Verbs [pages 494–497] Which of the following sets of principal parts is correct? (Each set should include the basic form, past form, and past participle.)

2. (a) blow, blowed, blewn (b) bite, bit, bitten (c) fling, flang, flung
   (d) bring, brang, brought (e) give, gave, gave
3. (a) freeze, froze, frozen (b) beat, beated, beat (c) bear, beared, bore (d) drink, drinked, drank (e) see, seen, saw

Tense of Verbs [pages 497–505] Indicate whether the underlined verb in each of the following sentences is (a) present, (b) past, (c) future or future perfect, (d) present perfect, or (e) past perfect.

4. Since the 1950s American poetry has undergone a great change.
5. Beat poets of the 1950s wrote a new type of poetry.
6. Beat poets had attracted national attention by 1956.
7. For many years to come, poetry will display the effect of these poets.

Compatibility of Tenses [pages 506–508]

8. In which of the following sentences are the tenses compatible?
   (a) After years of experimentation, the airplane will have come into commercial use.
   (b) When people first started using airplanes, they are frightened.
   (c) By the year 2000 the airplane will have been in use for nearly a century.

Voice of Verbs [page 508] Indicate whether the verb is (a) in the active voice or (b) in the passive voice.

9. Airplanes have been tested by daring pilots.
10. Airplane crashes are not as common today as in the past.

Writing for Review Write a paragraph relating an incident that happened to you as a child. Be sure to use verbs correctly.

CHAPTER 22 SUBJECT-VERB AGREEMENT

Agreement in Number [pages 510–519] Indicate the verb that agrees with its subject in each of the following sentences.

1. A butterfly or a moth (a) is/(b) are a member of the insect family.
2. There (a) is/(b) are many kinds of moths and butterflies.
3. One of the most common butterflies (a) is/(b) are the monarch.
4. Monarchs apparently have a bitter taste that (a) makes/(b) make birds avoid eating them.
5. A group of monarch butterflies (a) travels/(b) travel for many miles during migration.

Writing for Review Write a short description on a topic of your choice. Demonstrate your mastery of subject–verb agreement by including various compound subjects and intervening phrases.

CHAPTER 23 USING PRONOUNS CORRECTLY

Personal Pronoun Usage [pages 522–526] Indicate the correct case of the personal pronoun in each sentence.

1. Two of the busiest people are my sister and (a) I/(b) me.
2. My sister and (a) I/(b) me started a dog-walking service.
3. The fees are split between the two proprietors of the service, my sister and (a) I/(b) me.
4. A neighbor asked my sister and (a) I/(b) me to walk his dog.
5. The dog was bigger than (a) I/(b) me.

Who* and *Whom [pages 526–527] Indicate the correct case of the pronoun.

6. I wonder (a) who/(b) whom our substitute teacher will be.

Pronoun-Antecedent Agreement [pages 528–529] Indicate the correct pronoun.

7. The newest driver in our fleet of school buses obtained (a) their/(b) her job last week.

Agreement in Person [page 529]

8. In which does the pronoun agree in person with its antecedent?
   (a) A person has to be careful when they cross the street.
   (b) After Bill and Patsy visited Mexico, they studied Spanish.

Agreement with Indefinite Pronoun Antecedents [pages 530–531]

9. Which of the following sentences has correct agreement between pronouns?
   (a) Each of the critics expressed their opinions about the play.
   (b) Both of the critics wrote their articles for the local paper.
   (c) Neither of the critics liked having their words quoted.

Clear Pronoun Reference [pages 531–532]

10. In which sentence is the pronoun reference clear?
    (a) When the reporters met the politicians, they were polite.
    (b) The politicians answered the reporters' questions, which pleased the reporters.
    (c) One politician amused the crowd with a funny anecdote, which was quoted in the newspaper the next day.

Writing for Review Write a paragraph describing what you and your family do on Thanksgiving or another holiday. Include a variety of personal and indefinite pronouns in your paragraph.

CHAPTER 24 USING MODIFIERS CORRECTLY

The Three Degrees of Comparison [pages 534–535] Indicate the correct comparative or superlative form in each sentence.

1. Hydrogen is (a) lighter/(b) more light than oxygen.
2. Of the three books, I liked *Rebecca* (a) better/(b) best.
3. Amanda is the (a) secretivest/(b) most secretive person I know.

Double and Incomplete Comparisons [pages 537–538] Indicate the correct form of the modifier in each sentence.

4. The groceries were (a) heavier/(b) more heavier than I expected.
5. Al eats more than (a) anyone/(b) anyone else I know.
6. The crocuses bloomed earlier than (a) any/(b) any other flowers in my mother's garden.

Double Negatives [page 540] Indicate the correct usage.

7. I have (a) never eaten/(b) eaten nothing as spicy as my uncle Jasper's chicken curry.

Misplaced and Dangling Modifiers [pages 540–542] For each pair indicate the sentence in which modifiers are placed correctly.

8. (a) Watching television, boredom soon set in.
   (b) Watching television, we soon became bored.
9. (a) The mountains with their snowy peaks impressed us.
   (b) The mountains impressed us with their snowy peaks.
10. (a) Working around the clock, the deadline at last was met by the newspaper reporters.
    (b) Working around the clock, the newspaper reporters at last met the deadline.

Writing for Review Write a paragraph in which you compare one thing with another, such as winter with summer. In your paragraph use modifiers to make comparisons.

Preferred Usage [pages 544–555] Indicate the preferred usage of the choices given in each sentence.

1. The baseball game will start in (a) a while/(b) awhile.
2. A misanthrope is a person who exhibits (a) a/(b) an universal dislike of other human beings.
3. The actress (a) adapted/(b) adopted a childlike expression.
4. The toys were divided (a) between/(b) among the four children.
5. (a) A lot/(b) Alot of people visit the Smithsonian Institution.
6. I would like to (a) borrow/(b) lend/(c) loan your book about the history of flight.
7. All the planets (a) accept/(b) except Mercury rotate on an axis.
8. The health code states that workers (a) can/(b) may not wear open-toed shoes in this factory.
9. There were (a) fewer/(b) less questions on this week's current-events quiz than on last week's quiz.
10. The new seatbelt law (a) affects/(b) effects almost everyone.
11. Remember to (a) bring/(b) take your hat with you when you leave the restaurant.
12. The audience is so noisy that I (a) can scarcely/(b) can't scarcely hear the speaker.
13. I never feel comfortable in (a) this/(b) these kind of sandal.
14. The crew of the jumbo jet were (a) all ready/(b) already for the flight.
15. The rock concert was (a) all together/(b) altogether too loud.
16. (a) Being that/(b) Because you were ill, you will need to take a makeup test next Thursday.
17. Bluegrass music is different (a) from/(b) than country music.
18. Doctors now (a) advice/(b) advise their patients to eat less red meat.
19. Cynthia (a) doesn't/(b) don't study hard enough.
20. Maura (a) could have/(b) could of visited Canada last summer, but she decided to take a summer job instead.

Writing for Review Demonstrate your knowledge of the distinction between the words in each of the following pairs by writing a sentence for each word.

emigrate, immigrate	hanged, hung
farther, further	lay, lie

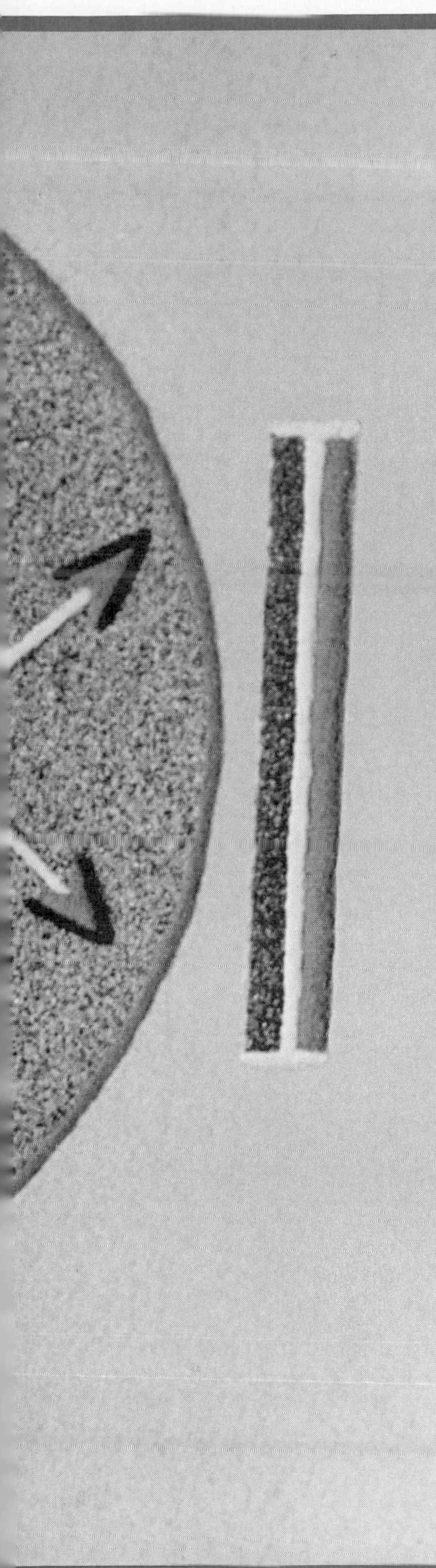

UNIT VIII

Mechanics

Thinking About Thinking: Recognizing a Symbol System

Mechanics—capitalization and punctuation—are part of a system of symbols that you use when you write. For example, this symbol—?—lets you and your reader know that someone is asking a question. These symbols help solve problems that get in the way of absolutely clear communication. In fact, you can think of the mechanics of writing as tools to use as you engage in the thinking process called problem solving.

Defining the Skill

In order to solve problems, it is often necessary to recognize that a symbol, or a whole system of symbols, is being used. For instance, if you see this symbol—÷—you know that one number is to be divided by another number. You can then proceed to solve the problem. If you see this symbol—𝄞—you know how to read the pitch of the notes on the musical staff. In each case, you are using the thinking skill called **RECOGNIZING A SYMBOL SYSTEM**.

Applying the Skill

Look at the photograph of the Native American sand painting. Together with a partner, identify what you think each of the symbols in the picture stands for. What story do you think the picture tells?

CHAPTER 26

Capitalization

Capitalization of Sentences

Capitalize the first word of every sentence, including the first word of a direct quotation that is a complete sentence.

> **O**ne of the first computers was so immense that it could occupy the space of a two-car garage.
>
> Henry Ford said, "**T**hinking is the hardest work there is, which is the probable reason why so few engage in it."

Capitalize the first word of a sentence in parentheses that stands by itself. Do not capitalize a sentence within parentheses that is contained within another sentence.

> Games can be tools for learning about computers. (**M**any programmers think that programming itself is the best game of all.)
>
> They were looking for software (**t**hey hoped to buy no more than three or four programs) that they could use in writing reports.

Do not capitalize the first word of a word group that cannot stand as a complete sentence.

> Astronauts must learn how to use computers, but they say that most astronauts are "**c**omputer users, not computer wizards."

Do not capitalize an indirect quotation. (An *indirect quotation* gives the meaning of an original statement without repeating it word for word. It is often introduced by the word *that.*)

> This letter from a computer camp states that **s**wimming, hiking, and archery will be offered this summer along with computer instruction.

EXERCISE 1 **Capitalizing Sentences.** Rewrite correctly any of the following sentences that have errors in capitalization. Write the word *Correct* if a sentence has no errors.

1. the colonial leader Patrick Henry summed up the American spirit when he said, "give me liberty, or give me death."
2. Margaret Mead (She was an anthropologist) wrote, "Today's children are the first generation to grow up in a world that has the power to destroy itself."
3. Eleanor Roosevelt wrote, "No one can make you feel inferior without your consent."

4. The civil rights leader Dr. Martin Luther King, Jr., wrote that nonviolence is a Powerful weapon. (he described nonviolence as a "sword that heals.")
5. The Russian-born sculptress Louise Nevelson said, "I never liked the middle ground—the most boring place in the world."
6. The Spanish philosopher and statesman José Ortega y Gasset wrote, "living is a constant process of deciding what we are going to do."
7. John F. Kennedy said, "A man may die, nations may rise and fall, but an idea lives on."
8. Albert Einstein wrote that Imagination is more important than knowledge.
9. The abolitionist Frederick Douglass wrote, "if there is no struggle, there is no progress."
10. Marie Curie, the French physicist who codiscovered radium (With her husband) wrote that the "True atmosphere of a laboratory" should be peaceful and meditative.

Capitalization of Proper Nouns

Capitalize a proper noun.

Do not capitalize a common noun unless it is the first word of a sentence.

In reviewing the following sections, remember to capitalize only the important words (excluding articles, coordinating conjunctions, and prepositions of under five letters) in proper nouns composed of several words.

1. Names of individuals

Seiji **O**zawa
Sally **R**ide
Mother **T**eresa
Sequoya
Chris **E**vert **L**loyd
Jesse **J**ackson

2. Titles of individuals

Capitalize titles used before a proper name and titles used in direct address (naming the person or persons to whom one is speaking).

Dr. **H**enry **R**amirez
Princess **D**iana
Bishop **T**utu
Congresswoman **B**ouquard
Chief **S**itting **B**ull
Aye, aye, **C**aptain [direct address]
Senator **D**ole
Prime **M**inister **G**andhi

Capitalize titles used after a proper name and titles that replace a proper name when you wish to show respect or indicate a high official. (For example, when referring to the current president of the United States, always capitalize the title.) Do not capitalize titles used as common nouns to refer to a general class or type.

the Democratic **R**epresentative from Alabama	*but*	the voting records of **r**epresentatives
Joseph, **C**hief of the Nez Percé	*but*	The **c**hiefs met with the President of the United States.

In general, capitalize the title of a family relationship used with or in place of a proper name. Do not capitalize the title if a possessive is used before it (unless it is considered part of the name).

Did you call **A**unt Flora? Please ask **G**randfather.	*but*	my **a**unt's travels your **g**randfather's business
What did you say, **M**other?	*and*	Quietly **M**other spoke.

3. Names of ethnic groups, national groups, and languages

Native **A**mericans	**M**exicans	**S**wahili
Laotians	**I**talian	**J**apanese

4. Organizations, institutions, political parties and their members, and firms

Food and **D**rug **A**dministration
Bank of **A**merica
the **C**ongress
the **D**emocratic party
a **R**epublican
Utah **S**tate **U**niversity

The word *party* is not capitalized. Do not capitalize common nouns such as court or university unless they are part of a proper noun.

She was appointed a judge of the **F**irst **D**istrict **C**ourt.
Mr. Tavares was a witness in **t**raffic **c**ourt.

5. Monuments, bridges, and buildings

Eiffel **T**ower
Vietnam **M**emorial
World **T**rade **C**enter
George **W**ashington **B**ridge
the **P**arthenon

6. **Trade names**

Chevrolet
Kleenex
Cheerios
Friskies cat food

7. **Documents, awards, and laws**

a Grammy
Fifth Amendment
Emancipation Proclamation
Pulitzer Prize
Bill of Rights
the Constitution

8. **Geographical terms**

Capitalize the name of continents, countries, states, counties, and cities, as well as specific bodies of water, topographical features, regions, and streets.

Orient
Times Square
Atlantic Ocean
Rio Grande
Middle East
Washington State
New England
Grand Avenue
Mississippi River
St. Louis
Tropic of Capricorn
Cape Cod
Lake Huron
Southern Hemisphere

9. **Planets and other heavenly bodies**

Pluto
Mars
the constellation Andromeda
North Star

Do not capitalize the words *sun* and *moon*. *Earth* is capitalized only when it is used in conjunction with the names of the other planets. It is never capitalized when used with the definite article *the*.

Venus and Mars are Earth's closest planetary neighbors.
The astronauts took many photographs of the earth.

10. **Compass points**

Capitalize the words *north, east, south,* and *west* when they refer to a specific area of the country or of the world or when they are part of a proper name. Do not capitalize them when they merely indicate direction.

the North	*but*	northern Portugal
the West Coast		the west coast of Oregon
South Pacific		south Maine

11. **Ships, planes, trains, and spacecraft**

Santa Maria
Columbia
Spirit of St. Louis
Yankee Clipper

12. Historical events, eras, and calendar items

Reconstruction	**L**abor **D**ay
Middle **A**ges	**I**ndustrial **R**evolution

Do not capitalize a historical period when it refers to a general span of time:

the twenties
the tenth century

Capitalize the days of the week and the months of the year, but do not capitalize the names of the seasons (*spring, summer, autumn, fall, winter*).

13. Religious terms

Capitalize names of deities, religions, denominations, and their adherents, words referring to a supreme deity, and religious books and events.

Christianity	**R**ussian **O**rthodox
Muslims	**P**rotestants
New **T**estament	**J**ews
Koran	**H**anukkah

14. School courses

Capitalize only those school courses that are the name of a language or the title of a specific course rather than the general name of a subject.

Spanish	*but*	**g**eometry
The **R**enaissance		**h**istory
Music 101		**m**usic

15. Titles of works

the ***O**dyssey*
"**T**he **G**ift of the **M**agi"
the ***L**os **A**ngeles **T**imes*
"**H**ome on the **R**ange"

Capitalize articles (*a, an,* and *the*) at the beginning of a title only when they are part of the title itself. It is preferred practice not to capitalize (nor to italicize) articles preceding the title of a newspaper or a periodical. In general, do not capitalize (or italicize) the word *magazine* following the title of a periodical.

"**T**he Fifty-First Dragon"	*but*	**t**he *Christian Science Monitor*
"**A** Marriage Proposal"		They read *Newsweek* **m**agazine.

EXERCISE 2 **Capitalizing Proper Nouns.** Rewrite the following sentences correctly, adding or dropping capital letters as necessary.

1. Early in the Seventeenth Century king george I of England gave the London company the right to settle in north america.
2. The settlers, among them captain John Smith, set sail in the Company's ships, the *godspeed,* the *discovery,* and the *sarah constant.*
3. After crossing the atlantic ocean, the Settlers established jamestown, Virginia, the first permanent British settlement on this Continent.
4. In 1619 a ship owned by holland brought the first africans to the English Colonies in america.
5. The pilgrims, a group of English puritans who disagreed with the church of england, landed North of Virginia at cape cod in 1620.
6. A member of the pawtuxet tribe named squanto helped the pilgrims survive their first Winter in the Settlement named plymouth.
7. In 1682 william penn and a group of quakers (members of the Society of friends) established the City of Philadelphia on the Delaware river.
8. In philadelphia people of all Religions were allowed to worship god and interpret the bible in their own way.
9. The Boston post road, which ran North from New York city to Boston, was completed in 1672.
10. In 1704 the first successful colonial newspaper, the *boston newsletter,* began publication.

Capitalization of Proper Adjectives

Capitalize proper adjectives (adjectives formed from proper nouns).

Most proper adjectives fit into the following categories:

1. **Adjectives formed from names of people**

   Napoleonic era
   Victorian customs
   Jacksonian ideals
   Marxist revolutionary

2. **Adjectives formed from place names and names of national, ethnic, and religious groups**

   Buddhist temple
   Chinese acupuncture
   African languages
   Hispanic studies
   Israeli dances
   Parisian accent

Many proper nouns do not undergo a change in form when used as an adjective.

United Nations calendar
New Orleans cooking
Suzuki recital
Passover meal

EXERCISE 3 **Capitalizing Proper Adjectives and Proper Nouns.** Rewrite the following sentences correctly, adding or dropping capital letters as necessary.

1. In 1790 the new american Government faced a huge debt as a result of the revolutionary war.
2. alexander hamilton wanted the Government to help settle the immense War Debt, but thomas jefferson disagreed with him.
3. Many Citizens in the north supported hamilton, who wanted to tax european and american products.
4. The jeffersonians (Supporters of Jefferson) did not want the Government to be involved in paying off the Debt.
5. Many of jefferson's Followers were southerners who wanted the National Capital moved farther South than new york city.
6. The Leaders of Congress approved hamilton's financial plans and agreed to move the Capital to washington, d.c., a city in the south.
7. When france went to war against great britain and spain in 1793, jefferson wanted to side with the french.
8. Hamilton wanted the united states government to support the british and the spanish.

9. The disagreements between these two renowned Statesmen eventually led to the formation of two opposing american Political Parties, forerunners of today's democrats and republicans.
10. The people who supported hamilton were called federalists, whereas jefferson and his supporters were known by the name democratic-republicans.

SUMMARY OF CAPITALIZATION RULES

CAPITALIZE	DO NOT CAPITALIZE
She gave us thirty pages of reading for homework. (**S**he said that we needed to do it.)	For homework (**s**he said we needed to catch up) she gave us thirty pages of reading.
He said, "**L**et me do those dishes."	He said that **h**e would do the dishes.
Father Time	My **f**ather wants to retire.
Captain **A**hab	The **c**aptain paced the deck.
Texas **S**tate **U**niversity	a **u**niversity in Texas
Lawrence **H**all of **S**cience	the **s**cience **m**useum in town
Prell shampoo; **I**vory **s**oap	Bring **s**oap and **s**hampoo.
Bill of **R**ights	an animal **b**ill of **r**ights
Pacific **O**cean; **G**hiradelli **S**quare; **S**anta **C**lara **A**venue	the **s**quare where the two **a**venues meet near the **o**cean
Neptune; **M**ercury; **E**arth	**s**un; **p**lanets; the **e**arth
the **K**orean **W**ar	Wage peace, not **w**ar.
Old **T**estament; **H**alloween	sacred **b**ook; **h**olidays
Russian; **E**nglish **L**iterature I	foreign **l**anguage; **l**iterature

SENTENCE WRITING **Creating Sentences with Capitalized Words.** (a) Write a sentence in which you include a quotation by a famous author. Be sure to mention the author's name. (b) Revise your first sentence by adding the nationality of the author. (c) Write a third sentence including the name of the work in which you originally found the quotation.

SAMPLE ANSWER (a) J. R. R. Tolkien wrote, "In a hole in the ground there lived a hobbit."

(b) The English author J. R. R. Tolkien wrote, "In a hole in the ground there lived a hobbit."

(c) The English author J. R. R. Tolkien began *The Hobbit* with these words: "In a hole in the ground there lived a hobbit."

REVIEW EXERCISE **Capitalization.** Write the letter of the one item that is correctly capitalized in each of the following pairs.

1. (a) James Baldwin wrote, "one cannot deny the humanity of another without diminishing one's own."
   (b) James Baldwin wrote, "One cannot deny the humanity of another without diminishing one's own."
2. (a) university of California
   (b) University of California
3. (a) General George Patton
   (b) general George Patton
4. (a) The English stage actress Rachel Kempson is the mother of Vanessa and Lynn Redgrave.
   (b) The English stage actress Rachel Kempson is the Mother of Vanessa and Lynn Redgrave.
5. (a) Georgia O'Keeffe's painting *New York night* is done mostly in dark colors.
   (b) Georgia O'Keeffe's painting *New York Night* is done mostly in dark colors.
6. (a) *A Raisin In The Sun*
   (b) *A Raisin in the Sun*
7. (a) European History I and physics
   (b) European History I and Physics
8. (a) a Buddhist temple
   (b) a buddhist temple
9. (a) But thy eternal summer shall not fade.
   (b) But thy eternal Summer shall not fade.
10. (a) West of the Colorado River
    (b) west of the Colorado River

CHAPTER 27

Punctuation, Abbreviations, and Numbers

Period

Use a period at the end of a declarative sentence and at the end of a polite command.

DECLARATIVE SENTENCE Track practice is held twice a week after school.
POLITE COMMAND Please sign up for two track events.

Exclamation Point

Use an exclamation point to show strong feeling and to indicate a forceful command.

Oh, no!
How polite you are!
What lovely weather!
Wake up!

Question Mark

Use a question mark to indicate a direct question.

Who would like a part-time job?
Which call should I answer first?

Do not place a question mark after an indirect question (one that is reworded as part of a statement).

The teacher asked whether anyone would like a part-time job.
He asked if I needed a work permit.

In general, do not place a question mark after a polite request.

Will you line up at the door.

EXERCISE 1 **Using End Punctuation.** Rewrite the following sentences correctly, adding periods, exclamation points, and question marks where they are needed.

1. Don't you think that everyone should learn about first aid
2. First aid is the immediate medical care given to an ill or injured person
3. Oh, if only people realized the importance of first aid So many lives could be saved

4. An instruction manual by John S. Kelly published by the U.S. Bureau of Mines has good information about first aid Will you get it from the library
5. The primary goals of first aid are to treat serious injuries, prevent infection, and make the injured or ill person as comfortable as possible
6. If you come upon an injured person, try to send for medical help right away Don't panic Try to stay calm
7. Are you the person best qualified to take charge If two of you know first aid, decide which one has the most experience and training The other one can assist
8. If people are crowding the injured person, make them stand at a distance
9. Once you have sent for help and the patient is lying still, ask yourself which injuries require immediate attention
10. Because an injured person may have broken bones or internal injuries, move someone only if it is absolutely necessary

Colon

COLONS TO INTRODUCE

1. Lists

Use a colon to introduce a list, especially after a statement that uses such words as *these, the following,* or *as follows.*

> The science test on Friday will cover these areas: the circulatory system, the digestive system, and the nervous system.
>
> To get to my house, follow these directions: (1) Drive north on Ashby Avenue. (2) After you pass the Claremont Hotel, take the first left, which will be Tunnel Road. (3) At the second stop sign, turn right onto Peralta Road. (4) Look for 248 Peralta, a brown shingled house with an oak tree in front of it.

Do not use a colon to introduce a list if the list immediately follows a verb or a preposition.

> The best nonanimal sources of protein are soybeans, wheat germ, brewer's yeast, nuts, seeds, and whole grains. [The list follows the verb *are.*]

2. Illustrations or restatements

Use a colon to introduce material that illustrates, explains, or restates the preceding material.

> I often wish that my parents had had more than one child: They worry too much about me.

COLONS BEFORE QUOTATIONS

Use a colon to introduce a long or a formal quotation. A formal quotation is often preceded by such words as *these, the following,* or *as follows.*

> Mrs. Hopkins asked the class to write an essay on the following traditional saying from the Hausa tribe of Africa: "It is the rainy season that gives wealth."

Poetry quotations of more than one line and prose quotations of more than several lines are generally written below the introductory statement (and indented on the page).

> In his long poem "The Other Pioneers" Roberto Felix Salazar writes:
>
> Now I must write
> Of those of mine who rode these plains
> Long years before the Saxon and the Irish came.
> Of those who plowed the land and built the towns
> And gave the towns soft-woven Spanish names.

OTHER USES OF COLONS

Use a colon between the hour and the minute in writing the time, between the chapter and the verse in making biblical references, and after the salutation of a business letter.

12:30 A.M.	Genesis 7:20–24	Sir:
4:00 P.M.	Ruth 1:16–18	Dear Ms. Snow:

EXERCISE 2 **Using the Colon.** Rewrite the following sentences correctly, adding colons where they are needed. For the sentence that does not need a colon, write *Correct.* Remember, colons are not needed when a list immediately follows a verb or a preposition.

1. Many people enjoy playing board games chess, checkers, and pachisi.
2. Chess may have spread from area to area in the following order India, Persia, and Spain.
3. There are several board games related to chess checkers, the Japanese game *go,* and Chinese checkers.
4. In chess each player has the following playing pieces one king, one queen, two bishops, two knights, two rooks, and eight pawns.
5. The qualities essential to a good chess player are a good memory, a quick mind, and foresight.
6. A chess army is in some ways like a real army It contains different types of "people" who do different jobs.

7. The *Encyclopaedia Britannica* notes that chess players use strategies of attack and defense aimed at the surrender of the opponent's king. The encyclopedia continues as follows "Nevertheless, the game is only a rather limited simulation of war or, in Freudian terms, a sublimation of that aggressive impulse."
8. The Old Testament has the following to say about war

    They shall beat their swords into plowshares
    and their spears into pruning-hooks:
    nation shall not lift up sword against nation,
    neither shall they learn war anymore.

    —Isaiah 2:4

9. A regional chess tournament typically takes place on a three-day weekend, with two rounds at the following times each day round 1 occurs from 11 00 A.M. to 1 00 P.M. and round 2 from 5 P.M. to 7 30 P.M.
10. In addition to the type of chess that most people play, here are some other types blindfold chess, lightning chess, postal chess, and computer chess.

Semicolon

SEMICOLON TO SEPARATE MAIN CLAUSES

Use a semicolon to separate main clauses that are not joined by the coordinating conjunctions *and, but, or, nor, yet,* and *for.*

> Nolan Bushnell worked his way through college by managing the midway games at an amusement park, **and** he has made and lost millions of dollars as the founder of Atari and Pizza Time Theaters.
>
> Nolan Bushnell worked his way through college by managing the midway games at an amusement park; he has made and lost millions of dollars as the founder of Atari and Pizza Time Theaters.

Use a semicolon to separate main clauses joined by a conjunctive adverb (such as *however, therefore, nevertheless, moreover, furthermore,* and *consequently*) or by an expression such as *for example* or *that is.*

In general, a conjunctive adverb or an expression such as *for example* is followed by a comma.

> Bushnell says that he wants to use technology to do "fun" things; for example, he wants to develop a robot that can be a combination household "pet" and servant.
>
> The video game industry seems to have collapsed; however, computer games have continued to grow in popularity.

SEMICOLONS AND COMMAS

Use a semicolon to separate the items in a series when these items contain commas.

> Some of the powerful African kingdoms that flourished before the sixteenth century were Kush, which dominated the eastern Sudan; Karanga, which was located around Zimbabwe in southern Africa; Ghana, Mali, and Songhai, which successively commanded the Niger River in West Africa; and Benin, which had its center in what is now Nigeria.

Use a semicolon to separate two main clauses joined by a coordinating conjunction when such clauses already contain several commas.

> The rule of Mansa Musa, the Muslim emperor of the African kingdom of Mali from 1312 to 1337, is remembered for military success, trade expansion, and Muslim scholarship; but it is probably most noteworthy as a golden age of peace and prosperity.

EXERCISE 3 **Using the Semicolon.** Rewrite the following sentences correctly, adding semicolons where they are needed.

1. The sculptor Louise Nevelson lived in Kiev, U.S.S.R., Rockland, Maine, Munich, Germany, and New York City.
2. At the age of five, Nevelson moved to Rockland with her family, she lived there for fifteen years.
3. Nevelson's family name was Berliawsky, at the age of twenty, she married Charles Nevelson and moved to New York.
4. Nevelson studied art in Germany under Hans Hofmann, the abstract painter who used primary colors in explosive contrasts, she also studied in Mexico with Diego Rivera, the muralist who used ancient methods to paint gigantic frescoes.
5. Many artists are not willing to struggle however, Louise Nevelson worked for years without money or fame.
6. Nevelson's first sculpture show was in 1940 after that she became world renowned
7. Nevelson makes sculptures with found objects her artworks are large and intricate.
8. Nevelson uses wood, metal, and plastic for her sculptures however, her wood assemblages in black, gold, and white are the most popular and the best known.
9. A pioneer in "environmental art," Nevelson created walls of framed sculptures her large-scale works sometimes take up an entire room.
10. Nevelson's art was influenced by multimedia sculpture along with the European movements of Cubism and Surrealism in addition, the art of Africa and pre-Columbian America affected her work.

Comma

As you study the rules for comma usage, keep in mind that to "separate" elements means to place a comma between two equal elements. To "set off" an element means to put commas *before* and *after* it. Of course, if the element set off occurs at the beginning or end of a sentence, only one comma is needed—either after it (for a beginning element) or before it (for a final element).

COMMAS AND COMPOUND SENTENCES

Use commas between the main clauses in a compound sentence.

Place a comma before a coordinating conjunction (*and, but, or, nor, yet,* or *for*) that joins two main clauses.

I am not going to the concert, for I am too busy.

Many of the prospectors searched for years, but others struck gold immediately, and some became quite rich.

You may omit the comma between very short main clauses that are connected by a coordinating conjunction unless the comma is needed to avoid confusion.

We heard a crash and the lights went out. [clear]

We visited Miami and the Everglades are next. [confusing]

We visited Miami, and the Everglades are next. [clear]

(For the use of semicolons before main clauses, see page 574.)

COMMAS IN A SERIES

Use commas to separate three or more words, phrases, or clauses in a series.

A chair, a table, and a sofa were the room's only furnishings.

It was a sunny, hot, humid day in July.

The cat ran out of the house, across the lawn, and down the street.

I rounded third, headed for home, and slid in safely.

Read carefully, take good notes, and outline the chapter.

No commas are necessary when all of the items are connected by conjunctions.

It was a sunny and hot and humid day in July.

Nouns used in pairs (*wind and rain, table and chairs, bagels and lox*) are considered single units and should not be divided by commas. The pairs must be set off from other nouns or groups of nouns in a series.

My favorite breakfast is bacon and eggs, toast, and milk.

COMMAS AND COORDINATE ADJECTIVES

Place a comma between coordinate adjectives preceding a noun.

Adjectives are coordinate if it would sound right to reverse their order or put the word *and* between them.

Pepper is a good, obedient, gentle dog.

Do not use a comma between adjectives preceding a noun if they sound unnatural with their order reversed or with *and* between them. Adjectives that do not need commas between them usually describe different aspects of the word to which they refer—for example, size, age, and material.

Jelani grew up in a small white frame house.

Commas may be needed between some of the adjectives in a series but not between others.

I like to read in our small, cozy family room.

In the preceding sentence *and* would sound natural between *small* and *cozy*, but it would not sound natural between *cozy* and *family*.

EXERCISE 4 **Using the Comma (Part 1).** Rewrite the following sentences correctly, adding commas where they are needed.

1. Many people think that hypnosis is a fakery and others think that it may be dangerous.
2. Some people claim that hypnosis can help you quit smoking stop overeating and build confidence.
3. Hypnosis may enable you to lessen an unreasonable unrelenting fear or it may help you ignore chronic debilitating pain.
4. Hypnosis can be done in a doctor's office in a patient's home or in any quiet setting.
5. Sitting on a chair in the office of a hypnotist is very pleasant relaxing and restful.
6. Many people imagine themselves on the beach in a forest or on a mountaintop.
7. Trusting the hypnotist relaxing fully and following instructions are keys to successful hypnosis.
8. The hypnotist will tell you to take a deep breath you will inhale slowly and your body will relax.
9. After hypnosis you may feel peaceful your life may be improved and your confidence may be increased.
10. Feeling comfortable relaxed and peaceful may be worth the price of a good hypnotist.

COMMAS AND NONESSENTIAL ELEMENTS

1. Participles, infinitives, and their phrases

Use commas to set off participles, infinitives, and their phrases if the words are not essential to the meaning of the sentence.

His old car, abandoned, rusted away in the back yard.

A customer stepped up to the counter, complaining loudly.

I have no idea, to be honest, what you would like for a graduation present.

Do not set off participles, infinitives, and their phrases if they are essential to the meaning.

The man standing by the door is my father. [participial phrase tells *which* man]

She went to medical school to become a doctor. [infinitive phrase tells *why*]

To become a doctor had been her goal for years. [infinitive phrase used as a subject]

2. Adjective clauses

Use commas to set off a nonessential adjective clause.

A nonessential (nonrestrictive) clause can be considered an *extra* clause because it gives additional information about a noun. An *extra* clause does not change, but adds to, the basic meaning of a sentence. Therefore, it is set off by commas.

Atlanta, which is the capital of Georgia, is the transportation center of the Southeast. [nonessential clause: *which is the capital of Georgia*]

Do not set off an essential adjective clause. An essential (restrictive) clause gives necessary information about a noun. It is needed to convey the exact meaning of the sentence.

People who are afraid of heights do not like to look down from high balconies. [essential clause: *who are afraid of heights*]

3. Appositives

Use commas to set off an appositive if it is not essential to the meaning of a sentence.

A nonessential (nonrestrictive) appositive can be considered an *extra* appositive; it calls for commas.

Indira Gandhi, the only child of a former Indian prime minister, was prime minister of India when she was assassinated in 1984.

My family has a problem, a tendency to overeat.

A nonessential appositive is sometimes placed before the word to which it refers.

An insurance executive, Charles Ives wrote music in his spare time.

An essential (restrictive) appositive gives necessary information about a noun and is not set off.

The word *fiesta* came into English from Spanish. [The appositive *fiesta* is needed to identify the word.]

COMMAS WITH INTERJECTIONS AND CONJUNCTIVE ADVERBS

Use commas to set off interjections (such as *yes, no,* and *well*), parenthetical expressions (such as *on the contrary, on the other hand, in fact, by the way, to be exact,* and *after all*), and conjunctive adverbs (such as *however, moreover,* and *consequently*).

Well, we'd better be going home.

No, we can't stay.

We have to leave, unfortunately.

Last night, on the other hand, we could have stayed longer.

We promised to be home by 9:00 P.M.; consequently, we must leave immediately.

You might want to come with us, however.

EXERCISE 5 **Using the Comma (Part 2).** Rewrite the following sentences correctly, adding commas where they are needed. For the sentence that needs no commas, write *Correct.*

1. Most Native American languages before the eighteenth century were not written down; consequently it was difficult for people to learn these languages.
2. A Cherokee Sequoyah saw the need for a written Cherokee language.
3. The Cherokees who had no system of writing thought that writing was the privilege of only certain people.
4. Like many other Native American groups in fact the Cherokees used smoke and drum signals to communicate with people some distance away.
5. Sequoyah however saw how valuable a written language would be to his tribe.
6. Sequoyah had been hurt in a hunting accident; therefore he had leisure to think about a writing system.

7. Sequoyah a grown man and a silversmith began to draw marks on twigs and stones in the forest.
8. People who once had laughed at Sequoyah's dream began to change their minds about him.
9. Sequoyah produced the first Cherokee alphabet making it possible for his tribe to write messages and record its history.
10. Sequoyah who had been successful despite the doubts of others was sent to Washington in 1828 to represent the Cherokees there.

COMMAS AND INTRODUCTORY PHRASES

1. Prepositional Phrases

Use a comma after a short introductory prepositional phrase if the sentence would be misread without the comma.

> To those outside, the house appeared deserted. [comma needed]
>
> At the last moment we decided not to go. [comma not needed]

Do not use a comma if the phrase is immediately followed by a verb.

> On the stone above the front door of the building was the date 1892.

Use a comma after a long prepositional phrase or after the final phrase in a succession of phrases.

> During the afternoon of the day of the game, we made a big banner.

2. Participles and participial phrases

Use commas to set off introductory participles and participial phrases.

> Purring, the kitten curled up in my lap.
> Sitting in a tree, my little sister called down to us.

COMMAS AND ADVERB CLAUSES

Use commas to set off all introductory adverb clauses. Use commas to set off internal adverb clauses that interrupt the flow of a sentence.

> Although I like country music, I did not want to hear his entire record collection.
>
> Until she arrived, I thought that no one was coming.
>
> Evan, after he thought about it awhile, agreed with our idea.

In general, do not set off an adverb clause at the end of a sentence unless the clause is parenthetical or the sentence would be misread without the comma.

COMMAS AND ANTITHETICAL PHRASES

Use commas to set off an antithetical phrase.

An antithetical phrase uses a word such as *not* or *unlike* to qualify what precedes it.

You, not I, deserve this honor.
Bicycles, unlike cars, cause no pollution.

EXERCISE 6 **Using the Comma (Part 3).** Rewrite the following sentences correctly, adding commas where they are needed. If a sentence is correct, write *Correct.*

1. To most people the name I. M. Pei means good taste and quality of design.
2. To be truthful Pei's name is one of the most respected in the field of architecture.
3. Because he combines a beautiful design with a practical budget Pei is considered a gifted architect.
4. Among Pei's most successful designs is the East Building of the National Gallery of Art in Washington, D.C.
5. Architects unlike artists must seek to harmonize a building's appearance with its purpose.
6. After a series of problems with the John Hancock Tower in Boston Pei's firm lost some business.
7. Once he replaced the windows in the John Hancock Tower Pei regained his reputation.
8. For a resort hotel in mainland China not on Taiwan Pei created a design that pleased everyone.
9. Having been born in China Pei was happy to design a structure for his native land.
10. Although Pei has become highly successful as an architect he continues to work hard.

COMMAS AND SPECIFYING WORDS AND PHRASES

Use commas to set off specifying words and phrases.

Specifying words and phrases add specific information about what precedes them.

1. Titles of people

Use commas to set off titles when they follow a person's name.

Alan Wong, M.D.
Martin Luther King, Jr.
Dianne Feinstein, Mayor of San Francisco
Cesar Gonzalez, Ph.D., will speak on Thursday.

2. Addresses, geographical terms, and dates

Use commas to separate the various parts of an address, a geographical term, or a date.

Anaheim, California, is the home of Disneyland.

During the summer my address will be 90 Sherwick Road, New Bedford, Massachusetts 02745, and my sister's address will be the same.

Friday, March 15, 1985, was the day I got my driver's license.

Use the following forms for letter writing:

90 Sherwick Road
New Bedford, Massachusetts 02745
July 7, 1985

Do not use commas if only the month and the day or only the month and the year are given.

October 31 September 1986

3. References

Use commas to set off the parts of a reference that direct the reader to the exact source.

Odysseus becomes reunited with his son Telemachus in the *Odyssey*, lines 859–905.

Please find three examples of extended metaphor in Act IV, scene i, of Shakespeare's *Romeo and Juliet*.

COMMAS AND DIRECT ADDRESS

Use commas to set off words or names used in direct address.

Tony, do you know where Kathleen is?
I can order the book for you, sir, if you like.
Thank you for the ride, Mrs. Salerno.

COMMAS AND TAG QUESTIONS

Use commas to set off a tag question.

A tag question (such as *shouldn't I?* or *have you?*) emphasizes an implied answer to the statement preceding it.

> You've already seen this film, haven't you?
> You won't repeat this, will you?

COMMAS IN LETTER WRITING

Place a comma after the salutation of an informal letter and after the closing of all letters.

Dear Maria,	Dear Uncle John,
Very truly yours,	Best wishes,

MISUSE OF COMMAS

Do not use a comma before a conjunction that connects a compound verb having only two parts.

INCORRECT She started the car X and drove down the hill.
CORRECT She started the car and drove down the hill.

The same rule applies to other compound elements.

INCORRECT The adults playing softball X and the children playing soccer argued in the field. [compound subject]
CORRECT The adults playing softball and the children playing soccer argued in the field.

Do not use only a comma to join two main clauses that are not part of a series. A sentence with this error is called a *run-on sentence* (or a *comma splice* or *comma fault*). Use a coordinating conjunction with the comma, or use a semicolon.

INCORRECT John Wayne worked in Hollywood for almost fifty years X he made more than two hundred films.
CORRECT John Wayne worked in Hollywood for almost fifty years, and he made more than two hundred films.

Do not use a comma between a subject and its verb or between a verb and its complement.

INCORRECT What you do with your money X is your business.
CORRECT What you do with your money is your business.
INCORRECT For the overnight camping trip you will need X a sleeping bag, a ground cloth, a towel, soap, and a toothbrush.
CORRECT For the overnight camping trip you will need a sleeping bag, a ground cloth, a towel, soap, and a toothbrush.

EXERCISE 7 **Using the Comma (Part 4).** Rewrite the following letter, adding commas where they are needed.

1516 Evergreen Road
Bonita California 92002
October 5 1988

Dear Melanie

Your mother has told me that you would like some advice about a good diet. She wrote that you want to lose about twenty pounds. I hope that she has misunderstood your weight goal Melanie because you would be quite thin if you lost that much weight wouldn't you?

I have enclosed a copy of an article about diet and weight loss that was published in the July 7 1987 issue of *Food for Health* page 59. The author is Ruth Zimmerman M.D. a specialist in nutritional disorders. In September 1986 I heard Dr. Zimmerman speak when I was in Washington D.C. and I have a great deal of respect for her knowledge in this area. You will read this article carefully won't you?

I am looking forward to visiting your family at Thanksgiving. I haven't seen any of you since I was in San Diego on May 14 1985 for a convention. When I visit this year I hope we'll be able to spend some time together Melanie.

Love
Aunt Elizabeth

Dash

Indicate the dash in typing by two hyphens (--). Do not place a comma, semicolon, colon, or period before or after a dash.

DASHES TO EMPHASIZE

Use a dash to set off and emphasize supplemental information or parenthetical comments.

It was a shiny new car—the first he had ever owned.

A shiny new car—the first he had ever owned—was his prize.

DASHES TO SIGNAL HESITATION

Use a dash to indicate an abrupt change in thought within a sentence or to show a hesitation or faltering in dialogue.

A small stand sells sugar loaves—the gift to bring when invited to dinner—sugar for the mint tea and for the sweet pastry, so flaky and light, that they bake.

—Anaïs Nin

Parentheses

Use parentheses to set off extra material.

Commas and dashes are also used for this purpose; the difference between the three marks is one of degree. Use commas for extra material that is fairly closely related to the rest of the sentence. Use parentheses for material that is not intended to be part of the main statement but is nevertheless important enough to include. Use dashes for material that more abruptly interrupts the sentence and that you wish to emphasize.

> Many contemporary women's fashions (business suits and low heels) show the influence of Gabrielle "Coco" Chanel (1883–1971).

A complete sentence within parentheses is not capitalized and needs no period if it is contained within another sentence. If a sentence in parentheses stands by itself, both a capital letter and a period are needed.

> The unisex trend (it still seems to be growing in popularity) was started by Chanel, who wore a man's trench coat.
>
> Chanel introduced the world's most famous perfume, Chanel Number 5. (This scent is still in great demand.)

PARENTHESES WITH OTHER MARKS OF PUNCTUATION

1. With a comma, semicolon, or colon

Always place a comma, semicolon, or colon *after* closing parentheses.

> Despite the simple clothes that Chanel designed and wore (the "little black dress" became her uniform), she became fabulously wealthy.
>
> In 1954 fashionable women wore long skirts with tiny waists and high heels (the Dior look); coming out of retirement, Chanel changed all that.

2. With a question mark or exclamation point

Place a question mark or an exclamation point *inside* parentheses if it is part of the parenthetical expression.

> Chanel believed that simplicity and practicality were more important (who would not agree today?) than obviously expensive, complicated-looking clothes.
>
> Although Chanel's influence on fashion lessened during World War II (1939–1945), she reopened her fashion house in 1954 (at the age of seventy!).

Place a question mark or an exclamation point *outside* parentheses if it is part of the entire sentence.

> Did you know that Chanel introduced many of today's fashion classics (sweaters, costume jewelry, sling-back shoes)**?**
>
> How amazed I was to find out that it was Chanel who made a suntan fashionable (in the 1930s)**!**

EXERCISE 8 **Using the Dash and Parentheses.** Rewrite the following sentences correctly, adding dashes and parentheses where needed. Remember that a dash is used to show emphasis or an interruption in thought, whereas parentheses are used to set off extra material.

1. In *Understanding Body Talk* Thomas Aylesworth the author of more than twenty-five books) discusses how body movements including gestures and facial expressions) communicate meaning.
2. Fiorello H. LaGuardia, who was mayor of New York City in the late thirties and early forties, made campaign speeches in English, Italian, and Yiddish. (LaGuardia Airport was named for him.
3. Aylesworth notes that when people watch a movie of Fiorello's speeches with the sound turned off—they can tell what language he was speaking. (Fiorello was a master of the art of body language!
4. Aylesworth explains that body movements are a kind of code a code used by animals as well as by humans.
5. Gestures whether learned or unlearned—can sometimes be misinterpreted with embarrassing—or even tragic results.
6. According to Dr. Edward T. Hall, depending on the situation intimate, personal, social, or public), people feel comfortable at specific distances from one another.
7. The personal distance Dr. Hall estimates this at 1.5 to 4 feet), for example, signals that the two people want privacy. (Dr. Hall calls this space a "small protective bubble" that people carry with them wherever they go.
8. Individuals of different backgrounds are comfortable at different distances. Some people even enjoy feeling crowded!)
9. Politicians must sometimes hire a drama coach to teach them how to project sincerity, intelligence, and strength. Can you think of a politician who needed no coaching?)
10. Although not everyone can learn to use body language effectively (some people seem to be born with the gift for it , all of us can learn to understand what people are expressing and communicating with body language and that is, perhaps, even more important than being able to use it.

Quotation Marks

QUOTATION MARKS FOR DIRECT QUOTATIONS

Use quotation marks to enclose a direct quotation.

Place quotation marks around the quotation *only*, not around purely introductory or explanatory remarks. Generally, separate such remarks from the actual quotation by using a comma.

A famous poster asks, "What if they gave a war and nobody came?"

A Pawnee poem advises us to remember "the sacredness of things."

Do not use a comma after a quotation that ends with an exclamation point or a question mark.

"What is the question?" Gertrude Stein asked.

(For the use of colons to introduce quotations, see page 573.)

When a quotation is interrupted by explanatory words such as *he said* or *she wrote,* use two sets of quotation marks.

Separate each part of the quotation from the interrupting phrase with two marks of punctuation, such as two commas or a comma and a period. If the second part of the quotation is a complete sentence, begin it with a capital letter.

"Over increasingly large areas of the United States," wrote Rachel Carson, "spring now comes unheralded by the return of the birds."

"It wasn't just that Babe Ruth hit more home runs than anybody else," said Red Smith. "He hit them better, higher, and farther."

Do not use quotation marks in an indirect quotation (a quotation that does not repeat the person's exact wording).

ORIGINAL QUOTATION	"Dance is life at its most glorious moment," said Pearl Lang.
INDIRECT QUOTATION	Pearl Lang described dance as life's most glorious moment.

Use single quotation marks around a quotation within a quotation.

President John F. Kennedy said, "I am one person who can truthfully say, 'I got my job through the *New York Times*.' "

In writing dialogue begin a new paragraph and use a new set of quotation marks every time the speaker changes.

He looked at me proudly. "Was it so hard to do, Daughter?"

"Not so hard as I thought." I pinned the brooch on my dress. "I'll wear it always," I said. "I'll keep it forever."

"Mama will be glad, Katrin."

—Kathryn Forbes

QUOTATION MARKS FOR TITLES OF SHORT WORKS

Use quotation marks to enclose titles of short works, such as short stories, short poems, essays, newspaper and magazine articles, book chapters, songs, and single episodes of a television series.

"The Legend of Sleepy Hollow" [short story]
"The Raven" [poem]
"On the Duty of Civil Disobedience" [essay]
"Woody Allen's Newest Film" [newspaper article]
"The 1980s in America" [chapter]
"If I Had a Hammer" [song]
"Division of the Spoils" [episode]

(For the use of italics with titles of longer works, see page 590.)

QUOTATION MARKS FOR UNUSUAL EXPRESSIONS

Use quotation marks to enclose unfamiliar slang and other unusual or original expressions.

My cousin uses the expression "the cat's meow" to describe something she likes.

QUOTATION MARKS WITH OTHER MARKS OF PUNCTUATION

1. With a comma or period

Always place a comma or a period *inside* closing quotation marks.

"The frog does not drink up the pond in which it lives," states a Native American proverb.

Henry David Thoreau humorously advises, "Beware of all enterprises that require new clothes."

2. With a semicolon or colon

Always place a semicolon or a colon *outside* closing quotation marks.

Her father said "yes"; her mother said "no"; her brother said that he did not know.

Portuguese and Spanish have similar words for "yes" and "no": The Portuguese say *sím* and *naõ*; the Spanish say *sí* and *no*.

3. With a question mark or exclamation point

Place the question mark or exclamation point *inside* the closing quotation marks when it is part of the quotation.

A famous sonnet by Shakespeare begins with these words: "Shall I compare thee to a summer's day?"

She said, "I never want to hear from you again!"

Place the question mark or exclamation point *outside* the quotation marks when it is part of the entire sentence.

I've finally memorized all of "Paul Revere's Ride"!

Why do you keep saying, "I'm sorry"?

If both the sentence and the quotation at the end of the sentence need a question mark (or an exclamation point), use only *one* punctuation mark *inside* the quotation marks.

When did he ask, "Would you like to go to the movies?"

We just heard someone shout, "Help!"

Who asked you, "Where is the fire?"

EXERCISE 9 **Using Quotation Marks.** Rewrite the following sentences correctly, adding quotation marks where they are needed. For the sentence that needs no changes, write *Correct.*

1. William P. Urschel's article, called History the Hard Way, about a trip to the American Southwest was published in *Quest* magazine.
2. Urschel said that he made the trip to find out how the American Southwest was explored.
3. Urschel said of his trip: My only companions will be my horse and a pack mule.
4. My only equipment, he said, will be what they can carry.
5. The loneliness of traveling alone outdoors is expressed in the song Home on the Range.
6. The question Where can I sleep tonight? was suddenly important.
7. At the end of the twelve-hundred-mile trip, Urschel asked himself, What have I learned?
8. What is important, wrote Urschel, I could not have learned in any number of shorter, weekend trips.
9. He added, I became aware of myself as a part of the environment.
10. Urschel concluded, What I conquered was fear and fatigue.

Italics (Underlining)

Italic type is a special slanted type that is used in printing. (*This is printed in italics.*) Indicate italics in typing or in handwriting by underlining. (This is underlined.)

ITALICS FOR TITLES

Italicize (underline) titles of novels and other books, lengthy poems and plays, film and television series, paintings and sculptures, and long musical compositions. Italicize the names of newspapers and magazines, ships, trains, airplanes, and spacecraft.

Foundation's Edge [novel]
Hamlet [play]
Wonderworks [television series]
Mediterranean [sculpture]
Consumer Reports [magazine]
U.S.S. *Enterprise** [ship]
Orient Express [train]
Snow-Bound [long poem]
Gone with the Wind [film]
Handball [painting]
Grand Canyon Suite [musical work]
the *Oakland Tribune* [newspaper]
Spirit of St. Louis [airplane]
Columbia [spacecraft]

Italicize (underline) and capitalize articles *(a, an, the)* written at the beginning of a title only when they are part of the title itself.

A Light in the Attic	*but*	a *National Geographic* article
An American Tragedy		an *Outdoor Life* article
The Red Badge of Courage		the *Chicago Tribune*

ITALICS FOR FOREIGN WORDS

Italicize (underline) foreign words and expressions that are not used frequently in English.

Do not italicize a foreign word or expression that is commonly used in English.

The ambassador's secretary was declared *persona non grata* and sent home.

I eat croissants for breakfast.

ITALICS FOR WORDS AND OTHER ITEMS USED TO REPRESENT THEMSELVES

Italicize (underline) words, letters, and numerals used to represent themselves.

His typewriter did not have the numeral *1*, so he used a small *L* in its place.

She was too superstitious to say it, so she handed the elevator operator a piece of paper on which she had written *13*.

Replace all of the number signs (#'s) with the word *number*.

---

*Do not italicize *U.S.S.* in the name of a ship.

EXERCISE 10 **Using Italics.** Rewrite the following sentences correctly, underlining the parts that should be italicized.

1. In the book Golden Girls by Carli Laklan, you will find information about women who won Olympic medals.
2. The ancient Greeks based the first Olympics on the concept of arete, which means excellence in every area of life, not just physical but also moral and intellectual superiority.
3. The author of Golden Girls notes that the earliest games featured just one event, the stade, a two-hundred-yard footrace; the English word stadium comes from the Greek word stade.
4. The word Olympics comes from Olympia, the name of the Greek city where the first Olympic games were held in 776 B.C.
5. Sonja Henie, who won three gold medals in figure skating at three successive Olympic games, became a movie star when her first film One in a Million was a big hit.
6. Peggy Fleming won a gold medal in figure skating at the 1968 Grenoble Olympics; she skated to Tchaikovsky's Pathétique.
7. With the financial backing of the publishers of the Chicago Tribune, Gertrude Ederle, who had won the gold medal for swimming in 1924, became the first woman to swim the English Channel in 1926; the French tug the Alsace followed her with a jazz band on board "to keep up her spirits."
8. Wilma Rudolph, who overcame an attack of polio, was the first American woman to win three gold medals in track and field; she later became a commentator for the radio series Olympic Odyssey.
9. After the 1984 Olympics, gold-medal winners Mary Lou Retton, Valerie Brisco-Hooks, and Joan Benoit were featured in Time, Life, Newsweek, The New York Times, and Sports Illustrated.
10. Many of the Olympic gold medalists have been on television shows ranging from What's My Line? to Evening Magazine.

Apostrophe

APOSTROPHES FOR POSSESSIVES

1. Pronouns

Use an apostrophe and s for the possessive of an indefinite pronoun that is singular.

Do not use an apostrophe with other possessive pronouns.

everybody**'s** problem **its** owner
each other**'s** parents **whose** talents

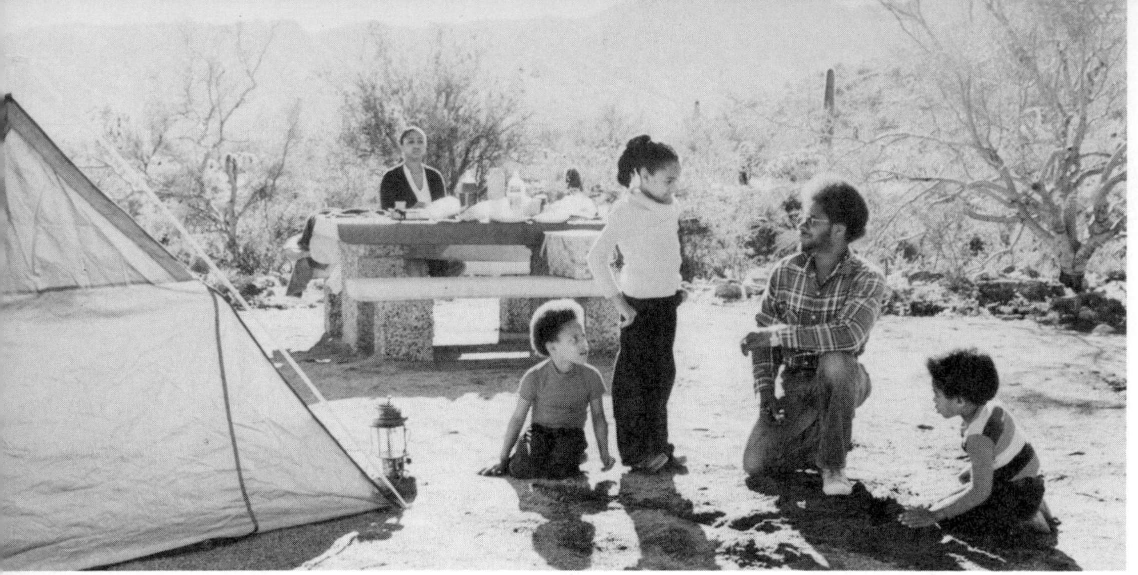

2. Nouns not ending in *s*

Use an apostrophe and *s* to form the possessive of a singular or plural noun not ending in *s*, whether common or proper.

Puerto Rico's cities
my sister's team
children's playground
women's hospital

3. Plural nouns ending in *s*

Use an apostrophe alone to form the possessive of a plural noun ending in *s*, whether common or proper.

the countries' treaty
Joneses' picnic
Azores Islands' airports
Campfire Girls' activities

4. Singular nouns ending in *s*

The possessive of a singular noun ending in *s* (or an *s* or *z* sound), whether common or proper, depends on the number of syllables in the noun.

If the noun has only one syllable, use an apostrophe and *s*. If the noun has more than one syllable, you can usually use an apostrophe alone.

the class's election
Robert Burns's poetry
the box's lettering
Groucho Marx's biography
Adele Davis' book
the princess' power
Grandma Moses' paintings
Euripides' plays

5. Compound nouns

Put only the last word of a compound noun in the possessive form.

my sister-in-law's office
the court-martial's effect
Cape Hatteras' beauty
the Chief of Staff's order

6. Joint possession versus separate possession

If two or more persons (or partners in a company) possess something jointly, use the possessive form for the last person named.

Larry and Louise's children
Johnson and Johnson's baby care products
Abbott and Costello's antics

If two or more persons (or companies) possess an item (or items) individually, put each one's name in the possessive form.

Tina Turner's and the Rolling Stones' songs
Chrysler's and the American Motor Company's cars

7. Expression of time and money

Use a possessive form to express amounts of money or time that modify a noun.

The modifier can also be expressed as a hyphenated adjective. In that case, no possessive form is used.

five minutes' drive	*but*	a five-minute drive
one dollar's worth		a one-dollar increase
ten days' wait		a ten-day visit

APOSTROPHES IN CONTRACTIONS

Use an apostrophe in place of letters omitted in contractions.

A contraction is a single word made up of two words that have been combined by omitting letters. Common contractions combine a subject and a verb or a verb and an adverb.

you'd	*formed from*	you had, you would
who's		who is, who has
it's		it is, it has
won't		will not

Use the apostrophe in place of omitted numerals in such expressions as "the class of '86" and "the '84 campaign."

APOSTROPHES FOR SPECIAL PLURALS

Use an apostrophe and s to form the plural of letters, numerals, symbols, and words used to represent themselves.

Italicize (underline) the letter, numeral, symbol, or word but not the apostrophe and the *s*.

Your *e*'s look like *l*'s and your *5*'s look like *50*'s.
She told me to replace the *henceforth*'s in my report with *therefore*'s.

EXERCISE 11 **Using the Apostrophe.** Rewrite the following sentences correctly, adding apostrophes where they are needed.

1. Many writers names are familiar to lovers of poetry and fiction.
2. Under the *As*, for example, youd list Louisa May Alcott, whos best known for *Little Women*.
3. No list of *The New Yorkers* poets would be complete without the name of Elizabeth Bishop.
4. The *Bs* would also include the names of Pearl S. Buck and Gwendolyn Brooks.
5. Pearl S. Bucks novels focus on the Chinese peoples culture, while Gwendolyn Brookss poems deal with Afro-Americans lives.
6. Nikki Giovanni is a poet whod be listed under the *Gs*; her works include *Black Feeling, Black Talk,* and *My House*.
7. At least four writers names would be listed under the *Ms*: Carson McCullers, Edna St. Vincent Millay, Margaret Mitchell, and Marianne Moore.
8. Millays and Moores names would be found on anyones list of talented poets; Mitchells and McCullers names are familiar to lovers of excellent prose.
9. Most people dont know that Margaret Mitchells *Gone with the Wind* took ten years effort to write; it was finally published in 36.
10. The novelist Katherine Ann Porters great-great-grandfathers name is also well known: Daniel Boone.

Hyphen

HYPHENS FOR PREFIXES AND SUFFIXES

A hyphen is not ordinarily used to join a prefix or a suffix to the beginning or end of a word. There are a few exceptions, however.

1. Prefixes

Use a hyphen after any prefix joined to a proper noun or proper adjective. Use a hyphen after the prefixes *all-*, ex- (meaning "former") and *self-* joined to any noun or adjective.

all-American	ex-coach
mid-Atlantic	self-confidence

Use a hyphen after the prefix *anti-* when it joins a word beginning with *i*. Also use a hyphen after the prefix *vice-* except in Vice President (of the United States).

anti-intellectual	vice-mayor

Use a hyphen to avoid confusion between words that look alike but are different in meaning and pronunciation.

re-cover the couch	*but*	recover the ball
re-store those cans		restore your confidence
re-lease the car		release the brake

2. Suffixes

Use a hyphen to join the suffix *-like* to a proper noun or to a word ending in *ll*.

a gull-like bird	*but*	an egglike stone
Alaska-like storm		a buttonlike nose

HYPHENS IN COMPOUND ADJECTIVES

Use a hyphen in a compound adjective that precedes a noun.

In general, a compound adjective that follows a noun is not hyphenated.

dark-green eyes	*but*	Her eyes are dark green.
a fifteen-year-old aunt		His aunt is fifteen years old.
a well-known reporter		That reporter is well known.

An expression made up of an adverb ending in *-ly* and an adjective is not hyphenated.

a nicely behaved dog	a fairly close race
a slightly rusted exterior	a hastily written report

HYPHENS IN NUMBERS

1. Compound numbers

Hyphenate any spelled-out cardinal or ordinal compound numbers up to ninety-nine and ninety-ninth.

sixty-four   thirty-fifth

2. Fractions used as adjectives

Hyphenate a fraction used as an adjective or adverb (but not one used as a noun).

one-eighth teaspoon	*but*	one eighth of a teaspoon
one-quarter cup	*but*	one quarter of a cup
one-half pound	*but*	one half of a pound

3. Connected numerals

Hyphenate two numerals to indicate a span.

pages 30-56   1986-1990

HYPHENS TO DIVIDE WORDS AT THE END OF A LINE

Words are generally divided between syllables or pronounceable parts. Because it is frequently difficult to determine where a word should be divided, check your dictionary.

In general, if a word contains two consonants occurring between two vowels or if it contains a double consonant, divide the word between the two consonants.

foun-tain	sup-per	tomor-row
lin-ger	struc-ture	profes-sor

If a suffix has been added to a complete word that ends in two consonants, divide the word after the two consonants.

kick-ing strong-est point-less

EXERCISE 12 **Using the Hyphen.** Write out the following sentences, adding hyphens where they are needed. Then make a list of the italicized words, showing where each would be divided if it had to be broken at the end of a line.

1. Sally Ride was thirty one in 1983 when she became the first American woman to *orbit* the earth.
2. She is also the *youngest* American astronaut to go into orbit.
3. At Swarthmore College, where she did her undergraduate work, Sally Ride won a national *tennis* tournament for *college* students.
4. Astronaut Ride received her *doctorate* from Stanford University.
5. Dr. Ride said that one third of the *scientists* at NASA are women.
6. A thirty four year old Russian woman, Svetlana Savitskaya, orbited the earth about eight months before Dr. Ride.
7. Astronauts are resourceful, self confident, healthy, highly educated, and experienced in their special fields of study.
8. By the year 2000, spaceflight may become *common;* within your lifetime thousands will be taking trips into space every year.
9. Ex astronauts such as John Glenn and Neil Armstrong were viewed as all American heroes for years after their *missions.*
10. Astronaut trainees must learn to live in an almost *weightless,* low gravity environment.

Abbreviations

Abbreviations are shortened forms of words. Abbreviations save space and time and prevent unnecessary wordiness. For instance, "M.D." is more concise and easier to write than "Medical Doctor." Most abbreviations take periods. Use a dictionary if necessary.

Use only one period if an abbreviation occurs at the end of a sentence that would ordinarily take a period of its own. If an abbreviation occurs at the end of a sentence that ends with a question mark or an exclamation point, use the period *and* the second mark of punctuation.

Gerry left at 8 **A.M.** Did she leave at 8 **A.M.?**

CAPITALIZATION OF ABBREVIATIONS

Capitalize abbreviations of proper nouns.

St. Cloud, Minnesota — **Rev.** Jesse Jackson
Shreveport, **La.** — **U.S.** Congress

Abbreviations of organizations and government agencies are often formed from the initial letters of the complete name. Such abbreviations omit periods.

YWCA **CORE** **IRS**
NASA **UNICEF** **CBS**

State names used in addressing mail may be abbreviated as shown in the following list. The official ZIP-code form consists of two capital letters with no periods.

Alabama **Ala.** **AL**
Alaska **AK**
Arizona **Ariz.** **AZ**
Arkansas **Ark.** **AR**
California **Calif.** **CA**
Colorado **Colo.** **CO**
Connecticut **Conn.** **CT**
Delaware **Del.** **DE**
Florida **Fla.** **FL**
Georgia **Ga.** **GA**
Hawaii **HI**
Idaho **ID**
Illinois **Ill.** **IL**
Indiana **Ind.** **IN**
Iowa **IA**
Kansas **Kans.** **KS**
Kentucky **Ky.** **KY**
Ohio **OH**
Oklahoma **Okla.** **OK**
Oregon **Oreg.** **OR**
Pennsylvania **Pa.** **PA**
Rhode Island **R.I.** **RI**
South Carolina **S.C.** **SC**
South Dakota **S.Dak.** **SD**
Tennessee **Tenn.** **TN**
Louisiana **La.** **LA**
Maine **ME**
Maryland **Md.** **MD**
Massachusetts **Mass.** **MA**
Michigan **Mich.** **MI**
Minnesota **Minn.** **MN**
Mississippi **Miss.** **MS**
Missouri **Mo.** **MO**
Montana **Mont.** **MT**
Nebraska **Nebr.** **NB**
Nevada **Nev.** **NV**
New Hampshire **N.H.** **NH**
New Jersey **N.J.** **NJ**
New Mexico **N.Mex.** **NM**
New York **N.Y.** **NY**
North Carolina **N.C.** **NC**
North Dakota **N.Dak.** **ND**
Texas **Tex.** **TX**
Utah **UT**
Vermont **Vt.** **VT**
Virginia **Va.** **VA**
Washington **Wash.** **WA**
West Virginia **W.Va.** **WV**
Wisconsin **Wis.** **WI**
Wyoming **Wyo.** **WY**

Capitalize the following abbreviations related to dates and times.

A.D. (*anno Domini*), "in the year of the Lord" (since the birth of Christ); place before the date: **A.D.** 5
B.C. (before Christ); place after the date: 1000 **B.C.**
B.C.E. (before the common era); place after the date: 4 **B.C.E.**
C.E. (common era); place after the date: 795 **C.E.**
A.M. (*ante meridiem*), "before noon"
P.M. (*post meridiem*), "afternoon"

ABBREVIATIONS OF TITLES OF PEOPLE

Use abbreviations for some personal titles.

Titles such as *Mrs., Mr., Ms.,* and *Jr.* and those indicating professions and academic degrees (*Dr., M.A., B.S.*) are almost always abbreviated. Titles of government and military officials and members of the clergy are frequently abbreviated when used before a full name.

Mrs. Reagan	**Gov.** Martha L. Collins
Desi Arnaz, **Jr.**	**Brig. Gen.** Dunlap
Dr. Rosalyn Yalow	Myron Lee, **D.D.S.**

ABBREVIATIONS OF UNITS OF MEASURE

Abbreviate units of measure used with numerals in technical or scientific writing but not in ordinary prose.

The abbreviations that follow stand for plural and singular units:

ENGLISH SYSTEM		METRIC SYSTEM	
ft.	foot	**cg**	centigram
gal.	gallon	**cl**	centiliter
in.	inch	**cm**	centimeter
lb.	pound	**g**	gram
mi.	mile	**kg**	kilogram
oz.	ounce	**km**	kilometer
pt.	pint	**l**	liter
qt.	quart	**m**	meter
tbsp.	tablespoon	**mg**	milligram
tsp.	teaspoon	**ml**	milliliter
yd.	yard	**mm**	millimeter

EXERCISE 13 **Using Abbreviations.** Write the abbreviations for the italicized words or phrases in the following sentences.

1. President Andrew Johnson's secretary of state William Seward purchased Alaska from Russia in *anno Domini* 1867.
2. *Senator* Bob Graham is the junior senator from Florida.

3. Many students attend summer school from 10 *ante meridiem* to 3 *post meridiem.*
4. The ZIP code for Waco, *Texas,* is 77005.
5. The *Internal Revenue Service* is responsible for collecting federal taxes.
6. W.E.B. DuBois founded the *National Association for the Advancement of Colored People* in 1909.
7. The Greek philosopher Aristotle lived in the fourth century *before Christ.*
8. *Doctor* Mary Walker, an army surgeon, won the Congressional Medal of Honor for her work with wounded soldiers during the American Civil War.
9. The architect's plans indicated that the garden would be 40 *feet* by 23 *feet* (12 *meters* by 7 *meters*).
10. *Saint* Louis, Missouri, is located on the Mississippi River.

Numbers and Numerals

In nontechnical writing some numbers are spelled out, and some are expressed in figures. Numbers expressed in figures are called *numerals.*

NUMBERS SPELLED OUT

In general, spell out cardinal and ordinal numbers that can be written in one or two words. Spell out any number that occurs at the beginning of a sentence.

New Hampshire is **one** of the original **thirteen** states.
There are **twenty-seven** students in the class.
Alaska was the **forty-ninth** state to join the Union.
Sixteen hundred and fifteen delegates attended.

NUMERALS

In general, use numerals to express numbers that would be written in more than two words.

Mount Mitchell, the highest mountain in the eastern United States, is **6,684** feet tall.

In 1790 the total population of the United States (according to the first census) was **3,929,214**.

In 1984 Joe W. Kittinger covered **3,535** miles in eighty-three hours and fifty-three minutes to set a new distance record for balloon flight.

Very large numbers are often written as a numeral followed by the word *million* or *billion*.

The area of the earth is close to **197 million** square miles.

If related numbers appear in the same sentence, use all numerals, even though you might spell out one if it appeared alone.

Bob ranked **65th** in the class; his brother ranked **119th**.

1. Money, decimals, and percentages

Use numerals to express amounts of money, decimals, and percentages.

$897,000,000 *or* **$897** million
$3.50
1.2 kilograms
5 percent

Amounts of money that can be expressed in one or two words, however, should be spelled out.

forty-five cents
two thousand dollars

2. Dates and times

Use numerals to express years and days in a date and for specific references to A.M. or P.M. time.

The Soviet Union launched *Sputnik I,* the first manufactured satellite to orbit the earth, on October **4, 1957**.

She went to her meeting at **4:15** P.M.

Spell out references to time used without the abbreviations A.M. or P.M. Spell out centuries and decades. Decades may be expressed as numerals if the century is included.

She set her alarm clock for **five** o'clock.

The Great Depression of the **thirties** (*or* **1930s**) was a severe national economic crisis.

3. Addresses

Use numerals for streets and avenues numbered above ten and for all house, apartment, and room numbers. Spell out numbered streets and avenues with numbers of ten or under.

165 West **66th** Street	**4** North Main Street
Apartment **8C**	Room **3**
30 East **15th** Street	**20 Second** Avenue

4. References

Use numerals to express page, line, act, and scene numbers.

Look on pages **20** and **59** for information about Pablo Casals.

Read lines **1–80** in Book **I** of the *Iliad.*

We rehearsed Act **2**, scenes **3** and **4**, of the graduation play.

EXERCISE 14 **Using Numbers and Numerals.** Write out the following sentences, making any necessary changes in the use of numbers and numerals.

1. Millions of Americans in the 80s have taken up jogging.
2. In the 19th century, however, walking was a popular sport.
3. In eighteen sixty-one, at the age of 22, Edward Payson Weston tried to walk from Boston to Washington in just 10 days.
4. Weston, who wanted to see Lincoln's inauguration in Washington, was 12 hours late.
5. 6 years later Weston won a prize of $10,000 for walking from Portland, Maine, to Chicago, Illinois.
6. Weston had covered more than 1,000 miles in 30 days.
7. When he was 71, Weston completed a walk from New York to San Francisco in 105 days; he walked back from Los Angeles to New York in 76 days.
8. Between April eleven and June third nineteen seventy-two, John Lees, who was born in England on February twenty-third, nineteen forty-five, walked from Los Angeles to New York City in fifty-three days, twelve hours, and fifteen minutes.
9. Tomas Carlos Pereira of Argentina spent 10 years (April six, nineteen sixty-eight, to April eight, nineteen seventy-eight) walking twenty-nine thousand eight hundred twenty-five miles around 5 continents.

Review

CHAPTERS 26–27 MECHANICS

CHAPTER 26 CAPITALIZATION

For each numbered item, indicate the correct capitalization.

Ursula LeGuin is an author of [1]fantasy and Science Fiction. A native of [2]berkeley, California, she writes books for adults and young people. The Taoist principles of the [3]chinese philosopher lao Tzu have greatly influenced her work. For the Earthsea trilogy she received many awards, including [4]the Hugo award. "Clarity and simplicity," she has said, [5]"are permanent virtues in a narrative."

1. (a) Fantasy and Science Fiction (b) fantasy and Science fiction (c) fantasy and Science Fiction (d) fantasy and science fiction
2. (a) Berkeley, California (b) Berkeley, california
3. (a) Chinese Philosopher Lao Tzu (b) Chinese philosopher Lao Tzu
4. (a) the Hugo Award (b) The Hugo Award (c) the Hugo award
5. (a) Are (b) are

Writing for Review Write a paragraph that includes several different kinds of proper nouns, proper adjectives, titles, and quotations.

CHAPTER 27 PUNCTUATION

For each numbered item, indicate the correct punctuation.

Gordon Parks, the noted [1]photographer is also an artist, [2]a filmmaker an author, and a painter. He has written [3]3 autobiographical novels (including [4]"The Learning Tree"), poetry, and [5]essays, he has also composed [6]music, and produced films. Now in his [7]'seventies, Parks says [8]that "there are many things he still wants to do. "I just want [9]the time, he said, [10]to do them carefully and with joy."

1. (a) photographer, (b) photographer (c) "photographer"
2. (a) a filmmaker an author (b) a filmmaker, an author,
3. (a) three autobiographical (b) 3 autobiographical
4. (a) *The Learning Tree*), (b) "The Learning Tree"), (c) "The Learning Tree,")
5. (a) essays, he (b) essays. he (c) essays; he (d) essays; He
6. (a) music, and (b) music and
7. (a) seventies (b) 'seventies (c) seventies'
8. (a) that "there (b) "that there (c) that there
9. (a) the time, he said (b) the time," he said (c) the time. he said
10. (a) "to do (b) to do

Writing for Review Write a paragraph that includes a dialogue.

Skills and Resources

PART

3

Printed and bound books: a resource for centuries

0
1
2
3
4
5
6
7
8
9

UNIT IX

Skills

Thinking About Thinking: Recalling

This unit focuses on several special language skills—vocabulary, spelling, speaking, listening, and test taking. Each of these aspects of using language engages you in the process of problem solving. As you strengthen your ability to think about how you solve problems with words, you will find that this kind of thinking will spill over into a great variety of situations. After all, thinking is not only a part of writing and using language. It is a part of living.

Defining the Skill

One of the most common thinking skills we use in solving problems, a skill that we often take for granted, is **RECALLING**. Vocabulary development and accurate spelling, for example, depend on being able to recall words you have seen before. Recalling makes it possible for you to build on past experiences to solve problems.

Applying the Skill

Look carefully at the photograph for one minute. Then close your book and list all the things you recall seeing in the photograph. With the entire class, make a list on the blackboard, adding to it until the class is satisfied that everything has been recalled. Then revise the list by examining the photograph again. Finally, erase the list from the board and try to recall the entire list again.

CHAPTER 28

Vocabulary Skills

A strong vocabulary is an important tool of effective communication. The more words you know, the more clearly you will be able to express yourself. This chapter looks at ways to build vocabulary. It focuses especially on helping you to improve the vocabulary you use in your writing.

Words in Context

Probably the most natural way of building your vocabulary is by reading. When you read, you are likely to come across many new words. Often you understand the meanings of these new words because the words occur in sentences and paragraphs; that is, they occur in *context.*

The **context** is the setting or surroundings in which a word appears.

By examining the context of an unfamiliar word, you can often figure out its meaning. You can also get an idea of how to use the word in your own writing. For example, look at these famous lines from Edgar Allan Poe's "The Bells":

> . . . the tintinnabulation that so musically wells
> From the bells, bells, bells, bells,
> Bells, bells, bells—
> From the jingling and the tinkling of the bells.

The word *tintinnabulation* is probably unfamiliar to you, but the context gives you a strong clue to its meaning. Since *tintinnabulation* is applied to bells and described as musical, you can figure out that it must mean "ringing."

When you are trying to determine the meaning of a word from its context, look for the following different types of context clues.

RESTATEMENT

Sometimes the context clarifies the meaning of an unfamiliar word by restating it in other, simpler words. Here is an example:

> A tsunami, or tidal wave, can cause great damage and loss of lives.

The context clarifies the meaning of *tsunami* by restating it in the simpler words "tidal wave." Notice that in this example the restatement interrupts the sentence and is set off with commas.

Not all restatements are set off with commas. Look at these two sentences, for example:

> From July through October, typhoons sometimes occur in the western Pacific Ocean. These severe tropical hurricanes have been responsible for the loss of many ships.

Here the restatement is a bit less obvious because it occurs in a second sentence. Yet you can still figure out that a *typhoon* is a severe tropical hurricane.

ILLUSTRATION OR EXAMPLE

Sometimes the context helps you understand an unfamiliar word by giving you one or more examples that illustrate the meaning of the word. Consider this sentence:

> Large felines include lions, tigers, and leopards.

The word *felines* may be unfamiliar, but a series of examples—lions, tigers, and leopards—helps you figure out that *felines* are members of the cat family.

One long example can also clarify the meaning of an unfamiliar word. For instance:

> After the Soviet invasion of Afghanistan, President Jimmy Carter instituted an embargo that prohibited Americans from selling wheat to the Soviet Union.

Here the single example about not selling wheat to the Soviet Union gives you a strong clue to what an *embargo* is. An *embargo* is a ban on trade.

Sometimes an unfamiliar word is one of the examples given. For instance:

> Italian chefs often season their dishes with ingredients such as salt, pepper, garlic, and oregano.

The word *oregano* may be unfamiliar, but it is listed along with three familiar seasonings—salt, pepper, and garlic. You can therefore figure out that *oregano* is also a seasoning.

COMPARISON AND CONTRAST

Sometimes the context compares an unfamiliar word to a familiar word or phrase. Here is an example:

> Chimpanzees are congenial creatures, and most small pet monkeys are also friendly.

Although you may not know what *congenial* means, the word *also* suggests that a comparison is being made. By examining the comparison you can figure out that *congenial* means "friendly."

Sometimes the context contrasts an unfamiliar word with a familiar word or phrase. Here is an example:

> Gorillas can be timorous, but chimpanzees are bold and confident.

Timorous may be unfamiliar, but the word *but* suggests that a contrast is being made. By examining the contrast you can figure out that *timorous* is the opposite of bold and confident. *Timorous* therefore must mean "meek and shy."

EXERCISE 1 **Determining Meanings from Context.** Each of the following ten passages contains an italicized word that may be unfamiliar to you. Determine the meaning of the italicized word by examining its context, or surroundings. Look for the different types of context clues—restatement, illustration or example, and comparison and contrast. Write the meaning of the word on your paper.

1. *Meteorology,* or weather forecasting, has grown more accurate since satellite pictures have become available.
2. Amelia Earhart was a famous *aviator* who broke many flying records before she and her plane disappeared mysteriously in 1937.
3. Mark Twain was noted for his *satire*. Much of his writing ridiculed the customs of his time.
4. Just as the sea can *erode* the sand, water can wear down a rock.
5. Many collections of semiprecious gemstones include topaz, opal, and *zircon*.
6. Many ships are equipped with *sextants*. These instruments determine latitude by measuring the height of the sun or a star.
7. Snails are known for being *sluggish,* but they can actually move quite rapidly when reentering their shells at signs of danger.
8. Many sailors had *scurvy,* a disease caused by lack of vitamin C.
9. Aspirin, although a useful drug, is not a *panacea*. People should not use it as a remedy for all pains and illnesses.
10. It is a *cliché* to say that it is raining cats and dogs. A more original expression might be that it is raining tigers and elephants.

SENTENCE WRITING **Using Vocabulary.** To show that the italicized words in Exercise 1 have become part of your writing vocabulary, use each word in a sentence of your own.

Word Parts

Another important way to build your vocabulary is to learn the meanings of the parts, or elements, that many English words contain. For example, when you look at the parts of the word *rechargeable,* you find *re-* ("again") + *charge* ("supply with electricity") + *-able* ("capable of"). You can therefore figure out that *rechargeable* means "capable of being supplied with electricity again."

When you write, you can put word parts together to make useful longer words. For instance, instead of writing "These batteries are capable of being charged again," you can write "These batteries are rechargeable." Notice how much stronger and clearer the second sentence is.

Prefixes

A **prefix** is a word part that is attached to the beginning of a word or another word part.

Many English words contain prefixes. For example, *rechargeable* contains the prefix *re-,* meaning "again." Knowing the meanings of common prefixes can help you figure out the meanings of words in which the prefixes appear. A knowledge of prefixes can also help you build new words to use in your writing.

Study the following chart of common prefixes:

PREFIX	MEANING	EXAMPLE
anti-	against, opposite	antiwar
co-	together with, joint	costar
de-	to reverse an action, to remove, to deprive of	decode, depopulate, devalue
dis-	not, opposite, to remove, to reverse an action	dishonest, dismount, disadvantage
ex-	previous, former	ex-convict, ex-star
in-, il-, im-, ir-	not, without, lacking	independent, illogical, imbalance, irregular
in-, im	in, into	inflame, immigrate
inter-	between, among	intercity
intra-	within	intracity

PREFIX	MEANING	EXAMPLE
mid-	in the middle of	midair, mid-May
mis-	wrongly, bad, astray	misread, mismatch
non-	not	nonviolent
out-	going beyond, better than	outgrow, outdo
over-	too much, outside, beyond	overspend, overcoat
post-	after	postseason
pre-	before	precooked
pro-	in favor of, for	pro-American, prolabor
re-	again, back	rethink, recheck
sub-	under, beneath, less than	subsoil, subcommittee
trans-	across	transatlantic
un-	not, opposite of, to reverse an action, to deprive of	unfriendly, unbutton, unseat
under-	too little, lower, beneath	underrate, underpass

EXERCISE 2 **Using Prefixes.** Rewrite each of the following fifteen sentences by replacing the awkward underlined phrase or clause with a single word that uses a prefix. Make sure the new word is placed so that your revision reads smoothly.

SAMPLE Some navy ships have guns that are to be used against enemy aircraft.

REVISION Some navy ships have antiaircraft guns.

1. Biographies are one type of writing that is not fiction.
2. Many hunting injuries are caused by rifles that have fired wrongly.
3. The first battle of the American Revolution was a skirmish before dawn on the Lexington Green.
4. Many communications between offices are made on an intercom system.
5. Many of the vitamins are lost if vegetables are cooked too much.
6. Parts of Minnesota often record temperatures below zero in winter.
7. Cheeses that are aged too little often have a bland taste.
8. Sports reporters often try to obtain interviews after a game with the winning coach.

9. Music of the fifties was introduced again in the seventies.
10. Britain's King James II was removed from the throne in 1688.
11. Tests in the middle of the term are given in many schools.
12. Former Presidents often have acted as the "elder statesmen" of their parties.
13. Charles Nordhoff and James Norman Hall are the joint authors of the novel *Mutiny on the Bounty*.
14. During the U.S. Civil War, Britain took a position in favor of the Confederate side.
15. A technical knockout, or TKO, indicates that a boxer has fought better than an opponent.

Suffixes

A **suffix** is a word part that is attached to the end of a word or another word part.

A suffix has a grammatical function as well as a specific meaning. For example, the suffix *-able* forms adjectives. In the word *chargeable* the suffix *-able* turns the verb *charge* into an adjective. In addition, the specific meaning of *-able* is "capable of." Thus *chargeable* is an adjective meaning "capable of being charged."

Knowing the meanings and grammatical functions of suffixes can help you build longer words to use in your writing. Study the following chart of common suffixes. The chart has been divided into sections that show the grammatical function of each suffix. Notice that a spelling change sometimes accompanies the addition of a suffix: for example, the *te* in *pirate* is dropped when the suffix *-acy* is added; in *rely*, the *y* changes to an *i* when *-ance* is added.

SUFFIXES THAT FORM NOUNS

SUFFIX	MEANING	ORIGINAL WORD	NEW NOUN
-acy, -cy	state, condition	pirate stagnant	piracy stagnancy
-age	result, process	bond	bondage
-al	action	dismiss	dismissal
-an, -ian	person from, person belonging to	America library	American librarian
-ance, -ence	state, quality	rely, differ	reliance, difference
-ant, -ent	agent, doer	attend, repel	attendant, repellent

SUFFIX	MEANING	ORIGINAL WORD	NEW NOUN
-ation, -ition, -ion	action, state, result	confirm, impose, infect	confirmation, imposition, infection
-ee	one receiving action	employ	employee
-eer	doer, worker, agent	puppet	puppeteer
-er, -or	doer, maker	write, elevate	writer, elevator
-hood	state, condition	brother	brotherhood
-ism	system, practice	critic	criticism
-ist	follower, doer	ideal	idealist
-ity	state, quality	electric	electricity
-ment	action, result	treat	treatment
-ness	quality, state	happy	happiness
-ship	state, condition	owner	ownership
-ure	act, result, means	fail	failure
-y	result, action	photograph	photography

SUFFIXES THAT FORM ADJECTIVES

SUFFIX	MEANING	ORIGINAL WORD	NEW ADJECTIVE
-able, -ible	able, capable of	wash, access	washable, accessible
-al	characteristic of	magic	magical
-en	made of, like	wool	woolen
-ful	full of, having	spite	spiteful
-ic	characteristic of	cube	cubic
-ish	like, characteristic	red	reddish
-ive	tending to	create	creative
-less	lacking, without	harm	harmless
-like	similar, like	life	lifelike
-ly	like, characteristic	man	manly
-ous	full of, marked by	fame	famous
-y	like, showing	greed	greedy

SUFFIXES THAT FORM VERBS

SUFFIX	MEANING	ORIGINAL WORD	NEW VERB
-ate	become, form, treat	valid	validate
-en	make, cause to be	sharp	sharpen
-fy, -ify	cause, make	simple	simplify
-ize	make, cause to be	standard	standardize

EXERCISE 3 **Using Suffixes.** For each of the following fifteen sentences, replace or revise the awkward underlined phrase or clause by using a word with a suffix. You may have to make other changes so that the new sentence you write reads smoothly. Remember that you sometimes have to make small spelling changes when you add suffixes.

SAMPLE Mark Twain often expressed views <u>characteristic of a pessimist</u>.

REVISION Mark Twain often expressed pessimistic views.

1. Newspapers often are thicker because of <u>what they advertise</u>.
2. Awkward compositions are sometimes lacking in <u>the state of being organized</u>.
3. In most gymnastics competitions ten points indicate a performance <u>without flaw</u>.
4. When water is heated, it <u>is made into vapor</u>.
5. Scientists <u>make classes of</u> rocks according to their hardness.
6. Many students now use electronic <u>instruments that calculate</u>.
7. <u>A quality of being aware</u> of the facts is necessary before you can reach a valid conclusion.
8. Some students receive awards for <u>the state of being a scholar</u>.
9. Many minor-league baseball players are <u>full of hope</u> about entering the major leagues
10. Sometimes there is a <u>discrepant condition</u> between the wording of a law and the intent of the law.
11. Actress Sissy Spacek often plays in roles that require an innocence <u>like that of a child</u>.
12. A <u>person who auctions things</u> traditionally speaks very rapidly.
13. In Greek mythology Jason searched for a fleece <u>made of gold</u>.
14. A sports team <u>marked by victory</u> often attracts more spectators than does a losing team.
15. A number of important American novels have been written about <u>people from Boston</u>.

Roots

A **root** is the central part, or core element, of a word, to which other word parts may be attached.

In the word *rechargeable* the prefix *re-* and the suffix *-able* have been attached to the root *-charge-*. While prefixes and suffixes can give you hints to a word's meaning, the real clue to a word's meaning is its root. Some roots, like *-charge-,* are also English words; others are not. For instance, the word *incredible* contains the prefix *in-* ("not") and the suffix *-ible* ("able"), but the key to its meaning is its root, *-cred-,* which is not an English word. Only if you know that *-cred-* is a Latin root meaning "believe" can you figure out that *incredible* is an adjective meaning "not able to be believed."

Many roots come to English from Latin, like *-cred-,* or from Greek. A knowledge of Greek and Latin roots can therefore help build your vocabulary. Study the following chart of Greek and Latin roots:

ROOT	MEANING	EXAMPLES
-aqu-	water	aqua, aquarium
-astro-, -aster-	star	astronaut, asterisk
-audi-	hear	audience, auditorium
-ben-	good, well	benefit, benevolent
-bio-	life	biography, bionic
-cent-	hundred	percent, century
-chron-	time	chronology, chronic
-cred-	believe	credible, credit
-fac-, -fec-	do, make	factory, perfect
-geo-	earth	geography, geology
-graph-, -gram-	write, writing	biography, telegram
-leg-, -lect-	read	legend, intellect
-log-	word, study	logic, geology
-man-	by hand	manuscript, manufacture
-metr-, -meter-	measure, instrument	metronome, barometer
-milli-	thousand	milligram, millennium
-mor-	die	mortuary, morbid
-ped-	foot	pedal, pedestrian
-phon-	sound	phonograph, telephone
-phot-	light	photography, photogenic
-port-	carry	portable, porter
-sci-	know	science, conscience
-scop-	examine, instrument	microscope, scope
-scrib-, -scrip-	write	scribble, script
-son-	sound	sonar, unison
-spect-	sight	spectator, spectacles

ROOT	MEANING	EXAMPLES
-tele-	far, distant	telephone, television
-therm-	heat	thermostat, thermal
-tract-	draw, pull	retract, extract
-uni-	one	unify, unique
-ven-, -vent-	come	convene, advent
-vid-, -vis-	see	evident, vision

EXERCISE 4 **Using Word Parts.** Using your knowledge of prefixes, suffixes, and Greek and Latin roots, write the meanings of the following fifteen words.

1. telescope
2. invisible
3. tractor
4. thermometer
5. telegraph
6. biology
7. manual
8. import
9. legible
10. sonic
11. mortal
12. intervene
13. inspect
14. distract
15. venture

SENTENCE WRITING **Using Vocabulary.** Write an original sentence for each word in Exercise 4

Word Origins

Latin and Greek are not the only languages that have influenced English. Many other languages have contributed words to the English vocabulary. Here are some examples:

FRENCH	beige, blouse, boutique, breeze, fiancé
SPANISH	alligator, barbecue, bonanza, tango
ITALIAN	ballot, carnival, salami, trio
NAHUATL (AZTEC)	avocado, chocolate, tomato
ALGONQUIAN	raccoon, squash, wampum
GERMAN	kindergarten, pretzel, waltz
NORSE/SCANDINAVIAN	ski, skin, sway
DUTCH	caboose, gruff, sloop
IRISH/GAELIC	bog, clan, plaid
HEBREW	kosher, sabbath, schwa
ARABIC	admiral, alcohol, alfalfa
HINDI (INDIAN)	bandanna, shampoo

Most dictionaries give the origins of a word in brackets or parentheses that appear either before or after the definitions of each word. (See Chapter 33.)

EXERCISE 5 **Examining Word Origins.** Refer to a dictionary to help you identify and write the meanings and origins of the following fifteen words.

1. balcony
2. boomerang
3. cargo
4. deluge
5. dinghy
6. geyser
7. ghoul
8. kiosk
9. maelstrom
10. mammoth
11. putsch
12. ransack
13. sabbatical
14. tycoon
15. woodchuck

SENTENCE WRITING **Using Vocabulary.** Write an original sentence for each word in Exercise 5.

Words from Proper Names

Some English words come from place names or from the names of people, fictional characters, or characters in Greek and Roman mythology. For instance, we use the word *cardigan* for a sweater that opens down the front. The word comes from the Earl of Cardigan, a nineteenth-century British army officer who popularized the garment. The word *denim* comes from a place name: The heavy cotton fabric we call denim was originally made in Nimes, France, and called *serge* ("fabric") *de* ("of") *Nîmes* (pronounced /nēm/). Eventually the expression became *denim.*

EXERCISE 6 **Examining Words from Proper Names.** Use a dictionary to discover and write the meanings and origins of the following fifteen words.

1. atlas
2. badminton
3. braille
4. cordovan
5. derrick
6. guppy
7. jovial
8. leotard
9. limerick
10. marathon
11. panic
12. shanghai
13. shrapnel
14. tangerine
15. watt

SENTENCE WRITING **Using Vocabulary.** Write an original sentence for each word in Exercise 6.

American Versus British English

From examining word origins you can see that vocabulary changes with time. It also changes with distance. Although English is spoken in both Britain and America, British English and American English have many differences in vocabulary. For example, in America we talk about the *hood* and the *trunk* of a car; in England these car parts are called the *bonnet* and the *boot.*

EXERCISE 7 **Examining British and American English.** In the following ten sentences, British words and expressions have been underlined. Rewrite the sentences in American English. Use context clues and a dictionary to help you figure out the meanings of unfamiliar British words and expressions.

1. Because of a lorry accident, there is a diversion on the motorway near the Watney roundabout.
2. While visiting London we queued up for the lift in the underground station.
3. Use the cloth serviettes at dinner tonight.
4. During the interval many theatergoers leave the stalls.
5. Popular vegetables at an English Sunday dinner include swedes, courgettes, and sprouts.
6. The mother wheeled the pram on the pavement and stopped to read the hoarding.

7. My friends in Britain watch the telly from a settee in their lounge.
8. While staying at Cambridge, we could not decide whether to lease a flat or live in a caravan.
9. In many English villages the chemist's stop, the ironmonger's, and the sweetshop are on the high street.
10. When we stopped for petrol, the attendant washed the windscreen, wiped the headlamps and looked under the bonnet with a torch.

Synonyms

Synonyms are words that have the same or nearly the same meanings.

A knowledge of synonyms can help you improve your writing. Instead of repeating the same word, you can use a synonym. For example, *hard* and *difficult* are synonyms.

WEAK REPETITION	Last week's history test was very hard because the essay questions were especially hard.
REVISED WITH SYNONYM	Last week's history test was very hard because the essay questions were especially difficult.

The first sentence sounds repetitious because *hard* is used twice. In the revised sentence the second *hard* is replaced with a synonym, *difficult.* Notice how much better the sentence sounds.

EXERCISE 8 **Using Synonyms.** Rewrite each of the following ten sentences by replacing the repetitious underlined word with its synonym. Choose the appropriate synonym from the following list. Use each word only once.

align	concede	emerge	solitary
assessed	conform (to)	ingenious	
commendable	diverse	intrepid	

1. The performance of an Olympic athlete is judged by a team of judges from different nations.
2. Agatha Christie is known for writing clever mysteries with clever solutions.
3. While film critics often praise actress Meryl Streep, they found her performance in *Sophie's Choice* especially praiseworthy.
4. Brave soldiers often win medals for bravery.

5. William Wordsworth wrote a poem about a lone reaper in the lonely Scottish highlands.
6. In order to protect themselves, small nations often ally themselves with powerful allies.
7. Some people refuse to follow society's dictates, while others are born followers.
8. Some people admit their mistakes, while others are unwilling to admit that they may be mistaken.
9. Various biographies report that Thomas Jefferson was a man of varied talents.
10. Many new scientific developments develop as a result of medical research.

Antonyms

Antonyms are words that have opposite or nearly opposite meanings.

A knowledge of antonyms can help you improve your writing vocabulary. Often you can strengthen a statement by using an antonym for a word expressed with a weak negative. *Hard* and *easy,* for example, are antonyms.

WEAK NEGATIVE	The math test was not hard.
REVISED WITH AN ANTONYM	The math test was easy.

Instead of using *not* + *hard,* the revised sentence uses an antonym for *hard, easy*. Notice that the revision is more direct and precise.

EXERCISE 9 **Using Antonyms.** Rewrite each of the following ten sentences by replacing the awkward underlined phrase or clause with an antonym for the italicized word. For example, in the first sentence provide an antonym for *reflect*. Be sure to place the antonym so that your revision reads smoothly. Choose the appropriate antonym from the list below. Use each word only once.

absorb	fruitless	manifest
accord	hectic	reluctant
artificial	indifferent	repugnant
bland	inflammatory	reputable
erratic	intense	timid

1. People avoid dark clothing in summer because dark colors do not *reflect* sunlight.
2. Speeches that are not *conciliatory* sometimes cause riots.

3. When you are buying or selling a home, it is important to choose a real estate agent who is not *untrustworthy*.
4. Laws passed by Congress must not *disagree* with the stipulations of the Constitution.
5. Lyric poems often reveal feelings that are not *weak*.
6. Some people avoid eating foods with ingredients that are not natural.
7. A traffic officer's day is often not *calm*.
8. Unlike most dogs, cats are not *eager* to enter water.
9. Despite their great size, mountain gorillas are not *bold* creatures.
10. While arbitration often solves labor-management disputes, sometimes efforts to avoid a strike are not *effective*.
11. The audience's reaction to the concert was not *enthusiastic*.
12. His command of the car's stick shift was not *steady*.
13. When she saw her good grades, her delight was not *hidden*.
14. I prefer Chinese dishes that are not *spicy*.
15. The realities of war shown in the film are not *appealing* to me.

Word List for Writers

The following list contains words that you will find useful in your writing. Try using each word in a sentence. If you have trouble at first, look up the meanings of unfamiliar words in a dictionary.

NOUNS

afterthought
ancestor
array
audacity

catastrophe
ceremony
column
comment
component
concept
conjecture

delusion
dismay
duty

episode
era

exile

fantasy
flattery

headway
homage

immaturity
impartiality
incentive
inequality
infection

mire

predecessor

regime

residence
rogue
routine
rubble

situation
skirmish
stamina
superstition
symbol

tactic
tension
transition
trifle
triumph
turmoil

zest

ADJECTIVES

absolute
absurd
academic
adverse
ambivalent
austere

belligerent
beneficient
boisterous

callous
cantankerous
ceaseless
compatible
complacent
cordial
crucial

deliberate
discreet
dormant
drab
durable
dynamic

eventual
explicit
extravagant

festive
forcible

glum

habitual
hideous

impeccable
imperfect
impractical
indestructible
ineffective
insufficient
invariable
inverse
involuntary
irresistible

melancholy

negligible
noble

oblivious
outmoded

partisan
perfunctory
peripheral
petty
pious
plaintive

quaint

reminiscent
robust

sensitive
sentimental
shabby
shrewd
simultaneous
sizable
slack
slovenly
spacious
sporadic
subjective

unbearable
unconditional
unimaginative
unpredictable

wholesome

VERBS

abolish
accelerate
accumulate
accuse
admire
analyze
antagonize
appall
assemble
assert
attain
attract

baffle
balk

compare
compensate
comprehend
conclude
confront

denounce
deny
detach
detest
deviate
dismiss
disparage
distort

elude
emphasize
enable
enact
enhance
enlighten

VERBS

enrich
enroll
entangle
evaluate
exaggerate

fascinate

identify
illustrate
immerse
immobilize
infiltrate
infuriate

insist
intend
inundate
involve

justify

lament

mock

overpower
overwhelm

precede

refute
resent

shirk
shun
stimulate

transform

underestimate

CHAPTER 29

Spelling Skills

Spelling is an important element in writing. Correct spelling is never noticed, but even one spelling error jars a reader and spoils a sentence. This chapter looks at some of the ways in which you can improve your spelling.

The spellings of many English words can be mastered with the help of the following spelling rules. Learning these rules and their exceptions will help you improve your spelling.

Adding Prefixes and Suffixes

When adding a prefix to a word, retain the spelling of the original word.

over- + rule = overrule
un- + natural = unnatural
mis- + understand = misunderstand
in- + accurate = inaccurate

EXERCISE 1 **Adding Prefixes.** Combine the following prefixes and words, and write the resulting words.

1. dis- + appearance
2. dis- + appoint
3. il- + legal
4. in- + exact
5. mis- + spell
6. over- + react
7. re- + commend
8. un- + necessary
9. un- + usual
10. under- + rate

Words That End in *-ness* and *-ly*

When adding *-ness* to a word that ends in *n*, keep the *n*.

sudden + -ness = suddenness
thin + -ness = thinness

When adding *-ly* to a word that ends in a single *l*, keep the *l*. When the word ends in a double *l*, drop one *l*. When the word ends in a consonant + *le*, drop the *le*.

beautiful + -ly = beautifully
cool + -ly = coolly
full + -ly = fully
horrible + -ly = horribly

EXERCISE 2 **Adding *-ness* and *-ly*.** Combine the following words and suffixes, and write the resulting words.

1. actual + -ly
2. favorable + -ly
3. green + -ness
4. incidental + -ly
5. intellectual + -ly
6. lean + -ness
7. mean + -ness
8. responsible + -ly
9. stubborn + -ness
10. subtle + -ly

Words That End in *y*

When adding a suffix to a word that ends in a consonant + *y*, generally change the *y* to *i*. Do not change the *y* to *i* when the suffix begins with *i*.

pity + -ed = pitied
pity + -ing = pitying
try + -ed = tried
try + -ing = trying

Exceptions include certain one-syllable words combined with certain suffixes: *dry* + *-ness* = *dryness,* for example. When in doubt, check a dictionary.

When adding a suffix to a word that ends in a vowel + *y*, generally keep the *y*.

boy + -hood = boyhood
play + -ful = playful

Exceptions include *day* + -ly = *daily, gay*+ *-ly* = *gaily*.

EXERCISE 3 **Adding Suffixes to Words That End in *y*.** Combine the following words and suffixes, and write the resulting words.

1. duty + -ful
2. extraordinary + -ly
3. happy + -ness
4. joy + -ful
5. lively + -ness
6. lonely + -ness
7. lovely + -er
8. play + -er
9. study + -ing
10. study + -ous

Words That End in Silent *e*

When adding a suffix that begins with a consonant to a word that ends in silent *e*, generally keep the *e*.

amuse + -ment = amusement
use + -less = useless

Exceptions include a number of one-syllable words and words that end in *dge* or two vowels; for example, *argue* + *-ment* = *argument, awe* + *-ful* = *awful, judge* + *ment* = *judgment, true* + *-ly* = *truly*. When in doubt, check a dictionary.

When adding a suffix that begins with a vowel (including -y pronounced e) to a word that ends in silent e, generally drop the e. However, when adding a suffix that begins with a or o to a word that ends in ce or ge, keep the e to retain the soft sound of the c or the g.

bite + -ing = biting
noise + -y = noisy
notice + -able = noticeable
change + -able = changeable

Exceptions include certain one-syllable words and words that end in two vowels; for instance, *canoe + -ing = canoeing, hoe + -ing = hoeing, mile + -age = mileage*. A few one-syllable words that end in *i* + silent *e* change the *ie* to *y* when adding *-ing;* for example, *lie + -ing = lying*. When in doubt, check a dictionary.

EXERCISE 4 **Adding Suffixes to Words That End in Silent *e*.** Combine the following words and suffixes, and write the resulting words. If you think that a word may be an exception, check its spelling in a dictionary.

1. arrange + -ment
2. bare + -ly
3. believe + -able
4. excite + -ment
5. guide + -ance
6. manage + -able
7. notice + -ing
8. taste + -less
9. use + -ful
10. use + -ing

Words That End in a Consonant

When adding a suffix that begins with a vowel to a word that ends in a single vowel + a single consonant, generally double the final consonant if (a) the original word is a one-syllable word or (b) the original word has its accent on the last syllable.

win + -ing = winning   com • mit′ + -ing = committing

Do not double the final consonant if the accent is not on the last syllable.

cov′er + -ed = covered   o′pen + -er = opener

Do not double the final consonant if it is preceded by two vowels or by another consonant.

treat + -ing = treating   rust + -y = rusty

When adding a suffix that begins with a consonant to a word that ends in a consonant, do not double the final consonant.

commit + -ment = commitment   win + -less = winless

EXERCISE 5 **Adding Suffixes to Words That End in a Consonant.** Combine these words and suffixes, and write the resulting words.

1. benefit + -ed
2. commit + -ing
3. confer + -ed
4. control + -ed
5. forget + -ful
6. forget + -ing
7. occur + -ence
8. profit + -able
9. quiz + -ing
10. regret + -ed

Spelling Plurals

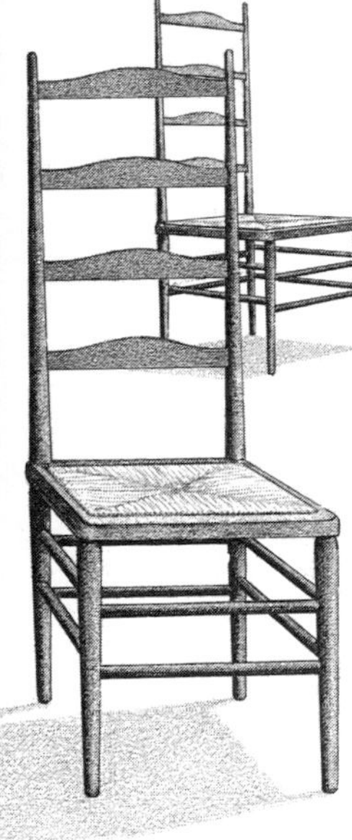

RULES	EXAMPLES
To form the plural of most nouns, including proper nouns, add *s*. For nouns ending in *ch, s, sh, x,* or *z,* add *es*.	chair, chairs Roth, Roths tax, taxes Rodriguez, Rodriguezes
To form the plural of common nouns ending in a consonant + *y*, change the *y* to *i* and add *es*.	army, armies city, cities rally, rallies
To form the plural of common nouns ending in a vowel + *y* and all proper nouns ending in *y*, add *s*.	toy, toys Cagney, Cagneys Kelly, Kellys
To form the plural of common nouns ending in a vowel + *o* and all proper nouns ending in *o*, add *s*.	radio, radios rodeo, rodeos Mongello, Mongellos
To form the plural of common nouns ending in a consonant + *o*, generally add *es*, but sometimes add *s*.	mosquito, moquitoes volcano, volcanoes halo, halos
To form the plural of most nouns ending in *f*, including all nouns ending in *ff*, add *s*. For some nouns ending in *f*, especially those ending in *lf*, change the *f* to *v* and add *es*.	belief, beliefs roof, roofs huff, huffs loaf, loaves calf, calves
To form the plural of some nouns ending in *fe*, change the *f* to *v* and add *s*.	knife, knives life, lives wife, wives

RULES	EXAMPLES
To form the plural of compound nouns written as one word, follow the above rules.	handful, handfuls huckleberry, huckleberries penknife, penknives
To form the plural of compound nouns that are hyphenated or written as more than one word, generally make the most important word plural.	editor in chief, editors in chief mother-in-law, mothers-in-law
Nouns with irregular plural forms do not follow any rules.	foot, feet mouse, mice
Some nouns are the same in the singular and the plural.	series, series sheep, sheep

EXERCISE 6 **Spelling Plurals.** Write the plural form of each of the following nouns. If you are uncertain of the plural form, check a dictionary. If a noun has no plural form listed in the dictionary, its plural is formed in accordance with the first plural rule on page 626.

1. basis
2. chief
3. chimney
4. commander in chief
5. Connery
6. cupful
7. fox
8. gas
9. gypsy
10. hairbrush
11. half
12. housewife
13. leaf
14. lunch
15. sister-in-law
16. solo
17. studio
18. technique
19. tendency
20. tomato

Spelling *ie* or *ei*

Write *i* before *e* except after *c*,
Or when sounded like *a* as in *neighbor* and *weigh*.

I BEFORE *E*	believe, niece, thief
EXCEPT AFTER *C*	conceit, deceive, receipt
SOUNDED LIKE *A*	eight, sleigh, vein

Exceptions to this famous rhyme include *efficient, either, foreign, height, leisure, neither, science, seize,* and *weird.*

EXERCISE 7 **Spelling *ie* or *ei*.** For each of the following, decide whether you should add *ie* or *ei,* and then write the complete word.

1. bel__f
2. c__ling
3. chandel__r
4. fr__nd
5. front__r
6. gr__f
7. rec__ve
8. repr__ve
9. shr__k
10. w__ght

Easily Confused Words

Some words with similar sounds are often confused. Learning the meanings and pronunciations of these words can help you avoid spelling problems. Study the following pairs of easily confused words:

accept to agree to take; to assume; to approve
except but

addition a joining; something added; an increase
edition the form in which something is published

affect to influence
effect a result

beside next to
besides in addition to; moreover

build to erect; to form
built erected; formed

choose [cho͞oz] to select
chose [chōz] selected

emit to give off; to discharge; to utter
omit to fail to include; to neglect

loose [lo͞os] free; not confined; not tight
lose [lo͞oz] to misplace; to drop

quiet [kwī′it] making little or no noise
quite [kwīt] completely; very; rather

than in comparison with
then at that time; next

EXERCISE 8 **Spelling Words with Similar Sounds.** In each of the following sentences, a choice of words is given in parentheses. Write the word that correctly completes the sentence.

1. Alaskan winters are (quiet/quite) cold.
2. (Accept/Except) for Ann, no one went to the dance.
3. The bridge was (build/built) ten years ago.
4. Events in Washington can (affect/effect) our lives.
5. We bought the late (addition/edition) of the newspaper.
6. The boy's front tooth is (loose/lose).
7. Helen (choose/chose) a seat near the door.

8. Some appliances (emit/omit) ultraviolet light.
9. A spider sat down (beside/besides) Miss Muffet.
10. Willie is two years older (than/then) Marie.

Homophones

Homophones are words that have the same pronunciation but different spellings and meanings.

For example, *be* ("exist") and *bee* ("an insect") are homophones. Learning the meanings of homophones can help you avoid spelling errors. Study the following homophones:

hear to be aware of sounds; to listen
here in this place

hoarse sounding deep and harsh or grating
horse a four-legged animal with hoofs, a mane, and a tail

its belonging to it
it's a contraction of *it is* or *it has*

peace a period of no war; calmness; absence of conflict
piece a portion or part of a whole

plain simple; not fancy; a flat expanse of ground
plane a flat surface; an airplane

role a function; a part performed by an actor
roll to move by turning; such a movement; a small loaf of bread

shone sent out light; gleamed
shown exposed to view; presented; made known; proved

their belonging to them
there in that place
they're a contraction of *they are*

threw tossed; cast; propelled into the air
through in one side and out the other; beginning to end; finished

weather atmospheric conditions
whether if

who's a contraction of *who is* or *who has*
whose the possessive case of *who*

your belonging to you
you're a contraction of *you are*

EXERCISE 9 **Spelling Homophones.** Write the word from the parentheses that correctly completes the sentence.

1. Anna spoke in a (hoarse/horse) whisper.
2. Buffaloes once roamed America's (plains/planes).
3. The warring nations signed a (peace/piece) treaty.
4. (Their/There/They're) lining up for the movie.
5. The sun (shone/shown) down on the sea.
6. (Your/You're) composition received an *A*.
7. (Who's/Whose) pen is this?
8. An actress must play many (roles/rolls).
9. The pitcher (threw/through) a curve ball.
10. Dogs can (hear/here) high-pitched sounds.

One or Two Words?

Some terms are written as one word in some contexts but as two separate words in other contexts:

all ready prepared; in final condition
already previously

At last we were *all ready* to leave.
We were *already* three hours late.

all together in one place; in one group
altogether completely; entirely

The cousins were *all together* at Christmas.
It is *altogether* impossible to meet the deadline.

all ways every way
always at all times; continually

She examined *all ways* of solving the problem.
She *always* tries to solve problems.

every day each day
everyday ordinary; usual

Every day we read a new chapter in the book.
The book is about the *everyday* lives of Eskimos.

The following should never be spelled as one word:

a lot no one

EXERCISE 10 **Spelling One or Two Words.** For the following words and expressions, write "no such word" if the term does not exist.

1. all ready, already
2. all together, altogether
3. all ways, always
4. a lot, alot no such word
5. every day, everyday
6. no one, noone no such word

SENTENCE WRITING **Spelling Correctly.** Write an original sentence for each correct word or expression in Exercise 10.

Frequently Misspelled Words

The following list contains words that are often misspelled by students in your grade. Master the words by (a) applying spelling rules where possible, (b) writing and rewriting the words, and (c) making up memory devices for problem words. For instance, if you have trouble remembering the *b* in *debt,* you might remember, "A debt must *b* repaid."

accidentally	afraid	always
accompany	again	ambassador
accomplish	against	answer
ache	airplane	appearance
achieve	all right	appreciate
across	almost	approach
actually	a lot	apricot
address	alphabet	apron
advertise	although	argue
affectionate	aluminum	argument

assistance
athlete
attitude
author
autumn
awful
awkward

balloon
ballot
banana
basically
basis
beggar
beginning
believe
beverage
blouse
bologna
boundary
burglar
business
butcher

calendar
camera
canoe
cantaloupe
capable
carton
celery
chalk
channel
character
chief
chili
chlorine
chocolate
chronological
cigar
cigarette
cinnamon
civilization
coffee
comfortable
competition
confidential
constitution
cooperate
corporation
correspond
cough
country
courtesy
criticize
crochet
curtain
curtsy

debt
deceit
definite
deny
despair
detergent
develop
diaper
dictionary
difference
dinner
dinosaur
disappearance
disappoint
disastrous
discipline
discuss
disease
disgusted
doubt
dumb
dynamic

earring
echoes
efficient
eighteen
eighth
either
elaborate
electrical
elegant
embarrass
emergency
emphasize
environment
equipped
equivalent
essential
exaggerate
excellent
excess
excitement
exercise
exhaust
existence
experience
extraordinary

familiar
fascinate
fatal
fatigue
favorable
favorite
February
festival
fiend
flirt
flourish
forehead
foreign
forty
fountain
fourteen
frankfurter
friend
fulfill

galaxy
garage
garbage
genius
gesture
ghastly
ghost

giraffe
gorgeous
government
gracious
grammar
grandfather
grandmother
grief
guess
guest
guidance
guide
gypsy

handkerchief
happiness
height
hippopotamus
humorous

icicle
icy
idea
ideal
ignorance
immediate
immense
impossible
impression
incidentally
incredible
inevitable
innocent
inquire
install
intellectual
intelligent
interfere
interpret
interrupt
island

jealous
jewel
jewelry

juice
juvenile

kindergarten
knead
kneel
knew
know
knowledge

landlord
laundry
leisure
length
leopard
lettuce
library
lightning
listen
liveliness
loneliness

magnificent
maintain
marriage
mathematics
meant
medal
medicine
metal
miniature
minute
mirror
misspell
modern
muscle
myth

narrator
necessary
necklace
nectar
neighbor
neither
nickel

niece
nightmare
nineteen
ninety
ninth
no one
noticing
nourish
nuclear
nuisance
numb

occasion
occurrence
offense
offered
official
often
omelet
once
opportunity
orchestra
origin

palm
panic
panicking
parallel
patrol
peanut
peasant
peculiar
pencil
perceive
performance
permanent
personal
perspiration
persuade
petition
phenomenon
phonograph
photograph
physical
physician

picnic
pillar
pilot
pirate
planet
pleasant
polar
pollution
possession
possible
potato
potatoes
practice
precede
pressure
primitive
prison
privilege
proceed
process
profession
pronunciation
proportion

quiet
quite
quizzed

realize
receive
recognize
recommend
region
rehearse
religion
repetition
representative
responsibility
restaurant
rhyme
rhythm
rind
rough

salad
salary
sandwich
science
scissors
senate
separate
serum
several
significant
silence
similar
sincerely
siren
spinach
spiral
spirit
sponsor
statue
status
stomach
suburb
sugar
suit
summary
sure
sweater
sword

technical
tendency
thorough
though
through
tiptoe
tired
tissue
today
tomato
tomatoes
tomb
tomorrow
tongue
tonight
tough
towel
transfer
trouble
truly
tulip
twelfth
tyrant

umbrella
useful
using

vacuum
vanilla
various
village
villain
visitor

wealth
Wednesday
weird
whisper
whistle
whole
width
wisdom
women
wrinkle

yolk
young

zero

CHAPTER 30

Business Communication Skills

This Chapter looks at business writing and related skills that you will need to know when you are searching for a job, applying to a college or another school, or making other business communications. The chapter opens with a section about the format and content of business letters. It then examines job applications and other forms that you must often fill out. It concludes with a presentation of valuable information about want ads, newspaper ads that you will often consult when you are job hunting.

Business Letters

A **business letter** is a formal letter written to communicate information or request action. You will find that a letter is often far more effective than a telephone conversation because it gives you an opportunity to organize your thoughts and to state them in specific, unmistakable terms. A letter also provides a dated written record that you can use for further reference or, occasionally, for legal proof of your communication. For these reasons, you should always keep a copy of each business letter you write, at least until the matter under consideration has been concluded.

Every business letter follows certain conventions of format and style. Generally, business letters should be neat, clear, courteous, brief, and easy to read. It is therefore advisable to *type* business letters whenever possible. Use single spacing, and leave an extra space between paragraphs and between the different parts of the letter. To make the letter visually pleasing to the reader, use wide margins and center the letter vertically on the page. In order to center the letter, you will probably have to type it once, examine its length, and then type a centered final draft. Be sure that your final draft is free of spelling, grammar, and punctuation errors, as well as messy erasures or typeovers.

The standard business letter is composed of six basic parts.

the heading	the body
the inside address	the closing
the salutation	the signature

On the following model business letter, the six parts are labeled. The model business letter is typed in **modified block style:** The inside address and the salutation align with the left-hand margin, while the heading, the closing, and the signature appear to the right of the center of the page and align on the left with each other. In modified block style each paragraph of the body may either align with the left margin or be indented. (Another example of a letter using modified block style appears on page 642.) In **block style** all six parts align with the left-hand margin. (You can find examples of letters using block style on page 643.)

The following subsections discuss each of the six parts of a business letter in detail. Study the information carefully and make use of the models in this chapter.

THE HEADING

The **heading** contains your mailing address and the date of the letter. The name of your city, town, or village should be followed by a comma, your state, and your ZIP code. Also put a comma between the day and the year in the date. Do not put a comma before the ZIP code. If you are using stationery with a letterhead that gives your address, your heading should consist of the date only.

In writing addresses, you should generally avoid abbreviations. However, it is permissible for you to use official post office abbreviations for the names of states in the heading of a business letter (see Chapter 27).

THE INSIDE ADDRESS

The **inside address** contains the name and address of the party to whom you are writing. It appears two lines below the heading. If you know the name of an individual to whom you should address your letter, put that person's name on the first line of the inside address. If you know the name of a room, a division, or a department to which you should send your letter, be certain to include this information as well as the name and address of the company or organization to which you are writing.

When you include the name of an individual in the inside address, use the person's full name preceeded by a **title of respect** if you know this information. In particular, four titles of respect—*Mr.*, *Mrs.*, *Ms.*, and *Dr.*—should always be abbreviated and must be written with periods. Most other titles of respect, including *Minister*, *Reverend*, and *Professor*, should be spelled out. The title *Miss* should never be followed by a period.

If you know the **business title** of the individual, you should usually put it on the same line as his or her name and separate it from the name with a comma. For example, in the model business letter, the business title *Manager* is included on the first line of the inside address after the name *Mr. Anthony Lisi.* If adding the business title makes the first line look too long, you may put it on a second line. In this case, no comma is used.

Robert Tallchief	or	Joanna Silver
Director of Marketing		Senior Vice President

MODEL BUSINESS LETTER (MODIFIED BLOCK STYLE)

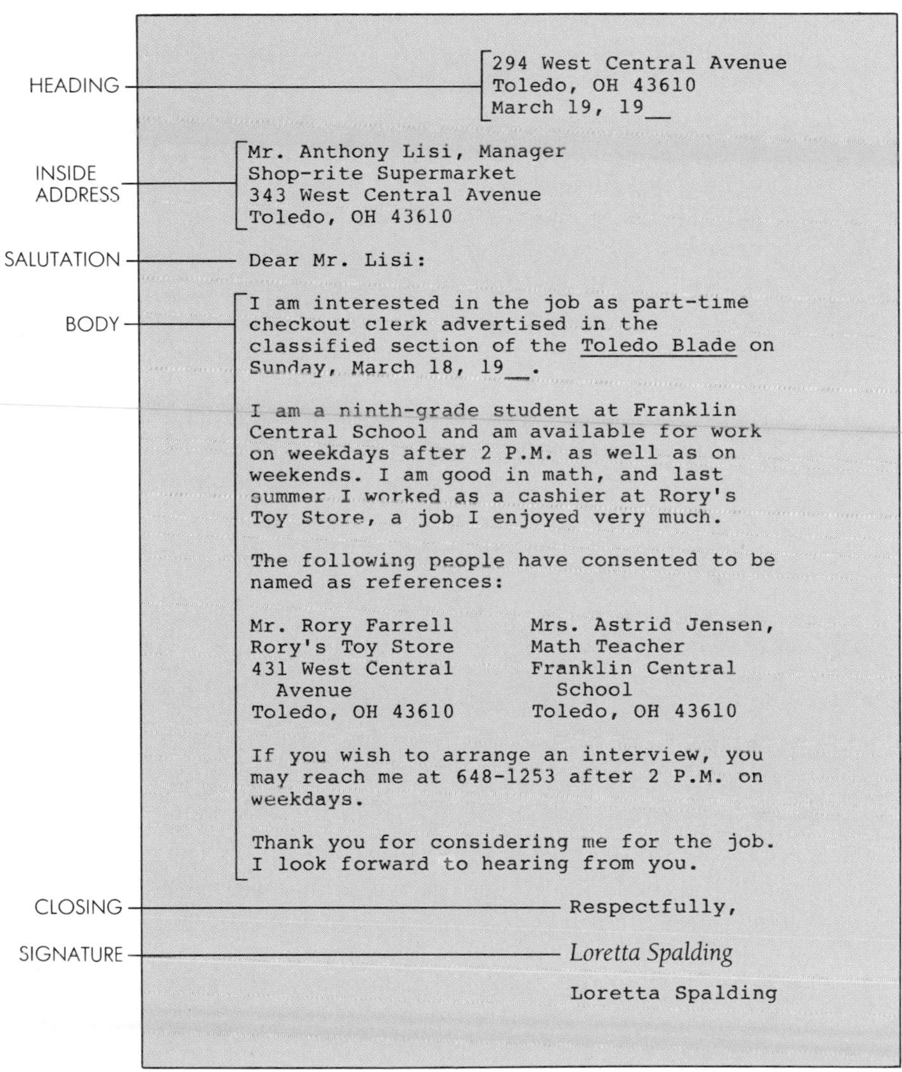

294 West Central Avenue
Toledo, OH 43610
March 19, 19__

Mr. Anthony Lisi, Manager
Shop-rite Supermarket
343 West Central Avenue
Toledo, OH 43610

Dear Mr. Lisi:

I am interested in the job as part-time checkout clerk advertised in the classified section of the Toledo Blade on Sunday, March 18, 19__.

I am a ninth-grade student at Franklin Central School and am available for work on weekdays after 2 P.M. as well as on weekends. I am good in math, and last summer I worked as a cashier at Rory's Toy Store, a job I enjoyed very much.

The following people have consented to be named as references:

Mr. Rory Farrell	Mrs. Astrid Jensen,
Rory's Toy Store	Math Teacher
431 West Central Avenue	Franklin Central School
Toledo, OH 43610	Toledo, OH 43610

If you wish to arrange an interview, you may reach me at 648-1253 after 2 P.M. on weekdays.

Thank you for considering me for the job. I look forward to hearing from you.

Respectfully,

Loretta Spalding

Loretta Spalding

The Salutation

The **saluation** is a formal greeting to the reader of your letter. It appears two lines below the inside address and is followed by a colon (:). Different kinds of salutations are used in different situations.

SITUATION	EXAMPLE
When writing a man whose name you know, use *Mr.* unless another title (such as *Reverend* or *Rabbi*) is appropriate.	*A letter to:* Mr. Lionel Black, Editor *Salutation:* Dear Mr. Black:
When writing to a woman whose name and title you know, use *Ms., Miss,* or *Mrs.* as she prefers unless another title (such as *Dr.*) is appropriate.	*A letter to:* Mrs. Simone Okaido *Salutation:* Dear Mrs. Okaido:
When writing to a woman whose name you know but whose title you do not know, generally use *Ms.* It is also possible to use her full name and omit the title of respect.	*A letter to:* Alma Jimenez, Director *Salutation:* Dear Ms. Jimenez: OR Dear Alma Jimenez:
When writing to a specific person whose name you do not know, generally use *Sir* or *Madam*. It is also possible to use the person's business title.	*A letter to:* Subscription Editor *Newsweek* magazine *Salutation:* Dear Sir or Madam: OR Dear Subscription Editor:
When writing to a company, an organization, a department, or a box number, generally use *Sir or Madam*. It is also possible to use the name of the company or organization.	*A letter to:* Pyramid Productions, Inc. *Salutation:* Dear Sir or Madam: OR Dear Pyramid Productions:

THE BODY

The **body** of a business letter communicates the information to the reader. It begins two lines below the salutation and should be single-spaced, with double spaces between paragraphs. Its contents will vary according to the kind of letter you are writing (see page 640) and the specific information that you wish to communicate. In general, however, the body should be brief, clear, and well organized. It should conclude with an expression of thanks or appreciation. If the letter follows up a previous letter or conversation, this fact should be mentioned in the opening paragraph.

THE CLOSING

The **closing** of a letter is a polite word or phrase that leads into your signature. It appears two lines below the body of the letter and is followed by a comma. If the closing consists of more than one word, only the first word should begin with a capital letter. The tone of the closing may be very formal or it may be a bit more personal, depending on your relationship with the reader of your letter or the particular tone you wish to achieve.

MORE FORMAL CLOSINGS	MORE PERSONAL CLOSINGS
Respectfully yours,	Sincerely yours,
Yours respectfully,	Sincerely,
Very truly yours,	Cordially,

THE SIGNATURE

Your full name should be signed in ink just below the closing. Beneath your signature you should type (or print) your name. If you have a business title, you may put it below your name, as Allen Davies does in the example that follows. A woman writer may also indicate how she wishes to be addressed by including a title of respect in parentheses before her name, as Elena Suarez does in the example that appears below.

Respectfully yours,	Yours truly,
Allen Davies	*Mrs. Elena Suarez*
Allen Davies Student President	(Mrs.) Elena Suarez

EXERCISE 1 **Using Business-Letter Format.** Write or type the appropriate heading, inside address, salutation, closing, and signature for letters to the following parties. Use modified block style, and draw lines to indicate the placement of the body of the letter. Use your address and today's date for the heading, and use your name for the signature.

1. Joyce Keating, Director, Hillcrest Photo Studios, 162 Del Paso Boulevard, Sacramento, California 95815
2. The Seacraft Company, 8500 Long Beach Road, Darien, Connecticut 06845
3. Professor Mark Mizner, English Department, Southern Methodist University, Dallas, Texas 75275
4. Manager, Cheyenne Sports Arena, Cheyenne, Wyoming 82002
5. Dr. Roberta Grandville, Director of Research, Kensington Institute for Advanced Studies, Lexington, Massachusetts 02173
6. the principal of your school

Addressing Envelopes

On the envelope of a business letter, put your **return address**—your own name and mailing address—in the upper left-hand corner. Put the **recipient's address**—the name and address of the party to whom you are writing—just below and to the right of the center of the envelope. Be sure to include ZIP codes in all addresses. The envelope for the model business letter would look like this:

```
Loretta Spalding
294 West Central Avenue
Toledo, OH 43610


                   Mr. Anthony Lisi, Manager
                   Shop-Rite Supermarket
                   343 West Central Avenue
                   Toledo, OH 43610
```

EXERCISE 2 **Addressing Envelopes.** Address the envelopes for three of the letters that you wrote for Exercise 1. Write or type the addresses on real envelopes or in rectangular boxes drawn on paper.

Kinds of Business Letters

Business letters are written for a number of different purposes. Among them are (1) to apply for a job or to a school, (2) to request information or services, (3) to place an order, and (4) to make a complaint or ask for an adjustment.

THE LETTER OF APPLICATION

Though most jobs and colleges require that you fill out a preprinted application form (see page 644), there are times when a letter of application may be all that is required. A **letter of application** asks that you be considered for a job, be allowed to enroll in a school or a course, or be permitted to join a club or another organization. An example is the model business letter in which Loretta Spalding applies for a job at a Shop-Rite Supermarket.

Follow these steps when you write a letter of application:

1. Identify the job or organization to which you are applying.
2. Identify yourself.
3. Include relevant information involving time, hours, and so on. For instance, if you are applying for a job, state the date that you can begin and the hours that you will be available. If you are hoping to

enroll in a special course, state the day, hours, and weeks or term during which the course is to be held.

4. Briefly explain your qualifications.
5. Include the names and addresses of people who may be contacted for references. If possible, give a **business reference**—a former employer or job supervisor—as well as at least one **personal reference**—a teacher, a neighbor, or another adult who knows you well. Always contact these people beforehand to make sure that they are willing to be named as references. Never list family members as references.
6. Include your telephone number and the best time at which you can be contacted.
7. Conclude courteously.

THE LETTER OF REQUEST

A **letter of request** asks for information or services from an organization or an individual. An example of a letter of request is the letter on page 642.

Follow these steps when you write a letter of request:

1. Identify yourself.
2. Explain the reason or reasons that you need assistance.
3. State a specific request. If you are requesting the services of a guest speaker or writing about another matter that involves a specific date, time, and place, be sure to specify the date, time, and place in your letter.
4. Conclude courteously.

THE ORDER LETTER

The **order letter** places an order for manufactured goods, magazines, or something else that requires payment. An example of an order letter is the first letter on page 643.

Follow these steps when you write an order letter:

1. Give the necessary information about the item or items that you are ordering. If you are ordering manufactured goods, specify the quantity, size, color, and price. If you are subscribing to a magazine, specify the time length of the subscription as well as the price.
2. If you are enclosing payment, state how much you are sending. Send a check or a money order; never mail cash.
3. Keep a copy of the check or money order as well as the letter until the order has been filled to your satisfaction.

THE LETTER OF ADJUSTMENT OR COMPLAINT

A **letter of adjustment or complaint** states a problem and asks that it be corrected. An example is the second letter on page 643, in which Jeffrey Wong complains about not receiving something he ordered.

Follow the steps listed below when you write a letter of adjustment or complaint:

1. Give all the necessary details of the situation.
2. Be polite but firm. A courteous tone is more likely to get a positive response than a rude tone.
3. Ask for specific action, and indicate that you assume that this action will be taken.

A LETTER OF REQUEST (MODIFIED BLOCK STYLE)

Brookdale High School
Kaysville, Utah 84037
January 18, 19__

Ms. Shirley Kanner
Town Supervisor
Kaysville, Utah 84037

Dear Supervisor Kanner:

I am writing to you on behalf of the ninth-grade class of Brookdale High School. On Monday, March 15, our history class is having a special assembly on the role of local government. The program will begin at 1:00 P.M. Our teacher, Mr. Roger Tindall, has suggested that we ask you to be our speaker.

We have been studying governmental responsibility at a local, state, and national level. We would like you to speak to us about the responsibility of local government to the town and to the state.

Please let me know if you can speak at our assembly program. If you need more information, I will be glad to supply it.

Thank you very much.

Yours truly,

David Smith

David Smith
Class Secretary

AN ORDER LETTER (BLOCK STYLE)

88 Main Avenue
Kenilworth, Illinois 60043
May 1, 19__

Athletic Center
Pleasantville High School
Pleasantville, Illinois 60048

Dear Sir or Madam:

Please send me four student tickets at $2.00 each for the Annual All-Star High School Football Game on June 23.

I am enclosing a money order for $8.00 and a return envelope.

Thank you very much.

Sincerely,

Irene Droziok

Irene Dorziok

A LETTER OF COMPLAINT OR ADJUSTMENT (BLOCK STYLE)

8 Circle Court
Glenrio, New Mexico 88423
October 14, 19__

Ms. Theodora Kneche
Customer Relations, Room 484
Five Star Music Company
52 Lakeview Road
Lansing, Michigan 48906

Dear Ms. Kaneche:

On August 20 I ordered a copy of the sheet music for the song "Fly Away" by Grant Ludlow. I enclosed with my letter a money order for $4.95.

It is now October, and I still have not received my copy of "Fly Away."

If the sheet music for the song is currently unavailable, please refund my payment. If the music is available, I expect to receive it shortly.

Thank you for your attention to this request.

Very truly yours,

Jeffrey Wong

Jeffrey Wong

EXERCISE 3 **Writing Business Letters.** Each of the following items asks you to write a different kind of business letter. For each letter that you write, use your home address, today's date, and your own name.

1. Write a letter of application to Jane Sullivan, Director, Silton Swim School, 1755 Atlantic Avenue, Manasquan, New Jersey 07232. You are applying for a summer job as a lifeguard. A friend told you about the job opening.
2. Write a letter requesting information about the conservation activities of the Forest Service. You need the information for a social studies project. Write to the United States Forest Service, Department of the Interior, Washington, DC 20242.
3. Write a letter ordering a sleeping bag, catalog number 4325, price $45.00, from Sports World, Inc., 92 Baldwin Avenue, Oakridge, Arizona 80508.
4. Write a letter complaining about the sleeping bag that you ordered for item 3. The bag arrived, but the zipper does not work.

Job Applications and Other Forms

There are many occasions on which you will have to fill out a form of one sort or another. For instance, you may have to fill out an application for a job or a school, a government form to report your income or obtain work papers, a bank form to open a savings or checking account, or an order form to order goods from a mail-order catalog.

Follow these steps when you fill out a form:

1. Examine the entire form before writing anything down. Read the directions, and look at each item of information that the form requests. Pay careful attention to directions about how you should fill out the form: Do the directions say to print or to type the information? To use blue or black ink? To use a pencil? If the form has no specific instructions about how to fill it out, use blue or black ink and print everything except your signature.
2. Gather together the supplies and information that you will need to fill out the form. In addition to your name, address, and telephone number, forms often ask you to list your social security number, your date and place of birth, your height and weight, your parents or guardians, information about your schooling, information about jobs that you may have held in the past, and the names and addresses of people who will provide you with references. In listing *personal* references, list teachers or other school officials, neigh-

bors, your family doctor, or other adults who know you well. Always contact these people beforehand to make sure that they are willing to be named as references. Never list family members as references.

3. Fill out the form item by item, paying careful attention to any specific instructions for the item to which you are responding. If a particular item requires a long or complicated response, write the response on a separate sheet of paper and revise it if necessary before copying it onto the form.
4. On most forms, if a particular item does not apply to you, write *N.A.* for "not applicable" or draw a line in the space provided. (The *N.A.* or line shows that you have not overlooked the item.) Only leave inapplicable items blank if the form directs you to do so.
5. In providing addresses, use commonly accepted abbreviations—like *St.* for *Street*—unless there is room to spell out all words. In providing dates, generally use a number for the month as well as the day and the year. Be careful not to confuse your birth date with the current date.
6. When you have finished filling out the form, read through it to check that you have followed all directions and left nothing out. Proofread your responses to make sure that they are free of grammar, spelling, and punctuation errors.

EXERCISE 4 **Filling Out Forms.** The following form is an application for a summer job as a counselor-in-training. The items on the application have been numbered and sometimes further subdivided with letters. Copy the appropriate numerals and letters for all items onto a separate sheet of paper. Next to each, write the information that you would provide if you were actually filling out the application.

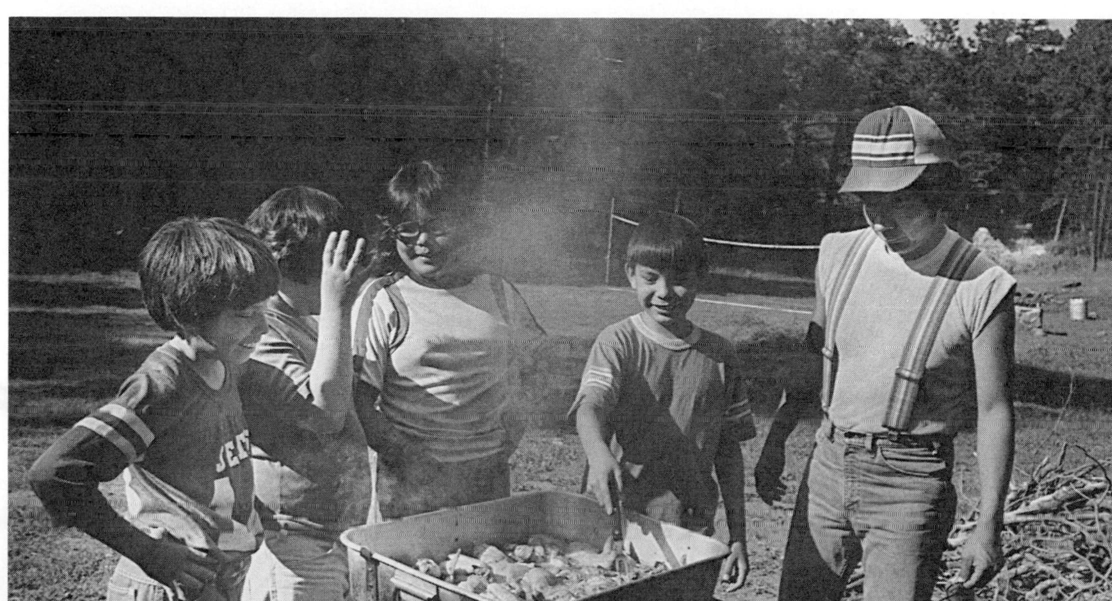

COUNSELOR-IN-TRAINING APPLICATION

1. Name ______________________ 2. Sex __________
3. Date of birth ____________ 4. Grade in school __________
5. Street address ______________________
6. City ____________ 7. State ________ 8. ZIP code ________
9. Telephone no. __________ 10. Social security no. __________
11. Have you ever attended a day camp? ____ 12. If so, where? ___
______________________ 13. For how many summers? ____
14. Have you ever attended a resident (sleep-away) camp? ____ 15. If so, where? ______________ 16. For how many summers? ____
17. What were your favorite camp activities? __________
18. Name of your school ____________ 19. Address of school ______________________
20. If you have an idea of what you want to do when you graduate, state your plans. ______________________
21. What are your favorite subjects? ______________
22. List any school clubs, teams, or organizations to which you belong or have belonged. ______________________
23. To what nonschool organizations (for example, Scouts, 4-H, church), if any, do you belong? ______________
24. What are your favorite hobbies? ______________
25. What is your swimming ability? (See list below.) __________
    Nonswimmer
    Beginner—able to swim but less than 100 yards
    Intermediate—strong swimmer but no knowledge of strokes
    Advanced—strong swimmer with at least five different strokes
26. Please list three references and their addresses.
a. ______________________
b. ______________________
c. ______________________
27. I affirm that all information provided is correct and complete.
a. Signature ______________________ b. Date __________

Want Ads

The **classified section** of your local newspaper is a good place to look when you are hunting for a job. In the classified section, usually under the heading **Help Wanted**, you will find the **want ads**, an alphabetical list of short advertisements for available jobs.

Because advertisers pay for space, want ads save space by using many abbreviations, some of which appear on page 647.

agcy agency
AM mornings
appt appointment
asst assistant
avail available
begnr beginner
btwn between
coll college
comm commission
dept department
equiv equivalent
eves evenings
exc, excl excellent
exec executive
exp, exper experience
fcty factory
5D five days
FT full-time
gd good
grad graduate
hr hour, hours
hrly hourly
h.s. high school
immed immediate
inq inquire
M/F male/female
mfg manufacturing
mgmt management
mgr manager
mo month
nec necessary
nt night, nights
oppty opportunity
pd vac paid vacation
perm permanent
PT part-time
reas reasonable
refs references
req required
respon responsible
sal salary
secty secretary
st start
temp temporary
w-, w/ with
wk week
wkly weekly
wpm words per minute
yr year
yrly yearly

Following are nine examples of want ads from the classified section of a local newspaper.

HELP WANTED

BAKER, nt hrs, exp nec. Gd sal, pd vac. Apply in person, Dandy Bake Shop, 231 Pine St.

COUNTER ASST, PT, fast-food. Will train respon person. Call for appt, 434-2180. Ask for mgr.

DOG WALKER, 5D/wk, AM & eves. Must be respon, gd w/ animals. Write to Ms. M. Lindstrom, 44 River Rd. Refs req.

GAS STATION ATTENDANTS, M/F, FT/PT, No exp req. Apply in person, ARCO station, Mill Rd.

RECEPTIONIST for dentist. Must type 35 wpm. Work Wed. & Sat. AM. Write to Wilma Rand, D.D.S., 143 Carter Blvd. Supply refs.

SALES MGR w/ exc oppty for advancement. Must be h.s. grad. Some travel nec. Phone for appt, 434-2990. Agcy.

SECTY for sales exec, 40 hr/wk. Must type 50 wpm. Sal depends on exp. Apply Box 34, Delaware Ave. Post Office.

STOCK CLERK, Hardware Dept. Will train. Exc oppty for respon begnr. Apply to Bill Harris, Asst Mgr, K-Mart, 14 Delaware Ave. No phone calls.

WAITRESS, eves, exp pref. Apply in person, La Paloma, 224 Mill Rd.

EXERCISE 5 **Interpreting Want Ads.** Write out the nine sample want ads. Use full words. Leave only the abbreviations *Ms.* and *D.D.S.*

EXERCISE 6 **Responding to a Want Ad.** Select an ad in Exercise 5 that requests a written response, and write an appropriate letter of application (see page 637). Use your own address and today's date in the heading of your letter, and use your own name in the signature. Since full addresses are not provided in the ads, complete the inside address in your letter with your own city, state, and ZIP code.

CHAPTER 31

Listening and Speaking Skills

Bore, *n. A person who talks when you wish him to listen.*

—*Ambrose Bierce*

How many times have you sat waiting impatiently for someone else to finish talking so that you could say what you wanted to say? Have you also been in the opposite situation, talking when you knew the other person was not really listening to you? In either case, what you were doing could not really be described as communication. Communication has two sides—speaking and listening—and one cannot occur without the other.

In this chapter, you will explore both of these aspects of communication. To improve your listening skills, you will learn to listen responsively, to follow oral directions, to distinguish fact from opinion, and to listen for main ideas and details. To improve your speaking skills, you will study your own voice and learn some techniques for using your voice more effectively. You will also find out how gestures and facial expressions can add to what you say, and you will examine the ways in which you should adapt your speech to different audiences.

After examining listening and speaking skills, you will apply them to a variety of situations: oral book reports, formal discussions such as panels, and conversations and informal discussions.

Throughout the chapter, you will be discovering that speaking and listening cannot be separated. A good speaker makes listening easier. A good listener makes speaking easier. When you are both a good speaker and a good listener, others will want to listen when you speak, and you will want to listen when others speak.

Improving Listening Skills

Listening is one of the most important ways we have of getting information, yet we rarely stop to think about what listening is. Does listening involve just using the ears, or is there more to listening than that? How does the way you listen affect what is being said and how it is being said? And, most important, what can you do to make yourself a better listener?

How often have you sat back and relaxed, thinking you had nothing more to do, the moment that a speaker's words reached your ears? In fact, though, the act of listening is just beginning then. If you are a responsive listener, you do more than hear what is being said. You focus on the speaker's words and block out distractions. You think along with the speaker by identifying the main points and supporting details and by evaluating what you hear. You also try to remain open to everything the speaker has to say instead of tuning out ahead of time because you think you know what is coming next or because you disagree with the speaker.

In addition, responsive listening means reacting to what you hear. Listening and speaking are part of a shared experience. Your responsibility as a listener is to let the speaker know that you are listening. An attentive expression and appropriate reactions to what is being said—laughing, nodding in agreement, frowning—will give the speaker positive feedback. A puzzled look if you do not understand something can help the speaker know that an idea needs to be repeated or explained in a different way. Even your posture and gestures can let the speaker know that you are paying attention. If you slouch in your chair or turn your head away from the speaker, your inattention will be obvious. If, on the other hand, you sit comfortably and look directly at the speaker, you will show that you are listening to what he or she has to say.

EXERCISE 1 **Learning to Focus.** Work in a group of four students. Take turns being the listener while the others in the group read different paragraphs from this book at the same time. As listener you should choose one of the three readers to listen to and focus on what that person is saying. When the readers have finished, you should repeat as much as you can of what was said by the person on whom you were focusing.

Listening to Directions

Learning to listen attentively to directions and to follow them accurately is an important survival skill both in school and out. These guidelines can make following directions easier for you:

1. Pay close attention to *all* the directions. Do not decide that you know how to do the job before you have heard everything.
2. Listen for time-order words like *first, second, before,* and *after* that tell you in what order things should be done. Also listen for words that name specific directions or actions—words such as *left, right, into, onto, turn, mix, cut, pour.*

3. Try to visualize each step as it is being described.
4. If the directions are long or complicated, jot down the important steps in a brief list.
5. To make sure that you understood what was said, repeat the directions in your own words. Use a phrase like "Let's see, the first thing I do is . . ." to introduce your restatement.
6. If anything seems confusing, politely ask the speaker to repeat that portion of the directions or to give more information.

EXERCISE 2 **Listening to Directions.** Working with a partner, take turns reading aloud the following set of directions while the other listens. As the listener, be sure to adhere to the six preceding guidelines for following directions. In particular, remember to ask questions about anything you do not understand and to repeat the directions in your own words.

1. Use two or three eggs to make an omelet for one person. Before you heat the pan, break the eggs into a mixing bowl. Then add salt and pepper, and beat the eggs with a fork. Do not beat them too much. Pour the eggs into a buttered, heated pan.
2. When the omelet has finished cooking, lift the pan by the handle and tilt it away from you. Run a fork around the edge of the pan, under the omelet, to loosen it. Then pick up a plate in your other hand. Tilt the pan and the plate against each other, and flip the omelet onto the plate.

Distinguishing Fact from Opinion

An important part of listening is being able to evaluate what someone has said. One way of evaluating the validity of a speaker's words is to determine which statements are facts and which are opinions. A **fact** is a statement that can be proved. An **opinion** is someone's own belief or feeling. It can be debated or challenged, but it cannot be proved true or false.

Sometimes opinions may be appropriate to an argument. "We should support the state's efforts to raise the reading level of high school graduates" is an opinion, but it is relevant to a speech arguing for educational improvement. However, if an opinion is stated, it should be supported with facts—concrete details, examples, and statistics—that make the opinion convincing. As a careful listener you should be alert for statements of opinion and, when they occur, you should decide if the opinions are appropriate to the speech and convincingly presented.

EXERCISE 3 **Distinguishing Fact from Opinion.** Each of the following sentences has two parts. One part is a statement of fact; the other part is a statement of opinion. Decide which part is fact and which part is opinion. Discuss your conclusions with the rest of the class.

1. Bobby's parents allow him to say up until 9:00 P.M., but young children should be in bed by 8:30.
2. *World Wide Press Conference* is hosted by Sharon Cornwell and Mike Burger; it is an interesting program.
3. We're probably one of the most generous communities in the state: Many of our residents have contributed to the United Charity Drive this year.
4. It's your own fault if you get a cold—I warned you not to go out in the rain last night.
5. Regular physical examinations are a good idea, and nine out of ten doctors recommend them.

Listening for Main Ideas and Details

When you listen to a speaker, you are often listening for information that you want to be able to understand and remember. You have to determine which information is most important and then absorb that information. Here are some tchniques for determining and absorbing a speaker's main ideas and important supporting details:

1. Be sure you understand the speaker's purpose. Is the speaker trying to inform you about a specific subject, to entertain you, or to persuade you to accept his or her beliefs? By understanding the speaker's purpose, you can focus on the information that supports the purpose.
2. Listen for words that tell you where the speaker is heading and how the ideas in the speech are connected. For example, some words indicate a time sequence (*first, then, last*); some show spatial relationships (*near, far, in the middle*); some indicate additional ideas (*besides, too, moreover*); some indicate contrasting ideas (*however, nevertheless*); and some signal results (*therefore, as a result, accordingly*).
3. As you listen, ask yourself questions to help identify the main ideas and supporting details. If, for instance, you have just heard two specific examples, you might ask yourself, "What main idea do these examples support?" By asking yourself questions, you will find that the relationships between the speaker's ideas will be clearer to you and the ideas themselves will be much easier for you to remember.

4. Listen for words and phrases that signal key terms and definitions—words and phrases such as *means, is called,* and *can be defined as.* Terms and their definitions are important details.
5. Pay attention to any visual aids that the speaker uses. For example, if a teacher writes a word or a list on the chalkboard as he or she is speaking, you can assume that the word or list is important.
6. As you listen, take notes on the important information. Taking notes will help you to organize the information and to remember it better. Do not try to write everything down; instead, focus on the information that you determine is important. Use abbreviations (if you will understand them later), and use words and phrases rather than full sentences. Organize your notes to show the relationships between main ideas and supporting details. A good way to organize your notes is to use outline form (see Chapter 32).

EXERCISE 4 **Listening for Main Ideas and Details.** While your teacher reads the following, take notes on the main ideas and important details.

Before we begin reading short stories, let's take a look at what a short story is. The writer Robert Penn Warren once asked, "Why do we read fiction? The answer," he said, "is simple. We read it because we like it. And we like it because fiction as an image of life stimulates and gratifies our interest in life."

A short story, like any work of fiction, is not a real-life account. It is the product of an author's imagination. Stories can therefore be written on a wide range of subjects. The only limit is length—a short story should be readable in one sitting. But if a short story is a work of fiction and not a real-life account, what did Robert Penn Warren mean when he said that fiction was an image of life? He meant that a good story presents enough lifelike qualities to help us better understand ourselves and our world. Some stories present quiet, ordinary-sounding events. Other stories carry us to faraway places and times. But one purpose of all good stories is to illustrate a truth—a generalization—about life.

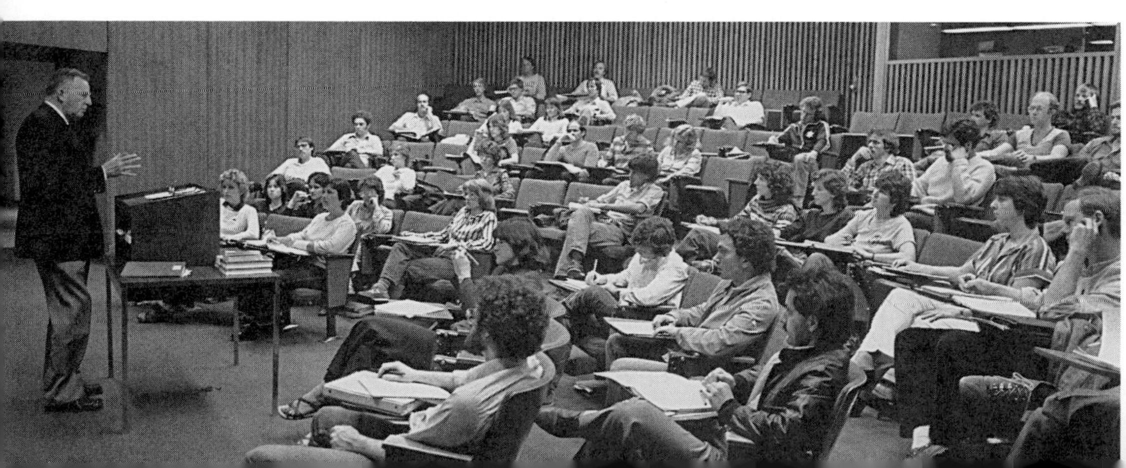

Improving Speaking Skills

The Student Government campaign is well under way, and the candidates are addressing the class. One candidate has a clear voice and a confident manner; the other slouches and mumbles. Which one is easier to listen to? Which one has better ideas? The answer to the first question is obvious. The second question probably cannot be answered fairly because no one heard the second speaker's message through the mumbles.

No matter how great an idea is, if it is not communicated properly, it cannot be made effective. Good speakers know this fact. They learn to use their voices and their bodies to get ideas across to their listeners.

When you learned to swim or to ride a bike, you were encouraged to practice the new skill. If you play a musical instrument or a sport, you spend a lot of time rehearsing or drilling. Your voice is the product of special sets of muscles in your throat, chest, and head. Like all muscles, they can be strengthened or trained through special exercises. First, however, you will have to find out what kind of training they need. In order to analyze your voice production, you should pay attention to these qualities:

pronunciation—the clarity or distinctness of your words
volume—the loudness or strength of your voice
tempo—the speed or rate at which you speak
pitch—the level or tone of your voice

EXERCISE 5 **Analyzing Your Voice Production.** Choose a favorite poem or passage from a story, and read it aloud to a partner or into a tape recorder. (You may wish to choose one of the literary pieces in the Sourcebook, pages 374–379.) Working with your partner or with the tape recording, use the following checklist to analyze your voice production.

1. Do you pronounce words clearly and distinctly?
2. Do you speak at a suitable volume, neither too loudly nor too softly?
3. Do you speak at a suitable tempo, neither too slowly nor too fast?
4. Is the pitch of your voice neither too high nor too low?

EXERCISE 6 **Improving Your Voice Production.** Go back to the passage that you read in Exercise 5, and again read it aloud to a partner or into a tape recorder. This time be aware of the answers that you gave to the checklist, and work on voice qualities that need improvement.

Improving Pronunciation

Learning to control pitch, volume, and tempo is often just a matter of concentration. Learning to pronounce words clearly and distinctly—so that you can avoid "the mumbles"—calls for greater awareness. Although running words together is common in everyday speech, slurring can become a habit that is hard to break. If you slur or swallow your words, your listeners will have trouble understanding you. Learn to separate your words just enough so that they can be heard. Pronounce them distinctly, and pay attention to the natural rise-and-fall rhythm of the language.

EXERCISE 7 **Improving Pronunciation.** Read the following sentences aloud at a volume and tempo that will allow everyone in the class to hear you. Say the words as clearly and distinctly as possible without losing the natural rise-and-fall rhythm of the language.

1. Which one do you want?
2. Leon broke his fingernail.
3. It's snowing in the mountains.
4. Are you going to help me?
5. That's very interesting.
6. When did you get here?
7. The President vetoed the bill.
8. Do you have to go now?
9. It's all right with me.
10. Helen jumped the high hurdles.

Speaking Expressively

As you become more comfortable with your voice, you will be able to control it so that it helps express the content of your speech or your feelings about what you are saying. For example, you might speak softly (but distinctly) when you read a poem about a child, while you might speak loudly when you read a poem about a baseball game.

EXERISE 8 **Speaking Expressively.** Choose one of the sentences in Exercise 7, and practice saying it in three different ways, each way expressing a different emotion. For example, you might read sentence 2 in an ordinary, matter-of-fact voice; in a voice filled with sorrow; and in a voice with a laugh in it. Ask the class to identify the emotions that you tried to express.

Using Body Language

When you talk to someone, you communicate not only through your words but through your **body language**—your posture, your gestures, and your facial expressions. Body language can add to what you are saying or distract your audience from your speech. Here are some guidelines for improving body language:

1. Stand up straight, but keep your posture relaxed and natural. Since the quality and tone of your voice are affected by your ability to breathe deeply and easily, standing straight makes you sound better as well as look better.
2. Keep in touch with your audience through eye contact. Move your gaze around the room, and look directly at as many people as possible. Eye contact makes people feel that you are talking *to* them and not *at* them.
3. Keep your face expressive—that is, show the emotions appropriate to your speech. A stony expression is like a monotonous voice, and it eventually bores the listener.
4. Use gestures and shifts of posture to emphasize ideas or statements that you wish to emphasize. When you are not using your hands to gesture, let them rest quietly.

EXERCISE 9 **Using Body Language.** Working with a partner, act out a situation in pantomime. For example, you might act out a diver preparing for a high dive, a tourist lost in a train station, or a cat stalking a bird. Use posture, eye contact, facial expressions, and gestures, but do not use words. Have your partner guess the situation or event that you are pantomiming.

Adapting Speaking Style to Audience

Without being aware of it, you change what you say and how you say it to fit your audience. Good speakers make this change consciously and adapt their speaking style to suit their listeners. Here are some guidelines for adapting your speech to suit your audience:

1. Use the pitch, tempo, and volume that you feel are appropriate. For example, if you want to calm down a crowd, keep the pitch or tone of your own voice calm; if you want to rouse an audience, use an enthusiastic pitch or tone.
2. Use words that suit your audience. The vocabulary that you use in talking to your English class, for example, would not be the same as the vocabulary that you use in speaking to a group of small children.
3. Suit your posture and gestures to your audience. For example, in an informal meeting with members of a sports team, you will adopt a more relaxed posture than you would if you were addressing the school assembly.

EXERCISE 10 **Adapting Speaking Style to Audience.** Working with a partner, role-play the following situation. Analyze each other's performances by noting how these elements change as the situation changes: (1) pitch, tempo, and volume of voice; (2) choice of works; and (3) posture and gestures.

SITUATION Ask each of the people below if you can postpone something that he or she has asked you to do.

your best friend	a student you do not know well
a small child	an important member of the community

Applying Listening and Speaking Skills in Formal Situations

Although formal listening and speaking tasks are more structured than informal ones, you use many of the same skills in both situations. Your job as a speaker is to be clear and interesting, both in what you say and in how you say it. As a listener, you have a responsibility to pay attention, to make sure you understand what is being said, and to determine how valid the speaker's statements are.

Oral Book Reports

Presenting a book report orally gives you an opportunity to share an experience directly with your audience. Your purpose is to entertain your listeners as well as to inform them about the book and to persuade them that the book is or is not worth reading. Follow these steps in preparing and delivering an oral book report:

1. Provide some background about the author. An interesting detail or a brief story about the author can help intrigue your listeners. You might use library resources (see Chapter 34) to find out more about the author than is contained on the jacket of the book. If appropriate, relate the author's life to the suject of the book.
2. If the book is a work of fiction, describe the setting, characters, main conflict, and highlights of the plot, but be sure not to give away the ending. If the book is nonfiction, provide examples of interesting information that the author uses to support the book's main idea. In either case, finish your description with a suggestion or a question that will make your listeners want to know more.
3. You may wish to read from or describe in detail one memorable passage in the book. Choose a passage that is central to the book's main idea or that is a good example of the author's style. If it is appropriate, you may also use visual aids to help illustrate the

book's main idea or simply to capture the attention of the audience. For example, you might show the book jacket, a photograph of the author, illustrations or maps from the book, or charts or diagrams that you yourself have prepared.

4. Explain the meaning of the title. Be sure your audience understands how the title is related to the main idea or overall theme.
5. Tell whether or not you liked the book. If you liked a work of fiction, tell which characters were believable and how the plot held your interest. If you liked a nonfiction book, mention specifically what you learned from it or why you think the ideas in it are important. If you disliked a work of fiction, explain why. Were the characters unrealistic? Was the plot predictable? If you disliked a nonfiction book, give reasons that will make your opinion believable. Did you feel that it was incomplete or poorly written? Was its point of view biased? Whether you liked the book or disliked it, provide specific examples from the book to back up your opinion.
6. Use note cards in preparing the book report. Do not write out the whole report. Write only the first and last paragraphs, and jot down the main points for the middle of the report. Refer to your note cards as you talk. If you are going to read from the book, mark the place ahead of time.
7. Practice giving your book report in advance. As you practice, use the following checklist:

   Are you speaking slowly, loudly, and clearly enough to be heard and understood?

   Are you using your voice and gestures to emphasize your meaning and to make your speech more interesting?

   Are you looking up to make eye contact with the audience rather than keeping your eyes glued to your note cards?

   If you are using visual aids, are you using them comfortably? Are you holding them so that everyone can see them? Have you worked them smoothly into your report?

8. When you actually give the report, relax, and remember that the listeners are your friends. You have something you want to tell them. If you enjoy what you are saying, your listeners will respond with enjoyment. You will not be speaking in isolation. You will have an audience that is reacting to you, and you will be reacting to your audience.

EXERCISE 11 **Preparing and Presenting an Oral Book Report.** Prepare and present to the class a five-minute oral report on a book that you have read recently. Follow the eight guidelines outlined above.

EXERCISE 12 **Evaluating an Oral Book Report.** As you listen to your classmates' reports, evaluate them in accordance with the preceding eight guidelines. Pay particular attention to the checklist in item 7.

Formal Discussions

When you give an oral book report, you are one person speaking to many people. You present your own ideas, and when you are finished, you just sit down and listen to someone else give a report. In formal discussions you also have an audience, but instead of having just one set of ideas presented, an exchange of ideas and opinions occurs, usually for the purpose of solving a particular problem or reaching a conclusion. The discussion is led by a discussion leader or moderator who sees that the flow of ideas is smooth and that everyone who wants to be heard gets a chance to speak. When only one speaker presents ideas, as in a forum, the question period provides the means for interaction.

TYPES OF FORMAL DISCUSSIONS

1. **Panel Discussion:** In a panel discussion, four to eight panel members, under the direction of a moderator, discuss one or more topics. You have probably seen panel discussions on television—perhaps a group of news commentators reviewing the week's major events. Panel discussions are often set up for the purpose of providing information or seeking ways to accomplish a particular goal. The panel members are chosen so that each one is knowledgeable about some aspect of the topic. Their presentations are unrehearsed, and they may disagree with each other and question each other's suggestions or statements. After all the speakers have had their turns, the moderator usually invites members of the audience to question the panelists. The following checklists describe the duties of the panelists and the moderator in a panel discussion:

   DUTIES OF PANELISTS

   Be knowledgeable. Prepare by reading and thinking, and choose one aspect of the topic to concentrate on.

   Be willing. An active panelist joins in whenever he or she can contribute something to the group.

   Be responsive. Listen to what the other panelists are saying, and react by asking questions or making statements.

   Be responsible. Back up your statements with facts, reasons, and other evidence.

   Be courteous. Listen to and respect different views.

   Be open. Keep listening; you might learn something.

DUTIES OF THE MODERATOR

Introduce the topic and the purpose.
Keep the discussion moving, and keep it focused.
See that everyone has a chance to speak.
Keep track of the time.
Ask good follow-up questions.
Help the group resolve conflicts.
Summarize major points at the end.

2. **Symposium:** A symposium is a formal discussion in which a group of speakers give prepared talks. The discussion is led by a moderator who presents each of the speakers in turn. It is customary to choose speakers who will represent each aspect of the subject under discussion. After the presentations are over, the participants may question each other. The moderator then invites oral or written questions from the audience.
3. **Forum:** In a forum, an audience asks questions of an individual who has just given a lecture, a speech, or another presentation. Usually a moderator calls on members of the audience to ask their questions or make their comments.
4. **Small Group Discussion:** A small-group discussion generally attempts to seek answers to a specific question or a solution to a particular problem. For instance, the chairperson of a club might divide the club members into small groups, each of which is responsible for answering a different question. One group might discuss ways to attract new members; another might talk about ways to raise money; and a third might discuss publicity. Each small group then chooses a representative to report its conclusions to the group as a whole.

EXERCISE 13 **Participating in a Formal Discussion.** With your classmates, choose a topic for one of the types of group discussions you have studied. Select students to be panelists or the moderator or to role-play reporters, politicians, or businesspeople. If you participate in a panel discussion, use the checklist that begins on page 658.

EXERCISE 14 **Analyzing a Formal Discussion.** Your teacher will divide the class into several groups, each of which should choose a TV panel-discussion news show to watch and analyze. The members of each group should then discuss answers to these questions:

1. What was the role of the moderator?
2. How did the moderator handle differences of opinions?
3. How did the panelists interact with one another?

Applying Listening and Speaking Skills in Informal Situations

Speaking informally may be easier than participating in a formal discussion, but, because we talk so naturally and so often, we are not always aware of what we do. If you learn and apply the skills of conversation and discussion, others will find your speech worthwhile.

Conversations

The English writer Samuel Johnson once described a happy conversation as one "where there is no competition, no vanity, but a calm, quiet exchange of sentiments." Translated into practical terms, his words might have produced these guidelines:

1. Be an active listener. Focus on what the other person says and not on what you want to say next. Pay special attention to the main ideas and important details of what you are hearing. Then think of a response that takes into account what was said.
2. Avoid talking only of yourself. If you want others to care about your feelings and ideas, you must show that you care about theirs. Ask questions that show your interests extend beyond yourself.
3. Do not monopolize the conversation, but do your share of the talking. Remember that conversation is an exchange of ideas.
4. Do not interrupt others when they are talking. Contribute your ideas at the proper time; interruptions annoy everyone.
5. Be courteous. A sharp wit is a weapon. It should never be used against another person, only against another idea.
6. Try to involve everyone in the conversation. Choose topics that will interest everyone in your group. When you speak, use eye contact to make everyone feel involved.
7. Change the topic if the conversation is dying. Be careful, however, not to change the topic while others are still interested in it.
8. Avoid arguments. If an issue cannot be resolved, at least agree that both sides have merit. Then move on to a new topic.
9. Read widely and have many interests. A good conversationalist can talk knowledgeably about many different topics.

EXERCISE 15 **Practicing Conversation Skills.** Work with a group of three to five students to have a conversation on one of these topics:

a movie you have all seen	a recent school event
a popular TV show	an important news event

Evaluate the conversation by using the nine criteria above.

Informal Discussions

Many discussions fall partway between the formality of a panel or symposium and the informality of a conversation. Such discussions may take place in a classroom after school, at a club meeting, or during another extracurricular activity. Unlike a conversation, an informal discussion has a specific purpose that the participants usually know ahead of time. For example, the purpose may be to provide information on a particular topic, to solve a problem, or to explore ways of achieving a goal. Unlike a formal discussion, everyone involved in an informal discussion is responsible for making sure that the discussion runs smoothly, that everyone has a chance to speak, and that participants stick to the topic.

Here are some guidelines for an informal discussion:

1. Remember that everyone taking part in a discussion is responsible for both listening and speaking. When others speak, you should listen as carefully as you would to any speaker in a more formal situation. If you feel it is helpful, take notes on what the speakers say. Try to evaluate what the other members of the group say so that you can respond intelligently. Are they presenting pertinent facts and ideas, or are they simply expressing opinions without backing them up? Are they responding to the questions of others, or are they just saying what they want to say? Are they accurately restating the ideas of other participants, or are they distorting what others have said?
2. When it is your turn to speak, you may introduce a new idea if it is appropriate or respond to an idea that has already been presented. If you are in agreement with an idea that has been presented, try to provide additional details to support the idea. If you disagree, state your reasons and back them up with supporting facts and convincing evidence.
3. Be courteous. Make an effort to be aware of how the other members of the group are reacting. Notice who is taking an active part and who is not, who tends to dominate the discussion, and who seems to be reluctant to participate. Try to draw out those who seem shy about speaking by asking them direct questions, inviting their responses, or referring to something they may have said earlier in the discussion.
4. Remember that the purpose of the discussion is to accomplish a specific task—to answer a question or solve a problem, for example. Prepare yourself as well as you can beforehand by reading and formulating ideas. Then make sure that everything you say helps the group to reach its goal.

5. Generally, address your remarks to the whole group. However, if you are responding to the ideas of another speaker, address your remarks directly to that person.
6. If the discussion seems to lose direction, introduce the main idea again. You might say something like, "We may be getting a little off the topic here."
7. If another speaker's ideas are not presented clearly, you can help move the discussion forward by politely restating what has been said, perhaps as a question: "Jon, you said . . . , didn't you?"
8. If someone disagrees with what you have said, defend yourself courteously and thoughtfully. A comment like "I think you may have misunderstood my position" or "Perhaps if I explain . . . , my point will be clearer" will help you avoid a confrontation and keep the discussion on track.

EXERCISE 16 **Being a Good Discussion Participant.** Suppose each of the following situations arose during a discussion. Discuss with your classmates the best way to respond in each case.

1. During a classroom discussion of a short story, a student interrupts a speaker to say she thinks the story is "dumb."
2. While someone else is speaking, another member of the class suddenly thinks of something important to say. He excitedly waves his hand for attention.
3. When asked if she agrees with the speaker's ideas, a third student apolizes, saying, "I'm sorry, but I wasn't listening."
4. At a meeting of the school newspaper's editorial committee, one of the editors responds to a suggestion of yours by saying, "That's not much of an idea."
5. During a discussion of ways to raise money for a class trip, a class member says, "Are we going to Boston again this year? Couldn't we go to Washington instead?"

EXERCISE 17 **Conducting an Informal Discussion.** Working in groups of six to eight students, conduct an informal discussion on a topic of your choice or on one of the topics provided below. Try to observe the eight preceding guidelines for successful discussions.

following fashion fads
getting a summer job
school dress codes or attendance policies
improving class discussions

CHAPTER 32

Study and Test-Taking Skills

This chapter will help you learn two skills that are very important to you as a student: how to study and how to take tests. In the first section you will learn ways to become a better listener, reader, and note-taker. In the second section you will examine the kinds of questions that appear on classroom and standardized tests, and you will learn strategies for answering these questions.

Study Skills

One of the most valuable skills you can learn in school is how to study effectively. Studying involves more than simply getting ready for tests. It includes all the other methods by which you learn, such as listening to your teachers' lectures, reading your textbooks, and taking notes on what you hear and read.

LISTENING SKILLS

Most students have no trouble *hearing* what their teachers say, but almost everyone has problems with *listening*. To be a good listener, you must be an *active listener*. That is, you must think about what you hear as you hear it. The following five suggestions will help you.

1. As you listen, think from time to time about the main points that the speaker has already made.
2. Try to think ahead of the speaker and to figure out the direction he or she is taking.
3. Consider what the speaker may be hinting or saying indirectly. In other words, listen "between the lines."
4. Try not to react emotionally to what the speaker is saying until you have heard all of it. If you start to think about how you feel about a statement, you may miss what the speaker is saying next.
5. Take notes on the important information.

SKILLS FOR READING TEXTBOOKS

Textbooks are another important source from which you are expected to gather information. Your textbooks are designed so that you can learn from them as easily as possible. The chapters and sections usually have titles or headings that identify the topics they cover. Main points are often summarized in introductions or conclusions. Review questions are often provided at the ends of chapters or sections. You will learn much more from your textbooks if you try to follow these suggestions when you read:

1. Before you begin reading, look at the chapter titles and other headings, the introduction and conclusion, and any review questions. These aids alert you to the main points and to other important information.
2. As you read, concentrate on the points mentioned in the headings, the introduction and conclusion, and the review questions.
3. Take notes on the important information. Review your notes to be sure they are clear enough for use at a later time.

TAKING NOTES

Whether you are gathering information by reading or by listening, taking notes will help you remember and understand the information. Notes have three important purposes. First, they help you learn the material, because the very act of writing something on paper helps to reinforce it in your mind. Second, taking notes forces you to organize the material and thus to understand it better. Third, your notes will serve as reminders when you use them later to study for tests.

In taking notes, try to follow these general suggestions:

1. Take notes in your own words. Putting ideas and information into your own language helps you learn the material.
2. Concentrate on the main ideas and important facts. Do not try to write down every word or detail.
3. Be sure to write down key terms and definitions.
4. To save time, use words and phrases rather than complete sentences, and use as many abbreviations and symbols as you can. However, be sure that your writing will make sense to you when you use the notes again.
5. Organize your notes, even if you must rewrite them. Put related points together, and put subordinate details below the main ideas that they support or illustrate. The most popular method of organizing notes is **outlining.** Follow these steps when you outline:

   I. Use Roman numerals for main ideas.
      A. Use capital letters for ideas supporting main ideas, and list them below the main ideas.
         1. Use Arabic numbers for detailed points supporting capital-letter ideas, and list them below the capital-letter ideas.

Read the following paragraphs from a literature textbook, and think about how you would outline the information that they contain. Then examine the sample outline that follows the paragraphs.

> A **biography** is the account of a person's life written by someone other than the subject. The key ingredient in a good biography is integrity—completeness and honesty. A biography with integrity is not simply hero worship or criticism but rather an effort to tell the truth about a life. . . .
>
> Many characteristics of good fiction appear also in a biography: lively recounting of events; crisp, authentic dialogue; richness of detail; many-sided characterization. Though rooted in fact, the biography does not just report a life but makes that life rewarding, entertaining reading.
>
> —*Understanding Literature* (Macmillan Literature Series)

I. Biography
- A. Account of person's life written by someone other than subject
- B. Integrity is key element
- C. Displays characteristics of fiction
  1. Lively recounting of events
  2. Crisp, authentic dialogue
  3. Richness of detail
  4. Many-sided characterization

EXERCISE 1 **Taking Notes.** Read the following paragraph from a social studies book, and take notes on the important information. Be sure that your notes are organized to show main ideas, supporting ideas, and supporting details. If you like, you may organize your notes by using outline form.

Improved education continued to be a chief goal of reformers in all sections of the country. During the 1850s, the legislatures of North Carolina and Kentucky passed laws providing for free public schooling. Several southern cities set up free public libraries for the first time. The legislature of Massachusetts in 1851 passed a law that allowed state money to be used for libraries. Several of the states of the South and Middle West set up state universities that provided college educations either free or at a very low cost. Colleges, both public and private, became especially numerous in the South. With a population less than half that of the North's to draw from, southern colleges had almost as many students each year. But schooling in the "three R's" continued to be neglected in the South. About one in five Southerners in 1850 could neither read nor write. This was true of only about one in fifty Northerners.

—Forcey and Posner, *A Strong and Free Nation*

Taking Tests

Throughout your school career, you will be required to take a number of tests in order to demonstrate what you have learned. Most of these will be **classroom tests**, tests prepared by your teachers to measure your understanding of the specific material that you have covered in class. Five types of questions that you will often encounter on classroom tests are **true-false questions**, **matching questions**, **multiple-choice questions**, **fill-in-the-blank questions**, and **essay questions.** True-false, matching, multiple-choice, and fill-in-the-blank questions require only short answers and test your ability to recall specific facts and information. Essay questions require longer answers and test your ability to think clearly and to organize facts and knowledge in coherent language.

The following sections examine the five common types of classroom test questions in detail.

True-False Questions

As the name suggests, **true-false questions** ask you to tell whether statements are true or false. Here is an example:

> Every rectangle has four equal sides and four right angles. True or False?

The answer to this question is *false*.

Follow these strategies when you answer a true-false question:

1. Remember that for a statement to be true, it must be completely true. If any part of the statement is false, the answer is *false*.
2. Be on the lookout for generalizing words that leave no room for exceptions—words like *always, none, every,* and *only*. These words sometimes make a statement false.

The preceding sample question illustrates the importance of looking for generalizing words. Every rectangle has four sides and four right angles, but only *some* rectangles—squares—have four *equal* sides. Therefore, the generalizing word *every* makes the statement false.

EXERCISE 2 **Answering True-False Questions.** Identify the statements below as true or false by writing *T* for *true* and *F* for *false*.

1. The only verb form that can act as a noun in a sentence is a gerund.
2. A comma may never be used to separate two clauses.
3. The predicate of a sentence includes the main verb.
4. Sentences that are commands always end with exclamation points.
5. An action verb that does not take a direct object is called an intransitive verb.

Matching Questions

Matching questions ask you to match items from two columns. Usually the two columns have the same number of items and each item is used only once. Sometimes, however, the second column contains some items that are not supposed to be used or some items that are supposed to be used more than once. Here is an example of a matching question in which the two columns contain the same number of items:

Column 1 lists three cities. Column 2 lists three countries. Match the cities with the countries in which they are located.

1. ___ Los Angeles	a. Italy
2. ___ Rome	b. Ethiopia
3. ___ Addis Ababa	c. United States

The answers are **1.** *c*, **2.** *a*, **3.** *b*.

Follow these strategies when you answer matching questions:

1. Read the directions carefully. The directions will clarify what is listed in column 1 and what is listed in column 2.
2. Read *all* the items in both columns before matching.
3. First match all the items about which you are sure. Then guess the matches for the remaining items. The more possibilities you eliminate in a matching exercise, the easier it will be to match the remaining items correctly. In order to keep track of items you have used and eliminated, cross them off the list.

The preceding sample questions illustrate the value of first matching all the items about which you are sure. You may not have known that Addis Ababa was in Ethiopia, but once you match *Los Angeles* with *United States* and *Rome* with *Italy*, you can figure out that the remaining item in column 1—*Addis Ababa*—matches the remaining item in column 2—*Ethiopia*.

EXERCISE 3 **Answering Matching Questions.** Column 1 lists short sentences in which one word is underlined. Column 2 lists parts of speech. Match the underlined word to its part of speech *as the word is used in the sentence.* (To make your matches, write down the number of each item in column 1 and next to it write the letter of the appropriate part of speech in column 2.) Use each part of speech only once.

1. __ Some cats are lazy.	a. noun
2. __ We often camp in the woods.	b. verb
3. __ The child wandered around.	c. adjective
4. __ She lives around the corner.	d. adverb
5. __ He attends a summer camp.	e. preposition

Multiple-Choice Questions

A **multiple-choice question** requires you to choose the correct answer from two or more possibilities. Usually, four or five possible answers are offered. Here is a sample multiple-choice question with four answer choices:

> In a research paper, a specific quotation from a reference source must be credited in a(n)
> (A) bibliography (C) subtitle
> (B) appendix (D) footnote

The correct answer is (D), *footnote.*

Use these strategies when answering multiple-choice questions:

1. Read *all* the choices before selecting your answer. Many multiple-choice questions are designed so that at first glance more than one answer seems correct.
2. Select the *best* answer from the choices given.
3. Use the process of elimination when you are unsure of an answer. That is, eliminate the choices that you are sure are wrong and then guess from the remaining choices. Cross off the choices you have eliminated so that you can concentrate on the remaining choices.

The preceding sample question illustrates the importance of reading all the choices given. Choice (A), *bibliography,* may at first seem like the right answer because reference sources in a research paper are indeed credited in a bibliography. However, if you had chosen (A) without reading the best of the choices, you would have chosen the wrong answer. A bibliography does not credit *specific* quotations from a source; that is done in a footnote. Choice (D) is therefore the *best* answer from the choices given.

EXERCISE 4 **Answering Multiple-Choice Questions.** Write the letter of the *best* answer from the choices given.

1. The kind of writing that tells about similarities is
   (A) narration
   (B) comparison
   (C) exposition
   (D) contrast
2. A word that names a person, a place, or a thing is a(n)
   (A) noun
   (B) verb
   (C) adjective
   (D) adverb
3. Which of the following punctuation marks cannot be used to end a sentence?
   (A) a period
   (B) a comma
   (C) a question mark
   (D) an exclamation point
4. The arrangement of the action in a story is called
   (A) foreshadowing
   (B) plot
   (C) an episode
   (D) the climax
5. Which of the following generally begins with a capital letter?
   (A) a transitive verb
   (B) an irregular verb
   (C) a proper noun
   (D) a gerund

Fill-in-the-Blank Questions

Fill-in-the-blank questions require you to supply a word or a phrase on your own. That is, in fill-in-the-blank questions—unlike true-false, matching, and multiple-choice questions—no possible answers are provided.

Many fill-in-the-blank questions ask you to provide a word or a phrase to complete a statement. Here is a typical example of this kind of question:

> The main idea of a paragraph is expressed in what is called the ____________ sentence.

The correct answer to this question is *topic*.

Sometimes the blank comes at the end of a question, and you must supply a word or a phrase that answers the question. For instance:

> In what kind of sentence is the main idea of a paragraph expressed?
>
> ____________

The correct answer to this question is *topic sentence*.

Observe the following guidelines when you answer fill-in-the-blank questions:

1. Read the entire sentence carefully to be sure you understand it.
2. Look for a key word or phrase in the sentence that gives a clue to the missing word.

In both of the preceding fill-in-the-blank sample questions, the key phrase is *main idea of a paragraph*. As you know, the main idea of a paragraph is expressed in a *topic sentence*.

Occasionally you will be given what appears to be a list of fill-in-the-blank questions, but your teacher will provide you with a separate list of possible answers. In such a case, what you really have are matching questions. Although you should continue to look for key words and phrases that guide you to the correct answers, you should also follow the procedure for answering matching questions (see page 667). In particular, remember to use and eliminate possible answers of which you are sure and then to guess the remaining answers.

EXERCISE 5 **Answering Fill-in-the-Blank Questions.** Write the word or phrase that completes each of the following sentences.

1. The direct words of a speaker are enclosed in punctuation called ____________ marks.
2. The mark of punctuation that can indicate the possessive of a noun is a(n) ____________.
3. ____________ is the kind of writing that tells a story, real or imagined.
4. ____________ are words that have the same pronunciation but different spellings and meanings.
5. ____________ are word parts that are added to the beginnings of words or other word parts.

Essay Questions

Essay questions require you to write answers of several paragraphs or longer. There may be one specific topic or a choice of topics. Directions may be general, or they may focus on a specific topic you have studied. Essay questions measure your ability to think clearly, to orga-

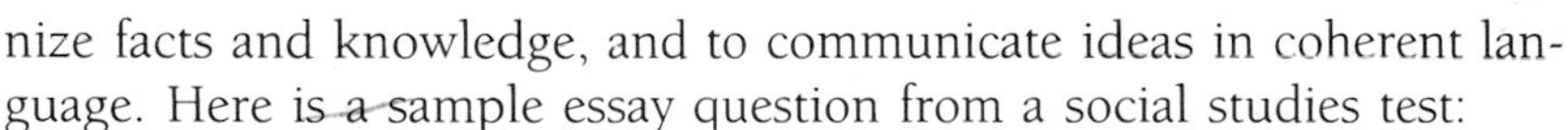

nize facts and knowledge, and to communicate ideas in coherent language. Here is a sample essay question from a social studies test:

> Explain three reasons for the outbreak of World War II. Be sure to support general statements with specific examples.

Follow these strategies when you answer an essay question:

1. Read the question carefully. Look for key words that tell you what you are expected to do—words like *compare, contrast, analyze, explain, describe, prove, define,* and *summarize*. Be sure to answer all parts of the question and to fulfill any requirements about the number of factors or examples you are to give.
2. Prewrite your answer by listing the information that you plan to cover. Use an extra sheet of paper or the inside cover of your exam booklet. You may find that the best way to list your information is to use outline form (see Chapter 11).
3. In your opening paragraph write a thesis statement that clearly states the general idea of your essay. Often your thesis statement will restate portions of the essay question. For instance, an essay answering the sample question might begin with this thesis statement: "Three reasons for the outbreak of World War II were *X, Y,* and *Z*."
4. Organize the body of your essay into paragraphs, each of which has a single main idea related to the thesis statement in your opening paragraph. For example, if you were answering the sample essay question and using the thesis statement suggested in item 3, the main idea of the first paragraph of the body of your essay would be that *X* was a reason for the outbreak of World War II; the main idea of the second paragraph of the body would be that *Y* was a reason for the outbreak of World War II; the main idea of the third paragraph of the body would be that *Z* was a reason for the outbreak of World War II. State the main idea of each paragraph of the body in a topic sentence (see Chapter 3). Then go on to support the main idea with specific facts and examples.
5. Use transitions like *thus, therefore, however, nevertheless, in addition, next,* and *last* so that sentences and paragraphs run together smoothly.
6. Conclude with a statement or a paragraph that summarizes the main ideas of your essay.
7. Reread your essay to see if it needs revision. Look especially for important points that you may have omitted.
8. Proofread your essay to make sure that grammar, usage, spelling, punctuation, and capitalization are all correct.

Standardized Reading and Vocabulary Tests

A **standardized test** is designed to measure your general knowledge and abilities. It is given to large numbers of students in a school district, a state, or even the entire nation. The participants start at a signal and are all judged by the same standards.

Standardized reading and vocabulary tests measure your comprehension of reading passages and the extent of your vocabulary. They often contain four types of multiple-choice questions: **reading-comprehension questions**, **synonym questions**, **antonym questions**, and **sentence-completion questions**.

Reading-Comprehension Questions

Reading-comprehension questions are based on reading passages of varying length and difficulty. They are usually designed to test your understanding of a passage in several specific ways. Each question will usually ask you to do one of the following:

1. Understand the main idea of the passage.
2. Recall or identify facts and ideas in the passage.
3. Make inferences, or conclusions, from the facts and ideas.
4. Evaluate the author's purpose, tone, or attitude.

Here is a sample passage and reading-comprehension questions:

> There are three kinds of lettuce. Loose-leaf lettuce is the most popular in home gardens and greenhouses. Almost all lettuce grown to be marketed in large quantities is head lettuce. The leaves in head lettuce fold tightly over one another to make a round ball, or head. A third type, called cos lettuce, or romaine, is popular in Europe. Its leaves curl inside one another to form a long roll.

Lettuce was first grown in Asia several thousand years ago. It was served to the kings of Persia five hundred years before Christ. It spread over Europe and was grown in England in 1345. Americans have raised lettuce since colonial days. All this lettuce was loose-leaf or cos-type lettuce.

Head lettuce was developed fairly recently. It became popular after the railroads built refrigerated cars for shipping. Then lettuce could be sent from California and Texas to the eastern markets. Today head lettuce can be eaten during every month of the year. Crisp head lettuce is also known as iceberg lettuce.

Leaf lettuce is easy to grow. The seeds are simply planted in shallow rows in the garden. When they sprout, the seedlings are thinned out so that the plants are about an inch apart. They grow very rapidly. Loose-leaf lettuce can stand frost very well, but not summer heat. Seeds are sown at intervals of two weeks in order to provide a constant supply of lettuce for the table.

1. Which of the following best explains the widespread sales of head lettuce?
   (A) fertile California soil
   (B) the refrigerated railroad car
   (C) resistance to frost damage
   (D) availability of a constant supply

Question 1 requires you to recall facts from the passage. For questions of factual detail, the answer is explicitly stated in the passage. In this case the third paragraph of the passage clearly states that the refrigerated railroad car is the reason that head lettuce became popular. The correct answer is therefore (B).

2. The most likely reason for the spread of cos lettuce from Asia to Europe in the fourteenth century is that
   (A) people learned to enjoy eating it.
   (B) there were no other vegetables to eat.
   (C) refrigerated railroad cars were used to ship it.
   (D) improving weather conditions aided its growth.

Question 2 requires you to make an inference. You must analyze factual information in the passage and reach a conclusion about the *most likely* reason for the spread of cos lettuce from Asia to Europe. You can eliminate choice (C) because there were no refrigerated railroad cars in the fourteenth century. Choice (B) is very unlikely. Choice (D) may sound reasonable, but there is no mention of weather conditions in the passage. The best answer is therefore choice (A). It is unlikely that lettuce would have been shipped or even grown if people had not come to enjoy eating it.

3. Which of the following best describes the main subject of the passage?
   (A) the popularity of head lettuce
   (B) the superiority of head lettuce over cos lettuce
   (C) various nations' cultivation of lettuce
   (D) varieties of lettuce and their development

Question 3 requires you to understand the main idea of the passage. To answer the question, you must differentiate between the main idea and secondary ideas contained in the passage. Choices (A) and (C) are discussed in the passage, but neither is the main subject of the passage as a whole. Choice (B) is not even suggested in the passage. The choice that best describes the main idea of the passage is choice (D).

4. The author's attitude toward the subject of lettuce is
   (A) humorous.
   (B) sarcastic.
   (C) objective.
   (D) personal.

Question 4 requires you to evaluate the author's tone, or attitude. You must look in the passage for clues about how the author feels about the subject. In this case there is no suggestion that the author regards lettuce with humor, sarcasm, or any other personal feeling. The correct answer is therefore (C), *objective*.

Follow these strategies when you answer reading-comprehension questions:

1. Before you read the passage, glance at the questions at the end to see what you should be looking for when you read.
2. As you read the passage, concentrate on *what* is being said and on *how* it is being said. Underline the main idea and key details so that you can find answers quickly.
3. In answering the questions, be sure to consider *all* the choices and to choose the *best* answer from the choices given.

Synonym Questions

Synonyms are words that have the same or nearly the same meaning. For example, *big* and *large* are synonyms. Many standardized tests use multiple-choice synonym questions to measure your vocabulary. These questions usually ask you to choose the word or phrase that is closest in meaning to a given word. Here is a sample synonym question:

BELLIGERENT (A) aggressive (B) annoyed (C) nervous (D) repugnant

The correct answer is (A), *aggressive*.

Follow these strategies when you answer a synonym question:

1. Read *all* the choices before selecting the answer.
2. Remember that few words are exact synonyms; you must decide which word is *closest* in meaning to the given word.
3. If none of the choices seems related to the given word, think about whether the given word has another meaning or can be used as another part of speech—as a verb rather than as a noun, for instance. Also consider whether the choices have other meanings or can be used as other parts of speech.
4. If you are uncertain of the answer, use the given word in a sentence. Replace it with each of the choices, and decide which choice best retains the meaning of the original sentence.

The preceding sample question illustrates the importance of choosing the word that is closest in meaning to the given word. A person who is *annoyed* may become belligerent, but *belligerent* suggests a much stronger attitude than annoyance. If you study all the choices, you will see that choice (A), *aggressive,* is *closest* in meaning to the given word.

EXERCISE 6 **Answering Synonym Questions.** Write the letter of the word *most nearly the same* in meaning as the word in capital letters.

1. STALE: (A) pleasant (B) old (C) cold (D) rough
2. RIVALRY: (A) friendliness (B) sympathy (C) competition (D) rigidity
3. ANTICIPATE: (A) expect (B) oppose (C) dismiss (D) procrastinate
4. ABRIDGED: (A) connected (B) undercut (C) cleansed (D) shortened
5. INSCRUTABLE: (A) discerned (B) rhetorical (C) enigmatic (D) chaotic

Antonym Questions

Antonyms are words that have opposite or nearly opposite meanings. For example, *start* and *finish* are antonyms. Standardized tests often use multiple-choice antonym questions to measure your vocabulary. These questions ask you to choose the word or phrase that is more nearly the opposite in meaning to a given word. Here is a sample antonym question:

SUPPRESS (A) ignore (B) understate (C) make haste
(D) make known

The correct answer is (D), *make known*.

Follow these strategies when you answer an antonym question:

1. Read *all* the choices before selecting the answer.
2. Remember that few words are exact antonyms; you must decide which word is *most nearly the opposite* of the given word.
3. Remember that many words have more than one meaning or can be used as more than one part of speech.

The preceding sample question illustrates the importance of considering alternative meanings. If you think only of the meaning "subdue or crush" for *suppress,* you might not realize that *make known* is an antonym of *suppress.* However, if you realize that *suppress* can also mean "prevent from becoming known," you will recognize that choice (D), *make known,* is the best answer.

EXERCISE 7 **Answering Antonym Questions.** Write the letter of the word or phrase that is *most nearly the opposite* of the given word.

1. CURIOUS: (A) happy (B) with energy (C) uninterested (D) lacking hope
2. TACTFUL: (A) insincere (B) with style (C) uncertain (D) indiscreet
3. FLOURISH: (A) displease (B) stabilize (C) lighten (D) decline
4. PLENITUDE: (A) scarcity (B) danger (C) supposition (D) vagueness
5. COSMOPOLITAN: (A) sophisticated (B) provincial (C) poor (D) earthly

Sentence-Completion Questions

A **sentence-completion question** consists of a sentence that is missing one or two words. You are to select the word or words that best complete the sentence. Your understanding of the incomplete sentence helps you fill in the blanks. Key words within the sentence control the possible word or words that can be substituted for the blanks.

Here is a sample question with one word missing:

> Many predatory animals are remarkably __________; they can stalk their prey for hours, waiting for the right moment to strike.
>
> (A) agile (C) patient
> (B) vigorous (D) fierce

The key words in this sentence are *waiting,* which suggests patience, and *remarkably,* which suggests that the missing quality is a surprising feature in predatory animals. The answer is therefore (C), *patient.*

Follow these strategies when you answer a sentence-completion question:

1. Be alert to the clues contained in the sentence. The given parts of the sentence will always provide clues to the correct answer.
2. If the sentence has two blanks, try to understand how the missing words are related to each other. For example, are they similar in meaning? Are they opposite? Does the second word reduce, increase, or negate a quality identified by the first word?
3. Be sure to consider *all* the choices before selecting the answer.

EXERCISE 8 **Answering Sentence-Completion Questions.** Write the letter of the word or words that *best* complete the meaning of each sentence. For items 2 and 3, the first words in the answer choices are for the first blank in the given sentences; the words after the three dots are for the second blank.

1. The __________ price controls on gasoline could mean a bonanza for the owners of service stations.
   (A) strengthening in
   (B) lifting of
   (C) certainty about
   (D) adoption of
2. __________, the captain of the girls gymnastics team performed well on the balance beam __________ her sprained wrist.
   (A) Discouraged . . . because of
   (B) Undaunted . . . in spite of
   (C) Courageously . . . resulting in
   (D) Regrettably . . . with the help of
3. Some of the telescopes in the observatories of the Southwest are slowly being __________ by the lights of the __________ expanding cities around them.
   (A) closed . . . gradually
   (B) enlarged . . . efficiently
   (C) blinded . . . relentlessly
   (D) enhanced . . . ever
4. Although it does not fly, the ostrich is surprisingly __________ when it runs; in fact, it is speedier than a cheetah.
   (A) awkward (C) lethargic
   (B) colorful (D) swift
5. The bottle was in a __________ position; we feared that it would topple and break.
   (A) precarious (C) humorous
   (B) secure (D) prime

Standardized Tests of Writing Ability

Another kind of standardized test that you may sometimes take is a standardized test of your writing ability. Such tests often include **capitalization-and-punctuation questions** and **grammar-and-usage questions.**

A capitalization-and-punctuation question requires you to recognize any errors in capitalization or punctuation in a given sentence. Here is an example:

> Francis Scott Key (A) wrote the words of "The (B) Star-Spangled Banner" during the war (C) of 1812. No error (D).

For this question, you would identify which underlined section—(A), (B), *or* (C)—contains an error in capitalization. If there is no error, you would choose (D). In this case, the error is in (C); the proper noun *War of 1812* should begin with a capital letter.

A **grammar-and-usage question** takes the same form as a capitalization-and-punctuation question but requires you to recognize errors in grammar or usage. For instance:

> Although (A) Ellen is a better tennis player than him (B), Henry has (C) occasionally beaten her. No error (D).

In this case, the error is in (B). The sentence begins with an adverb clause that leaves out the verb *is*. With the verb added, the clause would read *Although Ellen is a better tennis player than he* **is.** The pronoun is the subject of the implied verb *is*; therefore, the pronoun should be the subject pronoun *he*. *Him* is incorrect because it is an object pronoun.

EXERCISE 9 **Answering Questions That Test Writing Ability.** For each item, write the letter of the underlined section that contains an error in capitalization, punctuation, grammar, or usage. If there is no error, write **(D).**

1. Lester Short has observed birds in every state (A) except Hawaii (B) and has done ornithological studies in Europe, south (C) America, Africa, and the Cameroons. No error (D).
2. The Central Valley Water Project, with Shasta Dam as its key unit, (A) cost more than $400,000,000; (B) it was built to control floods (C) to supply fresh water for irrigation, and to generate power. No error (D).

3. Caribbean monk seals have not been (A) officially sighted since (B) 1952, and their survival remains an (C) open question. No error. (D)

4. No recent photograph (A) of the monk seals exists, although (B) local fishers periodically claim to have seen (C) the missing animals. No error. (D)

5. James Wilson Marshall discovered gold in 1848, (A) in the American River at Sutter's Mill, (B) an event that led to the famous (C) Gold Rush of 1849. No error. (D)

Review

CHAPTERS 28–32 SKILLS

CHAPTER 28 VOCABULARY SKILLS

Using Context Clues [pages 606–609] **and Greek and Latin Roots** [pages 614–615] Determine the meaning of each underlined word.

1. The Glee Club convened at two o'clock.
   (a) broke up (b) came between (c) came together (d) sang
2. A phonic system helps some young children learn to read.
   (a) math (b) memory (c) relating to sight (d) relating to sound

Using Prefixes and Suffixes [pages 609–613] Identify the word that could replace the awkward underlined portion of each sentence without changing the meaning of the sentence.

3. A person receiving work in this company receives many medical benefits.
   (a) employable (b) employee (c) employer (d) employment
4. Spaghetti that is cooked too much is limp and soggy.
   (a) overcooked (b) precooked (c) recooked (d) undercooked

Using Synonyms [pages 618–619] and **Words from Foreign Languages** [pages 615–616] Identify the synonym for each word given.

5. DELUGE: (a) delusion (b) flood (c) regime (d) tycoon
6. RANSACK: (a) baffle (b) cargo (c) infiltrate (d) plunder

Using Antonyms [pages 619–620] and **Words from Proper Names** [page 616]. Identify the antonym for each word given.

7. JOVIAL: (a) cordial (b) festive (c) melancholy (d) negligible
8. PANIC: (a) skirmish (b) tranquility (c) triumph (d) turmoil

CHAPTER 29 SPELLING SKILLS

Using Spelling Rules [pages 623–627] For each item, identify the one word that is spelled correctly.

1. (a) believeable (b) committment (c) neice (d) unnecessary
2. (a) lifes (b) manageable (c) occured (d) regretable

Distinguishing Between Easily Confused Words [pages 628–630] Identify the one underlined word that is spelled correctly in each of the following sentences.

3. As an actress, you should (a) chose (b) rolls that have a positive (c) effect on (d) you're future career.
4. He (a) build a lighthouse that (b) shown (c) it's beam (d) beside the dangerous rocks.

CHAPTER 30 BUSINESS COMMUNICATION SKILLS

Examining Business Letters[pages 635–644], **Forms** [pages 644–646], and **Want Ads** [pages 646–648] Select the answer that best completes each item.

1. A business letter should have a comma after the
   (a) salutation (b) closing (c) state name (d) ZIP code
2. A letter of adjustment or complaint should always
   (a) use block style
   (b) avoid a courteous tone
   (c) ask for specific action
   (d) be addressed to a specific person

CHAPTER 31 LISTENING AND SPEAKING SKILLS

Examining Listening Skills [pages 648–652] and **Speaking Skills** [pages 652–658]. Select the answer that best completes each of the following items.

1. A statement that can be proved true is called a
   (a) fact (b) forum (c) opinion (d) moderator
2. The loudness or strength of your voice is called the
   (a) pronunciation (b) volume (c) tempo (d) pitch

CHAPTER 32 STUDY AND TEST-TAKING SKILLS

Answering a Synonym Question [pages 674–675]. Identify the word that is *most nearly the same* in meaning as the word in capital letters.

1. PREDECESSOR: (a) forerunner (b) component (c) homage (d) rogue

Answering an Antonym Question [pages 675–676]. Identify the word that is *most nearly the opposite* of the word in capital letters.

2. JUSTIFY: (a) assert (b) baffle (c) insult (d) refute

Answering a Sentence-Completion Question [pages 676–677] Identify the word that *best* completes the following sentence.

3. Not all idealists are ____ dreamers, although many seem unreasonable.
   (a) cantankerous (b) complacent (c) dormant (d) impractical

Answering a Writing Question [pages 678–679] Identify the letter of the underlined sentence part that contains an error in capitalization, punctuation, grammar, or usage. If there is no error, choose *d*.

4. At Thanksgiving dinner (A) the family argues (B) with one another about sports, politics, (C) and other subjects. No error. (D)

UNIT X
Resources

Thinking About Thinking: Observing

As you grow as a writer, you will find yourself wanting more information than ever before. You will want more information about words themselves and more information about the world they describe. You will be faced with a great variety of "word problems": What does this word mean? Which word works better? Who wrote this? How can I find out? The dictionary, the thesaurus, and the library—the resources covered in this unit—are problem-solving tools you will use.

Defining the Skill

Suppose you want to write a report about the habitat of walruses. You need to find out certain items of information. First, however, you need to know *how* to find out what you need to find out. You need to be resourceful, to develop your ability to search, and most importantly, to learn to see what you did not know was there before. This is a specific thinking skill called **OBSERVING**.

Applying the Skill

This photograph does not easily reveal its subject. Talk with a partner about what each of you sees in the photograph. What do you observe first? How would you describe what you observe? What is hidden in the picture? What prevents you from observing the hidden part of the picture in the first place?

CHAPTER 33

The Dictionary and the Thesaurus

When you are writing, two reference books that you will find very helpful are a dictionary and a thesaurus. This chapter examines dictionaries, thesauruses, and the valuable information that they contain.

The Dictionary

A **dictionary of the English language** is an alphabetical list of words, their meanings, and other useful information about the words.

An unabridged dictionary is the largest and most complete kind of dictionary. It lists over 400,000 words and gives detailed information about their histories and usage. Two of the best-known unabridged dictionaries are the *Oxford English Dictionary,* or *OED,* and *Webster's Third New International Dictionary, Unabridged.* Because most unabridged dictionaries consist of many volumes and are quite expensive, people usually consult them at a library.

A **college dictionary**, also called a **collegiate dictionary** or a **desk dictionary,** is an abridgment, or shortened form, of an unabridged dictionary. It contains from 150,000 to 200,000 words and provides less detailed histories and examples of usage than an unabridged dictionary provides. College dictionaries are convenient for everyday use and adequate for most students' needs. Four of the most popular college dictionaries in America are *Webster's New World Dictionary of the American Language, Second College Edition; Webster's New Collegiate Dictionary;* the *Random House College Dictionary;* and the *American Heritage Dictionary.*

A **concise**, or **condensed, dictionary** is an abridgment of a college dictionary. Because it contains fewer words and often omits examples and word histories, a concise dictionary alone cannot meet the needs of most high school students.

While all college dictionaries contain similar information, no two dictionaries are exactly alike. For example, some dictionaries list place names in their main sections; others list them in a special **geographical section** near the back of the book. Some dictionaries use a star to indicate American words and expressions; others use a different symbol. To save time and get the most benefit from your dictionary, it is important to examine its general contents and its explanation of abbreviations and symbols used in the work. The **table of contents** and a **list of abbreviations and symbols** are usually found near the front of the dictionary.

The main part of a dictionary is composed of alphabetically arranged word **entries.** Although the style of these entries varies slightly from dictionary to dictionary, most entries contain the same valuable information. In the model dictionary entries that follow, the different kinds of information have been labeled. The following sections explain the labels in detail.

The Entry Word

The **entry word** is the word being examined. Entry words are listed alphabetically in the main section of a dictionary and appear in bold (dark) print. To make specific entries easier to find, some dictionaries have **thumb indexes** that show you where the entries for each new letter of the alphabet begin. Dictionaries also print two guide words at the top of each page. The **guide words** identify the first and last entry word on the page. All other entry words fall alphabetically between the two guide words.

Homographs, or words that have the same spellings but different origins and meanings, are listed separately with superscript (raised) numbers after each entry word. In the model, the entry word *rap*^{1}, *rap*^{2}, and *rap*^{3} are homographs.

As you can see from the model, names of people are listed with the last name first. Sometimes a dictionary does not list people in its main section but instead lists them in a separate **biographical section** near the back of the book.

The entry word shows you two important things about the word you are looking up—its **spelling** and its **syllabification.** It may also give you information about **capitalization.**

SPELLING

Dictionaries provide correct spellings for all entry words. You can therefore use a dictionary to check the spellings of words and to find out if compound words are solid, hyphenated, or two-word compounds. For example, entry words in the current edition of *Webster's New Collegiate Dictionary* indicate that *lighthearted* is a solid compound, *light-year* is a hyphenated compound, and *light bulb* is a two-word compound.

Dictionaries also tell you if a word has **variant spellings**, or more than one correct spelling, and indicate which variant, if any, is preferred. Methods for indicating preferred spellings vary from dictionary to dictionary. If a variant spelling is accepted only or mainly in Britain, an American dictionary will indicate that it is a British or chiefly British spelling.

MODEL DICTIONARY ENTRIES

ENTRY WORD — **ran•som** (ran′səm) ***n.*** [ME. *raunson* < *OFr. raençon* < L. *redemptio,* REDEMPTION] **1.** the redeeming or release of a captive or of seized property by payment of money or compliance with other demands **2.** the price thus paid or demanded **3.** [Archaic] a means of freeing from sin; redemption —***vt.*** **1.** to obtain the release of (a captive or property) by paying the demanded price **2.** [Now Rare] to release after such payment **3.** [Archaic] to free from sin; redeem—***SYN.*** see RESCUE —**ran′som•er** ***n.***

DEFINITIONS

ADDITIONAL FORM

SYNONYM

Ran•som (ran′səm), **John Crowe** (krō) 1888–1974; U.S. poet & critic

ETYMOLOGY — **rant** (rant) ***vi, vt.*** [< obs. Du. *ranten,* to rave, akin to G. *ranzen,* to be noisy, *anragzen,* to affront] to talk or say in a loud, wild, extravagant way; declaim violently; rave —

PART OF SPEECH — ***n.*** **1.** ranting speech **2.** [Scot. or Brit. Dial.] a boisterous merrymaking —**rant′er** ***n.*** —**rant′ing•ly** ***adv.***

PRONUNCIATION — **ra•nun•cu•lus** (rə nuŋ′kyoo ləs) ***n.,*** *pl.* **-lus•es, -li′** (-lī′) [ModL., name of the genus < L., tadpole, medicinal plant, dim. of *rana,* a frog] *same as* BUTTERCUP

INFLECTED FORMS — **rap**[1] (rap) ***vt.*** **rapped, rap′ping** [ME. *rappen,* prob. of echoic orig.] **1.** to strike quickly and sharply; tap ☆**2.** [Slang] to criticize sharply —***vi.*** **1.** to knock quickly and sharply ☆**2.** [Slang] a talking; chat ☆**3.** [Slang] blame or punishment; specif., a judicial sentence, as to a prison term: usually in **beat** (escape) or **take** (receive) **the rap**, or **bum** (unfair) **rap —rap on the knuckles** a mild reprimand or light sentence **—rap out** to say or utter sharply [to *rap out* an order]

USAGE LABEL

IDIOMS

EXAMPLE

rap[2] (rap) ***n.*** [< ?] **1.** orig., a counterfeit Irish halfpenny **2.** [Colloq.] the least bit: now usually in **not care** (or **give**) **a rap** not care (or give) anything at all

rap[3] (rap) ***vt.*** **rapped** or **rapt, rap′ping** [back-formation < RAPT] [Obs. or Rare] **1.** to seize; snatch **2.** to transport with rapture: now only in the pp.

—from *Webster's New World Dictionary, Second College Edition*

SYLLABIFICATION

Most dictionaries break multisyllabic entry words into syllables by using spaces or midline dots. For example, in the model, the two-syllable entry word *ransom* is broken into syllables indicated by midline dots. Thus, if you have to type *ransom* on two lines, the entry word tells you to hyphenate it after the *n*.

CAPITALIZATION

Dictionaries capitalize entry words that are always capitalized, as in the *Ransom, John Crowe,* entry in the model. For words that are sometimes but not always capitalized, a dictionary tells you when capital letters should be used. For instance, while the entry word *president* is not capitalized in *Webster's New World Dictionary,* the entry says [*often* **P-**], meaning "often capital *P*," before the definition "the chief executive of a republic." The entry for *congress* says [**C-**], meaning "always capital *C*," before the definition "the legislature of the U.S."

PRONUNCIATION

Dictionaries tell you the correct **pronunciation** of each entry word. If a word has more than one acceptable pronunciation, its different pronunciations will be provided. Usually the pronunciation is given in parentheses, brackets, or slanted lines right after the entry word. In the model, pronunciations are given in parentheses.

Because there are only twenty-six letters in the alphabet but over forty sounds in spoken English, dictionaries use a special set of symbols, called **phonetic symbols**, to represent these spoken sounds. Different dictionaries use different phonetic symbols; for example, one dictionary shows the pronunciation of *few* as [fyōō], while another shows it as [fū]. To understand the sounds represented by a dictionary's phonetic symbols, consult its **pronunciation key**. The full pronunciation key appears near the front of the dictionary, while a short form usually appears at the bottom of each right-hand page.

When a word contains more than one syllable, the pronunciation indicates the syllable or syllables that are **stressed**, or emphasized. To indicate stressed syllables, dictionaries use **accent marks** (**′**) either before or after the stressed syllables. For example, in the pronunciation for *ransom,* the accent mark shows that the first syllable is stressed.

PART OF SPEECH

Dictionaries tell you the **part of speech** of each entry word. Usually the part of speech is abbreviated and italicized. Abbreviations include *n.* for *noun, vt.* for *transitive verb, vi.* for *intransitive verb, adj.* for *adjective,* and *adv.* for *adverb*. The abbreviation is placed before the definition or definitions to which it applies. For example, in the entry for *ransom* in the model, the *n.* before the first three definitions indicates that these definitions are for *ransom* as a noun; a *vt.* then indicates that the next three definitions are for *ransom* as a transitive verb. Some dictionaries have separate entries for each part of speech.

INFLECTED FORMS

Inflected forms include plurals of nouns and the past tense, past participles, and present participles of verbs. When these forms are irregular or confusing, a dictionary lists them in bold print near the entry word. For example, since the double *p* in *rapped* and *rapping* may cause some confusion, the entry for *rap*[1] lists these verb forms after the entry word.

When comparative and superlative forms of two-syllable adjectives are not made by adding *more* or *most,* a dictionary usually lists these forms in bold print near the entry word. For instance, in the entry for the two-syllable adjective *lonely,* a dictionary most likely will list *lonelier* and *loneliest.*

ETYMOLOGY

The **etymology** is the origin and history of a word. Most dictionaries include a word's etymology in brackets or parentheses before or after its definitions. In the model, etymologies are given in brackets before the definitions. The etymology for *rant* indicates that the word comes from an obsolete Dutch word, *ranten,* which is related to two German words, *ranzen,* "to be noisy," and *anragzen,* "to affront."

SUBJECT AND USAGE LABELS

If a word or a definition is restricted in its use, many dictionaries include a subject or usage label explaining the restriction. **Subject labels** like *Botany* or *Skiing* indicate that a word or a definition is restricted to a particular field. **Usage labels** indicate other restrictions; for example, a word may be rare, archaic, obsolete, colloquial, slang, or restricted to a particular region or dialect. Subject and usage labels immediately precede the definition or definitions to which the restriction applies. They are often abbreviated and may be italicized or put in brackets or parentheses. In the entry for *rap*[1] the subject label [Slang] indicates that use of the word *rap* to mean "to talk" or "to chat" is restricted to **slang**, or informal, English. In the entry for *ransom,* the related archaic meanings for both the noun and the verb are given.

DEFINITIONS AND EXAMPLES

An important function of a dictionary is to provide the **definitions**, or meanings, of words. If a word has more than one definition, each definition is numbered. Definitions for each part of speech are numbered separately. For example, in the entry for *ransom,* the three definitions of the noun *ransom* are numbered 1 to 3; new numbers are given to the three definitions of the transitive verb *ransom.*

In order to illustrate a particular definition, dictionaries sometimes include examples showing the word used in context. For instance, to illustrate the definition of *rap out* in the entry for *rap[1],* the example "to *rap out* an order" is given in brackets. Sometimes dictionaries include diagrams or charts to illustrate definitions.

IDIOMS

Toward the end of an entry for a particular word, dictionaries may list and define common **idioms**, or expressions, in which the word is a key element. Usually these idioms appear in bold print. In the entry for *rap[1],* the dictionary lists and defines the expressions *rap on the knuckles* and *rap out.*

SYNONYMS AND ANTONYMS

Dictionaries sometimes list **synonyms** or **antonyms** for an entry word. Usually they are labeled *Syn.* or *Ant.* and are listed near the end of an entry. At the end of the entry for *ransom* in the model, a cross-reference to the synonym *rescue* indicates that more synonyms for *ransom* are given in the entry for *rescue.*

ADDITIONAL FORMS

At the end of an entry, dictionaries sometimes list **additional forms** of the entry word. These forms usually appear in bold print without definitions. For example, at the end of the entry for the verb *ransom*, the noun form *ransomer* is listed. From your knowledge of suffixes and from the definition of the verb *ransom*, you can figure out that a *ransomer* is "one who obtains the release of a captive or property by paying the demanded price."

EXERCISE 1 **Using a Dictionary.** Consult a college dictionary before writing your answers to each question.

1. Which of these words are spelled incorrectly? What are the correct spellings?
   (a) ecstasy (c) Poughkeepsie
   (b) polo bear (d) wild-flower
2. Is *usable* or *useable* the preferred American spelling?
3. Is *Purim* always capitalized? What does it mean? Where would you hyphenate the word?
4. Is the last vowel sound in *epitome* the same as the *o* in *home* or the *e* in *he*? Which syllable in *epitome* is stressed?
5. Can *low* be used as a verb? If so, with what meaning or meanings?
6. What are the different origins of the two homographs spelled *swim*? What are the past tense, past participle, and present participle of *swim*?
7. In what dialect or dialects is the word *kirk* used? What does it mean?
8. What does the idiom *out in left field* mean?
9. Does your dictionary list synonyms for the verb *lift*? If so, what are they?
10. Does your dictionary list an adverb form of *complaisant* in the entry for *complaisant*? If so, identify and define the adverb.

The Thesaurus

A **thesaurus** is a list of words, their synonyms, and sometimes their antonyms.

When you use a thesaurus, you start with a meaning and find a word. For instance, suppose you want to say that your sister is helpful but wish to use a word stronger than *helpful*. A thesaurus will help you find that word.

Many thesauruses arrange entries alphabetically. In these thesauruses you would simply look up *helpful* to find a stronger synonym. (If *helpful* were not listed, you would look up the basic form of the word, *help*.) Entries are subdivided according to part of speech and are followed by lists of synonyms. Antonyms may be listed as part of an entry, or a cross-reference may direct you to them.

Other thesauruses arrange entries in numbered categories based on the ideas they represent. Finding a word in this type of thesaurus is a two-step process. To find a stronger synonym for *helpful,* first look up *helpful* in the alphabetical index at the back of the thesaurus. In the index to the *Original Roget's Thesaurus,* you would find:

helpful *willing* 597adj.
cooperative 706adj.

Choosing *willing* as the word closest to the sense you are trying to convey, turn to the adjective section of item 597. There you would find a list of synonyms including *compliant, agreeable, obliging, eager,* and *reliable*. You can then choose the synonym that you feel is most appropriate. Before making your choice, you may need to look up the precise meanings of the synonyms in a dictionary.

EXERCISE 2 **Using a Thesaurus.** Use a thesaurus to find and write two synonyms for each word below.

1. bravery
2. difficult
3. dizzy
4. dry (adj.)
5. eager
6. fight (v.)
7. happy
8. moist
9. slender
10. wealthy

SENTENCE WRITING **Using Synonyms.** Write an original sentence that illustrates the meaning of each synonym in Exercise 2. Before writing your sentences, you may wish to consult a dictionary to find the precise meaning of each synonym.

CHAPTER 34

The Library

The library is a huge storehouse of information. Most **public libraries** and **school libraries** (sometimes called **learning resource centers** or **media centers**) contain a wide variety of materials that can help you with your research and writing. This chapter looks at the different types of materials available at libraries and explains how to find and use these materials.

Fiction and Nonfiction Books

Libraries have a large selection of **nonfiction** (fact-based) books as well as **fiction** (novels and stories). Most nonfiction books provide detailed information on particular topics and can be valuable tools in your research. To find out whether or not a library has the book you need, you have to look in the card catalog.

The Card Catalog

The **card catalog** is an alphabetical arrangement of individual file cards listing each of the books owned by a library.

Most fiction books in a library have two cards each, an **author card** and a **title card**. Most nonfiction books have three cards each, an **author card**, a **title card**, and a **subject card**. Usually the cards are kept in drawers of special filing cabinets. Subject cards are usually filed in separate drawers and form the **Subject Index** of the card catalog. Author cards and title cards are usually filed together and form the **Author/Title Index**. Some libraries do not use file cards but instead maintain **on-line**, or computerized, **catalogs** or print their catalogs in paperback volumes.

The main entry on an **author card** is the author of the book, with the last name first. Author cards are filed alphabetically by the author's last name. Thus, if you wanted to find author cards for books by Charles Dickens, you would look in the Author/Title Index under *D*.

The main entry on a **title card** is the title of the book. Title cards are filed alphabetically by the first word of the title, excluding *a, an,* and *the*. Thus, if you wanted to find the title card for *A Christmas Carol,* you would look in the Author/Title Index under *C*.

The main entry on a **subject card** is the general topic of the book. Subject cards are filed alphabetically by these general topics. Thus, if you were looking for subject cards for books about volcanoes, you would look in the Subject Index under *V*. If a book deals with more than one general topic, it will usually have more than one subject card.

The following examples of catalog cards show an author card, a title card, and a subject card for the same book. The three types of cards all provide basically the same information. They differ only in their main entries—the author, title, or subject. The important information on the subject card has been numbered 1 to 6. This information is

1. **Call number**: The **call number** is used to locate the book in the library. The number on the card corresponds to the number on the spine of the book. Library books are arranged by call number.
2. **Main entry**: The **main entry** is the primary heading on the catalog card. On this subject card, the subject *Space Exploration* is the main entry; the author and title come below it.
3. **Publishing information**: The **publishing information** includes the location and name of the publisher and the date of publication.
4. **Collation**: The **collation** gives the number of pages or the number of volumes. Sometimes it gives the physical dimensions of the book. Sometimes it indicates whether or not there are illustrations (abbreviated *ill.* or *illus.*).
5. **Notes entry**: The **notes entry**, when it occurs, tells whether the book has any special features, such as an introduction or a bibliography.
6. **Cross-references to the card catalog**: The **cross references** indicate the book's other subject cards and can help you get a better idea of the topics covered in the book.

Sometimes you will find a fourth type of card in the card catalog—a **cross-reference card**. Cross reference cards tell you to *see* or *see also* other cards in the catalog. For example, if you look up *American History* in the Subject Index, a card may tell you to "See *United States, History of*." This cross-reference means that subject cards for all books on American History are filed under the subject *United States, History of*. On the other hand, if you look up *Airplanes* in the Subject Index, a cross-reference card may tell you to "See also *Aviation*." This cross-reference means that while subject cards for books about airplanes are filed under the subject *Airplanes*, subject cards for related books are filed under the subject *Aviation*.

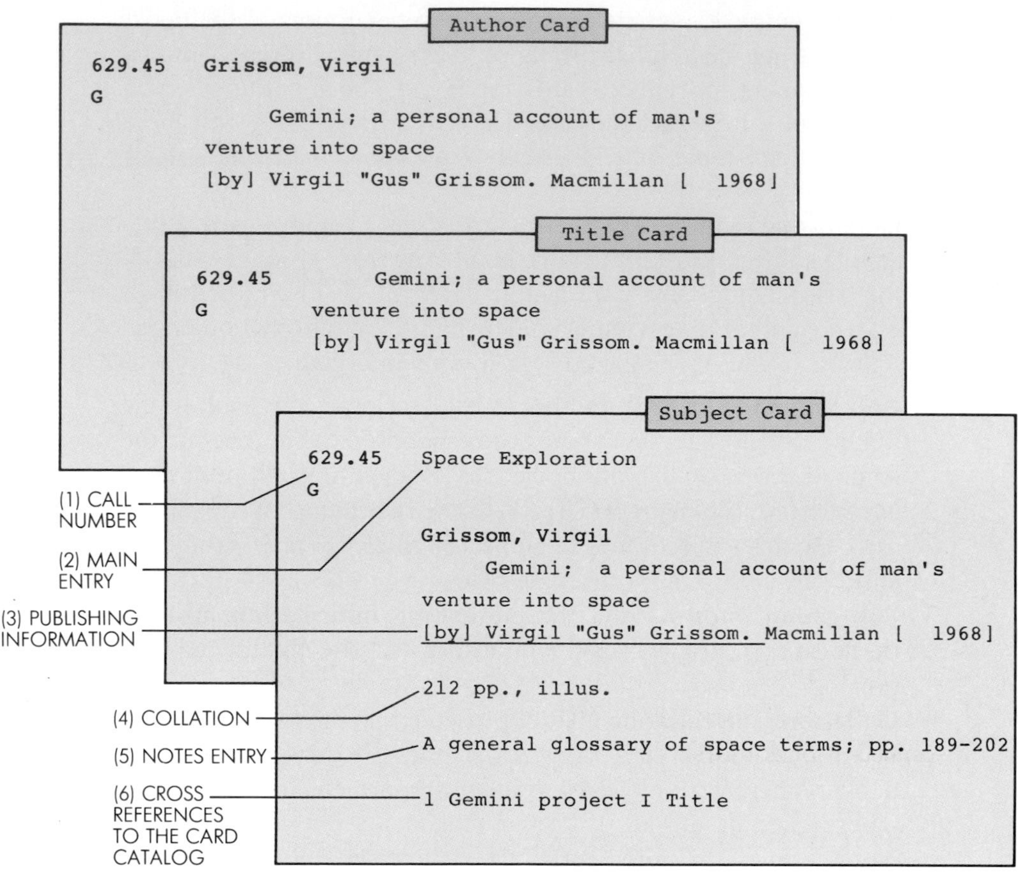

Author Card
629.45 Grissom, Virgil
G
Gemini; a personal account of man's
venture into space
[by] Virgil "Gus" Grissom. Macmillan [1968]
Title Card
629.45 Gemini; a personal account of man's
G venture into space
[by] Virgil "Gus" Grissom. Macmillan [1968]
Subject Card
629.45 Space Exploration
G
Grissom, Virgil
Gemini; a personal account of man's
venture into space
[by] Virgil "Gus" Grissom. Macmillan [1968]
212 pp., illus.
A general glossary of space terms; pp. 189-202
1 Gemini project I Title
(1) CALL NUMBER
(2) MAIN ENTRY
(3) PUBLISHING INFORMATION
(4) COLLATION
(5) NOTES ENTRY
(6) CROSS REFERENCES TO THE CARD CATALOG

EXERCISE 1 **Using Catalog Cards.** Refer to the sample catalog cards above in writing your answers to the following questions.

1. What is the book's call number?
2. Who wrote the book?
3. When was the book published? What company published it?
4. How long is the book?
5. Does the book contain illustrations?
6. According to the notes entry, what is the book's special section?
7. Under what subjects is the book listed in the Subject Index?

Classification and Arrangement of Library Books

The **call number**, found in the upper left corner of a book's catalog card and on the spine of the book, is based on the Dewey Decimal System, the Library of Congress System, or the library's own classification system. Library books are arranged by call number in accordance with the classification system that the library uses.

Most American libraries classify and arrange books according to either the Dewey Decimal System or the Library of Congress System.

THE DEWEY DECIMAL SYSTEM

The **Dewey Decimal System** arranges books numerically.

The Dewey Decimal System organizes books by subject into ten very broad categories designated by multiples of 100:

000	General Works	**500**	Pure Science
100	Philosophy	**600**	Technology and Applied Science
200	Religion	**700**	The Arts
300	Social Sciences	**800**	Literature
400	Language	**900**	Geography and History

Each category is then further divided into another ten subdivisions designated by multiples of ten. For example, Literature, the 800s section, is further divided into 810—American Literature, 820—English Literature, and so on.

In the Dewey Decimal System, most libraries do not assign call numbers to novels. Instead, novels are shelved in a separate Fiction Section and alphabetized by the authors' last names. Similarly, biographies are usually shelved separately and alphabetized by the last names of their subjects (not authors).

THE LIBRARY OF CONGRESS SYSTEM

In the **Library of Congress System,** the basic arrangement of library books is alphabetical.

The Library of Congress System classifies books by subject into twenty broad categories designated by letters of the alphabet:

A	General, Miscellaneous	**N**	Fine Arts
B	Philosophy, Religion	**P**	Language, Literature
C	History—Auxiliary Sciences	**Q**	Science
D	History, Topography	**R**	Medicine
E–F	America (including History)	**S**	Agriculture
G	Geography, Anthropology	**T**	Technology
H	Social Sciences	**U**	Military Science
J	Political Science	**V**	Naval Science
K	Law	**Z**	Bibliography, Library Science
L	Education		
M	Music		

Subdivisions of these categories are designated by using two letters; for example, *QB* indicates Astronomy.

EXERCISE 2 **Using Library Classification Systems.** Write the main Dewey Decimal (000 100, etc.) and Library of Congress (A, B, etc.) category for each of the following nonfiction books.

1. *The Complete Poems of Emily J. Brontë*
2. *The Story of Art,* Ernst H. Gombrich
3. *Those Amazing Computers!* Melvin Berger
4. *Exploring the Insect World,* Margaret J. Anderson
5. *Language and Its Structure,* Ronald W. Langacker

Locating Library Books

Use the **call number** to locate a book in the library.

The shelf area in which most books are kept is called the **stacks**. **Open stacks** are those that readers can enter in order to find books for themselves. Once you have obtained a list of books and their call numbers from the card catalog, you can go to open stacks to see if the books you want are available. **Closed stacks** are restricted to library personnel. If a library uses closed stacks, you will probably have to fill out a book-request slip and present it to a member of the library staff. The slip asks for information (such as the call number, title, and author of the book) that you can copy from a book's catalog card. If a book you want is not presently available in the library, you can often **reserve** the book by filling out a special card.

Most libraries have **circulating books** that you can borrow and take home for a given period of time. To borrow books, you will probably need a library card. Libraries also have **reference books** that you must use in the library. Reference books have *Ref* or *R* above their call numbers and are usually kept in a separate section or room of the library.

EXERCISE 3 **Locating Books in Your Library.** Visit your school library or a public library to answer the following questions. Write down your answers and the name and address of the library you visited.

1. Does the library use the Dewey Decimal System, the Library of Congress System, or a classification system of its own?
2. Does the library have a special reference section? If so, where in the library is it located?
3. Does the library assign call numbers to novels? If not, how are novels arranged?

4. What is the library's procedure for obtaining a library card and for borrowing books? For how long can most books be borrowed? Is there a fee for overdue books?
5. Use the card catalog to find out if the library has *Mythology* by Edith Hamilton. If the book has a catalog card, list **(a)** its call number, **(b)** its length, **(c)** its date of publication, and **(d)** its publisher.

Parts of a Book

Once you have found a copy of a book for which you were looking, you may want to examine it to see if it is suitable for your purposes. Certain parts of the book can help you find this valuable general information very quickly.

IF YOU WANT TO FIND	LOOK FOR THE
1. complete title, name of author, edition number, name of publisher, place of publication, date of publication, dates of previous editions	title page, copyright page
2. material explaining the nature, purpose, or scope of the book	preface, foreword, or introduction
3. a list of the general contents of the book and the page numbers on which the contents are found	table of contents
4. a list of the book's illustrations, charts, diagrams, maps, or tables	list of illustrations, maps, or tables
5. additional explanations not essential to the text itself	appendix
6. an alphabetical list of technical or unfamiliar terms used in the text	glossary
7. a list of the sources used by the author or additional readings suggested by the author	bibliography, references, or suggested readings
8. an alphabetical list of the specific subjects, names, and terms used in the text, given with all of the page numbers on which they are found	index

EXERCISE 4 **Using the Parts of a Book.** Refer to the parts of this textbook in writing answers to the following questions.

1. What is the precise title of the book?
2. In what year was this edition of the book published?
3. Does the book contain a chapter on listening and speaking? If so, how long is that chapter?
4. Does the book teach anything about suffixes? If so, on what page or pages?
5. Does the book teach anything about reference books? If so, on what page or pages?

Newspapers and Periodicals

Newspapers and **periodicals** (magazines and journals) contain short articles on specific topics and provide information that is usually up to date at the time of publication. By reading a selection of articles on a specific topic, you can examine different opinions and points of view in a relatively short time.

Most libraries keep current newspapers and periodicals on shelves or racks in a reading room or area. Usually newspapers are alphabetized by the name of their city of origin. Periodicals are generally alphabetized by title.

Back issues of newspapers are normally kept on microforms (see page 704). Back issues of periodicals are sometimes kept on microforms and sometimes bound together into hardcover volumes containing six months' or a year's issues. Recent periodicals are usually stored unbound on shelves or racks.

To find newspaper or periodical articles on a specific topic, you need to consult one or more indexes to newspapers or periodicals. These indexes are usually found in the reference section of the library. Among the most frequently used indexes are *The New York Times Index* and the *Readers' Guide to Periodical Literature*.

THE NEW YORK TIMES INDEX

The New York Times Index lists, alphabetically by subject and author, all articles published in *The New York Times* during the period covered by the issue of the index you consult.

Because *The New York Times* is a newspaper that contains many articles on national and international events, *The New York Times Index* is a useful source for articles on current events or history.

THE *READERS' GUIDE TO PERIODICAL LITERATURE*

The ***Readers' Guide to Periodical Literature*** lists, in alphabetical order by subject and author, all articles published in over 100 magazines during the period covered by the issue of the *Readers' Guide* you consult.

The *Readers' Guide* covers articles published in newsmagazines like *Newsweek* and *Time* and other general-interest magazines, such as *Mechanics Illustrated* and *Consumer Reports.* Issues of the *Readers' Guide* are published approximately every two weeks and are consolidated into bound volumes at a year's end. In the following sample column from the *Readers' Guide,* important parts are numbered. These parts are

1. **Main entry**: The **main entry** is the subject or the author of the article. In the sample from the *Readers' Guide,* the main entry "FOONER, Andrea" is the author of an article; the main entry "FOOT" is the subject of a number of articles. Main entries appear in bold print to the left of the column, and the first word of a main entry appears in capital letters.
2. **Subheading**: When the main entry is a subject heading, it is often further divided into smaller categories, each of which has its own **subheading.** Subheadings appear in bold print and are centered in the column.
3. **Title of article**: The **title** of the article is the first item in a listing.
4. **Author of article**: The **author's name**, if listed, follows the title of the article. Of course, when an entry appears under an author heading (like "FOONER, Andrea"), the author's name is not repeated after the title.
5. **Source of article**: The **source** includes the name of the periodical (often abbreviated), its volume number, the page numbers of the article, and the date of the issue. The highlighted source in the sample indicates that the article is illustrated (abbreviated *il*) and that it appeared in January 1979 in volume 9 of *Essence* on pages 30, 31, and following pages. (The plus sign indicates following pages.) All abbreviations used in the *Readers' Guide* are explained in the front of the guide.
6. ***See* reference**: A ***see* reference** directs you to a different main entry.
7. ***See also* reference**: A ***see also* reference** directs you to additional main entries that list articles related to the subject under which you have looked.

READERS' GUIDE TO PERIODICAL LITERATURE

SEE REFERENCE	**FOOD taboo.** See Taboo
	FOOD values
	Calorie counter, il Redbook 151:182+ O '78
	Confusing world of health foods. M. Stephenson. il FDA Consumer 12:18-22 Jl '78
	Nutrition in a nutshell: pocket guide to nutrients. il Consumer Rep 43:373-4 Jl '78
SEE ALSO REFERENCE	*See also*
	Diet
	Nutrition
	FOOD waste disposers. See Refuse grinders
MAIN ENTRIES — *(AUTHOR)*	**FOONER, Andrea**
	Countdown to fitness: how an astronaut stays in shape. por Redbook 151:112-13+ Je '78
	FOOT, Hugh Mackintosh, Baron Caradon. See Caradon, H. M. F.
MAIN ENTRIES — *(SUBJECT)*	**FOOT**
	Celebrating the American foot; exhibit at the Museum of Contemporary Crafts. B. S. Cornfeld. il Sat R 5:20-1 Je 24 '78
	Footin' it; Great American Foot show at the Museum of Contemporary Crafts in New York City. il Horizon 21:65 Ap '78
	Great American foot: does it have a leg to stand on? show at Museum of Contemporary Crafts. S. Moss. il Craft Horiz 38:58-63 AD '78
SUBHEADING	**Care and hygiene**
	Are your feet ready for sandal weather? il Glamour 76:53 My '78
	Best feet forward. il McCalls 106:79-80 N '78
	First-rate care for hands and feet. il Teen 22: 54-5 Ja '78
	Fitting room: do you need orthotics or cants? J. Wernick. il Skiing 30:26+ Spr '78
	Foot news. C. Ettlinger. il House & Gard 150:114-15* Je '78
	Footwork. il Mademoiselle 84:186-7 My '78
TITLE OF ARTICLE	Get yourself on a good footing. J. C. G. Conniff. il Read Digest 113:146-9 S '78
	Good healthy feet: what you need to know and do
AUTHOR OF ARTICLE	C. Kahn. Vogue 168:203-4+ O '78
	Help for feet that like to dance. il Glamour 76:72 N '78
	Look good/feel good. J. Lawrence and E. Lawrence. 50 Plus 18:63 D '78
SOURCE OF ARTICLE (NAME OF PERIODICAL, VOLUME NUMBER, PAGE NUMBERS, AND DATE)	Manicure & pedicure: you deserve the best. N. J. Darden. il Essence 9:30-1+ Ja'79
	See also
	Podiatry

EXERCISE 5 **Using the *Readers' Guide*.** Refer to the preceding *Readers' Guide* excerpt in writing your answers to the following questions.

1. In what magazine did the article "Footwork" appear?
2. Who wrote "Confusing World of Health Foods"?
3. When did the article "Look Good/Feel Good" appear?
4. In what volume of *Vogue* did C. Kahn's article about healthy feet appear? On what page or pages did this article appear?
5. Under what other main entry would you look for articles related to the subject of foot care and hygiene?

EXERCISE 6 **Using the *Readers' Guide*.** In a recent issue of the *Readers' Guide,* find the listings for two articles on each of the following topics. Write the issue or issues of the *Readers' Guide* you used and the author, title, periodical, volume number, page number or numbers, and date of each article.

1. backpacking
2. the United Nations
3. India
4. sports salaries
5. director Steven Spielberg

General Reference Works

The reference section of a library contains a number of **general reference works** that can help you obtain information useful for your research. Among the most frequently consulted reference works are encyclopedias, almanacs, atlases, and dictionaries.

Encyclopedias

Encyclopedias are collections of articles on thousands of general topics. Articles are arranged alphabetically by subject. If the subject is a person, the person is listed by last name.

Encyclopedias are a good place to begin a research project. They provide a brief summary of each topic and often include a bibliography referring you to other books on the topic. Four frequently used encyclopedias are the *Encyclopaedia Britannica,* the *Encyclopedia Americana, Collier's Encyclopedia,* and the *World Book Encyclopedia.*

To find a particular topic, look in the encyclopedia's index, which usually appears in a separate volume. The index arranges topics alphabetically and refers you to the subject headings of encyclopedia articles in which particular topics will be covered.

EXERCISE 7 **Using Encyclopedias.** Use one or more encyclopedias to find answers to the following questions. Write down your answers along with the sources of your information.

1. In what year did Alaska become the forty-ninth state?
2. Who isolated the element radium in 1910?
3. Which two people first reached the top of Mount Everest?
4. What does the Richter scale measure?
5. What were the six novels that Jane Austen completed?

Almanacs

Almanacs (also called **yearbooks**) are annual collections of facts and statistics on geography, history, current events, science, sports, entertainment, and the arts.

An almanac is a relatively up-to-date source of information. It covers material through the year preceding the year on its cover. Among the most popular almanacs are the *Official Associated Press Almanac*, the *World Almanac & Book of Facts*, and the *Information Please Almanac*. To locate information in an almanac, consult its index.

EXERCISE 8 **Using Almanacs.** Use one or more almanacs to find answers to the following questions. Write down your answers along with the sources of your information.

1. What is the world's longest river?
2. Who won the 1976 Nobel Peace Prize?
3. What are the four official languages spoken in Switzerland?
4. Who won the 1983 Academy Award for Best Actress?
5. What was the population of Oregon in 1980?

Atlases

Atlases are collections of maps that provide geographical data and information on topography, population, climate, and rainfall.

Some of the best-known atlases are the *Hammond Contemporary World Atlas*, the *National Geographic World Atlas*, the *Rand McNally Cosmopolitan World Atlas*, and the *Historical Atlas of the United States*.

EXERCISE 9 **Using Atlases.** Use one or more atlases to answer the following questions. Write down your answers along with the sources of your information.

1. What three states border California?
2. What is the capital of Venezuela?
3. Which is farther north, London, England, or Montreal, Canada?
4. At the tip of what continent is the Cape of Good Hope?
5. Of what European country is the island of Crete a part?

Other Useful Reference Works

The following list describes other types of library reference works that you may find useful when you do research.

LANGUAGE REFERENCE WORKS

Language reference works provide information about words and usage. They include English-language dictionaries and thesauruses (see Chapter 33), foreign-language dictionaries, and books on usage.

BIOGRAPHICAL REFERENCE WORKS

Biographical reference works give short life stories of noteworthy people. They include *Current Biography* and *Who's Who* books, *Dictionary of American Biography, Dictionary of National Biography, Who Was Who* books, and *Webster's Biographical Dictionary,* which gives basic biographical information about contemporary and historical personalities.

BOOKS OF QUOTATIONS

Books of quotations contain memorable quotations arranged by author, topic, or key word. Two well-known examples are the *Oxford Dictionary of Quotations* and *Bartlett's Familiar Quotations.*

LITERATURE HANDBOOKS

Literature handbooks include information about literary works and their authors. Examples are the *Oxford Companion to American Literature,* the *Oxford Companion to English Literature,* and the *Columbia Dictionary of Modern European Literature.*

HISTORY REFERENCE BOOKS

History reference books include the *Oxford Companion to American History* and the *Oxford Companion to World History.*

SCIENCE REFERENCE BOOKS

Science reference books include *Van Nostrand's Scientific Encyclopedia* and *A History of Technology.*

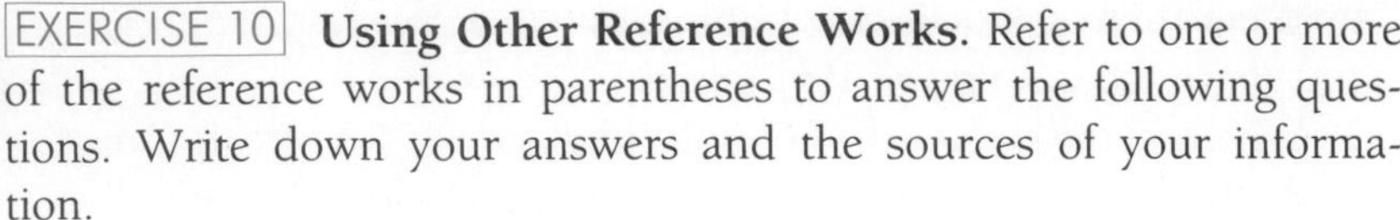

EXERCISE 10 **Using Other Reference Works.** Refer to one or more of the reference works in parentheses to answer the following questions. Write down your answers and the sources of your information.

1. What was novelist George Eliot's real name? (*Webster's Biographical Dictionary, Oxford Companion to English Literature*)
2. Who said, "Give me liberty or give me death"? (*Oxford Dictionary of Quotations, Bartlett's Familiar Quotations*)
3. What college did Geraldine Ferraro attend? (*Who's Who in America, Current Biography*)
4. What five tribes, or nations, originally comprised the Iroquois? (*Oxford Companion to American History*)
5. Who invented dynamite? (*Van Nostrand's Scientific Encyclopedia, A History of Technology*)

Other Library Resources

Microforms

Microforms are tiny photographs of printed pages that are stored on filmstrips **(microfilm)** or cards **(microfiche).**

Many libraries save space by using microforms. Materials that you are likely to find on microforms include newspapers and those magazines used frequently for reference, like *Newsweek* and *Time*. Microforms must be used with special projectors at the library. Projectors are not difficult to use, but you will probably need a demonstration before you use one.

The Vertical File

The **vertical file** is a collection of news clippings, magazine articles, photographs, pamphlets, and other brief material arranged alphabetically by subject.

The vertical file is a good source of up-to-date information on science, current events, and other changing fields. Most libraries keep a vertical file in a special cabinet in or near the reference section.

Nonprint Material

In addition to printed material and microforms, many libraries have **nonprint material** such as filmstrips, phonograph records, computer software, videocassettes, audiocassettes, and tapes. Consult a member of the library staff for information on how to use this material.

CHAPTERS 33–34 RESOURCES

CHAPTER 33 THE DICTIONARY AND THE THESAURUS

Using a Dictionary [pages 684–690] Examine the following dictionary entry, and then answer the questions that follow it.

> **rap•id** (rap′id) ***adj.*** [L. *rapidus* < *rapere,* to seize, rush: see RAPE[1]] moving, progressing, or occurring with speed; swift; fast; quick —☆***n.*** **1.** [*usually pl.*] a part of a river where the current is relatively swift, as because of a narrowing of the river bed **2.** a rapid transit car, train, or system—***SYN,*** see FAST[1] **—ra•pid•i•ty** (rə pid′ə tē), **rap′•id•ness** ***n.*** — **rap′id•ly** ***adv.***
>
> —from *Webster's New World Dictionary, Second College Edition*

1. What does *rapid* mean here: "We crossed the *rapids* in a raft"?
   (a) swift (b) swiftly flowing river part (c) subway (d) to rush
2. The word *rapid* should be
   (a) hyphenated after the *a*
   (b) stressed in the last syllable
   (c) pronounced with an *a* as in *cat*
   (d) Choices *a–c* are all correct.
3. To find synonyms for *rapid,* look under the first entry for
   (a) seize (b) swift (c) fast (d) quick

Using a Thesaurus [pages 690–691] Select the best answer.

4. All thesauruses include
   (a) synonyms for every entry
   (b) antonyms for every entry
   (c) definitions of entry words
   (d) an index of entry words

CHAPTER 34 THE LIBRARY

Using the Library [pages 692–704] Select the answer that best completes each of the following items.

1. Where is the catalog card for the novel *The Day of the Dolphin?*
   (a) the Author/Title Index under *T*
   (b) the Author/Title Index under *D*
   (c) the Subject Index under *D*
2. To find all the specific topics in a nonfiction book, consult its
   (a) table of contents (b) appendix (c) glossary (d) index
3. To find magazine articles on farming, consult
   (a) the *Readers' Guide*
   (b) *The New York Times Index*
   (c) the *Biography Index*
   (d) the card catalog
4. To find out last year's winner of the World Series, consult
   (a) an encyclopedia (b) an almanac (c) an atlas
   (d) the vertical file

Index

Writer's Sourcebook Credits

© AMERICA HURRAH ANTIQUES, N.Y.C.: p 363. ANIMALS/ANIMALS: © Anne Wertheim p 379T. PETER ARNOLD, INC.: © Y. Arthus Bertrand p 380. © CHRISTINE BENKERT: p 383TL. BRUCE COLEMAN, INC.: © Brandenburg p 362T; © Robert P. Carr p 362CL and BL. © COLOUR LIBRARY INTERNATIONAL, LTD.: p 360TL and TR, 360BL and BR. DPI: © Monty Monsees p 355TL. FREDRIC REMINGTON ART MUSEUM: p 358TL. THE IMAGE BANK: © Von Baich p 382TL. © WOLFGANG KAEHLER: p 381TL. © PETER B. KAPLAN: p 356BR. MAGNUM PHOTOS: © George Rodger p 381BL. © JOAN MARCUS: p 377TR. © MUSEUM OF AMERICAN FOLK ART: Gift of Dorothy and Leo Batkin, p 359TL. MUSEUM OF FINE ARTS, BOSTON: pp 354TL, 356TL, 357TL, 362TR. © 1985 by the New York Times, May 5, 1985, p 366. PHOTO RESEARCHERS, INC.: © Richard Hutchings pp 357BL, 362BR, 382BR; © George E. Jones p 364TL; © Edward Lettau p 364BR; © Susan McCartney p 367; © John G. Ross p 367B; © Lily Solmssen p 365BL; Van Bucher p 356BL; © C. Vargara p 354BR. KAY REESE & ASSOCIATES: © from Berlitz p 355CL. TIME: © 1984 Time, Inc. All rights reserved. Reprinted by permission of Time p 363BL. VANSCAN: ® by Daedalus Enterprises, Inc. pp 372–373T. WOODFIN CAMP & ASSOCIATES: © Craig Aurness p 355BL; © Tim Eagan p 380BL; © George Fischer/Visum, p 383BL; © Stephanie Maze p 365TL; © Momatiuk/Eastcott p 361TL, CL and BL.

Illustration Credits

© ROBERT JACKSON: pp 370–371T. © JOE LEMMONIER: p 372B. © LILY TANZER: p 369T.